THE MARKETING MANAGER'S HANDBOOK

THE KEYS TO SALES AND MARKETING SUCCESS

ERIC GAGNON

Internet Media Corporation

For inquiries related to this book, and book orders: (540) 349-2438
www.sellyourproduct.com

The Marketing Manager's Handbook
First Edition
ISBN 1-884640-04-4
© 2003 by Eric Gagnon.
All rights reserved. Published 2003.
Printed and bound in the United States of America.
Published by Internet Media Corp.

Author: Eric Gagnon
Designer: Chris Gagnon
Cover Design, Layout, and Production: Chris Gagnon

First Printing: May, 2003

TABLE OF CONTENTS

CHAPTER 3 • TOOLS OF THE TRADE: MARKETING METHODS, DELIVERABLES, AND MEDIA   47

Real Marketing

CHAPTER 4 • HOW TO WRITE ADVERTISING (OR MANAGE THOSE WHO DO): DISCOVERING, DEVELOPING AND PRESENTING YOUR PRODUCT'S MOST EFFECTIVE SALES MESSAGE   61

Contents

CHAPTER 7 • DIRECT MAIL TESTING: REDUCING MARKETING RISK AND EXPENSE IN YOUR COMPANY'S DIRECT MAIL PROJECTS 133

Contents

CHAPTER 13 • TRADE SHOW MARKETING: MAKING A SUCCESS OF YOUR COMPANY'S TRADE SHOW OPPORTUNITIES   299

Contents

Start-Ups • Product Launches • Marketing Turnarounds

CHAPTER 16 • START-UP MARKETING: MARKETING FOR START-UPS, NEW PRODUCT LAUNCHES, AND NEW MARKETS   389

What Went Right? Examining Where Marketing Projects Go Wrong: Common Causes of Poor Marketing Response 445

Marketing-Related Problems 445

Copy and Deliverable Problems...445

Market and Prospect Selection 448

Direct Mail...448

Sales Support 450

Print Advertising..452

Clarity 453

Boldness...454

Marketing Execution 456

Solving Execution Problems 458

Product-Related Problems...459

More and Better Marketing Skill Will Never Save a Bad Product 460

How to Get Product Feedback 460

Common Product-Related Causes of Poor Market Response 461

Crisis Marketing: Taking Action When the Product is Ahead of Its Time.........463

Saving a Product That is Ahead of its Time..................................464

Common Changes to Marketing Strategy and Deliverables When a Product is Retooled...465

Distribution and Market Size Problems 465

Common Distributor Problems 466

Solving Distributor Problems 467

Sales Meetings...467

Adding and Improving Distributor Sales and Marketing Deliverables 468

Greater Involvement, Training and Communication Improve Distributor Sales Performance 470

Uncontrollable Factors Revealed by Your Test................................470

Action is the Cure for Adverse Market Conditions............................472

APPENDIX   **473**

INDEX   **476**

ABOUT THE AUTHOR   **488**

PREFACE

"Do the thing and you will have the power."
—*Ralph Waldo Emerson*

This is a book for marketing managers who want to be *doers*, not dreamers:

- **If you're an experienced marketing manager** charged with the task of improving your company's sales through development of a more effective marketing program, this book will help you meet your goal;

- **If you're starting your career in marketing** or product management, and you need to learn how to execute any marketing project you'll face in your company, this book shows you how;

- **If you're launching a new product, or you're in a start-up,** and you need to get your new marketing program created, developed, and executed quickly, this book is your roadmap to developing a successful marketing program.

The practical methods of **marketing execution** detailed in this book have been proven in over 20 years of real-world experience in a wide variety of companies, of all kinds and sizes. Everything in this book is a result of field-proven experience, and the lessons learned from this experience, using actual examples of marketing projects produced for real, live clients in a variety of industries. These techniques have been responsible for the generation of millions of dollars in sales, and have acquired hundreds of thousands of new customers for the companies in which they have been implemented.

This book's emphasis on the need for marketing managers to become hands-on involved in the marketing methods and techniques of their marketing programs is a call for a return to basics in marketing management:

- **Tradecraft:** The need for marketing managers to gain the knowledge and skill required to *drive the process* of creating and executing the projects required for their marketing plans;

- **Presentation:** The importance of *salesmanship in marketing*, expressed in clear, unequivocal language readily understood by readers, viewers, and listeners;

- **Execution:** The importance of rapid, competent *marketing execution* in marketing projects, driven by the marketing manager's knowledge of the process of this execution, leading to *respect for the process.*

Since the 1970s, authors of books on marketing have made the subject far more complicated than it needs to be. Business writing on marketing has moved a far distance from the practical, into the world of generalized management theory and impenetrable business writing.

Plain, practical advice and "street wisdom" on marketing has been shoved aside by vague platitudes. Consider how the language of marketing has changed over the past 30 years. For example, discovering and developing a product's most *persuasive sales benefits* is now referred to as: "Creating Customer Value and Satisfaction." Developing a marketing plan to *sell a product* is now: "Setting the Product and Branding Strategy." And *detailing a product's competitive sales advantages* now requires twice as many words: "Positioning and Differentiating the Market Offering through the Product Life Cycle."

Pseudo-scientific efforts to reduce marketing management to the formulas, matrix charts, and case study analysis of many of today's marketing books results in *distancing the reader* from the clear understanding of the actual skills and methods required to run effective marketing programs. In many companies, this *obscurity by platitude* in marketing education has created an environment where those responsible for selling a company's products have become far removed from the techniques *actually required to sell their products.* A newly-minted college or MBA graduate, or a top sales rep, promoted to a marketing or product management position, will often find themselves ill-equipped to define, develop, and execute a timely and effective marketing program for their company.

Most marketing education in college and graduate-level business schools is also oriented toward teaching marketing management for mature, market-dominant global corporations, who can afford to carpet-bomb their large markets with saturation advertising to gain a few percentage points in market share. In these large corporations, responsibility for marketing and sales results is spread among a battalion of mid-level marketing and product managers, where direct accountability is easy to hide from, and where immense financial resources cover the many failures in marketing presentation or execution that would be fatal to any smaller company.

Big-company management theories and weak marketing platitudes are of little use to the marketing manager in a mid-sized trade, industrial, or business-to-business company, who must put together a sales mailing to his company's prospect list, or who must sketch out the key sales benefits for his company's upcoming advertising program or trade show, under deadline pressure. Marketing theory is of little use to the marketing manager struggling to increase his or her company's sales under an inept, lackluster marketing program, or who believes he isn't getting the best effort or work product from his company's ad agency or marketing team. Marketing managers who haven't been taught the tradecraft necessary to drive the content and execution of their marketing programs will, by default, leave these critical tasks to their ad agencies or marketing consultants, who may or may not be up to the job.

The further a marketing manager is removed from the *content* and *execution* of his marketing program, the less effective his marketing program will be. And the less effective the marketing program, the lower the sales result. However, the marketing manager who knows the elements required for effective presentation and execution of a marketing project—an ad, a mailing, a trade show opportunity, a Web site, or video, for example—and who can sketch out the essential sales benefits this project must communicate to the prospect, can work with his company's ad agency or marketing consultant to drive the project through to its timely completion.

Because he knows the most effective sales benefits of his company's products, knows how to translate these benefits into the form required for effective presentation in the "marketing media" of the project, and knows the critical steps required to execute the project, this marketing manager moves *closer to the process*, and increases its chance for success.

As a marketing manager, using the techniques outlined in this book will move you closer to the content and process of your own company's marketing program, through **Real Marketing**, this book's underlying principle:

> **Clear and direct presentation of your company's prime sales benefits in every marketing project, with every marketing deliverable, and in all marketing media, backed up with swift, forceful marketing execution.**

The only goal of your marketing program is to generate sales. And the best way to meet this goal is through clear and persuasive presentation of your product's most compelling sales benefits, and basic, down-on-the-ground marketing execution. This is Real Marketing.

In marketing programs, Real Marketing means hitting your product's most obvious, persuasive sales benefits—hard—in your company's advertising, direct mail, sales support programs, and everywhere else your company communicates to its market.

Most company marketing programs also require better marketing execution. Success is often determined where "the rubber meets the road"—working with your ad agency or marketing consultant to develop ads, mailings or other marketing deliverables, in the pressroom, where marketing collateral is printed, at a trade show, where your sales reps present to their prospects, or at the mailing house, where your company's direct mail packages are prepared for delivery to prospects in your market. A marketing manager who has knowledge of the process of marketing execution for each of these types of projects develops *respect for the process* and, in doing so, gains the confidence and trust of his marketing team.

As a marketing manager, you will also experience failures and adversity in your marketing projects. Despite your (and your team's) best efforts, your ads, mailings or other marketing projects will, at some point, generate poor sales response.

It is not the failure, but your response to the failure, that determines the ultimate outcome. Here, the skills developed by the practice of Real Marketing—the ability to present clearly and execute well in all marketing projects—will help you turn a failed or underperforming marketing program around.

There's no mystery to selling a product. There are but a handful of marketing methods (such as advertising, direct mail or sales force support) that can be used to reach the prospects in your company's market. As a marketing manager, your job is to apply the time-tested principles of effective marketing presentation and execution to these marketing activities in your company, and to make the changes to your program required by your market's response to your marketing effort. The faster you can execute these changes, the greater your chance for ultimate sales success.

In marketing, as in life: "Do the thing and you will have the power." To do is to act, and action always creates more options. And in these options you will often discover the new elements required to make your marketing program a success.

If you have a good product at a good price, and one that is wanted by the potential buyers of your market, the rest is just clear, effective, salesmanlike presentation and rapid, competent marketing execution. And I hope that this book will provide you with a practical plan of action for achieving success in your own company's marketing program.

Acknowledgements

Few efforts are ever accomplished alone, and I am grateful to many friends and business associates whose advice, support, and confidence have become of part of the many real-life "lessons learned" which have been incorporated in this book.

I thank my mentor Stan Cotton for providing me with important early inspiration, and for building my confidence to enter the advertising and marketing business over 20 years ago. I will always strive to measure up to the qualities of clear, powerful, honest expression that Stan pioneered in his more than 50 years in the business.

I am grateful to my friend and associate Jeff Hyman, whose steady friendship and support has bolstered us through many years, and to my friend Mike Walsh, who helped us to establish many of the important business relationships in our marketing consulting work (thanks also to Mike for his valuable contribution to the conference section in Chapter 13).

Thanks also to Glenn Hanna, one of our long-time clients who became our close friend, for his unwavering support and encouragement on this book. His review and contributions to this book have given it the important "reality check" only a veteran marketing manager like Glenn could provide.

Thanks to Martin Edelston, whose kindness, personal support, and enthusiasm for our projects has always been a source of encouragement, and whose innovations in direct mail promotion and publishing copy and presentation have, for many years, been an inspiration to my own work, and to the work of many others in the field. It's rare to find someone who is as generous, helpful, and supportive to as many others as Marty has been in his long and successful career.

Our business would not exist, of course, without the help and support of our clients, and the enjoyable and memorable relationships we have established with our contacts at these firms, most notably: Jeff Pulver, Marni Shapiro, Jim Bonan, Rosemary O'Brien, Rose Mary Casella, Greg Gudorf, Christopher Ryan, Patricia Ruggieri, and Angela Smith, among many others with whom we've worked in the past.

Thanks also to "our group," the members of our company's team, each of whom have been an important contibutor to our success in our company's consulting, product development, and publishing activities: Gary Goldberg, Ken Herrera, Carl Johnson, Jon Van Oast, Claire Wolfe, Paul Yovino; Bill Seward, Bill Ferinde, Brian Bryant, and the staff of All American Printing; James Dwyier, Helen Bauserman, and the staff of Dwyier Associates, Ford Prime, Heidi Prime, and Michael St. Pierre of Prime Signs and Tradeshowshop.com; Bonnie Burroughs, and her late husband (and our dear friend) Jim, of Innovative Projects, and Bruce Mackey of EU Services, for his inspiration and support. Thanks also to Jim Hood of the Oakton Press, who provided the valuable interview comments for this book's sidebar on broadcast video in Chapter 15.

Most of all, I owe whatever I've accomplished in life to my wife, best friend, and partner, Chris, who has worked with me, side-by-side, through every day in our many years together. This book, and virtually all of the examples of our company's work in this book, are the result of her extraordinary design skills. I have been blessed to share life with one as beautiful, kind, and talented as her.

Eric Gagnon (**eric@realmarkets.net**)

REAL MARKETING
CHAPTER 1
FIRST PRINCIPLES OF EFFECTIVE, SUCCESSFUL MARKETING MANAGEMENT

This book takes you deep inside the process of marketing, by covering the total array of marketing techniques, tools and processes that will increase your company's sales, if they are executed with speed, boldness, and intelligence.

This is not a book of untested theories or management platitudes. The step-by-step techniques of *marketing execution* documented in this book have been formed in the crucible of over 20 years' field marketing experience, and have been proven in actual use with companies of all sizes, in many different industries.

The techniques used in this book have generated millions of dollars' worth of sales for the companies that have employed them. They owe their success to common sense, and to the teachings of the famous masters of the advertising and marketing worlds: John Caples, Rosser Reeves, Claude Hopkins, Victor Schwab, Max Sackheim, and others, who have established the foundation for marketing success in business today.

Following the practical, how-to steps contained in this book will help you, as a marketing manager, increase sales in your company, by improving the effectiveness of your company's marketing program, and by improving the effectiveness of the "deliverables" used in your marketing plan—advertising, direct mail, sales support collateral, Web site, and other marketing tools. Following the instructions in this book will help you avoid many of the common errors in marketing presentation and day-to-day management that beset marketing managers in many companies today.

The Marketing Manager's Handbook concentrates on the practical, proven steps involved in planning, developing, and producing the major types of marketing projects that you, as a marketing manager, will be required to execute for your company. This book covers the process of marketing execution for the broad range of marketing projects required in any type of business: Small to mid-sized companies, entrepreneurial start-ups, and product-line divisions of large corporations.

If you are a marketing manager in any of these types of companies, and are responsible for selling your company's product or service by print advertising, direct mail, the Internet, trade show marketing, or with other types of marketing tools and media, you will find the practical information and advice you need here to successfully execute any marketing project, and to greatly enhance its chances for success in your company.

While the main focus of this book is on trade or industrial marketing, more commonly referred to as business-to-business marketing (i.e., companies whose products or services are marketed and sold to other companies, and not to the consumer or retail markets), much of this book's content can also be applied to the marketing of any product or service to the general consumer market.

Whether you are selling hydraulic products in Dayton, high-tech imaging systems in San Jose, industrial manufacturing products in Denver, or specialized information services in New York City, the universal sales and marketing principles detailed in this book apply to all types of products or services, in all markets, at all price levels, and sold to all kinds of buyers.

These techniques will help your company in good times and—*especially*—in more challenging economic conditions, by giving you the information and advice you need to create ads, mailings, brochures, and other marketing deliverables that generate sales for your company. The principles explained in this book will *eliminate any doubt that you could have done a better or more effective selling job on a marketing project*. These doubts are often caused by not knowing the most effective, proven ways to develop, present, and execute marketing projects. If you follow the procedures and practices outlined in this book, you will go a long way toward eliminating this doubt that your marketing projects could have been better implemented, or better executed.

As you read this book, you will discover that there's no mystery to the process of marketing. Most of the intellectual horsepower required to successfully market your company's products is already known by your company's best salespeople, or, if you're involved in a start-up or new product launch, can be obtained through the application of proven market testing principles, and salesmanship, to your marketing projects. A focus on *salesmanship in marketing*, combined with skilled marketing tradecraft and solid execution, can revive a poor marketing program in a company, or can make a good marketing program even better.

The Importance of Salesmanship in Marketing Management and Advertising

Over the last 25 years, there has been a substantial decline in the competence of, and (as a result) the effectiveness of, marketing programs in many companies selling products in business-to-business markets. The plain truth is that many companies don't create effective marketing programs, and they don't execute them very well, or on a timely basis. The final "marketing deliverable" of many marketing projects—the print display ad campaign, the direct mail program, Web site, or other marketing project—doesn't adequately inform or sell the prospect. This inevitably leads to a poor sales response (if anyone even thought to measure response in the first place).

Many companies bounce from one marketing approach to another, and from one advertising agency to another, not finding the right mix of sales copy messages, marketing tools and media that could help them establish successful, sales-generating marketing programs for their companies. Instead, these companies rely on their in-house sales force, distributors, or dealer networks, whose selling efforts cover a multitude of errors in the company's marketing program. The company's marketing program becomes a haphazard, expensive, poorly-executed chain of projects performed by the company's latest ad agency, consultant, or other outside expert brought on board to implement the company's current marketing program, promotion, or product launch. Sales are made on the backs of the company's sales force, *in spite of the company's marketing program*, and through whatever methods the company has accidentally discovered that help it sell its products.

Part of the cause of these problems is that somewhere along the way, many companies hired marketing managers who never actually learned how to *sell something*. Before the MBA became the express elevator to middle management in corporate America, marketing managers rose from street-level field sales positions in their companies, where success was measured by monthly sales performance, new accounts won, reorder rates increased. A marketing manager knew how to sketch out a list of his or her product's best sales benefits, *because they already knew them from years of personal field sales experience*.

Likewise, account executives at advertising agencies and consulting firms, who usually work with marketing managers to develop a company's marketing programs, often move straight out of college marketing and advertising design programs to positions at advertising agencies and PR firms, without the benefit of prior sales experience. Many ad agency people seem more interested in winning design awards than creating effective marketing programs that generate inquiries for sales reps or direct sales for clients. Instead, they come up with clever, "creative" ideas for ad campaigns, mailings, and layouts with the expectation that a sight gag, a funny headline, or some other magic bullet will move people to buy the client's product. The end result is an ad, brochure, direct mailing, or other marketing project that doesn't clearly tell the reader about the company's product, and fails to provide the reader with the product's known sales benefits, features, and potential applications, presented in a way that persuades the reader to take the action required by the marketing deliverable: To call the company's toll-free number, to fill out and mail a coupon, or link to the company's Web site.

A sales background (or sales experience) is an important requirement for any marketing manager or ad agency executive. Sales experience helps marketing managers understand the human motivations behind a prospect's reasons for buying, or not buying, and gives them the know-how to develop the presentation skills required to make the sale. A sales background also helps copywriters and account executives at ad agencies and consulting firms address the prospect's needs and wants in effective sales copy and layouts for advertising campaigns, mailings, and other marketing projects.

Marketing Managers and the Tradecraft of Marketing

In addition to lack of selling experience, many marketing managers know very little of the *tradecraft* of marketing: The process of creating, developing, producing and executing the elements of a marketing project.

Throughout this book we stress the importance of *execution* in marketing, the need to diligently complete the steps required to plan, produce and complete any marketing project on a timely basis. As a marketing manager, you may not have to write your own sales copy for a print ad, create the home page for your company's Web site, or produce the printed materials for your company's sales information kit. However, to be an effective marketing manager, you do need to know what makes an ad effective and persuasive, the elements that help turn visitors to your company's Web site into qualified sales prospects, and the best available content and presentation options for your company's sales kits, direct mail projects, and trade show opportunities.

You need to know all of these things because you, not your ad agency or other outside supplier, are ultimately responsible for marketing execution in your company. As a marketing manager, knowledge of the essential content required for any marketing "deliverable," such as an ad, brochure, direct mail piece, or any other marketing tool, helps you to start any marketing project off on the right track by creating a rough, working outline, or specification, of the sales benefits, features, applications, and other content required for any marketing project.

Moreover, knowledge of the process of execution required for each of the wide range of marketing projects in your marketing plan will make you a more effective marketing manager when working with your ad agency, marketing consultant, printer, Web developer, or other outside vendors to execute these marketing projects for your company. Knowledge of the tradecraft of marketing, combined with forceful execution of marketing projects, imparts speed and vigor to your marketing program. In doing so, it will improve the quality and effectiveness of your marketing projects, and will greatly improve their chances for sales success.

No one else in your company should care more about marketing than you: Marketing managers who fail to learn marketing tradecraft put their entire marketing programs at risk. If you ask your ad agency or marketing consultant to write and produce an ad or direct mail campaign, without first providing them with an outline of the essential sales copy benefit points that the ad or mailing must contain, you leave these critical decisions entirely to the agency's copywriter, who, without your leadership, is likely to produce a less effective ad, mailing piece, or other marketing deliverable.

Knowledge of marketing tradecraft builds respect for the process of marketing execution: Your knowledge of marketing tradecraft must also extend to day-to-day implementation of your marketing projects. For example, if you don't know the steps required to create and produce a direct mail project in your company, you leave its execution to chance. At best, this means you leave the timing and coordination of the project to outside vendors who are not as motivated as you are to see the project through to its speedy, competent completion.

At worst, lack of knowledge breeds a lack of **respect for the process** on the part of marketing managers. This is often shown by marketing managers who, for no good reason, ignore projects until the very last minute, and then put their ad agency or outside vendor through a disruptive "fire drill" to get the project implemented on a rush basis.

All non-emergency marketing projects require a certain amount of time to complete, and for the marketing manager who is inattentive to the process, or who makes every project a last-minute emergency, due to his or her own poor planning or lack of knowledge, demonstrates a lack of respect for the process. This is soon communicated to others throughout the project's chain of execution as a lack of respect for *them*, and for their efforts. This means that small problems that occur in any project, such as printing mistakes, shipping glitches, or mailing list processing errors, are not solved quickly, because anyone in the chain of execution who feels their time or effort is not respected will tend to find ways to return this disrespect up the chain of command.

A marketing manager who takes the time to learn how an ad campaign is developed and put into place, how a direct mail program is launched, or how a Web site, trade show, video production, or public relations effort is executed earns the respect of his or her marketing team. This mutual respect motivates all to do a first-rate job on any marketing project, and to finish it faster. If you know how a project is executed, you can set realistic deadlines for it, and save goodwill for those unavoidable events when a true marketing emergency arises and you need a project to be done on a rush basis. When this time comes, your demonstrated respect for the process, and for your marketing team, will be rewarded by a well-done marketing project, completed to meet your rush deadline.

Real Marketing: First Principles of Successful Marketing Programs

Using salesmanship in your marketing projects, and knowing the tradecraft of marketing execution are two important requirements for success in marketing. They are expanded further in ten key principles of **Real Marketing**, defined as:

Clear and direct presentation of your company's prime sales benefits in every marketing project, with every marketing deliverable, and in all marketing media, backed up with swift, forceful marketing execution.

Real Marketing is, in many ways, an updated method utilizing time-tested, proven ways of presenting your company's product or service to prospects in your market, using practical methods of marketing execution.

Real Marketing helps you:

- **Uncover the benefits, features, and applications** that motivate prospects to buy your company's product or service;

- **Present your product's key sales benefits** in plain, simple, effective language;

- **Select, plan, develop, and execute** your marketing projects as quickly and efficiently as possible;

- **React quickly** to correct failures in marketing projects, and to exploit new marketing opportunities.

The two major elements of Real Marketing, covered in detail in the next section, are:

Direct presentation of sales benefits: Real Marketing uses clear, simple, direct language to communicate the known sales benefits of your company's product in all marketing deliverables—advertising, direct mail, the Internet, or any other marketing tool—and using bold presentation and layout techniques to make the sales message as obvious as possible to the largest number of readers and viewers in your market;

Swift and forceful execution of marketing projects: Real Marketing makes you, the marketing manager, a key part of the process of execution for every marketing project, by revealing the practical tradecraft required to execute any marketing project. Once armed with this knowledge, you can manage and drive your company's marketing projects with greater confidence, in shorter time, and with higher likelihood for success.

Ten Principles of Real Marketing

1.) Execution is the most important part of marketing

For want of a nail, the shoe was lost;
For want of the shoe, the horse was lost;
For want of the horse, the rider was lost;
For want of the rider, the battle was lost;
For want of the battle, the kingdom was lost,
And all for the want of a nail.

Figure 1-1:

Developing The Execution Mindset

These eight important steps to better marketing and marketing execution will improve sales in almost any situation:

- ### If You Can't Sell Your 10 Best Prospects Over The Phone, You Don't Have a Business
Forget about "branding," focus groups and fancy logos: Take your best available mailing list of prospects and call the 10 best of these. If your best persuasive abilities can't convince them to buy your company's product, something's wrong. Advertising will never save a product nobody wants.

- ### Do You Suffer From "Brochure Paralysis?"
If you can't get a brochure produced in two weeks, you've got a problem. Beyond two weeks, you're losing business and your entire marketing effort has ground to a halt—it happens every time. Set a deadline. Go from color to black and white; xerox if you have to—but get your brochure out on the street! If you can't sell your best 10 prospects with a draft of your brochure, you won't sell them with the fancy one you're waiting on, either.

- ### Where's Your Phone Number?
Tack your company's brochure to a wall and start walking backwards. If you can't read your company's phone number on it from 10 feet, your prospect won't see it at arms' length. Put your company's phone number, address, URL, and how-to-buy info on every ad, mailing, brochure, and sales letter you send out. And don't hold back—give your prospect all the benefits and information he needs to buy your product. No ad copy is ever too long if it *tells* your product's story and *sells* your product.

- ### If You Can't Send Out Your Brochure The Same Day, You'll Never Fill The Order
Sales information must be sent out in response to an inquiry the very same day as received—period. If it's not happening for you now, see that it does. Meanwhile, e-mail a one-page .PDF sales sheet to the prospect within two hours of his call—you'll get his attention. And if you can't tell your story on a one-page sheet, you don't have a business, either.

- ### Your Best Market May Not Be The One You're In Now
Most huge companies that once were startups aren't now in the same businesses or markets in which they originally began. Most transformed themselves overnight when faced with imminent failure. Mix it up: Run a lead-generating ad in a targeted publication. Try a direct mail test. Push private-label deals with big companies. Market your product "in the box" with someone else's. Like any other investment, sales and marketing expenses work best when they are diversified.

- ### Why the Hell Didn't the Mailing Go Out?
It's a fact: Delays kill marketing execution, and poor execution kills sales. Take no prisoners when it comes to delays in marketing execution. Don't allow petty excuses to bleed your company. Set firm deadlines for mailings, from idea to lettershop, magazine, or sales force: Seven days for critical items and 14 days for everything else.

- ### Too Many Eyes Can Kill Your Company
Don't run marketing copy and ideas past 27 different people. There are just three people who should review all marketing copy and materials in your company: You, your sales manager, and your best current customer.

- ### "Creative" People Will Hose You Every Time
Beware the man in the $75 haircut who says he has the magic bullet for your advertising campaign. Advertising isn't rocket science. If you have a good product and a willing prospect, the rest is smart execution, follow-through, and common sense.

Swift and competent execution is the most important part of any marketing program, but poor execution is a common affliction in many marketing company programs. Missed ad deadlines, slipped mailing dates, important sales materials delayed at the printer due to gratuitous type changes or other production glitches are the enemies of good marketing execution.

"For want of a nail," poor execution leads to missed marketing opportunities. A critical mailing that's not ready to drop in time to support a company's peak selling season or a new product launch, a new Web site endlessly delayed, an important advertising placement missed in a key issue of a trade publication, poor or late advance promotion and slipshod production for a company's most important trade show appearance of the year. All are examples of missed selling opportunities caused by poor marketing execution, and are easily correctable by using the principles detailed in this book.

A marketing manager's passivity, lack of knowledge of tradecraft, and of the key steps required to execute marketing projects, are the primary causes of poor marketing execution. Marketing managers who treat the process of marketing execution as a "black box" will exercise questionable judgement and unrealistic expectations in their management of marketing programs. Marketing managers who have a working knowledge of the day-to-day steps involved in any marketing project gain credibility with, and earn the respect of, their ad agencies, marketing consultants, printers, outside vendors, and the other members of their marketing team, as well as the sales managers they support, and the executives they report to.

Developing the skill of fast and effective marketing execution requires you to learn the tradecraft of marketing, for all different types of marketing projects. Learning how a thing is done, even if this task will be performed by someone else, helps you to better manage the process, and gives you a more realistic expectation of how your project can be executed, and how long it takes to get it done. Marketing managers who learn the tradecraft of marketing develop better marketing plans, and execute them well, *because they know the process of marketing execution.*

Gaining the ability to execute fast and well not only means you get your marketing program under firm control, it also gives you the power to attack any promising new marketing opportunity that arises: Ad placements and mailings required for a push into an exciting new market or product launch, a last-minute booth space opening at a major trade show, a critical change required in sales copy for existing ads, brochures, or other deliverables in your marketing program. **A marketing manager and marketing team that execute well can exploit any sales opportunity, anytime, anywhere.**

2.) Any good marketing project, well-executed, beats any great marketing project, poorly executed

A well-executed marketing program that arrives in time to generate inquiries and sales for your company is infinitely more valuable than an even better one that is not there when needed, or is hobbled by rushed, slipshod, or late execution.

The techniques described in this book enable you and your team to create effective marketing deliverables for any marketing project. Once an ad layout, direct mail package, or any other marketing deliverable is produced using the techniques described in this book, the marketing manager must then shift his or her focus over to the task of executing the marketing project where the deliverable is to be used—i.e., the advertising schedule, the direct mail program, trade show, Web site, or other project.

"Don't let the best be the enemy of the good" is the battle cry for marketing deliverables and projects that are threatened by endless tweaking, reviewing, and other fiddling as important deadlines approach. This often occurs whenever layouts for ads or brochures are reviewed and corrected by too many people inside a company, or when trivial design changes are made to ad layouts and deliverables.

In addition to these problems, "thinking too much" is another common cause of poor marketing execution. Any marketing deliverable can be revised or edited to make it even better. Moreover, if time is unlimited, there is, theoretically, always a better ad campaign, a better direct mail program, or a better version of any other marketing deliverable that can be produced. A quest for a better advertising concept or layout that becomes a neurotic, nagging doubt in your marketing program is not only a threat to your marketing execution, the doubt created by "thinking too much" about your marketing projects threatens your entire marketing program by undermining the confidence of your marketing team.

Don't be afraid to "fail faster:" Sometimes, the only way to learn the most effective way to sell your company's product is to suck it up and execute your plan: Place your ads, send out your mailings, rent booth space at the trade show, or execute any other activity that requires a hard commitment of dollars, effort and time. Some of these projects may yield good sales results, and some may yield poor sales results.

While it's good to be prudent, and risk can be minimized through market testing (covered in Chapters 7 and 17), there is always a risk of failure in any marketing project. In many cases, factors *other* than the marketing deliverable (such as product features or price) may be the cause of failure, but you will only learn this by actual execution, with the best plan and deliverables you have at hand. However, if you execute quickly, you also "fail faster," and, in learning what went wrong, you often have enough time to make the necessary corrections to your marketing program based on this actual experience. If nothing's ever ventured, nothing good can be gained.

If, by faster execution, you can more quickly resolve the "unknowns" in your marketing program—i.e., will the new mailing work? Will these new ads pull?—you will have more time to assess what went wrong, fix the problem, and get your revised marketing projects back in the race. If, instead, you had wasted time tweaking and fussing over this marketing project, you probably would have met the same end result, but now you would have no time left to correct your marketing program.

Better to decide on a course of action, develop the best marketing deliverable for the time and effort allowed, and get it into action, when your company needs it. An ad, mailing, or other marketing deliverable that's "good and there" is always better than the ideal one which always seems just beyond your grasp.

3.) Marketing is not creativity, branding, or design. It's salesmanship

Many marketing people, and the ad agencies who serve them, have lost track of what's important in their marketing programs.

The only goal of your marketing program is to generate sales. This is defined as the generation of inquiries converted to sales by your company's sales reps, or direct sales from a marketing project. The talismans of modern marketing-speak: "Brand recognition," "reader scores," or "mindshare" do not generate sales for your company. *Salesmanship in marketing* does.

Your Market Wants Reality, Not Someone's Idea of Creativity

Creativity and the other side aspects of advertising and marketing—graphic design, layout, and copywriting—are tools used in the service of salesmanship in advertising and marketing projects. Creativity, in itself, will not sell your company's product or service. All of us are creative, more or less, and to some degree. While creativity does play a role in the "downstream" process of developing an ad campaign or other marketing project, you must focus on the **reality** of your company's products in the initial stages of developing sales copy and layouts for marketing deliverables. This means focusing on the benefits, features, and applications of your product, and how they can be described in a way that persuades the prospect to initiate an action that starts the selling process: Calling your company's toll-free number, going to your company's Web site, filling out a coupon, or calling a dealer or distributor.

Your Enthusiasm Sells Products

As any top salesman will tell you, having a genuine enthusiasm for a product, an enthusiasm that infuses every aspect of his or her sales presentation, is often the decisive element in making a sale.

Enthusiasm is contagious. A salesman who is genuinely fired up about his company's product line imparts a sense of enthusiasm to his sales prospects, which always has a positive influence on their view of the salesman, and of the products he represents.

But enthusiasm is not limited to face-to-face encounters. Your prospects can sense enthusiasm in your advertising and marketing programs by the sales copy they read, and in all of your company's marketing programs.

Before you sketch out your outline and notes for any marketing project, take a few minutes to whip up a sense of enthusiasm in your mind for the product or service you're preparing to write about. Once you develop that inner fire, that boiled-over compulsion to tell another human being that he really *needs* to use your company's products, the rest of the job—answering the reasons *why* he needs your products, suddenly becomes much easier.

The "branding" myth: Branding is another bad idea that has moved from the big-money world of major consumer products advertisers into the world of trade and business-to-business marketers. The need for branding and brand reinforcement generally applies only to that small handful of Fortune 500 corporations who need (and who can afford) to pour hundreds of millions of dollars into saturation advertising campaigns to promote widely-used consumer products, fighting over a few market share points each year with their competition in the market for toothpaste, automobiles, or laundry detergent.

In their work with small and mid-sized business trade advertisers, many ad agency types attempt to replicate the same promotional carpet-bombing techniques used by these consumer product mega-marketers. The end results are grossly over-produced, irrelevant, and ultimately ineffective advertising, and an obscene waste of money for clients. The Internet "Dot-Com" boom and bust of 1998-2000 was the most recent example of the use of advertising as an attempt to buy "branding" for several high-profile (now defunct) companies, by throwing millions of dollars into saturation advertising campaigns.

An effort to produce advertising to "brand" a company's product, instead of advertising that informs and persuades the reader, has an even greater likelihood of failure when used to sell high-technology-related products or services in vertical trade and industry markets. Companies selling complex products or services have an even greater need to make their advertising simple, plain-spoken and salesmanlike, by breaking down their products' benefits, features, and applications into language that can be grasped quickly by readers in their markets. All these readers want to know is what the company's product is, what it does, and what it can do for them.

The misapplication of branding strategy to marketing for trade and business-to-business advertisers is a misunderstanding of the true meaning of branding. The positive regard a customer has for your product, expressed by brand awareness and brand loyalty, can only be accomplished by a long-term history of selling an excellent product, using honest business practices and providing excellent customer service. No matter how much money you spend, branding can't be bought in a three-month ad campaign. It's the by-product of years of selling excellent products, and treating customers as you would want to be treated.

Other unfortunate ideas have corrupted the world of advertising in the past 25 years, such as the notion that advertising must generate an "emotional response," that determines how your potential customer "feels" about your product. The only response you want from your advertising is to generate sales. All other considerations are irrelevant and, at worst, can be fatal to your company's marketing program.

4.) Stamp out the "Y Factor" in your marketing program

The "Y Factor" can be defined by asking the question:

"Did our marketing deliverable effectively present the benefits of our product, in a way that motivates the reader to buy the product?"

The "Y Factor" is, in effect, *the doubt* that the sales copy and layout of an ad, a mailing, or any other marketing deliverable has expressed your product's key sales benefits, features, and applications with sufficient force and clarity to motivate the reader to take the action you want them to take: To call your company's toll-free number to speak to a sales rep, to fill out a coupon requesting more information, to visit your company's Web site, or to place an order.

If the sales copy elements in your marketing deliverables—headline, subheads, body copy, and "call to action"—satisfy you that they clearly and persuasively present and sell your company's product to prospects in your market, then you can be satisfied that you've eliminated the "Y Factor" in this marketing project.

Your job, and the job of other members of your marketing team, is to eliminate this "Y Factor" in all of your marketing programs. Following the general advice outlined in the next section (below), the sales copywriting techniques detailed in Chapter 4, and the many techniques discussed throughout this book will help you to identify and eliminate this doubt in all of your company's marketing programs.

5.) A plain, clear, persuasive sales message always eliminates the "Y Factor"

Clear, simple, direct presentation of your product's sales benefits, in plain language that appeals to the reader's motivations, is the surest, most effective way to sell your company's products.

This is especially true for companies involved in trade, industrial, and business-to-business marketing. Here, there is an even greater need for simplification and clarity, as the important aspects of complex products or services must be broken down, explained, and presented to prospects in specialized industries and markets. High-technology companies bear an even greater burden of presenting their product's major benefits, and explaining to prospects how they will be better off by using their company's products.

Plain Words and Basic Appeals Sell Products

By staying focused on salesmanship and reality in your advertising copy, you can make simple, plain, and direct ad sales approaches beat creative, "impactful," or emotional appeals every time.

Put yourself in your average prospect's shoes: Fighting traffic, late for work, inundated with meetings, besieged with phone calls, e-mail, late projects, and all the other stresses and interruptions of daily life. Next, add in the crazed media

---

Figure 1-2:

What Do You Want?

" Let's say you have $1,000,000 tied up in your little company and suddenly, for reasons unknown to you, your advertising isn't working and your sales are going down. And everything depends on it. Your future depends on it, your family's future depends on it, other people's families depend on it. And you walk in this office and talk to me, and you sit in that chair. Now, what do you want out of me? Fine writing? Do you want masterpieces? Do you want glowing things that can be framed by copywriters?

Or do you want to see the g*d-damned sales curve stop moving down and start moving up. What do you want? "

— *Rosser Reeves*
Chairman, Ted Bates & Co. (1940-1966)
Author, "Reality in Advertising" (1961)

---

kaleidoscope of words, images, sounds, and printed messages that attack all of us every day.

Quick—look at both of these headlines below:

Headline 1:	Headline 2:
Discover Efficiencies With Thermotron	**Cut Your Fuel Costs by 25% with Thermotron Insulators**

Which of these headlines seems more persuasive to you? If you picked the headline on the right, you get the point. The direct and obvious approach, using salesmanship, always wins. Simple, proven truths, plainly stated and simply presented, like a first-rate salesman at the top of his game, sell products in any market, and for every marketing project.

Few if any of your competitors will use this plain, direct, salesmanlike approach in their marketing programs. Your ads and other marketing projects will be even more effective wherever they are seen by prospects in your market, because your competitors won't be using the clear, obvious, approaches that answer the most common questions and concerns of the prospects in your market.

The purpose of the direct, salesmanlike approach to advertising is to insure that you have presented your product's very best sales benefits in your advertising, and that you have presented these benefits in a way that *eliminates any doubt* they could have been presented more clearly, or with any greater impact.

Figure 1-3:

"What You Say is More Important Than How You Say It." —*John Caples*

Clear, powerful, salesmanlike appeals generate interest and sales everywhere, whether printed in a full page ad in <u>Business Week</u>, or painted on a piece of plywood along the highway.

"People will not be bored in print. They want economy, beauty, labor saving, good things to eat and wear. They will never know it unless the headline or the picture tells them."

—*Claude Hopkins*

The goal of your sales copy and presentation is to eliminate this "Y Factor:" The doubt in your mind that your advertising could have been more salesmanlike, more persuasive, or harder-hitting.

Great Sales Copy Works in Any Marketing Project

While the techniques of writing clear, direct, salesmanlike copy are used most often in your company's print advertising, these very same principles apply just as well to any other type of copywriting and presentation task in any marketing project: Brochures and print collateral, direct mail packages, Web sites, multimedia presentations, trade show signage, and sales support materials. Once you develop the ability to recognize and outline effective sales copy, you can apply it to any other type of marketing project, in print, online, and in any multimedia form, such as video or audio.

As a marketing manager, you probably won't be writing your company's advertising copy, but you must know your product's major sales benefits well enough

Figure 1-4:

Sales Appeals to Basic Human Motivations are Timeless—and Always Effective: These classic ads, written and produced by America's most successful advertising copywriters, illustrate the value of using direct appeals to human motivations and desires, connected to the goal of selling products.

In their time, these famous ads launched companies and brand-new ways of doing business and selling products. Times may change, but people, and their motivations, don't. Any marketing program can be made more effective by using the same basic appeals, updated with modern production values.

Credits: Top (L. to R.): John Caples (all). Bottom (L. to R.): Max Sackheim, Victor Schwab, John Caples.

to write them in outline form, so you can communicate them to your ad agency's copywriter. You won't be laying out or producing your company's brochures, sales kits, trade show signage, Web site, or video presentations, but you must learn to recognize the elements of presentation that make any of these marketing deliverables successful, so you can impart these winning features to these deliverables in your own marketing projects.

Whenever you work with an outside ad agency or marketing consultant, you should arrive at every meeting armed with your own list of sales benefits and copy points, derived from practicing the steps outlined in Chapter 4, and elsewhere in this book. This will give your ad agency or marketing consultant the helpful starting points they need for their development of marketing deliverables for your company, and will help insure that every one of your company's marketing projects will be an effective, salesmanlike effort that eliminates the "Y Factor" throughout your entire marketing program.

6.) Learn to see with "New Eyes"

Learning to see with "New Eyes" means developing the ability to see all of your company's marketing deliverables as your readers see them. To do this, you must block out everything you know about your company and its product, and pretend you are looking at your company's ad, mailing piece, sales kit, or Web site as if you knew nothing about your company's product, and you are seeing it for the first time.

Seeing with new eyes also means viewing your marketing deliverables as your readers view them, which is not for very long, and with an attitude of disinterest and mild skepticism. Your potential prospects are disinterested because they have many other things on their mind, and skeptical because of the meaningless, time-wasting hype they see in all the other advertising around yours—which means it is all the more important to make your marketing deliverables clearer and more effective than the rest.

How readers see your company's advertising: A reader who sees your ad in a trade publication, or receives your mailing piece, visits your Web site, or walks by your booth at a trade show will scan your ad, mailing, or other marketing deliverable for just a few short seconds. While doing so, they make a split-second decision in their minds as to whether or not they're interested in your product enough to read more about it.

How readers become prospects: If your ad's headline, or other prominent visual feature of your direct mail piece, Web site, or trade show booth, is powerful enough to draw them in, your reader will then spend a few more seconds skim-reading the other elements of your deliverable—subheads, product photos, a few lines of your body copy. If your sales copy is effective, it will spark the reader to begin asking questions about your product, questions that must be answered immediately by the sales copy they read in the next few seconds. As the reader becomes more interested and intrigued by your sales copy's presentation, they read more—and when they become very interested, they look to see what they need to do next to find out more about your company's product, or buy it. This is the point when a reader becomes a prospect for your company's product or service. This is also the point where your company's "800" number, Web site, or e-mail address must jump out for the reader's attention.

During this time, the prospect is constantly deciding whether or not to continue reading your sales copy, or to turn their attention to something else. If, during this time, there are any gaps in your presentation—a key question not clearly answered, an important, expected product feature not provided, or any aspect of your presentation that falls flat, or does not ring true, the prospect stops reading, stops being a prospect, and moves on.

How to develop this ability: Plain, clear and persuasive sales messages, plainly presented in any marketing deliverable, help your marketing program cut through reader disinterest and skepticism. Once you and your marketing team have produced an ad, mailing piece, Web site or any other marketing deliverable using the techniques described in this book, the easiest way to develop the ability to look at your project with new eyes is to forget about the project for the rest of your workday, then make it the first thing you look at the next morning, ahead of any memo, newspaper, or anything else. It also helps to break your existing habits of reviewing your company's marketing materials. For example, print out laser proofs of ads, mailings, or layouts for other deliverables, take them home with you, and look at them while you eat breakfast.

Next, block out everything you know about your company and your product, and scan your layouts:

- Is your headline instantly readable and understandable?

- Does it boldly present your product's main sales benefit in a clear and obvious fashion?

- Does your layout help the clarity and readability of your sales copy?

- Do the subheads in your sales copy clearly hit each of your product's other key sales benefits?

- Does the body copy of your marketing deliverable answer the most important questions an average reader has about your company's product?

- Does the reader clearly see what he/she has to do next—i.e., call your toll free number, visit your Web site, or contact a dealer or distributor?

In the few seconds you look at your layout, take note of the impressions that form in your mind: Often you will discover parts of your ad's sales copy that could be written more clearly, or see missing product details that first-time readers should know, or most important—you may spot a glaring omission, such as an important sales benefit, or product feature, not otherwise seen in the layout.

Figure 1-5:

Basic Sales Appeals Applied to Classic Trade, Industrial, and Business-to-Business Advertising: *All of these famous, successful trade and industrial ads produced over the past 50 years used basic, direct appeals to sell their products to tough-minded business prospects.*

Plain, direct, salesmanlike presentation in advertising and all other marketing projects is always more certain to generate inquiries and sales than many "creative" approaches.

Credits: THIS PAGE, top (L. to R.): Oliver Darling, Robert F. Millar. Bottom (L. to R.): Fletcher/Mayo Associates, Joe Serkowich/Larry Roth. OPPOSITE PAGE: Top (L. to R.): ESNA, Michael Tesch/Ally & Gargano. Bottom (L. to R.): Dick Haddad, Rick Whittey/Mintz & Hoke, Ralph Watts (Rockwell), Joseph Paonessa, Elmer Mellebrand (Campbell-Ewald).

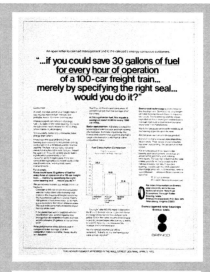

7.) Most marketing is ineffective in most markets, which is good for you

Bad marketing is all around you: Overstyled, ineffective advertising, weak direct mail pieces that go straight from the mail stack to the wastebasket, hard-to-navigate Web sites, and brochures that make the product a mystery to the reader. Everywhere you look, there's an emphasis on style and imagery over content, and a failure to provide the reader or viewer with solid product benefits and information.

Marketing programs in many companies have strayed far from the basic principles of salesmanship, and the clear and obvious presentation of their product's benefits. As mentioned previously, many companies succeed in spite of their marketing programs, by their size, by inertia, by luck, or on the backs of their sales reps. In other instances, marketers have been brainwashed by their ad agencies to believe that an ad with a clever headline, a shocking concept (see the Starbucks ad in **Figure 1-6**), or a provocative photo will sell their products.

The fact that most marketing is so bad is good for your company. If you follow the methods outlined in this book, any marketing deliverable you produce for your company, for any marketing project, and in any media, will be bolder, more persuasive, and more effective than most of the other ads or marketing deliverables from your competitors. Any ad or deliverable that uses the clear, direct, salesmanlike approaches outlined in this book will always generate more sales response than every other competitor's marketing message around it—in a trade publication, in a mailing, at a trade show, at a sales presentation, or on the Internet.

Following the methods described in this book, and learning to see your marketing projects with "new eyes," not only helps you produce better marketing projects for your company, it also helps you recognize all the bad marketing around you. And having the ability to see bad marketing helps you keep it out of your own company's marketing program.

8.) Always pick the boldest marketing option

Company marketing managers will often reject an advertising campaign or direct mail project featuring a bold headline, brutally honest sales copy, a fresh new sales message that tweaks the competition (or even their own company), in favor of the safe, watered-down version. This almost always turns out to be the wrong decision.

Any group effort, such as the development of marketing programs, tends to favor compromise and moderation. But whenever you are given the option of taking a bold step in your marketing program, remember that backing off and favoring the safe course usually does not yield a better result.

If you are fortunate enough to work with an ad agency or marketing consultant who knows how to create effective, salesmanlike marketing projects, and they've been brave enough to produce a bold marketing idea or deliverable that shakes up your company's established ways of selling its products and motivates prospects to buy, go with the boldest option they present to you.

Figure 1-6:

Stupid Marketing is Everywhere: *Bad advertising and poor marketing judgement, such as this Starbucks ad mocking the September 11th World Trade Center attacks, cost companies sales and customer goodwill*

NEWS **NYPOST.COM**

HOME | NEWS | COLUMNISTS | SPORTS | GOSSIP | POST OPINION | BUSINESS | ENTER

NATIONAL NEWS

STARBUCKS YANKS AD MOCKING 9/11

By JARED PAUL STERN and KATE SHEEHY

June 18, 2002 -- A Starbucks ad campaign has ground to a halt after concerns that its posters - including one displayed near Ground Zero - callously mimicked the Sept. 11 tragedy.

The tempest in a teapot revolved around 3,000 window displays touting summer tea brews by depicting two "twin" cups of the concoction standing side-by-side in tall, squared-off blades of grass with dragonflies dive-bombing into one of them.

CLUELESS IN SEATTLE:
This Starbucks ad near the WTC site takes a cheap shot at the Twin Towers.

The words "Collapse into Cool" are printed above the image.

If you believe that such an ad campaign, mailing, sales promotion or other deliverable has more than a good chance for success, and that any weaker alternative, or a compromised, watered-down version would generate weaker response, make this your rationale for defending your program to others in your company, and stand up for the bolder approach.

The need to execute bold marketing programs is even greater if your company is facing a critical sales and marketing situation, such as a major new competitor who threatens your company's market share, a major sales downturn, or an industry recession. Any adverse event requires new thinking, bold ideas, and aggressive action—and your company will be better off for having taken the bolder approach.

Of course, all bold marketing options also carry risk: A headline or layout that's stronger and more provocative than your company's usual advertising, a gutsy product feature comparison that stands your company's product right up to those of a much larger competitor, a new sales promotion that's never been tried before in your industry. And some bold marketing moves may pose too great a risk, such as a sales promotion that may threaten your company's successful and longstanding dealer and distributor networks.

However, when viewed in perspective, most of the risk of executing the bolder marketing option is outweighed by the potential upside gain your company can achieve. And in nearly every case, your company will be better off. Ask yourself: *What's the worst thing that could happen if we run with our boldest option?* You

Figure 1-7:

The Bolder Marketing Option is Nearly Always the Better Choice: When presented with a bold, out-of-the-box marketing concept (on left, below and on opposite page), each of these clients selected the safe, watered-down choice (at right) for their final version.

In retrospect, these clients would have been much better off had they selected the boldest options. Other clients, who selected the boldest options for marketing projects, usually achieved an increase in sales response.

The Bolder Option	*The Client's Final Choice*

The Bolder Option

The Client's Final Choice

The Bolder Option

The Client's Final Choice

might fail, but you probably would have failed anyway if you went with the weaker alternative. Worst case, your radical new sales promotion may generate less response than you had hoped, but there's an excellent chance that *what you learn from the experience* can be used to make your company's next, revised attempt a great success.

So, trust your marketing team. Stand fast, and have the courage and discipline to stick with the bold marketing concepts, deliverables, and other sales and marketing projects you believe in. Your company will be better for it, and the risk others see now will disappear in time.

9.) No matter how bleak the situation, there is always something you can do.

A marketing manager's career is never a continuous string of smooth and successful marketing projects. A new ad campaign or mailing may become a spectacular failure. A competitor introduces a surprise new product that may threaten your company's very existence. Adverse industry or economic conditions suppress the sales response of your marketing program.

Remember the words of Lt. General Harold G. "Hal" Moore (Ret.), who, as an American commander, successfully led his 395 men against 2,000 crack North Vietnamese Army regulars during the battle of Ia Drang, the first major battle of the Vietnam War.

His advice to his men: "Don't say 'there's nothing you can do.' There's always one more thing you can do."

When you are faced with a seemingly hopeless marketing situation, don't panic, or let yourself become paralyzed with fear: **Take action**. Most marketing projects are never complete failures. They usually contain one or two aspects that were either successful or, with modifications revealed by the project's outcome, could generate a better result in a new execution.

For example, prospect feedback from a mailing that generates poor response can tell you that a change in your product's pricing, or payment terms, could generate a better response next time. Re-targeting your marketing program to a new group of prospects, based on the comments you received from respondents to an ad placement that generated a poor response overall, could put your company's advertising program back on course. Uncover the parts of your marketing project that did work, build on these, and get a new series of marketing projects into action as fast as you can. The final chapter of this book (Chapter 18) covers the very specialized area of turnarounds in marketing programs in greater detail.

Every adversity, every failure, every heartache carries with it the seed of an equal or greater benefit.
—Napoleon Hill

Think like a man of action. Act like a man of thought.
—Henri Bergson

10.) Any marketing program can be improved by applying these principles

By focusing on swift and forceful marketing execution, by using clear, direct, salesmanlike sales copy and presentation in all of your marketing projects, and by applying the principles and techniques described in this book, a good marketing program can be made better, and an underperforming marketing effort can be dramatically improved. These efforts will yield equally dramatic improvements in sales response.

Of course, sometimes the problem has nothing to do with marketing. There are problems in companies, and with products, that are beyond the ability of any marketing manager, or any marketing program, to correct. A brilliant ad campaign or outstanding direct mail sales promotion won't save a bad product, or a product or service that no one wants to buy. In these cases, the problem goes beyond marketing, to product development, or into other areas of concern, such as company size, management's leadership ability, or financial standing.

However, if you take these first principles to heart, and work closely to the techniques described in this book, you will burn away the doubt in your mind that your marketing program could have been more clearly or forcefully presented, or could have been executed with greater competence or speed. Any good product, offered at a fair price, can be successfully marketed, using the techniques covered in this book.

How to Use this Book

If you have the time, you should read this book from cover to cover. Or, use *The Marketing Manager's Handbook* as a desk reference, and read it whenever you need information on executing any marketing project for your marketing program. For example, when you have a project that requires a direct mailing, or you need to plan and execute an advertising campaign or trade show, or any of the major types of marketing activities required in your marketing program, go to the relevant chapter in this book, and you will find the practical, step-by-step instructions you need to plan, specify, develop, and execute these projects for your marketing plan.

Unless otherwise noted, the examples used throughout this book to illustrate each type of marketing project are actual examples of work we have done for clients. In most cases, the marketing deliverables shown here have met or exceeded the goals of the clients for whom they were developed, generating positive sales and inquiry response. In all cases, they illustrate the proven concepts of bold, clear, salesmanlike presentation of products and services for trade, industrial, and business-to-business marketers. We encourage you to use the copy and layouts presented in these examples as "inspiration" in your own company's marketing projects.

Figure 1-8:

Plain, Direct, Salesmanlike Approaches are Always More Effective: The sales response for any ad, mailing, or other marketing deliverable can be increased dramatically by providing readers with clear, compelling sales benefits, and by giving them the feature and applications information that is relevant to what the prospect wants, instead of what your ad agency's copywriter thinks they need.

Before: An overproduced, underperforming trade ad

After: A better, more effective ad, using clear, powerful presentation

A Networked Digital Printer/Copier/Fax for Every Office, and a Zero Downtime Guarantee. . .

Small Office/ Home Office
1-5 employees

Mid-Sized Company
10-50 employees

Large Company /Department
75-150 employees

Pitney Bowes Office Systems is Now Imagistics. Lorem ipsum dolor sit amet, consectetur diam nonumy eiusmod tempor indidunt magna aliquam erat volupat. Ut enim ad mi nostrud exercitation ullamcorpor suscipit l ex ea commodo consequat. Lorem ipsum dolor sit amet, consectetur diam nonumy eiusmod tempor indidunt magna aliquam erat volupat. Ut enim ad mi nostrud exercitation ullamcorpor suscipit l ex ea commodo consequat.

Lorem ipsum dolor sit amet, consectetur diam nonumy eiusmod tempor indidunt magna aliquam erat volupat. Ut enim ad mi nostrud exercitation ullamcorpor suscipit l ex ea commodo consequat Lorem ipsum dolor sit amet, consectetur diam nonumy eiusmod tempor indidunt magna aliquam erat volupat. Ut enim ad mi nostrud exercitation ullamcorpor suscipit l ex ea commodo consequat.

Lorem ipsum dolor sit amet, consectetur diam nonumy eiusmod tempor.

Call 1-800-555-1234 or Link to www.imagistics.com

imagistics

Dependability is something to celebrate!

Use your Imagistics!

Corporate America has relied on Imagistics for office document solutions for more than 25 years. Imagistics (formerly Pitney Bowes Office Systems) delivers dependable digital copiers/printers, fans and multifunction document equipment, with impressive uptime and unparalleled direct service from over 1000 technicians nationwide. Document solutions from Imagistics help lower costs and improve productivity. For dependable document technology so...

Use your Imagistics!

imagistics

www.imagistics.com

COPIER/PRINTERS • FAXES • NETWORKED MULTIFUNCTION • XEROX • NATIONAL SERVICE & SUPPORT

YOUR MARKETING PLAN
CHAPTER 2
CHARTING THE COURSE
OF YOUR MARKETING PROGRAM

Your marketing plan is more than a static document, memo, or a spreadsheet: It's a plan of action that gives structure and direction to your company's marketing activities throughout the year.

In its most useful form, your marketing plan is a schedule that helps you keep your day-to-day management of all marketing projects on track. It helps you plan, execute, and manage the marketing projects that must be executed immediately, and, by providing a view toward the future, helps you anticipate and plan for marketing activities just over the horizon, so you can take important early steps necessary to insure the smooth execution of future marketing activities.

By helping you to determine which of your company's print ad layouts goes into next month's issue of what publication, which mailing must be developed and dropped to support an upcoming sales promotion three months from now, and what trade show must be planned for six months from now, your marketing plan gives you a clear view of all marketing activities both near, and further toward the horizon. Your marketing plan helps you to "stand above the action," indicating when you must turn your attention to the execution of any marketing project, far enough in advance to keep that project from becoming a last-minute fire drill that threatens the implementation of other important projects.

Every marketing plan should contain the following key elements:

- **The schedule of marketing projects**, by activity, of the company's marketing program, for a defined time period (by quarter, by year, or both);

- **A description of the marketing tools and marketing media**—the "marketing mix"—that will be used to execute these marketing projects;

- **The cost schedule of this program**, detailed by each activity in the marketing plan.

Your marketing plan serves the following goals in your job as a marketing manager:

As a company communication to senior management, your marketing plan is a documentation of the upcoming year's marketing projects required to meet your company's sales goals. The marketing plan keeps your senior management, sales, and finance staff aware and informed of the marketing projects that will be executed during the plan year;

As an action document for your staff, and for the other key outside members of your marketing team: Ad agency, marketing consultant, and other consultants and vendors. The marketing plan is the schedule of marketing activities that will take place in the upcoming year: The print advertising, by month, that must be scheduled, produced, and placed, the schedule of direct mail programs and promotions required for the year, production required for major trade shows during the year, and all other known marketing activities, scheduled as best as can be determined, for the upcoming year;

As a budget, the marketing plan details the cost of every marketing activity: Print display advertising costs, mailing, printing and postage costs, costs for creative, production, and execution services from ad agencies or marketing consultants, and all other costs directly related to the marketing plan. By setting the amount of expenditure for each activity in the plan, this allocation of funds in effect sets the priority of each activity for the upcoming year by your marketing team.

Developing Your Company's Marketing Plan

To the marketing manager, planning is a means, not an end: Your marketing efforts are handicapped without a plan, but marketing execution that generates sales response, not planning, is your job as a marketing manager. Planning is no substitute for marketing execution, since it is often the "best laid plans" that must be abandoned in the face of a sales downturn, a competitor's new product launch, or other unexpected business events.

The form or structure of your marketing plan is relatively unimportant. Your marketing plan may be a written narrative, like a business plan (in fact, many marketing plans are incorporated, verbatim, into business plans for start-ups and early-stage companies), or it may be as simple as a large spreadsheet, which is often the most useful form (see **Figure 2-2**). The most important background elements that underlie the content of any marketing plan are:

- **Marketing assessment**: The thinking and evaluation that goes into your plan before it is written, and serves as the underlying rationale for your plan;

- **The marketing mix:** The array of marketing tools, media, activities, and timing that comprise the plan;

- **Planning beyond your plan:** "Targets of opportunity," and other unexpected events that occur outside of your plan

In short, to develop your company's marketing plan, you must first assess your company, its products or services, its markets, current marketing activities, and your competition, use this assessment to shape your choice of the marketing activities required to meet your sales objectives, and allow for the unexpected events and opportunities that invariably occur while you are executing your plan.

1. Your Marketing Assessment

Your marketing assessment is the most important part of your marketing plan, and occurs before your marketing plan is even written. The marketing assessment is your personal evaluation of your products, markets, your company's current marketing activities, and where your company stands in its market, relative to the market, and your company's competitors. It is the process of thought and analysis that helps you to determine the "marketing mix" of marketing projects required to meet the requirements of the plan.

Your marketing assessment is a process of evaluating:

- **The existing methods** your company is using to market and sell its products or services;

- **The sales response** from these existing marketing efforts;

- **Changes and improvements required** to current marketing methods, deliverables, media or execution;

- **Upcoming, known marketing events**, such as product launches or sales promotions, that must be factored into your new plan;

- **Outline of other marketing efforts** required to support upcoming major new business development initiatives;

- **Changes and new developments in your market** having an impact on your marketing program;

- **Competitor assessment** and analysis

The degree of effort required for this assessment, and the extent of the changes that must be made when you develop your new marketing plan as a result of this assessment, depend on how well established your company is in its market, and on how well, or how poorly, your company's current marketing plan is performing.

In larger companies with long histories in their industries and markets, the shape, outlines, and content of their marketing plans may be fairly well established, reasonably successful, and, as a result, may require little change. For example, if you are a marketing manager in a well-established company, with proven methods of selling its products, there may be little wrong with your current marketing program. The only changes required in this situation usually involve improvements in marketing execution, and changes to a few marketing projects or deliverables to make them more effective, from a selling standpoint.

However, the marketing efforts in most companies, large or small, can always be improved. In fact, most marketing programs in most companies are, to some extent, damaged, and in need of repair. And this is nearly always true whenever a company hires a new marketing manager: Sales are down, the company's current run of marketing activities—ads, mailings, sales support—either aren't working, or aren't executed well, or on a timely basis. If you find yourself in this position as a newly-hired marketing manager, your marketing assessment will require more of your time, and will also require some early, stopgap measures to correct problems in your company's marketing deliverables or execution.

For start-up companies, or new product launches in new markets, there is no prior marketing program to assess, and you must therefore develop a marketing program from the ground up. Chapters 16 and 17 cover the special requirements of these marketing situations in extensive detail.

Companies in "turnaround" situations, with critical marketing, product, or sales problems, require special attention from marketing managers. The methods for identifying, evaluating, and reversing these more serious problems are covered extensively in Chapter 18.

Performing Your Marketing Assessment

1.) Identify the existing methods your company is using to market and sell its products or services, and assess the sales response from each of these existing marketing efforts

Identify all of the ways your company is currently marketing its products: Print ad campaigns, mailings, sales support, trade shows, Web site, PR. List any marketing activity your company has executed, requiring a hard-dollar expenditure, in the past year.

Next, assess the sales response from each marketing activity. Determine if any procedures were established to track sales response (inquiries generated or sales received) to advertising, mailing, Web site usage, trade show appearances, or any other marketing activity. Newly-hired marketing managers are often surprised to discover that their company's previous management did not think to track responses from ads, mailings, and other, easily-trackable marketing activities. In other cases, an ad agency was retained to run an "image" or "branding" advertising campaign at great expense, but with no provision made for tracking the response from the ads placed. Here, the lack of sales response to these campaigns is self-evident, since the ad agency has also been replaced, along with the marketing manager.

If no tracking system was put in place for ads or mailings, attempt to re-construct sales response by speaking with your company's sales reps or your sales manager. Usually, the best you can do is recall "anecdotal" information, such as instances where memory serves that a particular ad in a particular publication generated a greater number of calls than usual, or one sales promotion mailing generated many more inquiries than others. Anecdotal sales response information is better than none at all, so carefully note any instances where something has "gone right" with the marketing program. This may tell you that one or more trade publications, mailing lists, or other sales promotions have worked well in the past, and may be worth repeating in your new marketing plan.

Where a tracking system has been put in place and sales response can be measured, pull together the sales response (defined as inquiries generated or sales received) from each marketing activity in the prior plan year, from the following sources:

Ad placements and mailings: Records of sales response, tracked by each ad, for each issue. Reader service card inquiries received from ads in trade publications. Inquiries received from mailings, by mailing list, direct mail package, or direct mail sales promotion;

Trade shows: Number and quality of prospect booth inquiry coupons or business cards received from each trade show appearance. Other, anecdotal reports from sales reps and company management of major new sales accounts closed or business opportunities initiated from a trade show exhibition;

Web site: Total page views for your company's Web site, tracked by week and month. Page views, by key links/sections of your company's Web site (indicating the information site visitors view most often). Page views for specific Web links referenced in your company's advertising or direct mail programs;

Sales support: Average number of sales calls (phone, on-site, or both) required to close a sale ("calls to close" ratio). Duration of average "sales cycle," i.e., average time from first prospect inquiry to final sales close. Average time required for sales information kit to be mailed or e-mailed in response to prospect inquiries. Although the first two activities ("calls to close" and sales cycle) relate more to sales management, sales inquiry followup is an important marketing management issue, and delays in fulfillment of sales follow-up information kits and other materials (longer than same-day fulfillment to the interested prospect) are a common marketing problem;

PR and other "free media:" Sales response (inquiries or sales) received from trade and general business press coverage of your company and its products. Reader service card inquiries from articles, forwarded to your company from these publications.

Measure, compare, and analyze sales response for each marketing activity, comparing response within each activity (such as ad placements in one publication vs. others, mailings to one list vs, others) and response from one marketing activity to all others (print advertising vs. direct mail, etc.); all on a "cost-per-inquiry (or sale)" basis—i.e., cost of the activity divided by the number of inquiries (or sales) generated by that activity.

A side-by-side "by the numbers" analysis shows you the individual marketing activities that are more expensive, for results produced, than others, and the marketing activities within each category, such as an ad placement in a certain publication, or a trade show, that generated weaker response compared to other ad placements or trade shows.

As you evaluate your company's past marketing activities, you may discover that once again there are no results available for certain marketing activities previously described. Someone forgot to track them, or neglected to permanently record the results. On its own, this fact will point out the need for better response tracking in all future marketing projects.

2.) Changes and improvements required to current marketing methods, deliverables, media or execution

Ongoing analysis of sales response leads to your next step, an evaluation of the marketing activities that were executed in the previous plan.

Underperforming ads, mailings or other marketing projects are problems of:

Poor sales presentation in marketing deliverables: Lack of salesmanship, boldness, clarity, and simplicity in sales copy used in marketing deliverables, such as print advertising and brochure layouts, direct mail packages, and other tools used in your company's marketing activities. A related problem here also occurs when the lead sales benefit used in marketing deliverables is not recognized by your company's prospects as being meaningful or persuasive to them;

Poor prospect targeting: Sometimes, the wrong prospects, by job title, or even by entire industries or markets, have not been accurately targeted in the selection of trade publications, mailing lists, sales prospecting, and other marketing media used in the company's marketing mix;

Poor marketing execution: Often a major cause of poor sales response. Ad deadlines are missed, major mistakes and production errors occur in mailings, and in development of other marketing projects for the company. Poor marketing execution leads to delays, lost opportunities, and rushed, substandard final versions of marketing deliverables;

Poor allocation of dollars in the marketing mix: This occurs when a company spends too much of its total marketing budget on marketing activities that generate poor sales response. For example, a company will often spend substantial amounts of money on print display advertising, a notoriously risky marketing expense that often produces poor results. If the company had spent most of that amount on more direct mailings, or on booth spaces at more trade shows, it would probably generate a higher sales response for its marketing dollar.

In most cases, your company's ad agency, marketing consultant, and other outside vendors are responsible for the development and execution of marketing deliverables. Too many mistakes or delays in execution of marketing projects requires a close examination of how these problems occurred, or may even lead to replacement of your company's ad agency or marketing consultant.

Problems of poor sales response may also be caused by factors outside the area of marketing, such as a poorly-performing, overpriced, or uncompetitive product, insufficient financial resources, or poor selling skills or execution. These are fundamental business, financial, or market problems that may or may not be correctable by an improvement in marketing skill.

Solutions to many of these more extreme marketing problems, outlined above, are covered in further detail in Chapter 18.

3.) Upcoming, known marketing events, such as product launches or sales promotions, that must be factored into your new plan

Your new marketing plan must support any new major marketing events in your company during the upcoming plan year, such as product launches, sales promotions, seasonal promotions, and trade show exhibitions. Each of these new projects will require their own discrete marketing projects to support and promote the major marketing activity.

For example, new product launches will require specialized mailings to customers and prospects, display ad placements, and trade media announcements. Marketing support for sales promotions will require coordination with your company's sales manager, to time the execution of a specialized mailing to selected customers and prospects, and to allow for telephone follow-up by your company's sales reps to each individual on the mailing list. Booth spaces for trade shows must be reserved months in advance, and deliverables for the show, such as trade show booths, signage and collateral, must be developed in time, along with the advance planning required for mailings and specialized ad placements to support the show. **Figure 2-2** shows a method for scheduling special marketing events and incorporating them into your marketing plan.

4.) Outline of other marketing efforts required to support upcoming major new business development initiatives

You and the other members of your company's management team may have plans to launch major new business development initiatives, such as joint ventures with other companies in your industry, or a new marketing effort for your company's products in a new market.

To demonstrate your company's marketing capabilities during early joint venture and business development meetings with potential corporate partners, these efforts will require development of presentation materials for high-level meetings and presentations to senior management and boards of directors at partner companies, and development of prototype advertising campaigns and other marketing materials ("comps"). Once a joint venture or other joint marketing relationship has been established, you will often be responsible for working with your counterparts at these companies to plan and coordinate the execution of marketing projects to sell the products or services offered as part of the joint relationship: Media events and announcements, advertising campaigns, and sales meetings with dealers and distributors.

5.) Changes and new developments in your market having an impact on your marketing program

Identify new conditions or changes in your industry or market's business environment having an effect on your marketing plan in the new plan year.

Industry economic conditions: First among these are industry economic conditions. A booming industry requires an equally aggressive marketing program. A surging economy creates conditions that make it easier to sell your company's products, but it also masks a multitude of sins in company marketing programs. The longer an economic upswing, the more money wasted on unproductive marketing programs, such as corporate "image" advertising, and expensive launches into new and unproven marketing projects. Marketing managers need to be especially watchful of these lapses in discipline during boom periods, because they lead to the development of an attitude that assumes the boom times will go on forever, and denies the initial onset of poor marketing results that grow deeper as economic conditions decline.

Ironically, stagnant or poor economic conditions in your industry are the times when you must take the most risks, and be the most aggressive, in your marketing plan. Many companies have increased their sales and long-term market share by increasing their advertising and marketing budgets during recessions, while their competitors cut back on theirs.

During poor economic periods, companies also do well when they take a more aggressive stance in their marketing programs. Sales copy needs to be even more aggressive, and even more benefits-oriented, in all advertising, sales materials, and other marketing deliverables. In an industry downturn, buyers look for greater value, economy and productivity from the products and services they buy. If your company's product or service provides users with a cost savings in their operations, or higher productivity compared to current methods, systems, or processes, you must hit these benefits even harder in the sales copy and presentation of your marketing deliverables.

Also, during poor economic conditions in your company's market, give careful thought to developing new sales and pricing promotions for current customers and prospects, special pricing announcements, and other promotional ideas to boost sales during flat periods, as needed. Always better to have some special sales promotion mailings, ads, or e-mail announcements "in your pocket," ready to use whenever a slow sales month needs a boost.

Pricing and distribution: Pricing pressure on your company's products may force changes to your company's distribution structure, which also affects the form and direction of your new marketing plan. This often occurs in distribution of high-technology products where, as time passes, a product's price falls. As a product's price decreases, its distribution methods gradually evolve, from its original network of distributors, OEMs or dealers, to direct sales from the company to end users. This same change also occurs as a function of a company's length of time in business. As prospects in its market become familiar with a company, and as the company builds its reputation in its field, it eventually finds itself selling more of its products directly to end users, bypassing its distribution networks.

Changes in price pressure influencing distribution in your market may never occur, may occur slowly over several years, or may happen quickly and disruptively in response to technological innovations or other events. These potential changes in your market require extensive restructuring of your marketing plan. For example, a company's advertising, direct mail, and trade show marketing programs must shift their emphasis away from promoting sales to distributors, to sending prospects directly to one of your company's sales reps. A company's field distributor sales and support staff is transformed into an aggressive direct field sales force that must be supported by a marketing plan that drives interested prospects to these company sales reps. The company must establish other direct sales channels, such as direct sales from the company's Web site, or sales through the company's in-house telemarketing and customer support team. Each of these changes requires new marketing projects that must be incorporated into the new plan.

Changes to regulatory requirements and industry standards: New government regulations and other events, such as new industry-wide technical or engineering standards, may present new opportunities for your marketing program. For example, if your company's product helps your market meet a new regulatory requirement, or conform to a new industry standard, sales copy and marketing deliverables in your new marketing plan should reflect this new fact.

6.) Competitor assessment and analysis

As you develop your marketing plan, you should spend a substantial amount of your planning time assessing your competitors, their strengths and weaknesses, and, especially—how your competitors market their products, and what you can learn from them.

A close examination of your competitors shows where your company stands relative to all others in its field. For marketers, it helps reveal how your company should position its products, the best marketing media and methods your company should use to sell its products, and other tactics your company should use to exploit your market's current competitive situation.

Your first step in assessing your competitors is to gather as much intelligence on them as possible:

How your competition markets, advertises, and promotes their products: Research trade publications in your industry to reconstruct your competitors' space advertising schedules. Using a friend, your ad agency account executive, or a relative's name and address, request all of your competitors' sales information kits. Read and study how your competitors "talk" about their products in their sales copy used in advertising, sales materials, industry news articles, and other marketing channels;

Your competitors' reputations: Talk to your sales reps, customers, prospects, and others in your industry about your competition. Learn how well, or how poorly, they are regarded in your field. Anecdotal information may reveal weaknesses in a competitor's business area, such as poor customer service, that could be addressed, for example, by more forceful presentation of your company's superior customer service capabilities in your own company's advertising;

Public source information: Check out your competitors' Web sites, particularly their current news and new product announcement links. Run a Dun & Bradstreet report on your major competitors. Credit history and outstanding litigation will tell you about your competitors' financial condition and, in general, how they do business in your field. Other open-source information, such as public company SEC disclosure documents, often yields useful inside information, such as a company's assessment of its current products and marketing programs. Because of SEC disclosure requirements for public companies, this information is often more revealing than the information the company presents to its market.

Constant and careful examination of this background information will help you to know your competitors, their marketing programs, and their new product plans.

Do what your competitors are doing—and what they're not: One of the keys to developing a marketing plan that builds on your company's strengths and exploits competitors' weaknesses is to strike a balance between using marketing methods and media that have already been proven effective by your competitors, and executing new marketing projects, in new media, that your competitors aren't using.

For example, if your competitors run heavy advertising schedules, but no direct mail programs, you should explore direct mail as an option in your new marketing plan. A coordinated program of targeted direct mailings, followed up with phone calls from your company's sales reps, is usually a far more effective marketing technique than any competitor's print display advertising campaign.

A competitor who makes a splash by running a heavy schedule of new display ads for a few months isn't necessarily generating sales response from those ads. Companies hire and fire ad agencies, often in quick succession, so a new ad campaign that looks imposing in the first month may have run out its string a few months later. However, if many of your competitors have been running their advertising in your industry's major trade publications month after month, this is likely to be a sign that display advertising is effective for your type of product or service, and that your company should be "in there" with an ad schedule of its own.

Print advertising, however, carries high risk for trade and business-to-business marketers, and just because your competitors are running full pages in your industry's trade publications does not mean your company has to match them in size and frequency: Often, fractional ad sizes, such as half- and quarter-page sizes, can be just as effective as full pages (see Chapter 9 for full coverage of advertising execution and placement strategy).

This "hit 'em where they ain't" strategy can be applied to any area where you discover weaknesses in the competitor's product features, customer service, or marketing program. This can be a bold move, such as running ads and mailings pointing out the major product differences between your company's products and those of a named competitor. Other marketing options, such as improving the amount and quality of useful product and customer service information featured on your company's Web site, compared to your competitors' Web sites, can give your company an important advantage in its marketing presentation.

2. Determining Your Marketing Mix

Once you have evaluated your company's previous marketing plan and its sales results, by performing the marketing assessment detailed in the previous section, you are now ready to focus on the task of developing your company's new marketing plan.

The core of this new marketing plan is its **marketing mix**, the combination of:

- **Marketing projects:** Ad campaigns, direct mailings, sales support activities, or trade shows;

- **Marketing media**: Trade publications, mailing lists, trade shows and other third-party "distribution channels" that carry the marketing deliverables you execute for your plan;

- **Marketing deliverables:** Ad layouts, direct mail packages, brochures, Web pages and the other work products used in marketing projects;

- **Costs:** The cost of each marketing project in your plan.

Developing your company's marketing plan is, in effect, a process of deciding on the mix of marketing projects required to reach the prospects in the target markets you've selected for your company's marketing program. The importance of each marketing project in your plan is often defined by the amount of marketing dollars you devote to each type of "marketing media" in your plan. The marketing media and deliverables associated with each major type of marketing project are shown in **Figure 2-1.**

Determining Your Marketing Plan's Marketing Mix

For Well-Established Companies: Stable Planning, with a Focus on Continued Strong Presentation and Execution in the Marketing Mix

If you are a marketing manager in a stable, well-established company, your plan's marketing mix may already be quite well defined. Here, it's likely that you already know the trade publications in your industry that produce the best results for your print advertising, whether or not certain mailing lists or types of direct mail projects have worked to generate sales response, and, in general, the best ways to market and sell your company's products.

In well-established companies, if changes to marketing plans are made, it is likely they will be made to improve the company's **marketing presentation** or **marketing execution**: To better "tell the story" of your company's product or service, its benefits, features, and uses to potential buyers in your market, or to increase the speed and effectiveness of the marketing team's execution of its marketing projects.

The need for changes in marketing presentation can usually be identified by sales copy in print advertising, mailings, sales materials, and other marketing deliverables that doesn't persuasively convince readers to respond to the ad, mailing,

Figure 2-1:

The Marketing Mix— Marketing projects, media and deliverables used in most marketing plans

Marketing Project:	Marketing Media used for executing the marketing project:	Marketing Deliverables used in the execution of marketing projects:
Trade advertising	Major industry, trade, and business publications	Print advertising layouts
Direct mail	Mailing lists of potential prospects, rented from third-party list owners and list brokers, or self-compiled	Direct mail packages and associated elements: Brochures, cover letters, envelopes and reply coupons
Sales support	Your company's in-house and field sales force	Sales information kits: Brochures, flyers, sales videos, and other presentation materials
Dealer/distributor support	Your company's third-party dealers, distributors, and sales networks	Sales information kits: Catalog sheets, sales flyers, co-op advertising layouts
Trade shows	Major industry trade shows, conferences, and exhibitions	Trade show booth, signage, booth video, associated trade show flyers and handouts
Web site	The Internet serves as the electronic medium for your company's marketing efforts	Web page and interface design and development, CGI scripting, Web video and multimedia

or other marketing piece they are reading or viewing. These problems are revealed during your marketing assessment, when poor sales response leads you to the conclusion that the company's new advertising program doesn't pull as well as the company's previous advertising, when the company's sales materials tend to raise more questions from prospects than they answer, and when the company's sales reps criticize the company's marketing program for being "disconnected" from the true needs and wants of their prospects.

If a company has a well-established product and a solid sales track record for that product, and if there are no other external factors suppressing the response to your product (such as the recent introduction of a better product at a lower price from a competitor, or an industry downturn), sales response can often be improved by improving the **marketing presentation** of your company's marketing deliverables. This means using clear, forceful, salesmanlike presentation of the benefits of your company's products or services to its market. This is done by making the headlines, sales copy and layouts used in the company's marketing programs harder hitting, more persuasive, and more focused on *what your prospects want* from your product, instead of what your ad agency's copywriter or marketing consultant *thinks they need.*

The need for better marketing execution is apparent in the day-to-day implementation of your marketing program, where creative and production delays lead to missed deadlines, or where the quality of marketing deliverables has been compromised by being rushed to completion, because these deliverables weren't given sufficient time to be developed to their fullest potential. At best, constant, underlying, poor **marketing execution** saps the energy and enthusiasm of the company's marketing team like the common cold. At their worst, incidents of poor marketing execution—a critical ad placement that was missed, a serious production mistake in a mailing, an important, high-level sales presentation not properly supported, or production of trade show materials that missed the show date—are lost selling opportunities that ultimately represent lost sales revenue for your company.

Changes needed to correct problems due either to marketing presentation or marketing execution in your established marketing program are usually linked to your company's ad agency or marketing consultant, who is responsible for the creation, production, and day-to-day execution of your company's marketing projects. Your ad agency or consultant needs to do a better job of presenting and selling your company's product in marketing deliverables, needs to do a better job of marketing execution and follow-through, and, overall, needs to be more attentive to your company as a client. In many cases, and especially where poor deliverables have been produced for too long, or a ball has been dropped once too often, this may require you to replace your ad agency or marketing consultant with a firm that can do a better job for your company.

Adding new marketing projects to your plan: An established company fortunate enough not to experience major problems in either its marketing presentation or marketing execution can usually continue the execution of its existing marketing mix, largely unchanged, into the new plan year, with the exception of adding the new marketing projects required to support new product launches and other new business development initiatives for the company during the new plan year.

If new marketing projects are required to support the launch of new products within your company's existing product line, it is possible that the marketing media (such as trade publications and mailing lists) used to market these new products will be the same as those used for your company's existing products. However, new marketing deliverables must be developed to support these new projects, and the additional creative and production costs need to be included in your marketing plan's budget. Likewise, new marketing channels and new media should always be researched with any new product launch to determine alternative marketing options.

If your company is planning to launch a product in a new and unfamiliar market, or plans to launch other new business initiatives, such as a joint venture or joint marketing relationship with another company, the marketing mix of media, projects, and deliverables required to support these initiatives, to the extent they are known, must also be included in your new marketing plan.

Your new marketing plan will operate under your company's overall marketing budget, established on either a "percentage-of-sales" basis (see the budgeting section, further in this chapter), or under your own company's specific budgeting policies.

For Young, High-Growth Companies: New Business Development Requires Continuous Market Analysis and Changes to the Marketing Mix

Marketing managers in young companies with rapidly-growing sales, generated by the success of their current marketing mix, are usually faced with the challenge of scaling up their current success to achieve higher sales revenues in the new plan year.

From a planning perspective, there are two elements to the process of scaling up the marketing plan for the high-growth company. The first element involves increasing and broadening the number, frequency, and reach of the marketing projects in the company's current marketing mix. Second, and more important, new marketing projects must be executed to support new product launches and other new business development initiatives for this fast-growing company.

Expanding the current marketing mix: As a marketing manager in a high-growth company, you must make plans to scale up your company's current marketing mix in the new plan year. Below are some examples of how a company's existing use of major marketing media are scaled up in high-growth marketing plans:

- **Direct mail:** Mailing larger quantities to targeted mailing lists that have proven successful, and testing a broader range of new mailing lists;

- **Sales support:** As more sales reps are hired, for different business areas, their efforts must be supported by expanded prospect follow-up (sales kits, mailings);

- **Trade shows:** Expand the company's trade show booth exhibitions to other key trade shows in the industry;

- **Print advertising:** Run new ad schedules in new publications in your field and, as a lower priority, increase page sizes and frequencies of your company's existing print advertising schedule.

With some high-growth companies, the issue for the new plan year is not so much one of an increase in current marketing activities, but of expansion of the marketing mix into new marketing media. For example, if your company is currently using direct mail and trade shows in one year, you may decide to expand your marketing mix, by adding a print advertising campaign in your new marketing plan. You may also decide to add a series of press release mailings to promote story ideas for your company in your industry's trade press, establishing PR as a new element in your plan's marketing mix.

Planning for new business development: A substantial amount of a high-growth company's sales revenue is derived from new business development activities: Closing major new sales accounts, new product launches in existing and new markets, establishing joint ventures, private-label marketing deals, and major new marketing alliances with large corporations. It is likely you will be aware of the broad outline of at least some of these major new initiatives while developing your new plan, so you will need to consider the marketing projects needed to support these new initiatives, and incorporate these into your new marketing plan.

From a budgeting standpoint, many marketing managers in early-stage, high-growth companies hold an additional 10% of their total projected marketing budget, over and above their new plan's total marketing budget, as a reserve to fund the marketing efforts required to support these new business development projects.

For Start-Ups, New Product Launches, and Turnarounds: Bold Experimentation, Testing, _Reality_, and Response

Establishing a marketing mix for a start-up, or for established companies launching new products in unfamiliar new markets, is a process of bold experimentation, careful testing, and fast, forceful execution. This is often a process of trying the best variety of marketing options that a start-up's management team can conceive to market their product, realistically assessing the results, and then pushing harder with the marketing activities that work.

Since these initial marketing efforts often yield poor sales response, marketing managers in these types of companies must acknowledge the reality of their situation, and turn their marketing plans around quickly to adjust to the realities of this market response, changing their marketing deliverables, prospect targeting, distribution methods and other key factors to find more effective and successful ways to sell their company's products.

The marketing tradecraft necessary for marketing managers in start-ups, product launches, and turnaround situations is extensive and specialized. For this reason, the last three chapters of this book (Chapters 16-18) cover marketing planning, development, and execution in these special marketing situations.

Sample Marketing Plan

Figure 2-2 shows an actual example (in Microsoft Excel spreadsheet format) of a portion of a master marketing plan and schedule. Each of the major marketing projects and marketing media are shown for each market or business line addressed by the plan (for this example, the company's engineering market). Individual marketing projects, and the total costs for each project, are shown for each month of the plan, in summary form.

Figure 2-2:

Example Marketing Plan, Schedule, and Budget (Microsoft Excel spreadsheet format)

Sample PLAN (FINAL EXAMPLE)

Combined Marketing Plan and Budget

Version: 12/16/02

Engineering Market							
Project Description	**Unit Cost:**	**January** Activity	**Cost**	**February** Activity	**Cost**	**March** Activity	**Cost**
Direct Mail							
Standard - #10 pkg.	1.00	Custom Mapping Pkg. (to Existing Customers)	2000	Nat'l Soc Env. Consultants Test		1000 Prospects Since 2/94	2000
		Prospects - Since 8/93 (Custom Map Pkg.)	1000	TED	3000 TED		
		NAHB Mailing	2000			NAHB Mailing	2000
Display Advertising							
Hazmat 1/6 or L/S	900.00	P/E 1/6 or L/S	900.00	P/E 1/6 or L/S	900.00	Hazmat 1/6 or L/S	900
P/E 1/6 or L/S	900.00	NatEnvJnl Jan/Feb	900	Env. Pro. 1/6 or L/S		Env. Pro. 1/6 or L/S	900
Env. Pro. 1/6 or L/S	900.00	Nation's Building News	2500	Nation's Building News	2500	NatEnvJnl Ad Mar/Apr	900
NatEnvJnl Ad 1/6 or L/S	900.00					Land Development	400.00
Nation's Building News	2500.00						
Land Development	400.00						
FAX Broadcasting							
Est. @ 50/Msg.		Special Price On Custom Maps (to support mailing)	600	Custom Sales Rep Price Flyer (Like E.L. FAX)	600	Inactive Customer Special Pricing	600
		NAHB Promo					
Postcard Decks							
Hazmat (1X) MAR, MAY, JUL, NOV	1339.00						
P/E (1X) MAR, MAY, JUL, SEP, NOV	1800.00						
Env. Protection(1X) JAN, APR, JUL, OCT	1747.00	Env. Protection	1747				
Wiley Engr (VC) (1X) FEB, MAY, OCT	1767.00						
W/W & Env. (Wiley) Mar, Aug	1767.00						
Press Releases							
		NAHB Announcement	250		250	NAHB Announcement	250
		Custom Mapping Announcement	250	TED	250 TED		
Trade Show Support							
Booth Signage	1000.00	NAHB	4000	Hazmat South	4000	Hazmat Central	4000
Collateral/Other							
3/C Brochures	1.50	Print 3,500 3/C Bro.	5250		5250	Print 3,500 3/C Bro.	5250
Slide Guides	0.43	TBD	1000	TBD	1000	TBD	1000
Other/Targets of Opportunity	1000.00	Miscellaneous	1000	Miscellaneous	1000	Miscellaneous	1000
Miscellaneous	1000						
Agency							
GAA	3000	GAA	3000	GAA	3000	GAA	3000
Product Line Total (Engineering)			26997		18450		24200

Sheet1 / Sheet2 / Sheet3

• **The individual marketing projects shown in this plan**—direct mail, display advertising, postcard decks, etc.—constitute the marketing plan's marketing mix for one of this company's markets (engineering)

• **Monthly columns** show the marketing activities scheduled to occur in each month, and their costs. These include mailings and advertising for special sales promotions and new product launches in each given month

• **Single "Project Description" column** shows all marketing projects and marketing media scheduled for the year, and total costs for each project

This plan format provides a useful top-down view of all the company's marketing activities scheduled for the plan year. Totals and other key data lines from other, subsidiary worksheets, providing greater detail for each marketing activity, such as those for tracking response to direct mailings (shown in Chapter 7), and those for tracking advertising response (Chapter 9), can be linked to this master spreadsheet. This way, changes made to a more detailed spreadsheet covering a specific marketing activity, such as the company's schedule of direct mailings, their individual component costs, and response rates, can be linked into the summary cells in this overall marketing plan.

Budgeting for Your Marketing Plan

The total marketing budget required to fund your company's marketing plan can be established in one of three ways:

- **Convention:** Many small companies run ad hoc marketing programs, spending more or less the same amount on proven marketing activities (such as their Yellow Pages ads), mailings, trade shows, and other marketing efforts. They will spend more on marketing in one year, over another, depending on whether or not the business owner believes he/she is having a "good" year. In effect, these companies treat their entire marketing effort as one big target of opportunity, following the "we've always done it this way" school of hit-or-miss marketing planning;

- **Industry standards:** Many mid-sized businesses carefully observe their competitors' marketing programs, and combine this intelligence with whatever industry-standard data is available from trade associations or accounting sources, to arrive at an industry standard amount for their own company's marketing budget, usually expressed as a percentage of total annual sales. This ratio may be higher or lower in one industry compared to another, depending on the industry, and its maturity;

- **Percentage-of-sales:** Many start-ups and young, high-growth companies spend 15% of their projected yearly total sales on their "marketing and sales expense." This amount is often divided evenly between the company's "marketing expense" (the activities and media used to generate demand for the company's product, and to support the company's sales force), and the company's "sales expense," the personnel and other related cost of maintaining a sales force. A company may spend more than half on marketing, or more than half on sales, depending on whether or not it finds that it can generate more sales more efficiently by putting additional sales reps in the field, or by spending more on marketing activities to drive prospects to its existing sales force.

Of the three methods, the percentage-of-sales method offers the best approach to establishing a "stake in the ground" for your company's total marketing budget. Once the total marketing budget amount is established, the amount to be spent on each of the individual components of your company's marketing mix—advertising, direct mail, trade shows, etc.—are determined, depending on your type of company, its previous marketing track record, and the success or failure of those prior marketing efforts.

In addition to using the percentage-of-sales method for establishing their overall marketing budgets, many marketing managers also hold back up to 10% of this amount as a reserve to handle unexpected marketing events and various new, unforeseen "targets of opportunity" in their marketing plans (see next section).

3. Planning Beyond Your Plan: "Targets of Opportunity" and the Unexpected

Depending on the size and growth stage of your company—start-up, early growth phase, more established mid-sized company, or a well-established product line division of a large company—you must allow for the unexpected as you develop your marketing plan.

Events, both positive and negative, have a way of tossing your best-laid marketing plans:

- **A competitor slashes the price of his product**, forcing your company to counter with a series of special sales promotions for its own product line;

- **A major corporation wants to distribute your company's product**, and wants your company to handle the marketing execution for this new distribution deal;

- **Another major corporation enters your market** with a product directly competitive to yours, matched with a huge print advertising campaign in your industry's major trade publications;

- **An opportunity presents itself** to launch a new effort to market your company's products in an entirely new market, creating the need to develop and execute a new marketing program in this new market.

Each of these scenarios will force a change or addition to your marketing plan, and tests your imagination and fortitude as a marketing manager.

Positive developments, such as new business development and other "targets of opportunity," will often require that new, additional marketing programs be created, produced, and executed to sell products into these new opportunities, industries, and markets. You must draw on your skills in marketing execution to manage the development of the ad campaigns, mailings, sales collateral, and other deliverables required to market and sell your company's product in these new areas of opportunity.

Negative developments require even greater levels of courage, resourcefulness, and imagination. An advertising campaign that fails to generate response, a major competitive blow to your company's product, or declining sales from a trusted distribution channel place even greater emphasis on the need for skilled marketing execution.

In both positive and negative situations, knowledge of the marketer's tradecraft required to use all of the marketing tools available to your company, combined with skillful execution, help you make the needed changes to your marketing plan.

TOOLS OF THE TRADE
CHAPTER 3
MARKETING METHODS, DELIVERABLES, AND MEDIA

As a marketing manager, you must not only know how to execute your marketing plan, you must know the best marketing tools for selling your company's products. You'll need to know when to use them, and the right mix of marketing tools required for your plan's success. This is the first step in learning the tradecraft required to turn your company's marketing program from a risky expense, into an investment in higher sales.

This chapter is an overview of the marketing elements and deliverables described in detail in the next 12 chapters, and describes the thought processes that you must use as a marketing manager to evaluate the best ways to sell your company's product or service. This chapter covers the major types of marketing tools available to most marketing managers, evaluates their strengths and weaknesses, and starts you on the road to determining the right tools to use, in the right combinations, to turn individuals into prospects, and to turn prospects into buyers of your company's products.

To Find the Best Marketing Methods, Make Use of All Marketing Tools

There are usually one or two marketing methods that work best to sell a company's product, but these best approaches can only be found by using skillful marketing tradecraft and execution to test a variety of marketing methods. Once you find the one (sometimes two) best ways to generate sales response for your company, you must continue to test new marketing approaches in other marketing media, both as a means of continuing the process of building up your company's marketing mix to increase your company's sales response, and as a hedging strategy against the sudden decline in sales effectiveness of your best current marketing methods.

Marketing is the combination of different marketing projects, used in the "marketing media" of trade publications, mailing lists, trade shows, news coverage, and the Internet. Some companies, in some markets, will spend most of their marketing dollars on direct mail and trade shows, and less on display advertising. In these companies, advertising is used to reinforce the company's main marketing push in direct mail and trade show appearances. Other companies focus their marketing efforts in support of their company's field sales force, who carry most of the burden of selling the company's products, and use advertising, direct mail, and other marketing tools to generate leads for their sales reps. Some new Internet-based companies may generate most of their sales on their Web site, through "viral marketing," and may spend virtually no marketing dollars in traditional print advertising or direct mail. In most cases, companies can only find the best ways to market their products by trying all ways, and then finding out what works.

Developing a company's best "marketing mix" is a result of the company's experience in its industry, based on trial-and-error, or, in well-established companies, is based on the ways companies "have always done it" in their industries. Well-established companies tend to know the top trade publications in their field read by their prospects, the most-attended trade shows, their best standard promotional mailings, and these companies become accustomed to marketing and selling their products in these ways.

Established companies usually continue to do well until they become complacent, and allow their marketing programs to become less effective in their impact and less relevant to their markets. When this happens, the company's marketing plan becomes stagnant and unresponsive, its marketing deliverables soft and ineffective. This provides the perfect opportunity for an upstart competitor, using more aggressive sales copy and more imaginative marketing techniques, delivered with faster execution, to gain market share, snapping the older company out of its complacency. You could be the marketing manager in this upstart competitor, or the newly-hired marketing manager in the older, well-established company, charged with turning around the company's flagging sales. In either case, the marketing tools and techniques described in this book will help you to run a vigorous, effective marketing program.

The need for fast, flexible, skillful execution is even greater for start-ups, in young, high-growth companies, and for new product launches in established companies. Wherever a marketing program must be created from scratch, a knowledge of all of the marketing "tools of the trade," combined with skill in their execution, develops marketing programs that sell products.

Finding the Best Ways to Market Your Company's Products

Any new marketing project begins with a three-step process of:

- **Identifying the best sales prospects** for your company's product or service;

- **Locating those prospects** wherever they are;

- **Applying the best marketing tool(s)** to reach these prospects

As obvious as this may seem, many companies have wasted billions of dollars in marketing expense by making the wrong choice at any one of these steps—or in not following them at all.

Identifying Your Company's Sales Prospects

As you read this book, you will note the importance stressed on relying on your company's sales reps as an invaluable source of information, advice, and direction to your work as a marketing manager. When thinking about your company's best prospects, it helps to think like a salesman who has just been given the responsibility of selling your company's product or service. Here are the questions a salesman would typically ask when "scoping out" a new business-to-business sales assignment:

- **In what markets or industries** would we find the most likely buyers of our product?

- **Within these markets or industries**, what are the types of companies who would be the most likely buyers?

- **Who are these companies**, and where are they?

- **Within these companies, who would be the key person** most likely to buy our product?

- **What is the single characteristic, such as a job title**, or a prior history of using or buying products similar to ours, that identifies these prospective buyers?

You may already know this information, but if you're new to your company, you can get answers to these questions as you conduct your "sales rep's de-brief" in the sales copywriting steps detailed in the next chapter (Chapter 4). Although there may be more than one or two best answers to the questions above, you are looking for a consensus opinion from your company's sales reps that points you to your company's one or two best kinds of prospects, not a laundry list of all the prospects your company's sales reps call on.

Locating Your Company's Sales Prospects

Once these questions are answered, down to the level of identifying the likely prospects for your company's product, the next set of questions relate specifically to your role in developing and executing marketing projects to reach these prospects:

- What **trade publications** do these prospects subscribe to?

- What **trade shows** and conferences do they attend each year?

- What **trade associations** do they belong to?

- What **Web sites** do these prospects link to, or "visit," on a regular basis?

- How do our **competitors** currently market and sell their products to these prospects?

- What **other companies** currently sell products, complimentary to our company's products, to these prospects?

These are the essential questions asked by any experienced marketing manager. The answers to these questions reveal the resources available to your marketing program, and the marketing tools required to reach these prospects (such as these shown in **Figure 3-1**).

Every newly-hired marketing manager should spend their first week on the job collecting the information required to answer these questions. Once in hand, every successful marketing manager will carefully evaluate this information before developing their own marketing plan.

Applying the Best Marketing Tools to Reach the Prospects in Your Company's Market

After defining your prospects, and identifying the relevant marketing media (such as trade publications and mailing lists) and marketing tools used in these media to reach them, you are now ready to examine each marketing option available to you, and assess each marketing tool's importance and priority in your marketing plan.

The next section outlines the major marketing tools and marketing media used by trade and business-to-business marketers, how they're used, their advantages and disadvantages, and major issues and concerns for each.

Overview of Marketing Tools and Media

Direct Mail

Direct mail, also known as direct response, describes a wide range of marketing activities, from mailings of small numbers of direct mail packages to select, high-quality prospect lists, to mailings of large numbers of pieces to "rented" mailing lists

Figure 3-1:

Finding Prospects in Your Company's Market—Media and tools required for your marketing plan

Points of contact in your company's market:	**Marketing media and tools** used to reach these prospects in your company's market:
Trade publications read by prospects	Display advertising, subscriber mailing lists (direct mail), and editorial (PR)
Trade shows attended by prospects	Trade show booth space exhibit opportunities (trade shows)
Trade associations where these prospects can be found	Trade association mailing lists (direct mail) and conferences (trade shows)
Web sites visited by prospects	Content, design, and function of your company's Web site; Web video and audio (video and multimedia); possible online advertising or link-exchange opportunities with related industry Web sites
Competitors currently selling to these prospects	Analysis of competitors' marketing programs (all marketing tools and media)
Other companies selling complimentary products	Analysis of potential joint ventures, co-marketing deals, or other high-level business relationships (sales support)

of subscribers to trade publications in your industry, and mailings to customer lists to upsell or cross-sell your company's current customers with new product announcements or special offers.

The mailing list used in any direct mail project is its most important element, and is the most critical factor in the success or failure of any mailing. Mailing lists can be rented from third-party sources, such as publication subscriber lists, or from other companies, who rent out their own buyer lists.

However, the best, most effective lists for most trade and industrial marketers are self-compiled lists. These are highly-targeted prospect and customer lists that you compile on your own initiative, from trade association member lists, Internet research, publications (such as the *Thomas Register of Manufacturers*), and other sources, including your own customer lists. The most effective self-compiled lists are those where the prospect has been recently identified at the company, by name, job title, and phone number, via telephone follow-up from someone in your company who has called the company to gather this information for the list.

Mailings of hard-hitting direct mail packages to these highly targeted self-compiled mailing lists, combined with follow-up telephone contact from your company's sales reps, is often the best and most reliable marketing technique in a company's marketing plan, and is a common fixture in sales support marketing activities in many companies (see sales support, further in this section). Direct mail follow-up is also an important feature in print display advertising programs, where sales information kits are sent by mail to prospects who call or return reader response cards to request additional information in response to the company's ads.

In addition to the fact that it can be highly targeted to prospects in your market, direct mail's other benefits are the fact that mailings can be tested in small quantities to determine their sales effectiveness, and sales response from mailings can be tracked and measured from the prospect sales inquiries received from a mailing.

Direct mail planning, copy, production, testing, and execution are covered extensively in Chapters 6, 7, and 8.

Print Display Advertising

Trade publication advertising is another very common marketing method for reaching prospects in most industrial and business-to-business markets. Print advertising is used to generate sales inquiries (and sometimes direct sales) for a company and, secondarily, to build awareness of the company and its product among publication readers.

Of all marketing tools, print advertising is the most expensive, and is often misused by trade publication advertisers, who waste large amounts of their marketing budgets on ineffective advertising campaigns.

The most productive use of display advertising in your marketing plan are advertising programs designed to generate **measurable sales response**: Calls to your company's sales or customer service reps, links to your company's Web site, or any other requests for additional information on your company's products or services. If the price of your product is low enough, your company might also be able to generate sales directly from its advertising. In any case, however, advertising and direct mail can work very well together, with sales inquiries from display ads linked to follow-up direct mailings to improve sales response from your company's advertising.

Take a go-slow approach to print advertising if you are a newly-hired marketing manager involved in sales turnaround situations, or you're involved in a start-up company that has not yet used print advertising to market its products. Other marketing methods, such as direct mail and trade shows, are often more effective ways to test a company's sales copy and message in these situations, but at far less cost.

A company should *only* test a limited-scale advertising campaign after it has proven that it can present and sell its products in its markets using other less risky, less expensive, marketing methods. For example, a successful direct mail test to a trade publication's subscriber list is usually an accurate indicator of success for print advertising in that publication, if similar sales copy is used in the final print ad.

Many companies also overspend on the size and frequency of their advertising programs. Most full-page ads can be replaced by half-page (or even smaller) sizes that are often just as effective as larger ad sizes, if they are produced with benefits-oriented sales copy and a hard-hitting layout.

The planning and execution of print advertising programs is covered extensively in Chapter 9.

Trade Shows

As a way to get your company's product and sales presentation in front of hundreds, sometimes thousands, of real, live prospects in your market, trade shows are an unbeatable marketing and sales tool.

Trade shows are also an invaluable experience for marketing managers, because they allow you to see and hear the response to your sales message from the actual prospects in your market: These are the people who see your ads, receive your mailings, and view all the marketing projects you produce for your company. Unlike other, more expensive marketing tools, such as print advertising, trade shows give you the opportunity to learn what benefits sell your company's products, through direct, live interaction with prospects.

This feedback helps you find the appeals that work best to sell your company's products, and in doing so, helps you improve the presentation and effectiveness of the methods and deliverables you use in your marketing program. For marketing managers, there's no better way to get immediate feedback on the sales copy and benefits you are using to sell your company's product or service.

Trade shows require extensive advance planning and large up-front expense: Booth space rental, booth backdrop and signage development and production cost, and associated travel and lodging costs. Opportunities to rent space at some of the most popular trade shows may require reservations up to a year in advance, if booth space is even available. However, next to direct mail, trade shows are very effective marketing tools and should be included in most company marketing programs.

Trade show planning and execution is covered in Chapter 13.

Web Sites

Your company's Web site is often a "backstop" for the other marketing tools you use in your marketing plan, and serves as an information and communications resource for prospects who respond to the print advertising, direct mail, and the other marketing tools used in your marketing program.

Increasingly, potential customers use Internet search tools like Google to search for information on companies and their products. The quality, extent, and effectiveness of your company's Web presence often determines whether or not these potential customers will find your company on the Internet, or will find your Web site useful or persuasive enough for them to request additional information about your company's products.

Business-to-business Web sites take all forms, from basic, one or two-screen "Web brochure" sites, featuring minimal company sales and contact information, to elaborate online catalog sites that let your customers browse and purchase any of your company's products. Every company should have a Web site, but your company's product line, its complexity, your sales force structure and distribution channels will dictate the type of Web site that's best for your company.

Video and other multimedia-based formats, such as Flash and audio, enable you to provide site visitors with interactive sales videos and other highly effective ways to present and sell your company and its products.

Web sites also serve as useful communications channels to customers and prospects, through the use of free electronic e-mail newsletters, mass-mailed to customers, prospects, and other users who sign up for them on your company's Web site.

Web sites, the Internet, and video/multimedia production are covered extensively in Chapters 10-12, and 15.

Public Relations

Public relations, promoting your company and its products through "free" editorial coverage in trade, general business and consumer media outlets, can be a useful supplement to your marketing plan.

Coverage of your company's new product announcements and other news from your company can generate prospect inquiries for your company's products. News about your company can also attract the notice of other companies both inside and outside your industry, for potential joint venture and new business development opportunities.

However, using public relations as a marketing tool has two major disadvantages. First, with the exception of print advertising, companies tend to waste more of their marketing budgets on aimless PR programs that seem more focused on getting the names of the company's senior executives into the news instead of generating sales for the company.

The other disadvantage of PR is lack of control over the final outcome. You can distribute press releases, and work with trade publication editors and writers to help them on their articles, but you can never be sure whether your company will receive positive, negative, or marginal coverage in the final article printed in their publications. Moreover, even positive news coverage of your company's products in a trade publication article is no guarantee that the article will generate enough sales inquiries to make the effort worthwhile.

Because of this unpredictability, public relations should be viewed a secondary activity in your marketing program, used only to support the other, more controllable, and more effective, marketing tools available to your company, such as advertising, direct mail, trade shows, and your company's Web site.

Sales Support

Most companies selling products in trade, industrial, and business-to-business markets do so through a network of sales reps, either directly employed by the company, or working for third-party distributors, dealers, or rep firms on the company's behalf. When a sale is made in these companies, it has been made by a salesperson—by a field sales call, or over the phone.

The purpose of marketing in most trade and industrial companies is to provide the important sales support for the company's in-house (or outside) sales team. The goal of the marketing program is to use marketing "tools of the trade"—print advertising, direct mail, etc.—to generate as many qualified sales inquiries as possible, and to drive these interested prospects to the appropriate sales rep. This is standard marketing procedure in most companies selling their products in business-to-business markets.

All of the marketing tools and media described in this book can be used in service of this sales support function. For example, a print ad in a trade publication, or a mailing to a rented subscriber mailing list, generates phone calls to the company's inbound customer service or sales reps, who send the company's sales information kit to the interested prospect, and then route the inquiry to a phone or outside sales rep for an in-person sales call. At this point, other marketing deliverables, such as a company sales video, sales brochure or spec sheet, are presented to the prospect.

Your efforts in marketing to serve sales support also serve high-level sales presentations in discussions for joint ventures, major business alliances, and other major new business development opportunities for your company. Here, you will be asked to develop and present mockups of proposed ad campaigns, product packaging, and other marketing plans and deliverables to present and sell your company's proposed business or marketing relationship to the other company. Each of these new business relationships will require a marketing plan of its own, using the best marketing tools, media, and deliverables available for the task.

Evaluating the Marketing Tools Used in Your Company's Current Marketing Program

How sharp are your company's marketing tools? Every marketing manager is faced with the task of evaluating their company's marketing programs, and the most successful marketing managers do this constantly, with clear vision, to head off major problems before they start.

If you are a marketing manager in a well-established company, it is likely that you have already been running print advertising, that you have a direct mail program in place, your sales reps have their standard "sales information kit," your company already has a Web site, and your company attends at least one or two trade shows a year. It's also likely that, unless your company is experiencing serious sales or marketing problems, your company's marketing program is already generating sales.

But no matter how successful your company's marketing tools are at generating sales response, any marketing tool can be made even better, through either improved **presentation**, or by better marketing **execution**. In more critical situations, where a company is experiencing a sales slump, or finds itself in a turnaround situation, where drastic action must be taken *now* to save the company, more extensive corrective action must usually be taken (marketing turnarounds are covered in-depth in Chapter 18). However, as a starting point in each of these situations, you should always start with the current presentation and execution of the marketing tools used in your marketing program:

> **Presentation:** Presentation, or rather "marketing presentation," encompasses the sales benefits used in the headlines and copy of all your company's marketing deliverables—advertising, direct mail, sales kits, Web site, etc. The most common problems in marketing presentation are caused by lack of either **clarity** or **boldness**—or both. When this happens the selling copy used in the company's ads, mailings, brochures, or other marketing deliverables doesn't present the benefits, features, and uses of the company's product clearly or forcefully enough to break through to the average, disinterested reader (i.e., your prospect). Or, the major sales benefits used in these deliverables are not seen by your prospects as being the benefits that would move them to buy your product; i.e., they are not the benefits that are meaningful or relevant to them.

> Another common presentation problem is lack of clear and obvious sales presentation that obscures the key facts about your company's product to your reader. This includes failure to answer the most common questions a prospect would have about your product, failure to illustrate how your product is used, and most important, failure to tell the reader (or viewer) what you want them to do next—call your company to speak to a sales rep, fill out a coupon, contact a named dealer or distributor, or link to your Web site.

> **Execution:** If poor sales presentation is a "lack of sharpness" of marketing tools (your product's sales message), poor marketing execution can be thought

of as poor assembly and use of these tools, and it is the other major problem in many marketing programs. Poor marketing execution often begins when the marketing manager does not give their ad agency or marketing consultant a clear description and outline of the form and content of a marketing deliverable required for the project. For example, a print advertising program is required, but no clear sales benefits have been specified for inclusion in the final layout. Or, a Web site is needed, but the marketing manager doesn't offer his Web development team a clue as to what content must be featured on the site, and the order of importance of each type of content. Poor initial guidance often leads to poor execution, and produces a weak final marketing deliverable suffering from poor marketing presentation, described previously.

Poor execution also occurs frequently during the final production and implementation stages of marketing projects: Ads are delivered to magazines late, or without key art files or fonts, sales brochures and mailing packages are held up at the printer because of production delays or last-minute copy changes that should have been made earlier in the process. Time is wasted and important marketing opportunities are delayed (or lost) because of the marketing manager's poor understanding of the process of marketing execution, and failure to take firm control and clear, accountable oversight of the process.

Improvements to both sales presentation and marketing execution in your company's marketing program can mean the difference between a marketing program that yields only marginal, inconsistent sales response from one ad or mailing to the next, and marketing programs that generate a strong flow of inquiries and sales results across all marketing methods and media used in your marketing plan.

What are the Best Marketing Tools to Use in Your Company?

Most companies selling products in trade, industrial, and business-to-business markets do so with either field, or in-house (telemarketing-based) sales forces, or sometimes both. The marketing manager's role in these companies is to implement a marketing plan to generate inquiries from prospects who respond to ads, mailings, and other marketing tools used in the plan.

Generally speaking, the most effective marketing tools for trade and business-to-business marketing, in order of their effectiveness, and relative to cost, are as follows:

1.) Direct mail

For these companies, direct mail, and direct mail combined with telephone followup, are the least expensive, most effective tools for generating inquiries and sales from interested prospects in nearly any market or industry. Most companies with field or in-house sales forces combine their direct mail programs with telephone follow-up from their sales reps, with calls timed to closely follow the receipt of the company's mailing piece by the prospect.

There are an almost infinite number of ways to develop and execute direct mail marketing projects—for example, using rented lists or self-compiled lists, or using brochure self-mailers or letter-sized mailing pieces. However, regardless of the specifics of their execution, the combination of direct mail and telephone follow-up is the best and most effective marketing tool for companies utilizing a sales force to sell their products;

2.) Trade shows

Next to direct mail, your company's booth at a major trade show in your company's market or industry is the best, most cost-effective marketing tool for selling your company's product or service. If your company is attending the best show in your market, and if this show can draw solid attendance, as most major trade shows do, there is no substitute for putting your company's sales reps directly in front of thousands of qualified potential buyers in your market at the show;

3.) Print advertising

If your marketing program can generate solid sales response by direct mail and at trade shows, there is a reasonably good chance you can duplicate this success in print advertising, if you use the same proven sales benefits and copy in your print advertising that you have already used in your direct mailings. However, print advertising can be risky and expensive for most business-to-business marketers, and should be introduced to the company's marketing mix with caution. This is usually done by starting with a limited schedule of smaller, fractional page ads in the top one or two trade publications in your industry, and then carefully tracking and measuring sales response generated by these ads. The ad program is then expanded only if it can justified by the initial sales response;

4.) Other marketing tools: Web sites, PR, sales support

All other marketing tools, such as your company's Web site, and PR efforts to generate free publicity in your industry's trade press, are, generally, the parts of your company's marketing plan that support and serve other major marketing tools used in your plan (such as direct mail, sales support, or print advertising). In most cases, they cannot be relied upon by themselves to generate adequate sales response. For example, your company's Web site may draw interest from prospects who discover it during an Internet keyword search on Google, but most companies can't rely on their Web sites alone to generate the sales response they need. Editorial coverage on your company's products, appearing as a result of your company's PR efforts, may also generate sales inquiries, but not as steadily or reliably as direct mail, trade shows, or print advertising.

While each of these marketing tools are important, and many deserve a place in your marketing plan, they should either support other, more important marketing efforts, or serve as second-level additions to your marketing program. For example, your company's Web site supports other marketing efforts by providing more detailed information on your company's products, and a communications channel to prospects who receive your company's direct mailings or see your print advertising. Other marketing tools, such as public relations, are not reliable sales response generators, and are dependent on other, more forceful marketing methods (such as advertising or personal sales calls), and should be viewed as less-important parts of your plan.

Of course, this is a very generalized assessment of the power of these marketing tools, and will not be true in all instances. For example, some companies may work with third-party dealer or distributor networks instead of employing their own sales reps, and will use marketing efforts like co-op advertising campaigns, designed to drive prospect inquiries to these distributors. Other companies may be successful at selling their low-priced products by direct mail or advertising, without the need for sales reps at all. In the past few years, some new companies have even become very successful using their Web sites and e-mail as their exclusive marketing tools, operating as "Internet only" businesses.

The only way to determine which marketing tools work best in your company's marketing plan is to select the ones that you think will work best in your own company's situation, develop them using clear, forceful sales presentation, execute them to the best of your ability, and carefully track and measure the sales response from each marketing tool you use. You may experience different results from using these marketing tools than those described here.

If your company has a good product at a good price, and is selling in the right markets, all the rest is clear, obvious, salesmanlike presentation of your company's product, using skillful marketing execution and tradecraft, and hedging your marketing program by using as many marketing tools as your company can afford.

Professional Development for Marketing Managers

As a marketing manager, you will be working with your company's ad agency, marketing consultant, and other outside vendors on every aspect of the development and execution of the major marketing tools described in this chapter: Copywriting, layout, production, and the planning and final implementation of all your company's marketing projects, using all of the "tools of the trade" available to you as a marketer.

The next section of this book, consisting of 12 chapters, covers the key aspects of planning, development and execution of these major marketing tools, and provides you with the essential information you need as a marketing manager to successfully implement these marketing projects in your company's marketing plan.

Many of the action steps described in the next section of this book will be handled by your ad agency, marketing consultant, or outside vendors, but it is essential to your success as a marketing manager to know how these projects are developed, produced, and executed.

For example, your ad agency or marketing consultant will create, develop, and produce the key marketing deliverables that go into an ad, direct mail package, or other marketing project in your company's marketing program. While you may never write a line of advertising copy that appears in the final product, you do need to know what makes an ad effective, and how to discover, document, and organize the main sales benefits of your company's product or service, so you can provide your ad agency or consultant with a written outline, or "spec," of your company's major sales benefits that must be incorporated into the final print ad. You also need to know enough about the process to manage it, and to supply this same background sales copy information for any other printed marketing deliverable: A direct mail package, a sales brochure, a catalog sheet, or any other deliverable used in any marketing project.

You probably won't be creating your company's Web site, but you need to know what makes a business Web site successful in serving your marketing program, and how to manage the Web development process for your company's Internet projects. The same holds true for other marketing projects, such as video production, or the special marketing requirements for start-ups, new product launches, and turnaround situations. Your knowledge of the tradecraft of marketing improves the quality of your company's marketing projects and their execution, and is an important part of your professional development as a marketing manager.

HOW TO WRITE ADVERTISING (OR MANAGE THOSE WHO DO)
CHAPTER 4
DISCOVERING, DEVELOPING, AND PRESENTING YOUR PRODUCT'S MOST EFFECTIVE SALES MESSAGE

Developing effective advertising isn't a cookie-cutter approach, but it's not rocket science, either. The secret to writing effective ad copy is to find the major benefits of your product or service, and to fit the right benefit into the right element in the final structure of your ad, brochure, or other marketing deliverable.

This chapter focuses on the process of discovering these key benefits in your company's product or service, and turning these benefits into clear, effective, salesmanlike advertising—in print, online, or in any other media form.

Even though you may never write a word of your company's advertising copy, you'll need to have a solid working knowledge of the process, so you can recognize effective advertising copy that sells your company's products. Equally important, learning to write effective ad copy for any marketing assignment gives you the ability to recognize ineffective ad copy submitted by your outside ad agency. Sadly, you may experience this many times in your marketing career.

Developing the skill of ad copywriting helps you to know what you want when directing your ad agency, and to *drive the process forward*, insuring the fastest, most efficient execution of all marketing projects. You may not write copy for your ads or brochures, but these techniques will help you write down the essential sales copy benefits for any marketing deliverable, so you can supply these background notes to your ad agency or marketing consultant. And just like all good marketing managers should have once been good salesmen, as a marketing manager you should know how to write good, serviceable advertising for your company—even if this job is done by your ad agency or marketing consultant.

Learning How to Tell Your Product's Story—to Sell Your Product

Although we use the term "advertising" throughout this chapter, the process of identifying your product's key sales benefits, and the copywriting techniques covered here, apply to any form of marketing deliverable—brochure, catalog sheet, sales kit, Web site promotional page, trade show marketing, etc.). These techniques are highly effective in any marketing project, and in any form of media.

These techniques allow you to systematically discover and develop your product's major selling benefits, to develop marketing deliverables that present these benefits in the most effective way. The major benefit of using these techniques is that they eliminate the "Y Factor" in your marketing program, which is the *doubt* that an ad campaign or other marketing project conveys a clear, effective selling message to your market.

Whenever you, or your management, evaluates your company's advertising and marketing prior to its placement, you should always ask:

> *"Does this ad accurately and effectively communicate and present the major benefits of our product in a way that would motivate the prospect to buy our product?"*

By using the techniques described in these two chapters, you guarantee that your answer to this question is always: "Yes!"

Effective Ad Copywriting Means Research and Execution

There are three parts to the process of developing effective advertising:

Part 1: The information gathering stage, where you pull together every piece of information about your company's product or service, and its benefits to your prospective buyer;

Part 2: The writing stage, where you document the key sales benefits of your company's product or service, garnered from your research. These benefits are then ranked by their importance, with the most important benefit(s) becoming headlines, and with secondary sales benefits being incorporated into subheads and body copy;

Parts 3 and 4: The execution and layout stages, where you (or your agency) put this information together into a hard-hitting, effective advertising deliverable—a display ad campaign, a direct response package, multimedia presentation, or Web page. These important aspects of marketing execution will be covered in detail in the next chapter.

Again, the key steps covered in this chapter are not limited to writing display advertising alone. The same research, thinking exercises, and copywriting principles can be applied to any marketing project that requires sales copy—an ad, brochure, Web site, or video script.

Part 1: The Information-Gathering Stage

Before you sit down to write any advertising, you will begin by pulling together all the information on your company's product and its benefits, from these sources:

- **Your company's best salespeople;**
- **Your company's product development managers (or engineers);**
- **Your competitors;**
- **Open-source (public) information**

Step 1: Listen to Your Company's Sales Reps

Your company's best advertising copy comes from your company's best salespeople. Sales pros are a company's street-fighting foot soldiers, and they've learned from hard experience how to present your company's products to real prospects and buyers on a daily basis. And the best of them have learned how best to explain your company's products to the outside world in order to make the sale.

Since making sales is the sole mission of your company's advertising, it only makes sense to talk to (or "debrief") your company's salespeople as your first step in gathering the information you need to execute effective advertising deliverables.

Insiders in any company—Presidents, CEOs, Vice-Presidents, even marketing managers—are often dangerously insulated from how your company actually sells its products.

Above all else, a company's top salespeople know the most important thing about your company's product or service: Which feature, benefits, and applications work best to help them close the sale. Often, these features and benefits will be different, or expressed and positioned differently, than the benefits you, your management, or your ad agency have been presenting in your company's marketing program.

By listening to how your best sales reps actually sell your product, you can tap into this energy and bring it inside your company, to serve your efforts to market your company's products more effectively.

Talk to your sales reps, and talk to them often. They know what's really going on.

How to Debrief a Sales Rep

Your job here is to be an extremely attentive listener and intelligence gatherer. Call a meeting, or attend your company's next sales meeting. Take careful note as you listen to your company's sales reps talk about your company's products. Start out by asking your company sales reps to give you their best, standard sales presentation— as if *you* were the prospect on the other side of the desk.

Listen closely for the key benefits and those little "personal persuasion statements" that highly effective sales pros use to bolster their case. At this stage, you are looking for the real world-oriented, anecdotal, verbal selling points your salespeople use to convince the prospect. Also pay close attention to the "you" benefits—how the salesman personalizes the benefits of using your company's products or services, to you, the prospect:

- *"...our system is like a promotional coupon for your readers, but because it's Internet-based, the coupon promotion can change anytime your customer wants to change their promotion..."*

- *"...Mr. Jones, my customers tell me that since they put our company's updated K4000 pumps online, they're saving about 25% on their monthly fuel costs. I figure you could save about this much, too..."*

- *"...sure, we could match the price of [competitor X], but at that price, would you get the same service from them that you already know you can get from us?"*

- *"...our systems are in use by some pretty impressive companies, including [Big Companies X, Y and Z]..."*

- *"...if you want the biggest savings and the most efficiency for your money, go with our Model 3D4, that saves you half the regular price of the electronic control package, included in this upgrade..."*

Your company's sales reps will often drop these little gems into your lap, and each of these can be turned into an effective piece of sales copy for any marketing deliverable. **Figure 4-1** shows how each of these sales lines can be turned into a compelling piece of ad sales copy, or a headline.

An experienced marketer knows when he hears a new copy point he can use in his next ad or brochure—and by listening carefully you can develop a highly-tuned sense for detecting usable and effective sales points you can incorporate into your company's next sales promotions. All you have to do is listen, write them down, and pass them along to your ad agency or marketing consultant who writes your company's sales copy.

Learn Which Benefits Work Best

While you're listening to their presentations, ask your sales reps about each key benefit they present, and which benefit is the most important; then which one is the next important, etc. This helps you rank key all sales points in "Good/Better/Best" fashion:

- **"Good:"** *Sales benefits that belong in your company's ad copy, or elsewhere in promotional text;*

- **"Better:"** *Sales benefits that belong in bold-faced ad subheads, bullet points or in other, more prominent positions;*

Figure 4-1:

Listen to Your Sales Reps—Comments from your sales reps can be turned into effective ad copy or headlines:

What the Salesman Said:	Your Copy Point or Headline:
"... our system is like a promotional coupon for your readers, but because it's Internet-based, the coupon promotion can change anytime your customer wants to change their promotion . . ."	Our system combines the proven sales effectiveness of your current coupon-based programs with the speed of the Internet, by letting your customers change their coupon programs whenever they want.
"... Mr. Jones, my customers tell me that since they put our company's updated K4000 pumps online, they're saving about 25% on their monthly fuel costs. I figure you could save about this much, too . . ."	Save Up to 25% on Your Monthly Fuel Costs with the New K4000
"... sure, we could match the price of [competitor X], but at that price, would you get the same service from them that you already know you can get from us?"	Our price includes on-call service at no extra cost—remember this next time you need a new printing head installed in the middle of your best customer's next big production order.
"... our systems are in use by some pretty impressive companies, including [Big Companies X, Y and Z] . . ."	Join [Big Companies X, Y and Z]—All Satisfied Users of Our Company's Products
"... if you want the biggest savings and the most efficiency for your money, go with our Model 3D4, which saves you half the regular price of the electronic control package, included in this upgrade . . ."	Your Best Value: A 50% Savings ($XX,XXX) on our upgraded Model 3D4, which includes our electronic control package at no extra charge

- **"Best:"** *Key sales points that can stand alone as headlines in advertising, and major sales headlines for brochures, signage or other collateral.*

How Do Your Salespeople Counter Common Sales Objections?

Next, ask your company's sales reps about the **major objections** or questions a prospective customer will commonly raise against these stated benefits. You want your sales rep to verbalize what their prospects say to them, and how the sales rep counters the objection.

You can often incorporate these major sales "counters" in your company's advertising copy to pre-emptively anticipate and neutralize prospect objections. Answering objections in advance in your company's promotional messages helps soften the prospect's potential objections, and shortens the selling cycle.

What Else Do Your Salesmen Have to Say? (Plenty!)

Next, get as much free-form, anecdotal information from your salespeople on their experiences in presenting and selling your company's products in the field:

- **What are the prospect's other areas of resistance to buying your company's products?** For example: Is the price for certain products too high? Is a competitor's product better in some key respect? If so, ask your sales reps how they handle these varied, wild-card objections;

- **What other reasons do prospects have for saying "No?"** For example, do prospects have major problems getting your product included in their company's budget—if so, what (or who else) is the problem? This kind of objection often means your ad copy needs to address the concerns of other people in the prospect's company, or you need to be reaching these other contacts in addition to (or instead of) the current prospect's job responsibility;

- **What do your salesman *really* have to say about how your company's products, and how they stack up against those of your company's competitors?** Tease out any additional, off-the-record intelligence or other information that can be used in promotion, or that could help you head off big, potential marketing problems down the line, such as rumors of new product announcements or price cuts by your competitors. This kind of information reveals itself best during informal discussions with sales reps and other unguarded moments.

Ask Your Top Sales Reps: "What's Your "Elevator Pitch?"

When pitching a new movie idea, all movie producers have an "Elevator Pitch:" It's their latest project's brief, hard-hitting 15-second pitch they always have at the ready to give to a top Hollywood producer they hope to accidentally meet during a short elevator ride in an office building.

Elevator Pitches include some of the following techniques to pack the essential benefits of a movie pitch—or in your case, the key benefits of your company's product—into a concise selling statement that monopolizes your listener's attention and plants your product firmly in the prospect's mind.

Elevator Pitch Examples

- *"...our company sells environmental risk mapping services to engineers and real estate developers to determine any property's environmental risk or liability. Our customers find the cost of our reports is about one-third the price of doing it themselves, and anyone can get a report within 24 hours, for any property in the U.S...."*

- *"...our system is a new profit center for your newspaper that lets you link readers of your newspaper's classified ad section instantly to a photo of the item being advertised in the ad. A reader who sees an ad for a used car, for example, can just enter a short code that's printed right there in the ad, to go right to a photo, on the Internet, to see what the car looks like. It's like having eBay in your newspaper!"*

- *"...our Web site lets you download all kinds of talk radio programs and audiobooks right to your MP3 player, so now you can listen to Rush Limbaugh or Charlie Rose in your car, or whenever you want. Best of all, it's free..."*

- *"...I'm with [company X], and our monitoring systems are installed in most of the top companies in your industry. Our new system is a real quantum leap in the field, because all of our sensors are now linked wirelessly to each other, and each can be programmed by you, on site, so that a fault detected in one sensor will trigger any action that you set, which means no more machine shutdowns from false alarms..."*

Here are some common techniques used in the most effective Elevator Pitches:

- **Linking the familiar with the unfamiliar:** "Our service works just like your existing monitoring service, but at half the price, because there's no dedicated telecom lines or equipment;"

- **It's easy to do, and you won't risk much:** "Your people can train on our new system in a day or two, just like we did at Allied [his biggest competitor] last month;"

- **Catching a new wave:** "Our Web conversion systems position you for the future of wireless Net access over Internet appliance-type devices"

No doubt your own company's sales reps have their own Elevator Pitches—the short, sweet pitch that instantly *defines* your company's product. A competent advertising copywriter can usually pull a solid headline and the beginnings of good sales body copy for any advertising project from the Elevator Pitch alone.

Whether it's delivered in an elevator, in a short phone call, or in an office reception area as the salesman catches the prospect on their way to lunch, every one of your sales reps has an Elevator Pitch. Ask for theirs, and write it down, word for word.

What Do Your Sales Reps Think of Your Company's Marketing?

Ask your company's top sales reps what they like and don't like about your company's advertising and marketing programs—as they're practiced now, and as they've been implemented in the past. Salesmen complain about anything, but your job is to listen for true successes and mistakes in marketing presentation, product positioning, pricing, or (most important) marketing execution. Take the praise and criticism to heart, and avoid repeating these mistakes in your marketing program.

Figure 4-2:

Marketing in Start-Ups—Getting sales copy benefit information for start-ups

What if Your Company is a Start-up, or Doesn't Have a Sales Force?

For start-ups and new market launches: If your company is a start-up, or is launching a new product in a new market, create some mockups of a sample ad or brochure for your company's new product.

Next, go out and locate a handful of key decision-makers at companies in the market you are trying to reach. Send these mockups to these individuals, along with a personalized cover letter. Ask them to review the mockup and sample sales copy and let them know you will be calling them in a week to follow up and ask them their opinion of the piece.

People who are contacted in this way will be flattered that they're being asked for their opinion on such a high-level matter, and will take the time to review your materials and give you some thoughtful opinions. You'll also get critical information on

your product's features, whether or not the price is right, and other, possibly invaluable, info that could lead you to make important pricing or feature changes in your product or its marketing strategy, improving its chances of success.

For new product launches in established companies: If your company is planning to launch a new product to your existing customer base, contact your top half-dozen current customers. Contact the person there who made the purchasing decision. Ask them what the most compelling benefits were that persuaded them to buy your company's product.

If your company works through distributors or dealers, substitute the best contacts at these organizations in place of your salesmen, and ask them the questions we've previously outlined.

See Chapter 16 or more information on sales copy testing for start-ups, new product launches, and new market entries.

Finally, ask your sales reps about any missed opportunities in the past and present—mailings to key prospects that should have been sent out, but weren't, blown advertising opportunities in key publications, missed trade shows, or key high-level sales calls that were not properly supported by your marketing team. More new business opportunities arise from sales reps in the field than are created from on-high in your organization. And one of the most important aspects of your job as a marketing manager is to provide key support for helping to develop and to convert these opportunities into sales and new markets for your company.

Your company's sales force is your best source of worthwhile ad copy and marketing ideas. Keep in touch with your best reps on a regular basis, let them know that your door is always open, and they'll make your job as a marketing manager a lot easier.

Step 2: Check Your Competition

Next to talking to your company's top sales reps, watching what your company's competitors are doing in the marketplace—how your competitors position, present and promote their products, where they advertise, and how they support their sales forces—can be a great influence on your company's advertising, marketing and promotional efforts.

Just as important, competitors will often show you what *not* to do when it comes to marketing your own company's products. Since many ad campaigns, including, most likely, those of your competition, may not be very effective in their intended target markets, you may have a tremendous opportunity to top whatever your competitor has done, provided you know what *you're* doing.

Ask your company's sales reps about your competitors: Your company's sales reps see your competitor's marketing plans executed every day in the field. They see and hear what your competition's doing from their own account base, their new prospects, and even from their selling counterparts at your competitor's company. Ask them if they've seen anything that works, such as particularly effective advertising campaigns in your industry and good sales support efforts, such as targeted mailings or effective collateral pieces. Here, you are not asking your sales reps to be creative consultants on your advertising (this is always a mistake), you're gathering field intelligence that helps you do your job more effectively.

Step 3: Get Your Competitor's Sales Information Kit

Get your neighbor, friend or relative, or someone at another company in an office down the hall to call your competitor to request all sales information kits available on your competitors' products. You want to see what your competitors send to interested prospects, but without them knowing that you're requesting their sales information.

When this information arrives in your hands, review it carefully: Put yourself in the prospect's shoes, and take careful note of what you observe as good, persuasive sales copy points in your competitor's sales letter, brochure, response pieces, and other collateral material.

Notice the layout of your competitors' printed materials: If the headlines, subheads, and body copy, including copy points, are instantly readable and persuasive to you, that means your competitor is doing a good job in its ad copy presentation. Of course, this means you will have to be at least as good as they are when you develop your own company's marketing deliverables.

From a copy standpoint, take special notice of any sales promotions and "call to actions" your competitor uses to close the sale. If your competitor has been using certain promotions and closing tactics (such as free samples, trial offers, percent-off savings offers on the first order, and other inducements), it's a good bet that your competitor is using these techniques because they work. Which means you may also want to emulate some of these special promotions in your own company's marketing program.

Step 4: Research Trade Publications in Your Industry

Visit your local library or ask someone in your office where you can get a stack of back issues of the top two or three trade publications in your industry—a year's worth of back issues is a good start, and two years' worth is even better. Next, flip through the pages of each issue, and pretend you are a very busy, somewhat disinterested reader—i.e., the typical sales prospect you must reach with effective advertising and promotion.

Tear out any ads you see that you think do a particularly effective job of selling and explaining products in your company's line of business. Also take note of ads that repeat each and every month, taking special notice of small, fractional-page ads—the workhorses of the advertising business. Chances are, ads that repeat over long periods of time do so because they work. They pull in sales leads and new orders time after time.

This process of analyzing advertising placements over time also reveals the "creative" ad campaigns that run for only two or three issues, and then quietly disappear. Learning to identify the wrong-headed, big-dollar attempts at "branding" a company's product, executed by ad agencies for their clients, is an important part of your research. These are pretentious, one-shot ad campaigns devoid of compelling sales benefits relevant to their markets.

Step 5: Publicly-Available Information on Competitors & Markets

Your competitor's Web site: Obviously, the quickest way to see how your competitor sells their product is to go to their Web site. Study their Web site's promotional product copy, download their Acrobat .PDF brochures, check their press releases for new product announcements and sales copy. If your competition offers some type of free e-mail newsletter or update service so you can stay on top of their latest new product announcements, sign up for it (just remember to sign up for it using your private e-mail address to avoid detection as one of their competitors).

Gather as much information as you can on how your competitors talk about their products, and, without copying any of this outright, let the best of this information influence you when it's time to start your own copywriting process.

Public company information: While not strictly related to the topic of writing advertising copy, the financial information that public companies are required to file by the Securities and Exchange Commission (SEC) is also an excellent source of marketing and competitive information on any public company. Log on to the SEC's Web site (**www.sec.gov**) and search for any public company's 10K and 10Q public disclosure documents.

By law, the SEC law requires all publicly-traded companies companies to disclose any and all business information that may have a "material impact" on a company's financial condition. Companies will often describe certain details about their marketing, product development and other business development activities in these publicly-accessible documents that you won't see disclosed in a more "public" setting, such as by press release or on the company's Web site.

For example, you can often find information here that a company would not otherwise want to publicize, such as a company's assessment of its success (or lack of success) in the launch of a new product line, along with disclosure of key marketing expenditures, by amount.

Outside of a small circle of Wall Street financial wonks, company 10K statements are one of the best-kept secrets for getting marketing intelligence on publicly-traded companies.

Part 2: Writing Effective Advertising and Promotional Copy

There's no special mystery or hidden art to writing effective advertising copy for your company. Like most of life, creating good advertising is really a matter of putting one foot in front of the other—common sense and basic execution.

Claude Hopkins, one of the last century's most famous advertising pioneers, and the author of the advertising classics, *My Life in Advertising* and *Scientific Advertising*, once defined advertising as **salesmanship in print**. This is still the best definition of what advertising should be.

However, the purpose of advertising has been lost on many who work in the advertising business today. It's a sad fact of life that most people employed in all levels of advertising agencies never actually worked in professional sales positions in industrial or consumer goods companies at any point of their careers.

This lack of professional, down-on-the-street selling experience is all too obvious: Just flip through any business trade publication, magazine, or newspaper. If you judge all of the ads you see there from the strict standpoint of salesmanship—does the ad provide the facts and the benefits required to make a buying decision?—A majority of ads in any publication wouldn't make the cut.

That's because many people who work in ad agencies, including their "enablers" who hold marketing management positions at the companies they serve, have deluded themselves into the belief that advertising is some type of mysterious, "creative" process of trying to evoke an emotional "feeling" about the product, to reinforce the magical goal of "brand reinforcement."

How Prospects See Your Advertising

It's important for all marketing managers to understand how your average prospect really sees your advertising. Before you can get your reader to respond to an ad, you must get them to notice it. So before you plan any marketing project, keep the following thoughts in mind:

> **People are busy, and don't pay attention very well:** The most important rule of advertising is to acknowledge the fact that most people are way too busy and attention-deprived to read your company's advertising. According to the *Journal of Advertising Research*, the average American is exposed to over 500 different advertising messages each day.

The average reader's ability to pay attention has been degraded by work days and lives filled with wall-to-wall interruptions. A lifetime of watching television has also diminished the average person's ability to concentrate;

Most markets don't understand most advertising: To your audience, most advertising is a pretty picture they don't understand, and care even less about. That's because most advertising is over-produced eye candy created by people who never had to sell a real product to a real person.

Sometimes, ineffective advertising is created because it's supervised by marketing managers who have been gulled by their advertising agencies into running ineffective, criminally wasteful ad campaigns. In other cases, corporate inertia dictates that, since "we've always done it this way," the marketing manager must work with the company's designated ad agency, and that all ads must conform to "corporate branding guidelines," regardless of this policy's deadening impact on the effectiveness of their advertising. In other cases, and especially in smaller companies or start-ups, marketing managers may not be experienced enough to realize how ineffective their ad campaign is until they experience the effect of a poorly-performing ad campaign themselves.

The fact that most advertising is ineffective means the companies who produce the small number of effective, sales and inquiry-generating ads found in any publication will be rewarded with an even larger sales response, compared to their competitor's advertising. You want your company to be part of this successful minority.

You only have two seconds: According to W. Kroeber-Riel (as reported by Erik du Plessis for the Advertising Media Internet Center), the average reader will spend about 2.8 seconds viewing a double spread advertisement, 1.9 seconds viewing a 3/4 or full-page advertisement, and 0.6 seconds viewing a 1/2 page or smaller-sized ad. The average reader has lost most of his ability to sit still and focus on any one thing for longer than two seconds, so if your ad cannot stop a reader in less than three seconds, they will never read the rest of your ad. They are gone forever (or, at least until the next time you can spend more money to reach them).

Most people—not even those who become your company's customers after seeing your advertising—read every word of it. They "skim read," stopping to read your headline, then skipping down to a bold-face subhead, then down to the bottom of your ad, and then back up again to read some more ad copy.

This is not to say that all advertising should contain very little text, or that long-copy ads or sales collateral will not be effective. The average reader "takes in" your ad or other marketing piece, forming a general impression of your company and its product or service. Your advertising's ultimate success depends on how effectively all the elements of your advertising work together on the page—headline, subheads, body copy and call to action. Not only must each element support all the others, but they must all work together to *answer the most likely questions* your reader is asking about your company's product.

Anatomy of a Effective Ad

The four elements of any effective advertisement, or most any other marketing deliverable (such as a brochure, catalog sheet, or sales flyer) are:

- **Headline**
- **Subheads**
- **Body copy**
- **Call to action**

The techniques detailed in this chapter will show you how to develop the most effective advertising sales copy for each of these four elements.

Headline

The headline is the most important element of any print ad (or any other printed marketing deliverable).

A headline may be a single word, or two dozen words, but all headlines should have one—and only one—purpose: To make the prospect read the rest of your ad.

A headline should be a bold statement of your product's prime benefit to the reader. Writing headlines that hammer home your product's prime benefit provide clear and obvious sales presentation, and offer the lowest risk of failure.

Because of the headline's importance, it is crucial that the prime benefit expressed by the headline be seen as a key benefit by your prospect, and not the benefit that you, your management, or your ad agency *wish the prospect would see*.

This is a critical distinction. Often, and especially in start-up companies, advertising is created in a vacuum by a company that has become too dependent on its ad agency's "creative" approach. Or, a new product or service is placed before a focus group, whose participants will, more often than not, *tell you what they think you want to hear*, and not what they really think about your product.

Whether they arise through management consensus in your company, an ad agency's faulty creative impulse, or a focus group, a headline will not be effective if it contains a benefit that is not perceived by your readers as being an important benefit to *them*.

Headlines are often joined with an ad's visual element, such as a product photo, an illustration, or other imagery. Graphic elements used in ads should support and amplify the prime benefit expressed in the headline, and not distract the reader. Let the text be the star of your ad, and don't let the image take the attention away from your headline.

You should almost never use humor, irony, and sarcasm in headlines. What may strike you or your agency as a "funny" headline usually has no impact on an ad's effectiveness. Likewise, "edgy" approaches, or the use of visual sight gags and other

Figure 4-3:

Humor in Advertising

Humorous ads, like the ones below, are only effective if they don't lose sight of the ad's main mission—to sell your product.

gimmicks, may go over very well around your office, but will usually receive a cold sales reception in the market. Occasionally, humorous ads can succeed (see examples in **Figure 4-3**), but the risk of running these kinds of ads can often be greater than following a serious and more proven, benefits-oriented approach.

Subheads

The subheads in your ad or other marketing deliverable are lines of bold-faced text that communicate the other important benefits of your company's product, its **secondary benefits**.

Subheads are sentences or phrases interspersed throughout your ad copy, that outline your product's other key sales benefits to the reader.

Because most readers never read the complete text of an ad, subheads play an important role by communicating the other key benefits of your product. Ideally, your prospect should get the gist of your product's sales message by just skim-reading your ad's headline, its subheads, and its call to action.

Figure 4-4:

Long-Copy Ads—There's nothing wrong with using a lot of copy in your ads and brochures, if your copy *sells*

**The More
You Tell,
the More
You Sell:**
*Persuasive,
well-written
long copy ads
are particularly
effective when
you are selling
a product that
is entirely new
in concept, or a
product that
requires
extensive
explanation to
communicate
its benefits*

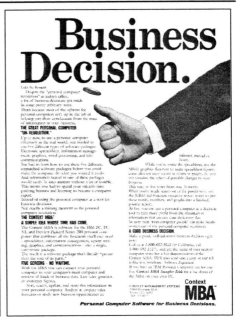

Body Copy

Whether long or short, the body copy of your ad communicates your product's major sales benefits. In long form, ad body copy can tell a complete sales story about a product, or in short form, conveys just two or three brief sentences tot get the reader to take the action you want them to take.

How long should your ad's body copy be? This depends on the length of your ad's headline and your ad's page size, but generally, copy length depends on *how much space you need to explain your product, and to sell its key features to your prospect.*

If your sales objective is to get the reader to pick up the phone and call your sales rep, or to visit your company's Web site to request a sales information kit, an ad with one or two short paragraphs of copy may be all that is needed. But if your company is selling a product or service that is radically different than its predecessors, or requires a more detailed technical explanation, an ad with longer copy may work even better than an ad that employs a couple of short lines of "teaser copy."

An interested prospect who has been drawn in by your headline and subhead wants to know more about your product—now. If it's persuasive and well written, long ad copy can be effective, even when your readers' attention spans may otherwise be short. So give them what they want—and take the space you need to describe and sell your company's product.

Call to Action

Your ad's call to action tells your reader what they must do next. It also answers the most likely questions your reader would have about your company's product or service:

- **How much does it cost?**
- **Where can I find it?**
- **How do I get it?**
- **Who do I call/where do I go for more information?**

A call to action may also include a promotional incentive to persuade the reader to act more quickly:

- **"Call us before (date) and save 10% on your first order"**
- **"Go to (Web site address) and get your free sample issue"**
- **"Call us at (phone number) for more information, and to discuss your project"**

All good salespeople know how to close a sale. After the presentation is made, and all the prospect's questions are answered, a good salesperson asks for the order. And like any good sales pro, once your ad's headline, subheads, and body copy have made their presentation, the call to action makes it clear to the prospect what they must do next, and then *asks* for the order or inquiry.

These elements should not be slavishly applied to any advertising project, for any product, and for every company. It would be foolish to "ask for the order" in an ad that's selling electrical turbines, or mainframe computers, heavy construction equipment, or any other high-dollar product or service, for example. However, it would be equally foolish not to feature a link to your company's Web site, in the closing sales copy at the bottom of the ad, where readers could get detailed technical descriptions and specifications on these high-dollar products.

Writing Effective Advertising: Three Advertising Copywriting Exercises

The next section covers three essential writing exercises that help you develop an advertising copywriter's mindset when writing about your company's products or services. It's the same process used, more or less, by every advertising copywriter who knows how to write effective sales copy, and forms the essential basis of all effective sales messages, in any advertising medium.

These exercises help you discover the key sales benefits of your company's products, and will teach you how to "talk" about them in different ways—short and telegraphic, or in a longer and more descriptive way. And by revealing the copywriter's art, these exercises help you set a firmer hand to the marketing process and make you a better marketing manager.

Step 1: The Laundry List

If you haven't done so already, gather your basic research from your sales rep debriefings, publications, etc., as already described in the first part of this chapter. Read it, digest it, and then put it aside for awhile. Like all creative projects, it helps to "sleep on it" and approach it again the next morning.

Next, on a new sheet of paper, make a Laundry List of your product's every possible benefit. This includes both features and benefits. At this stage it's not important to make a distinction between features and benefits; it is more important to list everything you can think of—good, descriptive, or indifferent about your company's product or service. You can separate the features from the benefits after you've completed this step.

Sales Benefit Attributes

Here are some "soup starters" to help you write your own Laundry List of sales benefits, including copy points that describe any of the following attributes of your company's product or service:

• Speed • Efficiency • Productivity

What aspects, functions, or processes of your company's product perform faster than comparable products? How are these important to your prospective customer?

If your company is a service business, does it perform its tasks more quickly than your competitors? If so, is this important to your customer, and how?

What is it about your company's product that helps your prospective buyer get more work done, or done more efficiently?

Can the efficiency of your company's product or service be measured using numbers (such as in time saved, or better use of materials, fuel, or power)? If so, then who says so? An independent trade group or outside research firm?

Does your product help your customer become more productive in their business? If so, how?

What other ways will your prospective customer find using your product to be better than the "old ways" he does business today?

• Quality • Comprehensiveness • Richness

What is it about your company's product that makes it <u>better</u> than those of your competitors?

What is it about your company that makes its products, or about how your company performs its services, distinctive or better than comparable products or services?

Are there key parts or components of your company's products or manufacturing processes that use better materials than other products in the same class, and are these materials known for their better quality or greater durability? If so, what are these parts or processes, and how are they better?

If your company provides a service (not a product), how experienced are those who perform the service? How many combined years of experience do they have? What is it about their backgrounds, or about the way they were selected or trained, that makes them more skilled, qualified, dependable, or competent than your competitors?

Do your company's products or services have attributes that make them the product leaders of your industry?

If so, then what are those recognized qualities?

Who else, such as leading companies who are also customers, or respected trade groups in your industry, recognizes these qualities?

If your company provides services, has it done exceptional work for any of your prospect's well-known competitors? If so, what do they say about your work (and would they say it in your company's advertising)? How should this past performance motivate a prospective customer to use your company's services?

How broad is your product line? Does it solve all of a potential customer's problems in the area of his need?

Can you provide a prospective customer with all the services he will need within the range of your business offering? If so, list all the services your company provides, and list your depth of experience in each type of service.

What other <u>aspects of quality</u> are there about your company's products that set them apart from the rest? Write down as many of these as you can.

• Low cost • Savings • Value for money

Can your customer save money or reduce their costs by using your company's product or service? If so, how?

How much can a customer save by using your product or service? How can the customer measure their savings (such as savings per month, or savings compared to using current products)?

Who says the customer can save money? Is there outside verification of these savings—like an industry trade group, or an independent research study?

How exactly would a customer be better off (saving money or cutting costs) if they use your company's product or service? For example, what aspects of their business would improve as a result of these savings?

Is your company able to make the customer a special offer so they can save money on their first purchase with your company? If so, what are the terms of this offer?

Low cost, savings, and value propositions are very important benefits for advertising copy, so write as many of these down as you can for your company's product.

• New • Updated • Improved • Upgraded • Different

Is this a new product? If so, how is it similar to other products known by your prospect?

How is your product different and better than these "older" products? How do these differences make current products look "old" or out-of-date by comparison?

If your product is radically new on the market, is there still some key aspect of it that operates like a product known to your prospect? If so, describe this aspect, and why your product's departure from it is superior to the "old" functionality. Likewise, if these older product aspects or features are valued by your prospects, and exist in your new product, make sure to mention them.

Has the product been upgraded from a previous model? If so, how does your prospect benefit from your product's upgraded features?

Are there aspects of your improved product or service that have never been done before, or represent a radical departure from current ways of doing business? If so, link these new ways (the unfamiliar) with the current ways your prospect uses products or services like yours (the familiar). List how they are similar, and for each, describe how your company's new approach is better for the prospect.

Step 2: The Park Bench Story

The Laundry List is your warmup for the next step: The Park Bench Story, which is a full-blown selling presentation incorporating the benefits you've just written down in your Laundry List.

However, instead of falling into the usual rut—writing this as the jargonized boilerplate that often passes for "marketing communications"—write this for a certain time, in a certain place, and to a certain person.

Take out a new sheet of paper and write this presentation as if you were talking to a perfect stranger sitting next to you on a park bench. Imagine this stranger as a well-dressed, elderly gentleman with bright eyes, and a kind, attentive, interested expression.

Figure 4-5:

The Simple Explanation

Just before they were about to present him with a verbal or written explanation of a very complex issue, President Eisenhower would tell his staff: ***"Now please explain this to me as if you were explaining it to a 5 year-old child."***

If it worked for the man in charge D-Day, the largest military invasion in history, it's also excellent advice for advertising copywriters, and those who oversee the process.

Stark simplicity of explanation, clarity of presentation, and delivery with enthusiasm and personal warmth make your advertising copy persuasive.

This gentleman knows nothing of your business or your company's product or service. But because he has all the time in the world, he wants to hear your story. He will not criticize you, but he will ask questions from time to time.

What to tell this man? Begin by telling him a little about your company, its history, and how long it has been in business.

Explain your company's product or service to this gentleman, bearing in mind that he doesn't know your industry or any of its buzzwords. Look at what you've just written: Would he understand what you wrote? If not, break down the explanation of your product or service in language he would understand.

Next, describe your company's range of products. Talk about your company's lowest-priced products or services, and what they do. What are the highest-priced products, and what do they do?

Who benefits by using your company's product or service, and what markets or industries are they in?

If there are aspects to your product or service that he might not understand because he's not in the field, then back up, re-write and explain those aspects. You can do this by using analogies known to the average person, or with language so basic even a child could understand.

Now comes the most important part: Tell this stranger how he would use your company's product or service. Most important tell him how his job, business, or life would be made better by using your company's product or service.

Next, tell him the things that you think make your company's products or services better and different from those of your competitors.

Imagine how you would say all of this to the kindly stranger on the park bench, and then write it down exactly as you would have said it (it even helps to start this exercise by speaking into a tape recorder and then writing it down later). Once you start talking (and writing), it becomes easier.

As you tell the story of your product, you'll find yourself unconsciously folding in the key benefits your wrote down in your previous Laundry List, and adding in new product features and benefits as they come to mind.

Finally, tell your imaginary listener what he has to do in order to buy your company's product. For example, if he needs to call your company's toll-free number to contact a sales representative, explain to him, in simple terms, how to do this.

If your product is sold through your company's Web site, tell him how to reach your Web site, and where he would go there to order your product. Anticipate any special concerns an average person may have ("is my credit card information safe if I order from your Web site?"). Talk it out in your mind, or out loud; then write it down.

When you are finished, your Park Bench Story should be simple and easily understood by anyone, especially someone with no prior knowledge of your company and its products.

Step 3: Your Elevator Pitch

As you practice these writing exercises, you gain experience by writing down all the product benefits you can think of (the Laundry list), and then "talking out" your product and its value (the Park Bench Story). All of these thoughts, now firmly planted in your mind, prepare you for the next exercise, where you condense the most important of these sales benefits into your product's "Elevator Pitch."

As you will recall from earlier in this chapter, the Elevator Pitch is the concise, 15-second sales pitch your best sales rep would give to his or her best prospect if they were both taking an elevator ride during a chance encounter at the prospect's office.

The elevator pitch puts the best one or two of your product's top benefits into a concisely-worded, do-or-die sales pitch.

If you weren't able to copy down the Elevator Pitches you heard from your sales reps in your debriefing, write your own Elevator Pitch by answering these four questions for your listener:

    1.) Who is your company?
    2.) What does your company sell?
    3.) What's so good about that?
    4.) What's in it for me?

Write down your responses to each of these questions, in the order above. Give only one answer to each of the four questions—the best answer is usually the first one that pops into your mind.

Combine these answers into a string of two or three sentences that, when spoken, create a forceful and compelling verbal statement. Do this by reading what you've just written, out loud. Rewrite if necessary, as new words or better ways of saying things occur to you as you're speaking.

When you're satisfied that what you've written is about as good as you can write and say it, then you've finished the writing exercises and are ready to move on to the next chapter, covering the process of writing sales copy and executing marketing deliverables.

What You Have Accomplished by Completing these Exercises

These three ad copywriting exercises give you the experience of writing about your company's products in three different forms:

- **Short:** The Elevator Pitch;

- **Medium:** The Laundry List;

- **Long:** The Park Bench Story

Even if your ad agency writes your company's advertising copy, practicing these exercises helps you:

- **Discover your product's major benefits**, which repeat themselves across two or more of the writing forms above;

- **Learn how to write sales copy** for large, medium, or small copy spaces, big ads or small ones, and other marketing deliverables, of all sizes (such as brochures, catalog sheets, fact sheets, postcards or any other project);

- **Give your ad agency guidance and direction** prior to their development and execution of your company's ad campaigns and marketing deliverables.

The last point above is the most important: To control your company's message and presentation, as a marketing manager it is your responsibility to keep your company's ad agency "on the message."

To do this you must take the initiative in developing your product's key sales copy benefits, and insist that these key sales benefits appear in all copy for your company's marketing deliverables.

> **Giving this control over to your ad agency, or letting your agency divine their own interpretation of your company's product benefits without your assistance, almost guarantees that your advertising will be less effective than it could have been.**

If they are doing their job, these are the same steps undertaken by your agency's advertising copywriter as he or she writes your advertising copy for your account. These exercises give you an extremely helpful and revealing view of how your sales message is developed. And by going through this process yourself, you will be able to speak with far more credibility and authority when dealing with your agency's account executive, creative director, and copywriter.

The next chapter covers the third and final aspect of ad copywriting, the process of writing and layout for advertising and other marketing deliverables.

MARKETING DELIVERABLES
CHAPTER 5
COPY, LAYOUT, & EXECUTION
OF EFFECTIVE ADS, MAILINGS, AND
PRINT COLLATERAL

Once you have completed the three-step Laundry List, Park Bench Story, and Elevator Pitch writing exercises in the previous chapter, you're ready to start the third and final step: The process of identifying your product's major benefits, features, and applications, hammering these benefits into sales copy for your ad or other marketing deliverable, and driving the final design and layout process.

We refer to print advertising in our examples, but these techniques apply equally to many other forms of marketing deliverables, such as brochures, direct mail packages, catalog flyers, even Web sites.

Part 3: The Execution Stage

This chapter isn't intended to be an in-depth tutorial on ad copywriting, design, and layout (see Appendix for a list of recommended books on this subject). However, it will illustrate to you the process of converting the results of the writing exercises in the previous chapter into the four basic elements required for any ad, brochure, or other marketing deliverable:

- **Headline**
- **Subhead**
- **Body copy**
- **Call to action**

These elements form the essential structure of nearly every marketing deliverable, and will help any sales communication be more effective to prospects in any marketplace, if the right sales benefits are used in each element. This section outlines a basic technique for matching the best sales benefit(s) to each element, and you can use this technique for outlining the sales copy notes you provide to your ad agency or marketing consultant who writes your company's sales copy. You can also use these techniques to write your own sales copy, if necessary.

Your Headline

Start by taking the sheets of paper containing the notes you made from your Laundry List, Park Bench Story, and Elevator Pitch (from the writing exercises in the previous chapter), and place them side by side.

As you read across each version you wrote, you'll often see a key benefit that's *repeated across all three written versions.*

Summarize this benefit in 20 words or less, and write it down. This is your product's **prime sales benefit,** and is (with some rewriting) your headline in your company's advertising or other marketing collateral.

Converting Benefits to Headlines: Examples

Here are some prime sales benefits, in raw form, that you might have written down as notes from the previous writing exercise examples, if you were a marketing manager in any one of the following industries:

- For a nationwide chain of hotels aimed at budget business travelers:

    Save about half the usual cost of business lodging—without having to stay at a "cheap" hotel

- For a company selling a new thin-film material for flat-screen digital displays:

    Industry experts say: Our material has 15% greater saturation and contrast

- For a software company selling a new ERP ("Enterprise Resource Planning") software system to accountants:

    Drive your inventory costs even lower and your manufacturing efficiency higher, with a single ERP system

- For a business leasing company specializing in computer systems:

    Guaranteed lease processing in 15 minutes or less via our Web site

- For a company selling a digital projector for displaying business presentations:

    No more clumsy laptop PC connections—start up your presentations instantly from the projector's built-in memory

- For a secure, off-site data backup facility that also offers sophisticated, mission-critical corporate data backup services:

> *Your data backup facility isn't worth anything if you don't back up your data in the first place*

- For a company selling miniature fiber-optic cameras to airline service companies:

  > *A 5-minute check with our scope prevents a 10-hour engine teardown*

Revealing sales headlines: There are sales-driving, stop-and-read-'em headlines just waiting to jump out of these prime benefits. Here are some headlines written from the previous benefit examples:

- **Prime Benefit:** Save about half the usual cost of business lodging—without having to stay at a "cheap" hotel…

  Headlines:

  How to Save Half the Cost of a Business Hotel, Without Staying at a Cheap Hotel

  (or)

  Save Half the Cost of Your Next Business Stay

- **Prime Benefit:** Your data backup facility isn't worth anything if you don't back up your data in the first place…

  Headlines:

  Super-Secure Data Facilities (Free Data Backups Included).

  (or)

  If Disaster Struck <u>Right Now</u>, Would You Have 100% Data Backup?

Your Subheads for Sales Copy

Next, take a red pen and circle any benefit that appears across any <u>two</u> of your three writing forms (Laundry List, Elevator Pitch, and within your Park Bench Story).

Write these benefit lines down, as complete sentences, line by line. You should end up with 3 to 6 benefits that repeat themselves across your three writing forms.

Read these benefits, and pick out the one that you think is the most important benefit of the group. Then, pick the second-most important benefit line, and so on, ranking the rest of them in order of their importance.

An example of a list of ranked benefits would look something like this example (for a nationwide chain of budget hotels targeting business travelers):

Rank:	*Benefit:*
1.	*Room rates cost just a little more than those of "econo"-type motels*
2.	*Our hotels are the same from city to city, so you know what to expect*
3.	*Our hotels have fast Internet hookups—check your e-mail and move big files around while you're on the road*
4.	*We have a hotel in most major cities—you can find one wherever you travel*
5.	*We have food service in most locations, so you don't have to drive around a strange city late at night, or first thing next morning, to find someplace to eat*
6.	*It's easy to reserve a room on our Web site*

Your Ad's Body Copy

Ranking your product's benefits not only provides you with a list of useful subheads, but forms the basis of an outline for the body copy of your ad.

Continuing with our previous example:

Benefit points:

- *Room rates cost just a little more than those of "Econo"-type motels*
- *Our hotels are the same from city to city, so you know what to expect*

Copy:

"At Four Points by Sheraton, you get a nice, business-class room for just a little more than one of those "econo" places, and without any unexpected surprises."

Benefit points:

- *Our hotels have fast Internet hookups at no extra cost—check your e-mail and move big files around while you're on the road*

- *We have a hotel in most major cities—you can find one wherever you travel*

Copy:

"Our rooms have broadband Net hookups for a modest additional fee, so you can check your e-mail and move those large files around in no time."

"Chances are, there's a Four Points by Sheraton at the next major city your business takes you."

Benefit points:

- **We have food service in most locations, so you don't have to drive around a strange city late at night, or first thing next morning, to find someplace to eat.**

- **It's easy to reserve a room on our Web site**

Copy:

"And most of our hotels have their own restaurants, so your next meal is never a mystery."

"It's easy to see our rooms, and make your next reservation anytime on our Web site, **www.fourpoints.com**."

Now, here are all the benefits put together into the final sales copy for the ad.

In this example, the length of the ad copy was short, so it includes just the top two subhead benefits in the final ad copy block, as shown here in the full copy block of the ad:

Get a Nice Room, at a Nice Rate—and No Surprises

At Four Points by Sheraton, you get a nice, business-class room for just a little more than one of those "econo" places, and without any unexpected surprises.

Our rooms have broadband Net hookups for a modest additional fee, so you can check your email and move those large files around in no time.

Find Us Everywhere You Go

Chances are, there's a Four Points by Sheraton at the next major city your business takes you.

And there's extended-hour food service in every location, so your next meal is never a mystery.

It's easy to see our rooms, and make your next reservation anytime on our Web site, **www.fourpoints.com**.

Call to Action

In a way, the last paragraph in the ad copy above is a call to action. But if you were the marketing manager at Sheraton, it might be smart to offer new customers an incentive to book a room right away on your Web site, right from the ad, and save 10%, with this call to action at the bottom of your ad:

> **Book a Room Online, Save 10%:** Save 10% on your first room reservation at Four Points by Sheraton—go to **www.fourpoints.com** and enter your special savings code: 98741

When possible, offering a special, trackable promotion in your ad's call to action not only increases response, but allows you to measure your advertising's effectiveness. Measurability is far easier now that consumers can go to dedicated Web links printed in your ads, brochures, and other sales materials.

This Writing Process Opens Infinite Possibilities

There are infinite variations to how any of the four elements derived from your rough sales benefit copy can be written. By forcing you to think, view, and describe your product's benefits in different ways, these writing techniques unlock the infinite creative possibilities found in your product's sales story.

For example, there are many ways to write a headline out of the prime selling benefit of your product. Moreover, with a little imagination, there are virtually limitless ways in which this benefit may be expressed and presented—in alternate headlines, copy, graphics, and many other, highly persuasive, ways. But this is where the job of the marketing manager usually ends, and your advertising agency's or marketing consultant's job begins.

Except that now, by performing these writing exercises on your company's products yourself, you're in a better position to direct the sales messages of your company's advertising projects, and to guide your ad agency to produce better ad campaigns and marketing deliverables for your company.

Your product's major selling benefits, when combined with the effective layout techniques described in the next section, will transform your advertising into a hard-hitting, response-generating selling tool for your company.

Part 4: The Layout Stage

The Rise of the Advertising Art Directors and the Decline of Advertising: All You Need to Know About Advertising Layout

One of the major reasons why advertising is not as effective as it once was is that ad agency art directors have too much control of the process of creating advertising and marketing deliverables.

In many cases, this happens because marketing managers and their management counterparts in ad agencies have simply not done their jobs. If neither the marketing manager nor ad agency head or account executive takes on the process of hammering down the product's key selling benefits, then this vacuum will be filled by those who follow in the next step of the process—the ad agency's art director, and other "creatives."

When marketing managers and agency account executives view salesmanship as a "creative" process, and pass the buck to art and creative directors at the agency, they nearly always doom their marketing projects to failure.

Why? The art director's primary career motivation is to create advertising that wins local or national design awards. Winning a "Best of Show" award in an ad design competition is a mark of pride and a resumé enhancer. Sales appeal used to be an important factor in the way show judges picked the winners of these design competitions, but no longer.

Like much of our culture, the art of advertising design has degraded such that striking (and sometimes shocking) visual imagery wins design awards. Think of the last time you saw one of those over-the-top Benetton ads, and you get the point: Many art directors view salesmanship as the ugly stepchild blocking the entrance hall to the design award ceremony.

If you compare the winning ads in any current issue of *CA* (*Communication Arts*), the leading professional publication for advertising art directors, to any issue of 15 or more years ago, you'll see this point. When viewed from the aspect of sales-oriented presentation—the only measure that counts—most any ad from any pre-1985 issue of CA would beat most any ad from a current issue.

Taking Back the Advertising Layout Process

When judged by inquiries or sales generated from an ad, advertising projects dominated by art directors nearly always fail. That's why most advertising is as poor and ineffective as it is today. If, as a marketing manager, you develop your product's sales benefits, and insist these benefits be effectively communicated all the way through to the final ad or deliverable, you will guide and influence the process, and you won't surrender this important role to your agency's art director.

This section covers the key techniques for producing effective ad layouts and, like the other techniques described in this chapter, they apply to any type of marketing deliverable—ads, brochures, sales flyers, etc. This chapter's purpose is not to make you an advertising layout designer, but to reveal some of the techniques sales-oriented layout designers use to dramatically increase the attention-getting power of their layouts. You will not go wrong if you utilize these techniques in all of your company's advertising, mailings, print collateral, or any other marketing project.

Figure 5-1:

Serif, Sans Serif Type Samples

Serif Type:

Aa Kk Mm Nn Ee

(notice the "feet," circled above)

Sans-Serif Type:

Aa Kk Mm Nn Ee

Headlines come first: Your ad's headline is your most important sales message—always. Headlines should be set in big, bold type so they're very readable, even at a distance. Graphical elements of an ad, such as photos or illustrations, should not distract the reader from your ad's headline, nor should they dominate your headline.

Sans-serif for headlines, serif for body copy: "Serif" type is any typeface with "feet"—i.e., short horizontal lines running out from the base of each letter. Sans-serif typefaces are, literally, "without feet."

Sans-serif typefaces, such as Franklin Gothic, Futura or Helvetica, work best for your ad's headlines and subheads, because they give the highest impact where the fewest words are used.

Serif typefaces, such as Times, Garamond, and New Century Schoolbook are more readable than sans-serif faces, and work better where more words are used, so they should be used in your ad's longer body copy.

While sans-serif type can also be used in body copy, and serif type can look just fine in a headline, the contrast generated between serif body copy type and sans-serif headlines and subheads makes for a more attention-getting ad.

Tight kerning is good: Kerning is the amount of spacing between the letters of the text of your ad. A headline with kerning set "tighter" than a headline with no kerning conveys a sense of greater urgency. Tighter kerning in long blocks of copy also allows you to fit more words in the same space.

Where's your phone number? It's surprising how much time and money companies spend on their advertising, yet at the end of their ads fail to tell the reader how to contact them. Don't repeat their mistake in your ads—always feature your company's phone number and Web and mailing addresses in big, bold type across the bottom of your advertising. Your prospects want to reach you, so why should you stop them?

White space is nice, but the black space does the selling: If your product requires long advertising copy, your ads should be long-copy ads. Don't let others criticize your ad layouts for having "too many words," if you believe that these words are well-written, tell your company's story, and **sell** your company's product. If your product's sales benefits are effectively communicated in your advertising copy, your prospects will read your advertising.

Let the *meaning* of your ad be the *master* of your layout.

"Busy" is good, if it's interesting: There's nothing wrong if, in addition to copy, your ad requires diagrams, sidebars, or thumbnail photos. These information-rich

---

Figure 5-2:

Kerning and Leading—Use tight letter-spacing (kerning) and line spacing (leading) in all of your headlines

---

Before: *The type in this headline is how it appears, without adjusting the kerning, as it is set from your font style list.*

No Kerning, Loose Leading:

Now You Can Save 20% on Your Next Shipment

After: *Adjusting the spacing between each letter of your type (kerning) improves the readability, impact and appearance of your headline or body copy, and makes your ads and brochures look tight and professional.*

Tight Kerning and Tight Leading:

Now You Can Save 20% on Your Next Shipment

---

layouts can work very well for products that require detailed explanations, or are aimed at people who are likely to have detailed questions about your product, such as engineers, programmers, or doctors. These layouts require extra skill on the part of your agency's ad layout person, and it always helps to have some examples for them to work from (see paragraph below).

If you see a good layout, copy it: Become a connoisseur of ad layouts. Buy and read the layout and design-related books listed in the Appendix. As you flip through trade publications, magazines and newspapers, keep an eye out for ad layouts that you think do an especially good job of presenting a product's sales benefits. Not "pretty" ads, or over-designed ones, but ads that attract you by their sales appeal, and the way the product is described and presented. Clip these ads and start a file folder, so you can refer back to them whenever you need a new idea for an ad for your company.

In ad agency art departments, these are called "reference files" and they're a source of ready inspiration for every art director. There is nothing wrong with adapting someone else's ad layout for your own projects. Obviously, we're not suggesting you steal their photos or art—just let another ad's layout "inspire" your own, as many artists have done throughout history.

Figure 5-3:

Ad Contact Info—Use taglines on all marketing collateral

Make it easy for prospects to contact your company, by putting your company's full contact information at the bottom of your company's ads, brochures, and other marketing deliverables.

My e-mail address is: _____

For More Info, Call **1-800-767-0403**

vistainfo
vistainfo.com

(800) 856-MEET

Collaborative Technologies Corporation

Team Conferencing For Better And Faster Business Decisions. Around The Table. Or Around The World.

■ A Lotus Notes Alliance Partner

8920 Business Park Drive, Suite 100
Austin, TX 78759
(512) 794-8858
FAX: (512) 794-8861

Call For Free Report On Any Site Of Your Choice:

(800)989-0403

E|R|I|S **ERIIScan**
Environmental Property Report

For more information, call Peter Gorog at (703) 834-9402 or Chris Lawlor at (301) 236-1729.

⊕ **Bell Atlantic ScanFone**
Being launched in the Washington Metro area in September

For More Information:
Tel: (786) 853-8947
www.whpwireless.com

whp wireless™ INC.
THE BRIDGE TO THE WIRELESS REVOLUTION ™

7 Taggart Drive, Suite I • Nashua, NH 03060

Learn to see with "new eyes:" It's likely your prospect has never heard of your company or product, and, when he sees your ad, will be seeing it for the first time. So develop the ability to see your ad layouts as your prospects see them. Put yourself in their position, and learn to see your ads and marketing deliverables as if your mind was a blank slate: Does your headline make sense if someone doesn't really know about your product? Could a reader get the gist of what your company's ad is selling just by scanning it from top to bottom? Look at your ad layouts first thing in the morning, after a good night's sleep; this helps to reveal missing details or points in your ad copy that could be expressed more clearly.

Using Color in Print Display Advertising

Should you use color? In certain instances, use of color in your company's advertising is mandatory—as hotels, travel advertisers, and big-ticket consumer products manufacturers (such as auto companies) have known for decades.

Advances in digital pre-press technology in recent years have enabled magazine production departments to reduce the added production costs of running four-color process ads. While this cost difference places color within the reach of many full-page advertisers, bear in mind that rates for four-color display advertising will

Figure 5-4:

Long Copy Sells—Use effective sales copy and interesting layouts, and prospects will read your advertising

"Busy" Ads Sell Better than Short-Copy Ads: Give your readers the information they need to make a buying decision on your company's product or service. Use bold subheads to highlight key sales benefits and product features, and a bold "call to action" at the bottom of your ad to tell readers what to do next.

generally average at least 10%-25% higher than for the same ad sizes in black and white.

If your company sells a product that will benefit by color presentation, a vivid color photo conveys an impression of quality. Technical diagrams and quality line art looks better in color as well. If there is any visual aspect of your company's product or service that could be communicated more effectively, or with greater impact, in color, then you should use color.

Just because color is used, doesn't mean that it should be overused in advertising projects, which frequently happens. For example, an advertising art director's placement of a photo or illustration that completely overwhelms the headline or body copy of your sales message suppresses the impact of your ad's sales message.

The most successful four-color advertising uses color sparingly, with a small, beautifully-executed color photograph, or an illustration teamed with competent type design. Good color ad layouts feature mostly plain-white page backgrounds or, going to the other extreme, solid, vivid background colors bleeding off the edges of a page.

The previous section described how marketing managers must sometimes re-take control of the layout and design process from the ad agency's art director. This is especially important when working with color in ad layouts. You may find it

---

Figure 5-5:

Advertising's Job is to Inform Your Prospects—Your job is to give them this information, in a persuasive way

"*I don't know who you are.*

I don't know your company.

I don't know your company's product.

I don't know what your company stands for.

I don't know your company's customers.

I don't know your company's record.

I don't know your company's reputation.

Now—what was it you wanted to sell me?"

The prospect's view, presented in this classic 1958 McGraw-Hill ad, is just as true today as it was then.

MORAL: Sales start before your salesman calls—with business publication advertising.

McGRAW-HILL MAGAZINES
BUSINESS•PROFESSIONAL•TECHNICAL

---

necessary to rein in the advertising art director's use of color, and restore to prominence what should always be the most important elements of your company's advertising—headline, subheads, body copy and call to action.

Remember, just because unlimited digital color design and production capabilities are now available at the click of a mouse doesn't mean they should all find their way into your company's advertising layouts.

Four-Color Advertising Layout Techniques

Judicious application of color: Limiting your use of four-color process art to jewel-like photos and line art illustrations of the highest production quality and resolution, combined with the same pro-grade typesetting design you'd use in any black and white ad, makes color work the way it works best—sparingly.

Color photographs must be sharp, vivid, and professionally executed. And sometimes even reality isn't good enough: For example, even the best, professionally photographed shots must sometimes be enhanced and digitally "airbrushed" to bring out their best features and highlights. When you are spending money on color, spend the extra money it sometimes requires to perfect your photos and other color art.

Figure 5-6:

Color in Display Advertising —Use color sparingly, and let your headline be the main focus to your reader

Small Color Photos and Graphics, combined with bold headlines, are an attractive and attention-getting way to use color in your print display ads

Full-color illustrations: Full-color illustrations work best when they are created by the best illustration artists your company can afford. Often, these artists still work largely in the non-digital mediums, such as watercolor, pen and ink, etc. This means your company will incur added costs to scan these illustrations on high-resolution scanners in your advertising's final production process. However, when working with color, the stunning end result, and the added punch it gives to your ad's selling power, makes the effort worthwhile.

Heavy solids and page bleeds: At the other extreme, another highly effective technique for using color in advertising is to use solid, primary color backgrounds (your printer calls them "heavy solids") that bleed off a publication's page on all three sides. This method only works in ads that use few (or no) photos or illustrations, and, most important, in ads that do not utilize an extensive amount of text. This works best with solid, primary colors—cool, dark blues, greens, dark reds—using bolder, sans-serif typefaces reversed out in white over these solid colors.

Keeping your ad designs to either of these ends of the four-color design and production spectrum gives your company's advertising the best opportunity to get noticed. You will make the best use of color in your advertising, and you will prevent color from overrunning your advertising's sales message.

Figure 5-7 :

Setting Headlines—Type display techniques have a tremendous effect on readability and sales impact

---

Now You Can
Save 20% on
Your Next Shipment

Not Effective: *Plain serif type headline*

**Now You Can
Save 20% on
Your Next Shipment**

Effective: *Bold, sans-serif display type, set with tight kerning and leading, makes an impact on your reader*

**Now You Can
Save 20% on
Your Next Shipment**

Even Better: *The same headline set in reverse type stands out even more in ads, brochures and other deliverables*

**Now You Can
Save 20% on
Your Next Shipment**

Tone Reverses: *You can tone down any reversed headline by using the same type on a 40% screen of solid black, without diminishing its impact to the reader*

Creative and Black and White Ad Design Options

There will be times when the option of using full-color will either be too expensive or, as in the case of newspaper advertising, unavailable. For example, if you decide to run fractional ad sizes, such as half- and quarter page ads, the additional costs for color on these smaller sizes will average 30%-50% higher than for the equivalent black and white ad size, which often makes four-color advertising in these sizes too expensive to consider. Or, you may be promoting a product that doesn't require color presentation, such as a newsletter or other information-based product or service.

You won't find a black and white ad to be a disadvantage, if it's produced well. Creative use of the "monochrome medium" of black and white in print advertising can often make a black and white ad even more effective than many, more expensive, four-color ads.

Use the following simple techniques to boost the visibility of black and white advertising:

Bold, graphical headlines: Big, bold, black type makes your headline sell: Using an extra-bold, sans-serif typeface such as Franklin Gothic Heavy, combined with artful line arrangement and tight leading, makes any black and

Figure 5-8:

Combining Product Photos and Sales Copy in Print Ads and Other Marketing Deliverables

Product Photos and Sales Copy: *Using the mask-and-shadow technique for photos, combined with type runarounds of text or bullet points, boosts readability and interest for both your product shot, and your sales copy*

white ad stand out on a page, and hits readers right between the eyes with your headline.

The secret to this technique of "graphical" headline type presentation consists of using line breaks to logically separate a longer headline into three or more easily readable, stacked lines (see **Figure 5-7**). Also make sure that the letter spacing, also known as "kerning," and the spacing between your lines, called "leading," are set "tight"—that is, so both letters and lines of type are squeezed as closely together as possible.

Setting headlines in this tight-and-stacked style can actually transform your headlines into an attention-getting graphical element in your ad. Even ads with no photos or illustrations will grab a reader's attention if the type layouts of their headlines are executed in this way.

Headline screens and reverses: Another smart variation when designing with type is to reverse your ad's headline, placing it as white on a 30 to 40% square or rectangular screen (see example in **Figure 5-7**). A bold, screened (or even black) field sitting behind a reversed white headline of sans-serif type makes a bold visual statement that demands attention.

Black and white photo presentation: Since photographs in your black-and-white ad must compete visually with full-color photos and illustrations in color ads, you must pay even greater attention to how your black-and-white photos look in your advertising. Always ask your ad agency for a printable **press proof** that gives you a very close approximation of how your ad will look in its final form. Since black-and-white photos often print darker in publications than they appear on your computer screen or in their original source photographs, it is important that you get an accurate picture of how your ad will look before it appears on the printed page.

Mask and shadow technique: If you are using photos of your company's products, the "Mask and Shadow" technique can often transform your product photo into a visually-arresting graphical shape (see example in **Figure 5-8**). Text set around the outlined shape of your photo (also called a "runaround"), combines the visually interesting shape of your product with tight, effective type design to produce a truly compelling black-and-white ad that draws your readers into your ad layouts.

Type—keep it tight throughout your ad: Make sure you extend this close attention to type design to the rest of your ad layout, not just to your headline alone. For example, and to increase the chances that they will pop off the page, the subheads of your ad's body copy should be set in the same (or same family of) typeface as your ad's headline. Tight, bold-faced subheads, written so they read as complete sentences, help skim-readers get the gist of your sales message even if (like most people) they don't read the entire text of your ad. Setting these subheads in the same typeface as your ad's headline helps busy readers get the essential message of your ad in the few short seconds their eyes spend on your ad, before their eyes dart away from your page.

The bold visual: A simple black-and-white shape, line drawing, or photo, when "amped up" beyond the rational proportions of where it "should" be sized within your ad, can often be so effective that it stops the reader—your prospect—so completely that they will focus their entire attention on the rest of your ad. Using simple, iconic figures, such as generic symbols or punctuation, can also be real traffic stoppers for readers when these line images are blown up to "unexpected" proportions in even the smallest black-and-white ads.

Use These Techniques, Trust Yourself, and Your Marketing Team

Your company is full of amateur art directors and creative dilettantes. Anyone who can hold a red pen thinks they know more about ad layouts than you do. It's a bad aspect of human nature that leads people to tear down or unduly criticize any creative work, and it's especially destructive when people don't know what they're talking about.

You'll find this to be especially true whenever you're working on advertising and layouts for other kinds of marketing deliverables in your company. In the development and final approval stages, limit the number of people who see your company's advertising, and above all, have confidence in your own abilities, those of your marketing team, and in your marketing projects and their direction.

Most of all, hold fast to the principles outlined in this chapter—they are proven, time-honored techniques that help you and your team create advertising that generates inquiries and sales for your company.

DIRECT MAIL PLANNING
CHAPTER 6
GENERATING INQUIRIES AND SALES THROUGH DIRECT MAIL AND DIRECT RESPONSE

In all its forms, direct mail is the mainstay of many business marketing activities, and your success or failure as a marketing manager often depends on putting your company's printed sales materials into the hands of the right prospects in your market.

Whether it's a high-volume mailing piece sent to 50,000 prospects using rented mailing lists, an expensive, personalized, high-end mailing distributed to a small, carefully-chosen list of CEOs among your company's best customers, or a postcard mailing to existing customers announcing a new product promotion, all direct mail marketing projects are a targeted, personal communication to an individual in your company's marketplace who may be a buyer for your company's product or service.

In planning and executing direct mail projects, your job as a marketing manager is to determine the general approach and marketing deliverables needed to persuade these individuals to take action: To call your company's sales reps for more information, to buy your company's product for the first time, to place a re-order, or respond to a special promotion.

Advantages of Direct Mail

Direct mail offers many important advantages to your marketing program:

Control: More than any other marketing activity, direct mail projects give you a high level of control. Unlike a trade show booth, or a display ad in a trade publication, you control your product's sales message in the direct mail package. Your product's sales appeal is not obscured by its placement in a magazine, by another competitor's larger ad, or by a poor booth location at a trade show. Unlike print display advertising, for example, direct mail projects can be executed anytime, anywhere, without regard to a publication's closing dates or its printing schedules. If you have a mailing package and a mailing list, you can get a mailing out in a matter of days;

Cost: Unlike advertising and trade shows, there is no minimum "buy-in" cost to put out a mailing. You determine the quantity of pieces to mail, and the cost of each piece, whether it's 100, or 100,000, mailing pieces. And once you've developed a direct mail package that works, you can achieve tremendous savings by printing higher quantities, in advance, for the printed pieces you use in your direct mail programs;

Flexibility: You can develop specialized direct mail packages to exploit, or respond to, virtually any new marketing situation or opportunity. You can put out a mailing designed to stimulate sales during a slow period, or to respond to a competitor's price cut with a special promotional offer;

Speed: A direct mail project can be developed and produced in a very short period of time. Any competent and dedicated ad agency or marketing consultant can turn out a direct mail package, start-to-finish, in a week, or two weeks at most. This fast turnaround lets you enter new markets quickly, and respond to marketing emergencies faster than any other marketing method. When you've developed an array of individual printed marketing deliverables for your company, you can increase your company's speed of execution even further. For example, once developed, an arsenal of printed pieces like direct mail brochures, reply cards, standard cover letters, and envelopes can be quickly modified and reassembled into a new direct mail package for a quick test in a new market, a fast mailing to a promising new prospect list, a mailing to kick off a new joint business relationship, or any other promising new business opportunity that needs to be acted upon—fast;

Personalization: The more you can personalize your direct mail piece to your prospect, the better your response. Database software and digital printing technology offer a wide range of personalization options to give your prospects highly targeted information on your company's products;

Precision: The technology of direct mail allows you to build mailing lists of customers or prospects by business size and type, number of employees, past purchases, or any other available field in your marketing database. These same profiling options are also available from rented mailing lists of potential prospects, available from outside sources. Once selected, today's high speed digital printing technologies enable you to tailor your sales message on the outer envelope, cover letter, and brochure of your direct mail package to appeal specifically to smaller and smaller groups of prospects within these lists, based on their profiles;

Unlimited creativity: In direct mail, there are virtually no limits to size, color options, individual printed elements, or other print or production-related options. Your materials can be as simple, or as elaborate, as your budget and judgment allow;

Testing and predictability: You can test a small portion of a mailing list and predict, with a reasonable measure of certainty, the results you'd likely receive if you were to mail the same mailing piece to the entire list. You can also create a "response curve" to predict the final response of a mailing list, based on the small number of initial responses received during the first several days of a mailing. And if you receive a favorable projected response to a mailing, you can start sooner to plan your follow-up mailing to larger portions of the list. Conversely, if you receive a poor projected early response, you can make plans to mail to other potentially more productive, lists, or move on to other more productive marketing activities sooner (testing and projection for direct mail projects is covered in detail in the next chapter).

Direct Mail Applications

The two major applications for direct mail in business-to-business marketing are:

Market coverage: Generating new inquiries and sales leads for your company's sales reps, through a program of regular, systematic mailings to both self-compiled mailing lists, and lists rented from outside sources, such as trade publications;

Sales support: Using mailings after the sales call to shorten the selling cycle. This involves close coordination with your company's sales reps and using sales contact management system software to time a series of regular mailings to prospects, designed to help your sales reps turn prospects into buyers. This may be just one follow-up mailing package, or it may be a series of two or more, rising in complexity, based on a prospect's qualifications, and personalized as a result of your sales rep's last sales call to that prospect.

There are almost no limits to how and where direct mail can be used in your company's marketing programs. Here are some examples:

- **Reach CEOs** with a highly personalized direct mail package, specially tailored to each recipient;

- **Reach key distributors and dealers** with new product announcements, new pricing options and ordering plans, or new product features and enhancements;

- **Communicate with your customers** on a regular basis, through your company's printed (or e-mail) applications newsletter, focusing on the latest industry developments and providing helpful product applications advice, weaving promotional information on your company's products or services into the content of these communications;

- **A mass mailing to a rented list of previous buyers** of another product, sold by another company, very similar to products sold by your company;

- **A mailing to a self-compiled list**, gathered from a telephone canvass of a trade association mailing list;

- **A questionnaire to your customer base**, seeking new application ideas for one of your company's new products or processes;

- **An announcement to your customers and prospects**, informing them of an important change in government regulation, and alerting them to the fact that one of your company's products will help them comply with this new regulation;

- **A direct mail market test**, featuring a mock-up or prototype of a product your company is planning to offer, mailed to key prospective buyers in a handful of important new retail channels;

- **A series of direct mail pieces, mailed weekly**, each focusing on a different attribute of your company's product;

- **A "downstream" mailing to dealers**, with tips on selling your company's product, designed to stimulate "upstream" sales and product re-order calls back to key distributors in your sales network;

- **A quick, live market test of your company's product**, mailed to a small sample of prospective buyers in a totally new and untried market, obtained from a rented subscriber list of a major trade publication in this market;

- **A mailing piece sent directly to prospective end-users** of your company's product, designed to test direct sales to users, bypassing your company's conventional dealer network;

- **A rapidly-executed mailing** sent out to your customers in response to a competitor's attention-getting price cut, emphasizing the fact that superior customer service and on-time delivery are often more important than a temporary price cut;

- **A "Member-Get-A-Member" promotion**, to encourage existing customers to refer new prospects to your company;

- **A mailing piece introducing a new sales representative** to customers in the rep's sales territory, featuring a laser-printed photo and message from the new rep;

- **A mailing highlighting a recent industry study** documenting a specific productivity gain experienced by companies using your company's product;

- **A mailing to trade show attendees**, inviting them to your company's booth seminar or hospitality suite.

Part 1: Mailing Lists: The Heart of Your Company's Direct Mail Marketing Activities

The mailing list is the most important part of any direct mail project. A good mailing list is more important than the most compelling sales headline, or the most persuasive sales letter in any direct mail piece. While a mediocre direct mail package sent to a great mailing list can sometimes be successful, a great direct mail package sent to a mediocre mailing list always yields a poor response. Despite this fact, mailing lists are the most overlooked aspect of many direct mail projects.

A company may spend thousands of dollars and hours of time preparing its direct mail piece, and yet will defer vitally important decisions on mailing list selection until the direct mail package is ready to go to the printer. At this point, the company's ad agency may thoughtlessly select a low-grade rental list of 20,000 names from a mailing list compiler, throwing in some additional names of prospects who responded to the company's most recent print ads. The piece is then mailed to this list, and the response is underwhelming. To add insult to injury, a large number of mailing pieces are returned with incorrect or outdated addresses, since no one gave any thought to checking the accuracy of the list before it was mailed. After one bad experience, the company's management has been turned against direct mail for good. This is what usually happens whenever a company's marketing manager says: "Oh, we've tried direct mail, but it just doesn't work." With a single failure, a company will close off a very important selling channel in its marketing program.

In direct mail, the mailing list *is* the market: A mailing list can take many forms. It may be a carefully profiled list of your customers, segmented by their overall sales volume or by product. It can be a rented list of subscribers to the leading trade publication in your industry, chosen as an Nth-name selection for testing purposes (more on this further in this chapter). A mailing list can also be a self-compiled list of prospects generated by a telephone research project in your company, or an industry executive directory gathered from a trade association. It may also be a list of prospects who have responded to your company's trade publication advertising over the past six months, key-coded by publication and area of product interest.

In every example just mentioned, the mailing list represents a market of individuals with a job title, previous purchasing history, or some other characteristic that could make them a future customer of your company. An effective mailing list not only defines the individuals whose names appear on that list, it defines the content and selling message of the direct mail package that's being mailed to it.

Assessing Mailing Lists

Before you execute any direct mail project, start with its most important aspect— the mailing list. As you assess any list, ask yourself the following questions:

• Where did this mailing list come from?

- How can I trust the quality and selection of the names that were gathered for this list?

- What are the underlying needs and wants of the individuals on this mailing list?

- Are these needs and wants sufficiently addressed by the sales benefits we're using in our company's existing direct mail package?

- If not, is there a more customized, more effective sales message we can develop that would appeal to the individuals on this list?

- What is the underlying qualification of the individuals on this list that would induce them to buy our company's products or services?

- Have the individuals on this list already purchased products that are either exactly like, or similar to, the products sold by our company? If so, how do we know this, and did the individuals on this list actually make the purchasing decision?

- In addition to special sales appeals or product descriptions, is there some type of special promotional offer our company can make to the individuals on this mailing list?

Your answers to these questions may mean you'll have to modify one of your company's existing direct mail packages to tailor its selling message more closely to the audience represented by the list. In many cases, the sales potential of a mailing list will warrant the creation of a direct mail package that's been specially developed to sell to that particular list.

Elements of a Winning Mailing List

The best prospect mailing lists share the following characteristics:

Previous buyers: Next to your company's own customer list, the best mailing lists are prospects who previously purchased products just like the ones sold by your company, or other products closely related to those produced by your company. Obviously, this would also include the mailing lists of your competitors, but these lists are rarely obtainable;

Qualification: The next important element of a successful mailing list is the makeup of the individuals on that list. Are the prospects named on this list the people at the companies who'd be qualified to make the decision to buy your company's product? In most cases, you can answer this question based on your company's current sales experience. For example, if many of your current customers are Vice-Presidents of Technology or Engineering, you should be selecting other mailing lists by these (and similar) job titles;

Timeliness: Are the individuals on the mailing list you're evaluating still working at their companies? Are the addresses listed the correct current addresses for these companies? Has the company changed its name, been acquired by, or merged with, some other company? Although this aspect of a mailing list's quality is largely a matter of "list maintenance," mailing lists can become outdated after only a few months;

Accuracy: How "clean" is the mailing list? Are all the fields of every record filled in? Simple mistakes, like missing or mis-entered "Mr." or "Ms." salutations, or misspelled names of major companies, can cause embarrassing problems for your mailings. Other problems, like missing state fields, may prevent your mailing piece from reaching its recipient.

Mailing Lists: Self-Compiled and Rented Mailing Lists

When obtaining mailing lists, you'll either build them (self-compiled lists) or buy them (rented lists).

Self-Compiled Mailing Lists

In business-to-business marketing, the very best mailing lists are the ones you build yourself. Self-compiled mailing lists are created by combing through public sources, like trade association member directories, Web sites, and industry directories, as well as your own company's prospect databases, to put together targeted mailing lists for your company's own direct mail projects

Self-compiled lists are usually created as a result of laborious, time-consuming, detailed research and telephone contact. In most companies this difficult and tedious job always seems to fall on the shoulders of the marketing manager—that would be you.

This is however, such an important job that if it's not done, or not done well, then you'll miss one of the best potential sales opportunities for your company. That's why you must always take charge of the task of self-compiling mailing lists in your company.

Self-Compiled Mailing List Sources

You can tap the following sources to develop self-compiled prospect mailing lists for your company:

Figure 6-1:

Trade Association Lists

Trade Association Web Sites often feature online member directories, making them a very useful source for self-compiled mailing list projects

Contact information gathered from trade association Web sites can be combined with research of WHOIS Web site records (see Figure 6-2) to obtain the specific names and titles of the people inside the companies you're trying to reach for your direct mail projects

Your company's prospect databases: Your company's own internal prospect and sales inquiry database is your first, best choice whenever you need a self-compiled mailing list for an upcoming mailing. This includes your company's main customer database, sales prospect contact management system database, and other sources, such as prospects who've recently responded to your company's advertising in trade publications, magazine reader service card inquiries, and prospect names gathered during your company's recent trade show appearances;

Trade associations: Many trade associations serving the industries for the markets you're trying to reach freely publish their entire member directories on their Web sites, or make them available at a modest additional cost when you order the association's annual print directory. Trade association membership directories are a valuable starting point for developing mailing lists for test mailings to new markets, or if you're involved in a start-up company. You can get more information on list availability by calling a trade association's own research department;

The Internet: The Internet is the best thing that's happened to information research since the invention of the printing press. Google (**www.google.com**) is by far the best search engine available on the Internet today, and it's also a wonderful list-building tool: Enter keywords for the companies and industries you're trying to gather contacts for, and Google will take you to the most relevant Web sites. You can usually find the names of a company's top managers at the company's Web site, under links marked "Corporate Profile," or "Management," to get the names of prospects to add to your self-compiled mailing lists (see Chapter 12 for more detail on using the Internet for research);

Your company's business relationships: Joint ventures and other top-level business relationships can be an important source for direct mail sales opportunities, and for new mailing lists arising from these business relationships. For example, one action item in a new joint marketing venture might be a mailing to your new partner's customer and prospect lists. Of course, you must abide by the terms of your agreement with the other company prior to utilizing their customer lists.

The "Dumb Assistant" List Compiling Method

Another technique for getting targeted names for your self-compiled lists is the "Dumb Assistant" method.

Here's how it works: Have your assistant, a temp, or some other person in your company call the main numbers at the companies you're trying to reach on your mailing list. Once they reach someone at the reception desk who answers the phone, have them say something like this:

Figure 6-2:

WHOIS—Very useful for finding the contact behind a company's Internet address

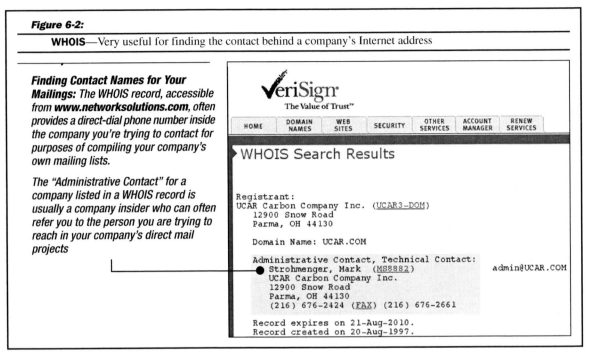

Finding Contact Names for Your Mailings: *The WHOIS record, accessible from **www.networksolutions.com**, often provides a direct-dial phone number inside the company you're trying to contact for purposes of compiling your company's own mailing lists.*

The "Administrative Contact" for a company listed in a WHOIS record is usually a company insider who can often refer you to the person you are trying to reach in your company's direct mail projects

> *"I've been asked to send materials to someone who handles engineering and technology [or any other generalized function] at your company, and I just don't know who to talk to. Could you please connect me to someone in that department at your company?"*

—your staffer will then be connected to an administrative assistant or some other lower-level employee in that department at the company. Your staffer should then ask that person:

> *"I don't know if you're the right person I should be speaking to about this, but I've been asked to send some information to someone in your company who handles airframe quality control [put your own company's very specific product application area here]—could you tell me who that person would be?"*

It may take your staffer three or four turns to get the name, phone number and address of the right person in the company, but once this contact is obtained, it's an extremely valuable addition to your company's self-compiled prospect mailing list.

Bypassing company voice mail systems: Automated voice mail can prevent you from reaching a real live human being at companies today. If your assistant hits a "voice mail receptionist" at the company's main number, there are other ways to get to someone inside the company:

Internet domain WHOIS: Click on the WHOIS link at **www.networksolutions.com** and enter the Internet domain for the company you're trying to reach. WHOIS is an Internet feature that gives you the full information on the people responsible for administering an Internet ".com" Web address at a company. These records usually list an "administrative contact," and that person's direct-dial phone number. This number usually bypasses the automated voice mail systems currently used in many companies, and puts you in touch with a back-office computer guy who can refer you to the right person or department you're looking for in his company.

Company press contacts: Another useful technique for getting the right contacts for your company's self-compiled prospect mailing lists is to call the published media contact listed at the bottom of a company's press release in its "News" or "Press releases" link on the company's own Web site. PR people are very helpful, and they will often be able to supply you with the contact name you need.

Self-compiling your company's own prospect mailing lists is laborious and time-consuming, but there's no better way to create your company's own mailing lists of the most highly-qualified sales prospects to use in your direct mail projects.

List Compilation: Set Your Database Up Right the First Time

If your company already uses a sales database or contact management system, this section probably doesn't apply to you. However, if you're with a start-up, and building your mailing lists from scratch, a little extra thought at the beginning of the process can save a lot of time and trouble later on. Plan your database ahead by incorporating all the required standard fields:

- **Salutation (Mr./Ms.);**
- **First name;**
- **Last name;**
- **Title;**
- **Company;**
- **Address;**
- **Address 2 (suite number, mail stop, etc.);**
- **City/State/ZIP;**
- **Phone/FAX/Cell phone/E-mail address**

Qualifying information: Depending on your own marketing objectives, you may want to add some additional fields to expand on certain characteristics of each record, such as:

- **List source** (a key code representing where the list came from—an ad, trade show, self-compiled list etc.);

Figure 6-3:

FileMaker Pro—A powerful, versatile, and easy-to-use database manager for mailing list projects

FileMaker Pro, available for both Windows and Macs, is a very easy to use database program that imports and exports in all formats, and is an excellent choice for your own mailing list maintenance and processing projects

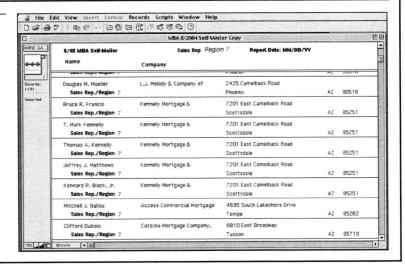

- **Prospect ranking** (a code describing the size of the prospect's company, its sales potential, or some other quantitative measure of the prospect's sales potential or level of interest);

- **Company size** (estimate if not known);

- **Number of employees** (estimate if not known);

- **Comments/Subjective info** (such as if the prospect is known to use your competitor's product or service)

Of course, you can create your own field descriptions and key code identifiers so you can retrieve names from your database by searching any of these fields. Make sure to incorporate a master legend in your database that matches the key codes and other identifiers you're using to a description of their source, so you won't forget your key code definitions when you need to select names by these key codes for your mailings at a later date.

You'll have to qualify each individual record when compiling your own mailing lists: Could this company be a major customer of your company's products, or is it likely they'd be a small customer? How many employees are at the company? Does the company pay its bills? Are they a major competitor of your biggest current customer, and, if so, how would contacting them affect your sales relationship with this big account? Review your prospect lists as they're compiled, to screen them against these more subjective characteristics.

Figure 6-4:

Standard Rate & Data *Direct Marketing List Source*

The SRDS Direct Marketing List Source print directory covers over 38,000 trade, business, and consumer mailing lists available for rental, and is an indispensable resource for any direct mail marketer

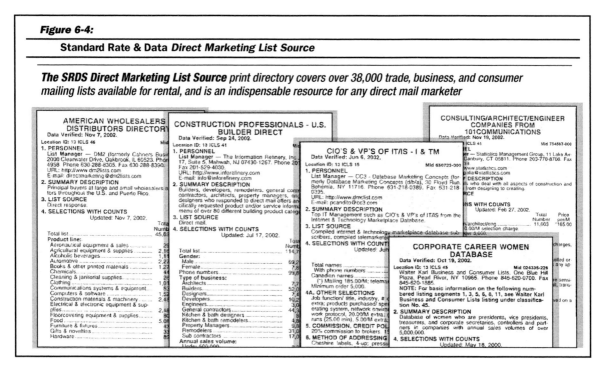

Rented Mailing Lists

In addition to self-compiled lists, you may also need to "rent" mailing lists of potential prospects from external mailing list sources, such as trade publications, newsletter publishers, trade show producers, and other companies who make their own mailing lists available to direct mailers, or from list compilers, who create mailing lists by processing them from other sources, such as telephone directories.

There's a sizeable industry devoted exclusively to the marketing, rental and trade of mailing lists for business and consumer direct mailers, and it's likely you'll be renting (via your ad agency or marketing consultant who produces your direct mail projects) mailing lists for your company's direct mail marketing projects.

Mailing list rental is usually done through a **list broker**, who is a third-party agent for the list owner, and who handles the processing, marketing and administrative chores for the list owner's mailing list rental activities. Mailing lists are rented on a one-time mailing use, at a rate that is based on a price-per-thousand names rented.

Mailing list rentals range in price from $50 per thousand names rented for low-quality compiled lists, to $300 or more per thousand names rented, for higher-quality buyer and subscription lists from top publications.

Advantages of rented mailing lists: There are two main reasons why you'd want to rent mailing lists from outside sources for your own company's direct mail projects:

Figure 6-5:

Standard Rate and Data Service *Direct Marketing List Source*

***Key Features** of a sample mailing list entry in the SRDS Direct Marketing List Source printed directory*

***List Manager:** Your key contact for renting the list. Usually a third-party broker representing the owner of the mailing list*

***Description and List Source:** List owner's summary description of the list, and source for the names on the list: Publication subscribers, product buyers, trade show attendees, card deck respondents, or compiled lists from databases and other sources*

***List Selections:** Breakouts and quantities by job title, function, geographic region, and other characteristics. Selections by job title are very useful for targeting specific groups of prospects in the list and can boost sales response for a mailing*

***Formats and Minimum Order:** Supported list delivery formats, rental policies, and minimum list order quantity*

	Total Number	Price per/M
Active subscribers	10,000	100.00
Former subscribers	50,000	70.00
Male	44,398	+5.00
Female	1,837	"
Unknown	10,770	"

Minimum order 5,000.

4A. OTHER SELECTIONS
State, Zip, SCF, gender, split, key coding, 5.00/M extra.

6. METHOD OF ADDRESSING
Cheshire labels, 4-up; pressure sensitive labels, 7.50/M extra; mag tape, nonrefundable, 25.00 fee; cartridge, 25.00 fee; 3.5 diskette, 60.00 fee; e-mail, 75.00 fee.

8. RESTRICTIONS
Two sample mailing pieces required.

ELECTRONIC SYSTEMS TECHNOLOGY & DESIGN

Data Verified: Nov 19, 2002.

Location ID: 13 ICLS 95 **Mid 025246-000**

1. PERSONNEL
List Manager — Statlistics Management Group, 11 Lake Avenue Ext., Danbury, CT 06811. Phone 203-778-8700. Fax 203-778-4839.
URL: http://www.statlistics.com
E-mail: j.papalia@statlistics.com

SUMMARY DESCRIPTION
Recipients of Computer Design Magazine: computer based systems designers and/or managers; classified primarily by engineering functions, systems they design, nature of organization, products specified/purchased, application/end product of systems designed.

3. LIST SOURCE
Controlled circ.

4. SELECTIONS WITH COUNTS
Updated: Oct 24, 2002.

	Total Number	Price per/M
Subscribers	85,224	125.00
Telemarketing	74,563	+50.00
Job function:		
Executive management	20,803	+10.00
Engineering management	26,531	"
Senior engineering	19,446	"
System engineering	13,906	"
Test/prod/mfg engineering	2,060	"
Other job title	1,562	"
Business/industry:		
Design or mfr comp/peripheral	17,390	+10.00
Design of mfr other electronics	29,703	"
Design of mfr prod in-house	13,218	"
Software house	20,417	"
Military/government	6,299	"
Research and dev/university	14,065	"
Design mgmt:		
Architecture/product def	43,910	+10.00
Dsgn ASICs/Program logic	23,725	"
Design sys/subsys or board-level products using ICs or ASICs	36,825	"
Design equip/sys using single board computers/other board prod	32,283	"
Design mix analog/digital ASICs/ICs board level sys/Subsys	25,660	"
Develop software embedded or used in company products	37,048	"
Dsgn using OEM computers	23,228	"
Integration of computers into larger system	27,517	"
Develop software for in-house use	32,955	"
Develop software for sale	23,907	"
Hard-/software integration	5,648	"
Testing/evaluation/QA	30,735	"
Design/test consulting	2,810	"
Applications engineering	24,991	"
Engineering education training	1,742	"
Products designed:		
Computers	26,125	+10.00
Computer Peripherals	27,845	"
Test/measurement equip	25,621	"
Data Acquisition control	30,251	"
Comm/networking equip.	30,209	"
RF/wireless equip	1,909	"
Office/bus equipment	12,139	"
Avionics/Navigation/guidance	10,899	"
Military/aerospace	4,667	"
CAE/CAD/CAM equipment	11,924	"
Graphics/simulation equip	14,513	"
Imaging/diagnostic equipment	13,855	"
Automotive/transportation	8,384	"
IC's/ASIC's/semiconductors	13,938	"
Consumer products	14,932	"
Education	1,710	"
Medical	2,213	"
Purchase influences: Integrated Circuit		
Integrated circuits:		
8/16-bit microprocessors/microcontrollers	37,904	+10.00
16 bit microprocessors	4,435	"
32/64-bit microprocessors/microcontrollers	40,699	"
64 bit microprocessor	2,866	"
ASICs (gate arrays, cells)	26,356	"
PLD, CPLD, FPGA	32,457	"
IP cores	1,662	"
Analog array/standard cell	16,583	"
Custom LSI/VLSI	15,135	"
RAM (Static, Dynamic)	44,295	"
SDRAM	17,273	"
PROM, EPROM, Flash	40,746	"
ROM	19,844	"
Communication/LAN/WAN ICS	280,490	"
Flash memory	21,495	"
Voice/image compression	16,655	"
RF/Wireless devices	19,639	"
Driver/interface ICs	28,491	"
Fiberoptic Interface ICs	15,414	"
Disk/tape controller ICs	14,263	"
Analog ICs	25,523	"
Mixed-signal ICs	14,666	"
Graphics ICs	10,551	"
DSP ICs	14,595	"
Chip sets	14,595	"
Power management ICs	10,251	"

	Total Number	Price per/M
Platforms:		
IBM PC	47,263	+10.00
PC Clone	56,020	"
Macintosh	15,366	"
Sun	26,974	"
HP	20,964	"
DEC	10,844	"
Other	4,086	"

Minimum order 5,000.

4A. OTHER SELECTIONS
SCF, Zip, state, run charges, 10.00/M extra; phones, 50.00/M extra; key coding, 3.00/M extra.

5. COMMISSION, CREDIT POLICY
20% commission to brokers. Cancel charges: Cancelled orders are subject to a 50.00 flat cancellation fee plus any applicable production charges.

6. METHOD OF ADDRESSING
Cheshire labels, 4-up; pressure sensitive labels, 10.00/M extra; mag tape, (9T 1600 BPI) non refundable, 25.00 fee.

8. RESTRICTIONS
Sample mailing piece required. All orders are approved a reciprocal rentals. Telemarketing now available.

9. TEST ARRANGEMENT
Minimum order quantity: 5,000. Continuations available.

ELECTRONIC SYSTEMS TECHNOLOGY & DESIGN DB EMAIL LIST

Data Verified: Nov 19, 2002.

Location ID: 13 ICLS 95 **Mid 755581-000**

1. PERSONNEL
List Manager — Statlistics Management Group, 11 Lake Avenue Ext., Danbury, CT 06811. Phone 203-778-8700. Fax 203-778-4839.
URL: http://www.statlistics.com
E-mail: j.papalia@statlistics.com

2. SUMMARY DESCRIPTION
Engineers, engineering managers and senior engineers responsible for the design concept, integrity and performance of computer and micro-processor-based original equipment (OEM) market products.

4. SELECTIONS WITH COUNTS
Updated: Oct 24, 2002.

	Total Number	Price per/M
US email addresses	44,664	"275.00
Job function:		
Executive management	5,576	+10.00
Engineering management	10,990	"
Senior engineer	7,990	"
Systems engineer	5,826	"
Test/product/manufacturing engineering	933	"
Other	770	"
Design management:		
Architecture/product definition	18,104	+10.00
Design ASICS/program logic	10,126	"
Design equip/system using single board	14,776	"
Design equipment/systems	11,979	"
Develop software embedded or used in company products	14,821	"
Design equipment/systems use OEM	6,107	"
Integration of computers into larger sys	10,146	"
Develop software for in-house use	12,625	"
Develop software for sale	9,166	"
Hardware/software integration	2,713	"
Testing/evaluation/quality assurance	11,606	"
Design or test consulting	1,219	"
Applications engineering	8,802	"
Engineering education/training	771	"
Design mix analog/digital ASICs/ICs board level system/subsystem	9,984	"
Purchasing influence:		
Integrated circuits:		
8/16 bit microprocessors/microcontrollers	14,560	+10.00
16 bit microprocessors/microcontrollers	1,989	"
32/64 bit microprocessors/microcontrollers	16,084	"
64 bit microprocessors/microcontrollers	1,212	"
ASICs	10,807	"
Programmable devices	13,004	"
PLDA, CPLD, FPGA, IP cores	738	"
Analog arrays/standard cell	5,925	"
Custom LSI/VLSI	5,876	"
Static/dynamic RAM	17,652	"
ROM	7,991	"
EEPROM/ROM/EEPROM/PROM	16,075	"
ROM	8,583	"
Communication/LAN/WAN/ICs	10,865	"
Flash memory	9,993	"
Voice/image compression/decompression ICs	6,173	"
RF/wireless devices	7,135	"
Driver/interface ICs	11,314	"
Fiberoptic interface ICVs	5,558	"
Disk/tape controller ICs	4,977	"
Analog ICs	9,914	"
Mixed signal ICs	5,751	"
Graphics ICs	3,986	"
DSP ICs	6,229	"
Chip sets	4,916	"
Power management ICs	3,912	"
Multichip modules (MCMs)	1,741	"
RISC	5,520	"
Cell based arrays	2,134	"
IC packaging	2,140	"
Sensors	871	"
System boards:		
CPU boards	13,764	+10.00
Embedded PC CPU boards	11,840	"
Memory boards	12,049	"
Disk/tape/peripheral controllers	8,950	"
Data acquisition boards	10,119	"
Network/communication controllers	10,376	"
Graphics controllers	9,049	"
Image processing boards	5,761	"
DSP boards	7,974	"
Systems design:		

Proven buyer lists: The best rental list you can find is a list of previous buyers of a product just like the one your company sells. Next to these lists, buyers of products in related categories close to those of your product can also be good prospects;

Trade publication subscriber lists: Nearly all trade publications in any industry rent their subscriber lists, and most of the larger trade publications can also provide you with mailing list "selects," which are custom selections of their subscriber mailing lists sorted by key characteristics, such as job titles or geographic regions. Publication mailing lists are the best choice when you have a direct mail project that requires you to "cover your market," by reaching the broadest possible number of qualified prospects in your industry. When combined with a display advertising schedule in the same publication, a mailing to the same readers who see your display ads always packs an extra wallop.

Where to Find Mailing Lists to Rent: SRDS Direct Mail List Source

Standard Rate and Data Service (SRDS), publishers of the advertising rate directories covered in Chapter 9, also publishes their SRDS *Direct Marketing List Source* directory, an invaluable tool for researching the wide range of mailing lists available for virtually every industry.

It's the standard mailing list reference used by ad agencies, mailing list brokers, and direct mail marketing consultants, covering the entire range of mailing lists, in every industry, and for every conceivable market and human interest. An hour spent flipping through the SRDS *Direct Marketing List Source* directory will really fire up any marketer's imagination, and it's a wonderful resource and idea-generator for your direct mail projects.

SRDS *Direct Marketing List Source* covers over 38,000 mailing lists in 223 standard industry categories, from "Advertising and Marketing" to "Woodworking." Each mailing list in SRDS is categorized by its industry classification, and contains a detailed description of the list, its owner, quantities and rental rates, plus details on special "selects," which are options to rent specific name selections from the list by job title or function, products purchased, company size, or geographic region. For each mailing list description, you'll also see contact information for the list broker who manages the rentals for that list.

How to Look for Mailing Lists in SRDS Direct Marketing List Source

Here are some list-selection pointers to follow as you scan through the pages of the SRDS mailing list directory.

Proven buyers: As previously mentioned, "buyer lists" are mailing lists of individuals who've already purchased or specified the products similar to ones sold by your company, and are usually derived from trade publication survey questionnaire results, lists of industrial or trade catalog buyers, or company warranty registration card lists. Individuals on a buyer list are also likely prospects of your own company's product or service. As such, they're the mailing lists that offer your own direct mail marketing programs the highest chance for success.

"Hotline" buyers: You'll often see references to "hotline" names, which refer to product buyers on mailing lists. "Hotline" names are individuals who've been recently added to the list owner's mailing list. These are individuals who've purchased the types of products described by the mailing list owner within a recent time period (such as during the past 90 days). On buyer lists, hotline names generally tend to be higher-quality prospects, since a recent buyer of a product similar to yours, or related to the product sold by your company, may be more receptive to an offer from your company.

Trade publication subscriber lists: Mailing lists of subscribers for the business trade publications listed in any SRDS industrial category account for the majority of mailing lists you'll see listed in SRDS. The "Two Publications Rule" described for selecting publications for advertising in Chapter 9 also applies to mailing lists: The best subscriber mailing lists in any business or trade category will nearly always be the subscriber lists for the top two trade publications in that category.

The leading trade publications also offer the largest mailing lists, and for the largest trade publications in a major field, such as banking or computers, offer further selection options. For example, because of their large subscriber bases, larger trade publications offer you the ability to select from their mailing lists by job title, company type, and geographical region. Additionally, many of these larger publications offer special "Hotline" selections of brand-new subscribers to their publications. These "hotline selects" give you the opportunity to sell your company's products to brand-new entrants to your industry, who will be the most receptive to learning more about products available in their fields, including those sold by your company. Check with your ad agency, marketing consultant, or mailing list broker to see if the mailing lists for the publications you are considering have a "hotline names" option.

Types of Trade Publication Mailing Lists

Trade publications fall into two categories:

- **Paid publications** have mailing lists of subscribers who've paid money to receive a subscription to the publication;

- **Controlled circulation** publications are sent free of charge to subscribers, but only after each subscriber has completed a detailed survey questionnaire, where they provide the publication with specific information on their role at their company, such as their job title, number of employees at their company, and their purchasing responsibilities for buying or specifying certain kinds of products within their companies.

"Paid" vs. "Controlled" circulation—which publication is better? While you could make the argument that subscribers who receive a publications for free may be

Figure 6-6:

Response Rates for Direct Mail Marketing Projects—Estimated responses for different types of mailings

Type of Mailing and List	Estimated Response Rate
Mailings to **current customers**–new product announcements, promotions, etc.	► **25% +**
Mailings of a sales kit in response to **prospects who call** as a result of accompanying display advertising	► **15%**
Mailings to **self-compiled lists**, created in-house by telephone surveys	► **10%**
Mailings to **rented lists** of buyers of a product the same as, or similar to, the mailer's product	► **1.5-3.5%**
Mailings to **trade publication subscriber lists**	► **1.0-3.0%**
Mailings to **compiled lists** rented from list brokers	► **0.5-1.5%**

"lower quality" prospects than those who pay money to receive a publication, there are many very successful and well established "controlled circ" trade publications that have worked very well for both trade advertisers and business direct mailers for many years.

Any perceived loss of subscriber loyalty or buying power—due to the effect of a controlled circulation subscriber not having to pay to subscribe to that publication—seems to be more than made up for by the fact that, as a direct mailer, you can obtain much more detailed information on controlled circulation subscriber buying habits than from mailing lists of subscribers to paid-circulation publications.

Other trade publication and mailing list options: In addition to the top publications you know in your field, you will probably notice other types of mailing lists offered in your industry's relevant category in SRDS. These include smaller-circulation publications addressing more specialized areas in your field, lists of subscribers to newsletters published by market research and consulting firms in your industry, and mailing lists of attendees of trade shows and conferences in your market.

Go with what (and who) you know: These more specialized mailing lists are definitely a high risk/high-reward proposition, so unless you have a very strong hunch that prospects on one of these lesser-known, or more specialized, mailing lists might be good prospects for your product, hold off on mailing to these lists until you've already had some experience mailing to some of the more well-recognized mailing lists in your industry (such as one or more major trade publication subscriber lists), and until you've tested and proven the overall effectiveness of your company's direct mail package and program (covered further in the next two chapters).

Compiled Mailing Lists

Compiled mailing lists are lists that have been assembled from other sources, usually by mailing list brokers. List brokers develop compiled lists by mining database records from electronic yellow and white pages telephone directories, product warranty cards, mail and telephone surveys, and other databases.

Compiled mailing lists have a well-deserved reputation for generating poor response for direct mailers. The main problem with compiled mailing lists is that the names on these lists lack a single, strong unifying characteristic. They're often not much more than a retrieval result from the mailing list broker's database, promoted as a targeted industry, market, or buyer list by brokers.

Because you don't know where they came from, you should avoid mailing to compiled lists, unless you are running a very large direct mail program and you must have access to the widest base of names to mail.

How Much Response Should You Get from Your Mailings?

It's hard to predict any given response rate, and as a direct mail marketer, you should never rely on response rate estimates printed in a book. Because there are many factors that affect response to mailings, response rates will vary widely. However, you should be able to form a general expectation of the response a mailing should generate, even if your company is new to direct mail.

Figure 6-6 shows the typical response rates for business direct mail, by type of project. These are only rough estimates based on previous experience, and your experience may be very different. While response rates like these can be used in your own financial projections, each product, market, and direct mail project is unique. Don't limit your horizons by any outsider's estimation of the response rates your own direct mail programs will produce—what really counts is the response your own company's mailings generate over time, and you can only achieve this by putting your own pieces in the mail.

Mailing List Rentals and Policies

In most cases, your advertising agency or direct mail marketing consultant will perform the tasks of ordering and processing mailing lists rented from outside sources for your company's mailings. They will communicate directly with the list broker representing the list, who will ship a computer tape or disk directly to your mailing house once the list owner has approved the order. The list owner will also ask to receive a sample of the mailing piece you plan to mail to their list, so they can review it and approve it.

Occasionally, and especially if the list owner happens to be a close competitor to your company, they may reject your order. This is to be expected, and there's no way around it, unless your company is willing to exchange its own customer mailing list with the list owner for one-time rental, which can sometimes be done.

Unless otherwise requested in your order, mailing lists are always rented for one-time use only, and computer tapes containing the mailing lists must be returned after the mailing is completed.

Part 2: Direct Mail Packages

Next to the mailing list, the direct mail package, or direct mail piece, is the most critical element in any direct mail project. "The package" can take many forms: From big, colorful, expensive 9 X 12-sized sales information kits sent to prospects who call your company's toll-free number asking for additional information on your company's products, to an inexpensive, high-volume, single-piece postcards sent to large numbers of prospects on rented mailing lists.

Chances are, in your role as marketing manager, you'll experiment with many of these different types of mailing pieces until you settle on a half-dozen or so formats that work best for each marketing situation you encounter in your company.

The type of direct mail package you send, and how much it costs, depends on three factors: List quality, level of interest, and quantity of pieces mailed. This means you always want to send your best direct mail package (i.e. your most expensive package) to your best mailing lists, such as interested prospects who've called your company's toll-free number, or e-mailed your company to receive additional information on your company's product or service. Quantities on your best mailing lists are usually smaller than those for lower-quality lists, so it follows that the higher the quality (and expense) of the mailing piece, the lower the quantities, and vice versa.

When mailing to rented mailing lists, where your sales message will be seen by a broader, and accordingly, somewhat less interested, markets, select a less-expensive mailing package, such as the "Classic" #10 size mailing. At the extreme, one day you may even find yourself mailing an ultra-cheap, two-cent printed postcard to a very large mailing list, where a very low response rate is expected.

Just as there are different tools for different projects, there are different direct mail packages that can be applied to different kinds of marketing projects.

Direct Mail Package Elements

The main elements found most often in direct mail packages are:

- **Outer envelope**
- **Sales letter**
- **Brochure**
- **Response/reply/order card**
- **Buck slip (optional)**

Figure 6-7:

Types of Direct Mail Packages, and How to Use Them

The most common kinds of direct mail packages, their specifications, and how to use them in your own company's marketing applications

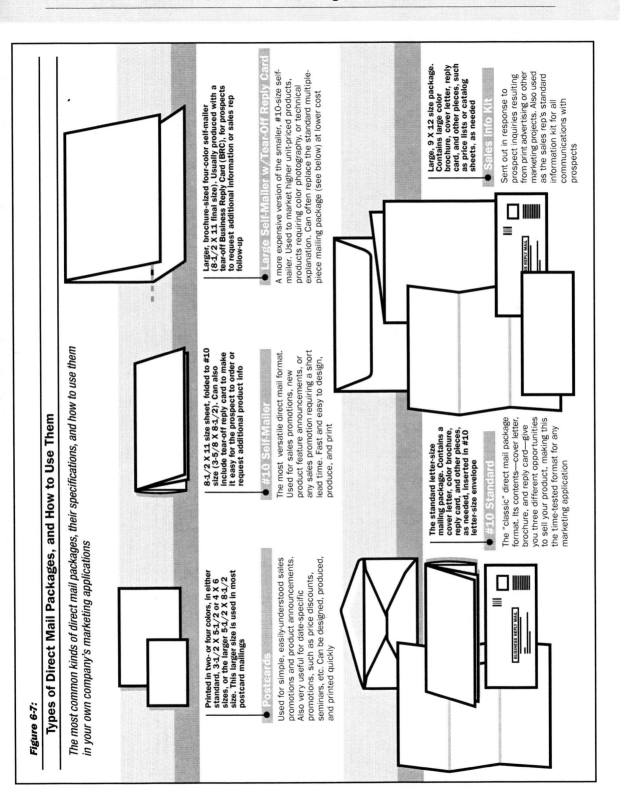

Larger, brochure-sized four-color self-mailer (8-1/2 X 11 final size). Usually produced with a tear-off Business Reply Card (BRC), for prospects to request additional information or sales rep follow-up

Large Self-Mailer w/ Tear-Off Reply Card

A more expensive version of the smaller, #10-size self-mailer. Used to market higher unit-priced products, products requiring color photography, or technical explanation. Can often replace the standard multiple-piece mailing package (see below) at lower cost

Large, 9 X 12 size package. Contains large color brochure, cover letter, reply card, and other pieces, such as price lists or catalog sheets, as needed

Sales Info Kit

Sent out in response to prospect inquiries resulting from print advertising or other marketing projects. Also used as the sales rep's standard information kit for all communications with prospects

8-1/2 X 11 size sheet, folded to #10 size (3-5/8 X 8-1/2). Can also include tear-off reply card to make it easy for the prospect to order or request additional product info

#10 Self-Mailer

The most versatile direct mail format. Used for sales promotions, new product feature announcements, or any sales promotion requiring a short lead time. Fast and easy to design, produce, and print

The standard letter-size mailing package. Contains a cover letter, color brochure, reply card, and other pieces, as needed, inserted in #10 letter-size envelope

#10 Standard

The "classic" direct mail package format. Its contents—cover letter, brochure, and reply card—give you three different opportunities to sell your product, making this the time-tested format for any marketing application

Printed in two- or four colors, in either standard, 3-1/2 X 5-1/2 or 4 X 6 sizes, or the larger 5-1/2 X 8-1/2 size. This larger size is used in most postcard mailings

Postcards

Used for simple, easily-understood sales promotions and product announcements. Also very useful for date-specific promotions, such as price discounts, seminars, etc. Can be designed, produced, and printed quickly

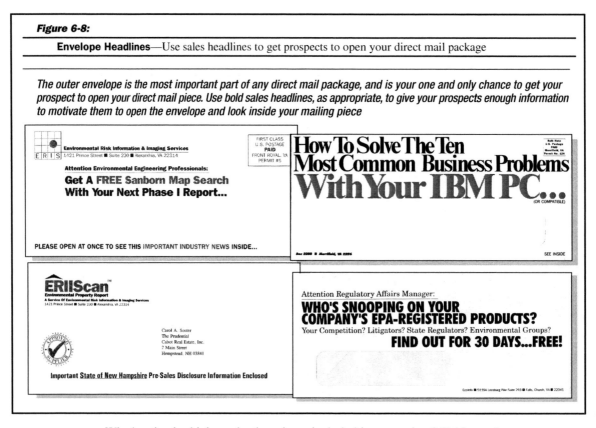

Figure 6-8:

Envelope Headlines—Use sales headlines to get prospects to open your direct mail package

The outer envelope is the most important part of any direct mail package, and is your one and only chance to get your prospect to open your direct mail piece. Use bold sales headlines, as appropriate, to give your prospects enough information to motivate them to open the envelope and look inside your mailing piece

Whether they're high production pieces included in expensive 9 X 12 envelopes used in sales response mailings, or less expensive, scaled-down versions used for higher volume #10 letter-size mailing packages, these standard elements have been used in mailing packages for decades.

The next several pages cover each of these elements in greater detail. Your ad agency or marketing consultant may be responsible for the task of actually writing and producing your company's direct mail packages, but you never know when you'll find yourself in the position of having to develop a mailing package on your own.

Even if you aren't directly responsible for writing or producing your company's direct mail pieces, you need to know how effective direct mail packages are created, so you can tell whether or not your ad agency or marketing consultant is producing a mailing piece that will generate solid sales response for your company.

Much of the material covered in the sales copywriting exercises of Chapter 4, combined with the special characteristics for each package element described in this section, can help you work with your ad agency or marketing consultant to create direct mail pieces for your company's mailing projects.

Outer Envelope

Your direct mail package's outer envelope delivers your first, best sales message, creating the first impression the prospect has of your company when he or she holds the piece in their hands. The address on the outer envelope should **always** be addressed to a person by name, and never addressed to a generic job title alone.

The most prominent feature of most outer envelopes in direct mail packages is the sales "grabber" headline. Its sole purpose is to seize the reader's attention and get him/her to open the envelope. While entire chapters of direct mail copywriting books are devoted to the art and craft of writing the envelope headline, most envelope headline copy essentially follows the "Tell me" approach:

Tell me what you've got;
Tell me what's good about it;
Tell me what to do next

Tell me what you've got: Busy prospects don't like to receive mysterious direct mail. So tell the reader what you're selling, so they'll know whether it's for them or not: The first part of your headline announces your company's product or service, in as few words as possible. For example: "New Imaging Systems for Line Quality Control;"

Tell me what's good about it: Use additional sales copy to link the description of your product to its prime sales benefit. Tell the recipient of your mailing package just enough about your product's main benefit to arouse their curiosity, so they'll open the envelope: "Faster Line Processing and Better Inspection Rates with VyComp Intelligent Imaging Systems;"

Tell me what to do next: After the prime sales benefit, add another line to tell your interested prospect what they need to do next, and, optionally, what reward they'll receive when they take this next step. The goal is to move the reader to open the envelope, so the best choice of words is often the simplest: "Open this envelope…" or, "Look inside for…"

This may seem to be so obvious as to be unnecessary, but readers actually *want* to be told what to do next, and will respond to this appeal. Also, if you're offering some type of special promotion or savings offer, then here is where to include this message. For example: "Open this envelope to find out how to save 20% on your first installation…"

There are many variations possible with the "tell me" approach, limited only by your imagination, and your direct mail copywriter's skill.

Should you use "loud" envelope headlines on business-to-business direct mail pieces? Don't be too concerned about being too bold or brash in the presentation of the headline and sales copy on the outer envelope of your direct mail package. It's a safe assumption that your prospects will accept a certain level of "loudness," or bombastic salesmanship, in an envelope headline. In fact, busy readers appreciate any sales communication that gets to the point, tells them what your product is, and what it can do for them.

There are some important exceptions. The promotional "volume level" of an outer envelope headline should vary inversely to the level of personalization of your mailing piece. An overtly promotional headline used on an envelope in a highly personalized mailing sent to a select audience of business prospects may work against itself.

For example, if your goal is to send a personalized communication to high-level prospects, such as a list of CEOs in your industry, an outer envelope that looks too promotional negates the personal connection you are trying to make; so "turn the volume down on" your outer envelope's headline accordingly, or leave it off and send your mailing out as person-to-person business correspondence—on your company's regular letterhead, imprinted with your company logo and return address only.

The Sales Letter

The sales letter is a long-form narrative that tells your product's story and explains its benefits to the reader. Like any written letter, a sales letter is a person-to-person communication. In the context of your direct mail package, it serves as a personal counterpoint to the more formal, promotional presentations your reader sees in the other sales pieces of your package, such as the sales brochure or reply card.

While in most cases the task of writing your company's direct mail sales letters will be done by a copywriter at your advertising agency, it's important that you know the time-tested elements of effective sales letters, and how they are written.

The general letter-writing techniques covered here will also help you create a solid working outline of the essential sales benefits and content to pass along to your ad agency or marketing consultant, when they write your company's sales letters.

Tone and writing style: The tone of a sales letter should be friendly and informal—much like the "Park Bench Story" writing exercise in Chapter 4. In fact, you should refer to this exercise as a general guideline before writing notes for any direct mail sales letter.

The more personalized, the better: A sales letter should be as personalized as possible, but there are often limitations to the level of personalization that can be incorporated into sales letters. For high-volume mailings, the level of personalization will be dictated by your budget, and by the amount of information you have for the prospects in your sales database or mailing list.

Today's high-volume laser printing technologies are much more affordable, so you should always strive to make your sales letters as personalized as possible. At the very least, most sales letters you produce should have the standard name, company, address, and the proper salutation on each sales letter. This personalization should extend to the end of your letter, with a graphic image file placed for the signature or,

Figure 6-9:

Sales Cover Letter Features

Boldface or Underline Key Sales Benefits, *and any other important "call to action" words, phrases and other sentence fragments. You can use either boldface type, or underlines, or (preferably) both; however, since boldface type stands out, use it to highlight the benefits and phrases for those who skim-read your letter*

Tabbed-in and Indented Paragraphs *make your sales letters visually interesting, and make key sales benefits and features stand out from the rest of text*

Formatting Caveat: *It's important to understand the difference between a* **personalized** *letter and a* **personal** *letter. Your use of various attention-getting formatting techniques should vary inversely to the personalization and targeting of your sales letter. While these formatting techniques can be very effective for highlighting your sales letter's key selling points, they aren't appropriate for personal sales letters. For example, if these techniques were used in a personal letter for a small mailing sent from your CEO to other CEOs, they may be perceived as being too "promotional" when seen by this high-level audience*

Signature: *Your sales letter will look more personalized if its signature is printed in a separate blue-ink color*

A "P.S." Line at the Bottom of Your Letter *serves the same purpose as a headline used at the top of a letter, and reinforces the key promotional benefit and "call to action" of your mailing*

ERIIScan™
Environmental Property Report
Environmental Risk Information & Imaging Services
1421 Prince Street, Suite 330 ■ Alexandria, VA 22314 ■ 1-800-989-0403 ■ (703) 836-0402 ■ FAX (703) 836-0468
May 17, 1994

Carol A. Souter
The Prudential
Cabot Real Estate, Inc.
2 Main Street
Hempstead, NH 03841

Dear Ms. Souter:

We are writing to tell you of important developments involving recently enacted mandatory state broker disclosure laws for the state of New Hampshire, which may have a significant impact on your Prudential Real Estate Affiliates Office.

Brokers and agents are now required by New Hampshire state law to provide full pre-sales disclosure of known potential environmental conditions with every home sale.

Under this recent "mandated property condition disclosure law," pre-sale disclosure of registered Federal and State environmentally hazardous conditions on and around a residential property is now a required step in the sales process, just like an appraisal or a termite inspection. Increasingly, owners of real estate brokerage offices may face the potential threat of legal liability for non-disclosure of potential environmental risks on home listings they represent, if this information is easily and inexpensively available.

Through an exclusive arrangement with Prudential Real Estate Affiliates, the ERIIScan Environmental Residential Property Report is now available to all Prudential brokers and agents for any residential property in the U.S. The ERIIScan Report meets recent industry-recognized standards, fulfilling your requirement to provide environmental disclosure on all your office's home sales.

Here's how ERIIScan Residential Property Reports help you:

● **Avoid Potential Legal Liability Expense:** The ERIIScan Property Report can be your important "first line of defense," providing you with the best state and industry-compliant tool you need for exercising the seller disclosure due diligence required under New Hampshire state law -- and protecting you and your sales office today from the potential threat of present or future non-disclosure liability legal expenses...

● **Meet State Disclosure Requirements, Affordably And Efficiently -- For Just $75 for each home report:** The ERIIScan Property Report is the fast, complete, affordable "professional compliance package," giving you a one-stop source for all the environmental government records review information you need to meet New Hampshire state disclosure requirements...

● **Meet National Environmental Information Standards, With The Industry**

(...next page, please...)

Sincerely,

Dan S. Prickett
President
Environmental Risk Information & Imaging Services, Inc.

P.S.: **To get your FREE complimentary ERIIScan Residential Property Report for any property of your choice, just call us now: 1-800-989-0403**...also, please let us know if you need us to send you additional copies of the enclosed materials for review by all the brokers and agents in your office...

even better, the signature printed in contrasting blue ink. Most lettershops use various signature imprinting methods, and can provide samples of the available options.

How long should a sales letter be? The shorter and more concise you make your sales letter, the better—but not at the expense of telling your product's complete sales story. Your sales letter should run no more than two individual, printed sheets (printed front and back); however, a one-page, one-sided sales letter is ideal.

Sales letter content: To recap, your sales letter's content should meet the following goals:

- **To serve as a personal address** to your prospect;
- **To summarize the sales benefits** of your product;
- **To introduce the other elements** of your direct mail package (such as your brochure and response coupon);
- **To guide the prospect to the next step; i.e.,** what you want them to do next

Elements of Successful Direct Mail Sales Letter Copy

The general copy structure of a sales letter contains three elements:

- **Lead paragraph;**
- **Key sales benefits and sales bullets;**
- **The close and call to action**

Lead Paragraph

Your sales letter's lead, or first paragraph, should pull the reader directly into your letter, or at least interest them enough so they'll skim-read your letter before moving on to the other pieces in your direct mail package. Sometimes, in more promotional letters, the sales lead paragraph is preceded by a two or three-line headline, printed in either boldface, or all caps, at the top of the letter.

Sample lead paragraph copy approaches: There are many different techniques direct mail copywriters use for writing lead paragraphs in sales letters. Two of the most common approaches are:

The direct approach:

> *Dear Mr. Smith:*
> *I'm writing to tell you about (your product), that can (your prime benefit)...*
>
> or,

The question:

> *Dear Mr. Jones:*
>
> *How would you like to save 25% on your next turbine overhaul? That's what our customers have saved, on average, by using (your product)...*

There are many ways to open a sales letter, but the common denominator of all great sales letter leads is the personal enthusiasm communicated by the letter writer to the reader. Enthusiasm is a vital element in all advertising copy, and especially so for sales letters. If the writer conveys a sense of excitement and enthusiasm about the company's product, this enthusiasm will be felt by the reader, and will influence his or her impression of your company and its products.

Key Sales Benefits and Sales Bullets

After the lead paragraph draws the reader into the beginning of your cover letter, it's usually followed by a short, one or two-sentence paragraph that introduces your company and its product's key sales benefit:

> *Yes, it's true: At Duramco we've been saving plant managers an average of 25% on their valve replacement costs, with our full line of titanium-sleeved pressure valves. Since 1969, thousands of your fellow plant managers around the world have come to rely on our line of surge valves and pumps in extreme-use environments.*

Once your lead grabs the reader and this "set up" paragraph introduces your company and its key sales benefit, you can then punch out your product's other key sales benefits in bulleted form, with short paragraphs introduced by short, telegraphic, boldface sales phrases. For example:

> Duramco valve systems help you:
>
> - **Cut ongoing maintenance costs:** Fewer replacements mean fewer hours spent by your plant repair crews;
>
> - **Reduce plant downtime:** Longer intervals between valve replacements mean fewer plant downtime periods and lower associated costs;
>
> - **Reduced heat operation:** Duramco's patented HiPro valves give your processes an average 5% decrease in materials flow heat rates, compared to other valves in its class. Lower flow drag means less heat, and less heat means less machinery wear

As you sketch out your sales letter, continue it as a kind of "selling conversation," drawing out the other features and benefits of your company's product.

Figure 6-10:

Eight Golden Guidelines for Writing the Perfect Sales Letter by Ray Jutkins

1.) The best way is the simple way. Write it like you say it. Don't worry about grammar. Don't concern yourself with punctuation (we overuse it anyway). Don't wordsmith every sentence. Make it human.

2.) The best mail is personal mail multiplied. Write to your Aunt Minnie (or if you don't like Auntie M., then your favorite somebody). And do it over and over and over to others. It works.

3.) If your audience is octogenarians in Oshkosh then you become an octogenarian in Oshkosh. Pretend you are the recipient and write to yourself.

Plumbers don't respond the same as doctors, teenagers differently from grandparents, presidents of large companies differently from those of smaller firms, women from men, musicians from architects.

Write to your audience, talk to them with whatever common denominator is available, Put yourself in your reader's frame of mind.

4.) Never, but NEVER talk down to your audience. Look them straight in the eye, aim at them directly. Or even better yet, look up to them.

5.) Do not tell a lie. Be honest, straightforward, up front, true. Tell a funny story, be entertaining, weave a theme to make your point, play games any way that will help your cause, but do not tell a lie. Ever.

6.) Have something to say. This may seem funny to have to say, but many letters don't say anything. Have something specific to say, a message, and then say it. Don't beat around the bush— come out with it.

7.) Make an offer. The offer says if you do this now these good things will happen to you now. The offer is the reason a certain percentage of your audience will respond—and it many times is the difference between success or failure. Move those "considering" you to your side with a good offer.

8.) Ask for the order! Be specific—ask your audience to do something. Don't just hint. Spell it out in spades.

Ray W. Jutkins (ray@rayjutkins.com) is an Arizona-based copywriter, speaker, and marketing consultant. Reprinted with permission.

Sales Letter Close and Call to Action

The close of a sales letter consists of two or more final paragraphs that tell the reader what he or she needs to do next, and usually contain the following information:

- **Restate** your product's prime benefit;

- **Assure the reader** they will be making a good decision by buying your company's product;

- (Optional) **Introduce the terms of any special savings** offer or promotional discounts as an extra incentive to the reader for "acting now;"

- **Tell the reader what to do next**—call your company's toll-free order number to speak to a sales rep, link to your company's Web site, send e-mail, etc.

How prospects read sales letters: Most readers of a sales cover letter will quickly read the first sentence of its lead paragraph, then glance down to its list of bulleted benefits, and then to the closing benefits of your letter. That's why the closing paragraphs of your sales cover letter should recap the essential sales benefit you want to communicate to the prospect.

Figure 6-11:

Self-Mailer Brochure Format—A versatile format for many direct mail marketing projects

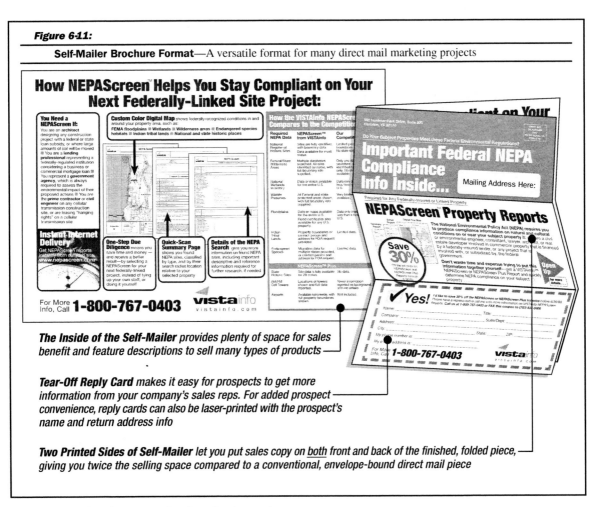

The Inside of the Self-Mailer provides plenty of space for sales benefit and feature descriptions to sell many types of products

Tear-Off Reply Card makes it easy for prospects to get more information from your company's sales reps. For added prospect convenience, reply cards can also be laser-printed with the prospect's name and return address info

Two Printed Sides of Self-Mailer let you put sales copy on both front and back of the finished, folded piece, giving you twice the selling space compared to a conventional, envelope-bound direct mail piece

Below is a example of a sales letter close:

> **Join thousands of plant engineers just like you** who are putting Duramco's industry-leading valve technology to work in their plant operations—reducing downtime, energy costs, and maintenance expense.
>
> **Call us today at 1-888-555-1234** to speak to a local Duramco sales engineer, and receive a free plant flow processing software program and custom plant analysis, with no further cost or obligation. Or, just fill out and drop the enclosed reply card in the mail to receive a sales kit.

Layout Tips for Sales Cover Letters

Historically, sales letter copywriters have employed a number of visual layout techniques designed to enhance readability, to magnify important sales benefits and product features, and to highlight key selling phrases. Some of these techniques include underlining key phrases or benefits, and setting important phrases in boldface type, to highlight your letter's important sales benefits to busy readers. The sales letter layout example in **Figure 6-9** shows some of these layout techniques.

Brochures for Direct Mail Packages

Every direct mail package you produce for your company should also contain a sales brochure for the product you're selling. The brochure is the centerpiece of any direct mail package, and the formal selling counterpoint to the more informal, personalized sales message of your package's sales cover letter. The sales brochure used in your company's direct mail pieces sets the tone for the entire package, and establishes a good impression of your company in the minds of your prospects.

Most brochures used in direct mail pieces are downsized, less-expensive versions of a company's tried-and-true standard product brochure. There's no reason why an effective brochure that works for your company's sales force would not work in a direct mail package, provided that the headlines, subheads, body text and other copy are concise, readable and clearly understood by the reader.

Modifications for direct mail brochures: In certain instances, you might have to modify your company's standard sales brochure to work in a direct mail package:

Cost: Often, it's too expensive to include your company's standard large, four-color sales brochure in high-quantity mailings to sales prospects. The standard four-color sales brochure that works well in your sales operation can, with some modifications, be produced at a low enough cost to make it economical for use in your company's direct mail promotions. For example, you can achieve substantial savings by printing your brochure on less-expensive glossy stock. Also, choose a more lightweight stock, to save postage cost on your mailings;

Four-color vs. two: Four-color brochures can, in many cases, be converted to two-color format, making use of black ink for the text and images, and a second color (such as blue or red) used for solid coverage on the cover of the brochure, and for accent coverage on the inside of the brochure;

Reducing size: If your company's best sales brochure is a large 9 X 12 size, and you're producing a letter-size direct mail package (also called a "#10 size" mailing), you'll most likely have to produce a sales brochure to fit this smaller size. Your ad agency or marketing consultant can lift the best headlines, subheads, sales copy and graphics from a larger brochure, adapting the sales content of your larger sales brochure to fit this smaller, business envelope-sized format.

Once produced, a good #10 size brochure can be the sales workhorse of all your company's direct mail projects. This brochure can be further modified to serve as a self-mailer for higher volume mailings (see **Figure 6-11**), where an single, very inexpensive printed piece is called for (more on self-mailers in the next section). It

Figure 6-12:

Reply Card Sales Copy—Your final opportunity to sell your product and ask for the inquiry or order

Tell Your Prospect What to Do Next on your mailing's reply card or coupon, and make it easy for the prospect to order, request more information, or ask a sales rep to call

can also be used by your company's sales reps as a piece of sales collateral to "leave behind" in their personal sales calls on prospects, and as a mailed insert for their follow-up "thank you" letters to these prospects.

Direct Mail Response/Business Reply Cards (BRCs)

The final piece found in most business and direct mail packages is the response card, also called the business reply card, or "BRC."

The BRC serves three key purposes:

Sales reinforcement: The BRC restates your product's prime selling benefit, and why this benefit is important to your prospect;

The offer and call to action: Next, the BRC restates the savings or terms of your mailing's special promotional offer (if any), and clearly explains to the reader what he or she needs to do to take the next step—either asking for one of your company's sales representatives to contact him, or explaining what he needs to do to buy your product;

The inquiry/order form: Your BRC should have a clearly laid-out area where your prospect can fill in his or her name, address, phone number, e-mail, company, and any other information you need from them. Make sure to provide plenty of space so that the average person can enter this information legibly (better yet, and if possible, you can pre-print the prospect's address information on the inquiry/order card to save them the effort).

Figure 6-13:

Value-Added Direct Mail Premiums—Give "something extra" to your sales prospects

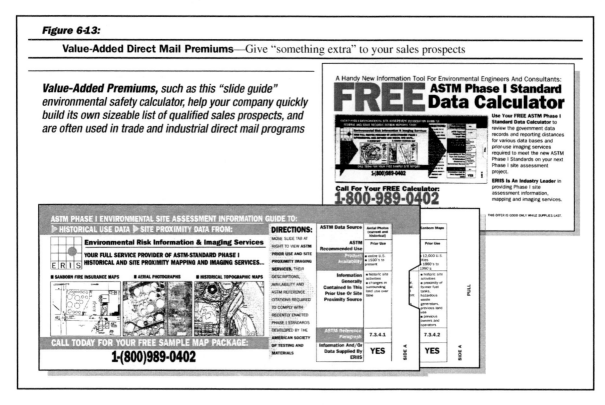

Design your BRC so it can sell all by itself: When reading their mail, a busy executive interested in your product will often discard all of your sales materials, except the BRC, saving it to fill out later—sometimes, several days later when they finally get around to it. This is why it's especially important to repeat your product's prime sales benefit, and the terms of any special promotional offer on the BRC, and, just as important, your company contact information—toll-free number, mailing address, Web site and e-mail address. Your BRC should be able to stand alone as a sales piece, delivering the most important sales message of your mailing.

The reverse side of your BRC displays your company's return mailing address, along with postage-paid free return postage, so all the prospect has to do is fill the card out and drop it in the mail.

The "Buck Slip"

An optional printed piece, sometimes included in a direct mail package, is called a "Buck Slip." A buck slip is a #10 size (or smaller), boldly-printed card that usually displays an attention-grabbing headline, or some type of startling headline.

A classic buck slip headline goes something like:

"Read this if you decided not to buy [your product here],"

Figure 6-14:

Large Four-Color Self-Mailers—This format can often replace a traditional envelope-bound mailing package

Large, Four-Color Self-Mailing Brochures combine all elements of a conventional direct mail package—outer envelope, cover letter, brochure, and reply card—into a single, dynamic mailing piece that's often more effective than the traditional direct mail package

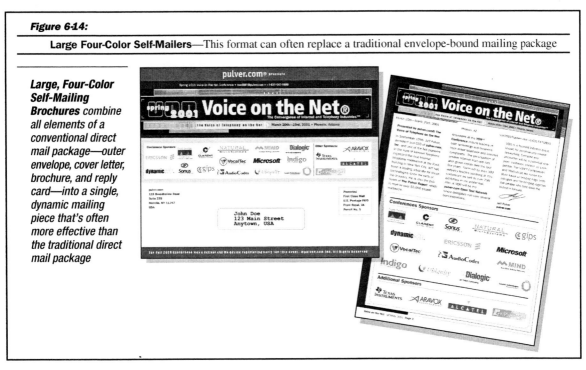

—followed by a brief, persuasive sentence that tries to overturn the most common sales objection to buying the company's product.

Buck slips aren't a mandatory requirement for most direct mail packages, but they have been known to increase response in direct mail sales, and can be a very effective, creative way to clear up common misperceptions or objections about your company's product. A buck slip can also be used to hammer home the main sales benefits of your company's product, serving as a quick-read counterpart to the longer sales story found in the brochure and sales cover letter in a direct mail package.

The Call to Action: Direct Mail Premiums to Get Inquiries and Orders

Sometimes even the most compelling presentation of your product's sales benefits isn't enough to overcome the prospect's inertia. That's when you need that "something extra" to get the prospect to pick up the phone, visit your Web site, or fill out and mail or FAX the order coupon. Incorporating an extra promotional incentive or premium into your direct mail package's call to action can mean the difference between a mildly positive response, or a solid success in a direct mail project.

Offer free, value-added information: Most executives in any industry are very receptive to receiving information that they think will help them do their job better, cheaper, faster or more productively—especially if this is truly useful information, not marketing hype.

When planning a mailing, you should strongly consider adding an offer for your prospect that gives them some kind of value-added information premium, such as a free informational report, video, DVD, or e-mail newsletter subscription.

For example, if you were marketing a specialized chemical coating to industrial clients, you could offer an "Industry Handbook" that would cover details involved in the surface preparation of various types of materials, special problems and challenges in these applications, useful data tables, materials weights and measurements, and conversion charts. The focus here is to provide information that's useful to your audience, and not just information having to do with your company's products (although this can be very subtly worked in to the content of your premium).

Value-added information premiums, like industry reports, handbooks, or other materials, benefit your prospect by giving them a handy reference tool they can use in their daily work, and most importantly, they help to establish your company as an authority or expert in your industry. This reputation then begins to attach itself to your company's products, to your company's benefit. If you take an honest, sincere approach to developing truly useful information premiums, you'll reap tremendous benefits in prospect goodwill—and sales will follow.

Other Promotional Offers for Direct Mailings

Here are other, proven promotional offers you can use to boost response in your company's direct mailing projects:

Special price promotions: Include a special price offer in the "call to action" portion of your BRC—list a special promotional price, along with a deadline date when this special price offer will end. Also, if your company expects to increase prices in the future, be sure to mention this in your direct mail promotions;

Bonus offers: Give something with something—if your prospect agrees to purchase your product by a certain date, give them a special 2-for-1 offer, but only if they agree to purchase by a certain date—and don't forget to define the specific dollar value of the additional item they'll be receiving;

Free samples: A mailing of a free sample can add interest to inherently "uninteresting" products, like industrial commodities and specialty materials. By printing your company sales message on these materials, or producing them in a unique way as a useful object, they can be offered as free premium samples in direct mail promotions;

Qualify respondents to these special offers: Make sure to capture important information, such as job title and company size, when offering a free premium in a direct mail promotion. Carefully screen inquiries, being careful to forward only qualified inquiries to your company's sales reps.

Figure 6-15:

Self-Mailing Postcards—Fast and easy to produce, print and mail to your prospects and customers

Large, Four-Color Postcards are excellent solutions for simple promotional announcements—trade show appearances, limited-time sales promotions, and other time-sensitive marketing opportunities

Self-Mailer Formats: Brochures, #10 Mailers and Four-Color Postcards

Increasingly, business mailers have been turning to various "self-mailer" formats for their direct mail packages—these are one-piece, mailable four-color brochures, produced in a wide variety of sizes and options.

Self-mailers do indeed represent the next wave of direct mail packages. For many applications, they offer a lower-cost, more easily produced alternative to the traditional multi-piece business direct mail package.

Advantages of self-mailer formats: A large-format (8-1/2 X 11) self-mailer direct mail piece has some important advantages over the traditional, multiple-element direct mail package:

Immediate impact: Self-mailers combine the best features of a sales brochure and outer envelope into a single mailing piece, putting the best elements of your company's sales message in front of your prospects—bold, compelling headlines, a bright, colorful cover, product photos and graphics, and other sales copy. You can put your company's best sales headlines on both sides of the self mailer, and your prospect can easily flip the piece open and start reading it on the spot—no envelope to open, and no other direct mail pieces to read;

Total presentation: With the self-mailer, you can put all of your product's features, benefits and sales points, as well as the BRC reply card, on a single printed piece. The all-in-one self-mailer is the perfect quick-reading mailing piece for today's busy readers, and for the upcoming raised-on-MTV generation of business prospects;

Cost: Self-mailers, even glossy, four-color pieces, can be produced for less than it usually costs to print four or more separate pieces for a conventional mailing package—sales letter, brochure, BRC, and outer envelope. Self-mailers also require much less preparation at your mailing house, since there are no multiple printed pieces to be inserted into envelopes, and (usually) no custom imprinting or personalization. In some cases, postage costs may also be less for self-mailers compared to more conventional direct mail packages.

Self-Mailing Postcards

Larger-format (5-1/2 X 8-1/2 inch) four-color postcards are easily-produced mailing pieces, ideal for many marketing projects. Postcards can be used to make important product announcements, such as price cuts or special promotions. Because they can be produced and printed in a matter of days, postcards are ideal for any company sales announcement that must be executed quickly, and for projects where a full-blown mailing package is not warranted.

For example, self-mailing postcards can be mailed out to a trade show attendee mailing list in advance of trade shows where your company will be exhibiting. An advance trade show postcard, featuring the date of the show, your company's trade show booth number, and some basic, bulleted sales copy, helps to put conference attendees on notice about your company and its products, and drives them to your company's booth at the show. Sometimes even smaller, standard-sized postcards, with preprinted color postage for a more personalized look, can be used to catch the prospect's attention.

When to use self-mailer formats: Self-mailers have many advantages, and you can use them in many mailing projects, replacing the traditional, four-pieces-in-the-envelope, letter-sized mailing piece. While you should definitely test both formats in your mailing programs (more on testing in the next chapter), let the value of the mailing, and of the prospects on your mailing list, guide your choice of which type of direct mail package to use. For example, if you're mailing to a top-quality mailing list and you don't want to leave anything to chance, a traditional, envelope-based direct mail piece should give you a higher chance for better response on the mailing. However, this can be a very close call, given the advantages of self-mailer formats.

DIRECT MAIL TESTING
CHAPTER 7
REDUCING MARKETING RISK AND EXPENSE IN YOUR COMPANY'S DIRECT MAIL PROJECTS

Testing and sampling techniques open many exciting opportunities for your company to expand its marketing efforts using direct mail. By sampling small portions of large mailing lists in your industry, you not only test the viability of using direct mail as a part of your company's marketing program, you can also test new markets, new promotions, new pricing plans, and sales copy.

Testing is a vital part of any direct mail marketing program. Tests of third-party mailing lists, available from list brokers, such as trade publication subscriber lists, trade show attendee lists, or third-party buyer lists (described in detail in the previous chapter) will account for most of your direct mail testing activities as a marketing manager. For example, a typical large trade publication subscriber mailing list may contain 200,000 names. It would be too risky to mail to this entire list at once, without knowing how much response you'd receive to this mailing.

However, you can "sample" a small portion of this list (for example, 2,500 pieces), by selecting every 80th name (called an "Nth-name select") and sending your direct mail piece to this sample. Then, you can use proven statistical measuring techniques to analyze the response received to this test mailing, and project, with a reasonable degree of certainty (95%) the response you'd receive if you were to mail to larger portions of the list, or to the entire list itself.

What You Can Test

You can test a wide range of elements in your direct mail marketing program:

Mailing lists: You can (and always should) test a small but statistically valid sample of any large mailing list, such as rented trade publication subscriber lists. You can apply your testing program across small samples of several different mailing lists at the same time, scaling up your subsequent mailings only to those lists that have tested well, and eliminating lists yielding poor response;

Direct mail packages: You can split-test two different direct mail packages sent to the same mailing list. You can also test the response to different mailing pieces, each containing different individual package elements, such as sales letters, brochures, or other separate inserts;

Promotions and pricing: You can test new promotional ideas and new product pricing options using small portions of your company's customer and prospect lists. For example, by testing you can determine whether or not a dramatically lower price will generate higher overall profit through increased sales volume, without disclosing this new, lower price offer to your entire customer or market base. Conversely, you can test your product at a higher price (usually along with some additional value-added feature) to assess whether or not your company could be selling its product at this higher price. You can also test new promotional offers to a small list sample of your existing customers or prospects, gauging the results of your test before making the offer available to a wider market. When done with discretion and tact, you can execute these tests in a more or less "private" environment, testing different promotional and pricing variations in a low profile manner, and reducing the risk of exposing these tests to major customers or prospects;

New products and markets: Direct mail testing is absolutely the best way to test sales response in new markets for both new and existing products. One or more relatively small and inexpensive direct mail tests prior to a large product launch, or entrance into a new market, can save your company substantial amounts of money in sales expenses in the long run. Since a poor response to a small and relatively inexpensive mailing test can provide you with a statistically valid response, testing is also an important tool for helping you decide whether or not to enter a new market (see Chapter 17 for more information on testing for start-ups and new product launches).

Typical Mailing Tests

There are "statistically correct" methods for determining how many names on a list constitute a valid sampling of a large list to mail (more on this further in this chapter), but as a practical matter, most of your mailing list tests will involve mailing either 2,500 or 5,000 names for each individual test, whether you're testing a new mailing list, a new direct mail piece, or some other aspect of your direct mail program. Tests of different mailing lists, or different direct mail packages, are usually grouped together and mailed at the same time to constitute a single test mailing project.

For example, a typical mailing test to rented, third-party mailing lists involves a mailing to at least 3-6 different lists, with quantities of 2,500 or 5,000 names mailed to each list, for a total quantity mailed between 7,500-30,000 names total (either 2,500 X 3 = 7,500, or 5,000 X 6 = 30,000 names total).

Once results are received, they're analyzed using statistical techniques (more on this in the next section) to determine their projected response if follow-up mailings were mailed to larger quantities on the same list. The mailing program is then "ramped up" on a staged basis, by mailing to larger portions of the list.

When to Test

Despite its advantages, many companies do not test as often, or as well, as they should. Generally speaking, direct mail testing should be done whenever:

- The financial risk of failure in mailing a large volume of direct mail pieces would be an unacceptable loss for your company, or;

- When your company seeks to minimize its risk prior to a new product launch, or entry into a new market.

You should view testing as a "marketing manager's insurance policy" that helps you minimize your marketing expenses, hedge your marketing options, and zero in on the most effective sales appeal for your company's product or service. Whenever you're faced with an important marketing decision, it's likely that you can structure a direct mail test to help you answer critically important questions about your prospect's buying behavior, your targeted market, and other critical pricing or promotion issues.

Deciding What to Test

Whenever you are setting up a test, it's very important to hammer down what, specifically, you want to test. This may seem obvious, but since you can test virtually anything in a direct mailing, and in a unlimited number of combinations, it's important to establish just one or two very clear goals for each direct mail test.

When running a test, you are usually testing one, two or all three of the following variables:

The direct mail piece: Testing sales benefit headlines on an outer envelope, brochure sales copy and formats, different sales copy for sales cover letters, special pricing or promotional offers on the response coupon;

The list: Mailing to a small sample of a large third-party mailing list (also known as an "Nth-name selection"), mailings to small segments of a list, selected by job title, purchasing responsibility, or geographic location, or mailings to samples of several different third-party lists in the same market;

Promotions and pricing: Testing various special promotions, such as percent-off discounts, discounts for first-time buyers, free premiums and other special offers, or different prices and pricing combinations.

How many variables you choose to test depends on your company's depth of experience in its market. For example, if your company is a start-up with no prior experience with its product in the market, or an established company launching its products in a brand-new market, you'll be testing several mailing pieces, several lists, and—at least during the early stages—different sales copy, pricing, and promotional offers.

If your company is well established, it's likely you are already using a proven direct mail piece that has generated solid sales results in prior mailings, so your testing variables will be limited to testing new mailing lists, and relatively minor modifications to your existing direct mail pieces, such as special promotions or price discounts.

Your Testing Benchmarks

Before you execute any direct mail test, it is also important to establish a benchmark that determines when a test is a success. This keeps everybody honest in the process, and prevents subjective, after-the-fact interpretations of results. Most companies usually use one or the other of the following measures to make this judgement:

Response rate: Established companies, or companies selling high-ticket products and services with longer sales cycles, measure success by the overall response rate to a mailing, usually compared to an average response rate received from past mailings. For example, if a well-established company that sells construction equipment in a mature market may receive an average 2% response rate from its mailings to the subscriber list of a leading construction industry publication (i.e., 2% of those who receive the company's mailing piece call or contact the company's sales reps for more product information). The response from any new direct mail test for this company would be measured against this established 2% response rate;

Break-even and cost-per-customer (CPC): You can also use basic financial measurements to measure response to your direct mail tests. In some instances, results are measured against the break-even costs of a mailing, that includes all related creative, production, printing, mailing list rental, lettershop and postage expenses for the test. Costs used in this break-even calculation are then adjusted to account for the reduced costs of mailing to larger portions of the same mailing list. Cost-per-customer calculations involve the comparison of test mailing responses to your company's established cost of acquiring a single customer. A mailing test result that generates response which is lower than the company's average CPC is a favorable result; likewise, a result that yields a higher CPC than average indicates a mailing that needs work.

Testing Sample Sizes: How Small is Too Small and How Big is Too Big?

One of direct mail testing's truly useful advantages is its ability to help you predict the likely response you'd receive on a mailing to a large mailing list, based on the actual results of a smaller test mailing sent to a small sample of this list. Any large mailing list, whether it's a rented publication subscriber list, or your company's sizeable prospect list, can be "sampled," by uniformly selecting a small number of names from the entire list, and mailing your direct mail package to this small list sample.

Using proven, well-established statistical sampling techniques, you can determine:

- **The smallest sample size** you need to mail in order to achieve your desired "confidence level," relative to the response you hope to generate by mailing to the larger list;

- **The projected response** of a mailing to the entire list, based on the results received from your initial test mailing, including an acceptable range of error.

The topics of list sampling and response projection fill many pages in direct mail marketing books, but this section provides the essential tools you need as a marketing manager to help you determine list test sample sizes, and to project response, as you work with your ad agency or marketing consultant to plan your company's direct mail marketing program.

Minimum List Sample Size

Before conducting any test mailing, you must determine the required sample size of the mailing. This is the minimum number of names required to mail in your test, to allow you to project your response in a mailing to the entire list; that is, the projected response you'd receive if you were to send the same mailing to the entire list.

There are two ways to determine your minimum list sample size: The "Statistics Professor" method, using standard statistical sampling methods to a select sample size for your mailing, and a "real world" method.

Finding List Sample Sizes: The "Statistics Professor" Method

First, determine the response rate you expect to receive from your test, from one of the "expected response" columns along the right-hand side of the table shown in **Figure 7-1**. If you're unsure, make an educated guess based on your prior experience, or select a desired response rate for your mailing. Select the percentage response rate in the column that's closest to your projected response rate, in one of the columns along the top of this table (see **Figure 7-1**).

Next, select a "plus or minus error" number along the left-side column on this table. This is the maximum amount of variation that you'll accept in your test results, expressed as a "plus or minus" variation of your expected response rate.

The intersection of the "plus or minus error" figure on the left-hand column, and your projected response rate, selected from one of the response rate columns in the table, gives you the **minimum sample size** you must mail in order to achieve the "confidence level" you desire for your test.

For example, if your desired response rate is 3.0%, and you can accept a plus-or-minus error variation of 0.5 (a final response that will vary no more than 2.5%-3.5% on your mailings, which is a variation of plus or minus .5), the intersection of the 0.5 figure in this row on the left-hand column of the table and the 3.0% expected response rate column, is 4,500 pieces. This means you must mail a sample of 4,500 pieces in your initial test, if you are projecting a 3.0% response rate, and you are willing to accept a margin of error of 0.5% on a mailing to the entire list.

In other words, if you are projecting a 3.0% response to your test mailing, and will accept a variation (margin of error) of 0.5%, from a statistical basis, the final response for a mailing to the entire list, based on a 3% response from your test mailing, may vary from as low as 2.5% (3.0% -0.5% = 2.5%), to a response as high as 3.5% (3.0% + 0.5% = 3.5%) for a mailing to the entire list.

This sample size of 4,500 pieces would be sufficient to test a mailing list of any size, and, if the mailing achieves a 3% response, the projected plus-or-minus variation is calculated to hold true at a 95% "confidence level," which means there is only a 5% probability of error in these results.

As you can see from the minimum sample size table, to reduce your range of error by even a few tenths of a response percentage point, you must mail a substantially larger number of pieces for your test. In the world of statistics, as it applies to direct mail, it always costs a lot more to be just a little more confident.

The "Real World" Sampling Method

In the direct mail field, test sample mailing sizes of around 1,000, 2,000, or 5,000 pieces are used for most test mailings. So, instead of using "error ranges" to determine sample sizes in the previous method, it's more realistic to mail a small number of pieces for your test (1,000, 2,000, or 5,000 pieces, for example), and then

Figure 7.1:

The "Statistics Professor" Table—Use this table to determine your range of error on test mailings

Expected Percentage of Return from Mailing

Plus or Minus Error on Expected % of Return	1.0%	1.5%	2.0%	2.5%	3.0%	3.5%	4.0%	4.5%	5.0%	5.5%	6.0%
.05	152,100	227,000	301,200	374,600	447,200	519,000	590,100	660,400	729,900	798,700	866,700
.1	38,000	56,800	75,300	93,600	111,800	129,800	147,500	165,100	182,500	199,700	216,700
.2	9,500	14,200	18,800	23,400	27,900	32,400	36,900	41,300	45,600	49,900	54,200
.3	4,200	6,300	8,400	10,400	12,400	14,400	16,400	18,300	20,300	22,200	24,100
.4	2,400	3,500	4,700	5,900	7,000	8,100	9,200	10,300	11,400	12,500	13,500
.5		2,300	3,000	3,700	4,500	5,200	5,900	6,600	7,300	8,000	8,700
.6				2,600	3,100	3,600	4,100	4,600	5,100	5,500	6,000
.7			2,100		2,300	2,600	3,000	3,400	3,700	4,100	4,400
.8						2,000	2,300	2,600	2,900	3,100	3,400
.9								2,000	2,300	2,500	2,700
1.0										2,000	2,200

measure your final test results against the *projected range of response* you'd likely receive if you were to mail the same piece to the entire list.

So, for "real world" test mailings, the response ranges shown in the table in **Figure 7-2** are a more practical way to project response from a test mailing. This table contains the projected ranges of response for the test quantities you'd most often mail, based on a confidence level of 95%. In other words, the results shown on this table would be correct 95% of the time, an acceptable level of risk for direct mail marketers.

For example, using this table for a test mailing of 5,000 pieces that generated a 3% actual response, there is a 95% chance that any subsequent, larger mailing to more names on this same list would generate a final response between 2.52% and 3.48%. The projections for sample sizes and expected response rates shown in both tables are valid for mailing lists of any size.

Use the table in **Figure 7-2** when you're mailing either a 1,000, 2,000 or 5,000-piece test sample, and you need to determine a response range based on the response you project (or have actually received) from your test. This is how you will be projecting results from your test mailings most of the time.

Since the table in **Figure 7-1** covers a broader range of mailing quantities, you can use it for subsequent, larger follow-on mailings (also called "extensions") after your smaller, initial test mailings, to calculate the margin of error at the projected response rate for your next mailing. To do this, find the number that is closest to the number of pieces you're planning to mail for your test under the column for the response you're projecting for this mailing, to find the plus-or-minus error.

List-Testing and Sampling: A Typical Example

Here's an example of how these sampling methods would be used in a test mailing. Let's say you recently mailed, or "dropped," a small test mailing of 1,000 pieces to test a large, 100,000-name subscriber list for a trade publication in your industry.

After tracking and measuring response, it looks like the test has generated 22 inquiries, or about a 2% response. After doing a cost-per-customer analysis, and comparing this to the other results you've received in your company's marketing efforts, you conclude that this is a pretty positive initial result. Once you're confident that you've received all of the responses you are going to get for this mailing (generally after about two weeks), you're ready to evaluate your results.

Using the table in **Figure 7-2**, match up your 1,000-piece test mailing with a 2% response. The table indicates that if you were to mail the same mailing piece to the entire 100,000-name subscriber list, you'd receive a response to your larger mailing ranging anywhere from 1.12%—2.88%.

Figure 7-2:

"Real World" Sampling Table—Use this table to project the response on test mailings to the entire list

① If the size of your test mailing is:	② ...and the % return on the test mailing is:	③ ...then 95 chances out of 100, the % response on the identical mailing to the whole list will be between:	① If the size of your test mailing is:	② ...and the % return on the test mailing is:	③ ...then 95 chances out of 100, the % response on the identical mailing to the whole list will be between:
100	1	0 & 2.99	250	1	0 & 2.26
100	2	0 & 4.80	250	2	.23 & 3.77
100	3	0 & 6.41	250	3	.84 & 5.16
100	4	.08 & 7.92	250	4	1.52 & 6.48
100	5	.64 & 9.36	250	5	2.24 & 7.76
100	10	4.00 & 16.00	250	10	6.20 & 13.80
100	20	12.00 & 28.00	250	20	14.94 & 25.00
500	1	.11 & 1.89	1,000	1	.37 & 1.63
500	2	.75 & 3.25	1,000	2	1.12 & 2.88
500	3	1.48 & 4.52	1,000	3	1.92 & 4.08
500	4	2.25 & 5.75	1,000	4	2.76 & 5.24
500	5	3.05 & 6.95	1,000	5	3.62 & 6.38
500	10	7.32 & 12.68	1,000	10	8.10 & 11.90
500	20	16.42 & 23.58	1,000	20	17.48 & 22.52
2,000	1	.55 & 1.45	5,000	1	.72 & 1.28
2,000	2	1.37 & 2.63	5,000	2	1.60 & 2.40
2,000	3	2.24 & 3.76	5,000	3	2.52 & 3.48
2,000	4	3.12 & 4.88	5,000	4	3.45 & 4.55
2,000	5	4.03 & 5.97	5,000	5	4.38 & 5.62
2,000	10	8.66 & 11.34	5,000	10	9.15 & 10.85
2,000	20	18.21 & 21.79	5,000	20	18.87 & 21.13
10,000	1	.80 & 1.20	100,000	1	.94 & 1.06
10,000	2	1.72 & 2.28	100,000	2	1.91 & 2.09
10,000	3	2.66 & 3.34	100,000	3	2.89 & 3.11
10,000	4	3.61 & 4.39	100,000	4	3.88 & 4.12
10,000	5	4.56 & 5.44	100,000	5	4.86 & 5.14
10,000	10	9.40 & 10.60	100,000	10	9.81 & 10.19
10,000	20	19.20 & 20.80	100,000	20	19.75 & 20.25

In a business where a half a percent can mean the difference between a profitable mailing and an unprofitable one, a 1.12%—2.88% range is a swing of almost two percentage points, and a very risky bet if you were to mail to the entire 100,000-name list based on your response to a 1,000-name test. And if your response to the larger mailing ended up being closer to the low end of this range (1.12%) than the high end, this mailing could be a very costly mistake.

Here's the point where you put away the statistical charts and exercise common sense. It would be a grave mistake to drop a 100,000-piece mailing by making a straight-line extrapolation of the results from a small, 1,000-piece test, regardless of how much response was received on this small test. Instead, send out another mailing of 2,000, 5,000, but no more than 10,000 pieces, to test the same list again.

Then, if the next test of 5,000 names still generates a 2% response, you know that you're working with a narrower margin of response for larger mailings, as shown on the table in **Figure 7-2**, a range of 1.60%—2.40%. A larger, 10,000-piece mailing generating a 2% response yields an even narrower margin (1.72%—2.28%), again proving that the more pieces you can afford to mail, the more confident you can afford to be.

Planning Your Direct Mail Test Program

For most business-to-business marketers, direct mail tests involve testing one or more different direct mail packages against several different mailing list samples, also known as "selects." You can start a direct mail program by testing a couple of top mailing lists for your industry, and then expand the scope of your testing as your mailings generate sales response, as you gain experience using direct mail as an element of your company's marketing program.

Selecting Mailing Lists to Test

Most direct mail testing activity involves tests of mailing lists from outside sources, such as trade publication subscriber lists, trade association member lists, and other lists available for rental or purchase from outside list brokers and other sources. Since the mailing list is the most important part of any direct mail project, you must select only the best mailing lists available for your direct mail program, paying close attention to the list assessment techniques covered in the previous chapter. Here are some of the typical mailing lists that business-to-business mailers use, and how they are tested:

> **Trade publication subscriber lists:** Mailing lists of subscribers to the two or three largest trade publications in your industry will usually form the cornerstone of your company's direct mail marketing program. Accordingly, you should begin any direct mail testing program by testing a small sample of each of these lists. For example, a typical test might consist of mailings to two or three of these lists, at a quantity of at least 2,500 names for each list;

Proven buyer lists: Lists of proven buyers, or individuals responsible for purchasing products similar to those sold by your company (also known as "specifiers"), are very desirable, if you can find them. These "compiled" buyer mailing lists are much less attractive to mailers, but worth testing if your budget will allow. A typical initial test of these lists might cover two test mailings of at least 2,500 names to each list;

Trade association member directories: Trade association member lists, identifying prospects in your industry by name, company, and job title, are often very good mailing lists to use for your company's direct mail projects;

"Wild card" lists: If possible, you should also include at least one small test of a list that represents an extension into a new prospect base, market, or some other promising target of opportunity. This could be a sample of a list of attendees to a recent trade show for your industry, selected by an appropriate job title, a high-end newsletter subscriber list obtained from a consulting and research firm well known to your industry, or even a test of a list for a publication in a related industry for a market you believe may hold new promise. Some very exciting and lucrative marketing opportunities have been created by throwing one or more of these "wild card" mailing lists into a test. If, for example, you are planning to test a half-dozen or more mailing lists of at least 2,500 names each, keep an eye out for an interesting wild card list to add to your mix.

"Nth-Name" Mailing List Selection

Any order for any segment of a mailing list that is a portion of the total size of the list should always be made on what is known as an "Nth-name" selection basis. With Nth-name selection, you can order a segment of a mailing list consisting of names that have been uniformly selected across the entire mailing list.

For example, if you are testing a list sample of 5,000 names from a 100,000-name mailing list, selecting every 20th name from the entire list (100,000/5,000 = 20) gives you a uniform, statistically valid sample of the larger list.

Nth-name selection is the standard method for ordering mailing lists, both for initial test mailings, and for subsequent reorders of larger quantities of the same list. If your initial test is successful, and you reorder a larger quantity of names from the same list, make sure to ask the list owner to *exclude* the names that you ordered from your previous Nth-name test, to avoid mailing twice to the same people on that list.

Testing Direct Mail Packages

You can also test different direct mail packages. For example, you might test two different envelope headlines on your mailing pieces, or a conventional, letter-size mailing piece containing a sales letter, brochure, and reply card, against a single, less-expensive, four-color self-mailer. By testing different direct mail packages, you can also discover the sales copy appeals that work best for your company's products.

In direct mail projects where you are testing for the very first time, it's usually best to begin testing with no more than two direct mail packages, each one being substantially different from the other. Usually this means testing the two best direct mail package concepts your advertising agency or marketing consultant produces for your company. As often happens in the process of creative development of direct mail programs, your ad agency will end up creating two very strong final candidates for your direct mail package. And whenever you are involved in any new marketing program, you should always hedge your bets by testing them both.

Each of these two direct mail packages should represent a different and distinctive creative selling approach to your company's product, each having their own, distinctive headlines, sales appeals, and internal elements (such as a different reply card used in each package).

Use a proven, existing direct mail piece as your "control:" For direct mail marketing projects where you have already been working with a proven direct mail package that produces good sales response, you will often want to test a new direct mail package against your existing one with a variety of lists, using your existing mailing piece as the control for your tests.

Testing Different Promotional Offers

You may also want to test various promotional offers across different mailing lists. This can be done by changing the headline on the outer envelope, and the sales copy in the cover letter and reply coupon of the mailing package.

Unless you are running a very large test, or your promotional offer is essential to your mailing, it's usually not necessary to test more than two different promotional offers. It's more important to test the other elements of your testing program— mailing lists and direct mail packages—so you get these more crucial aspects of your direct mail program "dialled in" before testing a multitude of offers.

Preparing Your Direct Mail Test

Once you and your ad agency or marketing consultant have chosen and developed your direct mail packages and selected your mailing lists, you'll need to plan the tracking and follow-through for your test.

Create a Test Panel Matrix

Using the format shown in **Figure 7-3**, organize your test mailings by the variables you are planning to test, and then assign a unique key code to each variable, as shown in this example Microsoft Excel spreadsheet.

This testing panel format is not only useful for helping you keep track of what you're testing, it's a must-have tool for tracking the response received from each

Figure 7-3:

Test Mailing Response Tracking

Use a Simple Spreadsheet to log responses to mailings, by key code, to analyze response by lists tested and different types of direct mail packages used

Direct Mail Packages Mailed (by type or contents)

Mailing Response (%)

Mailing List Test Panel

	A	B	C	D
1	**Company XYZ Mailing List Analysis**			
2				
3				
4			**Package**	**Package**	
5	**Mailing List**	**Mail Date:**	**"A"**	**"B"**	**Total**
6					
7	**Conventions Monthly**	11/20	2,500	2,500	5,000
8	Key Code		200	300	
9	Responses		63	38	101
10	Response (%)		**2.52%**	**1.52%**	**2.02%**
11					
12	**Better Meetings**	11/20	2,500	2,500	5,000
13	Key Code		400	500	
14	Responses		41	22	63
15	Response (%)		**1.64%**	**0.88%**	**1.26%**
16					
17	**Network Monthly**	11/20	2,500	2,500	5,000
18	Key Code		600	700	
19	Responses		83	62	145
20	Response (%)		**3.32%**	**2.48%**	**2.90%**
21					
22	**Total Test Responses**		187	122	309
23	**Average Response (%)**		**2.49%**	**1.63%**	**2.06%**
24					

"cell" in the test, since tracking by key codes is the only way to accurately measure response from a test. Of course, spreadsheets like this one are also very useful for helping you to manage and record responses received from test mailings.

Key-Coding Your Direct Mail Pieces

One of the greatest strengths of direct mail is its measurability. Unlike other forms of advertising media, direct mail gives you the ability to track where prospects come from, and how they become your customers. You can track your direct mail prospects by tracing them back to the mailing lists where they initially responded, the date of the mailing, the promotional offer, and the specific direct mail package they received. In fact, any aspect of your mailing that can be individually tracked can be measured in a direct mail program. But you cannot have measurability in your direct mail marketing programs until you know where the response is coming from—and this is where key-coding comes in.

Key-coding is the first, essential step toward measurability in direct mail programs, but it's a step that's often overlooked. In the rush to get a company's direct mail projects printed and mailed, many ad agencies and marketing managers forget to key code their mailings. As a result, information that is critically important for the next step beyond testing—expansion and rollout of a company's direct mail programs, is lost forever, because no one remembered to collect it in the first place.

Developing a Key Code System for Your Mailings

The most important thing to remember about creating your own key code system is to make it so simple that everyone will use it. This means that key codes must be short enough so your prospects will communicate them clearly to your company's phone sales staff, and easy for the people at your company who answer your phones, open your company's incoming mail, and administer your Web site, to collect and forward to you.

What to key code: the three most important things to track by key code in any mailing are:

- **The mailing list;**
- **Direct mail piece;**
- **The promotional offer**

A basic key-coding system consists of three to six digits, with each single or double digit key-coded to each direct mail element. For example, you can assign a simple, three-digit key code to your first test mailings:

123

—where "**1**" represents the key code assigned to each of your initial test **mailing lists** numbered 1 through 9;

—where "**2**" represents the key code assigned to each different **direct mail piece** used for the test mailing;

—and where "**3**" represents the keycode assigned for each type of **promotion** used in the test mailings.

Since each of these three fields are independent from one another, they will accommodate any combination of mailing list, package, or offer you want to test.

As you expand your direct mailing activities, you can expand this basic 3-digit key code system to 7 digits :

1230105

—where "123" represents the list/package/offer fields, and the last four digits are used for recording the month and year of your mailings.

Of course, you can modify these key-coding methods to suit your own marketing activities. For example, you can drop certain fields (such as promotional offers or direct mail packages), if you will not be testing these individual elements.

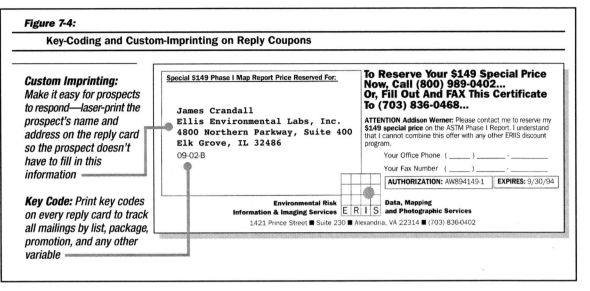

Figure 7-4:

Key-Coding and Custom-Imprinting on Reply Coupons

Custom Imprinting:
Make it easy for prospects
to respond—laser-print the
prospect's name and
address on the reply card
so the prospect doesn't
have to fill in this
information

Key Code: Print key codes
on every reply card to track
all mailings by list, package,
promotion, and any other
variable

Special $149 Phase I Map Report Price Reserved For:

James Crandall
Ellis Environmental Labs, Inc.
4800 Northern Parkway, Suite 400
Elk Grove, IL 32486
09-02-B

To Reserve Your $149 Special Price Now, Call (800) 989-0402... Or, Fill Out And FAX This Certificate To (703) 836-0468...

ATTENTION Addison Werner: Please contact me to reserve my **$149 special price** on the ASTM Phase I Report. I understand that I cannot combine this offer with any other ERIIS discount program.

Your Office Phone (_____) _____ - _____
Your Fax Number (_____) _____ - _____

AUTHORIZATION: AW894149-1 | **EXPIRES:** 9/30/94

Environmental Risk
Information & Imaging Services   E R I S   Data, Mapping and Photographic Services
1421 Prince Street ■ Suite 230 ■ Alexandria, VA 22314 ■ (703) 836-0402

Where to Print Key Codes

On the response coupon: Ideally, the best place to print a key code on your direct mail package is next to your company's phone number on your direct mail package's reply coupon.

Most lettershops can provide you with a number of flexible printing options for custom imprinting and personalization on your company's direct mail pieces. In addition to outer envelopes and sales letters, typical custom-imprint applications also include inkjet or laser imprinting on business reply cards or coupons. These materials may be supplied to your lettershop as partially pre-printed blanks, or may be printed entirely on the lettershop's high-speed printing equipment.

Since it is also a good idea, and a customer convenience, to print the recipient's name and address on the return address portion of the reply coupon of your mailing piece, a key code can also be printed next to the recipient's name on the reply card (see **Figure 7-4**). In business direct mailings, this additional imprinting step is done to save your prospects the added effort of having to write their names and addresses on the reply card. For a small additional setup charge, your lettershop can print a key code along with the return address, which can be tracked when prospects mail the reply cards back to your company, or are asked for the key code by your in-house sales and marketing staff when they call your company's toll-free number.

Mailing labels: If you can't print them on any piece that's inserted into the envelope, you can always print key codes on the mailing address block of the outer envelope mailed to the prospect. This form of key-code imprinting detracts from the personalized impression you are trying to create for your mailings, and some prospects who discard the outer envelope before they contact your company will be unable to provide a key code, but it's a better place to print a key code than not at all.

Figure 7-5:

Tracking Web Site Response on Ads and Mailings

Publication names, dates, or other short, simple, easy-to-enter identifiers can be appended to your Web site's URL in ads and mailings to track prospect links to your company's Web site

www.panasonic.com/broadcast
www.medcare.com/AMAJournal
www.tradex.com/Spring

Using dedicated Web addresses as key codes: In some instances, Web addresses can be used as key codes in your company's direct mail materials. For example, adding an easy-to-type code word after your company's main ".com" Web address can help you track response from prospects who link to those individual Web addresses.

Developing Procedures for Collecting and Reporting Key Codes

Once you've established your direct mail key-coding system, your next job is to get everyone else in your company's sales and customer service departments to start collecting key codes every time they receive a response from one of your mailings. Locate the people at your company who are responsible for receiving direct mail responses at every contact point:

- **By phone and FAX:** In-house sales and telemarketing reps, company receptionist, or field sales reps;
- **By mail:** Mailroom staff, administrative and secretarial staffs;
- **Internet:** Your company's IT/technical staff

Clue all of these individuals in on your new key-coding system, stressing to them the importance of asking prospects for key codes printed on all mailings. To simplify the task of gathering key codes at any point of contact, a key code entry field should be included in your company's sales contact-management software, and it's a simple task for your technical staff to add this field to your company's sales database.

If all else fails, and as a simple expedient, you can always create a xeroxed form and ask your phone sales staff and those who open and handle incoming mail to record these key codes by hand.

Developing a "Response Curve" for Your Mailings

Record the results your company receives from every mailing, sorted by key code, on a daily tally. By recording each day's mailing results for both mail and phone inquiries the day they are received, and for every mailing, you will eventually be able to develop a **response curve** for your mailings. This response curve can then be used

Figure 7-6:

Direct Mail Response Curve—A useful tool for projecting total response to any mailing

By Tracking Responses to Test Mailings, *by each day responses are received, you can build a **response curve** for your direct mail program. Using a spreadsheet like the one below to log responses to your company's mailings, over time you can develop an average response curve to help you make an early projection of a mailing's total response, based on the partial response received during the first few days*

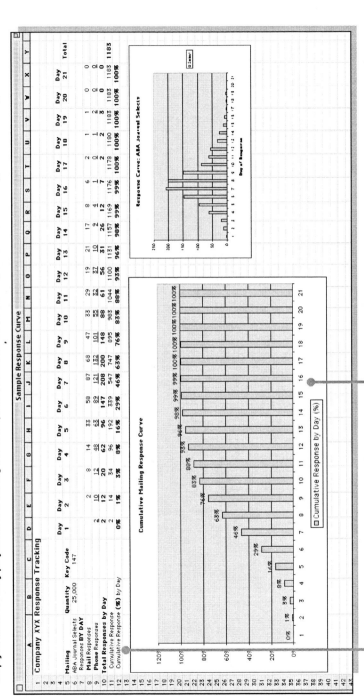

Cumulative Daily Response, *by percentage, helps you determine what total percentage of responses will be received, starting with the first day responses (inquiries or orders)*

The Response Curve *shows cumulative response to any mailing, when phone, mail, and Web responses are tracked by day. **Response curves for several mailings can be combined to develop an average response curve** that can be used as a general projection tool in your company's direct mail program* to project the total response to a mailing based on the first days' responses to that mailing. The key advantage to using response curves is that they save execution time on direct mail projects by helping you to make plans sooner to ramp up mailings that look like they will be successful.

A response curve is a measurement showing daily and cumulative response to a specific mailing, starting from the first day responses are received. Response curves for mailings are a distinctive inverted-"U" shape, as shown in **Figure 7-6**.

Using a Microsoft Excel spreadsheet graph, you can create your own response curves by entering the day-by-day responses for each mailing, starting from "Day One"—that is, the first day you receive responses on that mailing. Divide each day's responses into the total number of responses you received for the mailing to calculate the **daily percentage** of total responses, as shown in the chart above.

Next, add the percentage results for each day to create a **daily cumulative percentage response**, as shown. This cumulative daily percentage is the total percentage of responses received, as each day passes, for a mailing.

Once you've sent out at least a half-dozen or more mailings, and you've plotted a response curve for each mailing, *calculate an average* for each cumulative daily percentage, for all previous mailings. Since response curves will be different for mailings of different sizes, calculate your response curve averages only for mailings of roughly the same quantities, and use the response curve that most closely matches the quantity of the current mailing whose response you want to project.

For example, over time you'll likely develop an average response curve for a 5,000-piece test mailing, another average response curve for a 10,000-piece mailing, and so on. You can then use the response curve whose quantity most closely matches that of your current mailing to project its final response.

Making early projections using a response curve: By applying a response curve from previous mailings, you can make some fairly accurate response projections on early results that come in from a new mailing. If, for example, on this new mailing, by the end of the fourth day in which responses have been received, you've received 150 inquiries or orders from a mailing, and the response curve you've already calculated for a mailing of a similar quantity tells you that, on average, 25% of your total response arrives by day four, you can project that you will receive 600 total responses to this mailing (600/25% = 150).

The main benefit to using a response curve on mailings is that it dramatically shortens your decision-making time on your mailing programs. Instead of waiting the additional weeks required to collect and tabulate the total responses to a mailing, you can often make reasonably accurate calculations based on the first 5 to 8 days' response—and, if your mailing looks like it will be successful—prepare for a rollout and expanded schedule based on the results of this mailing. Likewise, if the early initial results look less than satisfactory, you will have extra time to test other lists. Either way, projecting total response based on early returns can save you 2-3 valuable weeks in your marketing plan. Shortening this "decision cycle" is a major benefit to any marketing program.

. **A note of caution on response curves:** While some direct mail books issue pronouncements on response curves, such as: "You'll receive 25% of your total responses after the first week of your mailing," you should always be skeptical of such broad statements. There are many factors that can affect response to a mailing—the mailing piece, the list, the offer, even the post office where the mailing is dropped. Response curves are different for different types of mailing pieces, and for different products. A response curve published in a book, or based on someone else's marketing experience, probably won't match yours.

That's why it's critical to track your own company's response to its mailings, and to accurately record these responses on a day-by-day basis, to create response curves unique to your company's direct mail marketing program. This takes time, but developing a tool that allows you to predict total response to mailings in your company, based on early returns, is a valuable tool indeed. When you're making decisions that affect the expenditure of many thousands of your company's marketing dollars, take the time required to build your own response curves. Until then, give your responses sufficient time to come in before making decisions on new mailing rollouts and extensions.

Analyzing Results of Your Test Mailings

Once you've allowed sufficient time for responses to arrive from your mailings (usually 30 to 45 days), it's time to analyze your results. If you've been carefully tracking and collecting the responses to your mailings by key code, the next analysis is relatively straightforward, and applies both to test mailings, and mailings in your ongoing direct mail program.

To perform a basic analysis of your mailing results, set up a Microsoft Excel spreadsheet, such as the one shown in **Figure 7-7**.

Choose your type of response: Before analyzing mailing results, you must first decide if your mailing program should be run on either a **cost-per-sale**, or a **cost-per-inquiry**, basis. As mentioned earlier, if your company sells a product that carries a high unit price, it usually requires a fairly long sales cycle—three to six months or longer. From a timing standpoint, it may be impractical for your planning process to tie the results of any one mailing to the sales generated from that mailing. Therefore, it's unacceptable to defer additional mailing decisions if you must wait three to six months to see if those sales have actually occurred.

Cost-per-inquiry: You should always use your best efforts to tie final sales results to the mailing that first drew the prospect, but since much time may have elapsed between the prospect's first inquiry and the final sale of the big-ticket product that resulted from that initial mailing many months earlier, most companies that sell high-dollar products operate their marketing programs on a **cost-per-inquiry** basis.

Figure 7-7:

Mailing Response Cost-Per-Inquiry Analysis

*Use a **Basic Worksheet** to calculate and compare mailing costs to sales response on your direct mail projects*

	Mailing List Return Analysis			
	A	B	C	D
1	Mailings & Worksheet & Analysis			
2	XYZ Corp.			
3				
4	Mailing			
5		Drop Date/		
6	Lists Mailed:	Package	Quantity Mailed	
7				
8	Conventions Monthly	1/15 Pkg. A	5,000	
9	Response			
10	Total Responses		127	
11	Response (%)		2.5%	
12				
13	Production Costs	Unit Costs:	Total Costs:	
14	Printing	1.34 $	6,700	
15	Mailing List Rental	0.10	500	
16	Postage	0.37	1,850	
17	Lettershop Expense	0.03	150	
18	Total Cost	$ 1.84 $	9,200	
19				
20	Cost Per Inquiry		$ 72.44	
21				

Cost-per-sale: If your company sells a relatively low unit price product (under $2,000), that can either be sold directly by mail or phone, and in a fairly short selling cycle (usually less than 60 days), you can frequently compute your direct mail marketing costs on a cost-per-sale basis.

Cost of the mailing: In either cost-per-inquiry or cost-per-sale mailing list analysis, make sure to accurately record the total direct unit cost for each mailing:

- **Printing cost**, calculated for each mailing piece;
- **Mailing list rental cost**, calculated for each mailing piece;
- **Lettershop cost**, by mailing;
- **Postage cost**, by mailing

Next, record the number of inquiries received for each mailing, by key code. If you are analyzing a series of test mailings in a single mailing test, or any other group of mailings that dropped at the same time (either of which is usually the case), perform your analysis of the mailings as a group, with each mailing broken out individually by its own key code.

Tracking "no code" responses: While gathering inquiry responses by key code, it's likely you will receive a number of responses where the prospect was unable to provide the key code for the mailing they received, so there's no way you can determine which list or mailing the prospect responded to. In this case, "unknown" key code inquiries are assigned proportionally to each individual, key-coded mailing, according to that mailing's *percentage of the total inquiries received*. For example, if a mailing with its own specific key code accounts for 20% of your total inquiries, assign 20% of these "no key code" inquiries to this key code, because it's likely that this share of inquiries were generated by this mailing anyway. Calculate the percentages for each key code received, and apportion your "no code" responses accordingly.

Response rate: Divide the total number of pieces mailed in each individual, key-coded mailing, by the total number of inquiries (or sales) generated by that mailing. This number is the **response rate** for the individual mailing, expressed as a percentage, and two decimal places.

Next, divide the total cost of each individual mailing by the number of individual key-coded inquiries (or sales) received for each mailing to calculate the **cost-per-inquiry** (or **cost-per-sale**) for each mailing, by key code.

In a cost-per-sale analysis, calculate total sales that are applied to each mailing by multiplying the number of sales received on each mailing by the unit sale, and then deduct the mailing cost (including postage cost, and the costs of "undeliverable" mailing pieces returned by the post office from your mailing) from total sales for each mailing to calculate total profit (or loss) for each mailing. This "gross sales" calculation will no doubt be disputed by your comptroller, who will subtract his or her own additional "overhead" expenses from this figure, but this is a battle you'll have to fight on your own.

Once you've calculated your response rates and cost-per-inquiry (or sale) figures, for each key-coded mailing, the winners and losers of your mailing test are revealed.

For example, what usually happens is that, out of a test mailing consisting of mailings to 6 different lists (6 test mailings):

- Two mailings will be clear winners, having generated solid response at or above your expectations;

- Two or more mailings will generate results somewhat below your expectations;

- Two mailings will generate unacceptably low response.

By careful collection and analysis of key-coded responses in your initial tests, you are ready and able to make an informed decision to roll out the successful mailings of your test to higher mailing quantities, to cautiously extend mailings that have generated less impressive test response, and to cut your losses on mailings that have generated poor response.

Direct Mail Troubleshooting: What To Do If Your Test Mailings Fail

Despite your best preparation and execution, you'll experience failures in some of your direct mail tests.

However, if a mailing test has been thoughtfully planned, executed, and carefully tested, it's likely it will not end in total failure. If not obviously successful, it's likely that the response results will enter into a "gray middle"—that is, a mailing test that generates enough results to keep it from being a costly failure, but whose results are still insufficient to justify a rollout to higher quantities. Outright failures in direct mailings do occur, but it is likely you will experience many more of these "gray middle" results in your marketing career.

What should you do when your direct mail program fails, or the results fall into the gray area of disappointing response? This section is an action plan for saving your direct mail marketing program, by improving response to your mailings.

Look at your lists: Did you test a sufficient variety of mailing lists in your test? When testing the viability of direct mail as a new marketing method for your company, when testing a new mailing package, or when testing new markets, a credible test will generally require a mailing of least three to six lists, at a minimum quantity of 2,500 names per list (7,500 to 15,000 names total) to generate adequate results. Many companies will mail a single test of 2,500 names to a single list, and, having received poor response from that list, declare: "Direct mail doesn't work for us." When the stakes are high, and you're testing the viability of using direct mail as an important element of your company's marketing program, don't hamstring the effort by testing an insufficient number of lists.

Choose better "selects" on your mailing lists: Upon reflection—and having received a poor response to a mailing—you need to consider whether or not your mailings are reaching the people you actually need to be reaching. Take another look at the lists of job-title selections available for the major mailing lists in your market, as well as other "selects" criteria, such as company size and geography, for example. A modified mailing piece, mailed to a person having a job responsibility more likely to make a buying decision on your product, can substantially improve your mailing response.

Too many "undeliverables:" A mailing that produces a larger-than-expected number of "undeliverable" mailing pieces returned by the U.S. Post Office, is a clear indicator that the list used in the mailing needs updating or other significant correction. A high number of returned, undeliverable mailing pieces are obviously a drain on response, since these pieces never reached your prospects in your mailing. Mailing lists can be "cleaned," either manually, or by running them against NCOA (National Change-of-Address) databases. The next chapter covers this process in greater detail.

Crank up the volume on your direct mail piece: Next to poor mailing list selection, most direct mail failures are caused by underperforming direct mail packages. Take another look at your direct mailing piece, especially now that you can see the results of your test mailing. Repeat the process of looking at your direct mail piece with "new eyes," as if you didn't know anything about your company and its products, and you were receiving the piece for the very first time. Do you think your product's major selling benefits were adequately communicated in your mailing piece? Take another look at the graphics and presentation of your mailing piece, especially the outer envelope and inside brochure: Do those headlines and main selling benefits pop right out so that your average, disinterested prospect can see them? Often, sales response can be increased substantially by "rediscovering" your product's key benefits, simplifying them, and then making the presentation and layout of these benefits in your mailing piece bigger and bolder.

Make a new offer: While re-examining your direct mail package, re-examine its promotional offer. Upon reflection, is your offer generous enough to move the recipients of your mailings to pick up the phone, fill out a coupon, or visit your Web site for further information? Are the terms of your offer compelling and easy to understand? If you're not offering a discount or other added-value promotional offer to your direct mail prospects, you're probably losing up to a third of the response you'd otherwise receive from your mailing.

Change the economics of your mailings: In some cases, a less expensive, one-piece self-mailer can do the job of a more expensive, conventional direct mail package (consisting of sales letter, brochure, reply card and outer envelope)—at 1/3 to 1/2 the cost. Self-mailers, such as larger, self-mailing brochures (or even large-format, self-mailing postcards), offer the advantage of selling your product and telling its story more quickly than the usual, envelope-bound mailing piece. All your prospect has to do is open your self-mailer brochure, turn it over and begin reading your sales headline—rather than having to slice open an envelope and sort through its contents to get to the key benefits of your product. Changing your mailing piece into a single, self-mailer format can change the costs of your mailings enough to make them profitable, and works especially well when the selling objective of your mailing is to draw sales inquiries, rather than direct orders, or when you are presenting a simple, compelling offer on a product that's relatively easy to explain.

If you've done everything you can do, then you'll have to do more: If, after carefully assessing the results of your mailing test, and carefully re-examining your mailing list choices and direct mail packages used for your test, you honestly believe there is no way you could have improved any of these elements of your direct mail program, then you must consider the possibility that direct mail sent out "cold" to your marketplace is not a viable marketing approach for your company.

Add telephone follow-up to your mailings: Direct mailings unaccompanied by follow-up calls from sales reps may not work with some kinds of products, or in some types of markets. The only way you'll know this is by testing.

Brand new categories of products sold by start-up companies, or complex products that require extensive explanation, are two other instances where standalone direct mailing programs may not be successful. Also, if your company's products require a long sales cycle, where many weeks or months may pass between your company's first contact with the prospect and the final sale (due to the need for your sales and engineering staffs to custom-fit your company's products and systems to your prospect's requirements, for example), one-shot direct mailings without telephone follow-up will not be successful.

In any of these cases, you'll have to obtain telephone numbers in addition to the standard name/company/address mailing list information, and integrate a series of follow-up sales phone calls by your company's sales reps as a part of your company's direct mail program.

Direct mail programs that require follow-up phone calls by skilled, knowledgeable sales representatives in your company also require very precise, timely mailing execution on your part, and close coordination with your company's sales manager to ensure that your company's sales reps will always have a steady supply of prospects for their follow-up calls, at the same time making sure that your sales staff is not overwhelmed by too many direct mail pieces being dropped at any one time. This means you'll be mailing smaller quantities of direct mail pieces much more frequently—usually, on a weekly basis.

Testing is a Continuous Process: Test Always, and Test Often

Because it plays such an important role in your company's direct mail marketing program, testing should be a continuing process. Even after you have launched a successful direct mail program in your company, you should always be testing new mailing lists, direct mail packages, promotional offers, and sales approaches.

You never know when the response of your best direct mail piece will begin to fail, or when your closest competitor will launch a new direct mail promotion that overshadows your mailing program. However, if you've been testing continuously, you can draw a new mailing piece, brochure mailer format, sales approach, or promotional offer from a prior test, and put it into action.

Testing provides knowledge, and it gives you options—and the more options you have in any marketing project, the better your chances for success.

Rolling Out: Scaling Up Your Mailings After Your Direct Mail Tests

As mentioned earlier, results from mailing tests are almost never "all good" or "all bad." In a typical test mailing, where you are testing a half-dozen or more different mailing lists, it's likely you will see two lists that have generated excellent response, one or two lists that have generated responses well below your expectations, and a couple of tests that fall right in the middle, where response is still below expectations—but close enough to warrant additional testing.

Scaling Up: Determining Your Range of Response to a Mailing

Once you have allowed sufficient time for all of your responses to arrive (usually about a month after your mailing), and you've received and tabulated all responses to your test mailings, calculate each mailing's projected response rate ranges from the statistical probability chart in **Figure 7-2**.

From the chart, select the quantity closest to the number of pieces mailed in each test, then move across the table to select the response rate that is closest to the actual response rate generated by your mailing. For example, if you mailed 2,000 pieces on a single test, and received a 2% response, then, according to the table, there is an extremely high probability (95%) your overall response from a follow-on mailing to a larger quantity on that list, or to the entire list, will generate a final response rate ranging between 1.37% and 2.63%.

You have now calculated your own best- and worst-case response rates for scaling up your mailings from your test results. While you will usually find that response rates rarely fall outside the projected ranges shown in this table, mailings of larger quantities often seem to yield slightly lower responses than the smaller original test. Nonetheless, these statistical response ranges serve as useful "guard rails," by helping you determine how well, or how poorly a list will perform when estimating the projected response from a test mailing as you scale it up to larger quantities mailed to the same list.

Test Mailing Rollouts: How Many Pieces to Mail Next?

The projected ranges of response you calculate for each test mailing will determine the boldness of the next stage in the rollout of your direct mail program. If your initial mailing tests have generated very favorable results, and the statistically-projected response ranges tell you that future mailings will likely exceed your goals, even at the low end of projected response, you can afford to take the risk of mailing much larger quantities as you scale up, or extend, your mailings to a particular list. Likewise, and more likely, your mailings will generate responses that are either slightly below your expectations, or slightly above them. In either case, the projected low-end response ranges for scaling up these types of mailings should serve as a caution to prevent you from taking the undue risk of mailing too many pieces to this list on your next rollout.

Best case—"very positive" response: If any of your test mailings generate responses whose statistical projection shown on the table indicates a very positive projected response, even at the low end of the projected response range, then, (theoretically at least) you could expand a successful test mailing of 2,500 or 5,000 pieces into a mailing of the entire list, regardless of the total size of that list— whether it's 100,000, or 1 million, names.

Practically speaking, there are two reasons why this "statistical validity" approach works better in theory than does in the real world. First, since there are always external factors that affect your mailings, such as seasonality (see **Figure 7-9**), a competitor's introduction of a new product that coincides with your mailings, or changes in your industry's market conditions, you should never let yourself be guided by statistical projection methods alone. Second, it's better to be conservative, especially when you're spending your company's money. Third, if your mailing depends on telephone follow-up by your company's sales reps, you do not want to mail a higher quantity of pieces than these sales reps can reasonably handle when they do their follow-up.

When rolling out, triple up: For test mailings where results were "positive," a good rule of thumb to follow is that you can safely mail **up to three times** the quantity of pieces you mailed in your initial test. For example, if you mailed 2,500 pieces in your test, and achieved a solidly positive response, you should then be able to safely mail up to 7,500 pieces on your first rollout, or extension, of that list (2,500 X 3 = 7,500).

This "triple up" rule works for all subsequent mailing extensions to the same list. Following our previous example, if your subsequent mailing of 7,500 pieces continued to generate a very positive response, you could then increase the quantity on your next mailing to 22,500 pieces (7,500 X 3 = 22,500); tripling up the quantity of each subsequent mailing extension if you continued to receive satisfactory response from each new mailing.

There's no complicated statistical reasoning behind the notion of tripling the quantities of your mailing tests. But it makes good sense because it can prevent you from suffering a financial loss from poor response after mailing far too many pieces on your extension, based on a positive response from a relatively small, initial test.

If you want to be even more prudent, you can mail just double the number of pieces of your original test. If on the other hand, you're willing to take the gamble, you can mail many more times this amount in your extension, but this is not recommended. Some mailers have been known to extend a series of 5,000-name mailing tests to mailings of 50,000 pieces on their very next extension (that's up to 10 times the original test), and their responses matched those of their original tests. In this case, however, these mailers had great confidence in their product and their marketing plan, were willing to take a big gamble, and were playing in a very competitive marketplace where timing was critical. Unless you're in a similar situation, it's unwise, and usually unnecessary, to be this aggressive.

"Mildly positive" response: If the low end of your projected response rate range, as indicated by your analysis, places the projected results of your mailing extension in negative territory—i.e., where, in a worst-case scenario, you wouldn't meet your financial goals if the response to your next mailing came in at the low end of the projections shown on the table in **Figure 7-2**, you need to take a more cautious approach when considering subsequent mailings to the same list.

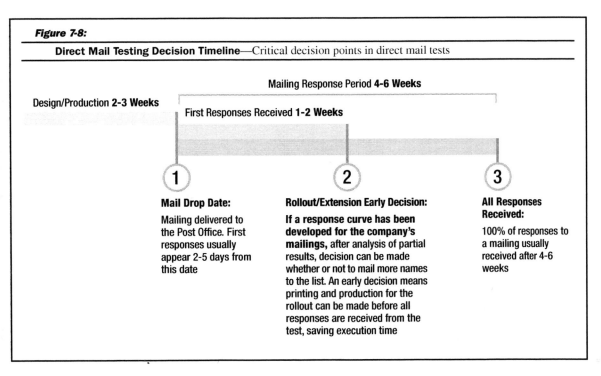

Figure 7-8:

Direct Mail Testing Decision Timeline—Critical decision points in direct mail tests

Mailing Response Period **4-6 Weeks**

Design/Production **2-3 Weeks**

First Responses Received **1-2 Weeks**

① Mail Drop Date:
Mailing delivered to the Post Office. First responses usually appear 2-5 days from this date

② Rollout/Extension Early Decision:
If a response curve has been developed for the company's mailings, after analysis of partial results, decision can be made whether or not to mail more names to the list. An early decision means printing and production for the rollout can be made before all responses are received from the test, saving execution time

③ All Responses Received:
100% of responses to a mailing usually received after 4-6 weeks

The most conservative approach to follow when your test results appear "mildly positive" is to mail only the same number of pieces on your extension as you mailed in your original test, to either validate or disprove the response from your initial test. However, if your projected response appears to be mostly positive, that is, where only a smaller portion of the total range of your projected response may fall below your mailing's chosen break-even point, you could mail a larger quantity of pieces on your extension; but in no case should you mail more than double the number of pieces of your initial test mailing.

"Gray area" mailings: You should move cautiously on extensions to a test whose response has fallen into the "gray area;" that is, where response falls somewhat below expectations, but may be worth additional testing. Continue with a mailing schedule of the same quantity of pieces as you mailed on your original test, carefully assessing the response from each mailing. Even if you must repeat these small mailings a few more times until you are confident enough in the results of these mailings, it's better to be conservative until response rates on these mailings prove themselves.

Extending Your Direct Mail Program: Timing and Execution

Once you've begun to receive results from your test mailings, and the early results from some of the lists you've mailed look promising, you must now plan and execute your rollouts, or extensions, to these mailing lists.

Figure 7-9:

Seasonality and Your Mailings

Seasonality—the time of year you execute a mailing—can have a significant impact on the response to your mailings.

It's a widely recognized fact that a mailing sent during the summer months **between June and August** (Memorial Day and Labor Day) will generate less response than if it were mailed either before or after this summer season.

To a lesser extent, a mailing that arrives during the **second half of December** also runs the risk of generating lower response, since many potential prospects who receive mailings during this time will be preoccupied with pre-Christmas and other holiday activities.

The impact of seasonality on your company's mailings may be slight or significant, but if you're launching a direct mail program for your company for the very first time, or otherwise need to eliminate the possibility that seasonality could lower the response of an important mailing, you should schedule your direct mail program to avoid mailing during these times of the year.

At this point, you must make some very important, and potentially very expensive, decisions. More direct mail pieces must be printed, and at higher quantities; more postage expense must be pre-paid to your lettershop, and larger quantities of names on the mailing lists you decide to run for your mailing extensions must now be ordered and paid for. All of these activities require additional lead time, as individual pieces of your mailing are printed, mailing lists are processed, and each of these important elements are trucked, shipped, and Fedexed to the places they need to go.

Now is the point when you must decide on either of two approaches for executing your rollouts to the lists that have generated the best response from your initial test:

Fast but risky: If you are operating in a fast-moving, turbulent market, and working against very smart, aggressive competition, time may not be on your side. Therefore, it's important to eliminate the additional three- to four-week wait generally needed to receive all the responses from your mailings. If you can't wait for all your responses to arrive and you must move quickly, you can reasonably predict the total returns to each of your mailing tests based on the first 10-14 days' worth of responses. Once you've gained some experience with direct mail in your marketplace, and developed a proven "response curve" for your mailings, it's likely that you will be able to predict your total responses to mailings in even less time—as little as three to five days.

This approach is risky if you have little experience using direct mail as part of your company's marketing efforts, and is not recommended for start-up companies introducing their new products to the marketplace. There are many factors beyond your control that can harm the response to your mailings, so projecting response from your mailings based on early returns always contains an element of risk, even for mature companies with extensive direct mail experience. Your mailings may encounter faster or slower postal delivery times in different areas of the country, and other factors, such as labor strikes, major news events, weather emergencies, or other unforeseen calamities may

---

Figure 7-10:

---

5 Rules for Direct Mail Testing:

1. Keep your testing simple and manageable. *Keep your testing objectives simple. Test mailing lists, and different direct mail packages, but don't let your testing program get out of control by testing too many variables—numerous sales letter variations, too many coupon offers, etc. Testing an infinite number of package combinations along with different mailing lists only makes your responses more difficult to track;*

2. Always use Nth-name selection for your mailing list tests. *Nth-name selection insures that you'll receive the most representative sampling of the entire list you're testing, and is the best possible statistical reflection of the overall list;*

3. Use a sufficient number of names in your test. *Use the statistical tables in this chapter to determine the sufficient number of pieces to mail for your test, to achieve your desired confidence level of projected response. While you should never mail more pieces than you need to, the impressions you may receive from mailing an insufficient number of pieces can be costly and misleading;*

4. When testing, mail all of your pieces at the same time. *When testing multiple lists or packages in a single testing project, make sure that your lettershop drops all the pieces for this test on the same day, so each of your tests have a common starting point. Postal delivery schedules, weather, and other unforeseen factors can change on a daily basis, and can warp your test results if mailings have been staggered over a few days;*

5. Act on your test results immediately. *If the results of your test mailings generate a significant response, such as a very positive response to a new price offer, or a profitable result to a new direct mail package, make an extension mailing for this test your top priority. Market and competitive conditions can change quickly, but only fast follow-up execution can turn a favorable test result into a solid tactical advantage.*

alter the rate your mailings are delivered, thereby changing the rates and quantities of final response you receive from your mailings.

Slow but sure: The safest course is to wait 4-5 weeks from your test mailing's original mailing date, allowing sufficient time for most of the responses to arrive from your mailing. At 2-3 weeks from your mailing date, your mailings will have generated enough response to allow you to start your preparations for rolling out the more successful list tests from your mailing, while waiting the additional two weeks beyond this point (a total of 4-5 weeks from your original mailing date), for the balance of your results to arrive before you actually make the financial commitment necessary to put your new mailings in motion.

Allowing for sufficient time to receive actual responses, rather than projecting (i.e. estimating) them in advance is the safer, and more financially responsible, way to plan your mailings. This approach will also prevent you from making hasty, and expensive, mailing decisions. On the downside, you must factor in a minimum 30-45 day time interval into all your test mailings, plus an additional two or three weeks beyond that, before the larger, and more profitable, rollout mailings are printed and mailed.

This "dead time" represents a true marketing opportunity cost you will have to weigh against the need to be financially prudent. In general, however, if your company's market conditions can tolerate this 30-45 day delay between your test mailing and its subsequent, larger rollout, the conservative approach is always preferable wherever timing and marketing conditions allow.

What to do: Most of the time, you will gain enough of an impression of your test mailing's overall response approximately 2-1/2 weeks after the mail date to know whether or not you should begin to plan for another, larger mailing to that list. If you receive strongly favorable initial results from a test during this time, experience has shown that it is more important to seize the initiative in your marketing efforts, and get that new extension mailing out there, as quickly as possible.

You may have to mail upwards of 20,000 to 25,000 total pieces in a series of one, two, three or more subsequent mailing list extensions to generate sufficient test response to satisfy yourself that you are comfortable with the final sales response from a list.

All marketing efforts contain a certain level of risk. While you are being fiscally prudent and waiting 30-45 days to count all of your responses, a risk-taking competitor can swoop in with a copycat mailing of their own. There is a balance between the necessary speed of execution and good judgement required in all marketing decisions. You'll find this balance in most of your direct mail planning decisions, without having to lose too much time—and opportunity—in the process.

DIRECT MAIL EXECUTION
CHAPTER 8
CREATING, DEVELOPING, AND EXECUTING SUCCESSFUL DIRECT MAIL PROJECTS

Direct mail marketing projects take many forms, both large and small: From mailings of expensive sales kits to small numbers of highly targeted executives, to high-volume mailings to thousands of potential prospects in your market, spread out over dozens of rented mailing lists.

In all its forms, direct mail is a common part of most trade, industrial, and business-to-business marketing programs. Because of this, knowledge of direct mail tradecraft and execution is essential for marketing managers. There are an unlimited variety of direct mail options available to your marketing program, but learning how to use direct mail to address the most common marketing situations will put you on the path to using direct mail most effectively, to generate inquiries and sales for your company.

Putting Direct Mail to Work: A Mailing for Most Every Marketing Situation

The first part of this chapter details some of the typical marketing scenarios where direct mail is used, the types of mailing pieces typically used in each of these marketing situations, and how they're executed. The second part of this chapter details the critical steps in the execution of direct mail projects, and how to manage this process.

Marketing Situation #1: Mailings to Rented Mailing Lists

The scenario: Mailings to "rented" lists, such as subscribers to industry trade publications, trade show and conference attendees, trade association members, industry newsletter subscribers, and compiled lists developed by list brokers. These mailings begin with the mailing list tests covered in the previous chapter, where a small, random sample of the total list (usually 1,000, 2,500, or 5,000 pieces) is mailed. If successful, these mailings are then rolled out, or "extended," to subsequent, larger mailings to more names on the list. For many trade and industrial marketers, direct mailings to rented mailing lists ranks third in importance to display advertising and trade shows as a company's major sales lead-generating activity.

Who receives this mailing: An individual who receives a direct mail piece as a result of their name being on a rented mailing list is the direct mail equivalent of the "cold call," in that they are receiving your direct mail piece without having first requested it, and in many cases they are learning about your company and its products for the very first time (that is, if the sales copy on the outside of your mailing piece was persuasive enough to get them to open it in the first place).

Also, recipients of direct mail packages mailed to rented lists have sometimes been "selected" by certain defining characteristics, such as job title, location, company size, or some type of "buyer/specifier" characteristic, such as their past purchase of a product similar to one sold by your company, or a previously-stated "intention to buy" a product such as yours. When using rented lists, you will usually match them against your company's own customer list and exclude any current customers from the rented list, to avoid sending promotional mailings to your company's established customers.

Mailing goals: The primary goal of mailings to rented lists is sales lead generation, to "cast a wide net" in the marketplace, gathering a sufficient number of respondents who have been compelled by the mailing piece to contact your company—by phone, mail, e-mail or fax, to request more information on your company and its products. For trade and business-to-business marketers, sales leads generated from these mailings are then followed up by the company's sales force, or by outside dealers or distributors.

Mailings to rented lists can also be used to sell a company's product directly from the mailing piece, if the price of the product is sufficiently low enough. Products having a unit price under $2,000 can usually be sold exclusively by direct mail, or by a combination of direct mail, accompanied by one or more follow-up phone calls by a sales telemarketing staff. Products having a unit price under $500 can usually be sold by direct mail alone, and often in a single mailing.

While you don't own any of the names you obtain by "renting" a mailing list, once an individual whose name was on a rented mailing list responds to your mailing piece by contacting your company, and provides you with his/her name, company, and other sales contact information, you may then "capture" this lead and include it

Figure 8-1:

Self-Mailer Formats

Large Self-Mailing Brochures, incorporating sales copy and inquiry request/order forms, such as this 8-1/2 X 14 piece, are a quick and versatile format for many direct mail projects

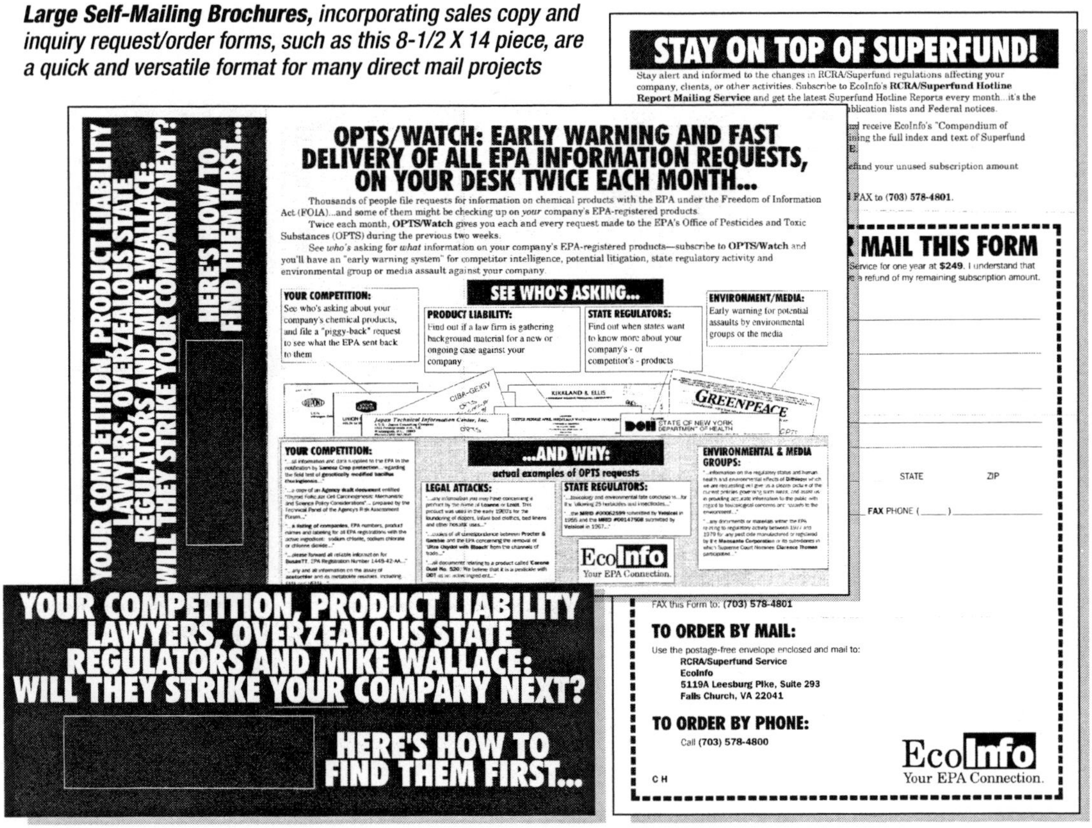

in your company's own sales and marketing database. Your company then "owns" this new sales lead, which then becomes part of your company's own mailing list.

Package elements and contents: The "classic" direct mail piece sent to rented mailing lists is typically either a letter-size (#10) or 9 X 12 ("catalog" size) mailing piece, containing the following elements:

- **One or two-page sales letter (personalized or generic);**
- **Color promotional sales brochure;**
- **Postage-paid reply card;**
- **Promotional card, or "buck slip" (optional)**

Figure 8-3:

New or Improved Product Feature Mailings—Use self-mailers to cut marketing execution time

Self-Mailer Formats, such as this piece, custom laser-printed for individual sales territories, are an excellent choice for new product feature announcements, special price promotions, and other marketing situations where fast turnaround is needed

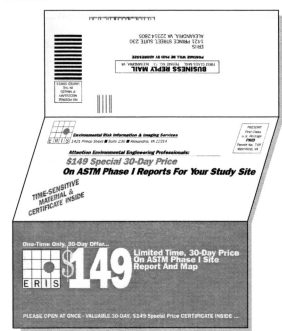

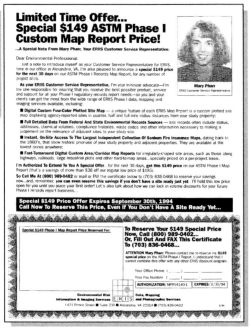

There are, of course unlimited creative styles and variations of the "classic" direct mail package: For example, outer envelopes can look like your company's traditional letterhead, or can be boldly emblazoned with big, promotional, eye-catching headlines; envelopes can be printed four-color, solid color, or plain white, depending on your ad agency's creative approach, and your marketing budget.

One-piece, self-mailer options: For many years, direct mail marketers clung to the "classic" direct mail format for mailings to rented mailing lists, because this was the proven, time-tested format that worked on past projects. Also, given the extra expense of mailings to rented mailing lists (about $50 to $100 or more per each thousand pieces added to the cost of a mailing), direct mail marketers stayed with this proven format to ensure the best possible chance of success when executing these more expensive mailings.

Over the past several years, however, various types of one-piece, self-mailer formats have proven themselves as effective alternatives to the traditional, letter-

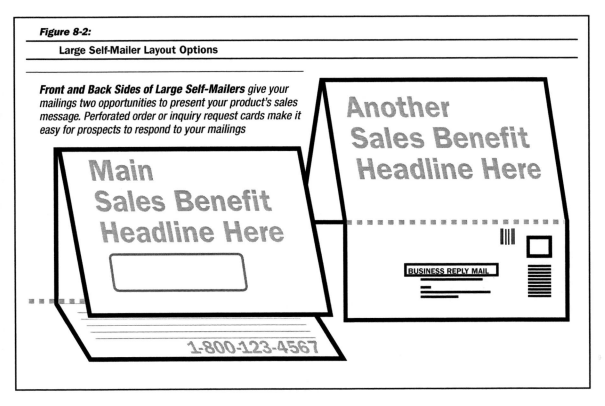

Figure 8-2:

Large Self-Mailer Layout Options

Front and Back Sides of Large Self-Mailers *give your mailings two opportunities to present your product's sales message. Perforated order or inquiry request cards make it easy for prospects to respond to your mailings*

Another
Sales Benefit
Headline Here

Main
Sales Benefit
Headline Here

BUSINESS REPLY MAIL

1-800-123-4567

format mailing piece. For example, large-format (8-1/2 X 11 folded size) 3-panel self-mailing brochures (approximately 28 X 11 inches in their unfolded, flat size) combine the selling power of the traditional, letter format's sales cover letter, color brochure and response card into a single, full-color, mailable printing piece that can be unfolded and read more quickly by prospects than an envelope-bound mailing piece. Postage-paid reply cards can also be integrated into these large-format self-mailers, and perforated so they can be readily removed, filled out and mailed in by prospects.

In addition to their sales impact, often equal to or better than a multiple-piece, envelope-bound direct mail package, there are fewer printed pieces that have to be designed, produced and printed with self-mailers (3-5 individual printed pieces for a letter-format mailing piece, vs. the self mailer's single printed piece). Depending on quantity, postage costs and lettershop expenses are also lower for self-mailers than for letter-format mailing packages.

Self-mailers can be produced in a variety of sizes, from the larger-format 11 X 17 sheets folded down to 8-1/2 X 11 size, or to 5-1/2 X 8-1/2 (folded) size, or to the smallest, letter-size format (#10 size), measuring approximately 4 X 8-1/4 inches in its final, folded size. However, large-format, 8-1/2 X 11 (final folded size) pieces account for the vast majority of self-mailer formats used on mailings to rented mailing lists.

Marketing Situation #2: Tactical Mailings for Sales Promotions, New Product Announcements, and Other "Targets of Opportunity"

The scenario: These types of mailings exploit various tactical "targets of opportunity," such as new product launches, new sales promotions and special pricing announcements, and tactical mailings designed to contrast your company's product with that of a major, named competitor.

Who receives these mailings: Sales promotion, announcement, and target-of-opportunity mailings are usually sent to your company's in-house customer and/or prospect lists, and, depending on the promotion, are sent to other special mailing lists that you compile in-house, such as trade association membership rosters, or specially-created lists of business executives at targeted companies or markets, compiled by the "Dumb Assistant" list compiling technique, described previously in Chapter 6.

Mailing goals: These special mailings are designed to achieve a *tactical effect*, and are usually used to stimulate short-term sales for your company. For example, if you know that your company faces a slow selling season during the upcoming summer months, a well-timed sales promotional mailing scheduled to arrive three weeks before Memorial Day can provide a lift to a slow sales period.

A tactical mailing can also boost sales by announcing sales promotions tied to improved product features, or announcing market changes benefiting your company. For example, the addition of a major, well-known company as one of your new customers, or an endorsement by a leading trade or professional organization in your industry can serve as the "hook," around which a mailing can be created.

Competitive mailings: Tactical mailings can also be used to favorably compare your company's products against those of your leading competitors. Direct, in-your-face sales headlines work best when you're putting out a mailing that is intended to stack your product's major benefits up against those of your major competitors: "Now 20% more efficient than [named competitor's product X]." Another common feature used in these kinds of mailings is a comparison table, listing key features and benefits of your company's products, alongside those of your major competitors, in a row-and-column table format.

New or improved product feature mailings: If your company has added a new, significant, or improved feature to its product or service, you can build a mailing around it. A tactical mailing to your company's own customer and prospect mailing lists, outlining the major user benefits of the new product improvement or feature, along with a reinforcement of your product's overall benefits, is a tremendous opportunity for keeping your company's products in front of your customers and prospects.

New and improved product feature mailings work best when you include a special, limited-time promotional offer, such as a percent-off discount, a special quantity price break, an added premium, or some other incentive for your customers and prospects to place a call to your sales reps, in response to your call to "Act Now!"

Package elements and content: Any common direct mail format can be used in a tactical mailing—from conventional letter-size mailings containing a cover letter, brochure and reply coupon, to self-mailer formats of any size—even postcards. Since these tactical opportunities often present themselves quickly, and require an equally rapid response, self-mailer formats in either 8-1/2 X 11 (folded) or 5-1/2 X 8-1/2 (folded) size formats are fast and easy to produce, print, and mail.

Options: Four-color, self-mailing postcards are also an excellent mailing format for simple, basic sales announcements, or any other tactical marketing event that can be easily communicated to your customer and prospect base. These include announcements of limited-time only sales discounts on products that are well-known to your customers. Other, easy-to-understand promotional offers, such as: "Buy One, Get One Free" can also be readily presented in a postcard format, and rapidly mailed to your customer and prospect lists. Four-color postcards in 5-1/2 X 8-1/2 size are an inexpensive, versatile format for many of these one-time-only promotional mailings.

Marketing Situation #3: Inquiry-Generation

The scenario: These mailing activities utilize postcard decks and magazine reader service responses to help you build and maintain a large inquiry mailing list, suitable for one or more subsequent re-mailings of a "bounceback" package mailing.

Postcard Decks

Postcard decks are individual postcards, inserted and mailed in a small, polyethylene or mylar bag, to business, professional, trade and industrial mailing lists, by third-party card deck marketing companies. These independent card deck mailers utilize a large number and variety of mailing lists for their mailings—trade publication subscriber lists, association member lists, as well as low-grade compiled lists put together from telephone directory listings, warranty card lists, and other sources.

There are hundreds of different postcard decks available for business, trade, and consumer marketers in the U.S., and there's at least one card deck covering every major industry, business, and trade category, including your company's market or industry. Many trade publications who rent their subscriber mailing lists also offer card deck mailing programs, consisting of one, two or more card deck mailings each year.

An executive or business professional who receives a card deck gets a thick packet of about 100 or more individual postcards, with each card promoting an advertiser's product or service targeted to that particular business category or industry. For example, there are postcard decks for engineers, marketing managers, and computer programmers. Most people who receive postcard decks in their business mail will at least open the packet and shuffle through the stack of cards; very few actually discard the stack unopened because card decks are perceived as being more substantial than the average piece of "junk mail."

Figure 8-5:

Postcard Decks—Use free, value-added premiums to build your own prospect mailing list

Postcard Deck Mailings, using free premiums that are relevant and useful to recipients in their market (such as these offers for data guides and wall maps for environmental engineers) are the best, fastest ways to build prospect mailing lists for your ongoing marketing projects

Postcard decks build big sales inquiry mailing lists—fast: As a business, trade, or industrial marketer, the sole reason to utilize card decks is to build and maintain a steady stream of sales leads to build your company's own prospect mailing list. When using a card deck, your goal is to get as many reasonably qualified recipients as possible to fill out your postcard with their name, company, and address information, and to drop this card back in the mail to you. As you build this list, you can then mail your company's "bounceback" mailing piece to the names on this list, for followup by your company's sales reps to further qualify each prospect.

Because they're mailed to large numbers of low-quality mailing list names in an industry, sales inquiries generated by postcard decks tend to be lower-quality sales leads than inquiries generated by your company's display advertising or other direct mail projects. However, what postcard deck mailings lack in quality is more than compensated for by the large quantity of sales leads they generate.

Postcard decks are an excellent way to "cover a market," and to build a large mailing list in a short period of time. Despite the low quality of the leads they generate, it's often worthwhile to send subsequent, additional follow-up promotional mailings to these names on a periodic basis (see below), with follow-up phone calls made by your company's in-house sales reps, to further qualify prospects after they've received the original sales premium.

Figure 8-4:

Tactical Postcard Self-Mailers—Best used for simple, fast marketing promotions

---

Full-Color Postcard-Size Self-Mailers are an excellent choice for market tests, product announcements, and easily-understood sales promotions

If your postcard is produced for maximum effect, a postcard deck can often generate a 5-10% response. This means that on a typical postcard deck mailed to 200,000 executives in your industry, you could receive 10,000 to 20,000 returned postcards. That's a great way to build a big list of prospects in a hurry, and it can be a substantial boost to your marketing program, if your sales reps can efficiently call and qualify these inquiries.

To get the highest postcard response, send something FREE: To get the largest possible number of inquiries from postcard decks, develop and promote a free offer for a tangible item with perceived value for prospects in your marketplace. A free offer or premium should make it easy to persuade a prospect to fill out the postcard and drop it in his company's outgoing mail bin back to you. Examples of proven, successful free card deck premium offers include:

- **Relevant industry or technical reports, booklets or videos;**
- **Printed premiums, such as wall maps or technical reference charts;**
- **Printed, specialized data reference and conversion slide charts or reference cards;**
- **Software on CD-ROM;**
- **Demonstration or product applications video on DVD**

The most successful card deck premium offers are those that are the most relevant to the business, technical or professional interests of the card deck's audience, items that are only available from your company, and ones having a high level of interest to your card deck's professional audience. If the premium is seen by the recipient as being a unique and interesting item that helps them solve a common problem in their business or profession, the greater the chances are they will fill out and mail the postcard.

Postcard layout for card decks: The single most important word on any postcard in a card deck is: **FREE!** Print the word "FREE!" as large as possible on the face of your card layout, in the upper left-hand corner of the card, followed by a boldface subhead describing the premium, and its major benefit to the reader. Below the word "FREE!," show a picture of the premium, along with a brief, descriptive paragraph that tells more about it, with some brief, descriptive benefits-oriented text on your company and its products. Make sure to print a "Call to action," along with your company's toll-free phone number and Web address in bold, readable type along the bottom edge of the card. See **Figure 8-5** for examples of successful postcard layouts.

Postcard deck "bounceback" mailing piece: Design and execution of an effective card for card decks is just the first step in successful card deck execution. As the "drop date" for the card deck mailing draws near, you should have a sufficient quantity of your "bounceback" response mailing pieces printed and ready to be mailed immediately to the interested prospects who send back cards from the card deck mailing.

A typical card deck sales bounceback package (see **Figure 8-6**) contains the following pieces:

- The premium item;
- Outer envelope, printed with a picture of the premium, along with the headline letting the prospect know what's inside: "Here's your free [Item] you requested…" (make sure to let them know they asked for the item);
- A brief, personalized or generic sales cover letter;
- Your company's standard product brochure;
- Response card with "call to action"

Don't ever let sales leads from card decks grow cold: Have your bounceback mailing packages printed, assembled, and ready to mail as soon as postcards begin to arrive at your company. The faster you can get the prospect's name and address entered into your company's sales database, and the bounceback package mailed back to that prospect, the more favorable your prospect's first impression of your company and its product will be. Fast response in marketing execution keeps your company's sales leads "hot."

When estimating the number of bounceback packages to have on hand, assume a response rate ranging from as low as 1%, to as high as 10% of the total quantity of

Figure 8-6:

Postcard Deck "Bounceback" Mailing Piece—Create a special "Requested Material" envelope

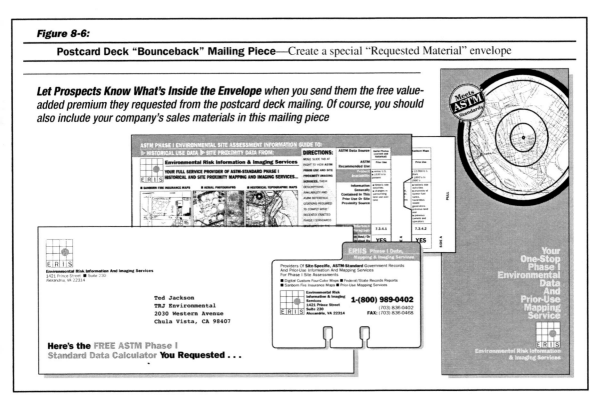

Let Prospects Know What's Inside the Envelope when you send them the free value-added premium they requested from the postcard deck mailing. Of course, you should also include your company's sales materials in this mailing piece

names being mailed in the card deck. For example, if a card deck is being mailed to 200,000 names, you should have at least 2,000 bounceback pieces (200,000 X 1% = 2,000) ready to go.

Many companies follow the one-two punch of the card deck/bounceback mailing piece with a telephone call from a company sales rep. This should also be done in a timely manner—no more than a week after the prospect has received the bounceback package.

Once you've received and entered a prospect's address information from a card deck mailing, you have "captured" this mailing list name, and it now belongs to your company. Having become part of your company's sales prospect mailing list, you can send additional, subsequent mailings to this prospect any time in the future, without having to pay additional list rental charges.

Reader Service card inquiries from display advertising: "Reader Service Card" inquiries are another source of mailing list names you'll receive from publications where your company's display advertising appears. As a service to their readers, many magazines insert a "Reader Service Card" bound into their publications, that readers can use to receive additional information from advertisers whose products are of interest, by checking off a box next to the advertiser's name. The publication then forwards this mailing list of respondents to its advertisers on a regular basis, usually monthly, or twice a month.

Reader Service Card inquiries have a well-deserved reputation for being low-quality sales leads, since these readers are less interested in your company's products than other readers of the publication who already saw your ad, and made the effort to pick up the phone and call your company (after all, how much effort is required to circle a number next to a company on a Reader Service Card?).

This is not to say that you shouldn't have Reader Service Card entries entered into your company's mailing list database. Just make sure they are key-coded to identify them, so they can be eliminated whenever you must filter out inquiries likely to be of lower quality and interest when generating a list from your sales database for a future mailing.

Marketing Situation #4: The Sales Rep's Sales Kit

The scenario: Every company that employs salespeople has its standard "sales information kit," usually prepared and mailed out, as a result of your sales rep's first phone contact with the prospect.

Who receives this mailing: Prospects who have contacted one of your company's sales reps in response to an ad, a mailing piece, or some other marketing effort executed by your company, or who have been contacted over the phone by one of your company's salespeople. This marketing scenario is usually the most "personal" form of sales communication, because it involves a direct contact between one of your company's sales reps and an individual prospect.

Mailing goals: This type of mailing consists of a direct mail package that is usually pre-assembled in small batches by support and administrative staff, and mailed out at the end of each workday, at the sales rep's request. This package is nearly always combined with a brief note or standard sales cover letter bearing the salesman's signature.

Speed of response is crucial in any mailing, but it's especially important that sales kits be mailed out to prospects on the very same day your prospect has spoken to one of your salespeople. Every day lost in sending your company's sales information package to an interested prospect is a day the prospect's interest grows colder. From an execution standpoint, this is largely a matter of good office organization: An ample supply of materials comprising your company's standard sales kits must always be printed and on hand, and your sales administrative staff must develop standing procedures to insure that sales kit materials are mailed out to interested prospects on the same day as the inquiry is received by your company's sales staff. It's your job, along with your company's sales manager, to impress upon your company's sales representatives and sales administrative staff the importance of getting sales kits out to interested prospects on the same day they call your company.

Package elements and contents: Because any sales contact that involves one of your company's sales people is usually the most expensive, from a cost-of-sales standpoint, the standard "company sales kit" is also usually a company's most expensive direct mail piece. Sales kits consist of one or more large format (8-1/2 X 11) four-color brochures usually inserted into a standard, die-cut sales presentation folder, along with other sales collateral material either you or your salesperson includes to meet the prospect's specific needs, such as price lists or technical spec sheets for certain products. The sales kit should also include a sales letter, signed by your sales rep, and/or a handwritten note from the sales rep, along with his or her business card.

You may also wish to include some type of "response vehicle," such as a reply card, for the prospect to fill out to indicate their continued level of interest in your company's product, or to provide your company with additional comments on their product needs or preferences.

Sales kits are usually sent by First Class Mail in your company's standard 9 X 12 - inch letterhead envelope, with your company's logo and return address printed on the envelope.

Marketing Situation #5: Sales Inquiry Bounceback Package

The scenario: This direct mail piece, usually less expensive than your company's full-blown sales rep's "sales kit," is mailed to prospects who respond (by phone, mail, fax, or e-mail) to your company's print advertising, or visit your company's Web site.

Who receives this mailing: Sales inquiry bounceback mailings are usually sent "cold" to larger numbers of prospects than those who receive your sales kit, and without the pre-qualification usually done by one of your company's sales reps during their initial phone contact to the prospect.

Mailing goals: The goal of your company's marketing and sales department should be to personally contact any prospect who wants to learn more about your company's products, and on a timely basis. However, if your company's advertising programs generate a larger number of inquiries than those that can be handled by your company's sales reps, or if you execute any other type of marketing project that generates many hundreds (or thousands) of prospect inquiries, the bounceback package gives these prospects the information they need on your company's products, while buying your sales staff the time they need to enter them into your company's sales contact database, and give them further attention.

Some marketing activities, such as the large number of inquiries typically generated by postcard deck mailings, require a bounceback mailing as an additional step to further qualify the prospect, since a typical postcard deck mailing may generate many lower-quality sales leads.

Package elements and contents: Bounceback direct mail packages are usually sized in either a larger, 9 X 12 inch format, or the smaller, letter-size version. The size you select depends on your budget, the amount of space required to tell your product's story and sell your product, and the number of pieces you are mailing.

Outer envelopes on bounceback packages should display some type of promotional tagline or other "teaser," such as: **"Here's the information you requested…"** It's very important to remind the prospect that the mailing piece is information they requested, as opposed to unsolicited business "junk mail."

Bounceback packages should also contain a sales cover letter introducing your company, its products, and their benefits. Wherever possible, this sales letter should be personalized with the prospect's name, address and salutation. However, depending on your budget, logistics, and quantity, a more generic sales letter salutation, such as "Dear Fellow Industry Professional:" is also acceptable.

In addition to a sales letter, bounceback direct mail packages contain a smaller, lower production-quality version of your company's standard product brochure, and a reply/response card for the prospect to complete and drop in the mail. To save on printing expense, this reply card is often printed as a perforated attachment to the brochure.

Self-mailer options: One-piece "self-mailer" mailing pieces are now being used with greater frequency as bounceback mailing packages, replacing the traditional "three pieces in an envelope" letter-size mailing package.

Self-mailer formats used as bounceback packages are sized so they can be folded down to either 8-1/2 X 11-inch, 5-1/2 X 8-1/2-inch, or standard letter size (approximately 4 X 9-1/4 inches). When folded down to any of these mailable sizes, one side of the self-mailer will display the required postage, address label (or address imprint), and your company's return address. The added advantage of a self-mailer over the traditional letter-oriented bounceback mailing package is the fact that a self-mailer allows you to place a sales headline or promotional message on *both* sides of the piece, effectively doubling the chance your prospect will see it.

Typically, the address side contains a message that alerts the prospect that this piece contains information they requested: "Here's the information you requested on [your product here]," with the reverse side of the piece listing your company's best benefit-oriented sales headline, product photo, and other sales text—essentially, you can set up the other side of the self-mailer to look like the front of your company's existing sales brochure.

Another feature that works very well in self-mailers is a postage-paid reply card perforated on the edge of the self-mailer. Like all reply cards, this tear-off reply card provides your prospects with a convenient way to respond to your company. For example, you can include a check-off box and option line ("Yes—Please have one of your sales reps call me") on a reply card to allow your prospect to easily indicate if they want one of your company's sales representatives to follow up with them by phone. Additionally, you can provide a number of check-off boxes to allow prospects to specify the types or individual models of your company's products of interest to them.

Executing Your Company's Direct Mail Projects

Next to a promising mailing list and a hard-hitting, effective direct mail package, rapid, timely execution and diligent oversight are the two most important factors in any direct mail project. By their nature, direct mailings require the coordinated effort of several members of your marketing team—your ad agency (or direct mail marketing consultant), and your mailing list broker, printer, and lettershop. As well, after the mailing is sent out, you will need the cooperation of your company's sales reps, customer service, and administrative staff to follow up, track, and respond to prospect inquiries from these mailings.

Direct mail packages must be developed, produced, and printed. While the direct mail package is being produced, mailing lists must be researched, selected, ordered, and then forwarded to your lettershop, where they will be processed for personalized output. Several suppliers may be involved in the execution of your direct mail projects, and your mailing projects will require certain key steps to be performed at critical times during the project. Each of these critical tasks relies on successful and timely completion of the previous step, so it, in turn, can be handed off to the next vendor. Close communication and coordination between the members of your direct mail marketing team—agency, printer, list broker, and lettershop—is the vital element that keeps a mailing project on schedule, a marketing program on track, and, ultimately, your company's sales growing at a steady rate.

In your role as a marketing manager, you may not have direct, hands-on involvement in the direct mail execution steps covered in this section. In most cases, your ad agency or direct mail consultant will be responsible for ordering mailing lists, producing the direct mail package for the mailing project, and day-to-day execution of the mailing. However, the most successful marketing managers in direct mail projects are those who stay closely engaged to the process. You must be familiar enough with each of the steps involved to know how each task is executed, and you must know why a particular task must be executed at a specific point in the project. The engaged, hands-on marketing manager who has a basic working knowledge of the process knows enough to anticipate problems in direct mail projects before they occur, and if necessary, will step in and take action to correct these problems before they lead to delays in execution.

The next several pages cover the steps required to execute direct mail projects for your marketing program.

Step 1: Mailing List Selection (Estimated Execution Time: 1- 2 Weeks)

All direct mail projects begin with a mailing list. Always decide on the mailing lists you're going to use before deciding on any other aspect of your mailing project. Your mailing list choices influence the other key elements of your mailing, such as how to shape and focus your sales message to the individuals targeted by the list, how to develop the content and makeup of the mailing piece sent to the list, and how to create the sales promotion used in this mailing piece for this list. Order your mailing lists before you begin work on the direct mail package, so your lettershop will have sufficient time to prepare those lists and have them ready by the time your direct mail package arrives at their shop.

A mailing list may also be the catalyst that initiates a direct mail opportunity. For example, your company may form a joint business venture with a strategic partner who provides your company with a valuable new mailing list of its customers and prospects, for which a direct mail package must be developed. In other cases, you'll have to execute a mailing to your own company's internal customer and sales prospects lists for a new sales promotion, or for a new product launch. And, of course, you will also be researching, selecting, and renting outside mailing lists for your company's ongoing sales lead and inquiry-generation direct mail programs.

Mailing lists for any direct mail project come from either an **internal** source, such as your company's own customer, prospect, and inquiry databases, or from **external** sources, such as rented lists from publications or mailing list brokers.

Internal Mailing Lists

The process of selecting mailing lists from internal sources, such as your company's own customer and prospect lists, is mostly one of thoughtful selection and competent database processing. Most mailing list processing tasks involving any single mailing list database having up to 50,000 names (this encompasses all types of business direct mail projects) can be readily managed, processed, and output from any desktop PC, using common database programs, such as Microsoft Excel or FileMaker Pro.

If you are in charge of marketing in a small to mid-sized company, and are responsible for maintaining your company's mailing lists, it's a good idea to develop some basic database processing skills, by learning to use programs like Microsoft Excel, or, better yet—a dedicated database program like FileMaker Pro.

If you are a marketing manager at a large or mid-sized company, it's likely your sales database is managed by your company's IT staff, and you will have to ask for a "database dump" whenever you need a mailing list. Even if you're not personally in control of your company's key sales databases, you'll need to provide your IT staff with very specific instructions for your mailing list request.

Timeliness: Timeliness of database records for a mailing is an important mailing list attribute. If it's important for you to select only those names of customers, prospects and inquiries who have been added to your company's database after a certain date, make this selection criteria very clear to your company's technical person handling your mailing list request. Most higher-end database software can tag a database entry by its "date created," so even if a specific field has not been created, these names can be selected according to the date they were added to your company's database. In some cases, you may want to mail to "inactive" customers, those customers who have not ordered from your company beyond a certain date, or older, "aged" prospects on your prospect or inquiry lists. In either case, the ability to retrieve names from your sales database by "date created" is critical.

Other selection criteria: When making your list request, you must give careful consideration to the characteristics of the customers and sales prospects you are selecting from your company's database. For example:

- **Customer sales volume:** Do you want your mailing to reach only those customers whose total annual sales volume with your company is greater than (or less than) a certain dollar amount?

- **Customer product orders:** Would your mailing be more effective if you only targeted previous customers who bought specific product models?

- **Screening customers:** Conversely, would your mailing be more effective if you *excluded* certain customers or prospects, such as those belonging to a certain business line or industry classification?

Because a single "inclusion" or "exclusion" of certain groups of customers and prospects from your company's database can make a significant difference in sales response generated from a mailing, you should carefully consider your desired selection criteria when developing mailing lists from your company's database.

Mailing list accuracy: To some degree, most companies suffer from poor data entry and inconsistent sales recordkeeping practices in their internal customer and prospect databases. These problems result in poorly spelled or mis-typed address information fields, out-of-date contact name and title fields, and major mailing list problems, such as undeliverable mailing addresses and transposed or missing fields. Most companies compound these errors by sending their mailing lists directly to their ad agency or lettershop without a careful visual inspection by the marketing manager or other responsible person. These problems are spotted only at the very last minute before a mailing list is to be processed, but not soon enough to avoid a significant mailing delay.

How to inspect a mailing list: It's essential that you take personal responsibility for visually inspecting every mailing list used in your company's direct mail projects. Regardless of database or media format, make sure to check every mailing list for the following:

- **Database fields:** Check for obvious database field problems, such as transposed fields (switched company and address fields, for example), and skipped or missing fields in the mailing list database;

- **Mailing addresses:** Check for old, out-of-date, or undeliverable mailing addresses on your mailing lists. It often helps to have your sales manager and sales reps visually inspect address information on their key customers and accounts as a part of this process;

- **Presentation:** Check for other obvious problems, such as incorrect salutations (Mr., Ms.), and misspelled names, companies, and cities, new people hired at companies on your list, incorrect Zip codes, etc.

At best, database-related problems with mailing lists are the leading cause of delays in direct mail projects. At their worst, undetected problems in mailing list databases can kill a mailing's sales and inquiry response rates.

External Mailings: List Execution for Rented Mailing Lists

List selection for rented mailing lists: If your direct mail project is an extension, or "rollout" of a successfully completed test mailing of a list rented from an external source, the specifications of your list order for the extension (such as job titles, company size, or other special list selection criteria) specified in your initial test should be duplicated exactly in your mailing extension, so your larger rollout reflects the identical profile that made your original test mailing a success.

In other words, don't change any of your list selection criteria when it's working: If your original test worked well with a list selection based on a job title selection for all "Vice Presidents of Marketing" available on the list, then order the same job title selection, as well as all other specific list selections, that you specified for the list order from your original test. Make changes to your selection criteria only when you have exhausted all available names matching your selection criteria, and then test these new selections of the list with a smaller test mailing.

Lists "excludes" from rented lists: If you are placing a new order for new names on a mailing list, as a result of a successful prior test mailing to that list, make sure to specify that the names you just mailed for your test be excluded on your new list order. To do this, make sure to include the following language on your mailing list order: "Exclude all names from previous list order of [date]." List brokers and their mailing list data-processing services keep track of the individual records on previously ordered lists, by customer and order, so it's a simple matter for them to exclude these names so these individuals won't receive your same mailing twice.

List rental order requirements: Mailing list owners or brokers require you to submit a sample of your direct mail piece along with your list order, at the time of your order. This can be an actual sample of the printed mailing piece, or a laser-printed proof copy, if it has not yet been printed. If you are ordering through a mailing list broker, this mailing sample is then passed along to the list owner for their review and approval. Mailing lists are rented for one-time use only, and are "seeded" with a few addresses known only to the list owner, so that the list owner or broker can monitor whether or not a list has been used more than once by any mailer.

Timing and mechanics of rented list orders: Mailing lists can generally be received and in-hand within 1-2 weeks of your list order and sample mailing piece submission. For their own "security purposes," list owners and mailing list brokers generally ship mailing lists only to lettershops, which makes it inconvenient for you to visually inspect the list. However, some mailing list brokers and list owners are more flexible on this point than others, so it doesn't hurt to ask them to send their mailing lists directly to you. As an alternative, you could also ask your lettershop to send you a copy of the mailing list file by e-mail for inspection purposes only once they receive the tape or disk from the list owner.

Inspecting rented mailing lists: Mailing lists rented from list brokers and other outside mailing list suppliers, like trade publications or industry associations, suffer far less from the mailing list inaccuracies, undeliverable addresses, and other common mishaps that often occur in a company's in-house processing of its own mailing list databases. This is because mailing list suppliers are indeed in the business of building, selling, and processing mailing lists, so their business depends on the delivery of accurate and reliable mailing lists. The fact that mailing list providers process and ship many mailing lists each day also helps them to achieve reliability through repetition. Nonetheless, you must be just as insistent on inspecting outside, rented mailing lists as you should be on inspecting your company's in-house mailing lists.

Mailing list media formats: Lists rented and ordered from external sources can be obtained in any one of the following media formats:

- 9-track computer tape (the large, old "computer tape" format still common in the mailing list industry);

- Zip or 3.5-inch computer diskette (containing files output in either tab-delimited or comma-delimited format);

- CD-ROM (standard, PC-format CD-ROMs that are "burned" with the mailing lists you've ordered, in either tab-delimited or comma-delimited format);

- E-mail (also sent in either tab- or comma-delimited file formats);

- Hard-copy, printed cheshire, or pressure-sensitive mailing labels

When ordering mailing lists from outside suppliers, you will nearly always request that lists be shipped to you in one of the above-mentioned electronic (as opposed to printed) formats, since it's almost certain that your mailing project will require additional processing on a list, such as added personalization for sales letters, or printing on outer envelopes of your mailing packages.

Since you should visually inspect all mailing lists used in your mailing projects, always request that lists be shipped in a media format that you can easily access on your desktop PC, so you can check each list. CD-ROMs are the most convenient format to import and view on your PC, followed by either Zip disks or 3.5-inch diskettes, or data files sent by e-mail. Once you have received a mailing list in any of these formats, it's easy to open or import it into a standard PC application, such as Microsoft Excel, or a database program like FileMaker Pro, where you can visually inspect the names and addresses on the list.

You may also want to sort copies of the mailing list by sales territory or region, and forward them to each of your company's sales reps for their follow-up, after the mailing has been sent.

When visually inspecting a rented mailing list, watch out for the same potential problems you would when inspecting one of your company's own, in-house mailing lists, such as proper spelling, and properly displayed database fields. Pay special attention to making sure that the output of the mailing list truly looks like the list you ordered. For example, closely inspect the company names and job titles shown on the mailing list: Are these companies known to you, and do they look like the companies you are trying to reach in your mailing? Are the job titles and functions listed for the individuals on this list the types of individuals you want to reach? Mailing list owners and brokers occasionally make mistakes, and will process and ship the wrong mailing list to the wrong company, so check the list you've received to make sure it's the list you originally ordered.

Step 2 : Direct Mail Package Design, Copy and Production (Estimated Execution Time: 1-3 Weeks)

Next to the mailing list, the direct mail package is the most important element in your company's direct mail projects. In the process of executing your direct mail projects, the copywriting, design, production and printing of direct mail packages consumes the most time of any other step in your direct mail projects. However, the process of creating, developing and finalizing your direct mail package can be executed concurrently with the mailing list selection process outlined in the previous step.

If your direct mail project is a brand-new mailing list test, or a new mailing to your company's customer and prospect lists, you must factor in the longer lead time required for your ad agency or direct mail consultant to develop a completely new direct mail package for this project. If you are "rolling out" from a successful direct mail test, and/or mailing one of your company's existing mailing pieces, the task of designing and producing your mailing's direct mail piece is already complete, so the time required to scale up your mailings is limited only by the time required to print more of these materials for the mailing.

Direct Mail Package Development for New Mailings

When developing a new direct mail package—that is, a mailing piece having mostly new and unproven elements, and being mailed for the very first time—your first step is to decide on the rough "shape" this direct mail piece should take.

Are you making a "big," or a "little," announcement? "Big," important mailings, such as new product launches and major sales promotions, generally require you to stay with the proven, envelope-bound direct mail formats, consisting of an outer envelope, sales cover letter, brochure, and reply card, in either letter-size (#10) or the larger 9 X 12 format. This is also the least risky and most proven format for mailings to outside, rented mailing lists, whose added list rental expense will raise the stakes on any mailing project.

When your marketing project requires that you present, explain, and sell the complex features and benefits of your company's product or service, the print "real estate" provided by the four individual elements of the letter-bound direct mail package—the envelope, cover letter, brochure, and reply coupon—give you four separate opportunities to get your sales message across to your prospects.

The self-mailer alternative: If, on the other hand, you are planning a mailing that has a "simple" story that can be easily and effectively explained in less space (and your mailing project does not bear the extra expense of renting outside mailing lists), your direct mail piece can take the form of the simpler, one-piece self-mailer format. Samples of these kinds of mailings would include seasonal or one-time sales promotion announcements to your company's existing customer or prospect lists, "news" announcements, such as industry awards given to your product or company, or other spot promotions and announcements mailed to your company's "captive" customer and prospect lists.

The default alternative: Whenever you are faced with the task of developing a direct mail piece for a completely new marketing project in your company—especially one that involves the launch of a brand-new product, or a product in a new and untested market, it's best to stay with the conventional, "three-pieces-in-an-envelope" letter-size (or larger) direct mail format. This format is not only the most proven direct mail format used in most mailing projects, it's also the format that allows you to develop all of the necessary sales copy approaches required to sell your company's products by direct mail—the outer envelope, the sales cover letter, the brochure, and the "call to action" reply card. These elements let you present your company's product or service in four different copywriting variations:

- **Short:** Outer envelope;
- **Conversational:** Sales cover letter;
- **Polished:** Sales brochure;
- **Telegraphic:** Reply coupon

The traditional, letter-format mailing piece gives you four different opportunities to present, explain, sell and "close" the recipients of your mailing and minimizes the risk of not providing your prospects with sufficient information to motivate them to buy.

Direct Mail Piece Development and Production: Timing and Mechanics

After you consider the general type of direct mail package required for an upcoming mailing, you need to discuss your ideas with your ad agency or direct mail consultant. This section covers the key steps involved in the planning, development, and execution of direct mail packages.

Step 1: Sketch Out the Requirements and Sales Copy Points of Your Direct Mail Package

As a marketing manager, your first task in developing a direct mail package is to sketch out the requirements and basic sales copy the mailing piece should contain. The point of this exercise is not to be doing your ad agency's job for them by writing the direct mail piece, but to lead the process by giving them a list of the minimum sales copy points to be included in the mailing piece, along with any other direction you think they will find helpful for the project. Your "package notes" should include the following information:

- **Who is the audience for the mailing?** Describe your mailing list(s) and the characteristics of the people whose names are on them—their job titles, demographics, and previous buying history with your company (if any);

- **Key sales benefits:** List the key sales benefits of the product or service offered in the mailing. Identify and describe the most important benefit, followed by next-important sales benefit, etc.;

- **Describe your offer terms and call to action:** What is the offer and call to action for this mailing? List the price of the product or service featured in the mailing piece, and (if offered) the special terms you're extending for the promotion. This can be stated as the answer to the question: "What special offer are you willing to make to the prospect if they are willing to respond to your mailing, right now, and what must they do to take advantage of this special offer?" Are there any other terms or limitations to this mailing's special offer (i.e., what language do your company's lawyers want you to include in this mailing)?

For this task, the writing exercises described in Chapter 4 should provide you with sufficient background for sketching out the key sales benefits and copy points of your mailing for your ad agency or marketing consultant.

Figure 8-7:

Adobe Acrobat .PDF Files—Eliminate the need for hard-copy print proofs in most marketing projects

Adobe Acrobat .PDF Proofs, sent by e-mail, are a very fast, efficient, and accurate way to review proofs of all your company's printed marketing deliverables

Step 2: Direct Mail Package Copy, Development and Production

Once you've handed over your sales copy outline and notes to your ad agency, the next one or two weeks are a process of going back and forth with your agency or marketing consultant, molding and refining the direct mail package for your mailing project.

Use .PDF proofs: The best, fastest way to work with your ad agency on layouts is to have them send their proof copies to you by e-mail as Adobe Acrobat .PDF proofs. The main benefit of using ".PDFs" is they allow you to see your layouts exactly as they will appear in their final, printed forms. Simply displaying a .PDF on your monitor gives you an excellent idea of how the final, printed piece will look, and printing .PDFs on your laser printer gives you a very good (black-and-white) approximation of how the final, printed piece appears when printed.

The Proofing Cycle

Once you receive a .PDF of your mailing package, print it out, read and review it, mark it up with your changes and edits, then FAX your changes back to your ad agency. This process will be repeated a few more times as you and your ad agency or marketing consultant work together to refine the mailing piece to its final form. At this stage, it's important not to run through too many of these proofing and correction cycles; once a deliverable is corrected more than three times, the process tends to devolve into an endless loop of unnecessary corrections that serve no purpose other than to delay your mailing.

Create a mockup of your direct mail piece: Once you believe your direct mail package is getting very close to its final form, print out the .PDFs of the individual elements of your direct mail package—envelope, sales letter, brochure, reply card, etc—and fold and assemble them to create a simple, printed mockup of the mailing package roughly approximating the piece you'll be mailing to your prospects. Tape the layout for the envelope to the front of a real envelope; then fold and assemble the pieces into the envelope exactly as they'd be prepared for the actual mailing.

Look at your mockup with "new eyes:" Put yourself in the shoes of the recipient of the mailing, and imagine that you are seeing this mailing piece for the very first time, having no prior knowledge of what's in it.

First, look at the outer envelope—does its sales copy intrigue you enough to open the envelope? Next, open the envelope of your mockup and examine the contents of the direct mail piece; especially how the individual pieces of your mailing package "fall out" of the envelope, into your hand. Pay close attention to the individual pieces of your mailing: Are the main, bold headlines on your brochure bold enough, and do they adequately convey the main sales message of your company's product? Do the sales copy points printed on the other individual pieces of your mailing communicate the other chief benefits of your company's product?

Get into the habit of printing out the .PDFs of the direct mail package elements, assembling them into mockups of their final, mailed form, and looking at these pieces with "new eyes." It's an invaluable exercise for helping you see your direct mail materials (and all other marketing collateral, for that matter) as your customers and prospects see them for the first time. The more you develop this skill, the more effective your company's marketing collateral will become.

Who else should review the mailing piece? Marketing managers often fall into the trap of letting too many other people review and comment on proof copies of direct mail and other marketing materials under development. This nearly always leads to additional delays in execution and production of your direct mail materials, resulting in lost marketing opportunities and, ultimately—lost sales. Wherever possible, keep your marketing copy and layouts away from all but the fewest number of people who need to review them. Ideally, marketing materials under development should only be reviewed by three people—you, your company's sales manager, and your company's CEO. At larger companies, the company lawyer must also review all marketing copy. Give all of your reviewers hard deadlines on their review of your project materials, and be careful not to let these deadlines slip.

Don't endlessly revise direct mail materials: Marketing projects often get delayed unnecessarily when companies fall into the endless loop of making revision upon revision to their direct mail (and other) marketing materials. Revising marketing materials many more times than is necessary can actually reduce the quality and effectiveness of your final product. Once you've cut back on the number of people who review your company's marketing materials, also cut the number of times your direct mail materials are reviewed, edited, and sent back to your ad agency for revision. There should be no more than two of these "revision cycles" for any direct mail project; any more than this, you're losing valuable time on your project.

Get a postage estimate from your lettershop: As soon as you've finalized the direct mail package for a mailing, send a mockup of the piece over to your lettershop, along with the other pertinent details of the mailing, such as the quantity of names to be mailed, and the postal rate (First-Class or bulk rate). Your lettershop can then estimate the total amount of the postage needed for your mailing. Since lettershops require your postage expenses be paid in advance of the mailing, it may take your accounting department a week or so to cut a postage check and send it to the lettershop, so start this process early enough to avoid a mailing delay.

Step 3: The Print Production Process

Once you've finalized and approved your direct mail piece, the final layout files are sent by your ad agency or marketing consultant to the printer. At the printer, the artwork files of your direct mail piece go through the printer's pre-press department, where the layouts are checked and prepared for printing.

Depending on the number, quantity, and complexity (such as four-color printing) of the pieces to be printed, your printer will generally require 1-2 weeks to produce, print, trim and fold the pieces that comprise the direct mail package for your mailing. If you're using a one-piece self-mailer, preparation time will be closer to one week, since this piece take less time to print.

Pre-press and proofing: At the printing pre-press stage, you have one final opportunity to check the layouts for your company's direct mail piece. For large, expensive, full-color mailings, it's a good idea to get a color "matchprint," a hard-copy, color proof that gives you an exact preview of how your printed materials will look in their final form. When checking a color matchprint or proof, you should only check for obvious printing problems, such as color match, dropped text, missing fonts, or other production glitches. You most definitely **do not**—except in extreme circumstances—want to be making copy changes on production proofs once your materials are at the printer. These changes should have been made prior to this final stage, and making them now only needlessly delays your mailing and increases production expense.

On smaller or less expensive mailings, or if you are very experienced in working with your ad agency and its printer, you may forego the steps of reviewing a hard-copy color matchprint proof. If your ad agency's printer is running a digital pre-press operation, they can e-mail you an Adobe Acrobat .PDF proof of your final layouts straight from their "direct-to-plate" digital pre-press system. These digital .PDF proofs give you an accurate representation of your direct mail package's final printed pieces, and, like any other .PDF, can be viewed, on-screen, and printed from your laser printer. Reviewing final proofs in this way saves at least two days on any direct mail project.

Printing quantities: As you (or your ad agency or marketing consultant) place your print order for your direct mail pieces, give some careful thought to the quantities you need for your project. Since you must have sufficient quantities of mailing packages to mail to every name on your mailing list, you don't want to run short of printed material for your mailing. This is especially important for multiple-piece direct mail packages, consisting of envelopes, cover letters, brochures, coupons, etc.; running short of any one of these pieces will mean that all or part of your mailing will be delayed until the additional quantities of these pieces are printed and delivered to your lettershop. Printers have their own standard policies regarding final quantities for print jobs, and usually give themselves an allowance to run up to 5% over (or under) the print quantities you specify in your order. However, printers will sometimes under-run a job, which means the lettershop may end up a few hundred printed pieces short on your mailing.

You can avoid this problem by making it clear to the printer that your mailing requires the exact quantities you have specified for your mailing. You, your printer, and your lettershop manager will appreciate not having to go through the fire drill of having to go back to the press to print a few hundred additional copies of a mailing piece, while the rest of your mailing is held back at the lettershop.

Where else could I use this direct mail piece? Another issue you need to consider when placing your print order are the other possible applications and projects for which you may have use for this package, apart from your current mailing. For example, you may want to print a few hundred extra pieces to send to your field dealers and distributors, or for use by your company's field sales reps as handouts on important, high-level sales presentations. You never know when you might need a few hundred (or even a few thousand) extra pieces of that direct mail package you're working on now. Smart marketing managers always keep an extra stock of their key mailing pieces handy, and having some extra copies printed on top of a large print run is always less expensive than having to run a smaller additional quantity at a later date.

Final packaging and delivery to the lettershop: If your direct mail package consists of two or more individual, printed pieces, ask your printer to clearly label and organize the individual printed pieces of your mailing as they are packed and made ready for delivery to your lettershop. This will help your lettershop to quickly and efficiently organize the individual pieces of your mailing on their production floor, once they receive the printed materials for your mailing.

Step 4: Lettershop and Mailing

Concurrently with the development of your direct mail package (described in the previous Step 2), and no later than the day your ad agency or marketing consultant sends their original layout files to the printer to begin the production and printing process for your mailing packages, you (or your ad agency) must contact your lettershop, who will be responsible for the final preparation, production, and physical delivery of your mailing to the Post Office.

Lettershops (also known as mailing houses) handle all of the final tasks involved in the actual mailing of your direct mail project, including:

- **Personalization** and high-speed printing of sales cover letters and other personalized materials;

- **Addressing** of outer envelopes;

- **Folding and insertion** of individual direct mail package elements, such as sales letter, brochure, reply card, etc.;

- **Delivery** of mailing pieces to the postal facility

Generally, lettershops require 1-2 weeks' advance notice of a mailing, so they can schedule the processing of your mailing in their production pipeline. If your mailing project is especially complicated—for example, if it has many thousands of cover letters that must be individually personalized, or special imprinting requirements, your lettershop will need additional time. Your lettershop will also need about one week extra if your mailing lists require additional computer processing (see next section).

Create a "nesting sample" of your mailing piece for your lettershop: If your direct mail package consists of individual, printed elements that are to be inserted in an envelope, the order, or the "nesting," of these printed pieces—that is, how they are to be inserted into your outer envelope, is an important consideration.

You do not want your carefully-written, designed, and printed pieces inserted, helter-skelter, into the outer envelope by your lettershop. What you do want are the individual printed pieces of your mailing package inserted in the envelope in such a way that when your prospect opens the envelope, he or she will see the individual pieces presented in a rational, organized fashion. In most cases, this means the first thing you want your prospects to see is your package's sales cover letter, then your color brochure, then your coupon, and then any other printed element of your direct mail package.

How to make a nesting sample: While your pieces are being printed, prepare a "nesting sample," a stapled-together mockup of your mailing piece that shows how the individual, printed pieces are to be inserted into the outer envelope. Generally, the nesting order of a conventional, envelope-inserted direct mail package is prepared as follows:

1.) Fold up and stack the individual, printed pieces of your mailing package from bottom to top, in the following order:

- **reply card (on the bottom of the stack);**
- **color brochure;**
- **cover letter (this should be at the top of this "stack," with address and salutation facing you)**

2.) Next, staple this stack of individual pieces together. The folded face of your package's sales cover letter should be facing UP on the top of this stack;

3.) Finally, staple the nested stack of the individual pieces you just stapled in step 2.) onto the **back** (reverse) side of your outer envelope. Now, looking at the pieces stapled to the back of this envelope the final, nested stack should now contain the following pieces, from top to bottom: Folded sales cover letter facing UP, brochure facing UP, reply card facing UP; all stapled onto the back of the outer envelope, that faces Front Side DOWN. This nesting sample shows your lettershop exactly how your pieces should be inserted.

Now, when prospects open your direct mail piece, the first thing they'll see is your cover letter, then your brochure, and then your reply coupon (and then, other pieces if there are more to be inserted into your mailing). This puts the pieces of your direct mail package into the hands of your prospects in the order they should be seen, and gives them the best possible presentation in your mailing.

Mailing List Processing

If you are renting mailing lists from outside list brokers or other third-party list owners for your mailing, and you've already selected and ordered these mailing lists as the very first step in your mailing project, your lettershop should have received these mailing lists well before the time your direct mail pieces have been printed.

In some cases, the mailing list as it has been delivered to your lettershop will require your lettershop to perform additional computer processing steps prior to the physical steps of folding, inserting, bundling, and "dropping" your mailing at the Post Office, such as:

Merge/purge: On large mailings (50,000 or more pieces) consisting of several mailing lists rented from different sources, but all within the same industry, there is a high probability that some of names on these lists will be duplicated across any two or more lists. To save the extra, unnecessary costs of mailing the same piece two or more times to the same individual, a lettershop can perform what is known as a "merge/purge" on your mailing lists, combining the several, different mailing lists they receive from list owners into a single computer file, then removing the duplicate names from this unified, larger mailing list file;

Personalization and custom imprinting: Many business-to-business direct mail projects use a personalized sales cover letter, where the date, recipient's name, company and address, and a personalized "Dear Mr. [Last Name]:" salutation, along with the body of the letter, are printed on the lettershop's high-speed laser printers, using your company's blank business letterhead stock. Quality options for custom letter imprinting range from fast, lower-quality inkjet printers, to best-quality (but slower) laser printers that produce the same high-quality letters as the ones you would print from your office

---

Figure 8-8:

Direct Mail Postage Options

In most of your business direct mail projects, you'll be faced with the decision to send your mailing by First-Class for bulk rate postage.

First-Class postage, *priced at 37¢ (up to one ounce) for a business letter-sized mailing piece (as of January, 2003) is the most expensive way to send business direct mail. When you are mailing fewer than 500 pieces, First-Class postage may be your only option, since bulk mail requires extra sorting and handling expense, and this may negate any savings gained from cheaper bulk mailing rates. For mailings where the personal touch is critical, such as a highly personalized mailing sent to a select group of corporate CEOs for example, First-Class mailing of these pieces is a must, since mailing*

these pieces by a lower postage rate may cause recipients to view the piece as promotional "junk mail;"

Bulk rate postage, *priced at 26.8¢ for a business letter-sized mailing piece, can be a very economical choice for high-quantity promotional mailings, especially for those mailings without personalized sales cover letters. Bulk postal rates depend on several factors, such as the weight of your mailing piece, and how many of your mailing pieces are being mailed within specific Zip Codes, or in "carrier routes," which are highly localized areas within Zip Codes. Extra sorting and special envelope imprinting is also required to take advantage of lower bulk postal rates, and mailings sent bulk-rate take longer to arrive at their destinations than those sent by First-Class mail.*

---

laser printer. Your lettershop will require at least a few extra days' lead time to execute any custom imprinting and personalization for direct mail sales letters, and may require up to a week for imprinting on large mailings of several thousand pieces;

Graphic signature file: Since the "Yours truly" or "Sincerely" close of your mailing's computer-generated letter will also require a signature, your lettershop will need a scanned-in graphics file of the signature of the person who will be "signing" this letter. Your lettershop can then place this signature file at the close of your sales letters as they're printed;

National Change of Address (NCOA) processing: According to the Small Business Administration, about 10% of all small companies go out of business each year. Even in larger companies, executives change jobs, and entire corporate divisions move to different locations. If your company has very large customer or prospect lists, containing many records that have been on the list for a year or more without being updated, you should strongly consider asking your lettershop to run your mailing list against the National Change of Address (NCOA) database. The NCOA database, maintained by the United States Postal Service (USPS), is a database of all individual and business addressees who have relocated in the past 48 months. Your lettershop can match your company's customer and prospect lists to the NCOA database to "clean" your own company's mailing list, providing updated addresses for most of the individuals and companies who have relocated over the past year or longer;

Mailing list salutations database: While working on mailings that have personalized, computer-generated cover letters, you may find that the "Mr./Ms." salutation fields may be missing from one or more of your mailing lists. This makes it impossible to send a cover letter using the proper "Dear Mr./Ms. Jones:" business letter salutation form. Most lettershops can process your mailing lists against "name gender database" software programs that automatically select the proper salutation field, based on the gender identification of the first name field;

Postage for your mailings: Last—but certainly not least—your lettershop will require a check for the full amount of your mailing's estimated postage expense, prior to their delivery of your mailing to the Post Office. Your lettershop can provide you with a very accurate postage estimate as soon as you know the size and type of mailing piece you'll be using, the number of names to be mailed, and the postage rate of the mailing. To prevent delays in your mailings, make sure your lettershop has your postage check no later than the day they receive the printed materials for your mailing.

ADVERTISING: PLANNING & EXECUTION
CHAPTER 9
MAKING TRADE PRINT ADVERTISING PAY OFF IN YOUR COMPANY'S MARKETING PROGRAM

Print advertising can be the riskiest, most expensive part of your company's marketing program. More companies waste more money running ineffective advertising than companies who make their advertising pay. Careful testing and conservative ad placements minimize your risk and expense on any new advertising project.

The Trouble with Advertising

Advertising campaigns require the most advance planning and longest lead times of any other marketing activity. For example, a targeted direct mail project can be planned, developed and executed in days, or a couple of weeks at most. However, executing a print advertising schedule places you at the mercy of the publications where your advertising will appear, and presents you with an added lag time of 30-45 days from the time your advertising order is placed in a monthly trade publication, until your ad appears in print.

This time delay plays havoc with your ability to determine whether or not your advertising is working. For example, while you can often project the results of a direct mailing within a week or two of its execution, your company may be on the hook for as long as two to three *months* before you can determine if your new print ad campaign was a success.

A lot can happen in two to three months. Your competitor can launch a new product with features and benefits not adequately addressed by the ad campaign you approved two months earlier. You may discover a new, better, or cheaper way to sell your company's products, but may not be able to expand this new activity immediately because you've already committed your company to a months-long advertising schedule in a print publication.

For start-up companies, the temptation to spend too much money, too soon, on print advertising can be a deadly mistake. Specialized marketing consultants and ad agencies are often called in to help start-up companies whose marketing program has been stalled by the effects of expensive, ill-conceived print advertising campaigns. In nearly every case, these companies were talked into running these campaigns by their previous agency, who pocketed large ad space commissions in exchange for a couple of weeks' easy work.

Advertising can be effective, and the fact that U.S. companies spend approximately $220 billion each year on it shows that advertising has a permanent place in our economy. But it's also true that a substantial portion of this outlay is a wasted expense, and many marketing managers won't admit it. Many companies have a tendency to overspend on their advertising budgets, and usually fail to hold their advertising accountable for its contribution to sales—and this is where you must be especially vigilant.

Should Your Company Be Advertising at All?

It's a fair question to ask as a marketing manager, and you're not running against the wind by asking it: There are many successful industrial and trade companies operating in business-to-business marketplaces who run little or no display advertising. Instead, these companies utilize direct mail and their on-the-street sales force (or telemarketing sales groups), along with trade shows, to increase their sales year over year.

These companies would rather spend their marketing dollars on activities that target their prospects more accurately, and can be executed immediately, like direct mail. These companies have also developed proven sales channels—their outside sales reps, in-house telemarketing staffs, or independent dealers and distributors— who may not require extensive print advertising support to generate leads and sales.

These factors can help you decide if your company should run a print advertising program:

> **Your company's age:** If your company is a start-up or early stage company, you should move very cautiously into advertising, if at all. There are other, more effective ways for a new company to break into its market, by direct mail and trade shows, for example.

> **Your competition:** If you are in a mid-sized company and are competing with other mid-sized companies who have been running advertising for some time, print advertising may be a viable option. The fact that your competition has been running the same type of advertising on a consistent basis can mean that their advertising is generating sales and inquiry response for them. Check with your company's sales reps, and other industry contacts, to determine if this is the case.

Figure 9-1:

Advertising: Common Pitfalls

Here are the most common ways advertising campaigns fail...

Failure to test: Most marketing executives simply don't realize that they can lower the risk and expense of their print advertising costs by starting small and testing for results: Smaller ads, and less-ambitious advertising schedules, can often be run, with response being carefully measured. Then, the print advertising schedule can be scaled up if results look promising.

The one-shot failure: Inept advertising agencies will typically convince executives at high-tech start-ups, or other managers charged with executing a new product launch, to sign off on an ill-conceived ad campaign based solely on a budget number established in a company's marketing budget.

The worst thing any marketing manager can say to an ad agency is: "I have $100,000 to spend on print advertising in the next quarter for our new product launch." Ad agencies are then given a free rein to spend this budget, and will take the path of least resistance, spending the minimum amount of time required on the campaign, and then delivering their creative director's half-baked vision of what he thinks will sell the company's products—usually a splashy, full-page color ad.

And just like the auto body shop whose charges for collision repair always matches the dollar amount the insurance company tells him they will pay, the agency has performed the least amount of work required, and has blown the company's entire print advertising ad budget on a senseless three-issue run in the industry's most expensive publication.

The ad agency's confident assurances, which resonated so well before the campaign—"We're building brand awareness!"—are a bitter lesson for the marketing manager who is left holding a failed sales quarter and a substantial out-of-pocket cost.

The permanent campaign: Larger, well-established companies who often run sizable print advertising programs do so simply because of institutional momentum: "We've always done it this way." Here, the company may be compelled to keep their print advertising schedule running year to year simply because their leading competitor is also running a heavy print advertising schedule. Upward pressure from sales reps, dealers and distributors may also compel the company to carry print ad schedules well beyond their level of benefit to the company's actual sales.

And of course, if a company grows to a very large size, it can afford to run vacuous "image advertising" to make its senior executive staff and board of directors feel better about themselves and their company, but your job is to sell products, not your company's image.

Whatever the cause, print advertising in a larger company often becomes a permanent, budgetary line item in a marketing manager's budget—a bloated and poorly-justified cost that, if deployed to other marketing activities, such as direct mail or down-on-the-street sales training and support, can be transformed into a measurable investment that increases sales for the company.

Regardless of the company's size, or years in business, ineffective print advertising campaigns can be overcome by better planning, execution and, above all, the application of salesmanship and common sense. As your company's marketing manager, it is your job to stand up to the institutional or ad agency pressure that may be pushing you to move too quickly into an expensive, poorly-considered print advertising program.

However, some companies are compelled to run advertising campaigns to satisfy the demands of their extensive dealer and distributor networks. These companies view advertising as their "ante" to maintain their position among their dealer base, with little thought given to whether their advertising programs actually work. Just because your competition is wasting their money running ineffective advertising doesn't mean your company has to follow;

Your product, and its market: For companies contemplating sales of products directly to end users from their advertising, the price of a product is the most important factor in determining whether or not it can be sold directly from an ad. The higher the product's price, the less likely your prospect will purchase it, based solely on the information they read in your advertising. However, if your company sells a product priced under $1,000, it's entirely possible to sell it directly from a display ad in a business-to-business marketplace. Products at higher prices will require you to use various multiple-step sales and marketing techniques to convert these prospects into customers.

Key Elements of Your Company's Print Advertising Program

The four major elements of your company's print advertising program are:

1.) The advertising layout (or deliverable);

2.) Ad size;

3.) Publication;

4.) Frequency

If you can successfully guide and grow your company's advertising into a program that generates proven and measurable sales response for your company, you will have succeeded in transforming your company's advertising from an expense into a measurable *investment* that generates a solid return for your company.

Your Advertising Program's Goals

Before planning an ad program, you should always back up and ask yourself, again, whether or not your company should be running an advertising program in the first place. Given the expense, and the risk, it's never wrong to take a second, or a third, hard look at any print advertising program.

Your company should run print display advertising *only* if it can accomplish one of these objectives:

Direct sales: Can you sell your company's products directly from a print ad? The ability to sell a product directly from an ad, without intervening sales calls and other costly follow-up, is the ideal for any marketing manager. However, direct sales from advertising can only be done with easily-explained, relatively low-priced products, and most trade and business-to-business advertisers do not sell these kinds of products;

Sales leads: Can your advertising program generate quality sales leads, and will you be able to measure the response from each ad placement? Sales lead generation, as opposed to direct sales, is the most common use of advertising in small to mid-sized companies. If you're a marketing manager in one of these businesses, you'll be working on advertising that is designed to generate inquiries and sales leads from your company's advertising programs. Response can usually be measured as requests for information on your company's toll-free number from interested prospects, visits to a Web site link, or calls to a local dealer or distributor.

If you believe your company can generate either enough sales leads (more likely) or direct sales (less likely) from print advertising to at least cover the cost of your company's advertising expense, then you should consider adding print advertising to your company's marketing program.

If, however, your company's print trade display advertising isn't generating sufficient sales or response to cover its costs, then it's your job as a marketing manager to stop any advertising your company is currently running, and fix the problem.

Planning Your Company's Print Advertising Programs

The next four sections of this chapter provide you with a roadmap for developing a successful advertising program for your company. The final section outlines the nuts-and-bolts process of working with your ad agency or marketing consultant to execute an advertising campaign.

Figure 9-2:

"Trade" vs. "Consumer" Advertising

As a marketing manager it's more likely you'll be more involved in management of business-to-business marketing functions—i.e., selling your company's products or services to other companies. Because of this, the focus of this chapter is on the development and execution of **trade print advertising**, as opposed to **consumer print advertising** (products and services marketed to the general consumer market).

This is, however, largely a semantic difference, since most of the techniques discussed here for trade print advertising execution will also apply if you are a marketing manager in a small to mid-sized consumer products company.

The major difference between trade and consumer advertising is that media buying costs to reach consumers are usually far greater than the costs of reaching business-to-business prospects. However, the same underlying rules of salesmanship, effective ad copy, and solid execution apply, whether you are selling direct to end-consumers, or to business buyers.

The Advertising Layout, or Deliverable

The advertising layout, also called a deliverable, is the print advertisement itself, the final work product created by your ad agency or marketing consultant. Hopefully, all of the content of the ad layouts produced for your company by your marketing team will be based on the initial direction and sales copy notes you have provided to them, as detailed in Chapters 4 and 5.

As you and your team work on the ad layout during the planning process, you'll also have to consider the goal of your advertising (usually generation of sales leads), how you want prospects to reach your company when they see your ads, how to test your new advertising program, and how to track responses to these ads.

Compared to the more exciting aspects of ad layout and copywriting, these are rather unglamorous, but extremely important, background elements of every advertising deliverable. They will certainly drive many of the decisions you and your team will make on the more "creative" aspects of ad development, such as headline and body copy.

The Goal of Your Print Display Ad: Direct Sales vs. Lead Generation

First, you'll need to consider whether or not you can generate sales from an ad, or if your ads should be designed specifically to generate sales leads (inquiries).

Can we sell our product directly from the ad? Simple, readily understood, low-ticket (under $1,000) business-to-business products and services, such as information services or reports, utility software programs, or trial subscriptions to a newsletter or other publication, can often be sold directly from print display advertising.

Usually, however, business-to-business products and services are costlier, more complex, and have much longer sales cycles, which usually means the goal of your advertising is to generate inquiries, passed along as sales leads to your company's sales force. Because lead-generation is the goal of most trade and business-to-business advertising, the primary emphasis of this chapter's coverage will focus on the planning and execution of advertising programs designed to generate sales leads.

Consider Your Lead-Generation Options

Can we get prospects to ask for more info by calling our company's "800" number or linking to our Web site? Most effective print advertising starts the sales cycle by generating a steady stream of quality sales inquiries to your company's toll-free 800 number, Web site or to other contacts, such as sales distributors or dealers. There, once the prospect reaches your toll-free number or Web site, they either receive a sales information kit in the mail, or view it on your company's Web site.

Once your advertising draws a prospect to your company's sales rep, by phone, or to your company's Web site, your next objective is to capture some basic information from the prospect—name, title, company, address, phone number, e-mail address, etc.

This prospect sales information then goes into your company contact database for further followup, where additional sales mailings, phone calls and other contacts are made, over time. By far, this method of selling from print advertising is the one that has been used most effectively by businesses across all industries, and is likely to be the most successful way to sell your own company's products and services.

Can we get a prospect to talk to a real live human being, right now? This advertising response is based on the telemarketing model, where prospects can be briefly screened and qualified (such as by state or region), and then transferred immediately to an in-house sales rep who is standing by. This is an even better scenario if your company sells technical, but readily understood, information products, such as newsletters, engineering services, specialized mapping products, or database services. These kinds of products or services can, with some additional explanation and support, often be sold directly over the telephone or the Internet without the need for on-site sales calls.

Can we offer the prospect an extra incentive to contact us right now? You can often boost response to lead-generating ads by giving the prospect an added inducement to contact your company. These incentives include:

- Special, date-sensitive **savings offers** for first-time buyers;

- **Free samples**, reports or other premiums having a stated dollar value;

- Offers of **free estimates** or consultations;

- Free, limited-time **trial offers;**

- Free **videos**, **books**, or **technical reports** (very effective for explaining and selling complex, big-ticket products).

An offer to save money, or to receive something of extra value or utility, gives your prospect an extra reason to contact your company, so you should always offer "something extra" in your advertising to stimulate an interested prospect to contact your company.

Always Test Every New Advertising Program

Testing your company's advertising often means the difference between success and failure in start-ups, new product launches, or whenever your company makes a substantial change to its advertising program. Testing is a fairly easy process, yet it's surprising how many companies fail to test their advertising.

New ad campaigns or publications: Never agree to an extensive advertising schedule for a new ad campaign, or for a new publication, until you run in three consecutive issues first. Midway through this "3X test," you will receive enough response to determine whether or not you should continue advertising in the publication.

Ad concepts: If your agency has developed a number of interesting advertising deliverables that you believe may express equally compelling, yet divergent, benefits of your company's product, consider testing the best two of these ads by running them alternately in the best trade publication in your industry. Some publications also offer an "A/B split," option, where each ad can be alternated evenly throughout the press run of the same issue.

Whenever You Run an Ad, Track It

Most advertisers in most publications spend vast amounts of money to produce and place their advertising, but only a very small number of advertisers set up their ads so they can track the inquiries generated from each ad placement.

If an ad placement in a publication can't be tracked, it can't be measured. And if it can't be measured, there's no way you can determine whether or not the ad paid for itself. If you can't track the sales response of an ad, your company shouldn't be advertising.

How to track response: The mechanics of ad tracking are fairly simple. Here are two ways you can track response to your ads:

> **Phone response:** When your inbound telemarketing department or sales staff receives phone calls from your advertising, they should always ask the caller where they heard about your company and its product. Sales contact database systems make it easy to trap this information, but a xeroxed paper form will suffice. The important thing is to get your company's salespeople to track the responses they receive from prospects who call as a result of seeing your company's ads;

> **Internet links:** You can set up each ad with a unique Web address that the prospect can enter to receive additional information about your product.

> Ad copy for a call-to-action and easy-to-enter Web URL would look like this:

>> To see our detailed, 29-page report, go to:
>> **www.yourco.com/report1**

Each ad you place for each publication can have its own simple, unique address, after the backslash—/report1, /report2, /report3, etc., with each URL pointing to the same report or online brochure. This is very easy to set up, and your company's technical staff can readily measure the response received at each separate URL to track each ad's sales response.

2. Ad Size: What's Best for Your Advertising Program?

Ad size is the most important cost-related factor in shaping your advertising program, but it is not the only factor to consider when budgeting for ad campaigns. The two other critical factors are **publication choice** and **frequency**.

Since your budget ultimately determines the scope of your advertising program, ad size is the more important factor, because it dictates the number of times you can afford to run your ad (frequency) and where you cover your market (publication choice).

As a marketing manager, your approach to the print advertising size and frequency issue should be to insist that ad sizes be no bigger than they need to be to get the job

Figure 9-4:

Best Fractional Ad Sizes—Best fractional print display ad sizes (approximate)

For Magazine-Format (8" W X 10" H) Publications

• **Half-page horizontal** (6-7/8" W X 4-7/8" H): For magazine-format publications, the half-page horizontal ad size is a very workable size for presenting all the elements of your company's advertising: headline, body copy, subheads, and call-to-action;

• **Half-page vertical** (4-5/8 W X 7-1/2" H): For layout purposes, the half-page vertical ad size is an even better size than the half-page horizontal size. Unfortunately, it's not as available in many publications—but it's a very good format and you should use it whenever you have the option;

• **One-third vertical** (2-1/4" W X 10" H): One-third vertical size ads cost approximately 25% less than half-page sizes. Because they run top to bottom on the printed page, one-third verticals tend to dominate pages where they appear, almost as well as larger page sizes. While its narrow width poses a challenge for fitting headlines and graphic elements, a good ad layout designer can usually overcome this problem;

• **Quarter-page vertical size** (3-3/38" W X 4-7/8" H): Quarter-page ads sizes generally run 40% less than half-page ad sizes, and are another very workable fractional ad size. Their square format makes them more efficient for layout purposes than one-third verticals, so your headlines and copy will read better;

• **One-eighth page** (2-1/4" W X 5" H): Usually the smallest available display ad size found in magazine-format publications, the 1/8 page ad size is the least presentable ad size for most trade marketing applications. However, if your company offers a relatively well known, or easily-understood product or service in your industry—such as information services or commodity products, this ad size can be used very much like a Rolodex card to communicate your company's Web address or toll-free order number.

For Tabloid-Size (10-1/2" W X 14-3/8" H) Publications:

Junior tabloid (7-3/8" W X 9" H) and **Quarter-page** (4-3/8" W X 3-1/2" H): For tabloid-size publications, the junior tabloid page size or the smaller quarter-page are very versatile fractional ad space sizes.

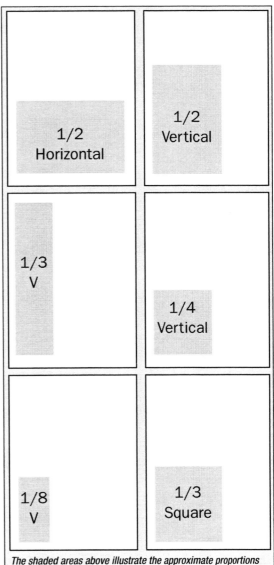

The shaded areas above illustrate the approximate proportions of the most common fractional ad page sizes.

In larger tabloid publications, sizes smaller than junior tabloids or quarter-pages tend to become buried next to other ads, since the larger tabloid size can accommodate more ads on a single page. Because of this, the quarter-page ad size is the smallest ad size your company should run in a tabloid-sized publication.

Figure 9-3:

Fractional Ads—Half-page, quarter-page, one-third page ad sizes

Fractional page ad sizes can be the inquiry- and sales-generating workhorses of your advertising program, often generating as many inquiries and sales leads as larger page sizes, but at far less cost

Protect Yourself
From Potential Buyer Liability

Now Available By PC On CARNET®

$39.50 For Any Property In CA.

Protect Your Home Buyer.

Reports In 24 Hours.

ERIIScan Environmental Property Reports are the fast, new, easy and inexpensive way to reduce the potential risk of lawsuits relating to registered hazardous environmental sites that may impair your property listings and expose your buyer to health and financial hazards.

ERIIScan—From Environmental Risk Information & Imaging Services In conjunction with the California Association of REALTORS®

1-(800) 989-0403

SEE YOU AT THE SHOW: Bring This Ad To BOOTH 601 At The California REALTOR® Expo To Receive A FREE ERIIScan Environmental Report On Any Site Of Your Choice

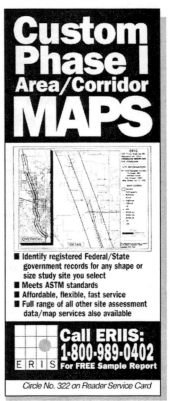

Custom Phase I
Area/Corridor
MAPS

■ Identify registered Federal/State government records for any shape or size study site you select
■ Meets ASTM standards
■ Affordable, flexible, fast service
■ Full range of all other site assessment data/map services also available

Call ERIIS:
1-800-989-0402
For FREE Sample Report

E R I I S

Circle No. 322 on Reader Service Card

done. You will often be pressured by ad agencies and publications to run larger ads, and to run them longer than prudently required. You will have to resist this pressure.

This role can place you in the unpopular position of having to tell your ad agency or marketing consultant to scale down a splashy, full-page, four-color advertising program to a more realistic schedule of smaller, fractional ads, timed to appear just before your company's peak business sales months.

Remember, by their nature, and the motivations of the people involved, print ad schedules have the potential to waste more money than any other marketing activity. Accordingly, this means you have to be tough and stingy with your ad agency on their print advertising schedule recommendations.

Figure 9-5

Fractional Ads—A smaller version of the same ad may pull just as well as the larger ad

	1/4 Page Ad Size	1/8 Page Ad Size
If a Half or Quarter-Page Ad works well for your company, test the next smaller ad size. Many fractional ads can often work just as well in even smaller sizes		

The Full-Page Ad Myth

Many marketing managers, as well as most people in the advertising business, believe that the only effective print advertising display size is the full-page ad. And since it serves their financial interests, many advertising agencies also promote this view.

For art directors at advertising agencies, what's not to like about the wide-open spaces afforded by the full-page, color display ad format? Ad designers use this space as their blank canvas to produce advertising to enhance their portfolios, and submit to design competitions.

Unfortunately, the world of your ad agency's art director is not the same world where you live. As a trade marketer, you must hold each and every ad placement accountable on a sales-generated, or inquiries-to-sales, basis.

While slick, four-color ads may look good to your company's CEO and board of directors, a plainer, harder-hitting series of black-and-white ads in half-page sizes often generates as much, or more, sales response, than a color advertising program.

There are instances when it's advisable to run full-page ads. If you have the budget and you need to make a splash with a new product launch, or you're launching in a new market, a full-page ad helps your company make the strongest impression possible, helping you to present the appearance of industry leadership. If your company can afford to make a splash, and can afford to keep splashing, in skillful hands, full-page ad sizes offer maximum impact (but at maximum cost).

Don't Run a Full Page Ad When a Smaller Size Will Do

If their copy and layout are well executed, ad sizes smaller than a full page can pull just as well, at less than half the cost. Because of this, your planning process should make the option of running full-page ads the exception, rather than the rule.

The size of your print ad should be the smallest size that holds the information required to generate a sales lead or make a sale. Often, instead of running a full-page ad, a half (or even smaller) page size can work just as well, or better.

A half-page ad with the same headline, ad copy and call-to-action often generates a higher return on investment than the same ad at a full-page size. This is a lesson that has already been learned by many seasoned marketing managers at well-established, successful trade and industrial companies.

Just scan through the pages of a couple of years' worth of issues in your industry's top trade publication. Notice that while many of the slick, colorful full-page ads appear and then mostly disappear by every third or fourth issue, the smaller, fractional-page ads continue to repeat, month to month, and year after year.

These successful fractional ads are the lead- and sales-generating workhorses for the companies they serve, generating solid returns every time they appear. They keep working every time, while most of their more colorful, full-page neighbors fade from view after a few issues.

Sales vs. Inquiries from the Ad: Best Fractional Ad Sizes

If your product is not too complicated, and its price is low enough, there is a good chance it can generate sales directly from an ad. And if you believe that you can generate direct sales from your advertising, you stand a better chance of doing so with at least a half-page ad size.

If, as in most companies, the goal of your advertising is to generate leads to be followed up by your company's sales reps, then ad sizes even smaller than a half-page can generate solid sales response.

While a good advertising agency or marketing consultant can make a half-page ad do the work of a full-page ad, a real pro can even make a quarter-page ad pull almost as well as a full page ad. Accordingly, in your ad planning stages, always ask your ad agency to produce at least two, preferably three, fractional ad sizes for the ad program you're producing.

For example, even if you are fairly confident that a half-page size is the smallest size you should run, ask your ad agency to produce the same ad in a quarter-page version as well. You may be pleasantly surprised to see that this smaller size, when skillfully produced, presents your sales message just as effectively, with minimal loss of impact due to size reduction (see **Figure 9-5**).

3. Publication (Trade Media) Choices: Where to Advertise?

According to the *Standard Rate & Data Service* (SRDS), there are over 9,300 individual publications in the vast constellation of trade and vertical-industry media. Reach—where to place your company's advertising to generate the greatest sales impact, can be an especially critical issue if you have been hired as a marketing manager in a new and unfamiliar industry, or if you are assigned the task of launching your company's product in a new industry or market.

Trade Media Placement in Your Industry: Usually, Two Publications Rule

Experienced marketing managers know that there are usually no more than two most-read, top-pulling trade publications in any industry. And between these top two, there is always a longstanding number-one trade publication, followed by a close runner-up.

This "two-publications rule" applies to most any industry or marketplace. A pass through Standard Rate & Data Service (SRDS), or asking your co-workers and customers, will confirm this fact.

In banking, it's *ABA Banking Journal* and *American Banker*; in computers, it's *Computerworld* and *CIO*. While there are exceptions to this rule, first-mover advantage and length of time in the industry usually lead to a condition where two publications will dominate the field, regardless of the industry.

This fact also greatly simplifies your media selection decisions as a marketing manager. Big circulation bases and must-read status among your prospects mean that the top two leading publications in your industry also make them the two best-pulling publications for your company's advertising.

While you or your ad agency will be contacted by ad sales reps for several other second- and third-tier publications in your industry, it's a safe bet that sales response from ad placements in these also-ran publications will be lower than for placements in your industry's leading publications.

Standard Rate & Data Service (SRDS)

Standard Rate & Data Service (SRDS) directories cover all U.S. magazines, trade publications, newspapers, direct mail lists, and TV/radio/cable outlets, sorted by standard industry classifications. The SRDS *Business Publication Advertising Source* lists over 9,300 trade publications for every industry classification, from "Air

Conditioning" to "Wire and Wire Products." SRDS is the standard reference used by media buyers at advertising agencies across the U.S.

An SRDS listing contains all the information you need to begin your media planning process, presented in a standardized format, and without the usual ad space salesman's marketing hype:

- **Publication name and contact information;**
- **Circulation base and demographic characteristics (such as job title, or responsibility);**
- **Display advertising space rates and ad closing dates;**
- **Special regional editions and editorial features**

SRDS is an indispensable publication research tool for planning your company's advertising campaign. Although its hefty annual subscription fee (up to $700 or more per year, per directory) makes it rather expensive, you can find the latest issues of SRDS in the business reference section of any major public library.

Use SRDS as your primary reference for targeting the key publications in your industry, and for locating the best publications in new markets your company may decide to enter in the future. You should familiarize yourself with the entire range of SRDS directories, but the ***Business Publication Advertising Source*** and ***Direct Marketing List Source*** directories are especially important for business-to-business marketers.

How to Select Publications

As you research various publications in SRDS, and request media kits for publications (more on this in the next section), pay close attention to each of the following elements for each publication's listing:

Circulation is generally the most important factor when evaluating publications as potential ad placement opportunities for your company. You will not only see that the highest circulation figures seem to cluster around two (and sometimes three) leading publications in an industry, you will also see references to two different types of circulation: "Controlled" vs. "paid," and it's important for you to know the differences between each type of circulation.

"Controlled" circulation: Publications with "controlled" circulations are mailed free of charge to business subscribers in an industry. To receive their free subscription, a subscriber must first complete a lengthy survey card that provides the publisher with important marketing information about the reader, such as job title, number of employees, type of business within the industry, etc. In this way, the publisher "controls" the circulation of its publication, sending it only to those individuals who actually work in the industry. These publications are commonly referred to as "controlled-circ" publications.

Figure 9-6:

Standard Rate and Data Service Business Publication Advertising Source

The SRDS Business Publication Advertising Source print directory covers over 9,300 industry and trade publications in over 223 industrial classifications, and is an invaluable information resource for trade advertisers

Industry Classification: *Publications are organized alphabetically in standard industrial classifications*

Editorial Profile: *Publisher's description of the publication*

Ad Sales Contact Info: *Your contact is usually the ad space sales rep for your region*

Ad Rates: *Rates are listed for various ad space sizes, by frequency and color options*

Color: *Added charges for color ads—four-color or spot (two-color) options*

Ad Dimensions: *Mechanical specifications and exact sizes for each ad space size*

Issue Closing Dates: *Space reservation and ad material submission deadline dates for each issue*

Issue Editorial Features: *Monthly "editorial focus" sections may provide added targeting opportunities or editorial coverage for your company's specific product or service*

Audited Circulation: *Publication circulation figures, verified and audited by independent, third-party BPA or ABM organizations, are a mandatory requirement for most trade advertisers*

"Paid" circulation: A publication with a "paid" circulation has a base of readers who pay an annual subscription fee to receive the publication, like most ordinary newspapers or magazines.

A controlled circulation publication generally provides you with far more extensive detail on its subscriber base than a paid publication, because readers must provide this information to the publication to receive their free subscription. This aspect of "controlled-circ" publications can be especially valuable when renting subscriber mailing lists from these publications, since list selections can be segmented in many very useful ways (as already covered in Chapters 6-8 on direct mail).

A publication with a paid circulation base is generally regarded as having "higher quality" readers in its subscriber base, and is therefore seen as a better choice for advertisers, since, as you would guess, there is greater perceived value among advertisers for readers who actually pay money to receive a publication.

However, either type of publication can work well for advertising your company's product, provided you have selected the industry leaders with the largest circulations, and that the circulations of these publications have been "audited" (see below).

BPA Audit Data: Business of Performing Audits (BPA) is a non-profit organization that provides objective standards and independent measurement of subscriber circulations for trade publications across all industries.

Founded in 1931, BPA is the most trusted source for accurate and objective circulation data for business, trade, and industrial publications. Most leading publications in any industry have been "BPA audited," and provide their BPA-audited circulation figures, which are also included in the publication's SRDS directory listing. (see **Figure 9-6**).

A BPA audit provides advertisers with independently verified information on a publication's circulation base, a more reliable figure than circulation numbers claimed by non-audited publications. As the "gold standard" for circulation data, if given a choice between a publication that is BPA-audited and one that is not, you should always select the BPA-audited publication.

Media Kits and Sample Issues

Once you've selected a list of publications that look like suitable candidates for your company's advertising program, call them, or link to their Web sites, and request their media kits, and (most important), a few sample issues.

A media kit is the publication's own sales information kit containing additional data on the publication, such as results of subscriber market research surveys, profiles of subscriber job titles and purchasing responsibilities, and additional survey data on the companies where their subscribers work, such as number of employees, annual sales volume, etc. Much of this data is market research paid for by the publisher, and, as you would expect, presents the publication in the most favorable light.

Evaluating sample issues: However, aside from information provided in the media kit (mostly duplicated from the publication's SRDS listing), it's more important to make a close study of as many sample back issues of the publication as you can. The publication will usually only send you a few recent issues, but 1-2 years' worth is ideal if they'll send you this many issues. Here's what to look for:

Number of ad pages: Take note of any change in the number of pages in each issue of a publication occurring over several months, or a year. Successful publications maintain a pretty steady level of ad pages per issue, and a substantial decline in ad pages is sometimes an indicator of a more serious circulation problem. Aside from general industry conditions, other factors leading to circulation drops may include changes in editorial focus, or the rise of some other, more competitive publication in the industry. Bear in mind, however, that in recent years there have also been some very severe recessions in the publishing industry, and during these periods even successful publications will experience declines in their ad page counts;

Your competition: Do your competitors advertise in the publication? This may tell you that your company should advertise there, too, if it's not already doing so. While it's true your competitors can waste their money on bad advertising placements just as well as your company can, if you notice several of your competitors' ads repeating month-to-month in a publication over a long time period, you can make a fair assumption that their advertising is working for them in that publication;

Repeat advertisers: Following the above, if you notice advertisers who are repeating their ads month after month, this is a good sign that their placements in the publication are working for them. It may also be a good sign that their ad layouts may be pulling especially well, too, so take note of any aspects of these ads, such as sales copy benefits, promotions, ad size, page placement, or layout that may "influence" the execution of your own company's advertising layouts.

While reviewing various publications in your industry, ask each publication's ad space sales rep to put you on their "comp" (complimentary) subscription list. These free subscriptions will help you keep on top of what's happening (and who's advertising) in your field, and will be a constant source of new ideas for your own company's advertising programs.

4. Frequency: How Often Should We Advertise?

It takes more than one insertion to build awareness in an advertising program. A reader may only glance at your ad in the first issue, may miss it entirely in the second, and may then respond to it by the third (or fourth) issue. A three-issue insertion, spread across any three consecutive issue dates of a publication (whether weekly, bi-monthly, or monthly) is the minimum length of time necessary to give your advertising the chance to build awareness in that publication.

When planning your advertising schedule, run the largest fractional ad size you can afford, at a minimum three-time insertion frequency, in the top two publications in your industry, based on the "two publications rule" covered in the previous section. Three placements (a "3X frequency") are sufficient to tell you whether or not your new advertising program will work.

For example, if you have a $30,000 print advertising budget, split more or less evenly between the top two publications in your industry, select the closest fractional ad size that allows you to spread each ad across three consecutive issues in each publication:

$30,000/3 insertions times 2 publications (6 placements total) = $5,000 per ad

Select the ad size closest to the amount ($5,000) calculated above for each ad placement. If this means you can afford full or half-page ad sizes, then these are the sizes you should run. However, in our example, even if the $5,000 per ad/placement figure pushes you down in size from a half-page horizontal to a smaller, one-third vertical or quarter-page, you should still be able to effectively tell your company's story and sell your company's product in these smaller sizes.

If, on the other hand, $5,000 per insertion would allow you to buy a full-page ad at a three-time frequency, you should, nonetheless, seriously consider a smaller ad size run as your initial test. Ask your ad agency to produce your ad in the smaller space size, run the ads, and track your results. After all, if you can make a half page ad pull the same response as a full-page, why would you spend nearly twice as much?

Ad sizes and testing: Skillful creation and smart placement of fractional ads is even more important when you are seeking to minimize your risk and expense by testing under the following conditions:

- **Response to an existing product in a new market;**
- **New products in new markets;**
- **New ad campaigns or selling approaches;**
- **Ad placements in new publications**

In any of these circumstances, starting conservatively with a 3-time frequency run of fractional ads will always give you a solid initial reading on a product's likely sales response from advertising. It also permits you to hold more marketing dollars in reserve, in case your ad campaign requires further adjustment, or if other marketing

---

Figure 9-7:

Flighting Your Advertising Schedule

Make a Limited Advertising Budget Go Further *by alternating, or "flighting," your ads across two or more publications*

	Jan	Feb	Mar	Apr	May	Jun	Jul	Aug	Sep	Oct	Nov	Dec
Publication 1	Half Page	Half Page	Half Page						Half Page	Half Page	Half Page	
Publication 2				Half Page	Half Page	Half Page						

---

methods (such as direct mail or trade shows) are found to make more efficient use of your company's marketing budget.

Other Advertising Planning Issues: Ad Scheduling, Positioning and Tracking Response

Your Advertising Schedule

Ideally, when planning the placement of your ads, you want to run a minimum three-time insertion schedule in your industry's top two publications. You can usually begin to tell whether an advertising program will be successful about 45 days after the first ad appears. Once your ads have had a chance to generate response, and once you've had the chance to measure and analyze this response, you can then expand your advertising schedule to more publications in your field, across longer frequency periods, while continuously tracking the response to each ad placement.

However, if you're in a start-up company, or if you want to move more slowly (i.e., you don't want to spend the extra advertising dollars too soon), you can "flight" your ad placements by running your first three ad placements in a single publication for the first three months (or issues) of your schedule, then switch to another publication for the next three-month (or issue) run.

For example, a typical ad annual schedule of ads, "flighted" by publication, might look like the table in **Figure 9-7**.

For Publication 1, half-page insertions are run in a three-issue spread (six insertions annually) from January-March, and September-November. After March, the next three-issue flight of ads runs in Publication 2 for April-June. Also note there are no placements in either publication during the summer vacation months of July and August, when advertising response in trade and business-to-business publications typically declines to the point of making any new ad placements a riskier bet.

In a variation of this schedule, since there would be sufficient time to measure response to ad placements in both publications from January to June, the advertiser might want to run in both publications from September to November, and not just in the flighted three-issue placement shown for Publication 1. This would give the advertiser an aggressive promotional front for the active business months of September to December, and with minimized risk, since, by this time, the ads would have had a full six months to prove their sales response in both publications.

This technique can be used for any number of publications, and in a variety of combinations, to minimize risk, and to stretch your advertising budget. Flighting offers the added benefit of giving your market's audience the impression you are advertising in all the publications in their industry simultaneously, without the cost of actually doing so.

Display Advertising Positioning

The positioning of your print display advertising—where your ad is placed in a publication—also plays a role in determining the sales response generated by your advertising.

For example, a display ad buried within the last 12 pages of a publication, or worse yet, a fractional ad buried "in the back of the book" along with other fractional ads near the classified ad-style "Marketplace" section, may generate a response up to 25% lower than if the same ad was moved up within the first 20 pages of the same issue.

The best positions for your display advertising in any publication are:

- **"Front of book:"** In the "front half" of the publication, or—even better still—within the first 20 pages of the publication;

- **Opposite relevant editorial:** A display ad receives a boost by being placed opposite an article that's highly relevant to the product or service being advertised. For example, an ad for a hydraulic pump placed opposite an article on the latest technical developments in the field of industrial hydraulics will usually get a nice "bump" in sales response by its proximity to this article;

- **Right-hand side pages:** Right-page ad placement is preferable anywhere in a publication, since right-hand side pages tend to stay open in the reader's hand, if the reader is right-handed (as most of us are).

A publication's production department usually controls the assignment and placement of all advertising space in a publication. A publication's top advertisers, who run full-color, full-page ads in every issue, usually receive the best positioning within a publication. It's an economic fact of life that your company's annual

Figure 9-8:

Publication Editorial Schedules—Useful for planning ad placements for upcoming issues

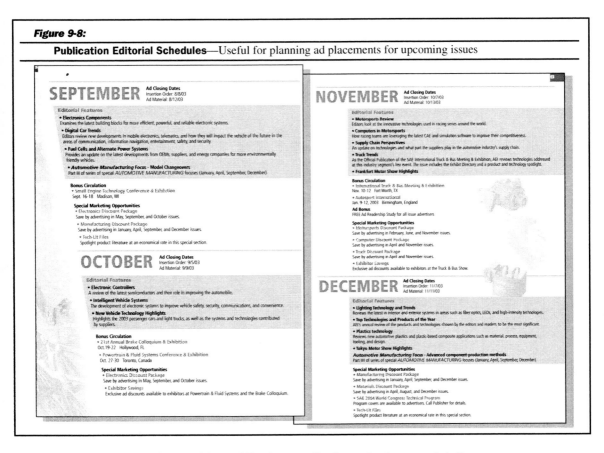

advertising expenditures with a publication usually determine how much influence you'll have in getting the most desirable placement for your company's advertising.

Fortunately, you can still exert some influence on ad positioning in a publication, even if your company isn't one of its top advertisers. Surprisingly, however, many advertisers and their ad agencies don't even try to negotiate better positioning placement for their smaller ads, but it's always possible.

Getting the Best Ad Position in a Publication

Even the smallest advertiser can exert some influence over where their ad will be placed in a publication, and smart advertisers in all page sizes do this all the time.

A publication's advertising sales representative is your best advocate for helping you receive better positioning on your company's ad placements. Since his economic livelihood depends on your continued ad placements in his publication, your ad sales rep is highly motivated to keep your company's advertising business.

As a marketing manager, you have the most influence with your ad sales rep at the time you are planning a new program of ad space placements with the rep's publication. This is the time you should push your ad sales rep the hardest, by pressing for one or more of these key ad placement terms:

- **Front half-of book positioning;**
- **Preferred placement, opposite relevant editorial (more on this below);**
- **Positioning several pages away from your leading competitors A, B, & C**

Although they'll never admit it, your ad sales rep can often exert influence with their publication's editorial and production departments to give your ad a better position, so the time to strike is when you're negotiating your initial advertising order with the sales rep; this is when everyone wants to insure the best possible chance of success for your company's new ad campaign.

Publication Editorial Schedules

Most trade publications publish, in advance, a month-by-month schedule covering the main editorial content of each upcoming issue of their publication (see **Figure 9-8**). Examples of editorial topics addressed on these "Editorial Calendars" include:

- **Key industry and regulatory issues;**
- **New products and technologies;**
- **Company/industry profiles and directories;**
- **Coverage of key, selected business markets and opportunities;**
- **Special, dedicated major annual trade show and convention editions**

When these special editorial opportunities arise, it pays to plan ahead. For example, if an industrial publication's main editorial feature for April covers plant automation, and your company sells plant automation software systems, you can modify your ad schedule by increasing your page size or placement for their April issue, so your ad appears in close proximity to a relevant, major article in this issue.

Special editorial editions can also provide your company with added editorial PR opportunities. Ad placements timed to appear alongside special editorial editions can also be paired with special press release distributions and story placement contacts to key editors, increasing your chances of receiving editorial coverage on your company and its products in that special edition as well (see Chapter 14).

Ad positioning—If you don't ask, you won't get: There's nothing to be lost by asking your ad sales rep what he or she can do to help your advertising get the best possible placement in his publication. The upside may well make the difference between a mediocre result from an ad placement, or a positive, profitable final result for your ad in the same issue. So if you don't ask for the positioning you want for your ad, you'll never know what your ad sales rep can do for you.

Figure 9-9:

Planning and Tracking Your Advertising Schedule—Use a spreadsheet to plan a yearly ad schedule

Publication Title and Ad Size/Type: In addition to the publication, note the title of the ad, if you are testing different ads, or ad sizes, in each publication (see below)

Schedule: Plan your advertising schedule out on a month-by-month basis, for the entire year. Extend as needed as you begin to plan for the next year's ad schedule

Important Dates: Track each publication's **space reservation** and **materials close** dates by month here, so you never miss an ad insertion or an opportunity to change your advertising placements

Leads and Cost per Lead: Track leads by each monthly ad insertion, and calculate your cost per lead (ad cost/number of leads) for each monthly insertion, by publication

Sample Ad Schedule & Worksheet

	A	B	C January	D February	E March	F April	G May	H June
1	Advertising Schedule & Worksheet							
2	XYZ Corp.							
3								
4	Publication Month		January	February	March	April	May	June
5								
6	Publications:	Ad Size/Type:						
7								
8	Conventions Monthly	Ad "Save Twice" (Full) $	3,824	3,824	3,824	3,824	3,824	3,824
9	Ad Space Reservation Date:		11/15	12/16	1/15	2/14	3/15	4/12
10	Materials Due By:		12/12	1/16	2/18	3/12	4/11	5/10
11	Leads		329	418	347	285	441	322
12	Cost per Lead	$	12	9	11	13	9	12
13								
14	Better Meetings	Ad "Save Twice" (Full)			4,752	4,752	4,752	
15	Ad Space Reservation Date:		10/9	11/4	12/9	1/4	2/14	3/9
16	Materials Due By:		11/4	12/2	1/5	2/6	3/7	4/12
17	Leads		0	0	502	643	602	47
18	Cost per Lead	$	-	0	9	7	8	0
19								
20	Network Monthly	Ad "Next Meeting" (Half $	1,793	1,793	1,793	1,793	1,793	
21	Ad Space Reservation Date:		10/21	11/1	12/18	1/19	2/16	3/19
22	Materials Due By:		11/14	12/18	1/5	2/21	3/17	4/20
23	Leads		58	72	43	89	61	47
24	Cost per Lead	$	31	25	42	20	29	0
25								
26	Total by Month	$	5,617	5,617	5,617	5,617	5,617	3,824
27								
28	Total Leads		387	490	892	1017	1104	416
29	Total Cost per Lead	$	15	11	6	6	5	9
30								

Tracking Your Ad Placement Schedule

As you plan your advertising schedule, you will need a simple, workable system for keeping track of the details of your company's advertising program, to track and measure the response your company receives from each ad.

The spreadsheet (shown in **Figure 9-9**) helps you keep track of all the pertinent details of your advertising schedule in a single worksheet. A copy of this file in Microsoft Excel format is also available from this book's companion Web site, **www.sellyourproduct.com**.

Key cells from this spreadsheet, such as cost totals and responses, can be combined with other spreadsheets to create a year-at-a-glance summary worksheet detailing costs, response rates, and other important information on your company's marketing activities.

Planning and Executing a New Print Advertising Campaign: Overview of Key Elements

Print advertising campaigns require longer lead planning times than any other element of your marketing plan. Since most trade publications run on monthly publishing schedules, the process of executing a print advertising program nearly always has a built-in lead-time of four to eight weeks from your final approval and placement of an ad, until you begin to see response from the ad in the publication.

This lead-time also assumes that you have finalized your print advertising deliverables (the "creative"), and that your advertising materials are already produced and ready to send to the publication. If not, then add two to four additional weeks in front of the publication's required lead time above.

There are always exceptions. For example, you are always able to make faster placements in a weekly or bi-monthly publication (about two to four weeks' lead time). Occasionally, you can even make emergency placements in monthly publications having last-minute "remainder space" opportunities in an issue that's ready to go to press. Nonetheless, count on your print advertising program as being the one element of your marketing plan requiring the longest advance planning.

The time estimates assigned here for each stage of the advertising development and execution process below are typical timeframes. They are very important, because they help you assign a definite time span to each stage of the process, and give discipline and focus to a task that is often plagued by unnecessary delays.

Advertising Creative Development and Production (1-4 Weeks)

For planning purposes, it will generally take your ad agency or marketing consultant one week (at the shortest), to four weeks (at the most) to create, develop and produce your company's ad campaign.

Step 1—Your De-Brief to the Agency

The process of creating a new advertising campaign begins with the presentation of your company's sales and product marketing objectives to your ad agency. This is when you provide your notes on sales benefits and copy points for your company's product (previously outlined in Chapter 4) to your agency, and all other background information they will need to create your advertising, and your initial publication placement suggestions for the advertising schedule.

At the end of this first meeting, your ad agency should have all the background information they need to get to work on your advertising layout ("deliverable").

Step 2—The Ad Agency Presentation

Roughly one to two weeks after your initial de-briefing, your ad agency should be prepared to present you with its ad "comps," semi-finished ad layouts illustrating the agency's choices of its best advertising layout, copy, and positioning concepts for your campaign.

Figure 9-10

National Print Media Options

As a marketing manager, your media buying will likely be focused on the leading trade publications within your industry. However, there are certain times when you need to reach a broader business market for your company's product or service.

For example, if your company decides to test-market a product directly to a general market of business end-users, the following leading business publications feature smaller, regional and vertical industry issue runs that are surprisingly affordable:

- *The Wall Street Journal*
- *USA Today*
- *Business Week*
- *Fortune*

Special business magazine editions are also available in special industry or vertical markets, such as engineering, manufacturing, electronics, energy, etc. These special editions allow you to reach prospects in your own industry, but also provide a broader reach than your usual schedule of vertical industry and trade-only publications.

Special Newspaper Editions: When You Have to Get to Market—Fast

Special national newspaper editions, such as *The Wall Street Journal*, *USA Today* and, to a lesser extent, *The New York Times,* allow you to test-market your company's products to specific U.S. regions or individual metropolitan areas. For business trade and industry marketers, special regional newspaper additions are useful whenever you need to reach a more generalized base of industry executives in one or more metropolitan areas.

For example, if you were testing whether or not your company's industrial product line had crossover potential to a more generalized market of business consumers, or your marketing program requires a regional focus (localized seminars, conferences or trade demonstrations), ad placements in newspaper regional editions are the fastest way to get into a market with print advertising.

While these publications generally would not be a part of your regular advertising schedule in most trade marketing applications, they do provide you with some useful options whenever you must test a product's broader business or regional appeal.

Using Regional Business Editions for Market Testing

Another very important benefit of regional editions is that they can be used as a testing ground prior to extending an ad campaign in more expensive editions of national business publications.

For example, even if one day you are faced with the prospect of spending $64,100 for a full page in *Business Week* (in the North American Edition of 950,000 subscribers), testing your advertising in *Business Week's* California edition, at a lower cost of $16,200 for a full-page color ad, with 135,000 subscribers, allows you to test in a smaller market at less cost, and can greatly reduce your marketing risk and expense before committing to a full, national advertising schedule.

Prior to this presentation, you should expect that your ad agency has evolved its own internal process of brainstorming, creative development, and layout on your advertising program to the point where it has created several potentially workable advertising campaign concepts. If your agency is talented enough to cull its own creative work prior to this meeting, it will have also eliminated some of its own ad concepts during the agency's internal creative process.

Ideally, if you have provided your agency with the required sales copy benefit information in your initial de-brief to them, and if your ad agency has incorporated these benefits into their work products, the successful result of this stage will allow you to make the final selection of the advertising concept or deliverable you're going to use for the ad campaign.

It's just as likely, however, that there will be some aspects of the selected ad that could be made better—missing product features or benefits, copy editing problems, and words or phrases in headlines or copy that could be improved.

This scenario often becomes the point of maximum danger for any advertising project. The longer an ad deliverable remains unfinished, the higher the probability is that it will never see the light of day. Our adage: "Too many eyes will kill your advertising," applies to this stage of advertising development, if you permit too many people within your company to add their comments and suggestions to your ad layouts.

Therefore, it's critical that you exercise the leadership required to finalize any remaining copy and layout issues in an ad, even if this means you must ignore suggestions that could further delay your primary task of marketing execution.

The "A/B split:" There are some instances where your ad agency will develop two equally good advertising approaches to a campaign. Both ad layouts will be so compelling that there will be no clear consensus on which ad campaign should go into print. This is always a blessing in disguise, since it provides the skilled marketing manager with an opportunity to test both advertising approaches, with an "A/B split."

If you have two strong ad concepts, have your ad agency or marketing consultant develop both as completed deliverables, place them alternately in each issue of your targeted publications, and then measure the response generated (inquiries or sales) by each ad.

Printing processes allow many publications to provide an A/B split within the same issue—that is, your ad "A" can be placed evenly throughout half of an issue's press run, and your second ad "B" can be placed evenly throughout the other half. By key-coding the call-to-action portion of your ad (see Chapter 17 on testing), and setting up a specific Web URL or response phone number for each, you can track response for each ad.

Figure 9-11:

Advertising Insertion Order—Standard form for reserving display advertising space in publications

GAA

3052 Railroad Vine
Fairfax, VA 22031
Telephone **(703) 255-9426**
FAX (703) 255-7237

Advertising Insertion Order

☐ If checked here this is a FIRM SPACE ORDER and BINDING unless cancelled before closing date*	DATE: **12/10/03**
☐ If checked here this is a SPACE RESERVATION	ORDER NO. **1202031**
☐ If checked here this is a CANCELLATION or change of:_____	Advertiser: **Internet Media Corp.**
	Product: **Internet Book**

To the publisher of:

Contract Year: **2004**

The Wall Street Journal
Attn: Advertising
8251 President's Drive
Orlando, FL 32809-7694
(407) 857-2600

Discount Level: **1X**

Edition (specify) National_____
           Regional_____
* Subject to conditions stated above and below

Issue Date	Space	Color/Bleed	Position	Frequency	Rate

Friday, 12/9   2 cols. X 56 lines (@$9.15/Line) B & W   Display Ad – **SOUTHERN CALIFORNIA REGION** 1X

NET RATE: $871.08

CHECK ENCLOSED

ADDITIONAL INSTRUCTIONS: ARTWORK ENCLOSED - CONTACT ERIC GAGNON AT (703) 255-9426 IF ANY QUESTIONS.

Payment:

Gross Space Cost:	$_____
Less Agency Commission_____:	$_____
Total Amount Enclosed:	$_____

Camera-Ready Materials, Copy & Instructions:

☐ To Follow   ☐ Enclosed With This Order

AGENCY CONTACT: Please Call Eric Gagnon at (703) 255-9426

CONFIRMATION: By:_____

_____
(Authorized Signature)   (Date)

Step 3—Final Ad Production (1-2 Weeks)

Once you and your ad agency have finalized your ad layout and placement schedule, your agency typically requires 1-2 weeks to complete the production of your ad deliverables, and to produce the final, "camera-ready" ads specifically sized to the production dimensions and requirements of the publications in which the advertising will be placed.

The time required to complete the production process has been dramatically reduced in recent years, with the advent of desktop publishing, digital pre-press systems and Internet ad delivery. Accordingly, this part of the project often runs closer to one week than a full two weeks.

Step 4—Space Reservations and Ad Submissions (Less than 1 Week)

If your company maintains the typical business relationship with its ad agency, where your agency places your company's advertising on its own, as your agent, and receives a 15% commission from the publication, the process of reserving ad space and placing your ads will be handled by your ad agency. It's still important to understand the process, so you can avoid any production delays that may occur during the final stages of ad placement.

Ad space close and space reservation due dates: Roughly four to five weeks before ad materials are due to be submitted, and two to three weeks before the publication date, a publication will require you to formally reserve ad space for the desired issue date of its publication. In most instances, all it takes is a phone call or a handshake to reserve space in the publication, with your agency's insertion order (see **Figure 9-11**) serving as the final written document that commits your company (through its ad agency) to an advertising schedule in the publication.

Major business and trade publications will, however, require you or your agency to fill out, sign, and submit the publication's own **advertising space order or reservation form**, in advance of submitting the insertion order.

Insertion orders: The filled-in insertion order, or "I.O.," is the formal business contract between you, your advertising agency, and the publication, for placement of all advertising in that publication. Technically, since your ad agency is drawing its usual 15% space commission from the publication, it is acting as your "agent," and is liable for all of your company's advertising space charges with the publication. The ad agency then invoices your company for the full amount of advertising it places on your behalf. Then, the agency pays the publication directly, deducting and pocketing its 15% commission from the "gross" ad space charge, once your company pays the ad agency for the full amount of its advertising expenses.

The insertion order sets forth all the pertinent details of the ad placement—the issue dates, frequency discount, ad sizes and specifications, and is usually signed by a principal at the ad agency. Insertion orders are usually issued by the ad agency, and are completed at the same time the verbal space reservation is made for the

---

Figure 9-12:

The House Agency Discount

How to Cut 15% Off Your Company's Advertising: The "House Agency" Option

Some companies have abandoned the traditional advertising space commission structure, and take the 15% ad agency commission as a discount from their advertising expenditures, utilizing the "House Agency Discount." This is a little-known secret of the advertising business that can save you 15% on all of your company's advertising expenditures.

How to get the House Agency Discount: Your company can print its own insertion order forms and insertion orders, with your company logo and address at the top of each form. Have your advertising agency or marketing consultant use these forms whenever they make space reservations and place advertising on your company's behalf.

The publication then invoices your company directly (instead of your ad agency) for the cost of your advertising, less the 15% ad agency discount. This amounts to a 15% savings on every ad placed by your company.

However, if you decide to go to this new arrangement, you will have to renegotiate your current business relationship with your ad agency, paying them higher fees on a per-project basis to compensate them for the income they lose from space commissions on your account.

Another very important advantage to the "House Agency" option is that, by eliminating the ad agency's built-in financial incentive to boost your company's advertising expenditures (they receive a 15% commission on your ad placements), this may reduce their incentive to push your company into spending more money on display advertising than is necessary.

The "House Agency" structure keeps your ad agency honest in its media recommendations to you, relieves your ad agency of its financial liability for the ad placements they make on your company's behalf, and gives your company a significant savings in its annual advertising expenditures.

---

publication (which usually makes it unnecessary to fill out the separate "ad space reservation" form supplied by the publication).

Ad Materials Submission

The Internet has combined with desktop publishing systems on Macs and PCs to revolutionize the process of submitting ad materials to most publications.

Most publications now allow ad agencies to submit ad files to a publication's production department over the Internet, either by direct mail, or Internet FTP (File Transfer Protocol). Most publications now accept the most common desktop publishing programs (QuarkXpress, Adobe Illustrator, Macromedia Freehand, etc.), and also accept electronic-format proofs of your ad in Adobe Acrobat .PDF file format.

All-electronic ad submission eliminates the need for, and the expense of, film negatives, overnight Fedex charges, and other back-end production charges for submitting ad materials. As a marketing manager, the major benefit of electronic submission gives your marketing program a dramatic increase in response time and flexibility. You now have more time before ad submission deadlines, and more flexibility if you must change, replace or reschedule your company's advertising.

Electronic Proofs of Your Advertising

You can proof all of your advertising and other printed materials, both on-screen, and in print (via your laser or color inkjet printer) with Adobe Acrobat .PDF-format files, also known as "PDFs." Acrobat PDFs are output from desktop publishing programs (such as QuarkXPress) and give you an exact visual representation of what an ad (or any other printed material) looks like in its final, printed form. Depending on how they are output, colors displayed on an ad on your PC's screen from an Acrobat .PDF proof bear a reasonable resemblance to the colors of the final printed piece.

Acrobat .PDF proofs print out very well on your office laser printer, and in most instances, black and white printouts of ads for text proofing, along with on-screen checks for color, are acceptable for most proofing tasks. Once you've done a few printing jobs or ad placements using .PDFs, and are comfortable with the final results in print, you and your ad agency or marketing consultant will never go back to the "old days" of just a few years ago, of proofing hard-copy bluelines and matchprints.

When you need film and a matchprint: There are still times, however, when you should order an ad to be submitted in the conventional fashion—film and a matchprint, a color proof produced from the actual film negatives sent to the publication:

- **When making a larger-than-usual advertising expenditure** with a big circulation business or general-interest publication, where it is imperative that you eliminate all possibility of minor mistakes or delays that may occur in electronic ad transmissions. In other words, if your usual ad placements are $5,000 pages in *Information Week*, but this quarter you're going with a full page in *Business Week* at $64,100—**get a matchprint**;

- **When color is critical:** Digital color matching is still not well-implemented by the production departments in some publications. If exact color matching in your ad is critical (as in photos or solid colors), get a matchprint made from your ad's film negatives.

Aside from these exceptions, all-electronic and Internet-based ad transmission gives a major boost to your company's speed of execution of its ad campaigns, and you should generally insist that all ads be proofed and transmitted electronically. See Chapter 12 for more information on using the Internet for production and execution of you company's marketing projects.

"Friction," those unneeded interruptions and delays to the smooth process of flawless execution of your company's ad campaigns, happens whenever production of your company's advertising files has to be stopped, then dumped to disk, output, handled, packed, messengered, couriered, and otherwise "messed with" in the real world. Use the Internet for what it's good for—fast, "frictionless" transmission of your marketing deliverables—and make it an important part of your marketing program.

WEB SITE PLANNING & DESIGN
CHAPTER 10
PLANNING YOUR COMPANY'S INTERNET STRATEGY

Your company's Web site is a very important marketing tool, an information and communications platform serving the other key elements of your marketing program. And, just like any other marketing deliverable, the presentation and content of your company's Web site has a direct impact on your company's sales.

As a marketing manager, you may not be directly responsible for design and implementation of your company's Web site, but given its importance to your company's marketing program, you must play an influential role in its planning, development, and execution.

The "Dot-Com" Bust Gives Way to a Slower, Quieter Internet Revolution

Despite the general sense of pessimism and gloom that is all-too pervasive in the Internet's post-bubble era, businesses and consumers continue to use the Internet to purchase products and services online. According to IDC Research, the worldwide value of business goods and services purchased online is projected to increase from $282 billion in 2000 to $4.3 trillion by 2005. The "old rules" of doing business that were supposed to have been swept away by the Internet are still with us, but it is now clear that changes in sales and distribution brought about by the Internet will happen more gradually.

However incremental these changes, the Internet has already had a significant impact on, and will continue to change, the way companies operate, their channels of distribution, and their methods of marketing, sales and promotion. For example, online travel Web sites are changing the way consumers purchase airline tickets and hotel rooms. Amazon.com has made a significant impact on the book sales industry.

Business-to-business marketers, such as Avnet Electronics Marketing (**www.avnet.com**), Grainger (**www.wwgrainger.com**), and many other Web sites are quietly revolutionizing many industrial manufacturing and distribution businesses.

Instead of sweeping the business practices of large, established businesses and entire industries aside in a few short years, the Internet will incrementally change the way prospects and customers interact with established companies in these industries. The Internet will serve, initially at least, as an *extension* of the ways existing companies market and sell their products. The more fundamental, radical changes, such as the elimination of old-line distribution channels and other middlemen, will happen more gradually over time.

The Marketing Manager's Role in a Company's Internet Strategy

In your work as a marketing manager, you will often be deeply involved in your company's Web site development projects. You may not have sole authority in deciding the form and content of your company's Web site and other Internet-related business activities, but you will play a very influential role in helping to steer the planning and development process of your company's Internet strategy in the direction that leads to higher sales, using the Internet to shorten your company's sales cycle by giving prospects the online information they need, to make purchasing decisions on your company's products.

The Internet's recent boom-and-bust cycle proved how foolhardy it was for any established company to abandon its current, successful channels of sales distribution in favor of all-Internet "e-commerce" business models, but every company can—and should—use the Internet in its marketing programs and strategy.

While strategic decisions about your company's direction, its technology, its overall ways of doing business and selling its products may be beyond the scope of your responsibilities as a marketing manager, your day-to-day responsibilities for your company's marketing efforts, combined with your own experience and common sense, and the guidance provided in this book, will help you steer your company's Internet-based marketing efforts in the right direction.

The Internet Extends a Company's Real-World Sales and Marketing Activities

If you are marketing manager for an established company, it's likely your company has been operating a Web site for some time now. During the Internet's gold-rush days, many companies threw large amounts of money at Web developers to create over-designed Web sites having little to do with the way these companies actually marketed and sold their products.

Many companies did, however, develop Web sites with sales promotion and marketing features much closer to the needs and wants of their prospects and customers. These companies have already incorporated the Internet as a successful part of their existing marketing programs. This chapter outlines the general techniques of marketing presentation that can be learned from these companies, who are quietly, successfully, reaping sales and marketing benefits from their Web sites.

How Your Company Can Use the Internet

The passage of time gives perspective, and in both the successes and the failures, some valuable, general principles can be learned from using the Internet as a marketing tool:

Established companies should see their Web sites as another marketing channel that serves the company's existing marketing programs and sales distribution networks. Web sites expand a company's online sales and marketing efforts, but not at the risk of threatening its established sales, dealer or distribution networks.

Web sites for most established companies can, at a minimum, shorten a company's sales cycle by providing interested prospects with the sales and product information they need, faster and more conveniently. Solid execution of this aspect alone can have an immediate, positive impact on sales for any established company;

Start-up companies have the advantage of being less restricted by the extent their Web sites serve their marketing and sales efforts, because they have no existing sales distribution and dealer networks to protect. Therefore, a new venture can move its marketing interactions with prospects, and sales processes for customers, as much, and as quickly, as its market and common sense allows.

However, very few start-ups can survive as Internet-only businesses. So, just as in established companies, the bulk of the marketing programs in most start-up companies require the expenditure of time, effort and money on conventional marketing efforts, such as print advertising campaigns, direct-mail, the organization of an on-the-street sales force, and the other, proven marketing methods of the "Old Economy."

For all companies, a Web site is an instant, two-way communications channel to interested prospects, current customers, the media, potential business partners, or anyone else with an interest in your company and its products. All Web sites should be platforms for experimentation, providing a company with instant, immediate feedback on its products, pricing, and marketing programs. The Internet is also a mechanism for helping a company to gradually transform the ways it markets and sells its products or services, to anticipate the slower, more gradual changes the Internet will gradually make in marketing and business practices.

Your Prospects and Customers Will Find Your Company on the Internet— Whether You Like It Or Not

The radical transformation the Internet is bringing about in business marketing is beyond your company's ability to control. If your company sells products to the consumer marketplace, for example, the slow-but-steady growth in Internet broadband access opens up the Internet's potential by making it a speedier and more pleasant experience for the user. Over the next few years, this will give your company many exciting new opportunities to present its products and services to consumers over the Internet, using high-bandwidth multimedia-based methods, such as high-quality video and audio, along with faster, more efficient methods of selling your company's products online.

For business-to-business marketers, new data interchange formats, such as XML, allow for the closely integrated exchange of information between your company and its customers, and especially for high-level integration, such as the interface of your company's product database with a customer's purchasing department. New types of wireless devices and other "Internet-anywhere" Net appliances will enable your company's prospects and customers to access extensive information about your company and its products from anywhere—the factory floor, a staff meeting, or on the road.

The tools and skills required for your company to serve prospects and customers in these new ways will be available for your company to develop and master, and there will be time for your company to adapt. If your company chooses not to, it will lose market share and key sales opportunities to its competitors who will take up the challenge.

Your interested prospects and customers are already using Google to search for your company, and for the kinds of products and services your company sells, on the Web. They will be visiting your company's Web site no matter how well, or how poorly, your company presents and sells its products there. Ready or not, your company must have a presence on the Internet, and it must develop this presence in a way that increases sales today, and sets the stage for the Internet's future role in your company's success.

The Web Spectrum: Types of Web Sites

You play a key role in influencing your company's Web strategy, helping your company develop a Web site that serves its strategic marketing and sales goals.

A Web site, of course, can be simple or highly complex, depending on:

- **Your company's financial resources;**
- **The complexity of your company's products;**
- **The price level of your company's products or services;**
- **The technical sophistication of your market base;**
- **Your company's current sales and distribution channels and methods**

The purpose, form, features, and capabilities of your company's Web site will fall somewhere along a spectrum of the following major types of Web sites:

The Web "brochure site:" The simplest, most basic of all Web sites, the "Web brochure site" consists of a few Web pages featuring your company's general sales information, some bulleted descriptions of your company's main product lines, your company's contact information, and not much more. Although derided by many Web developers, a Web brochure site can be a perfectly adequate Web presence for some companies, whose main, more effective, marketing efforts are better focused on other activities and media, such as print advertising campaigns and a large, active, on-the-ground national sales force. Web brochure sites also serve as "placeholder" Web sites for companies still finalizing their long-term Internet business strategies. At the very least, the Web brochure site provides site visitors with basic information on a company and its products, and more importantly, enables site visitors to contact a company, by providing additional e-mail, phone, and mailing address contact information;

A company showroom and library: The next stage in Web site development and complexity, and the most prevalent type of Web sites operated by most businesses on the Internet, are the online equivalents of "company showrooms," featuring extensive sales information on a company, its products, and their sales benefits. These sites also feature a company "library," with in-depth information on the features of a company's products, such as technical specifications, downloadable Adobe Acrobat .PDF "white papers," applications notes, and case histories, for interested prospects who want to know more about how the company's products can meet their needs.

Well-executed company showroom/library Web sites can dramatically shorten a company's sales cycle, by providing interested prospects with the in-depth technical information they need on the company's products, and in far less time than required to mail out a sales information kit, set up a sales presentation, or otherwise engage the task of informing, educating, and persuading interested prospects. How well this type of Web site works depends on how well the company presents the information that a prospect is likely to want, without making the prospect work too hard to find it;

A catalog and store: Higher still in development and complexity are company Web sites offering a full online catalog of the company's product line, combined with an online ordering system. If the price and complexity of a company's products are not too high, and existing sales networks are not threatened, the "online catalog and store" company Web site is the most highly-developed type of business Web site an established company can create.

An online selling capability can, over time, transform a company's sales channels, reduce its marketing and sales expenses, and fundamentally alter the relationship between the company and its prospects and customers.

For example, these Web sites can eliminate the need for a prospect to speak to a salesman before placing an order, or for a customer to call an account representative to place a reorder. This full-bore strategy is not suited for every company, and the more sure-footed of those that have developed successful Web catalogs have usually started with less-ambitious Internet goals, building up their site's capabilities and gradually evolving these into a direct-to-end-user sales capability;

The "all-virtual" presence: The highest form of Web evolution, these are Web sites created by companies that do all of their business on the Internet, such as Amazon.com and eBay. There are virtually no significant business-to-business companies selling physical products who operate in this rarified, "all virtual" environment, and interest among companies, entrepreneurs, and investors in reaching this highest level of engagement with the "virtual marketplaces" of the Internet has diminished with the collapse of the dot-com bubble. However, you can learn many valuable lessons from the few successes here, such as Amazon.com and eBay, by observing how these sites organize and present their "user experiences" for online shoppers and buyers.

What Should Your Company's Web Site Do?

If you're a marketing manager in an established company, the requirements and boundaries of your Web site may already be established. For example, if your company generates most of its sales volume from a few very large and influential distributors, establishing an online, full-range product catalog and direct-to-end-users online ordering capability would place your company in direct competition with your own distributors, threatening your company's established sales channels. Instead, your Web site should support your company's key distributors by providing the best, most persuasive information on your company's product line, combined with efficient capture of sales lead information collected on your Web site, and speedy referral of these leads to the appropriate distributor.

On the other hand, if your company is in the business of selling a line of relatively low-priced products on a repeating basis, and doesn't have established ties to key distributors or dealers in its sales channels, turning your Web site into an online product catalog with a secure, instant direct-order capability would be a plausible, and positive, move for your company.

Whatever type of business your company does, and wherever it may fall along this spectrum of possibilities, to the extent that you can influence its presentation and features, you will do no wrong if you can help your company develop a Web site that serves as an *extension* of the way your company currently markets and sells its product or service.

Generally, the best type of Web site for companies in trade and business-to-business markets is the "company showroom and library" Web site. This Web site helps your company shorten its sales cycle, without posing a threat to your company's established sales distribution channels. And as your company acquires more knowledge on how it can use its Web site to sell to its prospects and customers, it can always add more features and functionality.

Your Company's Web Site: Web Design and Production for Marketing Managers

This section covers the key aspects of creating or improving your company's Web site, by outlining the key Web design usability principles that help you increase the sales effectiveness of your company's Web site.

The purpose of this section is not to teach you how to be a Web site designer or producer, since this is not your job. However, just as this book brings you inside the creation, development and execution processes for other kinds of marketing projects, these two chapters cover the basic principles of presentation and marketing execution used in the Web design and development process.

As a marketing manager, you should know enough about Web site development to "drive a stake in the ground"—that is, to originate and execute a rough-but-plausible working initial design of your company's Web site that presents your company and its products effectively and convincingly online, to meet your company's sales and marketing goals. Hopefully, these two chapters will also de-mystify the Web design and production process, by providing you with some guiding principles to give direction to your staff and outside vendors, such as third-party Web site producers, to develop a Web site that shortens your company's selling cycle and sells your company's products.

A Web Site's Three Most Important Functions

The three most important functions a Web site can provide to any business are: Information, communications, and transactions.

1.) Information

Your company's Web site is an important extension of the way your company distributes information on its products and services. A well-executed Web site helps your company shorten its sales cycle, by providing interested prospects with the information they need on your company's product or service, prior to their purchasing decision.

Like it or not, today's smart, Web-savvy business customer is already using Internet search engines like Google to search for information on your company and its products. Your prospects are already forming judgements and making decisions on your company and its products based on the information they see on the Internet— from Net-based information sources other than your company's Web site, such as independent news articles written on your company and its products, and comments on Internet discussion groups. And if they don't find the information they're looking for on your company's Web site, they may well find it on your competitor's site and buy it there.

Give interested visitors and prospects all the information they require on your company's products and services: A "Frequently Asked Questions" (FAQ) file, an online product catalog, product photos, diagrams and explanatory graphics, or Adobe Acrobat .PDF format printable brochures. By enabling site visitors and prospects to self-select the information they want on your company's products, your Web site helps to shorten your company's sales cycle. Give an interested site visitor the information they want to see on your company and its products, and your Web site can turn them into a prospect who's ready to buy.

2.) Communications

Your Web site is an always-on, two-way communications channel to site visitors, prospects, customers, and the broader circle of those interested in your company— business and trade media, investors, analysts, and prospective business partners. At a minimum, you can begin to unlock this tremendous communications potential by publishing a free e-mail newsletter to send to interested prospects and customers, to keep your company's name in front of interested readers every time they receive a communication from your company.

You can extend this communications power beyond periodic e-mail newsletters to full-blown online discussion forums on your company's Web site, where customers and prospects can openly discuss your company's products and their applications with your own company's internal technical, marketing and support staffs. The sense of openness that is fostered by these more-or-less free, unedited online exchanges creates a positive image of your company in the minds of all site visitors, showing your company's respect for the views of its prospects and customers.

3.) Transactions

Of course, many business-to-business Web sites can also serve as online ordering and transaction points, where customers can purchase your company's products direct from your Web site. While this functionality represents the ideal, several key factors will influence whether or not a company can utilize its own Web site for online direct sales transactions of its products. For example, a company is more likely to be successful in selling its products direct from its Web site if it sells a relatively low-priced product, or a product that is a well-known commodity (for example, raw materials, or manufactured components well known to the buyer). Conversely, it is more difficult for a company to sell higher-priced products requiring extensive explanation and longer selling cycles, or products that are completely new and innovative in their brand categories.

Also, selling products direct from your company's Web site may pose an untenable risk if your company has already developed a well-established dealer or distributor sales network. In some cases, a direct Web site sales feature can co-exist with established dealer networks, if it is promoted as "merely" another customer service-oriented sales channel, and introduced in a low-key way to minimize disruption to established sales and distribution channels. While a transaction function may not be workable for every company's Web site, is certainly represents the ideal for many business marketers.

Characteristics of First-Rate Business Web Sites

Successful, marketing-oriented business Web sites share the following common characteristics:

Passing "The Ten-Second Test:" Anyone who reaches your company's Web site for the very first time should, within ten seconds, but able to understand what products your company sells, what these products do, and, in the most basic way, understand what your company's products can do for them. Simple presentation and clarity of expression on your Web site are the keys to meeting this "Ten-Second Test;" anything that gets in the way of this purpose, such as overproduced Web design, or irrelevant, gimmicky Flash intro screens (more on this later) only delays your interested prospects unnecessarily from their desire to learn more about your company's products, and ultimately has an adverse impact on your Web site's power to sell your product;

Intuitive access: Visitors to your site should be able to reach any feature of importance on it, easily, and without having to work too hard to figure out how to get the information they're looking for. The most important parts of your site—i.e., the places you want site visitors and prospects to reach at all times—should be the most prominently featured links on your site. These links must be displayed where the user expects to see them, and must not create confusion or difficulty for the user;

Top presentation quality: Like any other marketing deliverable, your company's Web site is a reflection of your company's image and character. Today's media-savvy business Web user will expect your Web site to meet a minimum level of presentation design quality that is at least equal to that of your company's main competitors. The key to good Web site design is to achieve a clean, functional, usable site design, without falling into the common trap of having your company's Web site appear "over-designed." This occurs when Web designers are too focused on your company's "brand image," and make decisions favoring design and style over content and usability.

Web Development Ground Rules : A Basic Design Template for Success

Contrary to what Web designers will tell you, the process of designing usable, functional and effective business Web sites is neither mysterious, nor especially complicated. In the decade that has passed since the initial, explosive growth of the Internet, Web design has evolved into the more-or-less "standardized" basic design format now being used for most business Web sites, where key links are displayed, top to bottom, along a left-hand sidebar, with other key navigation links displayed from left to right at the top and bottom of each Web page (see **Figure 10-1**).

This "left-hand sidebar layout" has proven itself to be a useful and easy-to-navigate format for Web users of every skill level. The vast number of business Web sites utilizing this design format have also conditioned Web users to look for the left-hand sidebar on every Web site they access. While some might say this homogenization of Web interfaces has taken some of the innovation out of Web design, the chief benefit of this "standard" format is that it helps all Web users anticipate key information and navigation links on a Web site, and gives users an immediate, intuitive sense of where everything is on the site, so they can quickly find what they're looking for.

Since there are many creative design possibilities available in this standard Web form, you should look on the left-hand sidebar format not as something that limits your creative options, but as a valuable convention that evolved on the Internet to boost the usability of Web sites for all, just as the "user interface" of the automobile evolved into the standard arrangement of gas pedal, brake pedal, steering wheel and speedometer, to make driving easier for everyone.

Basic Web Design, Layout and Production Techniques for Marketing Managers

As a marketing manager you aren't expected to be a Web site designer or producer, but you do play an important role in driving the process of developing and executing an effective, marketing-oriented Web site for your company, when working with your company's Web site production team, or with an outside Web site developer on your company's Web site projects.

Before you can drive this process, you must first decide what you want your company's Web site to do for your company, and then place your thoughts, ideas, and objectives into a form that can then be understood by your Web developers, and translated into a functional, successful Web site. As you start any Web site development project, you should prepare your own rough, initial outline and specification of the key functional elements you believe are important for your company's Web project.

Generally speaking, Web designers and developers are either "artists," or "techies," having little real-world sales experience, and minimal background

Figure 10-1:

Left-Hand Sidebar Navigation—A standard interface for many top business and consumer Web sites

The Left-Hand Navigation Sidebar *as shown on this sampling of business-to-business Web sites, has become a standard design format for many business, consumer, and industrial Web sites, providing a useful and efficient way to organize your Web site's information, services, and links*

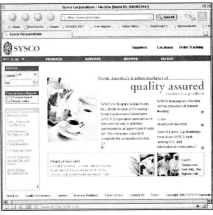

knowledge of your product's sales benefits or your company's marketing objectives. Your initial, outlined specification starts every Web project out on the right track, by keeping it firmly anchored in the reality of your company's marketing requirements.

This section details some basic techniques to help you prepare your initial Web site "spec," including a three-step Web design and production process that gives you the basic background knowledge needed to work with a Web developer to produce an effective Web site that meets your company's marketing and sales objectives.

These techniques apply both to the development of an entirely new Web site for your company, and ongoing revisions and improvements to your company's existing site.

Your Two Best Web Development Tools: Pencil and Paper

Start your Web outlining process by shutting off your computer and taking out your pencil and notepad. Quality Web site development should always begin as a low-tech task, which is the process of deciding:

- **What content you have;**
- **Where it should be placed on your Web site;**
- **What is most important for your audience to see first**

Translated into harder-hitting, marketing-oriented objectives, your own Web site specification should help your company's Web developers answer these questions:

- **What are we selling?**
- **How should this information be organized on our Web site?**
- **What is the most important thing we want our prospects to do when they visit our Web site?**

The end result of the exercises outlined in this section will help you to address these three important Web site marketing objectives in your outline/specification. This initial outline serves as your Web developer's starting point in their execution of your company's Web site. If you are working with a talented Web developer, it's also likely they will expand and enhance your initial vision of the site documented in your outline, adding their own creative, useful, and sales-enhancing ideas to the project along the way.

Creating a Rough Draft of a Web Site Layout

To begin the process of creating your own, basic Web site layout in rough draft form, start out by jotting down some notes to answer these three questions:

1.) What does our company do, what products do we sell, and what's the best thing about these products? Write this down, in 30 words or less. This is quite similar to the "Elevator Pitch" sales copywriting exercise covered in Chapter 4;

2.) What are the six most important things I want my market to KNOW about my company and its products? List the most important, general facts about your company, and the most important benefits of your company's product or service, as in the following examples:

- **Your company's product line;**
- **Product technical specs;**
- **On-line demo of your company's product in action;**
- **Product applications and how-to tips;**
- **Customer endorsements and testimonials;**
- **Company news;**
- **Management profiles/executive team;**
- **Downloadable, free software "helper applications;"**
- **Free e-mail newsletter**

Create your own list of six items, then rank them in order from 1 (most important), to 6 (least important), as a top-to-bottom list (or more than six items, if necessary);

3.) What are the three most important things I want prospects to DO when they access our company's Web site? Think of this as your "call to action" to interested potential buyers who visit your company's Web site. Select from the ideas below, or jot down any other "Do" steps that apply to your company and its market:

- **Order now;**
- **Visit our online store;**
- **Request an estimate;**
- **Request a print catalog;**
- **Contact us;**
- **See our best-selling products;**
- **Find a location near you;**
- **Get a free sample**

Write down your own list of these sales "action" steps, as simple two-to four-word sentences, similar to the ones above. Select no more than three of the most important of these, and rank them in 1-2-3… order, from most important to least important, left to right on a sheet of paper (you can use more than three "do" options, if necessary).

The result of 1.), 2.), and 3.) above forms the basis of your rough layout specification for your company's preliminary Web site design.

Figure 10-2:

Web Development Ground Rules:

- *Web site design has reached a level of maturity*

- *Net users have become accustomed to using Web sites in certain ways*

- *"Standard" Web design formats can make your Web site easy-to-use, right away*

- *Know what you want—don't be driven by your Web designers or developers*

- *Don't be taken in by the technology—let technology serve your goals*

Left-Hand Sidebar Layout: A "Standard" Site Template for the Web

Once you've sketched out the "Know" and "Do" options in the previous section, the template in **Figure 10-3** shows you where these options would fit, as clickable links by users, in a rough, working design for your Web site (a larger-sized, printable version of this template is available as an Adobe Acrobat .PDF file from this book's companion Web site at **www.sellyourproduct.com**):

The "KNOW" options (from previous step 2.) are the main content of your company's Web site. On the final version of your site, each of these "Know" options become links to their own, detailed information features on your site;

The "DO" options (from previous step 3.) are the top-priority action steps you want site visitors to take, once they've seen enough information on your Web site about your company, its products, and their applications and benefits (contained in the "Know" options above).

Write in the "Do" and "Know" options you've sketched out from the previous step into the blank spaces provided on the screen template in **Figure 10-3**. Write in the "Do" features, from the most-important on the left-hand side, to the less important on the right, on the top of the screen template. Likewise, the "Know" options should run most-important to less-important, from top to bottom on the left-hand sidebar.

The "Description" box, shown on the upper-right-hand side of the template, contains the brief summary of your company, its products, and its benefits (your "Elevator Pitch"), you've written from step 1.) of the previous exercise.

The "Know" and "Do" options are also repeated in two text-only rows along the bottom of the screen template, to provide users with immediate links to all of these important options on every page of your company's Web site.

Create a separate page for each of your site's "Know" and "Do" links: Once you have decided on your site outline's "Know" and "Do" links, devote a separate page in your notes for each of your "Know" and "Do" links, jotting down text notes for each of these items, further outlining the content and functionality of these individual links in your site outline.

The "Information Hole"

The main area for content on a Web page is its "Information hole," derived from "News hole," a term used by newspaper editors to describe the space used for the placement of news articles in a newspaper's layout template.

Your Web site's "Information Hole" is the area where text and other selling content is displayed for all the pages of your site. This is where the actual content for the "Know" and "Do" options for your site is displayed when selected by users as clickable links from any of the "Know" options along the left-hand sidebar on every screen of your Web site, or from any of the "Do" options at the top of every screen on your site.

Figure 10-3:

Left-Hand Sidebar Layout Template—Create a rough, effective, working design for your company's Web site

Use This Worksheet to Fill in the Essential Selling Content from **1**, **2**, *and* **3** *below to create a rough, initial working "spec" for your company's Web design team*

What does our company do, what products do we sell, and what's the best thing about these products? Write this down, in 30 words or less (similar to the "Elevator Pitch" sales copywriting exercise covered in Chapter 4)

What are the six most important things I want my market to KNOW about my company and its products? List the most important, general facts about your company that also describe the most important benefits of your company's product or service

What are the three most important things I want prospects to DO when they access our company's Web site? This is your "Call to action:" Tell interested potential buyers what you want them to do when they're on your company's Web site

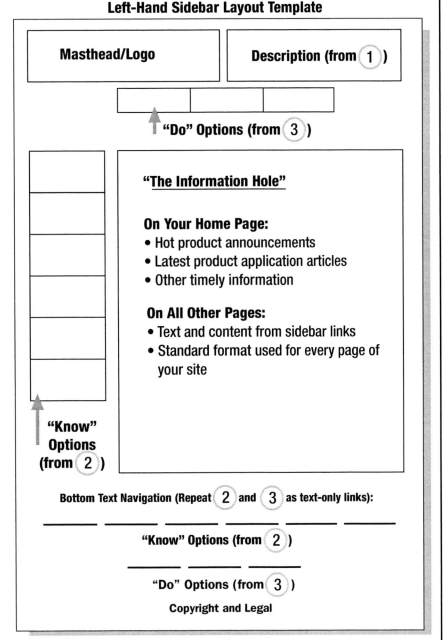

Left-Hand Sidebar Layout Template

| **Masthead/Logo** | **Description (from ①)** |

↑ **"Do" Options (from ③)**

"The Information Hole"

On Your Home Page:
• Hot product announcements
• Latest product application articles
• Other timely information

On All Other Pages:
• Text and content from sidebar links
• Standard format used for every page of your site

↑ **"Know" Options (from ②)**

Bottom Text Navigation (Repeat ② and ③ as text-only links):

_____ _____ _____ _____ _____

"Know" Options (from ②)

_____ _____ _____

"Do" Options (from ③)

Copyright and Legal

Figure 10-4:

Web Catalog Product Mini-Listing—Wrap text around photos, and include a "more info" link

Product Mini-Listings,
featuring short text
descriptions wrapped around
small product photos, with
links to in-depth information,
are a visually appealing way
to present product
information. This format is
also useful for presenting
many products on a single
Web page (product listing
shown here from
amazon.com)

Top Sellers in Electronics

Linksys Wireless 4-Port Cable/DSL Router

In the past, people creating a home network had to choose between stringing cheap Ethernet cable all over the house or spending tons of cash on a slow, unreliable wireless system. Products like the BEFW11S4 wireless four-port cable/DSL router from Linksys have changed all that. This unit works as an Internet gateway, traditional four-port Ethernet... Read more

Your Web Site's Home Page

Your site's home page is the most important part of your company's Web site. The sales copy, headlines, and graphics displayed here give your customers and prospects their first impression of your company and its products, and set the tone for all of your site's content, promotional features, and services.

Because of its importance, you should put considerable effort into the presentation of the home page on your company's Web site. Here, the "Ten Second Rule," mentioned earlier, applies the most, because this is where the overall impression created by your home page—in its descriptive text about your company, its sales copy, and the appeal generated by the product images and other visuals of your site— is formed, for better or worse, in the first few, short seconds a "visitor" spends scanning your site's home page.

Whenever you are involved in a Web site development project for your company, practice your ability to view your company's home page with "new eyes," putting yourself in the mind of your company's prospects, customers, and other visitors who form their impressions of your company and its products within the first few seconds of their initial visit to your company's Web site.

What's Your Key Selling Objective?

Once you've developed the "Know" and "Do" features outlined in the previous exercise to create a rough, working structure for your company's Web site, you must now give careful thought to the key selling objective of your company's site. This is the critical **sales content** displayed on your company's home page.

Of course, the key selling objective of your Web site's home page is driven by the type of products or services marketed by your company, its industry, your company's

---

Figure 10-5:

Your Web Site's FAQ (Frequently-Asked Question) File—An important sales tool on your Web site

By Answering the Most Common Questions Your Prospects Ask about your company's product or service, your Web site's FAQ file becomes a valuable selling tool on your Web site.

Start off your site's FAQ page with the list of questions in the FAQ file, set up as clickable links, and starting with the most common question. Then link the user to the answer to each question, further down on the same Web page

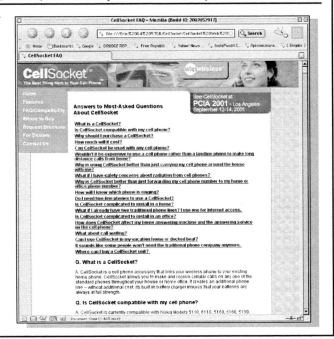

---

existing sales and marketing channels, and the prices of these products or services. Also, at this point in the Web development process you should have already resolved the key strategic marketing issues concerning your Web site's sales goals for your company, including the important decision on whether or not your company can (or should) sell its products to customers directly from its Web site.

How to Lead Off Your Home Page

Your choice of content to lead off your company's home page depends on the type of Web site you are developing. Here are some ideas for sales content and presentation on your home page, for the major types of business Web sites.

Online Product Catalog/Direct-Order Web Site

If you are selling your company's products direct from your Web site with an online product catalog, the most important goal of your home page is to *show your merchandise*—as much of it as possible, on your site's home page.

Start off your company's home page with its top-selling products, including thumbnail product shots for each product model, capsule descriptions for each product, and "more info…" links for users to click to get deeper into your company's catalog site (see **Figure 10-4**). Better yet, you can improve the timeliness of your site by leading off with updated, weekly product sales promotions or specials, using this condensed presentation format, at the top of your site's home page.

Service, or Information-Based, Web Site

If you're marketing a service business (publishing, information, consulting or professional services), the description of your company's services should obviously be the main focus of your home page. Give your interested site visitors the background information they need— describe those services and, if possible, make it easy for prospects to try your service with a demo, or on some other free, or limited-time, basis

Presentation techniques for information-based Web sites: You can use the following methods to present your site's most important sales information on your company's home page, to draw visitors into the rest of your site:

- **The big-type teaser paragraph:** You can start your home page off with a short, one or two-sentence text block introducing your company, mentioning your service, and teasing your reader into your service's main benefit as in this example:

    Space Design Services, Inc. helps America's leading architectural and property development firms to plan and execute economic, space-saving use of their building's core utility systems.

    We've saved major design firms and builders, on average, over 35% on their design and build-out expense for this critical construction area… **More...**

    The purpose of this teaser mini-paragraph is to draw your interested reader further into your site, by first giving them an engaging, easy-to-read, visually interesting introductory statement on your company and its service's main benefit.

    In direct-mail parlance, this is called an "involvement device." On the Internet, the mini-teaser serves the same purpose, drawing your site visitor further into your Web site, where they will either read more about your company and its services, or will click on the other descriptive, sales-oriented "Know" and "Do" links you already have waiting for them on your site;

- **Frequently-Asked-Question (FAQ) file:** FAQ files have become common fixtures of nearly every Web site, and for good reason: They put the answers to all of the most commonly-asked questions about a company, its services, its prices, and their features and benefits in one place. Web users—your prospects—expect to find the information they need and get answers to their questions, fast. This is especially true if your company offers a new or different type of service requiring extensive and detailed explanation. If so, then don't hesitate to lead off your site's home page with a FAQ file as the key information feature at the top of your home page, or below the teaser paragraph previously described.

The best way to lead off with an FAQ on your site's home page (or on any other page of your site), is to lead with a single "index" column that lists each of your FAQ's questions, set as links so site users can click on any question link to get the answer to their question, as shown in **Figure 10-5**.

Questions in FAQ files should be structured exactly along the lines of a standard sales presentation given by one of your company's sales reps, with each question revealing a new aspect of your company's service, and anticipating an interested prospect's next question or concern about your company's product or service.

Other Important Link Options for Information and Service-Based Sites

Who/what/where/how: Break down the salient features of your company's service or information product. Make it very plain to the reader what your service is, what your company does, what's good about it, how the reader would use your service, and what it can do for them.

Free samples: If your company is offering any type of information-based service, such as a newsletter, consulting, research, or advisory services, **open the curtain**— put up a collection of sample issues, articles, helpful features, and any other useful analysis or information content your company has developed. The Internet has truly revolutionized the information business, and its effects are still being felt by publishers, database providers, and other companies who provide specialized information services. Let interested prospects see what you are offering, by being generous with your proprietary information. They will soon return for more—and will pay money for your information once you convince them of its value by offering free samples.

Company News: If your company has an especially positive, major news announcement, such as an industry award, the winning of a major account, or a record sales performance, don't be afraid to lead with this news announcement on your company's home page. Everyone loves a winner—especially potential prospects for your firm's service or information products.

Industrial or Manufacturing Web Site (High Ticket, Long Selling Cycle):

If your company sells expensive, complex industrial products requiring a long sales cycle, many months, or a year or more, may pass from the time of the first sales contact to the final sale. More than other types of companies and products, Web sites for high-end industrial goods companies primarily serve an information and marketing support function, providing your company's interested prospects with the technical details, applications notes, case histories, and other background detail on the uses and applications of your company's products and systems.

Prospective buyers of high-end industrial products are technically-oriented individuals, such as engineers, who are used to dealing with the complex concepts underlying their technical fields and affecting their daily work. Unlike mass-market consumers, or buyers in other business-to-business markets, technical buyers will diligently read and study extensive technical information on your company's products. Accordingly, you can't give these potential buyers too much information.

To serve this requirement, place the most-requested technical information on your company's products as clickable left-hand sidebar links, organized by product line or application area. Additionally, links from your Web site's home page can provide your interested prospects with access to online repositories of your company's extensive line of technical documentation, posted on your Web site as printable, Adobe Acrobat .PDF format files.

Software, Systems, or High-Tech Product Web Site:

Many software products, systems, and other high-technology-related hardware products seek to change the way people do business, introducing new features and functionality. Even when a company's high-technology products, systems or software may not represent a revolutionary change, companies who market high-technology software and related products usually position them as offering users greater speed, power, efficiency, and productivity in their daily tasks.

If your company is in the software, systems, or other high-technology products field, you should view your Web site's home page as an opportunity to walk a prospective customer through your company's product, without overwhelming them with too much technical detail. The mini-teaser short paragraph, described previously—a simple, introductory benefit statement, combined with a visually arresting graphic, is a good way to lead off your home page, drawing interested prospects further into the features and benefits of your company's software, product, or system. Other compelling ways to lead off your software company's home page include:

- **Free download** of a trial version of your company's software;

- **Showcasing a satisfied current** user of your company's software or systems. Customer case histories or simply-presented human-interest product stories can be very compelling;

- **An aggressive comparison** of your company's software, system, or technology against that of a well-known, entrenched competitor in your industry—using numbers (i.e., "35% faster," "Less than half the cost…") or key feature-by-feature comparisons, leading with your product's most important differentiating feature. Don't be afraid to take on a big, top-name competitor if your company truly believes its product is better, and you can prove your claims.

Making Home Page Lead Sales Content Choices: An Overview

Your company and its products may not fit into any one of these examples, so here are some approaches for helping you determine the most important prospect sales information to lead off your home page and organize the sales content of your site:

Talk to your company's sales reps: A Web site serves a marketing and sales-support function for your company, like other marketing deliverables—a display ad, brochure, direct mail package, or other marketing collateral. And, just like any of these marketing projects, any Web site development project you undertake for your company would greatly benefit from the "sales rep debriefing" methods described in Chapter 4. Ask your company's sales reps to share the comments and suggestions they have heard regarding your Web site's features, services, and other content ideas requested by their prospects and customers.

Maybe there's a very effective printed sales piece your company's sales reps find especially persuasive in their presentations to prospects, such as your company's main product sales brochure. Copy points and other graphic elements can be "lifted" from this piece and adapted for use in your company's Web site.

Your sales reps are very plugged in to your market, and they can make many useful suggestions for new features for your company's Web site, such as an especially effective or compelling new feature recently introduced on a competitor's Web site. Talking to your company's sales reps can give you the wake-up call that's needed to sharpen the effectiveness and relevance of your company's Web development projects;

A word of caution: Salespeople, having the forceful personalities required to be good at their jobs, will sometimes champion their pet Web site ideas without regard to the idea's workability, or the "big picture" issues of your company's marketing strategy and direction. The purpose of your debriefing is to gather only as much raw intelligence as possible from those who work outside your company. Your function as marketing manager here, as in all other marketing projects, is to serve as gatekeeper, picking out the few good ideas and suggestions for your company's site, folding these ideas into your initial outline spec, then working with your Web development team to drive the project forward to completion. Just as you're not expected to be a Web designer, don't give your company's sales reps the power, or the responsibility, to specify the features of your company's Web site;

As a first Web site, there's nothing wrong with a "Web brochure site:" Web design critics look down their noses at "Web brochure" sites: Basic, three or four-page sites that are little more than online reproductions of a company's printed sales brochure. Web developers are quite right in expressing their professional frustration with companies who put up these minimal sites, and it's also true that companies with brochure sites may be missing out on potential sales growth opportunities by not placing greater emphasis on improving their Web sites.

However, something is always better than nothing—and, given the choice between throwing a brochure site together in a week, or having to wait two or more months with your company's Web URL pointing to an "Under Construction" page while you and your Web developers work to produce a more extensive site, a brochure site at least tells your company's promotional story and provides interested site visitors with a means to contact your company by e-mail.

There's nothing wrong with using your company's brochure as the inspiration and source of content for the initial version of your company's Web site, if it serves as the first step in the gradual evolution of a more effective Web site for your company.

When All Else Fails, Lead With Your "Elevator Pitch"

Stuck for a idea for the sales message to lead off your company's home page? You can always lead with your company's sales "Elevator Pitch," the short, hardest-hitting description of your company and your product's very best benefit to the prospect, described in Chapter 4. If you're drawing a blank when starting out on a new Web site project, and the ideas are come slowly or not all, you can do no wrong by penciling in your company's Elevator Pitch at the top of your home page sketch. Once you get this down on paper, you'll be surprised at how soon the "Know" and "Do" options (and other ideas) begin to pop out of your Elevator Pitch, once you write it down.

WEB SITE EXECUTION & LAUNCH
CHAPTER 11
RAPID PROTOTYPING, SKILLED EXECUTION, AND SMOOTH LAUNCHES OF WEB SITE PROJECTS

Once you've completed your rough Web site specification, you are ready to move on to the process of producing and launching your company's Web site.

Now is the time to bring in your Web designer, producer, or other third-party contractor who will be responsible for the hands-on development of your company's site project. Discuss your project, and the elements you've sketched out in your initial "spec." Make it clear to your Web development team that your specification is not chiseled in stone, nor is it your intent to close off any team member's own ideas or suggestions for your Web site. Your team should see your Web outline as a starting point, a set of minimal, functional requirements for the site project, with your team's participation in the project leading to enhancements of these features, and the creative addition of new features and capabilities as the development process continues. At this stage, everything's open for change, including your own rough outline.

Get a Prototype of Your Web Site Up, as Fast as You Can

Once you've discussed your initial Web specification with your team, and you've kicked around the ideas that came from the initial discussions, it's important that the rough specification you and your team are working on be turned into a rough, working online prototype as quickly as possible. This can be done in a few days, or under a week at most.

Your first, rough, online prototype is a crude, text-only version of your site project. At this stage, it won't contain any graphic elements or back-end functionality, such as CGI database links or other programming features. The prototype should, however, resemble the rough initial structure of your Web outline, containing links to all of the "Know" and "Do" pages you've sketched out, and whatever text content is available to fill in any of these "Know" and "Do" branches of your site. Check the sample prototypes shown in **Figure 11-1** to see an example of an actual first prototype for a Web site project.

Your Web site prototype serves three very important purposes:

> **The prototype helps develop your site's navigation and usability:** First, as an actual, functioning version of your Web site, the prototype lets you and your team test the usability of your site during the development process. The prototype answers important site navigation and organization questions, such as whether or not a specific section of your site should be accessible from one link, or from another;

> **The prototype gives your project a fixed location:** Second, since Web development projects are collaborative efforts, usually involving at least three or more individuals who may each be working at different locations, the prototype quickly becomes the central, working focus of your Web project; the "virtual location" where each team member can make changes and enhancements for others to see, test, and comment upon;

> **The prototype makes your project real:** Third, and most important, setting up a prototype in a fixed location makes every Web development project "real," providing your team members with a fixed, working (albeit rough) version of what will soon become the final version of your site.

The sooner you can get your first Web site prototype put together, the sooner you and your team can start to improve it, adding in more text and content, graphics, and other functionality as this prototype rapidly evolves into the final working version of your site. In Web development projects, you'll find that the "hurry up" effort you exert up-front to get your prototype established pays off by helping to make the rest of your project move along much faster.

Once Your Web Prototype is Up and Running, Push its Development Through to the Final Version

The other advantage of starting your Web development project with a rough outline or sketch based on a template, like the "Know" and "Do" template used in the previous chapter, is that it helps to streamline the process of moving your Web site from your initial, hand-written sketch, to your initial prototype, and then on to the first, graphically-based versions of your site.

Bear in mind that your use of this template is not intended to dictate the final appearance or functionality of your site. It is merely a tool that helps you lay down a marker for your Web project, an opening design concept meant to invite the constructive contribution of new ideas from members of your Web development team. If the graphic designer on your Web project is a cooperative, confident professional, they will appreciate having an initial starting point and set of ideas around which to base their own design interpretation of your site.

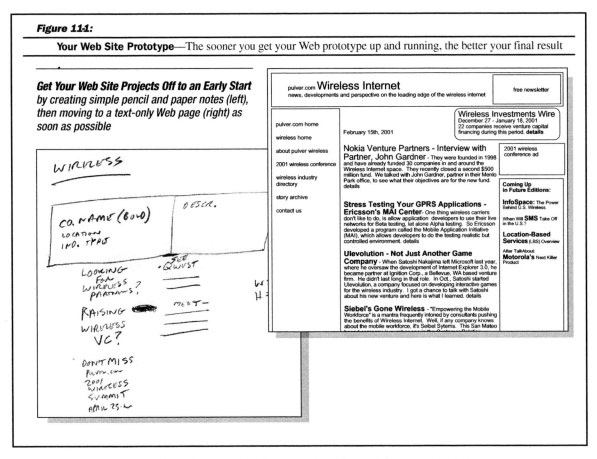

Figure 11-1:

Your Web Site Prototype—The sooner you get your Web prototype up and running, the better your final result

Get Your Web Site Projects Off to an Early Start by creating simple pencil and paper notes (left), then moving to a text-only Web page (right) as soon as possible

More than any print-oriented marketing project, Web development projects tend to be very fluid and fast-moving, so the final version of your Web site may look radically different than your initial sketch. As you, your Web development team, and your Web site's graphic designer work and brainstorm together, it is likely the members of your team will bring their own new ideas to the project. It's also likely that some of these new ideas will greatly improve the final version of your company's Web site, but may also mean that your original sketch design of the site will be changed, to a quite radical degree. While you must maintain a firm, steady grip on your Web development project, keep an open mind to these new ideas suggested by your team members, and don't be afraid to make changes—even major ones—to your Web project along the way.

Decide on the new ideas your Web team can implement now, and the ones to implement later: While you can, and should, be open-minded to new ideas for site changes that arise during the development process, be pragmatic enough to discriminate between the ideas that can be folded into your project immediately, and the ones that should be held aside for implementation on your site at a later date.

Figure 11-2:

From Rough Prototype to Completed Web Site—Early prototypes make better Web sites

Starting From a Quick Sketch and Hand-Written Notes, converted to a rough working Web prototype that evolves to the finished version, rapid prototyping helps you and your Web development team develop better Web sites, and complete them sooner.

By allowing your team to make a larger number of ongoing revisions to the prototype during the length of the project, early working prototypes also give your projects more time to evolve and mature; this leads to a better final product

| Rough Drawing | Prototype | Final Web Site |

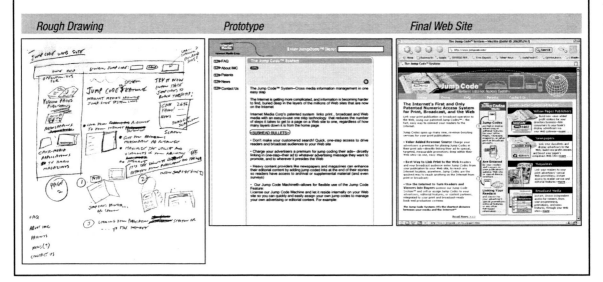

Any idea that improves the selling power of your company's Web site, without exceeding your project's timing or budget, is worthy of rapid adoption into your project. Conversely, any idea, even a good one, that doesn't meet the standard of increasing the sales and marketing potential of your company's Web site, or is too costly or time-consuming for the scope and schedule of your site project, should be put aside and added to a list of potential enhancements for "Phase Two" of your Web site; the next major revision to your Web site, implemented at some future date *after* your current Web development project goes "live." This keeps your current Web project on track, and prevents significant delays and cost overruns in your current project, while building up a useful storehouse of new and promising ideas to fold in to your site as "running changes" after your site goes live, or on its next major revision.

Start Testing Your Web Site Early in the Development Process

As your company's Web site prototype continues to evolve, one of your most important responsibilities as a marketing manager is to serve as a stand-in for the user—your company's prospects and customers. During the Web development process, you should be continuously testing this new Web site while it's being developed, checking for typos on site pages and other content glitches and, most important, checking your site's programming-related processes, such as order-entry forms, keyword search features, and other processes controlled by software programs or CGI scripts on your site (more on this further in this chapter).

The sooner you put yourself in your user's place in the development process, interacting with your Web site as your customers or prospects do, the more you'll be able to forestall any problems as your Web site reaches completion. Testing is covered in greater detail in the last section of this chapter.

Web Site Design Basics

While you work with your Web development team, creating and evolving your site prototype, adding in the text content for each section of your site, and the back-end CGI programming functionality (more on this in the next section), it's likely you'll either work directly with a Web graphics designer, or will be involved in the design process through an intermediary, such as an outside Web site development contractor or your company's ad agency. While no one expects you to be a Web designer (and non-designers shouldn't impose themselves on Web site design projects), you should know a little about Web site design, and the background execution of the process, so you can work constructively with your Web designer, helping them to do their job, without trying to do their job for them.

Initially, the graphic designer on your project usually works from an Adobe Photoshop or Macromedia Fireworks file to create the visual design for your site, that is then "sliced" and converted to the HTML-formatted Web pages of your site (see **Figure 11-3**). The crude, text-based screens of your initial Web prototype will soon be replaced by their graphically-oriented counterparts, moving your site closer in appearance to its final, working version.

Some Web designers are more "code oriented," in that they will first write the HTML code for your site, and then place the code for links to your site's graphics within the HTML-format table cells for their pages. While hand-coding of Web pages in HTML was, literally, the only way you could create a Web site before the advent of visually-based Web authoring programs like Macromedia Dreamweaver and Adobe GoLive, these authoring tools have opened up the Web design process, giving graphic designers the ability to design visually-appealing Web pages and create entire Web sites, without having to write a line of HTML code. In the first couple of years after their introduction, these visually-oriented Web authoring tools did tend to produce incorrectly-formatted Web Pages depending on which Web browsers were used to view them; this was caused by the way these programs generated the HTML code used to display the Web pages they created. However, these problems have been sorted out, and visual authoring systems are now the best tools for designing, developing and producing Web sites.

Web Site Design Tips for Non-Designers

It's usually a big mistake for non-designers to assume they know as much about design as the graphic designers on their Web development teams. People who don't know anything about design often try to do their Web designer's job for them, overriding a designer's thoughtful effort by making hasty, poorly considered, site design changes on a project. While no one expects you to be your company's Web designer, as a manager of any Web project, you should know enough to spot good Web design when you see it, to add to your own well-informed judgement on the design ideas and variations your site's graphic designer presents to you.

Here's some general advice to help you discriminate between good and bad Web design:

Easy navigation is good design: The purpose of Web design is to serve the navigation of your site, giving your site visitors the product information, benefits, and other features they're most interested in seeing within the first few seconds they link to your site. When someone goes to a Web site and can quickly find what they're looking for, just by stumbling through from the first link of the site's home page, that's good site navigation design. Web sites should always place the things that a site visitor is most interested in seeing right out in front on the site's home page, with visible, clearly-labeled links to help the user reach what they're most likely to want, without thinking too much or working too hard to get to it;

Avoid using Web site design elements executed for their own sake, such as Flash animations or other irrelevant or distracting graphic images. These get in the way of users (your prospects), and keep them from getting to the information they're most interested in seeing, right away, on your company's Web site. Good graphic design elements are those that inform the user, and get them quickly to the information they want to see. For example, on a site's online product catalog, small, jewel-like product images next to short, provocative thumbnail descriptions and clearly-labeled links add value to the information that's being displayed, by creating a visually interesting presentation of the company's product line, and displaying a wide variety of intriguing product options to the user;

When you see a Web site you like, bookmark it: When you use the Internet, do what professional graphic designers do: Create your own "Swipe File" of bookmarks for Web sites that have features or content you find especially useful. Save links for all types of Web sites whose design elements catch your

Figure 11-3:

Web Site Graphic Design—"Slicing" converts a Web page from graphics format to HTML Web pages

Many Web Page Designs are first created in graphics programs, such as Adobe Photoshop or Macromedia Fireworks (at right). Pages are then "sliced" into HTML-formatted tables (as shown) for conversion to Web pages

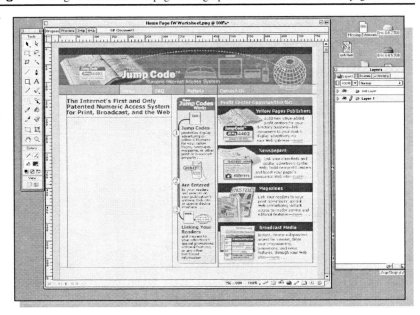

eye, and not just for Web sites in your line of business. Look for sites you not only think are well-designed, but for those with individual features that you think might work well in your company's own site. For example, if you come across a Web site with an especially well-executed process for signing users up to a free e-mail newsletter subscription offered on the site, or one with an especially clear and well-presented layout and organization of its product line, bookmark them so you can discuss these ideas with your Web development team.

"Borrowing" ideas from your competition is not a bad thing: All smart designers, including Web designers, create reference files (also called "swipe files") of Web sites having design ideas they find appealing, and that might be useful to them in a future project. Like artists, designers will allow that these ideas have "influenced" them on some of their own design projects.

The same holds true for interesting features or eye-catching presentation you see on any of your competitor's Web sites. If, for example, you notice an especially attractive and compelling graphic display on your competitor's Web site, such as a product description layout, or a visually appealing or informative feature article, technical schematic or applications chart, file these ideas away and consider how they could be adapted for use on your company's Web site.

Also, take note of any exceptional user navigation features you observe on a competitor's Web site. For example, if you believe your competitor's Web site features a truly intuitive, well thought-out online customer order entry process, chances are this process was not developed by accident, but through hard-won experience in learning from, and responding to, the actions and motivations of customers who order online; the final version being the result of an arduous trial-and-error process of dealing with the way real live customers actually use their Web site.

Certainly, you don't want to plagiarize someone else's content, or lift someone else's idea or Web interface wholesale. Use them as your starting point for executing a fresh, improved, or innovative adaptation in your own project. Train yourself to spot the best, most effective underlying techniques and methods your competitors employ on their Web sites to organize and present information on their products, develop an appreciation for their quality, and let these techniques inspire you on your own company's Web projects.

If you see something that is effective, or well-presented, and you can understand *why* it was done in this way, you are already more than halfway along in the process of improving upon this idea in your own execution. Let the best of these ideas guide your Web design, content, and process decisions.

In Web design, smaller is better: Like newspapers and magazines, the Web is a reader's medium. And on your company's Web site, text will always be the primary means of conveying information on your product and its benefits to the prospect. This fact should drive all of your Web design decisions. Images, such as icons, product shots, diagrams, tables, and link button graphics, should play a secondary role to the quality of the writing on your site, and should serve the understanding and readability of your site's text-based content, not detract from it.

Attractive on-screen fonts such as Arial, Verdana, and Times New Roman are now viewable by most major Web browsers, including Microsoft's Internet Explorer, the browser used by well over 80% of all Internet users. These fonts have essentially been "built in" to all Web browsers, so your Web developer can set the text and layout of your Web pages to look exactly as you want them to appear, specifying the font size and other attributes, such as leading, for your site text layout.

Text on Web pages looks best when set at 11 pixels (*not* points) for body text, and 14 pixels for larger subheads and headlines. While there are only a handful of universally-viewable typeface options available for designing text layouts on the Web, any capable Web page producer will know how to set up your Web pages using CSS stylesheets so your site's text layouts will appear exactly as you want it to be seen by users on your site.

Visual images, like product shots, graphic tables and charts, icons and logos, look best on the Web when displayed as small (1-1/2 to 2 inches wide), color images. And because the Web is a reader's medium, the text relating to each image should be placed closely alongside the image as a tight, narrow column.

Transferring your company's print colors to your Web site: If your company has already established a standard color scheme for the design of all of your company's print materials and advertising, the color choices used on your Web site should reflect this existing color scheme. If your company hasn't established its own standard color design, bear in mind that the same cool colors you see on television graphics and commercials—blues, greens, and dark reds—are also the best colors to use on the Web. These color choices also coincide with the same dark, cool, dignified colors used in most corporate design, such as the blues of General Motors and IBM, Xerox's burgundy, and Exxon Mobil Corp.'s dark red.

Figure 11-5:

Web Design Tips

- Form always follows function— design always follows site navigation

- Initial design and Web page format usually implemented by a designer working from your original pencil-and-paper spec

- During development, always work in quick prototypes of your Web pages—slap them together and try them out

- Graphic images and text: smaller is better

- Your site should look as good as your leading competitor's site

- "Cool" colors—blues, greens, dark reds—look better

- Verdana, Arial, and Times New Roman are attractive, universally-viewable typefaces

---

Trust Your Web Design and Production Team

Web designers can spend many hours, days even, agonizing over the smallest detail on a site, only to have the client make an offhand design change, without considering the fact that the Web designer likely had a very thoughtful and sound reason for making that design decision in the first place.

If you are fortunate enough to be working with talented Web developers on your team, and you are confident in your team's ability, don't make a snap judgment or speak out immediately with some suggestion for a change, without spending time to observe and consider what has just been shown to you. Take the time to review the newly-designed versions of your Web site and ask your Web design team why they made their choices. You may be pleasantly surprised to find your team may have anticipated user actions and design choices based on issues they have taken the time to uncover, consider, and resolve in their work—and that answer questions you *don't yet know to ask*. Show thoughtfulness and respect for the work of your Web design and development team, and your appreciation for their effort will be returned to you in the hard work, creativity and care they invest in your project.

Your Web Site's Multimedia Options: Video, Audio and Flash

Multimedia enhancements to your company's Web site, such as video, audio, and Flash graphics, can give your company's Web site tremendous additional sales appeal. A short, fast-paced video product demo with a tight, professional audio voiceover delivers tremendous sales impact on a Web page. Multimedia features, such as a video demo of your company's product, a short Flash graphic, or a brief audio voiceover file introducing your company, and played automatically for first-time visitors to your Web site, actively conveys the meaning of your company's products and their sales benefits to the user, without having to make them work too hard to read about it on your site.

Most companies never employ these powerful forms of media communication on their Web sites, or use them in trivial ways that don't convey meaningful information on their products or benefits. This is especially true for Macromedia Flash files, used on most company Web sites for little more than showing the novelty of a flying company logo, or other effect.

Web Video

When used to convey meaningful information on the benefits of your company's products, video can be a powerful and persuasive communications tool. On a broadband Internet connection, a short one- or two-minute video, properly set up for Web presentation, starts up almost instantaneously and plays smoothly without the bumps and glitches that were common in the Internet's early days of just a few years ago. Since, by now, most business Internet users access Web sites using higher-speed broadband connections and fast desktop computers, they're ready to see and hear the multimedia files you present to them.

It's unfortunate that video is not used very often on business-to-business Web sites, and when it's used, it's often pretty boring. For example, video on many business Web sites feature dull, talking-head speeches from the company CEO. Basic technical implementation of video on a Web site is another problem area. Videos are often placed on Web sites in file formats that require additional Web plug-in programs to view them. For this reason alone, many Web users have grown tired of having to hunt for an updated version of the latest streaming multimedia plug-in just to view a simple 30-second Web video, and will tune out if it's not easy for them to see the video with a single mouse click.

Examples of Web Site Video Applications

One or more video spots, integrated with your company's Web site, can be tremendous information and sales-boosters for your Web site. Inexpensive digital-video gear and desktop video editing systems put pro-quality video production techniques well within reach of most companies (more on this in Chapter 15). While production costs for a full-blown corporate video, such as a sales video or video news release can be expensive, a video doesn't have to be. Here are some applications where Web video can add substantial information and sales value to your company's Web site:

Product sales presentations and demos: A brief, one or two-minute video spot on your company's Web site that presents and explains your product's leading sales benefits, and shows your site's visitors how your product helps them solve their problems, can be extremely effective in boosting the sales appeal of your company and its products. Keep the production values simple and pay close attention to the quality of your script (see below);

Company home page intro: A short (about 30 seconds) introductory video, set to start automatically in a pop-up window when a new visitor accesses your company's Web site, tells first-time visitors what they need to know about your company. Control this presentation by placing a "cookie" in the user's Web browser (see further in this chapter), to determine whether or not a user is visiting your company's Web site for the first time, and to skip the automatic display of this video the next time the user links to your site;

Product applications: Live video of your product in action in real-world situations, combined with an informative audio presentation and supporting bullet-text copy points, adds depth and information value to your product's story. Better yet, you can add to the impact of your product's applications story by including live-video testimonials from your company's satisfied customers;

Technical and how-to explanation: Web video can add a whole new dimension to the presentation of complex, technically-oriented information on your company's Web site. For example, an animated product schematic or animated table with an explanatory audio soundtrack can communicate difficult-to-explain technologies and concepts more quickly, and with less effort required on the part of Web users, than multiple text screens or printable "white papers" in Adobe acrobat .PDF format. Video can also help your company improve its after-the-sale customer satisfaction, by providing customers with Web-based how-to video tutorials, video demonstrations of the product in use, and other instruction for using your company's products.

Web Video Content: All You Need is Simple Presentation, and a Great Script

One of the little-known secrets of video production is that the most important part of any video presentation is not the video, but the *audio*—the spoken word. Next time you watch TV, try watching it with the volume turned all the way down and you'll realize that the bulk of the information contained in any video presentation is communicated by its spoken audio soundtrack.

Start your Web video out with a great script: The spoken audio soundtrack carries the content of any video presentation, and every effective audio presentation begins with a very good script. The essential elements of good corporate video scriptwriting and audio presentations are covered in greater detail in Chapter 15, but the process of writing effective, persuasive audio scripts is very similar to the process of writing effective print advertising copy described in Chapter 4.

Stay as closely involved in the Web video production process for your company's Web site as you are for the production of any print ad campaign or other deliverable. To do this, you must be involved in the Web video production process at the script level. Here's what to watch for when reviewing audio narration voiceover scripts prepared by your ad agency or video producer for a Web video project:

> **Lead with your product's most important benefit:** Skip the use of video eye candy or other introductory video effects, and dive right into the major, compelling benefit of your company's product or service to the listener. You only have a few seconds to engage your viewers, so the script of your Web video should be "front-loaded" with a bold, clear statement of your product's most compelling benefit to the listener;

> **Tell the "why" and show the "how:"** Tell the listener, in extremely clear and simple language, why they should use your company's product or service.

> As in all of your company's promotional copy, keep your script's copy free of strange technical jargon (such as "network-centric"), tired buzz phrases ("an industry compliant, total solution"), and other overused phrases that have become the bone-tired substitutes for persuasive marketing sales copy these days.

> Also, the more complex or technically-oriented your product, the simpler the explanation of your product must be—even if your script speaks to a technically-minded audience. A technically-oriented person may know the technology and terms of art of your industry, but he or she is also very busy, and may not be giving their full attention to your video. Break down the use of your company's product into a series of individual, easy-to-explain steps, and explain how the listener benefits at each step. Here, the visual images in your video are especially important because they must support the spoken "how" audio of your script: Show your company's products in use, and explain to the listener how they benefit, by using bulleted-text, and on-screen captions as needed to support your audio narration;

> **Use a friendly, personal tone:** Because of bandwidth limitations and PC screen layouts, your Web video will likely be seen in a small, 320-by-240 pixel screen on your company's Web site. The small size of your video presentation has a way of magnifying any pomposity in the tone or substance of your script when heard by the listener. When overseeing the scriptwriting process on your Web video, make sure the tone of your script is friendly and simple.

To paraphrase the old producer's adage from the 1950s' "Golden Age" of television, your script should read and sound as if your announcer is an invited guest in the prospect's office, telling your product's story and its benefits. This story should be told in your script as if it were being told by one person (your narrator) to another (your prospect), without pretense, complication, or cleverness.

When reading a script, read it aloud: When you receive a draft of your Web video's script from your ad agency or Web producer, read it aloud: Is the tone natural, friendly, and conversational? Does it sound as if it's one person speaking to another? Most important, after reading the script out loud, do you believe that its presentation of your product, its uses, and its benefits would be readily understood by someone who is listening to your video for the very first time? As with every other marketing deliverable seen by those outside your company, an important part of your job as a marketing manager is to train yourself to "see things with new eyes." For this is how viewers of your Web video would see (and hear) your company's sales presentations.

Which Comes First, the Video, or the Script?

Like most visually-oriented people, video producers think in images, not words. Visual thinking is fine for purely consumer-oriented video work, such as television commercials or music videos, but when there is a need to explain complex topics and communicate persuasive selling arguments to a business audience, the script—and the narrated audio soundtrack produced from this script—always comes first. Work with your ad agency or video producer to write the best script you can, and the rest will follow. Once you have a great script, the live video and other visual images fall quickly into place.

Web Video Production: The Video Track

After you and your Web production team finalize the script for your Web site's video, the next step is to develop and execute the visual imagery, such as live-action video, text, superimposed graphics, and other visual effects to accompany the underlying, narrated soundtrack of your video. Since the audio portion of your video (i.e., the spoken word), carries most of the burden of informing and persuading your viewer, the purpose of the video track is to support the informational sales copy points made by your video's narrator, creating a strong, positive, professional impression of your company and its products or services.

Producing Web video for computer display: Your Web site's video is a presentation specifically intended to supplement, and complement, the rest of the content on your company's Web site. From a production standpoint, this means that videos produced exclusively for your Web site should be conceived, produced, and implemented solely for display on a Web site and, by extension, a personal computer.

For example, your Web site's video will be displayed in a screen size much smaller than television's standard 640-by-480 line screen size, and at slower speeds than television's standard 29.97 frames-per-second (fps) frame rates. The flashy video effects that look great on television, or on a big-screen display, don't come off as well when resized for the Web's smaller screen size. This means that video produced for display on your company's Web site should not attempt to mimic the high-end production values usually seen in corporate promotional videos displayed on your conference room's 42-inch flat-panel television. Most of the time these effects can make your video look like a weak version of your company's standard corporate promotional video, and not an effective sales video developed for the new medium of the Internet.

When Thinking Web Video, Think: "Slide Show"

Where the on-screen text content and images of your site's Web pages provide site visitors with the opportunity to read about your company, its products, and their benefits, your site's Web video should *repeat* and *reinforce* this sales and informational content, using the power of the spoken word, aided by moving images and bulleted text, to make it easier for viewers to understand your product and its appeal, and to move them one step closer to buying your company's product.

When discussing the look and production layout of your Web video with your ad agency or Web producer, encourage them to think of your Web video as a slide show or PowerPoint presentation, accompanied by a well-written, professionally-narrated, audio soundtrack.

The shot list: Since their lower production values make Web videos less of a "production" than a full-blown corporate video, there is no need for your ad agency or video producer to create elaborate storyboards during this step of the process, as they would in a conventional video project. All you need to see at this stage are the graphic screens used to illustrate the presentation, and to give you some idea of how the various parts of your video will look, and a "shot list," an item-by-item list of live-action video shots (clips), still images, and visual effects that will be needed for your project. The individual video clips and other images on the shot list are then matched precisely to the underlying sentences of the narrated script of your Web video. An example of a shot list and script are shown in **Figure 11-6**.

Graphic formats for Web video: During the time your script is being written, your Web video development team's graphic designer should be preparing the graphic screen formats for the various segments of your Web video. These include:

- **Intro and ending screen designs:** For most projects, these are the "bookends" that open and close your Web video, and usually feature your company's logo against a dark, solid color background. If any video effects are used, these are the places they are likely to appear;

Figure 11-6:

Video Script and Shot List—Your starting point for Web video projects

Your Video's Script and Shot List *(below) help you and your team develop and organize video projects for your company's Web site*

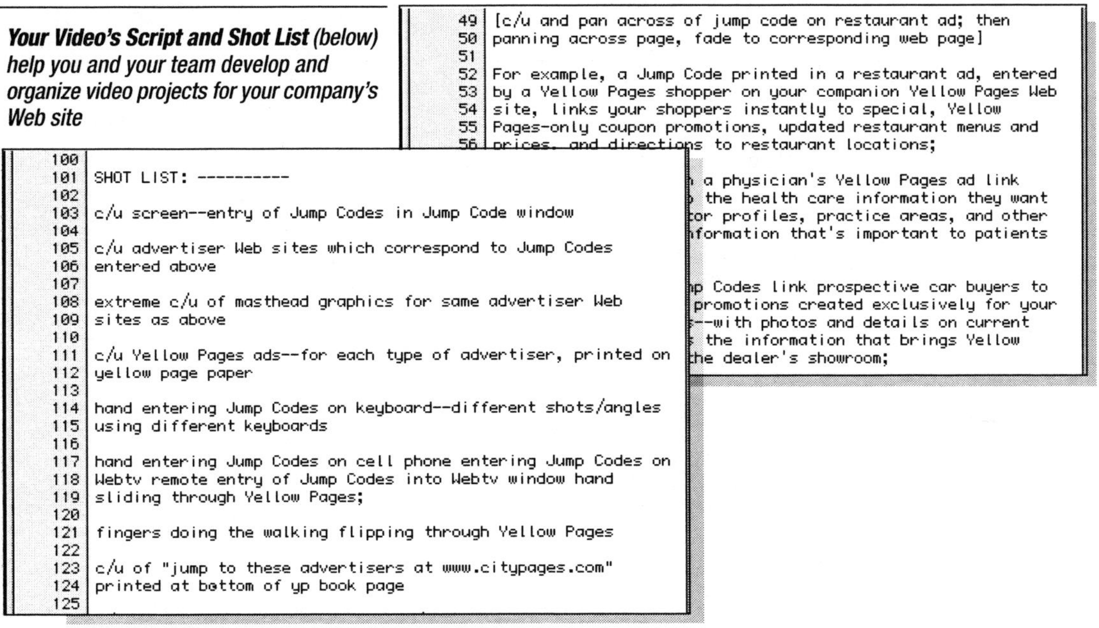

```
49  [c/u and pan across of jump code on restaurant ad; then
50  panning across page, fade to corresponding web page]
51
52  For example, a Jump Code printed in a restaurant ad, entered
53  by a Yellow Pages shopper on your companion Yellow Pages Web
54  site, links your shoppers instantly to special, Yellow
55  Pages-only coupon promotions, updated restaurant menus and
56  prices, and directions to restaurant locations;
```

```
100
101  SHOT LIST: ----------
102
103  c/u screen--entry of Jump Codes in Jump Code window
104
105  c/u advertiser Web sites which correspond to Jump Codes
106  entered above
107
108  extreme c/u of masthead graphics for same advertiser Web
109  sites as above
110
111  c/u Yellow Pages ads--for each type of advertiser, printed on
112  yellow page paper
113
114  hand entering Jump Codes on keyboard--different shots/angles
115  using different keyboards
116
117  hand entering Jump Codes on cell phone entering Jump Codes on
118  Webtv remote entry of Jump Codes into Webtv window hand
119  sliding through Yellow Pages;
120
121  fingers doing the walking flipping through Yellow Pages
122
123  c/u of "jump to these advertisers at www.citypages.com"
124  printed at bottom of yp book page
125
```

(partially obscured text:)
```
  a physician's Yellow Pages ad link
  the health care information they want
or profiles, practice areas, and other
nformation that's important to patients

p Codes link prospective car buyers to
promotions created exclusively for your
r--with photos and details on current
 the information that brings Yellow
he dealer's showroom;
```

- **Caption screen format:** Most Web videos are accompanied by superimposed captions at the bottom of the screen, highlighting the key selling points being made by the narrator of your video's audio soundtrack. Ask your video designer to work up a sample template for this screen (with dummy text inserted for a caption), so you can see how these screens will look;

- **Split-screen video and bulleted text:** For segments of your video requiring in-depth explanation, or at points where your script's copy builds a point-by-point case, such as a spoken enumeration of your product's sales benefits, a split-screen format combining bulleted text and live video can be very effective. For example, a "60/40" split screen format, with a dark, solid-color background covering 60% of one side of the screen, and live video or still images displayed in the remaining 40% area on the other side, is a very effective way of displaying a series of brief, bulleted text points in support of your soundtrack's spoken script (see **Figure 11-7**). This sizing works especially well when produced in 16:9 letterbox format (see below). The cut-in points (the changes from one video clip to another) for the clips in the live video running on the live video side of the screen can also be synchronized to support each new text point, or the live video can continue to roll on at its

Figure 11-7:

Letterbox (16:9) Video Format—A versatile digital video format for both Web sites and DVD

Letterbox Digital Video Format, used on product sales videos combining text sidebar bullets for sales copy, is a versatile format for displaying your video both on your Web site, and on DVD

A New Profit Center for Your Yellow Pages

For Advertisers:
• Faster Buyer Response
• Promotion Flexibility
• Competitive Display Edge

own pace. You and your project's video editor can experiment with different timing and editing options for bulleted text in this screen format;

• **Special effects:** Developing special effects for video is an extremely expensive and time consuming task, and for the most part, they are unnecessary for Web video projects. The flashy special video effects that look so impressive on television and larger-screen displays will be lost on viewers when displayed in the smaller screen sizes for video on your Web site, so use them with a very light touch, if at all. Video used on your Web site should enhance your site visitors' understanding of your company's products and their benefits, not distract them with MTV-style video effects. There's also a great temptation on the part of those who work with video to become overly attached to special effects, and to produce them on any project just because they can do it. Try to keep these impulses under control among your Web development team, without stifling their creative energy or enthusiasm;

• **Web video screen size and placement:** Unlike conventional television-based video production, there are no standard screen sizes for Web video. This gives your video production team a wide range of creative options for setting the screen size of your project. You can produce your Web video to fill a uniquely-sized area within a Web page, or the video can be displayed in its own pop-up window. You can also produce your Web video in a letterbox format (also known as "16:9," and pronounced "sixteen by nine"), an

---

Figure 11-8:

The Desktop and Digital Video Revolution — Lower costs and unlimited creative options

---

The past few years have seen tremendous growth in the use of Macintosh and PC-based desktop video production and editing systems, fueled by the introduction of digital-video cameras, with image quality closely rivaling that of much more expensive, professional-grade broadcast equipment.

Desktop video production and editing systems and software, such as Apple's Final Cut Pro and Adobe's After Effects, give your Web video production team the editing and video production capabilities that, just a few short years ago, were only available to those companies that could afford the services of a high-priced corporate video production outfit. Today, a $10,000 desktop digital video editing system can

produce better video, in a shorter period of time, than older, analog-bound editing suites of just a few short years ago, costing over $100,000.

To marketing managers, this revolutionary drop in the cost of video production provides two major advantages. First, it provides you with many more opportunities to utilize video on your company's Web site, whenever you believe that a sales presentation or other marketing communications project is best expressed in the medium of video. Second, and just as important, video producers using desktop digital systems can often pass their lower overhead costs to you on video projects. (Photos from www.panasonic.com and www.apple.com)

---

attractive screen format used to display movies on DVD. This rectangular letterbox format looks good on personal computer screens, and also works better when using a screen format that combines bulleted text and live video.

If, at some future time, your Web videos are to be displayed on conventional 640-by-480 television screens, they should be scaled down to a proportional measure of the 640-by-480 screen standard for Web display; usually half-scale (320-by-240), or a smaller proportional measurement.

What About Flash?

Macromedia's Flash, a popular multimedia file format for the Web, enables Web multimedia producers to create moving text and image effects that can also be combined with underlying audio soundtracks. Because Flash files pack a lot of multimedia action into a very small file size, they load very quickly into the user's Web browser. Another factor leading to the widespread use of Flash files on Web sites is the fact that the software "player," that allows Flash files to be run automatically when a Web page is displayed, is fully integrated into the newer versions of the most popular Web browsers, such as Internet Explorer, Mozilla, and Netscape. This means that a Flash file can run automatically when

Figure 11-9:

Using Flash on Your Company's Web Site—The best use of Flash is for display of text, not splashy graphics

Use Flash to Display simple, text-only selling points or other rotating announcements (as shown in the "Comdex" tab on right).

Using Flash for displaying text in slide-show fashion puts your key sales messages in front of site users, and helps them to understand key concepts and information in a shorter period of time

displayed in the user's Web browser, without forcing the user to go through the steps of selecting and running a separate Flash player program to view the file.

For these reasons, Flash has become the most used and, some would say, misused, Web multimedia format. This is because it has been used mostly to create flashy introductory graphic "splash screens," and other meaningless and irrelevant animated graphics on Web sites, causing the vast majority of Web users to condition themselves to either ignore Flash files, or to impatiently click through them to get through to a site's main content screen. In short, Flash has been used on most Web sites more to satisfy the egos of Web site designers and their clients than to improve the Web user's understanding of the information being presented on these sites.

This is unfortunate, because Flash has tremendous potential for helping users to better and more quickly understand the concepts being explained on the Web sites they're viewing. For example, the time required for Web users to grasp a complex technical concept or application surrounding a company's product can be dramatically shortened by the use of an animated Flash slide show combining bulleted text, graphic images, and voiceover narration into a short, slide show-like Flash animation. Likewise, a company's basic spoken sales presentation can be made into a compelling, Flash-based animated screen on a Web page, featuring a professionally-narrated audio soundtrack synchronized to the visual presentation of product images and bulleted text points.

Any Web-based presentation where you see the need to shorten the time it takes for the user to understand the meaning of the concept you are trying to communicate can be enhanced by implementing a Flash-format presentation, in addition to the conventional, on-screen text and images used on your company's Web site.

Audio on Your Web Site

Audio-only playback of spoken audio soundtracks is a rarely-used feature on business Web sites, but there can be some interesting uses for audio here. For example, a quick-loading .MP3-format audio file can be "embedded" in any Web page, and set to play automatically for new visitors to your company's Web site, providing first-time site visitors with a brief, spoken description of the types of products or services your company offers, announcements of your company's new products, or new product promotions.

Audio files are also helpful for providing your site visitors with additional, spoken instructions. For example, audio on your Web site's on-screen order form can be set up to give users additional spoken instructions for ordering products from your company's Web site. You can also add spoken information and instructions to other areas of your Web site, wherever additional explanation would be helpful to your site's users: E-mail newsletter entry screens, entry and registration screens for software downloads, or special product pricing announcements.

Audio and "cookies:" Audio files used on Web sites should only be played when a user views that page for the first time—and not on any of their subsequent visits to that page. This is done by using "cookies" placed from a simple CGI script (more on these two topics further in this chapter) to determine if the user is viewing this page for the first time, or if they are a return visitor. This ensures that your site visitors won't be annoyed by having to hear the same audio over and over again each time they link to this page on your site.

Establishing Connections with Your Web Site's Visitors: Your Site's E-Mail Newsletter

One of the true benefits of the Internet is the power it gives to your company to establish an ongoing communications dialogue with your prospects, customers, industry media contacts, and other interested site visitors. One of the most effective ways to establish and build an ongoing connection to your company's prospects and customers is to create a free e-mail newsletter, sent on a periodic basis to prospects and customers who sign up to receive it.

If you can make it interesting and informative to subscribers, an e-mail newsletter can help your company attract and build an online following of interested prospects, customers, key industry contacts, trade media editors, and other influential industry figures who have an interest in your company's products or services. By establishing a regular, open communications channel to these online subscribers, your company's e-mail newsletter also provides you with the opportunity to promote your company's products and services by informing and educating these online readers.

Figure 11-10:

Audio Voiceovers for Web Pages—Spoken instructions played on Web pages help site users

Audio Voiceover Sound Files, set to play automatically when Web pages are displayed, add tremendous information value in certain Web applications, such as user registration screens (shown on right), and for other uses where additional instructions or explanation would be helpful to your site visitors

Topics and Content for Your Company's E-Mail Newsletter

Here are a few examples of topics and content you can include in your company's e-mail newsletter:

General applications and advice: Everyone's interested in any information and advice that can help them do their job in a better, more efficient, or less costly, way. Make a habit of bookmarking interesting news items and feature articles that you read online in your industry, and feature these links in the next issue of your e-mail newsletter, prefacing each link with a short headline (see **Figure 11-11**). You can also publish brief, one-sentence capsule descriptions of these articles in your newsletter, along with clickable links to the online article sources;

Novel/noteworthy applications of your company's products: Readers are interested in new and novel applications for products in their industry, especially if these applications give them ideas for managing their own tasks more productively. If, for example, your company sells productivity-boosting systems used by industrial manufacturers in their assembly-line processes, and one of your customers has developed an especially novel use of your company's system, this is information that could be published in your e-mail newsletter;

Industry and market opinion: Top executives in your company have their own viewpoints and opinions on the latest trends in your industry. The best of these opinions may be of interest to your e-mail newsletter readers. For example, if

Figure 11.11:

E-Mail Newsletters—Establish a free E-Mail newsletter for interested visitors to your company's Web site

E-Mail Newsletters, sent in either plain text, or more visually appealing HTML format, are a low-key but effective way to open a communication channel to your customers and prospects, by sending informative news of your company's products and services, embedded with promotional messages on your company's products

Text Format	HTML Format
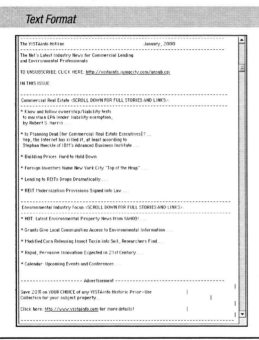	

your company's VP of Engineering has some interesting views on technical trends in the industry served by your company, these remarks can be hammered together into a concise, two or three-paragraph blurb for your next newsletter issue. Your e-mail newsletter readers will find these insider comments and observations on your company's industry or marketplace to be interesting and readable;

Industry events: Publish a series of one-line reminders of upcoming industry trade shows, conferences, seminars, or other professional development opportunities your readers may find of interest, with links to each event's Web site.

How to work your company's promotional information into your e-mail newsletter: Promotion of your company's products is, of course, the main reason to publish an e-mail newsletter. However, you'll disappoint readers if your newsletter appears to be overly self-serving, or contains too many promotional messages from your company. Readers will delete your e-mail next time, or "unsubscribe" from your newsletter's mailing list, so you must work promotional content into your newsletter with a very light touch. For each issue of your newsletter, limit promotional announcements to no more than three very short, one- or two-line mentions of a new product, special price promotion, or other sales copy (see examples on **Figure 11-11**). Place a clickable Web link after each of these short sales copy lines so readers can link to the Web page on your site featuring more extensive information on the product or promotion being described. These short, promotional announcements can be interspersed throughout the body text of your e-mail newsletter.

Keep it simple: The task of writing and producing a monthly e-mail newsletter needn't be an elaborate or time-consuming project. A concise, readable newsletter, consisting of a minimum of 8-10 short paragraphs, with links to other referenced Web sites (including links to your company's Web site), can be written and produced by you, your ad agency, or marketing consultant in around 4-6 hours each month. Keep your newsletter informative and useful, keep the sales promotion light-handed, and readers—your prospects and customers—will look forward to receiving it in their e-mail each month. And they won't forget your company when the time comes to make their purchasing decision, or reorder from your company.

Implementing an E-Mail Newsletter on Your Company's Web Site

Collecting e-mail addresses for your company's newsletter: One of the most effective ways to provide site visitors with the opportunity to subscribe to your company's free e-mail newsletter, especially during its launch, is to use a pop-up Web browser window, controlled by a CGI script (more on this below) that "pops up" over your Web site's home page when the user first links to your site.

This pop-up window contains promotional copy announcing the newsletter, describing its content and sample features, with an entry form for site visitors to fill in their e-mail addresses (see **Figure 11-12**). It's also very important to let would-be subscribers know that your company will not be renting out or otherwise using the subscriber's e-mail address for any other purpose. While you could also ask for other information in your entry form, such as name, title, company, etc., many users will find this to be annoying and intrusive. Your company will sign up many more subscribers if your entry form only asks for the user's e-mail address, so it pays to limit your marketer's desire to obtain more prospect information here.

The pop-up window should be controlled by a CGI script that places and reads a "cookie" in the user's Web browser, and blocks display of the pop-up window for site visitors who've already subscribed to your newsletter. This keeps the recurring pop-up entry window out of the faces of users who've already subscribed, the next time they link to your company's Web site.

Distributing your e-mail newsletter: The Web programmer on your site development team will utilize a bulk automailer program that automates the task of mailing many

Figure 11.12:

E-Mail Signup Window—A pop-up window on your site's home page makes it easy for site visitors to subscribe

Use a Pop-Up Window on your site's home page to get the most subscriptions to your company's free E-Mail newsletter.

Use a cookie-setting script to turn off this pop-up for site visitors who have already signed up for this newsletter

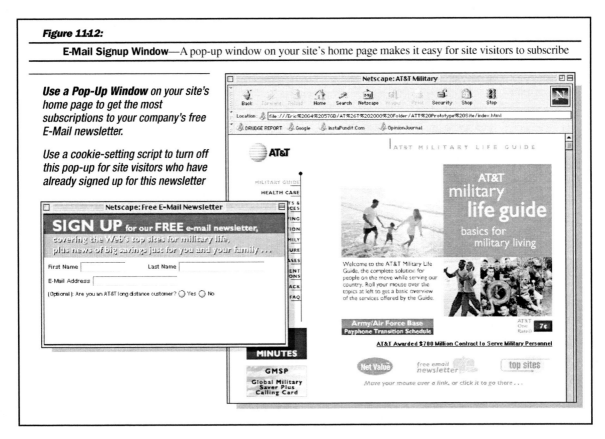

thousands, or hundreds of thousands, of e-mail newsletter copies to your online subscribers. This bulk e-mail distribution program should also include an "unsubscribe" link to enable users to remove their e-mail addresses from your subscriber database.

Promote your e-mail newsletter all over your company's Web site: Promote your e-mail newsletter by placing permanent links on the left-hand sidebar and/or bottom-page text links on every page of your company's site, so site visitors can easily subscribe to your company's newsletter at any time, wherever they are on your site.

CGI Scripting and Your Company's Web Site: What Marketing Managers Should Know

CGI, the abbreviation for "Common Gateway Interface," is a generic term describing the variety of ways Web sites can be programmed, or "scripted," to handle or process information, beyond the simple display of Web pages.

CGI scripts are computer programs, stored on your Web site's host computer, or embedded in the HTML text of your site's Web pages. CGI scripts can be written in a number of software languages, but the most common CGI scripting language used on the Internet is called PERL (the acronym for "Practical Extraction and Report Language"), a popular scripting language used by many Web programmers for CGI programming projects.

For example, CGI script that writes, places, reads, and processes cookies (see below) for a site visitor can create a Web page that's custom-tailored to the preferences of that user, based on the search keywords or product numbers they just entered into your Web site's online catalog. CGI scripts are also used to collect and store database entry information from users who order products from your site, or to collect and store a user's e-mail address in a database on your company's server for your site's e-mail newsletter feature.

Although there are a growing number of "shrink-wrapped," ready-to-use software applications that streamline many of the database and site automation functions that previously required custom CGI programming, there are still many instances where your Web programmer must write custom CGI scripts to handle a specific Web-based marketing application for your company's Web site.

In your own company's Web marketing applications, CGI scripts are used most often in combination with cookies to "identify" a user by the links they've selected on your company's Web site, to tailor the display of Web pages for that user's buying preferences, or to display different pages to the user based on the information that is passed to the CGI script by the cookie placed in the user's Web browser. CGI scripts are also used to build databases, or link to your company's existing product inventory or order entry databases.

Although off-the-shelf applications and SQL databases have supplanted many Web database functions that were formerly developed using CGI scripts, CGI is still very useful for creating simple databases on your company's Web site. Whenever you're faced with the task of developing a relatively simple database—such as a simple Web survey entry form for gathering information from prospects who visit your company's Web site—the Web programmer on your Web development team will usually write a short CGI script to handle this task.

Using Cookies on Your Company's Web Site

Web "cookies" are alpha and numeric character strings generated by your Web site's CGI scripts, and written to a file on your site visitors' hard drives, where they can be stored for a fairly long time. Think of a cookie as a kind of unique "serial number" your Web site can apply to each and every user who visits your Web site, which can be written, read, and processed by your site's CGI scripts. A cookie can be automatically, invisibly written to or read from the user's Web browser by CGI scripts on your company's Web site, in response to any action a user takes on your site, such as clicking on a product link, or entering a search keyword.

Each letter or number in the cookie can represent an action taken by the user on your Web site, in effect "profiling" a user's activity on your site. By reading cookies

Figure 11.13:

Cookies Set in a Web Browser—Many Web sites write cookies in most Internet users' Web browsers

Cookies are short strings of text, like serial numbers, set by programs, called scripts, on Web sites, and written into a special file on a site visitor's Web browser.

A list of Web sites that have written cookies to a Web user's browser is shown in the top part of the screen on the right. The browser cookie information set by amazon.com during a visit to the Amazon site is displayed at the bottom of this screen

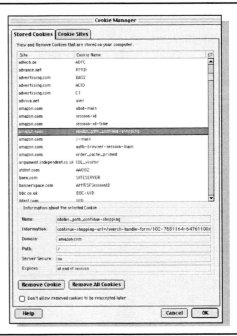

placed in a user's Web browser while that user is browsing specific items in your company's online catalog, your site's CGI scripts can identify that user's individual preferences—for example, identifying the specific products the user is browsing—by reading the information encoded in the cookie.

When combined with CGI scripts, cookies can give prospects custom-tailored information from your company's Web site. For example, if a user visits an online catalog site selling shoes and boots, and links to the "men's hiking boots" section of this site, a CGI program on this site can place a cookie in this user's Web browser during his initial site visit. Then, the next time the shopper visits this site, by reading the information in the cookie that was previously placed in the user's Web browser by the script, the script then dynamically generates a Web page featuring the latest sales promotions on men's hiking boots, created especially for this user.

Your company's use of cookies can be quite extensive, and can provide a great deal of highly personalized Web page customization features for your Web site's visitors. For example, Amazon.com makes extensive use of cookies placed in users' Web browsers to track each Web user's perusal—and preferences for—books, music and other merchandise on its site, dynamically building a customized Web page, in real time, specifically tailored to the subject area or type of merchandise items the user was just browsing. The next time you search for books on Amazon.com, notice that the pages display recommendations of book titles related to the topic areas you just browsed on the Amazon site. These new, personalized pages were dynamically created just for you. On Amazon, it's all done with cookies—and some very powerful dynamic Web page-creation programs working with back-end databases on Amazon.com's Web servers.

Adobe Acrobat .PDF Files

Using Adobe's .PDF (Portable Document Format) files, you can provide visitors to your company's Web site with high-quality, printable marketing materials and other documents. Site visitors can download these files from your Web site and view them on-screen, or print them on their own laser or inkjet printers.

The main advantage to .PDF files is that any of your company's printed marketing materials, when converted into .PDF format, can look as good as their original, printed versions (with the exception being that most .PDF files will be printed by Web users on their black-and-white laser printers). A .PDF file looks just as good on anyone else's personal computer screen or printer as it does on yours, regardless of the user's operating system or printer type.

For marketing managers, the two main advantages of .PDF "document portability" are presentation and speed. You control the appearance of your company's printed materials, providing interested prospects who visit your Web site with printable versions of your company's marketing materials that look almost as good as their original, printed versions. This helps you avoid the design limitations and other inconsistencies you'd encounter if you attempted to duplicate the design of these printed materials as Web pages. The most important advantage to .PDFs is that prospects who visit your company's Web site can download any of your company's print-ready marketing materials almost instantaneously, view them on screen, or print them out, without having to wait a week for them to arrive in the mail.

In many instances, providing prospects with your company's printed sales materials—even as black-and-white pages they can print from their own laser printers—helps shorten the sales cycle by giving prospects who visit your company's Web site enough sales information to address their initial questions about your products, before they are contacted by one of your company's sales reps.

Selecting Printed Marketing Materials for Use as Adobe Acrobat .PDF Files on Your Web Site

Which of your company's printed materials are best suited for distribution as .PDF files on your company's Web site? The obvious choices are your company's printed marketing materials, such as brochures, sales flyers, etc., but any printed material produced by your company that has immediate information value to your prospects and other site visitors can be made available on your Web site in .PDF form, including:

Figure 11.14:

Common Cookie Myths

There's still a great deal of unfounded fear and misunderstanding concerning the alleged privacy threats posed to Web users by a company's use of cookies on its Web site. At some point in your work as a marketing manager, you may be confronted by your company's prospects and customers on some of these issues, so it's important that you have the answers to these most common misconceptions about cookies:

Myth #1—"A cookie can steal my e-mail address off my computer:" To the contrary (and to the disappointment of many marketers), there is no way that the interaction between cookies, your company's Web site, its back-end CGI programming, and the user's Web-browser can reveal that user's Internet e-mail address to the owner of the Web site that placed the cookie in the user's browser. Cookies can be written only to a specific file on the user's hard drive, and once written, there is no other way that a site's CGI cookie-placing programs can "look around" on the user's hard drive for any other information;

Myth #2—"Companies can steal information off my computer's hard drive by using cookies:" Further to Myth #1, the software controlling a Web browser makes it impossible for the programming that reads and writes cookies to do anything else but read and write this cookie's character string into a single, specific file on the user's hard drive. While there have been several well-known instances where computer viruses have hijacked certain e-mail programs to play havoc with users' e-mail address files, or to crash a user's hard drive, it's simply not possible to do this by reading and writing cookies to or from a user's Web browser;

Myth #3—"Companies can use cookies to swap private information about me:" A Web site owner (your company) can only read or write cookies placed into the user's Web browser by your own company's Web site. Neither your company, nor anyone else, can read, write, swap, or otherwise access cookie information placed into a user's browser by any other Web sites visited by the user. Also, the information contained in cookies is a string of codes that only makes sense to the back-end CGI programs that operate on the Web site of the company that placed the cookie to the user's hard drive. Even if cookies could be revealed, they would be indecipherable by the other Web site, because there would be no way to decode the information in the cookie.

Company product brochures: Most of your company's printed brochures can be easily converted to Adobe Acrobat .PDF files just as they are, with no resizing or other conversion necessary. When converted into .PDF files, the added design elements of your company's printed brochures, such as photographs, product illustrations, technical diagrams, schematics, fonts, and layout enhance the quality of your company's sales presentation. Print materials give prospects a better visual impression of your company and its products than the most well-designed Web pages. Even when they can see the same sales information presented on your company's Web site, your interested prospects will always have an inborn need to "take a look at the brochure" before they buy—*so give them what they want;*

Your product's technical spec sheets: If your company sells products requiring extensive technical explanation and specifications, your prospects will want to see and print this information immediately, and read it at their convenience. If you make all of your company's printed spec sheets and other technical data sheets available on your Web site for immediate download by interested prospects, you'll save your company time and money, and you'll also help your sales reps by providing interested potential buyers with much of the background information they need to know, prior to their purchasing decision;

Product user manuals and instruction sheets: In addition to being a handy and convenient resource for your existing customers, posting your company's product instruction manuals as .PDFs to your Web site is also a compelling sales tool for prospects. A well-written, helpful, informative user manual, or well-designed product instruction sheet, not only helps your prospects answer some of the questions they may have on your company's products, but actually helps your prospects visualize how they would use your company's product—always a very good thing;

Dealer and distributor sales materials: .PDFs provide your company's dealers, distributors, and outside sales reps with the convenience of being able to download and print your company's sales flyers, catalog sheets, and the other materials they need, whenever they need them from your company's Web site. This is also an effective way to attract new dealers for your company's products, since it demonstrates the quality of your company's sales and marketing presentation;

As you can see, the marketing potential provided by converting your company's existing printed materials to .PDF format goes well beyond the most obvious, initial notion of posting your company's printed sales brochures to your Web site. The more information you provide for prospects and other interested visitors to your company's Web site, the more you'll improve your site's power to sell your company's products.

The Final Step: Testing, Staging, and Launching Your Company's Web Site

The final stage of any Web development project involves thorough testing of your company's new Web site, so you and your team can execute a smooth, reasonably uneventful launch of your new site. These steps also apply to the testing and launch of new site pages or features, if you are modifying or enhancing an established site.

As your Web site quickly evolves from your first, rough spec, to the first prototype, and then on to each generation of prototype, quickly evolving into its final, finished form, you and your Web development team must perform several key execution steps before bringing your company's Web site "live" on the Internet.

"Staging" your Web site: Once your Web site project is almost complete, and has been tested as thoroughly as possible by you and your Web development team, your site can be moved to a password-protected server location, where it can be tested by a larger circle of people inside, and outside, your company. These individuals include your company management, staff, and other outside business partners, such as key dealers, a major distributor, a joint-venture partner, or others whom you believe have a need to see the Web site before it moves into full public view on the Internet.

What to Test

The purpose of this final stage of testing, which can be performed in about one week, is to uncover and fix any unexpected technical bugs, content glitches, and site navigation or usability issues, such as:

- **Wrong, missing, or dead site links;**
- **Bugs in order entry forms and associated back-end software;**
- **Typos, misspellings, and factual errors in Web site text and promotional copy;**
- **Miscellaneous formatting problems, dropped text, or missing graphic images on Web pages**

At this stage it's also assumed that you and your Web development team have been continuously checking and testing your site during its development, catching the more obvious or major problems that always come up during this stage. Therefore the purpose of this final stage of testing is to trap any remaining bugs, or resolve any other problems that may be uncovered by bringing more people into your project.

You are the point of contact for testing: As you bring more people into this final testing stage, however, keep control of the process by acting as the sole point of contact for "bug reports" and all other comments and suggestions for the project. By acting as the gatekeeper for testing, you can separate the legitimate fixes that need to be made on the project from the other, less useful, comments or suggestions you are also likely to receive. You do not want your testers to be peppering other members of your Web development team with bug reports or, even worse, suggestions for unworkable or off-the-wall site changes that needlessly delay the execution of your project.

In this respect, final site testing is very much like circulating a final draft of a display advertising campaign, print brochure, or any other marketing deliverable. As you evaluate the comments and suggestions you receive from people who are testing your company's Web site during this final stage, keep your Web site project moving forward by learning how to identify and separate the more useful and important testing comments from the many arbitrary, irrelevant, or unnecessary suggestions that will also come your way. Remember that the purpose of this final testing stage is to resolve any final, unforeseen problems in your Web site under its current design; not to hamstring your project with a series of major, 11th-hour design changes.

Do-It-Yourself Web Site Testing

In most cases, you'll be able to enlist the aid of several people, both inside and outside your company, to assist in the final testing of your Web site, but you can never be completely certain that they will test it as thoroughly as you want them to. Unlike large technology companies, who can devote entire departments to the task of testing their Web sites, most small to mid-sized companies must rely on an ad-hoc, informal group of "regular people" for testing.

Final testing of your new Web site project is another task where you must assume the final responsibility, because, in the end, problems with your company's Web site usually turn into marketing problems for you. You must not only be actively involved in the Web site testing process, you must assure yourself that your Web project has been tested as thoroughly as possible. And the only way to gain this assurance is to do it yourself.

How—and What—to Test

There is no mystery to the Web site testing process, and no special skills are required. Testing a Web site requires thoroughness, attention to detail, and devotion of sufficient "quality time" to the process. Here are some guidelines to follow when testing a Web site on your own:

Test every link, from every page: Starting from the home page of your Web site, click on every sidebar, and every top and bottom navigation link, making sure these links go to the pages they're supposed to go on your site. Think of the structure of your Web site as being like that of a tree, and test your site as if you were climbing this tree: Start from your site's home page (the "trunk"), click on each of its main sections ("limbs"), and then to all the "branches"— each and every sequential page on your site. Take careful note of any site navigation links you invariably find that link you to the wrong page, or nowhere at all. Of course, this happens more often on larger site projects having many individual links and pages;

Check browser compatibility: Since Microsoft's Internet Explorer Web browser (IE) accounts for 80% or more of the market share for all Web browsers, the lion's share of your testing should be done using a recent version of IE. Market share of the Web's second-most popular browser, Netscape Navigator, has declined substantially over the past few years, and is slipping fast—with the exception of America Online (AOL) subscribers, where Navigator is used as AOL's default Web browser (AOL acquired Netscape some years ago, and has integrated the Netscape Navigator browser into the AOL service). So while most of your testing should be done using Internet Explorer, you should also test your company's Web site using a recent version of Netscape Navigator, since it is also likely your site will be visited by AOL subscribers, even in business-to-business markets.

Check your site on both browsers, making sure that font sizes used on your pages aren't too small when viewed on Netscape or AOL browsers. This is a common problem for the growing number of sites utilizing CSS ("Cascading Style Sheets"), a Web design technique that allows for more uniform display of text on Web pages seen by site viewers, but one that is not well implemented in Netscape browsers.

This doesn't mean you should twist your development effort around to accommodate the small minority of Web users who will be viewing your site on Netscape, and the handful of other obscure Web browsers. Make your Web site look and work well for the vast majority of Web users who are using Internet Explorer, and just make sure that your site's pages are nominally tight and readable when viewed using Netscape browsers;

On-screen entry forms, error-checking, and other programming-driven features: Test any and all screens that require your prospects and customers to type information into on-screen forms on your site, such as order forms, brochure request screens, and e-mail newsletter subscription windows. Go to these areas on your site, and enter the information just as a user would, paying extra-close attention to the "error-checking" behind these forms.

If, for example, you enter your name, address, and product info on your site's order screen, but you leave the Zip Code entry field blank, and then hit the "Submit Order" button, how does your site's order entry programming respond? If your site's order entry program re-displays a completely blank order form that requires your customers to re-enter all their customer information over again, someone on your Web site programming team should have anticipated this, and some reprogramming will be needed. If, on the other hand, your order process re-displays a screen that *only* asks the user to fill in their Zip Code (or other incomplete fields), this is the right way to handle the issue.

Keep repeating this blank-field entry process for every single field, for all the forms and other user entry windows on your site, repeating the process of hitting the "Send Order," "Submit," or "Subscribe Now" buttons, just as your customers and prospects would, to test the quality of your Web site's error-checking features, and to flush out any bugs in your site's back-end software. Also enter invalid or incorrect information, such as mis-typed product numbers, and see what happens: If there are any bugs in the software or CGI scripts used in your site's order entry and other back-end programming processes, your site users—your company's prospects and customers—will surely find them. Better for you to find them now, than for your customers to find them later.

Flipping the Switch: Bringing Your Company's Web Site "Live" on the Internet

After you, your Web development team, and your testing group have tested your site (or, your modifications to an existing site) and you are satisfied you've found and corrected any remaining site glitches, the site can now be moved to your company's Web server, linked to your company's own ".com" Internet domain, and made "live" for everyone on the Internet.

The first few weeks after a major site is brought online is a very busy time for Web developers. Additional bugs and glitches are often found by site users, and must be fixed by your team. Stay vigilant at the time of your launch, and afterward, be alert to these problems, and make sure bugs and other glitches are fixed.

Include a "bug report" link on every page of your site: The best way for you to know everything that can go wrong (or right) with a newly-launched Web site is to include a link at the bottom of every page on your company's Web site:

Problems? Comments? Questions? Contact our Webmaster

Users who click on this link can report problems with your company's Web site to your company's Webmaster, but your Webmaster can also set up this link so that you will be automatically copied on all e-mails received from this link for the first month or so after a site launch. This way, you'll know right away if there are any major problems on your company's new Web site, and will be able to deal with them appropriately from both a marketing, as well as technical, standpoint.

INTERNET RESEARCH & EXECUTION
CHAPTER 12
USING THE INTERNET AS A SALES PROSPECTING, RESEARCH, AND PRODUCTION TOOL

The Internet is an indispensable tool for many marketing research tasks, for gathering information on your company's competition, and for executing critical production steps in your marketing program.

For marketing managers, using the Internet for research doesn't mean sitting around in your office surfing the Internet, or checking a few industry news sites each morning. For example, in your role as marketing manager, you'll be called on to create a new mailing list of prospects for a new sales promotion. You'll be asked to line up a new booth for an upcoming trade show your company is attending. Your CEO may ask you to prepare a memo outlining the competitive outlook and opportunities for entry in a new and promising market, or your company's Business Development VP will ask you to locate a key contact at a company considered to be a potential strategic partner.

Using the Internet for Research

You can turn to the Internet to search for and find new sales contacts and opportunities, to research important strategic information, and to establish contact with people who can help your company. The Internet is a research tool that can help you exploit new marketing opportunities and increase your company's sales.

Just a decade ago, the power to skillfully locate business and sales contact information online belonged exclusively to large corporations, who could afford expensive, specialized online databases and other costly information services to conduct strategic research, compile new sales contact lists, and quickly locate other information for new marketing projects. The information in these expensive online databases was accessible to managers working at arm's length with specially-trained "corporate librarians," or "search specialists" at their companies, who mastered arcane, specialized "database query languages" to patiently extract needed information for managers, who always left the exchange feeling as if they still weren't seeing the full picture of the information they really wanted, or believed they might not have asked the right questions in the first place.

Fortunately, the explosive growth of the Internet has now made most of the same kind of information once available only to a few, at very high cost, freely available on the Net to anyone who can find it. But this information is only available to those who know where to look for it, and who know a few simple searching techniques to help them find what they're looking for, more efficiently, and in less time.

What You Can Find on the Internet—and How to Find It

For marketing managers using the Internet, the Net's top search site, Google (**www.google.com**) can help you find the information you need to perform a variety of important research tasks, including:

Assessing new markets and sales opportunities: Marketing managers are often asked to look into new markets and sales opportunities for their companies in unfamiliar new industries, or in unknown new marketplaces. You can use the Internet as a quick-reference information tool for scoping out the depth of potential new business opportunities for your company, and to acquire a quick, basic working knowledge of any new industry or market. A ten-minute Google search of some news and information sources can tell you a lot more about a new industry or market;

Sales prospecting: The Internet is an unbeatable sales prospecting tool, and is especially useful for gathering personal contact information for high-level presentations and proposals for new business development projects. It also plays a very important role in day-to-day sales prospecting tasks, such as compilation of mailing lists and sales contact records copied from Web sites in your market. Through the use of the WHOIS feature (covered further in this chapter), you can use the Internet to cut through the telephone "voice mail curtain" now in place in many companies, to identify and establish initial contact with the key person at the company 'you are trying to reach;

Competitive analysis: You can, of course, use the Internet to check out your competitors' Web sites, but checking out some of your competitor's deeper links on their Web site, such as company news releases, management team profiles, and financial/investor information, can often yield valuable competitive intelligence for your company and its marketing efforts;

Trade and industry news gathering: You can use the Google search site to search for the latest, most relevant and useful news in your industry or market, and to locate the major trade news Web sites covering your industry. For example, sites like ClNet's **news.com** and **ZDNet.com** provide up-to-the-minute news and information for the computing and high-technology fields. For any industry, there are usually several leading online news sites providing the latest news of your industry on a more timely basis than conventional trade print publications. These online news sites also have their own search features that enable you to retrieve relevant, older news stories from their searchable archives;

Product, vendor, and supplier research: You can use Google to quickly and easily find online suppliers of key marketing-related products and services needed by your company. If, for example, you were planning a trade show, a keyword search for "trade show displays" on Google would yield many useful links to suppliers who sell trade show booths online. The Internet is especially useful for finding hard-to-locate suppliers of specialty items needed by all marketers, such as sign producers, retail and specialty packaging suppliers, etc. The Internet is also an invaluable aid for helping you increase the speed of your marketing execution in dealing with online vendors. For example, by using e-mail to get online price quotes, for establishing online electronic file delivery connections, exchanging shipping instructions, and the other key, day-to-day online execution steps required for time-critical marketing projects;

Customer and product feedback: You can check Internet discussion newsgroups to see what customers, prospects and others in the marketplace are saying about your company and its products or services, and what they're saying about your competitor's products.

But before you can find what you're searching for, you must first learn how to find it. Every marketing manager should take the time to learn a few, basic keyword searching skills, to save time and increase the accuracy and quality of the information they collect when they search the Internet.

Google: The Go-To Site for any Internet Research Task

Most of your Net-based research tasks will involve the use of the Google search site, so most of the search techniques covered in this chapter describe the best ways to keyword search on Google, the Internet's best search site.

Started in 1995 by Stanford University students Larry Page and Sergey Brin, Google is a search site (also known as a "search engine") that indexes over 2 billion Web links, and responds to over 150 million daily search requests. Google is a search site like Yahoo! or AltaVista, but its killer application is its Web site analysis and ranking system, called PageRank™, which uses a proprietary software technology to retrieve and rank the most useful and relevant sites found in your search, by counting the number of *other Web sites* that link to each site found by your search, and ranking these sites by this characteristic.

Google was the first search site to recognize that an important measure of the quality of any Web site's content are the number of other Web sites linking to it, and who would post a link to this site on their own pages. Page ranking is based on the sensible notion that the quality of a Web site—i.e., the measure of its relevance and content—can be determined by measuring how popular it is, and thus, how many other Web sites "vote" for this page by featuring links to it from their own Web pages.

Google has become so popular that most people make it their first online stop anytime they need to find something—anything—on the Internet. And, you can usually find the information you're looking for on the first page of results of your Google search.

Keyword Searching on Google

Using Google couldn't be simpler—just enter a few keywords to find what you're looking for. But if you give some thought to the keywords you use, and the way you use Google, you'll get better, more accurate results, faster and more often.

For example, searching by a two-word phrase, entered within quotation marks, generates more accurate search results than entering the same two words without quotes, because Google finds only those sites that contain the entire phrase, instead of the larger number of sites that contain either of the two individual keywords. Also, you can often learn new and different keywords, such as technical terms or product names, by scanning the first few pages of your initial Google search results, and then entering these newly-found terms as new keywords in subsequent searches, to zero-in on the exact information you're searching for.

How to Develop Keywords for Your Google Search

The quality of the results you get from any Google search depends entirely on the quality of the **keywords** or **phrases** you use in your searches. Using keywords that are too general yields too many unwanted search results, and using keywords that are too specific in your initial Google search may cause you to miss some critically important information. So, think about the keywords you need to use in your search, and the best keywords to use first.

Step 1: Ask a Question

The quickest, easiest way to begin generating keywords for your search is to ask a question:

- What is the size of the U.S. market for **robotic imaging** and **identification systems** in the U.S.?
- Where are **video production** companies based in **Atlanta, GA**?
- What is the **U.S. balance of trade** with **China**?

- What **public companies** are involved in the **development** of **amorphous alloys**?
- Where can I learn about **industrial design** used in **personal computers**?
- Where can I find **legal forms**, like a **sample licensing agreement**?
- Where can I make **reservations** for a **hotel** in **San Francisco**?

Step 2: Enter the Question, or Find and Enter Just the Keywords

Once you've framed your search in the form of a question, you can begin your search by simply typing your question into the Google search window. However, a more effective way is to pull the key phrases and nouns out of your question, and enter each two or three-word phrase within quotation marks, followed by one, single keyword (or another two-word phrase) to further narrow the scope of the information you're searching. Here are the relevant keywords and search phrases, pulled out from each of the previous questions, and ready to enter into Google's search window:

> "robotic imaging" identification
> "video production" "Atlanta GA"
> "U.S. balance of trade" China
> "public companies" "amorphous alloys" development
> "industrial design" "personal computers"
> "legal forms" "sample licensing agreement"
> "San Francisco" hotel reservations

A keyword phrase within quotes increases search accuracy: Compared to the entry of a single keyword, entering an exact phrase within quotation marks is a more specific way to search, and yields a smaller number of search results, since Google will return only those Web sites matching the exact phrase you've entered.

Adding a single keyword or phrase narrows your search results even further: Adding a single keyword to the two or three-word phrase within quotes, as shown in the previous example, helps you to "triangulate" your search by adding this third keyword or phrase.

General keywords and phrases produce less relevant search results: For example, entering too-general phrases, like "sales data," "steel producers," or "real estate," retrieves far more—but far less relevant—results than using a more-specific search phrase:

Too-General Phrase	Better Search Phrase
"sales data"	"market share"
"steel producers"	"steel mini-mills"
"real estate"	"real estate broker"
"brooklyn new york"	"brooklyn heights"

Step 3: "Reading" Your Keyword Search Results

After you enter keywords, and keyword phrases, and click the "Google Search" button, Google generates a list of the search results it finds, ranking each Web page by its relevancy—the number of other Web sites that link to it.

If you properly structure your first keyword search, using keyword phrases specific enough to the topics you're searching, you'll often find the answer to your question among the first few search results returned by Google, and often in the first, second, or third result at the top of the first page of results.

Scanning the first page of Google search results: Scan the titles and abstracts on your first page of search results on Google, and train yourself to filter the results you are seeing, before clicking on every search result. By looking at the title, the abstract, and the Web URL, ask yourself: Does the source of the retrieved information appear to be a credible?

Trust your instincts when scanning titles and abstracts: On the Internet, *where* information comes from, and how it got there, is almost as important as the information itself. If, for example, you're searching for time-sensitive information, like current market size data for an industry, chances are a search result from a university, or a corporate Web site, would be less relevant or credible than a more recently-published article from a business news publication or newspaper Web site.

Location is important: A Google search usually generates a list of search results from Web sites all around the world, but search results from sites outside of the U.S. would be less timely or credible if, say, you were searching for information on a topic related specifically to a U.S.-based business market. Conversely, if you're doing some business research on the telecommunications industry of Great Britain, a search result from a U.K.-based Web site may be more timely or relevant than search results from Web sites based elsewhere.

Context adds to relevance: Observe the *context* of the information in your search results: Pay close attention to who's behind the link, and the descriptiveness of the information shown in the two-line Google abstract for each search result. For example, if you're searching for information on a specific electronics product, a search result from the manufacturer of that product is more relevant than a passing reference to that product found on a dealer's Web site.

Check the dates on the pages you're reading: For fast-changing business and market information, the more timely the search result, the better the information. Pay very close attention to the dates shown in Google search results, and on the Web pages you're reading from these Google searches. There are many "ghost" Web sites that haven't been updated since the dot-com bust, so if you're looking at sales contact information on a Web site having a "Last Updated: March 14th, 1999" line on the bottom of the page, it's probably out of date.

The Two-Page Rule: If It's Not on the First Two Pages of Your Google Search, Search Again

Your average Google search could generate 350, 3,500, or 3.5 million search hits across dozens, or thousands, of pages, but this obviously doesn't mean you must look at every page. Because of Google's page-ranking technology, it's a safe bet that the information you're looking for will appear somewhere within the first two pages of your Google search results, and usually on the very first page if you use the right keywords.

Following this "two-page rule" saves you a significant amount of time on your Internet searches, because if you didn't find what you were searching for on the first two pages of your search results, don't waste more time going to pages 3, 4, or 5—start over and refine your search using different, or more specific, keywords. The results you get from viewing the first two pages of your search tells you how well the search results you're getting match up with the keywords you're using. Cutting your losses after the second page, and starting a new search by entering new keywords saves you time and gets you closer to the information you're searching for.

Step 4: Search and Learn, and Then Search Again

Your first keyword search often leads you to another search: Keyword searching is equal parts art and skill. As such, it's often an imprecise, hit-or-miss process. One of the secrets to successful keyword searching is accepting the fact that it may take two, three, four, or more search attempts to find the answer to your question.

Keyword searching is a reiterative learning process: Because each search reveals new pieces of information and gives you new keywords to use for your next search, the results you see from your first, second, or subsequent keyword searches give you important feedback for your next search. And each new search reveals even better, more relevant, keywords and phrases. The information you see on search result pages, even if it's not what you're looking for, often provides you with the clues you need for your next search.

Start General, Then Go Specific

Searching the Internet is like taking a picture with a camera. There are many ways to photograph a single scene that's in front of you. You can walk closer to take a picture of a person or object in your view, or you can walk way back to capture the entire landscape. Or, you can step to one side or another to take the same picture from a different angle.

Think of the Internet as a vast landscape of information. The number, type, and quality of keywords you use helps you move closer to the most relevant and specific information available in your search. Or, using more generalized keywords, it moves you further away, which helps you to get a sense of the **context** of the information you've found.

The sense of context is an important aspect of all of your Internet searches. When starting a keyword search, it's best to start "general"—that is, using the keywords or phrases you think give you a sense of the big picture of the topic you're searching, before you begin to narrow your search by adding more (or more specific) keywords or phrases.

There are, of course, exceptions to this rule. For example, if you're searching for tomorrow's Portland, Oregon weather forecast, you'll want to do a keyword search that is as quick and as precise as possible. In most cases, however, this "general-to-specific" rule insures that you won't miss any important information that can help your search along the way. This rule also works in reverse: If your too-specific search yields too few results, you can always remove a keyword, or search by a more general keyword to retrieve more information on your topic.

Internet Newsgroup Searching

When you're trying to find information on the Internet, Internet newsgroups (also called Usenet newsgroups) are one of the Internet's best kept secrets. An Internet newsgroup is an online discussion area featuring text-based messages posted by individual Internet users, relating to the newsgroup's specific subject.

Newsgroups are one of the Internet's oldest features, and they were used long before Web browsers allowed for display of the more visually exciting Web pages we see today. However, their lack of glamour and visual appeal in no way detracts from their utility as a valuable Internet information resource.

The range of topics covered by newsgroups is virtually unlimited. There are over 30,000 individual newsgroups on almost as many individual topics—everything from talk on the latest movies and music, to tips and advice on car repair, to PC technical help, and serious discussions on specific health and medical conditions. Google also maintains the best online archive of Internet newsgroups, with over 700 million individual postings, going back to 1981. If there's a topic—any topic—you want to get more information on, it's certain there's somebody, somewhere on the Internet who's talked about it, online, in an Internet newsgroup.

You can access and keyword-search any of the more than 30,000 available Internet newsgroups to read recent messages, also called **postings**, contributed by other Internet users. You can post your own question, inquiry, or comment to a newsgroup, or comment on a message you've just read. Discussions in many newsgroup postings often turn into **threads**, which are ongoing, back-and-forth conversations on a single subject within a newsgroup.

Because newsgroups have been overshadowed by Web sites, most Internet users only stumble onto Internet newsgroups after they've been on the Internet for a while, if ever. Newsgroups are self-administered by their participants, and sometimes by "moderators," who edit the messages posted to a newsgroup.

Figure 12-1:

What To Do When You Can't Find It On the Internet (Yet)

Now let's say you've already done your keyword search, clicked on a few pages of search results, and you still haven't found the information you're looking for. It's a safe bet that the keywords you were using were either too general, too specific, or you were using the wrong keywords in the first place.

Too general: Searches using keywords that are too general produce too many, and less relevant, search results. If this happens to you during a search, don't waste any more time scanning through more pages of search results. Instead, add another single keyword to the end of your keyword or search phrase and try again. Adding more keywords to a search always reduces the number of search results, but dramatically increases the relevancy of these results.

Too specific: Generally, "specific is good" when it comes to Internet searches. But sometimes you will find that your search gives you a feeling that you're missing some other information out there that could be relevant to your search. Or, maybe your search generated a smaller-than-expected number of hits. The easiest remedy for a search that is too specific is to drop one of your keywords from the string of search keywords you're using, and try again. If you can

think of other, somewhat more general, keywords to use in your new search, this also produces better search results.

No results/poor results: If you're not getting the results you want from a search, the first thing to do is double-check your spelling of the keywords you've entered: Are your keywords spelled correctly? Did you put quotes around a keyword search phrase? Did any mis-typed characters find their way into the keyword search window when you entered those keywords? Typos happen to the most experienced Net searchers.

Learn new keywords from your found search results: If you've entered your keywords correctly, and you still aren't getting the results you want, you're using the wrong keywords. Take a minute and write down other keywords and phrases that can get you closer to the information you're seeking. It often helps to take a que from the more relevant information you see on the Web sites you've already turned up in your first search: Some of the proper nouns, phrases and other terms of art you see there may supply you with additional, more meaningful, keywords and phrases to sharpen your next search.

You can also use Google to keyword search every Internet newsgroup, to retrieve lists of individual newsgroup messages containing the search keywords or phrases you've entered. Google also lets you search newsgroup archives containing stored newsgroup content going back to 1981, quite useful for searching for information on obscure topics.

Benefits of Searching Internet Discussion Newsgroups

Unlike Web sites, which in many cases, are professionally-produced and edited information sources, Internet newsgroups let you tap the unfiltered "street wisdom" of other Internet users on an unlimited range of topics.

Newsgroups contain subjective information—opinions, comments, and observations. For example, newsgroups tell you what people think about a particular product, or personal observations from someone who's already visited a certain travel destination. You should always be skeptical when reading newsgroup messages, because "one man's opinion" in a newsgroup message may be completely wrong or off-the-wall. It helps to read multiple messages from different newsgroup participants on the same topic (in a "thread") to get a consensus viewpoint on that topic.

If you know what to look for, and how to look for it, you'll find newsgroups to be a wonderful resource for finding information:

Common interests: Newsgroups bring people together by their common interests. You can use newsgroups to get information, ask questions, and swap comments with other Internet users on any one of thousands of discussion topics;

Research and rumors: Net newsgroups are a useful "ear to the ground" for getting fast information on a topic you're researching, and for gleaning important information that often slips below the radar of conventional media sources. Whatever the topic, it's a good bet that a 20-minute newsgroup search can give you a rudimentary working knowledge of that topic. It's easy to learn how to access and search Internet newsgroups, and newsgroup searching is an important addition to your Internet searching skills;

A warning: As with all information you read on the Internet, you must be especially careful when viewing and evaluating any information you read on Net newsgroups. Since anyone can post a message to a newsgroup— anonymously, or even under a false name—you are likely to see many misleading or erroneous postings on Internet newsgroups.

Unlike newspapers, TV networks, and other forms of the "traditional" press, the Internet is a medium that is unfiltered by editors or censors. This is both a good and a bad thing. Because of this, it's especially important to be alert when reading advice and information you see posted to newsgroups.

The free flow of information that makes the Internet such a useful resource also imposes a greater responsibility on you, the reader, to exercise judgement and good sense. It is your responsibility to judge the credibility and worth of the information you find in a newsgroup, because the task of sorting ignorant, malicious, or plainly wrong information you see on newsgroups is entirely up to you.

Newsgroup Search Examples

Next to Web sites, newsgroups can be an excellent information resource for marketing managers. Here are some examples of useful marketing and sales information that can be found on newsgroups:

Product and company feedback: Newsgroups can be an excellent source of free, uncensored opinions on virtually any product or service used in consumer, technical, or business-to-business marketplaces. Newsgroup participants can be extremely outspoken in their views on companies, industries, and products and services in these industries; the results often evolve (or devolve) into free-wheeling, wide-open discussions.

Simply typing in a product name and model number into a Google newsgroup search window can generate hundreds of interesting, readable, and revealing comments concerning your own company's products, or those of your competitors;

Market information: You can search newsgroups to find how people are using particular products, and to discover interesting new uses for these products. For example, a company selling mapping services to the insurance industry was surprised to find participants on Internet genealogy-related newsgroups recommending this company's historical maps of towns and cities for use in genealogy searches. This discovery opened up a new and potentially very lucrative market for this company's mapping services.

Using Google to Search Newsgroups

In addition to its powerful and highly accurate Web site search features, Google also maintains the Web's most extensive online search capability and archive for Internet newsgroups, ranking the search results that appear to be most relevant to the keywords you've entered.

To search Internet newsgroups on Google, simply enter your keywords in Google's search window, and click on the "Groups" tab at the top of the Google home page. You will then see pages of search results, displayed much like the way Google displays Web site search results. These search results show individual newsgroup messages, called **posts**, containing the keywords or phrases you've entered. By skim-reading the individual subject lines and abstracts for the posts Google displays for each found search result, you can then click and read the newsgroup posts that look like they'd contain the most relevant information on your search.

Reading Newsgroup Threads in Google

A newsgroup **thread** is a collection of ongoing replies to an original newsgroup posting—comments, opinions, or (usually) other relevant facts posted by other Internet users. Newsgroup threads may continue for days, weeks, or months, as one Internet user after another posts their comments to the newsgroup thread.

A thread is like a dinner party conversation, where anyone may ask a question or make a comment. This often starts a conversation that goes on for the rest of the evening, meandering into all kinds of interesting, even unrelated, topics. This also happens in newsgroup threads, as comments posted by newsgroup participants spark new, and sometimes irrelevant, comments from other users.

To read newsgroup threads on Google, simply click the "View thread" link on the lower right below each newsgroup search result. You'll then see a split-screen window with a one-line listing of each of the posts in the thread on the left-hand side, with the individual newsgroup comments displayed in the larger, right-hand portion of the screen (see **Figure 12-2**). Clicking the individual comments on the left-hand side of the screen from top to bottom takes you chronologically through this discussion thread, from the first, earliest posted comment at the top, through the last, most recently-posted comment at the bottom.

As long as you're willing to spend some time wading through the sometimes-irrelevant comments posted on newsgroup discussions in order to find the one or two truly meaningful comments in a thread, you'll find Internet newsgroups to be a valuable source of insightful, street-smart advice, comments, and information to help you in your business and marketing research-related tasks.

WHOIS: The Salesman's (and Marketer's) Best Friend

Another important Internet research tool for marketing managers is the WHOIS database, an online repository of names, addresses, phone numbers and other contact information for the over 40 million registered ".com" Internet domains registered in the U.S. and around the world.

The WHOIS database is operated by VeriSign, a company that has been assigned the task of registering and managing Internet domains by the Federal government. VeriSign acts like a kind of "Department of Motor Vehicles" for the Internet, serving as a clearinghouse for companies, individuals, or groups who register their company or Web site domain names with Network Solutions for an annual fee.

The WHOIS database (accessible from **www.networksolutions.com**) is the Net's centralized repository of all .com Web domain names, and all of these domain registration records are available on the Internet. A WHOIS listing tells you who registered the site, their e-mail and physical mailing addresses, and best of all, the phone number of the person responsible for setting up or administering that domain (usually) at the company.

The WHOIS database is an extremely useful tool for cracking the wall of telephone voice mail systems used today in many companies, which often makes it very difficult for your company's salespeople to reach the right individual at the prospect's company. This inability to get through to a real live person at many companies also prevents you from compiling mailing list and sales contact information for your company's direct mail projects.

WHOIS is wonderful for finding who's behind the Web site you're looking for, and for getting to a real, live person behind a company's main-number voice mail system. For example, if you are building a sales contact database for your company, or you've been given the task of locating names and contact information for key contacts at potential joint-venture partners prior to a high-level sales contact by your company, searching WHOIS gets you on the path to finding the right person at the company you're researching.

The process of registering an Internet domain in any company is an important task. For small companies, this task is usually handled by a company owner or senior

Figure 12-2:

Internet Newsgroups—Newsgroup searches on Google are a very useful research tool

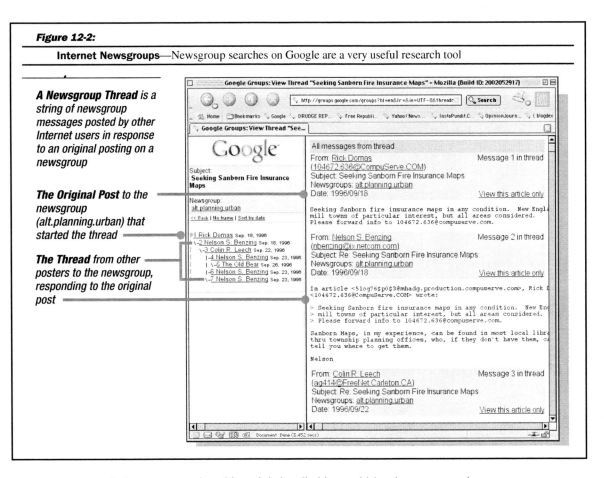

A Newsgroup Thread is a string of newsgroup messages posted by other Internet users in response to an original posting on a newsgroup

The Original Post to the newsgroup (alt.planning.urban) that started the thread

The Thread from other posters to the newsgroup, responding to the original post

manager. In larger companies, this task is handled by a mid-level manager, or by some other responsible "company insider." A WHOIS domain search not only gives you the names of these individuals—usually listed under "administrative" or "technical" contacts, but in many cases, it even gives you this person's direct-dial phone number.

From here, getting additional information, such as finding out who's in charge of the department or business function concerning your inquiry, is simply a matter of placing a direct phone call to the person found in the WHOIS search. For your company's sales reps, this means no more looping through endless voice-mail menus, and no more run-ins with snooty phone receptionists (see Chapter 6 for more information on using WHOIS for mailing list compilation).

The Internet as a Marketing Execution Tool

The Internet's instant communications capabilities allow you, your ad agency, your Web development team, and all of your company's marketing vendors—your printer, lettershop, mailing list broker, outside consultants, and advertising production managers at print publications—to use the Internet for rapid distribution of print advertising and collateral proof files, submission of electronic files for trade publication advertising placements, and the efficient, instant transfer and review of any file, in any format, to anyone. This ability to instantly move both work-in-progress project files, as well as files for completed marketing projects (such as print advertising layouts) adds tremendous power, speed and flexibility to your company's day-to-day marketing execution.

Even though, as a marketing manager, you won't be directly involved in the hands-on part of the processing and delivery of electronic files to meet a publication deadline, you will be involved in the initial part of this process. For example, it's likely you'll be using the Internet to proof electronic-format Adobe Acrobat .PDF files sent by your ad agency and other outside suppliers. Moreover, you may find yourself in the position of having to act as the champion in your company for promoting the use of the Internet in your company's back-end marketing execution process, if the other members of your marketing team, such as your ad agency, printer, or other key vendors are not yet using the Internet to its fullest potential for the processing and transmission of your company's marketing deliverables.

To be a proponent for this process, you must first understand its benefits, and become familiar with the ways the Internet can help your company's marketing execution, as described in this section.

Advantages of the Internet for Marketing Execution

Using the Internet in back-end marketing production tasks for faster marketing execution offers many advantages:

> **Print advertising:** Electronic file submission of your company's print advertising extends deadlines, and gives you the additional time you may need to execute or change your company's print advertising programs. You can use electronic file transmission to make last-minute changes to your company's print advertising, on-the-fly—to improve headlines and sales copy in response to feedback from prospects who respond to earlier ad placements, to clarify information on key product features, or to modify your print advertising to anticipate or react to unforeseen events, such as a new advertising campaign launched by a major competitor. Keeping all of your company's print advertising in electronic form, right up to the minute it is transmitted over the Internet to the print publication's Web or FTP site, gives you the power to turn your print advertising campaigns "on a dime" to exploit new sales opportunities;

Printed marketing materials: Using the Internet, all of your company's printed marketing collateral can be developed, designed, reviewed, and then transmitted to your printer's Web or FTP site. Unless your print project involves very large and expensive quantities of printed materials, you can view electronic versions of working and pre-press proofs sent to you by Internet
e-mail from your ad agency or printer, instead of waiting days to see hard-copy proofs and color matchprints.

Using the Internet to develop and transmit your company's printed marketing deliverables is a much faster, more efficient means of print production. Working with these files in electronic form all the way through to their final delivery to the printer substantially reduces the time required to design, develop and produce any print project, by eliminating the need to review hard-copy proofs with each new set of copy and layout revisions—no more Fedex, messenger, or proof-printing expenses. And because Internet transmission and delivery eliminates the need for you to review bluelines or matchprints of your company's print projects, your projects move more quickly through your printer's pipeline. This is especially true if your company's printer has an all-digital direct-to-plate prepress system;

The "virtual circle:" The Internet dramatically increases the speed and efficiency of your day-to-day working relationships with your marketing team. Of course, e-mail is the primary vehicle for your daily communications with members of your marketing team, but other Net-based features, such as file delivery through Web or FTP (file transfer protocol) sites, are extremely useful for reviewing and submitting files for marketing collateral, Web site design ideas, print advertising layouts, or any other deliverable required for any marketing project.

The best way use the Internet in your day-to-day work on marketing projects is to use e-mail to form a "virtual circle" of no more than two other key individuals at a time (three, including yourself) to work on any marketing project. When reviewing a proposed layout for a new print ad sent by your advertising agency, for example, your e-mail loop on this project would include you, your agency's account executive, and your company's Sales VP. Your ad agency's account executive starts by sending the ad layout to you by e-mail, as an attached Adobe Acrobat .PDF file. You then forward this ad file, along with your comments, to your company's Sales VP, who e-mails his comments back to you within 45 minutes. Next, you interpret the VP's suggested copy and layout changes, and include them along with your own comments, attaching a brief, point-by-point e-mail reply back to your agency's account executive.

This entire exchange occurred in a cycle of a few Internet e-mail messages, and the task at hand was resolved in a very short time. This exchange can take place in as little as 15 minutes to a half-hour if everyone happens to be sitting in front of their computers. More likely, the task will be completed between meetings, phone calls, appointments and other projects in a few hours during a typical business day.

If each of the three members of your "virtual circle" perform their task, and respond to you on a timely basis, this e-mail loop eliminates the "friction" that slows marketing projects down to a crawl: Voicemail telephone tag, printed memos lost in someone's in-box, yellow Post-it notes missing from hard-copy brochure proofs, and lost Fedex packages, all of which cause unnecessary delays whenever a marketing project leaves the Internet and has to be handled in the "real world." At best, these are minor annoyances that frustrate the execution of a marketing project; at worst, they result in lost sales opportunities because a critical marketing project was significantly delayed, or collapsed in a death by a thousand cuts.

Using the Internet as a Tool for Executing Common Marketing Projects

As a means of accelerating the day-to-day completion of your company's marketing projects, the Internet is not a hard tool to master. For most, it involves simple changes in mindset and habits. For others on your marketing team, the change may be somewhat more difficult. However, once people start using the Internet to do their work on marketing projects in this new, "frictionless" way, they never go back to the tedious, frustrating ways they had to work on marketing projects in those pre-Internet days: Leaving the third telephone message of the day with the printer, writing a paper note to attach to a blueline, or filling out the Fedex ticket to send a Zip disk containing your company's latest print ad, due by tomorrow's publication deadline.

Keep it Digital—Until it Meets a Printing Press

The secret to using the Internet for the day-to-day, back-end execution of your marketing projects is to keep all of your marketing deliverables in their digital, all-electronic form during the entire process of designing, revising, and final production, all the way through to their final destination. For example, as you and your ad agency develop your company's new advertising program, the layout files should move from their on-screen .PDF proof stages, directly to a publication's Internet FTP site for final ad delivery. Likewise, once you approve the digital .PDF proofs, the layout files for your company's next direct-mail package should be transferred to your printer by e-mail, or uploaded directly to your printer's FTP server.

Keep all of your files in digital format, and avoid using hard-copy proofs wherever possible. The forward motion of any deliverable on any marketing project usually grinds to a halt whenever it must be converted to any tangible, non-digital form, such as a hard-copy color matchprint, prior to completion. If your contact at a key supplier hasn't yet figured out how to open Adobe Acrobat .PDF files on his computer, and you must ask your ad agency to send him a printed proof by FAX or Fedex, that's one day lost on a marketing project. If an administrative contact at a trade publication insists your ad agency send her a disk with your company's advertising layout overnight by Fedex, instead of a file that could have been easily transferred by e-mail in two minutes, that's another unnecessary delay.

Of course, there are important exceptions to the "keep it digital" rule. For example, the best way for you, (and you alone) to review and correct any marketing deliverable sent to you as an Adobe Acrobat .PDF proof is to print it out, mark up your text and copy changes on your hard copy, and FAX it back to your ad agency. Likewise, good judgement dictates that you should order a color matchprint for any unusually expensive advertising placement for your company, or for any other expensive printing project.

Adobe Acrobat .PDFs can be easily attached to e-mail messages sent by your ad agency or your printer, and their color reproduction is quite satisfactory for most printed materials when viewed on-screen, and yields acceptable results on many color inkjet printers.

Making edit changes directly to the .PDF file: Although Adobe does provide a version of Acrobat that allows for direct, on-screen editability of .PDF files, the changes you make to text or layout on a .PDF can't be carried over to the applications in which they were originally created, such as QuarkXPress or Adobe Illustrator. This drawback defeats any time-saving advantages gained in making edits directly to the .PDF proof.

The best way to work with .PDF files is to print out the .PDF when you receive it, review it, making all of your markup changes directly on the printed copy, and then fax the printed .PDF back to your ad agency or printer. This also happens to be the way your agency or printer would prefer you to work with the .PDF files they send you, letting them make the final changes from your marked-up fax copy to their own, original layout, using the original application program in which the layout was created. Of course, for those minor, final revisions to a marketing deliverable, you can skip this fax markup process and phone or e-mail your few remaining changes to your ad agency or marketing consultant.

Electronic Advertising Transmission and Submission

Electronic ad submission services provided by nearly every print trade publication provide a quantum boost to the speed and power of your company's marketing execution on print advertising campaigns.

Become "electronic submission-aware:" The easiest way to institute Internet-based submission of your company's advertising placements is to encourage your ad agency or marketing consultant to submit your advertising to publications electronically, by pointing out the "electronic ad submission guidelines" found in the mechanical specifications section of a publication's advertising media kit, in the printed media kit, or on the publication's Web site.

Most publications offer Internet transmission, either by dedicated Web site link, an FTP link, or Internet e-mail; your company's advertising materials can be readily transmitted by any of these methods. As a courtesy, most advertising agencies will call the production departments of a publication to verify that the publication received the materials the ad agency just uploaded to them. This simple step can sometimes head off file transmission problems, such as missing fonts and damaged graphics files, before they lead to delays in ad submissions.

For some publications whose production departments check their e-mail regularly, verifications can be done by e-mail, which makes things easier for everyone. In either case, make sure to let your ad agency or marketing consultant know that you want to be cc'd in the e-mail loop on all of your company's advertising submissions, so you'll know when an ad has been submitted to a publication, if any problems occurred on the publication's side, and if those problems were corrected.

Check, and save, the final .PDF proof of the submitted ad: Your ad agency should also send you a final Adobe Acrobat .PDF proof made from the original application file in which your company's advertising layout layout was made (usually QuarkXpress, Adobe InDesign, Illustrator, or Macromedia Freehand). This final proof is a fairly exact, benchmark representation of how your ad is to appear in the publication. Although you should have carefully proofed the earlier versions of the .PDFs sent by your agency, review this proof again just to make sure, and save it on your computer in case there are any problems with the ad after it appears in the publication.

A publication's production department rarely makes mistakes when printing advertising, because they are usually very good at detecting problems in the ad files they receive before their press date, and will promptly notify your ad agency to ask them to correct the problem. Just in case, you can always show the publication your final .PDF proof of the ad in question if there are problems, so you can get the ad corrected for the next issue, or—if there are major problems—possibly receive a discount or a "make-good," which is an additional placement of the ad at no cost. The latter is rarely given, unless you and your agency can prove that the production mistake was the fault of the publication, and not a problem with the original, submitted ad layout.

Sending your ad to the printer in an emergency: Where Internet ad submission really pays off is when you must place a print display ad beyond a publication's "official" advertising materials close date, and even beyond their "unofficial" deadline, which is usually the day the publication's production department collects their layout files and advertising materials for their final overnight shipment or messenger run to their printer.

Figure 12-3:

Electronic File Transmission Tips:

Human-readable filenames: *Make sure that compressed archive files have filenames that readily identify the project. "Acme-Co-Ad-Ind-Week-Nov-06.ZIP" is a better and more understandable filename than "BigAd.ZIP." A file with a human-readable name helps the production staffs at publications and printing companies identify and match each file to each project;*

Don't forget to send ALL the files: *Production managers will tell you that the most common reason digital output files are held up at a publication or printer are that they were sent with fonts or graphics missing. Make sure all layouts have been "collected for output," meaning that all type fonts and image files used in a layout have been included in the folder of the final, compressed archive that is being sent to the publication, printer or other vendor;*

The "final" .PDF proof means FINAL: *The final Adobe Acrobat .PDF sent to the publication or printer along with the original application layout file (and all the fonts and image files associated with this application file) should be an exact reflection of the actual layout application file that is being sent for output to the publication or the printer;*

The printer will use the final .PDF proof to compare against the pre-press proofs they generate from the actual application file being output to negatives or press plates. *Any few, final tweaks, such as type changes, image adjustments, etc. which were subsequently made to the final application file effectively make your so-called "Final .PDF proof" an out-of-date, incorrect version, and creates added confusion at the printer. There's nothing wrong with making last-minute type changes or corrections to a layout, just make sure that your ad agency or marketing consultant produces another final .PDF proof that reflects the most recent changes made to the master application's layout, before transmitting both to the publication or printer.*

Sometimes, you must place an ad in a publication past the materials closing date—to take advantage of a new selling opportunity in your market, to make important changes to an ad that's currently running, or to substitute a new ad for an old one. With some help from the publication, you can frequently submit your ad directly to *their* printer, sending it by e-mail or uploading it to the printer's Internet FTP site.

A publication may have as much as an additional week beyond its "unofficial" ad materials deadline. This is the time when the publication's layout files are working their way through the printer's pre-press department. With knowledge of this fact, and honest pleas by either you, or your ad agency, a last-minute ad transmission can sometimes be made directly to the publication's printer—provided, of course, that you can convince the publication's production manager to let you do this.

This is, admittedly, a last-ditch measure, and you and your ad agency won't be too popular with the publication's production manager if you let this happen repeatedly. Because it's disruptive to their production process, some publications won't let their printers accept ad file transmissions under any circumstances. However, when you find yourself in this situation, you don't have any other choice, so there's no harm in asking.

When you or your ad agency are performing these 11th-hour miracles for your company, make sure that your ad agency takes special care in the preparation and transmission of your ad files, making sure there will be no problems with the new job files once they are opened by the printer. Sending your ad files directly to the printer is always an emergency measure, and a special favor granted to you as an advertiser by the publication, so make sure the ad files are correct.

Internet File Transmission Options

You and your advertising agency can move electronic files to publications, printers, or to other key contacts and suppliers, by one of four different methods:

Internet e-mail: The quickest, easiest way to transmit files is to send them as compressed attachments to ordinary e-mail messages. Ad layouts and printed materials files are compressed using either .ZIP (PC) or StuffIt .SIT (Macintosh) formats, sent as attached files in ordinary Internet e-mail messages to the publication, printer, or other key contact or vendor.

Electronic files sent as e-mail attachments work very well, except for transmission of very large attached files (usually over 5 megabytes), since many Internet mail servers have difficulty handling very large file attachments. Check with the publication or printer before sending large attachments, or send them by the Internet FTP or Web file-transfer methods detailed below;

Internet FTP site: An Internet FTP (file transfer protocol) site is an Internet server owned ("hosted") by the recipient of your electronically transmitted file: A trade publication, a printer, or another key contact or vendor. The main advantage of Internet FTP transmission is that it allows for the speedy transfer of files of virtually any size, including very large file archives, such as QuickTime video files and other large digital multimedia files.

To transfer a compressed archive file to an FTP site, you can usually just enter the FTP link into your Web browser (as you would a regular Web address); then drag and drop the file onto the open browser window to begin transmission. A more efficient approach is to use what is known as an "FTP client," such as Fetch for the Macintosh, or AbsoluteFTP for Windows, to transfer the file to the recipient's FTP server. Some FTP servers require a user ID and password for access, so contact the recipient by e-mail in advance when asking for their FTP link, to ask if any special account setup is required. If a publication or vendor hosts a "public FTP" site, usually no special account or password is required; however, sometimes public FTP servers still require you to sign on, using "anonymous" as your user name, and your email address as your password (and you can always try this on any FTP server if you're at a loss for how to get in);

Your own FTP server: Another method your company or your ad agency can use is to establish its own FTP host. This is a relatively simple task, and allows you to affirmatively provide any publication or vendor with your own FTP link for retrieving a file from your own FTP server;

Web browser: You can also transfer files by entering the FTP address in your Web browser, then dragging and dropping the file archive onto the open browser window. This method can be somewhat less reliable than using a dedicated FTP client software program, since some server operating system

Figure 12-4

Top Web Sites for Marketers

Here are some useful and interesting Web sites for marketing professionals:

Google (http://www.google.com): An indispensable tool for searching both Web sites and online Internet discussion newsgroups, Google should be your first stop for any Internet research task;

Yahoo! Business News (http://dailynews.yahoo.com/h/bs/): A concise, constantly-updated daily business news site, featuring top business news stories from the Reuters businesss news wire. Keep a browser window open with this site link on your desktop PC, then hit reload from time to time on your Web browser to see the latest updated business news stories and stock market action;

News.com (http://news.com.com/): If you are involved in high-tech—computers, software, systems, or IT—CINet's News.com is your news page. Updated throughout the day, just like the Yahoo! business news site;

The Securities and Exchange Commission EDGAR Site (http://www.sec.gov): The SEC's EDGAR public documents site is a very useful tool for researching important corporate insider information, marketing initiatives, product news, and for learning more about the business activities and financial condition of all public companies required to file these comprehensive, and sometimes very revealing, disclosure documents with the United States Securities and Exchange Commission;

Thomas Register (http://www.thomasregister.com/): The Thomas Register manufacturing directory Web site includes the online version of the venerable print directory, and is an excellent source of information for marketers. Companies can be keyword searched by SIC code, industry, and manufactured products. This site can be an an excellent first-look information source for locating prospects in new markets for your company;

Yahoo! Buzz Index (http://buzz.yahoo.com/): Every marketer wants to know what people want, and Yahoo! tracks the most-clicked links selected by users on the Yahoo! site every day, and displays them here. News on celebrities, the most popular TV shows and movies, daily controversies, etc., this site is also a good window on what people are searching for on the Internet;

***The Wall Street Journal* Online (http://www.wsj.com/)**: The online version of *The Wall Street Journal* requires an additional subscription fee to access the full online version of the print newspaper (worth it), but many interesting business and editorial features are accessible on this site for free. If it's worth it to you to get access to the Journal before the print edition hits the streets, this is how to do it;

Refdesk.com (http://www.refdesk.com): A handy all-in-one Web reference page, containing links to many useful and interesting Net information resources: Newspaper Web sites around the U.S. and around the world, online research databases, business facts and figures, online encyclopedias, and many other specialized online reference sources;

The Cluetrain Manifesto (http://www.cluetrain.com): A provocative view of the Internet's effect on markets, Cluetrain takes on the tired, ineffective ways companies market their products to their customers. Many of the statements you'll find here are too unrealistic to implement in real-world cases, but they are quite thought-provoking to anyone in the marketing field;

Amazon.com (http://www.amazon.com) and **Avnet.com (http://www.avnet.com)**: Two of the best examples of online catalog and e-commerce Web sites. If your company is planning to develop or improve its own Web product catalog and online ordering capabilities, check these sites to see how these two highly successful Web marketers do it.

settings may not work reliably with browser access. If you plan to be transmitting file archives on your own from time to time, your best bet is to download an FTP client (the most popular ones are available freely as shareware) and invest a little time in learning how to transfer files using an FTP client, instead of your browser.

TRADE SHOW MARKETING
CHAPTER 13
MAKING A SUCCESS OF YOUR COMPANY'S TRADE SHOW OPPORTUNITIES

As a marketing manager, you'll often be involved in selecting, organizing, and executing your company's trade show marketing activities, with an emphasis on <u>execution</u>. Good execution is even more critical in trade shows than with any other marketing project, because there is no time slippage allowed.

All of the activities associated with orchestrating a successful trade show appearance for your company: Design, development, and production of your company's booth, printed materials, pre-show promotion, and the incidental logistics of the show, must be planned, executed and coordinated so they all come together in time for the first day of the show. A day's delay on any one of these items can be a major embarrassment; a week later, the value of most trade show deliverables falls to zero.

Trade Shows: Where Markets Come Alive

For a few days every year, an industry's major trade show is the place where its market comes to life. At a trade show, companies, products, competitors, prospects and customers aren't names scribbled on a white board, or words and pictures in a brochure—they're living, breathing people working their booths and walking the aisles. Walk around any trade show floor in any industry and you'll see markets at work: Sales reps and executives at hundreds of companies, vying for the attention of thousands of potential buyers attending the show.

Trade shows provide opportunities to present and sell products in ways that can't be duplicated by advertising, direct mail, or other forms of marketing. A successful trade show appearance has launched many a successful young company, and for certain types of businesses in certain industries, such as wholesale suppliers to retail markets, where a company writes sales orders for most of its annual business in a few days, trade shows are a make-or-break sales opportunity.

Trade Shows Keep Marketing Managers Sharp

As a marketing manager, trade shows are an invaluable experience because they put you face-to-face with your own prospects and customers—the very people who will see the ads, mailings, and other deliverables in your marketing program. A trade show is the one marketing event where your prospects come to see you, and to hear what your company has to say about its product.

Marketing managers should work a trade show booth just their company's sales reps do, speaking to interested prospects and presenting your company's product or service. There is no better way for you to learn the features and attributes of your company's product or service that are the most (or least) compelling, and how best to present these attributes, than by talking to real live prospects at your company's next trade show.

As you present your company's product to many different prospects during the show, you find that your sales presentation gets better and better, as you refine it, based on how prospects respond, and as you repeat your description of your product's benefits and features.

Giving sales presentations directly to prospects at a trade show can make a tremendous improvement in how you develop your company's marketing programs and deliverables. By interacting with real prospects, and assessing their response to each of the product sales benefits and features you present, you learn the best sales approaches to use in your print advertising and direct-mail sales copy, and how your product's sales copy points and product feature descriptions should be presented and positioned in your company's marketing deliverables. Performers always say there's nothing like a live audience, and for marketing managers, there's nothing like talking to real prospects to help you keep your product's marketing message on target.

Like other marketing projects, there's no mystery to trade shows, just good planning, effective presentation, and solid execution. This chapter covers all of the aspects you'll need to know to successfully execute any trade show project for your company.

Locating the Best Trade Shows in Your Market

In every industry, there always seem to be more trade shows than a company could ever afford to attend in a year. There's also a great tendency for the sales and marketing types in your company, who enjoy the travel and excitement associated with trade shows, to push you to exhibit at every show. However, the experienced marketing manager knows that most of the sales potential in any market comes from the top one or two trade shows in an industry, and they will only focus their trade show activities on these top events.

Trade shows seem to follow the same pattern as trade publications. Just like there are usually no more than two major trade publications that offer the best, broadest advertising coverage in each industry, there are usually just one or two major trade shows each year that represent the best sales opportunities for your company. And, because of their busy work schedules and the added travel expense, most of the potential customers in your industry will also limit their attendance to the one or two major trade shows in your field.

If you've worked in your industry awhile, you probably already know which trade shows are the best sales and marketing opportunities for your company. However, if you're a recently-hired marketing manager who's new to the industry, or you're launching a new product in a new market, you can locate the best trade show opportunities by checking the following sources:

Your company's sales reps talk to prospects and customers every day, so they know the top one or two shows their prospects and customers attend each year;

Trade association contacts, such as membership directors, are usually well-connected in their industries, and will point you to an industry's best trade shows in their fields;

The major trade publications in your industry feature advertising and editorial announcements of upcoming trade shows in your company's marketplace. Flipping through a year's worth of your industry's leading trade publications will help you build a list of the top trade show opportunities;

Your competitors in any new market have usually sniffed out the best trade shows, and will be in attendance there.

Trade Show Timing and Planning

When scheduling a trade show project for your company, it's important to realize that most shows require a very long lead time—often, at least 6 months (and, usually 12 months) to plan in advance of the show date. This means that any trade show producers require you to reserve your booth at least 6-12 months in advance, and some of the most popular trade shows even sell out *before* the end of the current year's show.

Start all trade show production at least 60 days in advance: Because you must reserve a trade show booth months before the show, the production of many of the associated marketing deliverables required for your show—your trade show display backdrop, signage, collateral, and other marketing materials—often gets pushed to the back burner in the intervening months between the time you sign your company up for the show, and your show date.

What usually happens next is that execution of important trade show projects, such as design and production of your booth backdrop, becomes a mad scramble begun just a few weeks before the show. Avoid this by starting your trade show execution activities at least 60 days before the show date. This allows plenty of time for you and your ad agency or marketing consultant to put some quality work into all the marketing deliverables associated with the show, without turning it into an unnecessary fire drill.

Evaluating Trade Show Opportunities

Once you've identified the top trade shows in your field, contact the producers of these shows and ask for their exhibitor sales kits. You can also get a lot of the basic information you need, such as rates, last year's attendees, etc., from the show producers' Web sites.

Here are the questions you need to ask your trade show's sales rep:

Number and mix of attendees: How many people attended last year's show? How does attendance look for the current show? What types of individuals, by job title, attend the show? If you ask for it, many show sponsors will send you, free of charge, a printout or electronic file of their last year's attendee list, showing *only the job titles and company names* for all attendees. This gives you a good idea of the mix of attendees, and whether or not attendees at the show match the types of prospects you're trying to reach with your company's marketing program;

Other exhibitors: Who else is exhibiting at the show? You can often get a list of last year's exhibitors from the show producer's Web site, and your sales rep can tell you the exhibitors who've already signed up for the upcoming show. If the major corporate players in your industry will be exhibiting at the show, this usually indicates that a show is worthwhile. And if your competitors are going to be at the show, then your company should probably be there, too;

Conference program content: Review the show's **conference show guide**, which outlines the content being covered at the show conference. Now would also be a very good time to ask your show sales rep for the name of the person at his company who handles speaker selection for their conference sessions, since there may be opportunities to get your company's key executives placed as conference speakers at the show (more on this in **Figure 13-16**);

Rates and availability: Of course, you need to find out how much it costs to rent booth space at the show, and what booth spaces are available. Trade shows produced by trade associations often have higher booth space rates for non-members vs. members, so you'll have to consider whether or not it's cheaper, or more advantageous, for your company to join the association to attend the show as an exhibitor.

Once you've nailed down the essential information on your company's best show opportunities, and you've made your decision to exhibit at the show, you can now move on to the next two steps: Selecting a booth location, and producing your booth.

Figure 13-1:

Trade Show Booth Diagram—A must for evaluating and planning any trade show opportunity

Ask the Trade Show's Producer for their booth diagram to check the best locations for your booth at the show

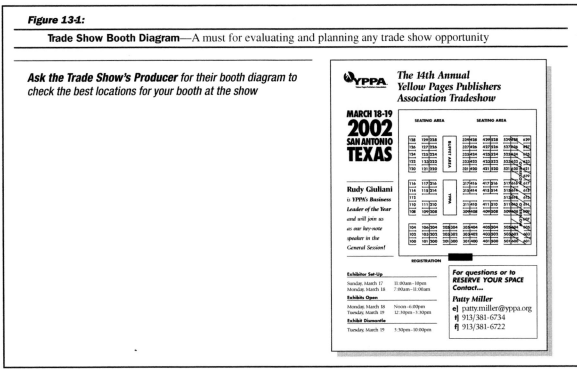

Selecting a Trade Show Booth: Location and Size

Your choice of booth size and location are critical. Of the two, you booth's location is more important than its size, because booth location plays a major role in the quality and amount of visitor traffic your company receives at the show.

Choosing the Best Trade Show Booth Location

Ask your show's sales rep for a booth diagram, showing the booth spaces available for the show. Your show's sales rep can also send you an up-to-date version of this diagram, showing the companies that have already reserved booth spaces at the show.

From this diagram, you'll want to note where the major exhibitors are located, and where your competitors are. Major exhibitors are generally your industry's biggest movers and shakers, and they usually take the biggest booth spaces and best locations at the show. If there's a major strategic advantage for your company to be positioned near one of these big companies—if for example, one of them is a major joint venture partner—this should play a role in your booth location decision. If possible, you'll also want to locate your booth far enough away from any of your company's direct competitors: Better that your sales staff spend their time staying focused on talking to prospects in your booth, than being worried about who's visiting your competitor's booth across the aisle.

The best booth space locations in a trade show are:

In the front row facing the show entrance: This is the best space for your booth: When show visitors walk on to the show floor, your booth is one of the first they will see. Out in front, you'll have the opportunity to pull these visitors in before any other exhibitor. While these positions are often taken by the biggest exhibitors, try to reserve a booth space here, if at all possible;

At the end of an aisle, front half of exhibit floor: The next best position is space at the end of an aisle, preferably as close to the entrance of the exhibit floor as possible, or at least within the front half of the entire show floor. Since booth spaces at the end of an aisle place your booth at the intersection of two aisles, this location makes your booth visible from at least two sides (or all three sides if your booth fills an entire corner);

Center interior row, front half of exhibit floor: If neither front or corner booth positions are available, the third best position, and the best option if your company is selecting the "standard" 10' X 10' minimum booth size, is any space in any *interior* row in the front half of the show floor. These spaces are usually the ones most available to exhibitors taking the minimum-size booth spaces, and they're a default choice if you can't get a space in the other two positions. If you're unable to reserve a space toward the front half of the floor closest to the show's main entrance, any other booth space in any interior row will do;

Outer perimeter locations: The least desirable booth space positions are those along the outer perimeter of the show floor. Booths in these locations attract much less traffic than other locations. Since they are the least-popular spaces, they are usually the last to sell out, and may be your only option if you are trying to get into a show on short notice. If this is your only space option, avoid booth spaces at the end of a row, or by fire exits; these are the loneliest booth spaces of them all.

As you make your final booth choice, pay close attention to who your "neighbors" will be, on either side of, and directly across from, your booth, to avoid getting a booth space next to a competitor, or any other exhibitor whose presence close to your booth may reflect poorly on your company.

Selecting Your Booth Size

A bigger booth space rarely translates to better sales results at a trade show. Since location is far more important than booth size, and doubling your booth size roughly doubles your booth cost (and other direct show costs, such as your booth backdrop display and related signage), there's little downside risk to keeping your booth space to a minimum.

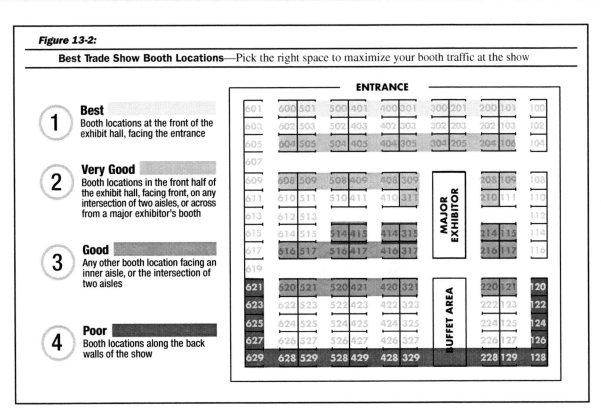

Figure 13-2:

Best Trade Show Booth Locations—Pick the right space to maximize your booth traffic at the show

1   **Best**
Booth locations at the front of the exhibit hall, facing the entrance

2   **Very Good**
Booth locations in the front half of the exhibit hall, facing front, on any intersection of two aisles, or across from a major exhibitor's booth

3   **Good**
Any other booth location facing an inner aisle, or the intersection of two aisles

4   **Poor**
Booth locations along the back walls of the show

Trade show producers usually offer booth space in 10' X 10' size, the minimum booth space available for exhibitors. This size is adequate for most small to medium-size companies, and can comfortably accommodate three or four of your company's sales reps and prospects who visit your booth. You can go for a larger booth space, by joining two or more of these 10' X 10' spaces together, or by renting larger booth sizes, which often gets you a better location on the show floor, such as near the main entrance, or on the end of an aisle.

While a company can always spend too much by renting more booth space than it needs, marketing managers rarely regret having rented a booth space that was too small. There is really no justification for a larger booth space, unless your company's size, the size of your product line, or the number of sales reps in your company requires it.

Getting Your Company Into the Show

Once you've selected and reserved your company's booth space and location, your next step is to handle the other important show planning steps required for your trade show project.

Reserving your booth and related services: Show producers require you to make a formal reservation for your booth space location, and often require a deposit of part (or all) of the booth space fee prior to the show. In the exhibitor's kit provided by the show producer, you'll also find a series of forms to fill out to obtain various additional, important, services provided by the show producer. The prices for these additional show services always seem rather expensive. Some services, like electrical hookups, are costly because they're a monopoly, and other services, such as audio/visual equipment and booth cleaning, are costly because suppliers of these services think they can get away with it (in some cases, however, there are alternatives, covered further in this section).

Here are the services you'll need for your booth:

Electricity and phone/Internet hookups: If you need electrical hookups for demonstrating computers or other equipment, now's the time to secure the outlets and voltages you need. The same goes for phone and Internet hookups. This service is only available from the contractor hired by the show producer or the exhibit hall, so you'll have to pay their price for what you need;

Booth carpeting, furniture and cleaning: Some shows will include carpeting for your booth space in the price of booth rental, and others charge extra, but in either case, you need a carpet for your booth. Since carpet is very heavy to ship, you usually end up having to pay what they're asking to rent a carpet for your booth. However, booth "cleaning" (vacuuming, actually) can cost your company up to *$150 a day extra*. Bring along a small vacuum and an extension cord (a Dirt Devil is perfect) and do the job yourself when no one's looking; you'll save your company several hundred dollars;

Audio/visual equipment (A/V): Rental of PCs, TV monitors, DVD players, etc. is another overpriced exhibitor service, but you can always find a less expensive A/V rental vendor if you look for one yourself in the city where the show is being held;

Booth set-up/breakdown and shipping: Added booth setup and breakdown fees are common in union-controlled exhibition halls. You can avoid these needless costs by making your own shipping arrangements and getting a modular booth backdrop that you and your team can wheel in to the exhibit hall by yourselves (more on these modular booth displays further in this chapter).

Plan ahead for these very important show preparations, because it's always much more expensive if these services have to be arranged on a rush basis just before the show. Also, make sure to keep copies of all the paperwork used to set up these services, and take them with you to the show in case there's a problem. You may need to document your order for any one of these services with a show vendor.

Trade Show Booth Options

The biggest marketing-related project you'll undertake for any trade show appearance is the production and execution of your company's booth display, or "backdrop." Your booth backdrop is a kind of wall that stands at the rear of your booth space, displaying your company's logo, text, and other visual imagery.

Your backdrop is, in effect, "packaging" for your company and its product at the show. It's the first impression your company gives to show attendees who've never heard of your company, and you should put as much care into its design as you would any of your company's own product packaging, printed materials, or any other marketing deliverable.

While you could spend as much money for a custom-built trade show display as you would for a small house, most small to mid-sized companies (even many large ones) use standardized, manufactured trade show exhibits available from companies such as Skyline Exhibits (**www.skylinedisplays.com**), or Prime Signs (**www.tradeshowshop.com**), who produce and sell a range of trade show displays for all applications and booth spaces.

There are many possible variations in booth layouts for large areas, but since it's likely that all of your company's trade show projects will use either standard 10' X 10' or the larger 10' X 20' booth spaces, your booth layout will likely consist of your backdrop, some additional smaller signs, and, ideally, a large flat-panel video display unit (more on this further in this chapter). Additionally, you can incorporate some counter units or display pedestals to your booth layout if your company has a product line to display at the show.

Trade Show Booth Backdrop

Next to design appeal and affordability, the most important features for any trade show booth backdrop are light weight and compact size. For most trade show applications, the ideal unit is one that doesn't cost a lot to ship, and can be taken along by your marketing and sales team by plane or car to any show location.

Fortunately, this is one marketing deliverable where there's a single, easy answer. The best backdrop for both 10' X 10' and 10' X 20' booth space sizes are modular "pop-up" backdrop units, such as those manufactured by Skyline Exhibits, and several other companies.

Pop-up displays use lightweight, custom-printed, four-color panels that are fastened to an aluminum frame unit designed to fold down to a very compact size. These aluminum frames are a show all by themselves: Consisting of a networked superstructure of many hinged, lightweight aluminum rods, these frames miraculously expand from their fully-folded shipping size of about 40" high by 12" square to create a standing 8' X 10' backdrop.

Figure 13-3:

Pop-Up Trade Show Displays—An affordable and attractive trade show backdrop for your company

Pop-Up Trade Show Displays can be easily transported in small, lightweight shipping containers, and use expandable frames and colorful graphics to create a visually attractive trade show backdrop

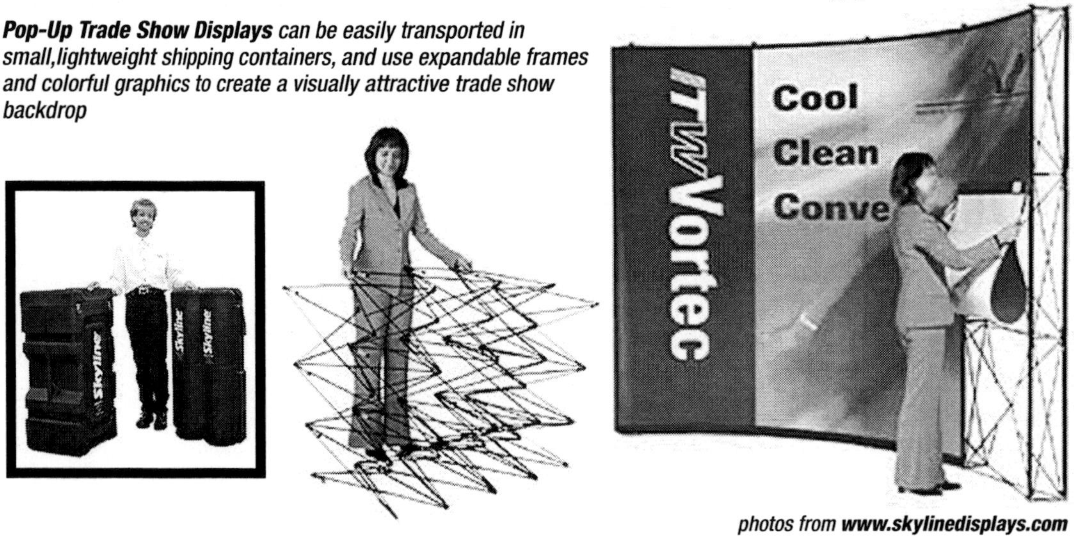

photos from www.skylinedisplays.com

The graphic panels of your backdrop are printed in full color on a matte or gloss vinyl-like material called Lexan, and are invisibly fastened to the front of this aluminum frame with special clips. You can print different panels, each with different graphics or sales copy, to use for different shows, or to highlight certain products or sales benefits targeted to the market served by each show. The panels are sturdy enough to be rolled up and packed into the plastic shipping case for the unit.

The graphics for these front panels can be produced from artwork created by any desktop publishing program, and offer you unlimited creative options for the design of your backdrop. Art for these front panels can be output as a single, continuous design, which means you can think of your backdrop as a single large canvas for displaying your company's logo, tagline, sales headline, imagery, photos, and background textures, in full color and high resolution.

The entire backdrop—frame, front panels and associated hardware, stows neatly in one or two sturdy, specially-designed, wheeled shipping cases, small enough to be checked as airline baggage, put into a car trunk or back seat, or shipped by any standard shipping method. This gives you the logistical option of shipping your booth by regular UPS or Fedex to your hotel at a relatively affordable price, or—if you're running on a tight schedule—taking your booth with you when you travel to the show by air or by car.

With either option, you get a higher degree of confidence that your booth will be waiting for you at your hotel, or traveling along with you as checked baggage (less confidence there, for sure). But in either case, you avoid the potential nightmare of shipping show materials directly to the bulk receiving area of the exhibition hall, where they're further out of your control, and where you won't know whether they arrived or not until the day you arrive at the show location

Cost and delivery: A pop-up backdrop display for a 10' X 10' booth size costs $3,000-4,000, including output of front-panel graphics, plus your ad agency or marketing consultant's design and production costs for the backdrop's graphic panels.

How Show Attendees Wander a Trade Show—and How to Get Them to Your Booth

The objective for any trade show is to draw as many *qualified* prospects to your company's booth as possible. Many marketers who think that traffic volume alone measures the success of a trade show resort to various gimmicks, like giveaways, contests, or other distractions to draw as many visitors to their booth as possible. Marketers who use these tactics will draw more traffic to their booths, and their salespeople will be very busy trying to qualify them. However, they won't draw as many qualified prospects as they would have if they had done a better job of rapidly familiarizing them with their products, so these prospects could qualify themselves.

Here's how a casual, disinterested show visitor, walking down the aisle at the show, sees your booth for the first time—and the booth elements required to draw show visitors to your booth:

Booth backdrop: The first thing most show visitors notice about your booth is the backdrop. If it has a simple layout that communicates your company name, and a brief tagline that describes your product, both set big enough so they're easy to see from 30 feet away, the initial message communicated by your booth backdrop will register in the prospect's mind. Once this happens, the prospect makes a very subtle mental calculation as to whether or not he or she can use your company's product or service. If the prospect is immediately interested, he'll draw closer to your booth right away. If he's undecided (like most show visitors), he'll start to walk directly past your booth space, his eyes now shifting to the smaller signs along the front of your booth;

Smaller signs: As your prospect walks alongside your booth, his eyes briefly wander across the bulleted sales benefit copy points you've printed on the smaller, easel-mounted signs you've placed in front of your booth, right along the aisle. These signs are critical because they must slow the prospect down long enough so he'll read more of them, and shift his attention to your video display;

Video display: This is a continuously running, 1-2 minute, professionally-narrated video sales presentation on your product, shown on a 42' flat-panel plasma display at the front of your booth. For about 10 seconds, your prospect hears a polished, letter-perfect sales presentation about your product in the voiceover of the video as he watches it on screen. Once prospects see the video, your company's sales reps can then engage the prospect, by introducing themselves and talking to them about their needs (that is, if the show visitor hasn't already approached your rep on their own).

Each of these three critical elements of your booth—backdrop, small signs, and video display—work at a distance that is appropriate to them, doing what each does best to draw qualified prospects to your booth. As your prospects see your backdrop, and are drawn closer to your booth, they get a better look at your smaller signs. Then, they see your video presentation, and overhear your sales reps talking about your product to other booth visitors.

In a few seconds, they build an impression in their mind of your company, and your product. As more time passes, they become more interested in your product to the point where, by their eye contact or proximity, they initiate contact with one of your sales reps working the booth—that is, if your sales rep hasn't already made contact. This is how prospects are drawn to your booth.

If any of these three elements are missing, or aren't strong enough to hold your viewer's attention as well as they should, you run the risk of losing show visitors who could be prospects.

Good booth elements help show visitors qualify themselves: If all of your booth elements work well, a visitor sees your booth backdrop, skim-reads your smaller signs, listens to your video, but then walks away from your booth has, by his action, told you he's not a qualified prospect. In doing this, he allows your sales reps to focus their attention on the interested prospects who remain in your booth.

This is not to say that your company's sales reps shouldn't try to collar potential prospects as they walk by, or that you shouldn't have a contest or a giveaway to draw booth visitors. The important point is that when you and your team are working on a trade show project, you should always focus on developing persuasive content and presentation that respects your potential customers as intelligent, reasoning human beings, instead of relying on the usual show gimmicks that treat show attendees as freeloaders on the lookout for another booth giveaway to stash in their tote bags.

The next section covers the execution of the critical trade show elements, and describes the presentation techniques you can use to drive qualified prospects to your booth.

Producing Your Company's Trade Show Backdrop Design

Your trade show booth's backdrop is the marketing element that performs the first, most important job of attracting the attention of show visitors. Like the headline of a print ad, or an outer envelope of a direct mail piece, it uses text, or text in combination with a visual element (your company logo, product shot, or both) to hook the viewer, and draw him closer to your booth space.

Figure 13-4:

Trade Show Booth Visibility—Carefully consider your trade show booth's first impression

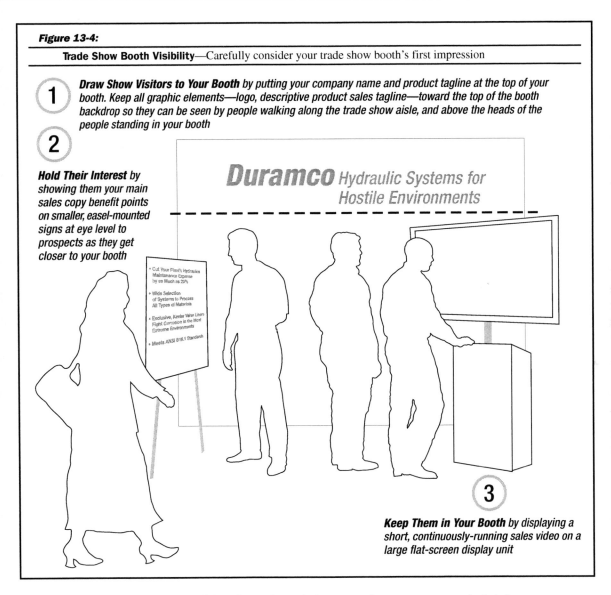

1 *Draw Show Visitors to Your Booth* by putting your company name and product tagline at the top of your booth. Keep all graphic elements—logo, descriptive product sales tagline—toward the top of the booth backdrop so they can be seen by people walking along the trade show aisle, and above the heads of the people standing in your booth

2 *Hold Their Interest* by showing them your main sales copy benefit points on smaller, easel-mounted signs at eye level to prospects as they get closer to your booth

Duramco Hydraulic Systems for Hostile Environments

* Cut Your Plant's Hydraulics Maintenance Expense by as Much as 20%

* Wide Selection of Systems to Process All Types of Materials

* Exclusive, Kevlar Valve Liners Fight Corrosion in the Most Extreme Environments

* Meets ANSI B16.1 Standards

3 *Keep Them in Your Booth* by displaying a short, continuously-running sales video on a large flat-screen display unit

The purpose of your backdrop is to telegraph the name of your company and a brief sales description of your product or service to the casual, uninterested viewer—your potential prospect—walking down the aisle along your booth space. To meet this goal, these text and visual elements must be placed high enough on your backdrop so they can be seen clearly from 30 feet, and above the heads of the people standing in your booth.

The key to specifying the design of your booth backdrop to your ad agency or marketing consultant is to keep it simple: If you are working in the standard 10' X 10' booth space, the only visual elements that should be featured on your backdrop are your company logo, a sales tagline describing your product or service, and some visual imagery, such as a photo of your product. Your company logo and sales tagline should be set in the top third of your booth backdrop, high enough so they can be seen over the head of someone who is standing in your booth (that is, about four feet in front of the backdrop).

When working in the standard 10' X 10' booth space, don't place any other sales copy, like bulleted product benefits or features, on your backdrop, since any copy placed below the top third of your backdrop will be blocked from view by the people standing in the booth. Instead, put these sales copy points on one or two smaller easel-mounted signs to be displayed close to the aisle at the front of your booth (see **Figure 13-4**). However, if you are working on a backdrop for a 10' X 20' or larger booth space, the extra booth space gives you more flexibility in your design options and allows you to place bulleted sales copy directly on your backdrop panels (see **Figure 13-7**).

Backdrop sales tagline copy: Give some careful thought to the sales tagline you use on your backdrop. Your sales tagline should concisely answer any two of the following three questions, in 12 words or less:

- **What is your product or service?**
- **Who is it for?**
- **What does it do for them?**

The backdrop's sales tagline is a brief, simple statement that mostly describes what your company sells. If you can, try to incorporate a few "benefit" words (such as "low-cost," "intelligent") into your tagline; if you can include your product's main benefit, that's even better, but not necessary.

Here are a few sample booth backdrop sales taglines:

- **One-Stop Environmental Mapping Services for Engineering Professionals**
- **The Low-Cost Newswire Alternative for Your Radio News Operation**
- **Intelligent Vision Systems for Robotic Assembly Operations**

The only purpose of the sales tagline on your backdrop is to cut through the noise and confusion of the show by sparking your prospect's attention as he or she walks down the aisle. The main selling job of your booth is handled by the other booth elements—the smaller signs at the front of your booth, and your sales video.

Small Booth Aisle Signs

To communicate your product's most important benefits and features to show visitors who approach your booth at close range, place one or two easel-mounted signs by the aisle at the front of your booth. These signs give show visitors clear, telegraphic sales information on your product and, since they are mounted on free-

---

Figure 13-5:

Expedient Trade Show Backdrop—A lower-cost alternative to modular pop-up trade show displays

---

Expedient Backdrops, *using Lexan or less-expensive laminated graphic backdrops hung from aluminum photographic background stands, are a low-cost alternative to pop-up display units*

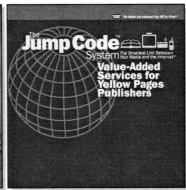

---

standing easels, can be put anywhere, and angled in any direction, to catch the eye of as many show visitors as possible who walk by your booth.

Compared to other trade show deliverables, booth aisle signs are quick and inexpensive to produce. This is a big advantage, because it allows you to change the bulleted sales copy used on these signs to target your company's product for each audience at each new trade show your company attends. These signs can also be produced at any sign shop, which means you can even re-work them *during* a show if necessary, to produce new signs that present new, more effective sales benefit points as you discover them, by listening to prospects at the show.

Sign options: Depending on your booth size and layout, you can use two signs, each measuring 16" wide by 20" high, or a single, larger sign, measuring 22" wide by 30" high.

Sales copy for aisle signs: Set about 3 to 6 bulleted copy points on each sign. Copy for this bullet text can be adapted from the bulleted copy you use in your brochures and other printed collateral. Determine the best features and benefits to use in this copy by performing the sales copywriting exercises covered in the "Laundry List" writing exercise in Chapter 4. If your company's product or service has an interesting visual presentation, you can also include it on your aisle sign in the form of a large, arresting photo or graphic.

Sales benefits: Here are some examples of sales benefits that would work well on aisle signs:

- **Increase output in all of your assembly operations**
- **Reduce product defects before they reach QA**
- **Highest resolution imaging and fastest image processing in its class**

Figure 13-6:

Easel-Mounted Aisle Signs—These hard-hitting signs do the most selling work in your trade show booth

Aisle Sign Options: You can use two signs, each measuring 16" wide by 20" high, or a single, larger sign, measuring 22" wide by 30" high, to put your product's key sales benefits right in front of trade show visitors

Mount these signs on either floor-standing or tabletop easels, and position them so they can be seen by the largest number of show visitors

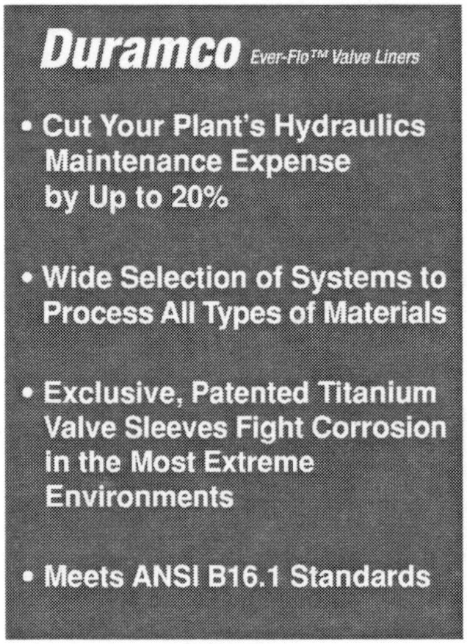

Duramco Ever-Flo™ Valve Liners

• Cut Your Plant's Hydraulics Maintenance Expense by Up to 20%

• Wide Selection of Systems to Process All Types of Materials

• Exclusive, Patented Titanium Valve Sleeves Fight Corrosion in the Most Extreme Environments

• Meets ANSI B16.1 Standards

Duramco Ever-Flo™ Valve Liners

• Cut Maintenance Expense Up to 20%

• Wide Selection of Systems

• Titanium Valve Sleeves Fight Corrosion

• Meets ANSI B16.1

22" W X 30" H 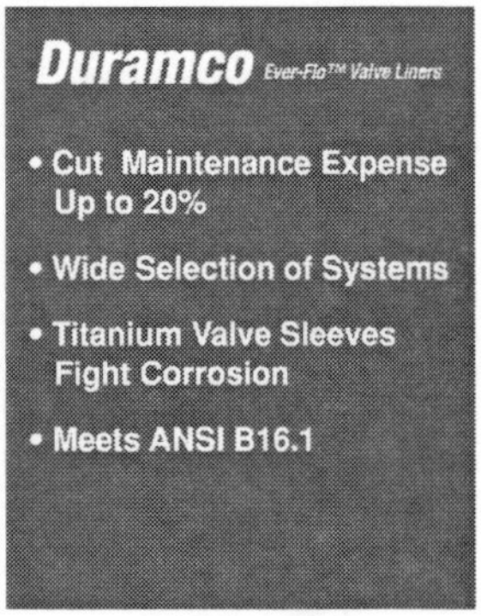   *16" W X 20" H*

Product features: Here are some examples of product features, written as aisle sign bullet points:

• **Full-color, 12 megapixel CCD imaging display**
• **Ruggedized, mil-spec control unit for adverse shop floor environments**
• **Meets ANSI R15.06 requirements**

If you already have bullet-point sales copy from your sales brochures and other printed marketing collateral, your ad agency or marketing consultant can readily adapt this copy for use on these aisle signs. Select the most important benefits and features from your sales materials, and boil these down to the fewest words possible.

Sign copy layout: If you're using two smaller signs (16" wide X 20" high), you can make one sign the "benefits" sign, with 4 to 6 of your product's top, bulleted sales benefits, and the other sign the "features," sign, with 4 to 6 bullets listing your product's top features. If you're using a single, larger sign (22" wide by 30" high), you can combine benefits and features on the same sign, starting with 3 to 6 benefits at the top of the sign, and 3 to 6 features below.

Maximum readability: Clear visibility and impact are the key goals for booth aisle signs. Make sure that copy on these signs is readable from a distance of 8 feet—the average, centerline distance from where most show visitors walking down the center aisle of the show will see your booth.

Figure 13-7:

Larger Booth Backdrops—Larger booth spaces provide more space options for sales copy and graphics

On Larger Booth Spaces, such as this backdrop for a 20' wide booth, sales copy bullet points and other sales text can be printed directly on the backdrop (see inset below)

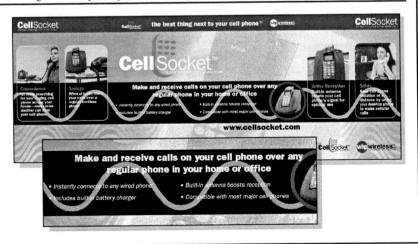

To accomplish this, text used on these signs should be set at about 90 points (about 1-1/4" inches tall). Sans-serif typefaces, such as Helvetica or Franklin Gothic, provide the best readability for all signage applications.

Sign design and production: Signs can be set either as black type on a plain white background, or in reversed white type on a dark color background. For signage applications, your ad agency or marketing consultant will have these signs output by a sign production shop on an inkjet printer and mounted on 1/4" or thicker foam-core mounting board (also known as "Gatorfoam").

Sign placement: Arrange easel-mounted signs so they can be seen by the most people walking by your booth at the show.

The most common placement for these signs is about six inches away from the front edge of your booth, facing out from your booth. If you are using two signs, and space in your 10' X 10' booth is tight, then, facing the front of your booth, you can angle the right sign about 35° clockwise, and the left sign about 35° counter-clockwise (i.e., both signs angled slightly toward the inside of your booth), to give people more space to move around in your booth. This also gives these signs more side-facing exposure to site visitors walking down either side of the aisle in front of your booth.

To get the best visibility for signs in your booth, experiment with sign placement during the show. For example, if the flow of show attendees seems to be moving more in one direction than another, angle your signs to face this flow of foot traffic.

Easel mounting options: You can select from a variety of floor-standing easels (such as Stanrite easels, made by The Testrite Company of Newark, NJ) to display

Figure 13-8:

Booth Signage Layout Options—Typical layouts shown for both standard and corner booth spaces

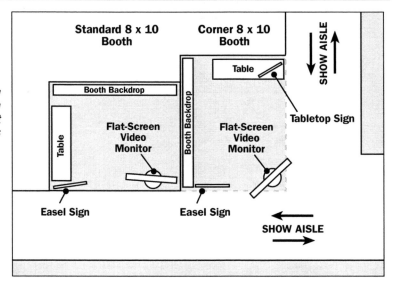

Arrange Your Booth's Signage and other features, such as video display units or product displays, for maximum visibility at the show.

Use a combination of floor-standing and tabletop signs to put your main sales benefit bullet points in front of the largest number of attendees at the show. Signs can be angled to face toward the best flows of show traffic

aisle-mounted signs in your booth. Most booths are supplied with a 2' X 6' folding table, so you can use a tabletop easel to mount one of your booth signs on the table, to save floor space in your booth.

Sign options for larger booth spaces: If you're using a 10' X 20' or larger booth space, this larger space gives show visitors a clearer view of your entire backdrop, and allows them to see sales copy printed lower down on the backdrop. Because of this, you can incorporate bulleted-text sales copy directly on the lower portion of your booth backdrop, either as a part of the original backdrop design, or on separate, detachable signs, mounted with velcro on your backdrop, so that sales copy can be changed with each show, or for shows in new markets (see **Figure 13-7**). Even for larger booth spaces, small, freestanding, text-bullet signs give your company's sales message an added boost.

Trade Show Sales Video on Flat-Panel Display

A continuously-running sales video, shown on a 42" flat-panel video display in your booth, is a powerful trade show marketing tool. This one- to two-minute video presentation, incorporating a professionally-narrated audio voiceover to give a letter-perfect sales presentation on your company's product or service, draws visitors to your booth, and holds them there while they listen and watch.

Figure 13-9:

Trade Show Booth Video—Use the power of video—and audio—to keep prospects in your booth at the show

A Trade Show Booth Video, shown on a large flat-panel display in your booth, holds prospects in your booth by making a polished, high-quality sales presentation for your company's product or service.

When shown on flat-panel plasma display units (inset, left), trade show videos are produced in wide-screen letterbox format, and played back on a continuously-running DVD

There isn't a more effective tool for drawing qualified prospects to your booth, and holding their attention. A booth video gives your sales reps the perfect opportunity to engage show visitors who are watching it, and frequently prompts show visitors to approach your sales reps on their own, after seeing and hearing a small portion of the video presentation.

Trade Show Video Production: Video is, in reality, an *audio* medium. People don't really "watch" TV, so much as listen to it. The most important part of your booth's sales video is its voiceover narration, which should be adapted from your company's standard sales presentation, and should use all of the key sales benefits and product features your sales reps use in their own sales presentations.

Since the audio portion of the video carries most of the load of presenting and selling your product, the video portion of this project needn't be an elaborate production. Often, all that is needed are some video clips of your product in use, mixed in with some PowerPoint-style text slides synchronized over your audio to reinforce your product's key benefits, as shown in **Figure 13-10**.

Animation, visual effects, and other eye candy always adds a "wow" factor, but don't let these hold up your project, or get in the way of delivering your sales message. Any visual imagery, no matter how spectacular, will never be as effective as the content presented in your project's spoken *audio*. Keep it simple, and put most of your effort into making sure that the voiceover track clearly presents and sells your product.

Figure 13-10:

Trade Show Booth Video Production—Use PowerPoint-style text bullets, along with audio, to sell your product

Use Both Sales Text Bullet Points and Audio to support your trade show booth video's sales presentation. This short (under 3 minutes) video holds interested prospects in your booth long enough to be engaged by your company's sales reps

Your ad agency, marketing consultant, or video production company should be able to adapt your company's sales presentation into a suitable trade show video. For further information on managing video projects, see Chapter 15.

Execution: Trade show videos should be mastered on DVD to run as a continuous loop. Make four copies of your DVD—one for your booth, and three copies as backups, in case a glitch develops on any of your DVDs during the show. You may not think you'd need this many backups, but DVDs will sometimes break down after many hours of continuous playback in your booth. This can happen at the worst possible moment, so be prepared.

Production cost: A one- to two-minute trade show booth video costs from $2,500-$5,000 to produce, depending on how much original video needs to be shot for your project, and how much time is spent producing and tweaking the special effects used on it. When you consider the fact that there is no more effective marketing tool for drawing traffic to your booth and holding it there, a sales video more than justifies its production cost.

And once produced, your sales video has additional uses beyond your trade show. For example, with slight formatting changes, it can be placed on your company's Web site to give site visitors a quick view of your product's key sales benefits and features, and it can also be used by your company's sales reps as a selling aid when they make field sales presentations.

Renting a flat-panel display: Because they're such effective trade show traffic builders, flat-panel displays are have become quite popular at trade shows. This wider use has dramatically cut rental prices for these units. A local audio/visual (A/V) rental company can usually provide these units for less cost than the "official" audio visual supplier designated by the show sponsor. Rental cost for a 42" flat-panel display, with a metal stand and DVD player, rented from a local A/V rental company, runs between $250-$350 per day. Do a Google search on the Internet, or go to your public library and check the local Yellow Pages for the city where the show is taking place, to locate a local A/V rental supplier for these units.

Trade Show Pre-Marketing: What to Do Before the Show

The promotional activities you execute prior to the show date are almost as important as the marketing activities done during the show. Since these projects must often be started well in advance of a show (about 6-8 weeks), they're often lost in the stampede of the marketing manager's other day-to-day marketing projects. Nonetheless, experienced marketing managers know the importance of pre-show promotion, and will make the time to get it done.

The goal of pre-show promotion is simple: You want to let show visitors know about your product and your company, by giving them just enough information about both, so they'll remember your company when they're at the show.

As a show exhibitor, you can obtain a mailing list of registered show attendees from the show's management, to send out a mailing (both hard-copy and e-mail) timed to arrive approximately 1-1/2 weeks before the show date.

A pre-show mailing is the most effective way to get the word out on your company and its product before the trade show, by reaching attendees in the relative peace and quiet of their own offices. By imprinting your company's sales message in the mind of your prospect ahead of the show, you give your company a better chance of cutting through the noise and confusion created by the hundreds of other companies who will be competing for attention once the show is underway. All you need to accomplish with pre-show promotion is to make show attendees mildly aware of your company and your product, so when they see your booth at the show they'll know a little more about you than they do about the other companies around you.

Trade Show Postcard Mailings

The best printed marketing deliverable to use for a pre-show mailing is a 5-1/2" high X 8-1/2" wide four-color gloss postcard, mailed to the show attendee mailing list by First Class Mail so it arrives approximately 1-1/2 weeks (eight business days) before the first day of the show. This allows just enough time for your prospect to see your postcard before the show, without arriving so early that your prospects will forget about it by the time they get to the show.

Key postcard elements: The goal of the sales copy benefits and features used in your pre-show promotion postcard is to give prospects just enough information about

Figure 13-11:

Trade Show Postcard Mailing—Mail a postcard to the mailing list of show attendees before the show date

Let Show Attendees Know You'll be Exhibiting at the Show by sending a postcard two weeks before the show date. These four-color, 5-1/2" x 8-1/2" color postcards, printed with your company's sales copy and booth number, make show visitors aware of your company and its products before they arrive at the show

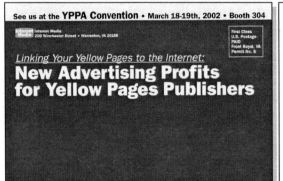

your company's product in bulleted form, so that some of the key benefits or features will "stick" in the mind of your prospect when he's walking down your aisle at the show. Your postcard should contain these elements:

• **Show name and date:** Let the prospect know that your postcard pertains to his upcoming attendance at the show, which is already important to him because it's on his travel itinerary;

• **Your booth number:** This is important and obvious, but it's surprising how many marketers forget to print their company's booth number on pre-show promotion deliverables. Tell your prospects where your company will be at the show, so they'll know where to find you;

• **Sales headline on front of card:** As with any direct mail piece, lead the front of your card with your product's main sales benefit;

• **Bulleted sales benefits and product features:** Put enough of your product's key sales benefits and product features on the reverse side of the card to "tease" the reader, by briefly describing your company, its product, and their benefits to the prospect. Set key benefits in boldface type, so they stand out from the rest of the text, and are skim-readable;

• **Contact info, Web site, and booth number:** Put your company's phone number, Web address, and e-mail address on the back of the card, so prospects who are very interested in your product can check out your company in

---

Figure 13-12:

E-Mail Trade Show Invitation—A low-cost way to invite your customers and prospects to your booth

---

Promote Your Company's Show Appearance by Sending Interested Customers and Prospects a colorful, HTML-format E-mail invitation before the show.

E-mail invitations are an inexpensive way to let both existing customers and current sales prospects know where to find your company at the show.

Personalization, as shown in this example, is always better, if your technical staff can do the necessary programming

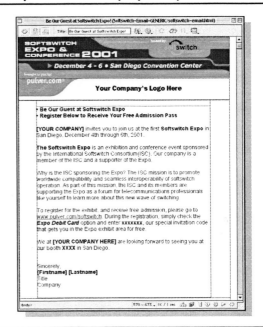

---

advance of the show. Repeat the name of the show and your company's booth number on this address block;

- **Free premium:** Optionally, you can offer the postcard recipient a free sample of your company's product, or some other free gift or premium, when they visit your booth at the show.

When specifying a trade show postcard to your ad agency or marketing consultant, think of it as a quick-reading, condensed version of your company's larger, standard product sales brochure. In fact, when you are writing your outline, or "spec" for your agency, you can lift and adapt key benefits and other sales copy from your sales brochure and use it on the postcard.

Timing and execution: With a generous allowance for scheduling, if you allow one week for printing, one week in your lettershop (for affixing of mailing labels or imprinting of addresses), and one week for arrival to attendees, your postcard artwork should be completed by your ad agency or marketing consultant, and ready for the printer 4-1/2 weeks before the date of the show. This will insure that your postcard will arrive approximately 1-1/2 weeks before the show date.

Figure 13-13:

Print Display Ads in Trade Show Dailies and Show Guides—Another trade show promotional opportunity

Larger Trade Shows Offer Additional Advertising Opportunities for Exhibitors with print trade show daily publications and show guide programs, distributed to attendees at the show.

Show attendees are often too busy to read advertising in show dailies and show guides, so keep your sales message to a few basic copy points and (most important) your booth number, so your ad can be skim-read by show attendees

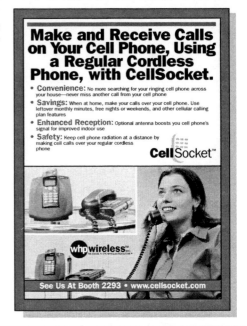

E-Mailing Show Announcements/Invitations to Existing Sales Prospects

Trade shows are a unique opportunity for your sales reps to meet with their existing sales prospects, and to close sales at the show. It's likely that many of your company's existing prospects and customers, whose contact information is already stored in your company's sales and marketing database, will also be attending the show.

In addition to mailing your pre-show promotional postcard, you should also plan on sending out an HTML-format e-mail announcement to this group of prospects and customers in your sales database (see **Figure 13-12**). The announcement should take the form of an invitation from your sales rep to the prospect or customer to visit your company's booth at the show. It requires extra programming on the part of your Web staff, but the e-mail invitation should, if possible, be personally addressed to the prospect in the body of the e-mail message.

Like printed postcards, e-mail promotional invitations should be sent to your current prospect and customer lists so they arrive approximately 1-1/2 weeks before the show date. While you may also be tempted to send these e-mail messages to the attendee list you receive from the trade show management, it's not a good idea, since attendees are likely to view your message as unsolicited spam e-mail.

Figure 13-14:

Single-Sheet Trade Show Flyers—A lower-cost alternative to using expensive marketing brochures at the show

Reduce Your Printing Costs for Trade Show Marketing Collateral by printing low-cost single-sheet sales flyers for your company's sales reps to hand out at the show.

These single-sheet flyers are inexpensive to print at higher volumes, and can be used to highlight specific products, benefits, and applications of your products, with sales copy targeted to specific kinds of prospects

Advertising in Trade Show Dailies

Some of the largest trade shows, such as COMDEX, publish "show dailies," newspaper-format publications distributed to attendees once (or each day) during the show. Although this is an added promotional opportunity for your company, ad show dailies aren't read by many attendees at the show, and they probably aren't worth the extra expense compared to postcard mailings or other targeted show marketing activities.

Sometimes trade show exhibitors are given a free ad placement in the show daily or show guide, which is included in the booth space rental for the show. If this is the case for your show, or if you've decided to pay the extra cost to advertise in the show daily, spec out a basic "tombstone" ad for this placement opportunity.

Because they're being handed out to readers who are more preoccupied with attending the show than reading your ad, ads for show dailies and other printed show guides shouldn't contain a lot of sales copy text: Just print your company name, logo, 4 or 5 sales bullet points, your company contact info, and booth number (see **Figure 13-13**).

Printed Marketing Collateral for Trade Shows

As you prepare for your trade show, you'll need to consider the print marketing deliverables for your company's sales reps to hand out at the show. If your company is exhibiting at a major trade show with thousands of attendees, handing out thousands of copies of your company's high-end, four-color 11 X 17 sales brochure could become a big expense.

Single-sheet flyers: A lower-cost alternative is a single-sheet flyer highlighting your company's product, or a series of flyers, each covering a specific product, or group of products. These one-sided flyers can be printed in four-color on gloss stock for a relatively low price, at quantities of at least 5,000 copies.

These flyers are inexpensive enough so you can place a stack of them out on the table of your trade show booth for show attendees to pick up as they pass by your booth. You can then reserve a stash of your company's higher-quality sales brochures for your sales reps to give to the more qualified prospects they speak to at the show.

You can also produce other types of single-sheet flyers to address certain aspects of your product's sales benefits, functionality, or applications. For example, you could produce a "Q & A" sheet to answer the most-asked questions about your company's product, or a series of single-sheet "Applications Profile" flyers to highlight the most common ways a prospect would use your product. Here, the idea is to have an inexpensive printed piece that a sales rep can hand out in your booth, on the spot, when the prospect asks the question that's answered by the flyer (see **Figure 13-14**).

Prospect inquiry coupon: Produce printed coupons for show attendees to fill in to receive additional information on your company's products. One type of card layout that works well here is a perforated card that presents your company's basic promotional information on one half, and the fill-in portion for the prospect's contact info on the other. Your prospect fills in the card, drops it off at your booth, and keeps the promotional half of the card. These cards can also be used in combination with a contest drawing, to provide an extra incentive for people to fill them out (see **Figure 13-15**).

Trade Show Premiums and Drawings

When making show preparations, consider what, if any, trade show incentives to provide to attendees who visit your booth at the show. These generally fall into two categories:

Figure 13-15:

Prospect Inquiry Cards and Promotions—An effective way to collect sales leads at the show

Prospect Inquiry Cards enable your sales reps to collect all-important prospect mailing list information for follow-up contacts after the show.

Show inquiry cards (below) can be used along with a contest drawing, (shown on booth sign at right), to encourage prospects to fill them out and leave them with your company's sales reps

Show premiums are "giveaways" imprinted with your company's logo, handed out to anyone who visits your booth—T-shirts, coffee mugs, pens, etc.;

Show drawings are for more expensive items that a lucky attendee wins if they fill in and drop off one of your prospect inquiry cards, or drop their business card into a fishbowl at your booth. If they win the drawing, either at the end of each show day, or at the end of the entire show, they win the prize.

Many marketers feel obligated to hand out freebies and other premiums to anyone who visits their booth. These giveaways do nothing to help you collect mailing list information from interested prospects, and attract the kind of show visitors who go from booth to booth, trolling for free stuff, and who aren't really interested in your product. If you'd like to hand out some premium giveaway items, by all means do so—but *only* for attendees who've provided contact info for your drawing.

A show drawing is a much better marketing incentive, in that there's an equal exchange between your company and the prospect: You get the prospect's contact info, and the prospect gets a chance to win the item. You may end up with contacts who aren't currently prospects for your company's products, but some of them may become prospects after receiving one of your standard follow-up mailings in the future.

Items used for show drawings needn't be expensive. Generally, any hot, high-tech gadget or sporting item that can be purchased for under $500 (such as a hand-held GPS receiver, iPod, or fancy golf driver) that motivates your prospects to fill out an inquiry coupon, or drop their business cards in a fishbowl at your booth, will do.

Drawing table sign: If you're having a drawing, you'll also need an easel-backed table sign, such as the one in **Figure 13-15**, to place next to the fishbowl for the table in your booth.

Trade Show Logistics

Once you've developed and produced your trade show booth, and all the other associated materials needed for the show, your job is only half finished. It's likely you'll also be handling all of the important logistics-related details involved with your company's show project: Shipping, booth utilities, booth setup and breakdown, and other important details involved in trade show execution.

Getting Your Booth and Materials to the Show

Trade show producers usually work with private shipping/trucking companies to provide you with the additional service of shipping your trade show booth and associated signage and printed materials to the show. Once these materials arrive, they end up in a staging area somewhere in the loading dock of the exhibition hall, and are rolled over to your booth space on the show setup day.

These services work for most exhibitors, most of the time. However, when compared to using a first-rate commercial shipper like Fedex or UPS, there's a greater chance your booth and other marketing materials might become lost in the show shipper's distribution system, or they might not get to the show at all. Either situation could be a marketing disaster, and a far greater cost than if you'd exercised greater control over shipping your company's show materials on your own, and spent the extra money to send your materials by Fedex or UPS.

Take personal responsibility for shipping your booth materials: If your company will be exhibiting in a standard 10' X 10' booth space, and is using a collapsible, modular pop-up booth backdrop, you can (and should) avoid using the standard show shipping service. Instead, either ship the unit yourself by Fedex, UPS, or another courier service that has real-time airbill tracking, or carry the unit aboard with you when you fly to the show. It's worth the few hundred dollars extra in shipping to keep control of your booth, and to avoid the possibility of your booth and marketing materials being lost somewhere in the show shipper's distribution pipeline the day before the show.

Figure 13-16

How to Get Your Company's Executives on Conference Session Panels

In addition to your company's trade show exhibit, another way to lift your company's profile and credibility at the show is to get one or more of your company's key executives lined up as a speaker or panel participant on one of the show's conference sessions.

A speaking engagement at a trade show conference session by one of your company executives is a tremendous opportunity for exposure for your company and its products, and confers great credibility on your company. In addition to opening new sales opportunities at the show, conference participation can also spark new joint ventures and other high-level business opportunities from members of the panel audience who see and hear your company's executives speak on a panel session.

How to begin: Conference producers are always seeking to improve the content of their conferences. Make their job easier by helping them do their jobs. The best way to get "your people" on as speakers or panelists is to propose an entirely new session topic and speaker panel for their next show. Select a topic where your company has proven credibility as a recognized industry leader. Then, in addition to featuring one of your company's key executives on the panel, propose the other participants who you think should be on this panel, and who represent viewpoints from all sides of the issues addressed by the panel.

These could be executives in partner companies, trade associations, or other influential executives who can speak knowledgeably on the panel topic. Company identification is more important here than name identification for these other panel participants. Your objective here is to form a "neutral" panel, whose participants will substantively address the panel's topic, without resorting to a sales pitch for their company's product, or other marketing hype.

Get in contact with these other panel speakers, indicating to them that "_____ (your own company's executive) suggested you'd be a great speaker for this panel at the next conference." Everyone is flattered to be asked to participate on a conference panel at a major trade show, so you should be easy to get a tentative agreement from other participants.

Next, get back in touch with the conference producer, and outline the content of the panel session and the

backgrounds of the speakers you've lined up for it. If he/she is interested in your idea, the conference producer will then begin to take ownership of your panel session idea and will finalize the details on their own.

When to begin: The best time to propose a new panel topic for the next trade show is during the current show. Study the panel topics in the current show's conference, and try to identify content gaps—new technologies, new industry issues, and new business developments—not addressed on panel discussions at the current show. Query the show producer a couple of weeks after the show ends with your first proposal for your new panel idea and participants. Once you get a go-ahead, you can then line up the other participants.

Many conference also issue "invitations to speakers," outlining topics they'd like to address in panels for future conferences. Also, ask the conference producer about the new topics he or she is interested in covering for their next conference.

Do not delegate this panel-formation task to your PR firm. Since you are essentially marketing your company's credibility on the panel topic, take charge of this project yourself. Most conference producers have been burned too many times by PR firms who overpromise and under-deliver on speaker qualifications and panel content, so they'd prefer to keep PR firms out of their conference content.

Tips for panel presenters: Make sure that your company executive sticks to the topic of the panel and that his/her presentation provides information that is truly useful to the panel audience. Nothing turns audiences off more than hearing someone's standard company sales pitch, so you should emphasize to the executive that the purpose of his/her appearance at the panel session is for "the good of the industry," and not to overtly promote the company's product or service. Although the measure of success for any speaker on a session panel is the number of business cards they collect from interested audience members who approach them after the show, many interested panel audience members won't approach speakers after the panel ends, so make sure that your speaker's PowerPoint presentations contain their full company contact info.

Ship your booth and marketing materials to the hotel: Since a hotel manager has a greater incentive to guard your property than some teamster at an exhibition hall, the best and easiest route is to ship your booth and printed marketing materials to the front desk of the hotel where you'll be staying. You can use a "three-day shipping" option with either Fedex or UPS, and time the delivery of these materials so they arrive two days before you arrive at the show. This way, you'll have some extra time to track the shipment, or send replacement materials, in case any part of your shipment gets lost.

A modular booth backdrop, plus enough boxed brochures and sales materials for a show, can be shipped anywhere in the U.S. at a cost of a a few hundred dollars. Once it arrives at your hotel, the whole shipment fits compactly in the corner of the hotel's shipping room, or behind the front desk, awaiting your arrival. Bring a small, folding hand truck with you to the show, so you and your co-workers can wheel these materials to the show exhibition hall.

If your booth requires computers, large product samples, or other large or heavy items, you may have no choice but to utilize the show's shipping service, or a commercial freight service. However, even if there is a mixup in getting your computers or equipment to the show on time, if you take control of getting your booth backdrop and marketing materials to the show, at least your sales reps will have a booth to work from, and brochures to give to prospects.

No one should care more about your company's marketing than you. Make trade show logistics your responsibility by taking personal control of your company's critical show-related marketing materials, and you'll avoid most show disasters.

Booth Setup Day

Booth setup usually occurs the day before the opening day of the show. Here is where all the hard work, planning and coordination for your show pays off. If your booth and all other marketing materials arrive when and where they're supposed to, "setup day" usually gives you ample time to get your booth set up and ready for business by the show opening. But this is also the time when the real world kicks in, so be prepared for show emergencies, both large and small, that can happen before and during the show.

Your trade show kit: You'll need to assemble a "marketing manager's trade show kit" containing all the items you'll need for setting up your booth and handling the minor emergencies that always crop up during the show.

A trade show kit helps you deal with the little things that can go wrong at the show: A torn booth panel that needs to be patched, protruding electrical wires that need to be tied down, or any other item that must be taped, cut, lengthened, shortened, joined, or otherwise forced into compliance. Your kit should also contain a small hand-held vacuum cleaner, so you and your co-workers can avoid the $150 per day fee show exhibition services charge to quickly run a vacuum across the carpet in your booth each night, by having you or your co-workers do the job.

Your trade show kit should contain the following:

- **Instructions and diagram for setting up and arranging booth elements**
- **Small, folding hand truck**
- **Clear shipping tape**
- **Box cutter**
- **Steel wire (for heavy hanging or fastening jobs)**
- **Monofilament fishing line (for invisible sign hanging or repairs)**
- **Duct tape**
- **Nylon tie-down straps**
- **Inline electrical power strips**
- **Extension cords**
- **Magic markers**
- **Paper towels and glass cleaner**
- **Dirt Devil or other small hand-held vacuum cleaner**
- **Rubber bands**
- **Leatherman or other multi-tool with needlenose pliers and pocket knife**
- **Small first aid kit**
- **One-time use camera and film (for taking pictures of your booth)**

Your kit can be shipped ahead with your booth, brochures, and the rest of your marketing materials, or you can take it with you when you fly or drive to the show.

Major Trade Show Emergencies

Despite your best planning and execution, major trade show emergencies happen, usually without warning, and at the worst possible times: Your booth can be lost by the airline, shipper, or hotel during the first day of the show, a box of your important sales brochures is lost, or arrives damaged beyond use, or all of your booth signs arrive with two inches of daylight punched through the middle.

Any of these glitches, if they can be solved with minimal disruption, end up as a funny story when you return to your office, but they're not very funny at the time they happen, and they will always force you to "go to Plan B"—you just have to know what your own "Plan B" is.

Here are some useful resources to keep in the back of your mind to address any major emergency threatening a trade show:

Same-day emergency shipping: Most show emergencies involve lost marketing materials, such as brochures, sales flyers, or signage, for which replacements are available—if they can get to your show on time. Airline counter-to-counter services, such as those provided by any major airline, can get your parcel on a scheduled passenger flight to the airport of your show city;

Local printing services: Kinko's (**www.kinkos.com**) has over 1,100 locations across the U.S., and is an excellent resource for emergency color copying and color digital printing of brochures, flyers, and small signs. Your ad agency or marketing consultant can transmit electronic files for your company's sales and marketing deliverables by e-mail to any Kinko's near your show location, where they can be printed and picked up. Also, it's a good idea to bring Adobe Acrobat .PDF copies of all your company's marketing materials with you on your laptop computer, in case you need to have these printed at a Kinko's in your show city;

Local sign production: If you need additional signage right away, your ad agency or marketing consultant can transmit electronic sign files to a local sign producer, such as FastSigns (**www.fastsigns.com**), a nationwide sign-printing chain, that specializes in printing and mounting of your new or replacement show signs.

The added shipping and production costs of show emergencies are expensive, but they're always a fraction of the downside cost of lost sales and marketing opportunities your company would otherwise experience. Your ad agency or marketing consultant can be a great help to you during these emergency situations, so let them know they should be "on call" to assist you in case of a show emergency.

The Show Begins: How to Work a Trade Show

Once the show opens, spend time in your company's booth, talking to attendees, customers, and prospects. This is the most exciting part of being a marketing manager at a trade show, because it's the time when you actually see and hear how prospects are responding to the sales message you've helped to develop for your company's product. You'll never have a better opportunity to assess the clarity and power of the sales "story" you've helped to create for your company's marketing program.

The customers and prospects you meet at the show give you priceless marketing feedback on your product's sales benefits and features. As you talk about your company's product to booth visitors, you'll learn which benefits seem to appeal more than others, and how certain features of your product could have been explained more clearly to your company's prospects. By their reactions and comments, and by the questions they ask during your conversations with them in your booth, prospects give you the valuable feedback you need to improve the sales copy and direction of your company's marketing program.

In addition to their response to your company's sales story, visitors to your booth can give you valuable insight on other aspects of your marketing program, such as:

- **Trade publications and trade shows:** Show attendees can tell you which trade publications they read most often in their fields, and why, and which trade shows they attend each year. This helps you plan your company's future advertising and trade show marketing projects;

- **Your competition:** Attendees give you their unvarnished opinions of your company's products, and how they stack up to those of your competitors. This information can sometimes point out how your sales copy could do a better job of highlighting the benefits of your company's products, compared to those of your competitors;

- **New marketing opportunities:** Show attendees often give you contacts for new marketing opportunities, suggestions for new uses for your company's products, and other insights that can lead to many interesting new marketing ideas.

When you talk to prospects and customers at the show, keep listening. They will give you the answers to many key marketing issues and problems, if you're paying attention.

Check out your competition at the show: Make sure to check out your competition at the show. If possible, try to slip in to your competitors' booths and listen to their sales reps talk to prospects, and pick up their printed marketing materials.

See the show: Take the time to walk the aisles of the show floor, and watch out for interesting booth designs, signage, product displays, multimedia presentations and other marketing techniques exhibitors use to drive traffic to their booths. Make a point of visiting your customers' and prospects' booths at the show, and introduce yourself to the new sales contacts you will meet there. Don't forget to bring a camera along, so you can get pictures of your company's booth, and other booths at the show for ideas to make your company's next trade show project more effective. Also, pick up any sales brochures and other marketing collateral you find especially interesting or persuasive.

When the Show Ends

Packing up and shipping your booth: At the end of a long show, tired sales reps are often careless about packing up your company's booth exhibit, and your booth and signage may arrive damaged if not properly packed. So, just as you took responsibility for shipping your booth and sales materials to the show, you should take charge of the task of breaking down and packing up your booth, and getting it back to your office.

Collecting sales leads from the show: You should also take charge of collecting, holding, and shipping the prospect inquiry coupons and business cards your company has collected in its booth. Ship these out by Fedex overnight back to your office, so they won't get lost in the shuffle when you break down your booth. For larger shows, you'll have enough collected leads at the end of each show day to justify sending them out on a daily basis. These leads are literally as good as gold, and represent the reason your company is at the show. Guard them carefully, and make sure they get back to your office so they can be entered into your company's sales database, for follow-up mailings after the show.

PUBLIC RELATIONS
CHAPTER 14
USING TRADE AND BUSINESS MEDIA
TO GENERATE INQUIRIES AND SALES
IN YOUR MARKETING PROGRAM

Positive news coverage and product reviews in your industry's trade media can boost your company's sales, if you make your public relations program serve the other, more important elements of your company's marketing program.

In many companies, however, public relations is often the most-misused, least effective marketing activity. Next to print display advertising, more companies in trade and business-to-business markets waste more money on ineffective PR efforts than on any other marketing activity.

The blame for ineffective PR execution can be shared equally between the PR firms that practice it, and the companies that hire them. Half the time, the company is not managing its PR firm effectively, and the other half the PR firm is making big promises to justify its monthly retainer, but failing to deliver measurable sales results.

Public Relations Serves Marketing, But By Itself, Public Relations is Not Marketing

The problem of ineffective public relations is partly caused by inexperienced marketing managers, who mistakenly believe that paying a PR firm to promote the company in trade publications means they are running a marketing program. This condition is aided in part by the egos of CEOs and senior managers, who like to see their names in print, regardless of any measurable sales effect. In any case, most of the money spent with PR firms could be more wisely redirected into other conventional marketing projects, where it would generate additional sales for the company.

Also, because of your inability to control its outcome, PR is the least effective element of your marketing program, compared to other marketing activities. First, PR puts you and your company at the mercy of an editor's decision on whether or not to cover your company's latest news, or new product announcement. Second, even if an editor decides to cover your story, you can't ever know whether this coverage will be favorable, negative, or somewhere in between. Even favorable coverage may not generate additional sales for your company.

Another contributor to ineffective PR is a simple lack of common courtesy and respect for trade publication editors by PR reps at ad agencies and PR firms. Every day, editors and writers receive hundreds of press releases sent by PR firms, containing announcements that are either not appropriate for the publication, or aren't newsworthy enough to have been turned into a press release in the first place.

Editors and staff writers who receive these press releases and followup phone calls by the clueless reps at the PR firms who sent them, resent having their time wasted, and rightly so. Having had an unpleasant first contact with a company via that company's PR rep, they will not be inclined to look at subsequent press releases from this company in a favorable light.

Benefits of PR and Media Management

All of this, however, is not to say that PR doesn't work, or that it doesn't have its place in your company's marketing program. An effectively-managed PR campaign that leads to a favorable article on your company's new product can produce sensational results, leading to thousands of new prospect inquiries, and setting a positive tone for all subsequent media coverage of your company and its products.

This coverage can be worth many thousands of dollars in free advertising for your company, and, equally important, can attract the notice of other companies seeking joint venture and business development opportunities with your firm. For these reasons, a well-executed, continuing PR program that keeps your company's name and news of its products out there in your market's trade media can be a major benefit. After all, PR is a medium of exchange: Editors, writers, and reporters rely on the steady flow of news announcements from companies like yours to fill their publications, and your company needs coverage of its products or services to supplement its other marketing efforts.

Your company will get PR, whether you want it or not: Even if your company has decided not to have an ongoing PR program, one day an event will occur that affects your company, and the media will come knocking on your door: A product recall, a lawsuit or adverse court decision affecting your company, or any other major event involving your company, either negative or positive, will spark media inquiries. You will then have no choice but to respond, and the truth and clarity of your initial response may mean the difference between a crisis that can be defused, or one that spirals out of control. A company that knows how to manage its media exposure through an effective PR response can neutralize a potentially negative publicity situation, or exploit a favorable PR opportunity.

How Trade and Industry News Is Made

One of the keys to using PR effectively as part of a company's marketing campaign is knowing how news is made in industry publications:

By press release: The press release is the spark that creates news coverage for companies in business-to-business marketplaces. Even though editors complain about the large mass of press releases they receive every day, and even though they will only cover a small number of press releases sent to them, editors know they couldn't operate without this flow of information. Press release mailings are the key means of distribution that keeps a company's name and product line in front of editors at trade and business publications, and companies keep sending press releases because they know, at some point, this continued exposure will lead to coverage;

By story pitch: Editors and writers also rely on reps at PR firms who call them with a "story pitch," an idea for an article that involves their client company. A PR firm earns its fees by the nature of its relationships with editors and reporters at publications, and by the quality and credibility of the story pitches it makes to editors and reporters on behalf of its clients. If the editor or writer thinks a story idea is newsworthy, or that it addresses an issue that's on-target for the publication, the company (or its product) receives coverage in that publication;

By the writer's initiative: Of course, many of the articles written in publications come about either because an editor assigned the story to a writer or reporter, or the writer came up with the idea on their own. Companies and the PR firms who represent them don't have the power to control the content of articles, but they do have some ability to influence how these articles are written. For example, if it can keep its name and product line in front of the editor and writer at a publication by continuing to send press releases and making the occasional story pitch, a company may stand a good chance of receiving coverage when the writer eventually decides to write a piece on a topic that relates to the company or its product.

There are other, unlikely ways your company can get media coverage: For example, your company could develop a product that becomes a major, industry-changing news event, attracting the notice of the trade media in your industry, without a public relations effort on your part, or your PR firm could dream up a brilliant publicity stunt that gets coverage by its sheer audacity. These events do happen, but they won't provide you with the year-round media coverage your company needs to support an ongoing marketing program.

The only way to get steady coverage that supports your company's sales efforts, is to develop and execute a continuous public relations program that

keeps a constant flow of relevant, high-quality press releases in distribution to your industry's top trade media, combined with thoughtfully-developed story pitches to the key editors at these publications.

How to Use PR in Your Marketing Program

Implementing a competent, successful public relations campaign for your company requires hands-on involvement on your part. You may not be involved in the day-to-day aspects of writing press releases, and contacting writers, reporters, and editors in the trade media, but you'll have to know enough about the process to keep it focused on your company's marketing goals, making sure that your public relations program doesn't lapse into costly irrelevance, as many company PR programs do.

First Principles of Successful Public Relations in Your Company

Execution of your company's ongoing PR program should be guided by three principles:

- **To send out press releases and announcements *only* when your company has something to talk about;**
- **To think of how your press release or announcement will be received by the writers or editors on the other side of the exchange;**
- **To make a press announcement only if the announcement sells your product, or if it can contribute to sales**

As simple and obvious as this advice may sound, the first two points above are the two biggest complaints of editors at trade publications, magazines, newspapers and other media sources concerning company PR efforts. Nothing travels from an editor's desk to their wastebasket faster than a press release that is either not relevant to the publication, or shouldn't have been sent to them in the first place. The third point above, the relationship of your PR announcement to your company's sales, is covered in greater detail in the next section.

Send out a news release only when you have news: Once you've established a PR program in your company, you'll find it becomes very easy to write and distribute press releases to the media. And now that anyone can send a press release by e-mail, where distribution cost is zero, the final barrier to self-restraint has been broken.

At many companies, what happens next is that *anything* that happens becomes another press release, and is distributed to the company's entire media list in a scattershot fashion. While your local business press might be interested in the news that your company won a quality award from a local trade group, *Business Week* isn't. Not every executive promotion, new account, product feature improvement, or sales promotion should be a press release. Even if it is published, chances are that a minor announcement in the back of a trade publication of a new account closed by your sales staff, for example, will only be read your sales manager and the rep who made the sale. Was it worth the $1,500 in hourly billing costs from your PR firm to write and distribute the press release? Probably not.

Create a minimum news threshold in your company, and stick to it. Your CEO or senior management may think every minor development in your company deserves a press release, but if you do, you'll soon wear out your welcome with editors in your industry's trade media, and train them to ignore every release they see from your company. Hold your fire until you have something more important to announce to these editors. When you do, they'll be listening.

Think of the Person Who Will Be Reading Your Press Release

One of the quickest ways to lose the attention of trade publication editors and writers in your industry is to do something that wastes their time, slows them down, or otherwise irritates them. Many PR firms are notoriously disrespectful of media people in these ways, and anything that shows a lack of consideration for an editor, writer, or media contact makes it very hard to win them back once have they turned against your company.

Put yourself in the place of an editor or writer at a major trade publication, magazine, or newspaper. In your average workday, you receive scores, maybe hundreds, of press releases. It's clear to you that many of these press releases have been sent to you just because your name is on a PR firm's media mailing list, not in consideration of any relevance to the areas you cover at your publication. Moreover, while you're trying to finish a piece for your publication's deadline this afternoon, you keep getting phone calls and e-mails from PR people asking if you got their press releases.

If you were this editor, wouldn't you appreciate a company and PR firm that didn't waste your time by bombarding you with irrelevant press releases? Wouldn't you want to talk more with PR reps and companies who had press releases and story ideas that would help you in your coverage of the industry? Much of this boils down to common sense, but you'll be surprised how looking at your news announcements from the other guy's perspective can improve your press coverage.

Here are some useful guidelines for developing and distributing news announcements for your company's PR programs, as seen from the perspective of writers and editors at trade publications and other media outlets:

> **Will they be interested?** Your first step is deciding who on your media list should get the press release of your news announcement, and who shouldn't. Look at your press release, then look at each editor or other contact on your list: Would your story be interesting to them? Is it something they'd be interested in covering for their readers? If not, then sending your press release to this person is like sending them junk mail—*don't do it*;

> **Have you filled in the *context* of your story?** Editors are always looking for news announcements that key into important business issues in your field,

such as hot new industry trends, emerging technologies, productivity, or government regulation of your industry. Your news announcement always gets more attention if you can tie some aspect of it to a major issue everyone's talking about in your industry. For example, if there is a proposed EPA air pollution regulation that has your industry up in arms, and if your company's new product feature can help a manufacturer improve their monitoring or reduce plant emissions, then your new product announcement should be wrapped around this issue. Think of the top issues and trends that everyone's talking about in your industry, and see if your company's news announcement could be credibly linked to one of these issues;

Have you given them all the details they need to write their story? If you've met these first two guidelines, think about everything else the editor or writer needs to write their story, and *give it to them*: Product spec sheets in Adobe Acrobat .PDF format, company history and background, high-resolution product photos on your Web site. Most important, make it easy for the writer or editor to contact you, by putting your personal company contact info on all PR materials.

The next two sections cover the typical company events that trigger news announcements to the trade and business media, and the distribution techniques you can use for each.

Will Your News Contribute to Sales? Deciding What Makes News in Your Company

It's your job as a marketing manager to decide what company developments are newsworthy enough to turn into press releases and story idea pitches for the business and trade media contacts in your industry. Inept public relations programs begin whenever this decision is delegated to your ad agency, PR firm, or marketing consultant, and anything becomes news to justify the PR firm's monthly retainer.

There's no mystery to making the decision on what's newsworthy, since any major development in your company, such as the launch of a new product line, or any major new business initiative, will make itself known, and should always prompt the addition of a PR campaign to your list of marketing projects for this event. The key is to discriminate between the company events that are worthy of aggressive PR promotion as news in your industry, those that should be treated in a more routine way, and those that shouldn't be announced at all. Treating every event in your company as an event that requires your PR reps to hit the phones to press your media contacts for coverage is a waste of your marketing dollars, and wears out your welcome with editors and writers.

An event should be announced as news by your company only if it sells your product, or if it can lead to sales. This is the sole factor you should consider when deciding whether a company event is worthy of a news announcement by your company.

Once you've made this initial newsworthiness decision, you should then consider whether your PR announcement should be handled as a major announcement, or as a less-important, secondary announcement.

Major News Events

If you can envision that your announcement for this event, after being written up in a trade magazine, business publication, broadcast outlet, or newspaper, would be compelling enough to sell your company's product or service directly from the article, you've got a major news event that deserves a strong, dedicated PR effort.

Examples of news events that can lead to sales directly from media coverage are:

Major new product launches: Favorable reviews of new products in trade publications can generate many sales directly from the article;

Major product upgrades and improvements: Likewise, a major upgrade to a product line can generate sales from trade and business media coverage;

New market entries: After initial market testing has been done, a PR program that runs parallel to the launch of your product or service in a new market can also lead to sales and prospect inquiries from readers who hear about your product for the first time.

Secondary News Events

Other events in your company may be newsworthy, but, when covered by the media, may not lead to sales in and of themselves. For example, if you judge that a news announcement, when run in connection with other marketing activities—print advertising, direct mailings, and direct selling—would have a positive, indirect influence only when your prospect sees it running alongside any of these paid promotional efforts, this is an announcement that should be made in a more routine way, with less intensity and cost than a major news event.

Examples of secondary news announcements, where media coverage would only influence sales when helped along by your paid marketing efforts, include:

New promotions, price changes, and minor product updates: Many of the press releases announcing these kinds of secondary news events wind up as two and three-column inch blurbs in the "New Product News" sections at the back of trade and industry publications, and may spark readers to contact your company for further information. Because they usually happen more frequently in your company than major news events, they may well account for the majority of your day-to-day PR efforts. If your promotion, price change, or update is significant, or is noteworthy in some other way, your PR rep can also follow up with a phone call to the publication to jog the editor's attention;

Noteworthy new product applications: New, novel, or unique uses of your product in your industry make interesting stories in trade publications. Make sure your press release has some good quotes from this new application's users, along with product photos and other information helpful to editors writing the story;

Major new account sales: Issuing a press release whenever your company closes a major sale, or lands a big, well-known customer, is another secondary PR opportunity, because news of your company landing a big new account with a major company in your field may attract notice from other large prospects in your industry. You can sometimes get the larger, more well-known company to issue their own press release on this announcement to their media contacts; if the other company is big and famous enough, this may lead to even wider media coverage for your company in general business publications;

New survey, report, or white paper: If it addresses a hot industry issue or market trend, a news release reporting on the results of a market survey conducted by your company (or research by an outside industry research firm paid for by your company) can be a sure-fire news opportunity. For example, information obtained by surveying your customers for their opinions on an important industry trend, or polling them on their major applications for your product, can be turned into a press release if it generates interesting and newsworthy results. If you're working in a technology-related field, intriguing reports or white papers written by your company's research staff on the technology or processes underlying your company's products are always well-received by the trade media, and helps to position your company as a thought leader and innovator in its field.

News that Doesn't Lead to Sales

The following news events inside your company do not generate sales, and should not be a part of your company's press release program:

Executive promotions: Press releases accompanied by head shots of executives who've been recently hired or promoted may make it into the back pages of a trade publication, but these announcements don't increase your company's sales;

Charity involvement or sponsorship: Companies often issue press releases touting corporate sponsorship or participation in charity and fund-raising events. Announcements of these events don't increase sales, and sending press releases out on them is a luxury your company can't afford.

Judge the importance of every news event in your company and assess whether or not its publication would realistically lead to, or influence, sales for your company. If not, you should kill the announcement and focus on your paid marketing efforts until you can develop a promotable news event for your company.

How to Write a Press Release (or Manage Those Who Do)

The press release is the key deliverable of every public relations project. A well-presented, well-written press release plays a major role in convincing media contacts to cover your news announcement, and provides the essential information editors and staff writers need to cover your announcement in their publications.

A press release has a formal structure governed by well-established writing rules. These guidelines mirror those of the "Five W's" of writing for newspaper reporters: "Who, What, When, Where, and Why." A good press release should read like a brief, well-written newspaper article, giving the reader the basic information on the news announcement in the first paragraph, then drawing them into the rest of the story with the use of interesting factual statements that fill in the outline created by the lead paragraph.

Like any front-page newspaper story, a press release never draws attention to itself, for example, by using the overtly promotional language that belongs in your company's sales brochure. Instead, your press release serves as the objective *platform* for conveying the essential facts of your company's news announcement to the reader as quickly as possible.

While you may not be responsible for writing press releases in your company, you will need to know how to develop and execute PR projects as a part of your marketing program. To do this, you must be able to specify the *essential content* that must go into a press release for any company product announcement or news event. This way, you can supply your ad agency, PR firm, or marketing consultant with the information they need to write a press release that accurately communicates your company's news announcement.

Turning Your Company News Into a Press Release

Before outlining the information required for your press release, think about how your news announcement will be seen by the editors or writers at the publications receiving your press release.

1. Think Like an Editor

Put yourself in the place of an editor or a writer for a trade or business publication in your field. Every week, they receive hundreds of press releases from companies just like yours, touting new product announcements, minor and major product upgrades, and other corporate and industry news, both large and small.

While there may be many exciting details about your new product announcement, product upgrade, new joint venture or other company news event, they can't all be instantaneously understood by an editor, writer, or reporter at the publication contacted by your PR firm.

To enhance the editor's understanding of your news announcement, distill your announcement into a single fact that is compelling enough for the editor who reads your press release to decide to cover your story, and then give the editor the additional facts that they will need to make the story interesting to their readers.

Questions editors ask: When an editor scans your press release for the first time, they put it through their own mental screening process, asking the following questions:

"Who are these guys? Have I heard of this company before?" Editors are very status-conscious when it comes to companies. News announcements from big, high-profile companies grab their eye more than releases from small and mid-sized ones. This automatically puts most news announcements from smaller companies at the bottom of their heap, unless the editor has been seeing a steady stream of relevant, interesting press releases coming from your company. This is what you need to be doing anyway, and it will help you overcome this hurdle and get your company noticed more often;

"Does this have anything to do with anything I'm working on right now?" After scanning the headline and lead paragraph of your release, every editor runs it past their own mental list of the stories they're working on for the next issue of their publication. If they're writing a story on Web security for the banking industry, and you're announcing a new Web-based secure account transaction system, you're in luck. Otherwise, your release goes back to the bottom of the stack, or into the back pages of the publication's "New Products and Services" section as a three-paragraph filler item. A skillful PR firm with reps who are in constant contact with the top editors and writers in your field will often know who's working on what, and can figuratively walk a press release right into the staff writer's story, if it fits;

"Hmmmm. [trend or issue] is a hot topic with my readers. Maybe I'll look into this some more." Editors and writers in any industry always follow the same new trends, issues and developments. For example, if there's a string of major oil refinery fires, then, one after another, oil industry publications will write stories on refinery fire prevention systems and related safety issues. The high-tech press is also well known for talking up certain technologies, communications protocols, and programming languages in lockstep, and then moving on just as quickly to the next hot new technology.

Your press release has an excellent chance of getting the editor's attention if you know the hot trends in your field, and if you can credibly link your announcement to one of these trends. For example, if a big issue in your field, like a dramatic increase in foreign manufacturers' imports that puts pressure on domestic companies to upgrade their manufacturing efficiency, leading them to buy systems such as those made by your company, your press release should lead with this issue, instead of a being just another plain-Jane new product announcement. However, this linkage must be credible: Editors and

Figure 14-1

A Few Hints for PR People . . .

by Hiawatha Bray
Technology Reporter, *The Boston Globe*

In certain circles, I have a reputation for being rather harsh to PR people. Well, sometimes. The ones with a proven knack for doing their jobs badly do get on my last available nerve. The good ones, however, are a joy to work with, and they make my life far easier.

So which do you want to be—a good 'un or a bad 'un?

I thought as much. That's why I'm going to help you out, with information about what to do and what not to do if you want me to write about you or your company.

First and foremost, don't phone the Globe at 5 pm with some bright idea for a red-hot feature. I work at a morning newspaper. By mid-afternoon, I've got better things to do than listen to your pitches.

In the morning, however, I don't at all mind listening. Well, maybe I mind sometimes, but don't worry. I'll get over it. So if you want to call, do it early rather than late.

In any case, you're far better off sending e-mail to bray@globe.com. For one thing, you can provide details that'll help me decide whether you have an interesting story. For another, I'll have a semi-permanent record of our interactions. I often forget about phone calls. I forget about e-mails too, but I can look them up and refresh my memory. So use e-mail. Don't write it in HTML, either. Just plain old ASCII text for me.

And don't phone me after sending me the message. I'll get back to you, if it strikes me as worthwhile. If not...better luck next time.

Some of you send me snail-mail press releases. Who reads such dreck? Not I. In this business, a postage stamp is God's way of telling me it's not important. If it really was important, you'd have phoned or e-mailed or even faxed. (The number is 617-929-3183.) I usually throw away mail without even peeking, unless it's a magazine.

So use e-mail. But don't use attachments unless I've agreed to accept them. Just put your pitch into plain old ASCII text and send it along. From time to time, you may feel obligated to send something a bit bulkier. Write me a plain e-mail first and try to talk me into it. Attachments are usually a waste of bandwidth and time.

Especially if they're really, really big. I've had people send me multi-megabyte PowerPoint slide shows once too often. I already hate PowerPoint—the focus of evil in the modern world—and PowerPoint slides glued to e-mail messages are even worse. Don't you dare attach something like that to an e-mail addressed to me. It'll go straight into the bit bucket.

You should include lots of contact information— phone, e-mail, pager, cell phone, preferably posted at the top of the message. If you can attach a vCard, please do. Some journalists don't care for them, but I like 'em fine. With a click, I can plug them into my address book for future reference. And if you've got sense enough to use vCards, I may well want to keep you as a future reference. I always did like people with brains...

By the by, why do so many corporate Web sites lack basic contact information, or bury it in an obscure spot? Time and again, I visit sites, hoping to write about a firm, only to find that their Web site has no phone number listed, or an e-mail address or even the name of a contact person. So I shrug, decide they don't want any media coverage, and find a more informative firm to write about. Such a fate could well await your company if you don't put this kind of contact info in an easy-to-find location on your site.

As a matter of fact, a good corporate site should include other goodies, like names and bios of the top execs and downloadable high-resolution photos of the firm's products.

Now, about your pitch. If you don't know what the heck it is you're talking about, how will I? Understand your product or service, and explain it to me in a sentence. And be sure that sentence appears in the first paragraph of your message—or at least the second. Don't waste my time with a cute lead-in, just get to the point. Remember, that's how newspaper people write, by putting the key information at the top of the story. Go and do thou likewise.

And of course, don't bother me with a pitch for a story that would never, ever appear in the Boston Globe. This is a newspaper, not a technical trade rag. Your hot new breakthrough in supply chain management may wow them at the next convention of the International Warehouse Logistics Association, but the readers of the *Boston Globe* won't give a rip. So keep it to yourself, okay? Unless it's that rare situation where an obscure innovation really would matter to our thousands of ordinary readers. In that case, give it a shot. The worst that can happen is that I'll mock you and and make disparaging comments about your ancestors.

This guide to the perplexed is a work in progress. I'll probably add more brilliant insights in days to come. But if you follow the advice contained herein, you won't go too far wrong.

Hiawatha Bray (watha@monitortan.com). Reprinted with permission from www.monitortan.com.

writers have finely-tuned "BS detectors," and they can always spot a company that is using a trend to push a product that doesn't belong there.

"_____ **handles this. I'll pass it along to him.**" One of the primary functions of editors in a publication is to route press releases to the writers who cover certain technologies, business lines, and markets in the industry covered by the publication. You can save a step here by making sure your press release goes directly to the person at the publication who writes about the area covered by your product. During their follow-up calls or e-mails to the publication, your PR rep can locate the right person at the publication who should be receiving your press releases;

"**Everyone knows that _____ . How is what you're doing any different than this?**" Working for a leading trade publication exposes editors and writers to everything that goes on in their industry—good, bad, and ugly. This exposure often causes editors to form cynical opinions on industry issues and trends, based on the new events they've already covered up close in the past. If a company recently failed in a major market push with a product or technology somewhat similar to yours, the editor may well write off your product announcement in this light. You must anticipate the common objections, both fair and unfair, that editors and writers may have to your news announcements, and get these responses out there in the press release, and positioned so they can rationally counteract the prejudices of editors and writers at these publications.

If your press release contains an important single fact, or **lead**, that passes the editor's mental gauntlet—and especially if you can link your news announcement to a hot trend or issue in your field—you'll put your press release ahead of the many others that land on the editor's desk or e-mail every day.

2. Answer the Big Questions

Start the process of sketching out the content and positioning of your press release by answering the important background questions on the news event you're planning to announce. The answers to these questions will help you and your ad agency or PR firm write a better press release—and helps your PR rep do a better job when they follow up with their media contacts by phone, or by e-mail.

Who is your company, where is it located, and what did it just do?

Start with the simplest questions. Briefly describe, in general, what your company does, where it's based, and your news event. This brief thumbnail description of your company begins to position your company in the editor's mind:

> "Dyalogix, Inc., of Houston, TX, one of the largest suppliers of electronic building security systems for the banking industry, today announced the introduction of…"

"Tricon Systems, of San Jose, CA, supplier of smart-card verification hardware and services, announces the release of Version 8.0 of its popular…"

What is it most single important thing about our announcement that readers need to know?

Focus on the single most important fact that readers need to know about your company news announcement. For example, if you're introducing a new product or service, what is its single most important and unique feature? In what way does your product make a dramatic improvement in some aspect of the potential customer's business? If you're announcing an upgrade to a product, state the most important aspect about the upgrade: Is it the first time this new feature has been introduced to the market? Is it now available at a lower cost? Is there no other feature like it available in competing products?

What are the main benefits to readers of your news announcement, and why are these important?

Once you've created the "news" of your announcement, fill in the reasons *why* this news is important to readers of the publications in your industry. DO NOT make the common mistake of recycling the sales copy benefits in your company's product brochure. This will make your press release read like marketing copy, and marketing copy cannot be easily re-written into a business news feature.

Instead, talk through each of these reasons in a low-key way, as if you were a third-person observer. Here are three different examples:

"…by giving plant operators more immediate response than previous models, the Dymax 4000 switch controller saves up to 6% on bulk liquid materials cost, according to the company."

"…the company's new scoring system allows insurance underwriters to quickly and inexpensively screen large commercial property portfolios for their potential environmental risk, to select only those properties requiring further investigation, and minimizing the high cost of on-site environmental surveys."

"…the new system generates higher injection pressure and provides more accurate control of very small volumes of fuel, allowing for better engine combustion and cleaner diesel engine operation."

Describe each of the main benefits of your news announcement in a detached, factual manner. Conforming to this business news-writing style makes it easier for writers and editors to adapt your press release to their own publications. At the very least, even if your press release is not picked up for a feature article, producing it in virtually ready-to-print business news-writing style makes it very easy for a writer or editor to lift the text of your press release wholesale and publish it as a smaller piece in the "New Product News" section of their publication, which is often done for news announcements not deemed important enough to become standalone news articles.

What is the context of this announcement? How does it fit in with your industry, and your competitors?

Now, put your news announcement in perspective, by positioning it within the context of your industry, and your competition. How beneficial is your product improvement to the industry? Is it substantially better than, or different from, products offered by your competitors, and, from a strategic basis, how does this put your company ahead of your competition?

What you are looking for is a high-concept statement that will make editors stop and think about how your news announcement fits in with the changes occurring in the industry. As mentioned earlier, if you can link your news announcement to a significant market trend or other industry issue, here's where to do it:

> "…the company's clean-burning diesel engine technology helps vehicle manufacturers meet increasingly strict Federal and state emissions standards."

> "…the system, now available for the first time to the insurance industry, puts powerful database risk screening capabilities within reach of every property transaction."

> "For long-range future technologies such as fuel cells, Hyperdrive technology is fully compatible and represents a natural evolutionary step…"

> "Lenders may face increased potential environmental liability risk as a result of a recent federal appeals court ruling…."

3. Press Release Lead Paragraph

The lead paragraph, or "lead," is the most important part of your press release. It boils down all of the essential facts of your news announcement into a concise paragraph containing all of the required Who/What/When/Where/Why information, fully summarizing the entire press release.

The lead of a press release should be so self-contained that it would give a reader the gist of your news announcement, if it were to be lifted from the rest of the press release and printed by itself. In fact, lead paragraphs for press releases are intended for this purpose, allowing editors and writers to literally copy and paste the first paragraph of a release into one-paragraph news announcements for their publications.

The lead paragraph of your press release should be written to conform to the standard press release format shown in **Figure 14-2**. However, when you're

Figure 14-2:

Press Release Structure—Key elements of a one-page press release

PRESS RELEASE   **Environmental Risk Information & Imaging Services**

505 Huntmar Park Drive, Suite 200
Herndon, VA 22070
Telephone (703) 834-0600
1-800-989-0402
FAX (703) 834-0606

E R I S

FOR IMMEDIATE RELEASE: June 24, 1994

Contact Info ▬▬ **CONTACT:** Glenn Hanna,
Vice President, ERIIS: (703) 836-0402

Headline ▬▬ **New Environmental Scoring System Helps Lenders Assess Risks On Large Property Portfolios**

Lead Paragraph ▬ **Environmental Risk Information & Imaging Services(ERIIS)** of Alexandria, Virginia, an industry-leading supplier of property-specific environmental due-diligence information to the engineering, financial, legal, insurance, investment and real estate markets, has introduced a new environmental information service and property scoring system which allows lenders, insurance underwriters and other holders of large real estate property portfolios to quickly and inexpensively screen multiple properties for potential environmental liability risk.

This new service, called the ERIIScore Environmental Property Portfolio Report, is available in print, FAX and electronic delivery formats, and depicts each of the many different properties in a real estate portfolio relative to their proximity to different types of potentially hazardous registered Federal and State sites.

A new environmental risk scoring system developed by the company, called the ERIIScore, calculated for every property in a portfolio report, is a weighted-average index of the number of potentially hazardous sites, the nature of these sites, and their distance from each specific study property address in the portfolio report. An ERIIScore is also calculated for four additional sites related to each portfolio property, each at a one-half mile distance along the north, south, east, and west axis from the portfolio property. These four "Neighborhood ERIIScores" provide a useful basis of comparison to judge a selected property's relative risk potential to other sites in its area, as well as to other properties in the portfolio. A neighborhood ERIIScore which is higher or lower than the portfolio study property's ERIIScore indicates a positive, negative, or neutral relationship of the portfolio property to its immediate surrounding area. The ERIIScore is designed to measure comparable risk potential, as opposed to contamination levels of selected properties.

Lenders may face increased potential environmental liability risk as a result of a recent federal appeals court ruling striking down a prior exemption granted to commercial lenders by the U.S. Environmental Protection Agency. This ruling has created some confusion in the lending, insurance and real estate development fields as lenders, insurance underwriters and attorneys seek out new ways to defend their interests against the potentially increased threat of Superfund site cleanup expenses.

By using environmental risk information services such as the new ERIIScore Portfolio Report, lenders can quickly and inexpensively screen large portfolios for potential environmental problems using information which conforms to industry defined standards. For example, a bank can use ERIIScore Portfolio Reports to screen trust or loan properties in its various portfolios to "select out" only those properties which may require a more detailed review by an environmental engineering professional, thus minimizing the costs of environmental site assessments. Rating agencies and insurance firms can use ERIIScore Portfolio Reports to screen and compare property portfolios prior to securitization or the underwriting of environmental liability insurance policies. Developers can use ERIIScore Reports to screen potential development properties prior to purchase.

Closing ▬▬ **For more information on the new ERIIScore Environmental Portfolio Property Report and ERIIS' complete product line** of environmental information and mapping services, call Glenn Hanna, vice president, ERIIS at **(800) 989-0402**.

Company and Product Background — Environmental Risk Information & Imaging Services:

Backgrounder ▬▬ **ERIIS is one of the industry's leading suppliers** of Federal, State and local environmental site assessment and local regulatory records data, mapping, and photographic services to the consulting, insurance, legal and lending industries, as well as providing environmental property reports for residential properties to home buyers. All ERIIS services provide those involved with environmental due diligence, related to property transactions, with the most accurate and timely background information available for their selected property sites anywhere in the U.S.

sketching out a lead for your company's press release that will be rewritten by your ad agency or PR firm, you only need to combine the notes you've already jotted down in the four previous steps:

1.) **Who/where is your company**, and what it just did;

2.) **The single most important fact** about your news announcement;

3.) **The main benefits** of your announcement, and why/how these are important;

4.) **The context** of how your announcement fits with your industry and your competition (this is optional for a lead paragraph, but should be worked into the body of your press release)

Press release lead paragraph format: These essential facts can now be re-written by you, or by your PR firm, into a single press release lead paragraph that strings together the information above in the following order:

• **Who/Where:** "Company name, of city, state" from **1.)** above;

• **What:** Brief background description of your company, from **1.)** above;

• **When:** News action—"announces/has now introduced… " etc. from **2.)** above;

• **Why:** Single most important fact from **2.)** above;

• **How:** Main benefits from **3.)** above;

• **(Optional):** Context information, from **4.)** above

Here is an example lead paragraph for a press release, with the "who/what/when/where/why" and factual news information combined into a concise lead paragraph for a press release:

"Environmental Risk Information and Imaging Services (ERIIS) of Alexandria, VA, an industry-leading supplier of property-specific environmental due-diligence information to the engineering, financial, legal, insurance, investment, and real estate markets, has introduced a new environmental information service and property scoring system that allows lenders, insurance underwriters and other holders of large real estate property portfolios to quickly and inexpensively screen multiple properties for environmental liability risk."

By itself, the lead gives an editor or writer at a publication enough information about the new product to decide whether or not it's of interest. The rest of the release (shown in **Figure 14-2**) tells the rest of the story and fills in the other essential product details, applications, and benefits.

If you're writing your press releases for your company, link to PR Newswire (**www.prnewswire.com**), to see thousands of examples of press releases for companies in a wide range of industries. Read press releases here for some good ideas and inspiration for writing your own company's press releases.

4. Filling In the Details: The Body of Your Press Release

After your lead, the body of your press release tells the story of your news announcement by expanding the essential facts summarized in your lead paragraph. If your ad agency, PR firm or marketing consultant is writing your company's press release, they can use your outline notes covered in the previous two sections as background material for writing the final release.

If you are writing your own press release, once you've written a solid lead paragraph, you will find that writing the rest of the release is essentially a process of expanding each of the key facts of your news announcement and arranging them in order of their importance.

The inverted pyramid: Like the "5W's" rule used for writing the lead paragraph of your press release, the format of the body of your release borrows from the "inverted pyramid" newspaper writing style, where the most important fact is discussed in the first paragraph after the lead, the second-most important fact is covered next, and so on.

This writing format puts the most important content of your press release "up front" in the first few paragraphs. Just like it helps busy newspaper readers get the essential details of an article by reading the first few paragraphs, the inverted pyramid style gives busy editors and writers the most important pieces of information in your release quickly, as they decide whether or not to cover your story.

Expand the key facts you've sketched out for your press release: Start writing the body copy of your press release by expanding on each of the key facts—the statements, features, and benefits—you've already sketched out for your news announcement. Answering the following questions about each fact helps you generate the information you'll need to fill in the body text of your press release:

- **How does this fact add value** to your existing product or service?

- **How does this fact help potential users** of your company's product?

- **How do current users benefit** from this fact?

- **Is this fact important to more than one type of user** in your market? If so, who are these other users, and how do each of them benefit?

- How does this fact **add value to your company**?

- **How does this fact make your product or service unique**, or different from, your competitors' products?

- **How does this distinctiveness improve the industry** or marketplace served by your product?

You'll notice some of these questions are variations on the same "What are the benefits?" question, but each are posed in a slightly different way. Writing a specific answer to each of these questions helps you to write about the benefits of your news announcement in a way that goes beyond the promotionally-oriented language of your company's sales copy, and helps you extract every important detail from each essential fact of your news announcement.

Since these are also the kinds of questions that an editor or reporter at a trade publication would ask you about your announcement, answering them in your press release provides the editor or writer with all the detail they need to help them write their story in a way that's interesting to their readers, increasing the odds that your news will be covered in their publication.

Write these answers out in a narrative form, as if you were telling them to someone sitting next to you. As you fill in the detail, each fact becomes a paragraph of its own. When you read each finished paragraph, certain important points may jump out—a key aspect of your news announcement, or a major reader benefit that an editor or writer should see. These should be moved to the head of each paragraph and reworded to make them into the lead sentences for each paragraph.

After you've expanded each of the essential facts, organize them in your release, from most-important to least-important fact, after your lead paragraph. Next, read your entire press release with "new eyes," as if you knew nothing about your company or product, and you were an editor or writer reading it for the very first time:

- **Do I get the gist of the announcement** from reading most of the lead paragraph, and the first sentence in each of the first few paragraphs?

- **Does it answer the most commonly-asked questions** a reader would be likely to ask about the announcement?

- **Have I made it easy for a busy reader to understand,** by minimizing unnecessary technical jargon, marketing buzzwords, and other barriers to readability?

- **Have I "walked the reader" through my announcement,** clearly presenting each essential fact, eliminating all doubt that any key fact has been omitted, or not explained well enough?

Writing Style Tips for Press Releases

Whether you are writing your own company's press releases, or assigning this task to your outside ad agency or PR firm, here are some additional pointers on press release presentation style:

Write for publication: The more you can make your press release read as if it were a news article, the higher the chance it will attract the notice of the editors and writers who cover your industry. The most effective press releases are written in a dry, factual style, as if the writer of the release was an outsider assigned to report the news your company is announcing. Your press release should read so much like a news article that an editor or writer could lift entire paragraphs from it wholesale and use it in their publications, as many do;

It's news, not hype: Banish all marketing hype, buzzwords, and unnecessary technical jargon from your press releases. Marketing managers and their PR firms fall into the habit of stringing together marketing buzz-phrases into meaningless, shopworn boilerplate. Editors grow tired of reading press releases from "growth-oriented" companies whose products are "industry compliant," and that provide a "complete solution." Nothing dooms a company's news announcement more than a press release peppered with wall-to-wall marketing buzzwords.

Writing Your Press Release Headline

The headline is a very important part of your press release. Like a headline to a news story, it is a concise summary of your company's news announcement. When used in a press release, your headline helps the editor or writer at the publication make a quick, yes-or-no decision on whether your announcement falls in their area of interest, and if they should take a closer look.

If you're writing your own press release, write its headline *after* you've written your press release. This way, you'll be better able to distill your news announcement into the single best sentence that describes it, using the fewest words possible.

The most common way to write a headline for your press release is to join the "who/what" parts of your news announcement, as in *who* is the company, and *what* has it done:

- **Tyrell Corp. Adds New Imaging System to its VyComp Metallurgical Inspection System**

- **Metacortex Announces Windows NT 15.0 Compatibility to its TM Supply Chain Management System**

Another option is to substitute your product or service for the *who*, and then combine it with the *what* that describes it:

- **New Cell Phone Accessory Lets Users Make and Receive Wireless Calls from Wired Home Phone Systems**

- **New Fuel Cell System Adds Low-Cost Backup Power Options for the Utility Industry**

While the "who/what" method of headline writing is the one used most often in press releases, you can develop some very interesting and eye-catching headlines by picking out and forming different combinations of any two (and sometimes three) of the "who/what/why/how" parts of your press release. Whichever way you go, the most effective headline is usually the shortest one that best summarizes the content of your news announcement.

Other Press Release Elements

To put your press release into final form, add the following elements:

Contact heading and date: Place the following text above the headline of your press release:

> **FOR IMMEDIATE RELEASE:** [Current date here]
>
> Contact: [Your name and title, or PR firm contact name and title]
> [Contact phone number and e-mail]

Put the name and phone number of the person responsible for speaking to the media about this announcement. This is usually the PR rep, if your ad agency or PR firm is handling PR for your company; or it's you if you're handling your company's PR effort. The date of your release tells editors and writers how current your announcement is, and serves as a kind of "date stamp" for older press releases posted in the "News" link on your company's Web site.

Contact closing paragraph: As the last paragraph of your press release, let editors and writers know where they can call or e-mail to get more detail on your announcement:

> "For more information on _____ , call [name, title] of [company/PR firm] at [phone number and e-mail]."

The time when a busy editor is working against a same-day publication deadline and wants to cover your news announcement always seems to be the time when they've lost your contact information, so make sure to include it as the last paragraph of your press release.

Backgrounder: At the bottom of your press release, and set in small type, print a single paragraph that gives writers and editors a brief, general description of your company, its background, the markets and industries it serves, and any other information that fills in the details on your company and its product line (see bottom of sample press release in **Figure 14-2**).

Length of press release: Generally, a press release should fill just one side of a letter-size page (about 500 words). Any longer than this, and it's likely that only the first page will be read.

Quoting company executives in press releases: When quoting executives for company news announcements, many PR firms literally fabricate quotes from company executives in the press release. Editors and writers can always spot a ghost-written quote, so this is always a mistake, because it weakens the credibility of your company's news announcement.

If you need a quote for your press release, have your PR rep conduct a brief interview of the company executive in charge of the topic covered by your news release, asking for his or her comments on the announcement, just as a reporter would. This gives your press release the authenticity it needs, and communicates the executive's sense of enthusiasm and excitement on the news announcement in your press release.

Developing Media Contact Lists

Every effective PR effort begins by developing and maintaining up-to-date media contact lists for your company. Where you focus your PR efforts with the announcement of your company's new product launch or other news event determines whether or not these efforts will have an impact on your company's sales.

Whether you're handling public relations on your own for your company, or if this task is being handled by your company's outside PR firm, concentrating your efforts on the trade media publications in your industry that can give you the highest likelihood of media coverage is a critical part of any public relations effort.

Your Media Contact List

Your company's media contact list consists of the editors, writers, and reporters who will be receiving your company's press releases and story ideas for news events announced by your company, and is organized as follows:

Top trade media contacts: The smallest list, but the most important one. These are the editors and writers at the major, vertical-market trade publications for your industry or market, who are most likely to cover your company's news announcements on a consistent basis, and includes editors and writers who have already written about your company and its products. If you are handling PR for your company, you'll be talking to these contacts every time your company has a significant news announcement. Otherwise, your PR rep will be in contact with them as a part of your ongoing PR effort;

Business media: Beyond your top trade media contacts, you (or your PR firm) should compile a contact list of editors and writers in the general business media. These contacts include general-interest business publications, such as *Business Week* or *The Wall Street Journal*, as well as editors at more specialized business publications indirectly related to your industry, who may be worthwhile media contacts, depending on your news announcement;

Local business press: Business editors, writers and reporters for local media outlets in your city may be interested in news about your company and its products. Generally speaking, local media coverage has less sales impact than national coverage in trade or industry-specific publications, but it doesn't hurt to include the local business press for certain announcements, if appropriate;

General media: Because it's highly unlikely they will cover your trade or industry news announcement (and even more unlikely that such coverage will lead to sales), you probably won't have a need to develop press lists for general-interest media outlets, such as newspapers, consumer magazines, or local broadcasters. These media outlets do not cover specialized company and product announcements unless your product and its underlying technology have a broader appeal to their general-interest audiences;

Media "targets of opportunity:" Occasionally, there may be a news event in your company that requires you to develop a specialized media contact list. A push into a new market or industry, or a product launch in an entirely new market, is often accompanied by a PR effort directed to the trade and business media covering this new market. You can use outside sources, such as Bacon's, and Standard Rate and Data Service (SRDS), to develop media contact lists for any industry or market (more on this further in this section).

Making personal contact with your media list: The level of personal contact required to follow-up with each group of contacts on your media list depends on their closeness to your industry, and the significance of your news announcement. For example, with a major new product announcement or product upgrade, you (or your PR firm's rep) will likely follow up, by phone or e-mail, with everyone on your list of "top trade media contacts," after they receive your press release.

Other contacts who receive the same press release, such as general business media writers or reporters, usually won't receive a follow-up call, since it's less likely they will be interested in covering your story. Nonetheless, the goal here is to keep sending your press releases to these broader media contacts to keep your company's name and products in front of them, so they'll remember your company on the day you have a news announcement they do decide to cover.

Regardless of who's responsible in your company for day-to-day implementation of your company's public relations program—you, or your outside PR rep—as a marketing manager, you should always make it a point to establish working contacts with the top trade publication writers and editors in your industry. You'll never know when you'll have to talk to a trade publication editor to pitch a story idea (more on this in the next section), or when you may have to pre-emptively call a staff writer to head off a potentially harmful negative review of one of your company's products.

Compiling Your Company's Media Contact Lists

If your ad agency, PR firm, or marketing consultant is handling your PR program, they will likely be responsible for developing your company's media contact lists, (using the methods described here), or working from their existing contact lists established by developing prior relationships with media contacts in your field. Either way, you need to know who's on your company's media contact list, and who's receiving a press release for your news announcement.

Creating your company's own media contact list is both a process of compiling your own lists, and obtaining media contacts from outside sources, such as Bacon's or Standard Rate & Data Service (SRDS). This section details the key steps for compiling your company's media contact lists, for each category of media contact previously described.

Establishing Top Trade Media Contacts

This media contact list contains your most important contacts for the trade and industry publications read by customers and prospects in your marketplace, and constitutes your "A" List of top contacts. If your company has already been covered in any of these publications, the writer of the previous article should be your primary media contact there. These writers will have a natural interest in receiving any new announcements from your company, so they are your best contacts at these publications.

When in doubt, go to the managing editor: If your company is new to PR, and has not yet received coverage in your industry's trade publications, check the publication's editorial masthead (found within the first few pages in the front of the publication) and locate the publication's managing editor (see **Figure 14-3**). Managing editors serve as gatekeepers for deciding what stories get covered, who covers them, and for pushing these stories into upcoming issues. When the managing editor receives your company's press release, they'll route it to the person at the publication they feel is most qualified to write about it.

If you're developing your company's own media contact lists, it's a good idea to contact the managing editors at these publications to introduce yourself, and describe your company and its products to them. In public relations, personal contact always improves your chances of getting coverage, so it's always a good idea to get to know who will be covering your company at the publication. Ask the managing editor who should receive your news announcements at their publication; this person, and the managing editor, should then receive press releases for all of your company's subsequent news announcements.

Figure 14-3:

Media Contacts

When in doubt, send your company's press releases to the Managing Editors at the trade publications on your media contact list. These contacts are found on the masthead at the front of the publication

Figure 14-4:

New Product News Sections—A useful source of sales leads for your company's new product press releases

New Product News Sections, found in many trade and industry publications, give your company's products or services valuable free media coverage, and generate sales leads from interested readers of these publications

"New product news" sections: Many trade publications also have an editor in charge of the "new product news" sections in their publications (see **Figure 14-4**). These new product sections feature small, three column-inch blurbs, often accompanied by small product photos submitted by the company with their press release. Many new product announcements end up here if the managing editor doesn't think the press release announcement warrants a standalone article. It's likely that many of your company's new product and product upgrade announcements fall into this category, so it's better to send them directly to the "new product news editor" at the publication, and get some minor coverage for them, than it is to try for bigger story placement with an announcement that (at least in the editor's mind) doesn't deserve it.

Establishing Contacts in General Business Media

You can repeat the process of checking the mastheads of publications for general business magazines, and in the business sections of your city's local newspapers, to compile contacts for the larger "B" Lists of general-interest business publications.

Both the managing editor and new product news editors should be added to your media contact list for each of these publications. If your company is involved in the high-technology field, add the publication's "technology editor" to your contact list.

When adding a contact for your local newspaper's business section, select the paper's "business editor."

Getting broader media coverage: If your company does business in one or more industries or vertical markets, it's likely you'll have to expand the scope of your company's public relations efforts. For example, if your company enters a new market, you'll need to execute a PR program to attract media coverage from trade publications in this new industry. Your company may even have a news announcement that would be appropriate for wider, general-interest media coverage, such as broadcast TV, cable, radio, or daily newspapers.

When you need to expand the reach of your public relations program, the Bacon's media directories (at **www.bacons.com**) can provide you with full contact information on newspapers, business media, TV, radio, and any other media source in the U.S. Average cost for the hard-copy Bacon's directories is around $400 each, but you can order and download specific groups of media contacts from their Web site, using their MediaLists Online service, for a $100 minimum charge per order.

For most of your company's public relations activities, however, you'll be focusing your efforts on the trade publications of your industry or marketplace. For example, if your company has developed a new model hydraulic pump for industrial plants, it's a safe bet that *The New York Times*, *Forbes*, or *The Washington Post* isn't interested. Keep your program focused on your industry, develop good working relationships with the editors at the top publications there, and you'll get coverage that boosts sales of your company's products.

Fitting Your News to the Size of the Story: Types of PR Announcements

Some PR firms make the mistake of treating every company news announcement, large or small, in the same way. They make follow-up phone calls to busy editors to promote relatively minor company announcements, not realizing that the small amount of coverage that may be generated by their effort isn't worth the strain they've added to their relationships with these editors.

Your company's news announcements aren't all alike, and not every news event from your company should be announced to the world in the same way. So, in addition to maintaining a threshold for "what is news" in your company, you'll have to decide what type of PR promotion to give to each news announcement from your company, and how much promotional effort each announcement deserves.

Minor (secondary) company news announcements: Minor, or secondary, announcements are the "everyday" news events that occur most frequently in companies, and account for the most promotion by companies and their PR firms.

These include:

- **Minor product upgrades**

- **Product price changes**
- **New account sales**
- **Product sales promotions**
- **Industry awards and recognition**

Minor news events are announced by a one-page press release sent either by mail or e-mail, and usually without a follow-up phone call. These announcements usually receive a few column-inches of coverage in trade publications, and many end up as two-or three-paragraph "filler" items in the back pages of these publications. They provide some help to your sales efforts by keeping your company and its product in front of prospects in your industry, but their most important benefit is that they keep your name in the minds of the *editors* at these publications until your company's next *major* news announcement.

Major company news announcements: Major news events in your company are events that justify coverage as individual articles in publications. Examples of major announcements include:

- **New product announcements**
- **New product reviews**
- **New market entries**
- **Major product upgrades**
- **Corporate mergers and acquisitions**
- **Corporate joint ventures**

Execution of major news announcements ranges from distribution of a press release, with phone follow-up by your PR rep, all the way up to special, big-city news conferences and other elaborate events requiring very sophisticated PR support. However, most major news announcements consist of a press release or press kit mailing (or e-mail distribution) and follow-up contact with editors by your PR firm. Also, "story pitches" may be made to business and trade publication editors to wrap a major industry trend or issue around the company's news announcement (more on story pitches further in this section).

PR announcements of major company news events are also timed to support and to coincide with the execution of other marketing projects, such as a print advertising or direct mail campaign for a new product launch. You can also time major PR announcements for new product launches to coincide with your company's exhibit at a major trade show for your industry, where this product will be introduced.

Execution of Your Company's PR Program

When planning your company's ongoing public relations program, it helps to plan the specifics of each of your projected news announcements out as far in advance as possible, to anticipate and support all of your company's marketing projects.

Plan ahead for major announcements: Since the press release is the main marketing deliverable all PR projects are built around, it helps to think of the major news announcements in your PR program as a series of press release mailings, or "distributions," timed to coincide with your company's major marketing initiatives throughout the year. For example, if your company plans a fall launch of its major product line, you need to have a press release distribution in place to support this launch. Major announcements require more background effort (such as creating and executing story pitches) than minor ones, so give your ad agency, PR firm or marketing consultant enough advance notice so they can prepare for these projects.

Establish "meat grinder" press release distributions for minor announcements: Your PR program must also provide for the continuous distribution of minor news announcements that need to be written up as press releases and distributed as they occur. These announcements, also known as "meat grinder" press release distributions, are minor news announcements in your company that usually arise immediately, and are handled just as quickly, by a rapid press release distribution to your company's trade media contacts. Again, the purpose of getting your minor PR announcements out is not so much to support sales (although there may be some effect here), as it is to keep your company's name in front of editors, writers and other media contacts, so they'll know who your company is when your PR firm calls them with your major news announcements.

In addition to these minor news announcements, you'll never know when an exciting new business opportunity or a novel product application in your company will present a useful opportunity for media coverage. These unforeseen events will require you to respond with either a minor or a major news announcement, so be ready to handle these opportunities in your PR program.

Countdown to a News Announcement: Execution Steps for Public Relations Projects

This section is a start-to-finish checklist and summary of the key steps involved in executing PR news announcements in your company.

Is it news?

Whenever a potential company news event presents itself, first decide whether or not it should even be a news announcement from your company. As mentioned earlier, some events, like executive promotions, charity contributions, or minor new account sales, simply don't justify the time and effort of a press release distribution. An event should be announced only if you believe it can have a positive effect on sales—either directly, by leading to sales from the press coverage, or indirectly, by creating a favorable impression alongside other marketing efforts, such as advertising and direct mail programs.

Is it a minor or major news event?

Judge the importance of the event: Does it justify more attention and effort, such as phone follow-up contacts, or story pitches? PR firms have a tendency to treat every client's news announcement with the same level of effort, unless you force the distinction. If it's a minor news event, put it in your "meat grinder"—have it written it up as a press release, and distribute it by e-mail to your media contact list, where some of these contacts may decide to cover it in their publications.

Should we use a story pitch?

A story pitch (also known as a "story hook") wraps your company news announcement inside of an industry trend or issue. For example, if Internet hacker attacks have been in the news, your company's announcement of its Web server software's upgraded security features could be presented in the context of the network security issue when your PR rep speaks to an editor at a trade publication. An example of a verbal story pitch for this announcement might be:

> *"You know, server and network security is a big topic these days, especially in light of last month's 'denial of service' Internet server attacks. The recent attacks on Yahoo!'s site were caused by _____; Rezware's IBX system prevents these kinds of attacks. If you'd be interested in doing a story on network server security, I'd be glad to supply you with some contacts in the industry who could talk about it..."*

Of course, a few of the "contacts in the industry" referred to above would include your company's CEO or VP of Technology (in addition to some other, more objective, contacts). Many articles in trade publications get published as a result of these story pitches, and editors and writers rely on skilled PR reps to provide them with the interview sources, industry research, and the other key contacts they need to write their stories.

Story pitches are made for significant company news events: These include new product launches, major new business or market investments and initiatives, or major product upgrades. Your PR rep makes the story pitch by e-mail or (preferably) telephone. Of course, when using story pitches, the accompanying press release should specifically address the topic of the story pitch.

Story Pitch Examples:

Most industries have hot-button issues and trends that become the focus of major articles in their publications:

- The quest for higher productivity;
- Increasing plant efficiency;
- More efficient energy consumption;
- Internet privacy and security;
- Using consultants to reduce personnel costs;
- Plant and workplace safety;
- Software moving to Web-based systems and services;
- Effects of growing numbers of seniors in the U.S.;
- Outsourcing to reduce overhead expenses;
- Electronic payment systems;
- Terrorism and domestic security

You can judge the quality of your PR firm by the quality and relevance of the story pitches they use. The best PR firms constantly develop fresh and imaginative story pitch angles featuring your company or product.

Much of what a PR firm brings to its relationship with your company are its own contacts and relationships between its PR reps and their contacts in the media: A PR rep who gets to know which staff writer covers what particular topics at a publication can tailor their story pitches to the interests of that writer or reporter.

Trade publication editorial calendars: Many trade publications plan out their editorial coverage in advance on key industry topics, in their editorial calendars. Story pitches—especially those tied in with key industry trends and issues—can be developed to meet the needs of a publication's editorial calendar. For example, the cover story and lead articles for three issues of a banking industry publication's editorial calendar might look like this:

January:	New trends in Web security
February:	Smart card technology and consumer acceptance
March:	Streamlining back-office loan processing operations

Many publications in many different industries publish editorial calendars, usually found in their advertising media kits, detailing the publication's planned editorial coverage in each issue, by month, up to a year in advance. Thoughtful development of story pitches featuring your product, if they are relevant to the story topics in the publication's editorial calendar, can open major trade press coverage opportunities for your company.

Trade and business writers appreciate having high-concept "hooks" to write their stories around, such as how your company's product changes the status quo of the industry, or how your product stands in contrast to your competitors' products. Even if you decide that a news announcement doesn't need a story pitch, the press release that covers your announcement should appeal to the desire of editors and writers to exploit conflict, contrast, and change in their coverage of your industry.

Should I give an exclusive to a publication?

Staff writers and editors at one publication compete with other publications to cover the news of their industry. If you have a fairly significant product announcement, such as a new product launch, or an entry into a major new market, you (or your PR firm) may want to consider negotiating for prime coverage in a publication by agreeing to give the writer or editor an exclusive to cover your story. This means that they will be the first and only writer and publication to break the story for an agreed time period, if you agree to hold off on issuing your broader press release distribution to any other publication until after they publish their story covering your announcement.

Since you can never be certain how much coverage your news announcement will receive, the sure bet of getting prominent coverage in a leading publication is often preferable to the greater uncertainty of taking your chances with broader distribution of your announcement. If you have a major announcement, you can propose this to your PR firm, who can then check with their best contact to negotiate an exclusive on it.

What information do I need for the press release?

As you're planning your company's announcement, you'll need to get started on the press release. If you're writing your own company's press release, follow the instructions in the first part of this chapter.

If your ad agency, PR firm or marketing consultant is writing the press release, provide them with some background notes to sketch out these essential details:

- **Summary:** What your company just did;
- **Main benefits** of your news announcement;
- **Why** these benefits are important to readers;
- **Context** of the announcement—industry and market impact, competitive aspects, etc.

Remember to keep your press release to one side of a letter-size sheet of paper (500 words maximum). The final version of the release includes all of the form elements editors look for—contact information, background paragraph,

press release date, etc., covered previously in this chapter and shown in
Figure 14-2.

What other deliverables do we need along with our press release?

If this is a major news announcement, put together a **press kit** that includes
the press release, and all of the additional information editors need to fill in
the background detail on your company. Background materials are important
additions to your PR program, and should be sent along with your press
releases on major news announcements. On minor press releases, these
materials should be posted to your company's Web site and made freely
available to the media as clickable Web links.

For each news announcement you're planning, think of the other background
deliverables to be provided to editors in the press release distribution:

> **Photos:** If you're announcing news about a product launch or upgrade,
> supply at least one product shot with the release, and make additional
> photos available to editors on your company's Web site: Action shots of
> the product in use, closeups of key features, and any other variations, as
> needed;

> **Software:** If your company is in the software business, or sells any
> related electronic or information product, you can provide editors with a
> CD-ROM containing a demo version of your software, for their review;

> **Backgrounders:** If this is a major company news announcement, include
> some additional pieces of information on your company, distributed as
> single-sheet "backgrounders" to your media contact list:

>> • **Product Q & A**: Answers to most-asked questions about the
>> product;

>> • **Executive profiles:** Supply a sheet listing brief, one-paragraph
>> profiles of your company's senior management;

>> • **Company history:** If yours is a long-established company, editors
>> are always interested in seeing some interesting or historic
>> background on your company and its business activities.

Previous major trade articles: Include copies of any major articles previously
published on your company or its products: Product reviews, company
profiles, business features, etc.

These background materials are a must for any PR program. Put these
together at the earliest opportunity, and make them freely available to any
media contact.

When do we make our news announcement?

Think about the timing of your announcement. Should it be made immediately, or are their good reasons for making your announcement at a later date? Usually, speed is critical in news announcements: A new product needs to be announced ahead of a competitor's product, or a press release that ties your company's product in with an important new market trend, must go out immediately to capitalize on the currency of this trend.

Trade shows: Delaying a news announcement sometimes provides your company with an added sales benefit. For example, you might consider delaying a major product announcement until the date of an upcoming trade show, to get maximum exposure for your product from the key contacts in trade and business media attending the show. Trade shows are also excellent opportunities to schedule press conferences or other events, to present your company's new product announcement to the key contacts you've invited in advance.

For minor news events, however, it's more important to get the announcement out there in the media as soon as the press release is written, and to keep a steady stream of these minor news announcements flowing, so your media contacts know who your company is when they receive a major news release from your company.

Trade publication editorial calendars: You may also decide to delay the publication of a news announcement so you can present it to an editor as a story pitch for an upcoming issue listed in the publication's editorial calendar. While almost never done for new product announcements, an interesting story idea featuring your company's product can often be held until it's covered in an upcoming "cover story" issue of the publication dealing with the subject or trend matching your story idea's subject.

Unlike other marketing activities, PR is dependent on external, uncontrollable factors, such as the whims and agendas of trade publication editors. Because of these facts, always consider whether a news announcement should be made immediately, or held back for a more favorable time, when it could better serve your company's marketing activities.

Who should be contacted for the news announcement?

Consider the scope of distribution for your company's news announcement. Most industry and trade news announcements are of interest only to those involved in the industry, so should only be sent to media contacts within that industry.

However, if your news announcement has broader appeal, you can include contacts for general business publications, such *The Wall Street Journal* or *Business Week*, in your distribution for the announcement.

Developing story angles that enlarge the scope of your company's products can also help broaden the appeal of your potential media coverage to a wider audience in the general business press. You can often receive broader coverage if you can plausibly tie your company or products to current events or trends having broader appeal in general business life, such as an interesting new technology used to manufacture your product, or a regulatory concern addressed by your company's service.

However, be warned that coverage of vertical-market companies and products in general business publications often has **no impact** on sales of your company's products. The average *Business Week* reader is probably not a prospect for your specialized industrial product announcement, so focus your distribution to the media contacts in your immediate industry, unless your news announcement is either a major industry event, or is interesting enough to warrant space for readers of general-interest business publications.

How should the media be contacted? By mail or e-mail? Should follow-up phone calls be made?

Send minor announcements by e-mail: Editors and writers at trade publications have Internet e-mail, and they check it continuously throughout the day. Press releases for minor news announcements can be sent exclusively by e-mail to contacts on your trade media list, along with a Web link for access to background materials, such as product photos, on your company's Web site. E-mail communications should always be introduced with a short, personal note from your company's PR rep.

Major press release announcements can be sent simultaneously, as both an e-mail communication and a hard copy press kit, which also contains product photos and other background pieces. If your company is in the high-tech field, you are just as well off sending press releases for *every* news announcement by e-mail, since this has become the accepted form of PR communications in the technology trade press.

Follow-up major news announcements by phone: Follow-up phone calls to trade media contacts by your PR firm are an excellent way to promote your company's major news announcements. A follow-up call to jog an editor's memory on the press release that was sent a few days earlier can often move your story higher on the editor's agenda. PR reps can also use follow-up calls to answer an editor's questions, and fill in additional detail on your company's news announcement.

Limit telephone follow-ups by your PR reps only to your company's major news announcements. Follow-up phone calls are unnecessary for minor news events. Editors and writers at trade publications know a minor news announcement when they see one, and they've already made up their mind on whether or not they'll cover your story when they first received your e-mailed press release. They get annoyed when they receive unnecessary phone calls from PR reps following up on a minor news releases, so don't risk turning them off when you'll need their goodwill for your more significant news announcements at a later date.

Where else should the press release be distributed?

As you finalize the essential details of your press release announcement, give some thought to where else your press release can be distributed, in addition to sending it to your media contact lists.

For example, you can send your press release (for an additional cost) to PR Newswire (**www.prnewswire.com**), a service that distributes your press release to thousands of contacts at media outlets who've agreed to receive press releases from PR Newswire. The PR Newswire Web site has a constantly-updated, keyword-searchable archive of all corporate press releases it distributes, which is sometimes used by editors and writers as an online research tool to search for background news items on the companies and industries they cover.

In general, you are far better off focusing your PR efforts on your own company's trade media contact lists than paying the extra expense (around $1,400 per release) to distribute your press release on PR Newswire. While some editors and writers pay attention to PR Newswire releases, they will pay more attention to a press release they receive from your company or your PR firm, especially if this release is followed up with a personal contact. If you have the money in your marketing budget, you can take your chances and put your press release out on PR Newswire, but bear in mind that this is often just a little better than doing nothing.

The final, very important, action step in a PR project is to put your press release up on your company's Web site. If you haven't already done so, create a "Company News" link on the home page of your company's Web site, and use this as your company's online press release archive, arranged by date.

Posting your press releases to your company's Web site can be a tremendously valuable promotional tool for your company: Potential strategic and joint venture partners, key sales prospects at other companies, major customers, media contacts, and others who are interested in your company and its products can learn more about them by reading your press releases here.

VIDEO & MULTIMEDIA
CHAPTER 15
USING THE POWER OF SPOKEN WORDS AND MOVING IMAGES TO SELL YOUR COMPANY'S PRODUCTS

In addition to the other elements of your company's marketing program, video and other multimedia-related projects play an important role in your marketing program, allowing you to reach prospects in a way that only the power of audio and video can match.

In typical marketing applications for small and mid-sized companies, video projects shown and distributed on VHS and DVD are also being used in other new ways. These new applications, loosely termed "multimedia," also include Web-based video and audio projects, interactive CD-ROMs, and other exciting new marketing opportunities using new devices, such as Net-accessible digital TVs, enhanced cell phones, and Internet broadband services.

Typical Video and Multimedia Applications

While there are differences between traditional video and multimedia, most of these relate to relatively minor issues, such as distribution (DVD vs. streaming Web video), or presentation (screen size or sound quality desired for the presentation of the final project). As a marketing manager, your task is to stay focused on using the power of multimedia to tell your product's story and sell your product, leaving these technical, presentation and distribution issues to your ad agency, marketing consultant, or video producer. Here are some typical uses for video and multimedia-based marketing deliverables in your company's marketing program:

Sales videos: A professionally-produced sales video presenting your company, its products, and their benefits, shown to prospects by your company's sales reps during sales calls, creates a very positive beginning to any sales presentation. Your product is seen in its most favorable light, and your sales

Figure 15-1:

Future Marketing Opportunities Using Multimedia—Multimedia plays an increasingly important role

New Products and Services Using Broadband Internet Access, *such as set-top boxes and other Net-capable devices, will open many profitable new sales opportunities for smart marketing professionals who use video, audio, and other forms of multimedia*

video answers the most common questions your prospects ask about your company's product or service;

Trade shows: A continuously-running video, shown on a large, flat-panel video display in your company's trade show booth, draws show visitors in to your booth, and introduces them to the essential facts on your company and its product, in a very short time. A trade show video that clearly and persuasively presents your product also performs the task of helping show visitors "pre-qualify" themselves in your booth: Visitors who are prospects will be engaged by your video, and will tend to signal this interest by lingering in front of your video long enough to be approached by one of your company's sales reps; others, who are not prospects, will watch your video and move on;

Web video: Most of the prospects in your market will be accessing your company's Web sites on fast broadband Internet connections. This higher bandwidth creates exciting new opportunities for using video as a selling tool in your company's marketing program. A sales video introducing your company and its product, set to run automatically on your company's home page for first-time site visitors (using "cookies," so that a site visitor only sees it once, when linking to your site for the first time) brings site visitors up to speed on your company and its product more quickly than expecting site visitors to click on the right information link to read more about your company's product;

Figure 15-2:

How-To Videos Boost Sales and Customer Satisfaction

Product How-To and Instructional Videos can help your company improve customer satisfaction, reduce customer service expenses, and provide a competitive advantage to your company's product before the sale

Video news releases: If the right "story hook" is created around your product or service, it has the potential to be covered in multiple local broadcast news markets, or on a major cable news and business/financial network. A video news release, also called a "VNR," is a video news "package" produced and distributed by your company to local and network broadcast news directors and producers, and supplies these news directors with the background video clips they need to cover your story;

How-to videos: Although not directly related to marketing and sales, instructional how-to-use videos on your company's products can be an important selling feature, generating higher new customer satisfaction rates for your product, and leading to higher sales reorder rates and repeat business.

High-End Vs. "Industrial" Video Projects

The production value of any video project—the level of craft and creative skill put into its camera work, editing, audio and effects—is, more than any other type of marketing project, dictated by the amount of money your company can afford to spend on the project.

For example, your company could spend up to $30,000 (or more) to hire a top-flight video production company to produce a three-minute sales video for your company. In any major city, there are usually a small number of top video production companies who command the highest rates, because they do the best work: First-rate commercials for major local and national consumer brands, splashy institutional video for large corporations, and other, high-dollar video work usually done in connection with the largest, most prominent advertising agencies in your area.

By contrast, there are also a large number of less-expensive, "industrial" video production firms, whose rates for a similar project may run one-half to one-third the cost of top video producers. Whether or not one of them can deliver a work product that is as effective as the work of a top video production firm depends, of course, on the firm, and on the guidance you give them on your project.

The Desktop Video Revolution

The introduction of powerful digital desktop video editing systems (such as Apple's Final Cut Pro) combined with less-expensive "prosumer" digital video (DV) cameras, have brought high-quality video production capabilities to any high-end personal computer. As a result, the desktop video revolution has drawn many new entrants to the video production field: Web developers, print designers, and ad agency in-house creative departments.

The final output quality of desktop video systems can rival that of broadcast-quality systems costing ten times as much, and is sufficient for many corporate video applications. Like any tool, however, the quality of the final project produced on desktop video is totally dependent on the experience, creativity, and skill of the user. And, given the virtually unlimited creative options offered by digital video systems, the quality of the end product is also dependent on the user's *restraint*: For example, overuse of editing transitions, effects and other available creative options is a common misuse of desktop video on many corporate video projects.

In the right hands, however, a digital desktop video editing system dramatically reduces the cost and execution time of video production, and opens up many new opportunities for using video as a marketing tool in your company. By slashing the cost of video production, and dramatically increasing its speed of execution, desktop video production offers the same revolutionary new possibilities for video and multimedia production that desktop publishing has already given to the design, production, and execution of brochures and other printed marketing deliverables.

Digital video also allows you to use video in more marketing opportunities than the far more expensive, old-school "film crew and editing suite" style of production, using costly, broadcast-quality video gear and high-priced labor. For example, if you can get a trade show video produced for your company's booth in time for next month's show, you might be able to increase your booth traffic by 25% or more. A talented digital video producer using "prosumer"-level DV camera gear and a desktop editing system can get a basic video shot, edited, and output to DVD in two weeks or less, for around $5,000. Another video producer using expensive, conventional approaches, might charge two to three times as much and take twice as long, which would put this marketing opportunity out of reach.

Everything depends on who is behind the DV camera and the digital desktop editing system. An inexperienced Web designer using your project as his first opportunity to create a digital video is likely to produce a final result that's worse than no video at all. This chapter covers some of the ways you can evaluate a video producer's work to make sure it's right for your project, along with some general pointers for working with producers on your own video and multimedia projects.

The Video Producer

The heart of every video project, whether it's a conventional sales video shown to potential prospects during a sales call, a streaming video on your company's Web site, or a "video news release" distributed to a cable news channel, is the **video production**—the combination of live video image clips, audio narration, on-screen text and captions, and special effects. The "project," or video production, is the main marketing deliverable of any marketing activity using video.

The **video producer** is responsible for developing, executing, and overseeing every aspect of the process—from sketching out the basic concepts for the video project, to working with a film crew to shoot the video necessary for the project, and on to the final editing process.

How to find a video producer: Video production is a highly specialized craft. Video producers usually work as third-party subcontractors to ad agencies, marketing consultants, and PR firms, so if you are already working with one of these kinds of firms, they will usually know the best video producer for your project.

Video producers usually fall into one of two categories: Elite producers of expensive, high-end projects, who mostly work for the large corporations and other organizations that can afford to pay for expensive video productions, and "industrial" video producers, who handle the majority of corporate video applications for small and mid-sized companies.

While the total costs for projects produced by high-end video producers can be very expensive (averaging $10,000-$15,000 per final minute of video produced), their work reflects the best production values available, and the quality of their final product is comparable to the best examples you would see on national cable and network television.

Industrial producers may have backgrounds in local television (news or commercial production), or they may be ad agencies or Web site developers using the latest desktop video editing equipment and digital video gear. Industrial producers generally charge between $2,000-$5,000 per final minute of video on a project. The quality of their work will vary widely, so you should always ask to see any producer's "demo reel" (see below) of their past work to judge whether or not it meets your needs.

How to Evaluate the Producer's Demo Reel

All video producers can supply you with their "demo reel," a videotape, CD, or DVD of their best previous work. Like an ad agency's portfolio, or a graphic designer's "book," the producer's demo reel shows you what kind of work the producer has done in the past, and for what kinds of companies.

Production value: When looking at a producer's demo reel, first look at the production values of their work. Does it come close to, or match, the quality of video you're used to watching on TV, such as the commercials or programming most of us watch on cable or financial news channels? All scenes should be well-lit, without harsh glare, and camera movements (if any) should be smooth and appropriate to the shot.

Special effects: The quality of special effects should also be comparable to what you see on a broadcast and cable news program every day. Informational tables and graphics should enhance your understanding of the concepts being explained in the video, without distracting you with the flashiness of the effects being used. Nowadays, with a little practice, anyone can use programs like Adobe After Effects to make a company logo zoom to the front of the screen, but only the best effects people know how to do it without making it obvious, or pushing the effect into the viewer's face: These are the people you want working on your company's video projects.

Pacing and editing: Do the clips in the producer's projects move along at a quick pace, or do you get the feeling that certain scenes and clips are staying on the screen too long? Viewers today can absorb quite a lot of visual information, and video images that don't change in some way every two seconds risks losing the viewer's attention. A first-rate video producer uses skillful editing that moves the viewer through the material being covered, using simple, quick cuts that build the viewer's interest as the presentation moves quickly from one shot to another, mixing in other visual effects, such as on-screen text bullets or captions, to reinforce the sales messages being presented. To paraphrase former AP broadcast editor Jim Hood (see interview in **Figure 15-5**), the best edit, transition, or effect is one that the viewer doesn't even notice.

How to be Your Own Executive Producer

Like any other marketing craft, video production requires skill, experience, and talent. While no one in your company expects you to be a video producer, knowing something about the video production process, and knowing the individual elements required to produce an effective sales video for your particular marketing application, helps you work more effectively with a video producer on your company's video projects.

Most of us have already watched enough television in our lives to make us familiar with the technical and creative aspects of video production. No doubt you're also able to sense the difference between good production values and poor ones, and to recognize the various elements that go into any television production: Video clips, the audio soundtrack accompanying the video, as well as text, captions, graphics, and other video effects.

Your role as a marketing manager is similar to that of an executive producer, who puts together a production for television or film. Like an executive producer, after establishing the key application and objectives of your video project, you will be broadly responsible for overseeing its content and direction. You must know enough about the process to communicate your goals to your ad agency, marketing consultant, or video production company, to specify the sales message and content of the project, and to supply your video producer with the elements required to execute and complete the project.

Decide on Your Video Project's Application and Goals

The nature and content of any video project depends on where it's to be used, its viewing audience, its length, and the sales message it must deliver. This section describes the major types of corporate sales video projects, their characteristics, and guidelines for producing each type of project.

Trade Show Booth Videos

A trade show video runs continuously on a large, flat-screen video display in your company's booth at the show. More than any other type of video project, a trade show video must grab and hold the attention of show visitors walking down the aisle in front of your booth, and must quickly communicate your product's essential benefits to these visitors during the brief time it can hold their attention.

Trade shows are noisy environments, so the audio narration of a trade show video may not be heard clearly enough by show visitors. Because of this, most trade show videos also display PowerPoint-style bulleted text, on-screen, to communicate and reinforce the important sales benefits and features of your company's product for show visitors who can't hear the audio. As a test of your trade show video's ability to communicate its sales message exclusively by the text, images, and graphics displayed on-screen, you should be able to clearly understand your product's essential content and sales benefits with the sound of your video turned *off*.

Trade show booth videos have short running times, usually ranging from just 30 seconds in length to no more than about 3 minutes, averaging in the one- to two-minute range. Because they're brief, and designed to accommodate the short attention spans of trade show visitors, a trade show video can be mildly reworked for use on your company's Web site, to accommodate the equally short attention spans of visitors to your company's Web site.

Sales Videos

Corporate sales videos can be used by your company's field sales force to kick off sales presentations to their prospects. Corporate sales videos range in length from 3-10 minutes and tell the story of your company, its products, their benefits and applications.

Figure 15-3:

Repurposing Video for the Web—Most video projects can be readily converted for use on your Web site

Sales or Trade Show Booth Videos can be easily converted for use on your company's Web site, using the power of video and audio to speed the process of presenting and explaining your product or service to site visitors

The purpose of a sales video is to present the viewer with the essential details on your company and its products, using first-rate production values, fast-paced editing, professional voiceover narration, video effects, a compelling musical score, and other aspects of the video producer's art to create a positive impression in the mind of the prospect, and to answer the common questions your prospect is most likely to ask about your company's products.

When shown before your company's sales reps begin their personal sales presentations to prospects, a sales video insures that all prospects receive the same basic sales message on your company's product, with no essential sales information left out of the presentation. The use of first-class production values also insures that prospects who see your video will be viewing your company's sales message in its most favorable light.

Because of their longer running times and higher production values, sales videos can be the most expensive video projects to produce, costing anywhere from $3,000 to $10,000 per minute to produce. While this can be expensive, a first-rate sales video often earns back many times its original cost in the additional sales it can generate for your company. And like trade show videos, a sales video can be modified for reuse on your company's Web site, with some of its footage used for other kinds of video projects, such as sales training videos and video news releases (see below).

Video News Releases

Video news releases, also called "VNRs," are corporate video "news packages"

Figure 15-4:

Value-Added Customer How-To Videos

Videos Distributed or Sold as Value-Added Product Premiums to Customers boost product satisfaction, cut customer service expense, and help your company differentiate its product from other, similar products sold by your competitors

distributed to broadcast, cable, and local television news operations. The video equivalent of a conventional press release, VNRs are used to promote broadcast news and feature coverage on a company's products, technologies, trends, or related issues. VNRs are distributed, either physically, or by satellite feed, to local television news operations, cable financial news channels, network broadcast news operations, and other cable or broadcast television outlets where there may be the potential for widespread national exposure.

The most successful video news releases build a story around a company and its product, designed to appeal to television news directors at cable networks and local news operations. VNRs can be viewed as an extension of your company's ongoing public relations efforts, and are linked to the press release mailings and story pitches your company uses to promote itself and its product.

Do you have a story fit for broadcast? First, develop your story pitch, or "hook;" then decide whether or not your PR project will work as a video news release, based on the following criteria:

Does this fit into the "usual" local news categories? In local TV news operations, most VNRs are picked up and run as general-interest consumer, health, or technology segments, so whatever story angle you use must have similar broad appeal, and must be relevant to one of these categories;

Is there a local or regional angle? If your company or product has a local or regional angle, it stands a greater chance of getting picked up by stations in those areas. For example, if your company's product addresses a local problem that's a hot current topic in a particular city, like traffic congestion, or crumbling road or bridge infrastructure, you can develop a story pitch and supply video in your VNR "package" to a local news station for possible coverage;

Can you see it running on CNBC, or on a CNN/MSNBC/FOX business segment? You can also get national coverage if your product and its related story pitch are novel, exciting, or topical. If your company is involved in an exciting new technology area, or if your product helps to address a hot current business trend or issue—such as a new computer application, or a telecom, digital media, anti-terrorism, or productivity-boosting product—it can be pitched as a business, technology, or financial segment to a cable news channel.

The purpose of a video news release is to supply television news operations with the basic content they need to broadcast a story featuring your company's product. This includes generic video clips of the product in use (called "B-Roll" video), talking-head interview clips featuring company executives and outside experts speaking about your company's products, explanatory product animation and graphics, and other content that a local and cable news producer can re-use or edit into the news segments they produce.

Video news release distribution: The best way to distribute VNRs is by personal contact, with your ad agency or PR firm making story pitches to news producers at television news operations. At extra cost ($5,000-$10,000 per VNR), VNRs can also be distributed on open satellite feeds to many hundreds of broadcast outlets, where there is a small chance they may be picked up by local stations. Because of the low chance of success in satellite VNR distribution, you're better off creating more highly-targeted story pitches and having your ad agency or PR firm's rep make personal contact with TV news producers to pitch these stories on your company's behalf.

Video news releases generally run 3-5 minutes in length, and are accompanied by other materials, such as suggested story "talking points," and contact follow-up information for the individuals covered in on-screen interviews in your B-Roll video clips (for more information on VNRs, see **Figure 15-5**).

Writing The Script: What Marketing Managers Should Know

The heart of any corporate video presentation is its spoken audio soundtrack. And the heart of every audio soundtrack is the script. For sales videos, the persuasiveness of your video script presents an enthusiastic vision of your company and its product, and tells the listener, in plain language, why they need it, much like the persuasive sales benefit copy used in your company's ads, brochures, and direct mail deliverables.

The script is the most important part of any video presentation. It's the foundation on which all the other elements of your video—live action shots, still images, and text bullet points—are built. Since the script drives the content and presentation of the visual imagery used in your project, it should always be the first step in your video project, and should be completed before any other visually-oriented work on your project begins.

The exception to this rule is found in expensive, high-end corporate video projects, where video producers, who are generally more image-oriented, shoot all of the images they need for a project first, and then develop the script as they edit their shots down to their final form. However, for many less-ambitious projects, and especially for lower-cost projects executed on desktop video systems, the script is the essential blueprint which guides the rest of the project.

What to Look for in a Video Script

As a marketing manager, it's unlikely you'll be writing the script for your video. However, you do still need to know what makes a video script effective, and you need to understand the scriptwriting process well enough to be able to sketch out some basic notes to define the minimum sales content required for your video project. Your ad agency, marketing consultant, or video producer will appreciate this initial guidance, and you'll be more pleased with the final result.

This section covers the basic process of video scriptwriting, to give you the background you need to "spec out" the content of a script, or to write the script yourself, if you ever find yourself in the position of having to produce a corporate video project on your own. Whether you're working with an outside video producer, or you're doing it yourself, here are some pointers to help you specify, develop and evaluate a script for your video project:

> **Answer your listener's most common questions:** Since the goal of most corporate videos is to sell your company's product or service, your video script should read like a somewhat more formal-sounding version of the sales presentation made for the product by your company's sales reps. Your script should anticipate and answer the most commonly-asked questions a typical listener would have about your product or service, describe its typical uses and applications, and its tone should emphasize your product's sales benefits with energy and enthusiasm. Like any other good sales copy, the goal of your script is to answer all the questions a person would ask about your company, its products, or other topics addressed by the video.
>
> Don't think that your viewers will be overwhelmed if you cover every key benefit of your sales presentation in your video. Between the images they see and what they hear, viewers can absorb a tremendous amount of information in a video, especially if you employ common video presentation techniques,

such as on-screen, PowerPoint-style text bullet points, to simultaneously reinforce the spoken sales points made in your soundtrack;

Keep your script friendly and conversational: The writing style of your script should use a friendly, conversational tone. Your script should read like someone is speaking—literally. The style of writing for a script is very much like the "Park Bench Story" sales copywriting exercise in Chapter 4. When reviewing a script (or writing your own), it helps to "sound out" your script by reading it aloud. Use simple, one and two-syllable words, and continue reading your script draft aloud to catch any words or phrases that sound too formal or unnatural when spoken;

Follow a logical structure: Generally speaking, the structure of a script for a corporate sales video follows the old speechwriting adage:

> **1.) Tell them what you're going to tell them;**
>
> **2.) Tell them;**
>
> **3.) Tell them what you've just told them.**

You script should have a structure that walks the viewer logically through your product's sales presentation, with each new point building on the previous one. An outline for a typical sales video might look something like this:

- Intro: Product summary and major benefit

- Product description

- How the product works

- Product key benefits 1, 2, 3…

- Who can use the product (examples)

- Who we are, and why you should buy from us

- Who else says we're good—comments from customers, outside experts, etc.

- Close: Recap main benefits, give contact info

Tell your story first—the images will come later: Because we're all attracted by compelling video images and special effects, it's easy to make the mistake of being drawn in by, and thinking too much about, the imagery and special effects you'd like to see in your project, before you've even outlined your script. Finish your script first, and make it the *best verbal presentation* that explains and sells your product. Then you can think about the video clips and other images that fit the script, and let the script be the foundation for the video clips and other imagery for your project;

Break down complex topics by talking them through: If you must describe a complex process or concept in connection with your product, break this description down into small parts, and explain each part in simple, clear language to the listener, as if they were sitting right next to you. It also helps to use examples or metaphors to explain these complex ideas. Focus on using the spoken word to explain the abstractions of your product, and then use animations and other visuals, as needed, to support your explanation;

How long is the script? A professional voiceover announcer can speak at a rate of around 154 words per minute (2.6 words per second). This is a good rule of thumb for estimating the final length of your video project, based on your script's final word count. As you review or write a script, pay close attention to its length, or running time. Most sales videos have running times ranging from 1-5 minutes, and average 2-3 minutes in length; a video for a trade show booth generally runs 1-2 minutes. Scripts often run longer than expected, and need to be cut and rewritten to fit the shorter time requirement. To prevent production problems down the line, once you've finalized your script, make sure that it fits your project's desired length.

Basic Sales Video Script Structure

While there are infinite variations in the structure, pace, and content of video scripts, one of the most common ways to organize a script for a basic, one, two, or three-minute sales video is to use the "Intro/Body/Close" structure:

Intro: "Tell them what you're going to tell them," by putting the essential information about your product and its major benefit into the first one or two sentences of your script. Tell your viewer what your product is, what it does, and its main benefit. A good technique is to write your intro *after* you've written the body and close of your script, because it's easier to create a better and more concise summary of your product's description and its major benefit once you've had the experience of writing about your product at some length in the body of your script;

Body: "Tell them," by presenting your product's essential features, benefits, and applications. The body of your script should sound like a verbal sales presentation for your product, but should be written in the somewhat more formal tone of the professional voiceover announcer—not extremely loose or conversational, but tight and polished, without being cold or unfriendly. Cover the information and answer the questions that most people ask about your company's product: Its main benefits, how it's used, compatibility issues, and key features;

Close: "Tell them what you've just told them," by either reinforcing your product's single major benefit, or by summing up a few of its leading benefits in the final one or two sentences of your script. Depending on your video's application (for example, if it's being distributed as a standalone DVD), include a "call to action" in your close by telling the viewer how they can contact your company, and what they need to do next to get more information on your company's product.

Even if you're not writing your own script, this structure helps you organize your notes as you write down the essential sales points and other content that the final script, to be written by your ad agency or video consultant, must contain.

Your Video Production Checklist: Executing Video Projects

As a rather technical and specialized marketing art, a video project requires you to use a more "hands-off" relationship with your video producer than with most other types of marketing projects, such as print advertising, Web site development, or direct mail. No one expects (or wants) you to take an active, day-to-day role in managing the highly specialized tasks involved in a video project—shooting, editing, etc. This is especially true for expensive, high-end video projects, where greater involvement by people who aren't skilled video producers only increases the expensive hourly costs of video production. The best video projects occur when a video producer can be allowed to work independently, guided occasionally by the marketing manager's light hand.

General goals for any video project: Once you've laid out the key sales message and written some notes on the required content for the project, trust your ad agency or video producer to keep your project on-message, and limit your involvement to periodic reviews of work in progress. Here are some general guidelines to follow when sketching out your key sales message and the other required content for the video:

> **Content:** Remember, *what you say is more important than how you say it.* Stay focused on the effectiveness of the **sales content** of your video project— the sales benefits, feature descriptions, and other key points you are communicating in your sales message to the viewer;

> **Visuals:** Next, suggest the most important and compelling visuals you believe should be included in your project, such as live-action shots of your company's product or service in use;

> **Execution:** Keep your video production team focused on clean, powerful presentation of your sales content and visuals. Techniques of video craft, such as editing and video effects, should serve the content of your video, not detract from it by drawing attention to themselves.

Figure 15-6:

The Audio Soundtrack—Audio is often the starting point for many video projects

The Audio Soundtrack (below, right) often serves as the foundation for the rest of the video project. Video clips, titles, and effects are then added in, "over" the audio soundtrack, in digital video editing systems like Apple's Final Cut Pro (right)

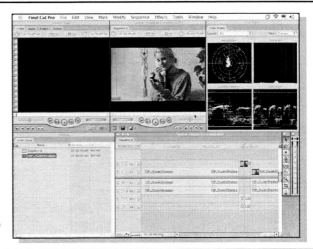

(Photo from www.apple.com)

Basic Elements of a Video Project

Whether you're working on a large video project, or a smaller, less expensive, one, you'll need to know the basic elements of any video project, and how your product's essential sales benefits and features can be incorporated into the content of this project.

The script: The script is the most important element of any video project. Your video's script drives the other elements of your project, such as the choice, presentation, and content of the video clips used in your project, and other elements, such as on-screen sales text bullet points used to reinforce the sales message of your script. The script also governs the overall pace and timing of the project.

Since your video project's script will be written by a scriptwriter at your ad agency or video production firm, it's likely you'll never have to write a script for a video project. However, you should supply the scriptwriter with the essential sales copy points and feature descriptions that should be included in the script, so the final voiceover narration will include your product's proven sales content.

Do this by jotting down some notes on the essential sales benefits and other content you believe are important enough to be included in your script. For smaller video projects, you should have a near-final draft of your script in hand before your video production team starts filming your project. Larger, more expensive projects are usually a "shoot first, write later" proposition, relying on the creative talent of the producer and editor to film the imagery for the project, and then assemble it into a tight, final production, with the script being incorporated at a later stage in the process.

Figure 15-5

A Broadcaster's Advice to Marketing Managers

Jim Hood, Washington, DC-based communications consultant and owner of The Oakton Press (www.oaktonpress.com) has an extensive background in broadcast news journalism, as former Deputy Director and General Broadcast Editor of The Associated Press, and as co-author of the AP Broadcast News Handbook. His most recent project is "& Thou Shalt Honor," a PBS documentary.

Here are his views on selecting a video producer for a big-budget project, how TV news producers evaluate potential stories for broadcast, and the role of the marketing manager in the video production process.

On different kinds of video production firms, and which one is right for your company:

"There are several different kinds of video production companies: First, there are hundreds, maybe thousands of companies out there that do what's basically called industrial video—this is what most of us would think of as the 'Army training film' school of video production . . . fairly drab, not the best production values and not a lot of show biz.

Second would be a rapidly-growing field of people who are basically coming at it from the computer and Web side of the business, using the new digital cameras and doing it all on Mac-based equipment, who are not really television people; they're sort of computer video people.

And then the third group are the high-end video production companies that are owned by someone who comes out of network television or the movie business or, generally speaking, entertainment and broadcast journalism fields. Those are the guys who really know how to put the 'sizzle on the steak,' who use world-class production values, and understand how to keep the viewer's eye, and hopefully their minds, engaged.

I really think this last category in the high-end broadcast video side of the business are the only ones a marketing manager should consider using for important video projects. The [work of the] rest looks amateurish to the trained eye, and to the untrained eye it just looks boring and uninteresting and people who see it are going to move on to something else."

How to judge the quality of a prospective video producer's work:

"The American consumer today is highly sophisticated in what he looks for today in video. People sit in their recliners with their remotes flipping through 250 television channels and if they don't see something in the first 1.3 seconds that catches their eye, you've lost them.

If they're walking down the aisle of an exhibit hall at a trade show it may be a slightly different situation, but the same principles apply: Their eyes will go to the monitor and stay on it for a second or two and then if it doesn't engage them, they're gone. The easiest way to look at a video and tell something about the producer of it, is to say to yourself: How often do the scenes change? If the video doesn't change every couple of seconds, then the person who put it together isn't a high-end, broadcast-standard producer. The video image has to be constantly changing in order to be compelling, and that's what the consumer has been 'trained' to look for.

You also want to ask yourself whether or not you are conscious of the transitions from one shot to another, and from one scene to another. If you say to yourself: 'Gee, that's a really interesting way they were able to make one image fade into another,' chances are it's an amateurish piece of work because you should never be conscious of any of the editing done in a video.

People shown on-screen should be wearing makeup. You shouldn't see the makeup, but you should notice that if someone is bald, their bald heads don't shine, that they don't have bags under their eyes, etc. Also, you should never see the camera jiggle, and everything should be a professionally lit."

Where marketing managers can find a top-quality video production firm for a big-budget project:

"If you're doing a big-budget video project, and you're in a major city, there are usually three or four companies that do the high-end work that everybody else knows about, and undoubtedly they're going to be the most expensive, but they're also the ones who've done the work that really stands out.

You can usually find them by asking around in advertising circles. For example, ad agencies use these guys and that's probably the best way to find them. They might also be in the Yellow Pages, but since they're business-to-business it's not likely they do a lot of consumer-level advertising."

On video news releases (VNRs) sent out by wide satellite distribution:

"Sending out video news releases has been compared to dropping leaflets out of airplanes during wartime. People spend a lot of money on video news releases and most of them never get on the air, anywhere. There's no way to guarantee that these things will be used, although there are a lot of ways you can guarantee that they will *not* be used.

For example, the first flaw that most video news releases display is that they're just totally inappropriate, they're presented as something that looks like a straight news story when in fact it's obviously a program-length commercial. A lot of this really gets into public relations, and how to best present your company to the market.

Satellite distribution of your VNR is the equivalent of putting your news release out on PRNewswire. Chances are it's really not going to get you very much. It's better than doing nothing, but not much better."

On how to best position and package your company's video projects for coverage by TV news and business programs:

"You've got to find what it is about your company or product that is actually newsworthy, which may not be the thing that you as a marketing manager love about it, or even the thing that you're trying to promote about it.

When reporters go out to cover something, they sort of back up and ask: 'What's the hook in this? What's going to hook the viewer and make them want to find out more about it, what problems does this solve, what shocking new disclosure does it make, how does this help people live better, longer, etc.' So that's really what you have to ask yourself, and until you've answered those questions, you can't even start to think about anything else regarding the video news release.

Another very important question to ask is: 'Who are you trying to reach with this?' If it's a regional product, for example, like a product that gets ice off of windshields faster, then you know that you're basically interested in the northern-tier states, and you can then localize it even more by saying: 'This is something that melts ice off windshields even when it's 30 below.' Then you know that you should be looking into getting local coverage in places like Minnesota, North Dakota, etc.

The more local something is, by definition, the more newsworthy it is. Staying with the de-icer example, if you have something you can take to a station in Duluth and say: 'Here's a really good story about our new windshield de-icer,' then maybe they're going to take a look at it.

The second thing to consider is how you're going to package your story. What a lot of companies pay extra for is to have the video production company take a person that they say is a 'reporter,' make them up like a news reporter, spray his or her hair, and put him up there, in serious tones and have them do a stand-up, with some cutaway video in it, and then send this around to news stations. Most stations that are any good won't even dream about using this video because your 'reporter' is obviously a shill, and he's not somebody who's known to their viewers.

Figure 15-5 (continued)

If they use it at all, most likely they're going to pick out the video cutaways anyway and use those instead. Not everyone would agree with me on this, but you have more credibility if you only send the 'B-Roll'—the actual videotape of someone using your product, and a couple of cutaways of people talking about it.

Ideally, it should be a scientist, a doctor, a high-ranking government official, or someone else who can lend some credibility saying: 'This is something that fills a void' in a very good way. Then the station can use it any way they want. You can also send them a transcript of everything that's on the video, along with a suggested story they can use along with it, and a number they can call to interview someone else with your company if they want to. This has a lot of possibilities if it also meets the other news criteria we just discussed, and you can focus it with the usual things stations are looking for—news, consumer and health tips, etc. You'll also have to persuade the news producers that this is a legitimate story, and not just someone hawking their product.

The best thing that can happen is that someone at a news station gets your tape, or your offer to send the tape, and says: 'This is a story we'd like to do ourselves.' It's ironic that you can spend all this time and money doing your own video and you're very proud of it, but what you really want to have happen is for the station, or better yet, the network to come out and shoot their own story; then they're going to use it. They may use a couple of pieces of your tape in that story, but if they come out to shoot their own stories, then it becomes their own story and they're much more likely to use it."

Working day-to-day with a video producer on a project:

"It's probably a mistake for most marketing managers to actually try to 'manage the production' of a video in terms of playing a day-by-day role in the content of the video. I know they want to do that, but the fact is they're not content producers or they'd be in that business.

Marketing managers should be able to point the producer to the contacts they need to do the show, and that's really about it, until periodic reviews start to come back. Ideally, once a week or every couple of weeks, the marketing manager and video producer should meet, and the producer shows him/her what he shot so far to give him some feeling for how the project is shaping up, but really that's about it. The way that big-budget video productions are made is how Fellini made movies—they go out there and shoot hours and hours of video to make a 3-minute project, and then they spend hours and hours in a production facility coming up with a final edit of the video that's really sizzling.

It's not going to work if the marketing manager's going to spend a couple of weeks out in the field with the production crew, dictating the shots, etc. and what to do next. This is the way to spend an awful lot of money, especially if the producer's working on an hourly basis as they often are, and to come up with a product that's not as good as if the marketing manager had taken a more hands-off approach. If you have a 3-man film crew out in the field you're spending about $1,200 an hour, and anything you do that stretches out this time is really going to bust your budget.

Using video as a sales tool:

"I would never *send* a videotape to someone as a sales tool; you've got to *show* it to them. If it's Fedexed or mailed, I can almost guarantee you they'll never look at it—they'll intend to look at it, but chances are they never will. You've got to get the person to sit down and look at it or they're not ever going to look at it on their own. I think every salesperson who represents your company should have with them some device that lets them show this video—a laptop, or a small television set with a built-in video player. "

Voiceover narration: After the final version of your script is complete, it will be passed to a professional announcer to produce the narration, or voiceover, for your video project. On smaller, less-expensive projects (such as those produced on desktop video editing systems), the voiceover is produced first, so it can serve as the foundation for the project. Here, the project's voiceover track is laid down in a digital editing system, with the other elements of your video—live-action video clips, captions, music tracks, etc.—cut and assembled over this audio soundtrack during the final editing process (see **Figure 15-6**). On more ambitious and expensive video projects, the voiceover narration is done later in the process, to match the assembled video clips and pacing of the more finalized, edited version of the project.

Video clips: The live video shots for your project are included in the "shot list," a checklist used by your video producer that covers all the video required for the project. For example, shots for a typical sales video or video news release would include different views of your product, clips of your product being used in the field, and on-screen "talking head" interview clips with your company's top executives, satisfied customers, and outside experts talking about your company and its product or service.

When planning a video project, make note of the images you believe are important to include in the shot list for your project. Don't attempt to "storyboard" the project, or to do your video producer's job for them—just note the key images that, in your opinion, should be included. For example, if your product can be demonstrated in a particularly effective way, write these ideas down so you can discuss them with your video producer.

Of course, the on-screen portion of any video project supplies the main content of your project seen by viewers, and will account for most of the work done by your video production team. Video producers will spend a considerable amount of time with a film crew to get all the shots they need, and end up using only a small fraction of the total footage they shoot for your project. On average, a video producer's film crew shoots an hour of video for each minute of the final project. For example, a three-minute video will require about three hours' worth of video, which is then edited down to the small number of final clips required for the project. On a high-end video project, the average three-person film crew (cameraman, soundman, tech) rents out for around $1,200 an hour—a good rule-of-thumb for figuring the costs for shooting each minute of a high-end video project.

On-screen text: Take note of your product's major sales copy benefits as you make your script notes. Your video producer can execute these sales points as PowerPoint-style text bullets appearing on-screen, and matched with the spoken narration of your video. On-screen text adds tremendous information value to your project, and is especially useful in trade show applications, where high noise levels on the show floor may drown out your video's audio soundtrack. Use white text on a black or blue background for the best readability.

Figure 15-7:

On-Screen Text Reinforces Your Product's Key Sales Benefits

Use On-Screen Text and Bulleted Sales Copy Points, superimposed over live video, to reinforce key sales benefit points in your video projects.

Sales videos should be understandable to viewers with or without an audio soundtrack

Special effects: Flashy, eye-catching video effects and other motion graphics are very time-consuming (and therefore very expensive) to produce, and should be used sparingly, if at all. When executed with a high degree of professional skill, special effects do indeed give your video project an extremely polished, "broadcast-quality" look, but you should be prepared to pay the costs required to do it right; poorly-executed special effects not only look amateurish, they can degrade the sales impact of your entire project. The best special-effects require enormous amounts of time to perfect, with each second of a special effect requiring at least *two hours* to create, execute, and refine. Don't forget that you will be paying for this time at a rate of around $350 per hour. This is one aspect you should leave to your video producer's discretion, since there is little else you can contribute in this area as a marketing manager, aside from setting the total budget for the project.

The Final Edit: Working with a Video Producer

After the video is shot, and as other elements, such as titles, graphics, and effects edge closer to completion, your video project goes to the editing booth, where it is edited, or "cut," to its final form. A skilled editor is just as valuable to your production as a skilled cameraman; in fact, a well-done editing job can often save a poorly-shot project. Your video producer will often edit your project himself, but occasionally an outside editor will be brought in to work on the project.

High-end projects are edited in expensive, sophisticated "editing bays" at professional video production facilities, that rent out for around of $400-$500 per hour. Lower-tier projects produced on desktop video editing systems generally cost less, but in either case, a video project may require up to 10 hours' editing time for each final minute of video produced.

On most projects, your producer will show you periodic, work-in-progress versions of the project for your review. Here's what to look out for when reviewing these interim versions of your video project:

Watch your video with "new eyes:" Pretend you are watching (and listening) to the video for the very first time, as a potential customer, a trade show visitor, TV news editor, or other member of the audience you are targeting for the video. Do the video clips work together with the voiceover to walk the viewer through the sales presentation for your product? Does the voiceover clearly explain your company's product or service? Does it answer the questions your target viewer is most likely to have on your company and its product?

Check the pacing: To hold your viewer's interest, the images they see should change every couple of seconds. Do a repeating "one-two" count in your mind as you're watching the video: There should be an edit (i.e., a cut from one clip to another), a new caption, a change in movement, or some other change in the image every time you hit "two" in your count. On longer clips, such as talking-head interviews, there still should be something moving or appearing, every two seconds, to hold the viewer's eye, such as a caption, or a scrolling background texture. Long, visually uninteresting clips create dead spots where the viewer loses interest, so keep it moving;

Listen: As you watch the video with "new eyes," you should also listen to it with "new ears." Is the announcer's tone appropriate to the material being covered? For example, a narration for a sales video should have a warmer, friendlier tone than a video news release, which should use the TV news reporter's dry, factual tone. Is the announcer rushing over certain parts of the script, when he should be slowing down a little, so people can understand the concepts being covered in the video clip?

Clean, well-edited video clips, cut and mixed with clear, readily-understood sales text bullets, set over a clearly-spoken, persuasive, and professionally-narrated audio track that sells your product, will always be more effective than a flashier, less direct approach. Clarity of presentation should always be your goal in all of your company's video production projects.

START-UP MARKETING
CHAPTER 16
MARKETING FOR START-UPS, NEW PRODUCT LAUNCHES, AND NEW MARKETS

Marketing managers in start-up companies must be bolder and more adaptable to rapid change than their counterparts in larger companies. As a marketer in a new venture, or in an established company launching a new product or entering a new market, this quick-march tempo forces you to respond, instantaneously, to the twists and turns occurring every day in start-ups and new product launches.

Riding the Tiger

If you're a marketing manager in a brand-new start-up, or an established company launching a new product, you'll be using all of the marketing tools covered in this book—development and execution of print advertising campaigns, direct mail projects, sales force support, and Web site development—but you'll be using them at a much faster pace, under greater time pressure, and with a higher risk of failure.

The unique marketing environment found in start-ups is also found in new product launches in established companies, and in the introduction of existing products into new markets. Because of this, use of the term "start-up" in the last three chapters of this book also applies to new product launches and new market introductions for established companies.

The three chapters in this final section of this book cover the three major stages of a marketing program in a start-up or a new product launch. This chapter details the process of assessing new markets and identifying market gaps for your start-up or new product launch, and developing the most compelling sales benefits for your start-up's product or service in its targeted market. The next chapter (Chapter 17) covers the critical process

of incremental testing of your start-up's new marketing program, and the launch of your company's new product. The final chapter (Chapter 18) covers the critically important area of marketing turnarounds: What to do when your start-up or new product launch generates less-than-favorable market response—which frequently happens.

Markets Turn on a Dime in Every Start-Up or New Product Launch—So Be Ready

Many start-ups or product launches that eventually succeed will do so using new and unexpected marketing techniques, and often in markets that end up being completely different from the market the company originally targeted. A start-up or new product launch that succeeds despite early adversity is a tribute to the quick-thinking, fast-moving founders of these companies, and also to the marketing managers who play critical roles in their success.

But those companies are the lucky ones: The business press is full of stories of well-funded start-ups spending lavishly on high-profile advertising campaigns who were unable to detect (or, which is more often the case, unwilling to acknowledge) the early warning signs of their failing marketing programs in time to make the necessary and sometimes radical changes that might have dramatically changed the outcome of the venture.

The purpose of these last three chapters is to help you avoid the pitfalls experienced by those who have failed in start-up companies and new product launches, and show how you can execute the specialized marketing techniques required to lead a turnaround in underperforming start-up and new product launch marketing programs.

Marketing in Start-Ups and New Product Launches Means Continuous Testing

The three most important things any marketing manager in a start-up or new product launch must do are:

1.) Research, evaluate and assess the start-up's (or new product launch) markets, and the opportunities in these markets;

2.) Test the market response of the start-up's product or service;

3.) Correct the problems uncovered by the test, re-test if necessary, and launch the product

Market-testing prevents the needless expenditure of precious start-up capital on bad marketing decisions. Testing identifies problems in a start-up's product positioning, its sales copy, its product, its distribution, or any combination of these factors that can be fatal to the start-up as it continues to move forward, and as more money is poured into the venture.

Testing for any start-up or new product launch is, in most cases, not a one-time occurrence, but rather a process of *continuous testing.* Usually, the first test yields mixed results: Some aspects of the test look very promising, others don't, and the rest fall somewhere in between. Sometimes the results of the initial market test are even worse than expected.

When this happens, experienced marketing managers know better than to panic in the face of poor initial test results. They know that a poor test result doesn't mean the start-up or the new product won't sell. They understand that most of the time this only means that the marketing manager and his/her team just *haven't yet found the best ways to market the product.*

The old Napoleon Hill quote, "every failure carries with it the seed of an equal or greater benefit" could have been written to describe the market testing process. The skilled marketing manager carefully examines the results of a test, especially the lessons learned from talking to potential customers in the company's market, and then tests again; the next time, with improved sales copy and marketing deliverables (direct mail, sales support materials, advertising, or Web site), and sometimes by targeting new prospects or new markets—all based on the lessons learned in the first test.

The next test usually generates better results, and certain parts that do well—such as a successful test mailing to a list, or a very positive response from an ad placed in a trade publication—are expanded immediately to exploit the opportunities opened by the test. More lessons are learned, sales copy continues to be refined, and the marketing manager and his/her team continue to test new marketing methods as they execute the expansion of the successful marketing programs revealed by the previous test. In effect, the start-up or new product launch is *testing continuously* as it ramps up its marketing launch program.

If you and your team carefully examine and thoughtfully reflect upon your test results, and then continue to aggressively execute each new marketing move with vigor and enthusiasm, most of the time you'll find the marketing opportunities that do exist for your product or service, and you'll be able to successfully exploit those opportunities to generate sales for your start-up or new product launch.

The ultimate success or failure of a start-up is not dependent on events, but upon *your response to these events*, and your ability to act decisively and to execute well in the face of adversity: This is the difference between success and failure in a start-up, or in any new product launch.

The Federal Express Story: Fast Response and Marketing Execution Saves the Day

The story of Federal Express is one of the better-known examples of a new venture that, under pressure, made a radical shift in its marketing plan during its initial start-up phase. By now, you've likely heard the story of how the company that became Federal Express originated from company founder Fred Smith's Yale term paper describing his vision of a dedicated, nationwide, overnight small package air delivery service.

What most people don't know is that the original market opportunity that motivated Fred Smith to start Federal Express was far different from the Federal Express we all know today. Six years after he received a "C" grade on his Yale term paper, Fred Smith originally started Federal Express with a fleet of small executive jets to serve as an overnight air delivery service shipping cancelled checks overnight for the Federal Reserve Board (that's what put the "Federal" in Federal Express).

The Federal Reserve project fell through shortly after the company's initial purchase of its first two Dassault Falcon executive jets. Fred Smith and his founder's team decided to move ahead with plans to begin overnight package delivery service to a limited number of cities. Federal Express would go through several major changes in its marketing approach and business plan over the next few years before it ultimately became the success it is today.

In a start-up, adversity is a challenge to its founders, and strengthens their abilities to adapt and change their company's direction. Many times, an initial setback reveals an even greater opportunity. In retrospect, if its original business plan had gone forward, Federal Express might have ended up as an obscure government contractor, a canceled-check air delivery service, instead of the phenomenal success it is today.

Fred Smith and the other members of his management team were to be challenged again, and soon. Federal Express' initial market launch on March 12, 1973 was a disappointing failure: Only six packages were shipped that night through the company's initial, 11-city network. Mike Fitzgerald, who was in charge of the Federal Express field sales force commented: "We realized then that we didn't have enough cities and people hadn't heard of us. This introduction was a bust." [1]

Federal Express' management team went back to the drawing boards, revamping their distribution network and sales promotion programs, expanding their network from 11 to 25 cities, and most important, changing the focus of their sales and marketing efforts from small, single-package shippers to larger, higher-volume industrial prospects. In a matter of months, their nightly package volume increased dramatically.

---

[1] Sigafoos, Robert. *Absolutely Positively Overnight.* St. Luke's Press, 1983

There were to be many more struggles until the company turned a profit, but the early history of Federal Express is a classic example of how the founders of a start-up had the ability to quickly spot and accept their marketing and sales problems, and the willingness to respond quickly and change their marketing direction to force a turnaround.

Anecdotes like these are common in many start-ups that become successful, fully-grown companies, and they emphasize the importance of vigilance, courage, and flexibility for any marketing professional willing to "ride the tiger" in a start-up or new product launch.

Start-Up and New Product Marketing: The Important Thing is Knowing What You Don't Know

When you join a start-up as a marketing manager, or become involved in a new product or new market launch, there is often more that you don't know about your market, what motivates prospects in this market, and the best ways to reach these prospects. To the smart marketer, *knowing what you don't know* is the first step toward developing a successful marketing plan.

Initial market assessment: The next step is learning what questions need to be asked. There are three steps involved in the process of developing your start-up's initial marketing program:

> **1.) Market gap analysis**
> **2.) General market assessment**
> **3.) Marketer's analysis and action plan**

This three-step process helps you develop your start-up's initial marketing plan, which is then executed as a one-two marketing punch—one or more small, quick, informal market tests, followed by a more formalized, "live" market test, executed before, or incorporated into, your start-up's final launch.

Marketing action plan: Once you've completed this three-step process of researching your market, you will then have to consider the marketing tools needed to execute your marketing plan:

> • **Print display advertising;**
> • **Direct mail;**
> • **Sales force support;**
> • **Dealer/distributor networks;**
> • **Trade shows;**
> • **The Internet;**
> • **Video and multimedia;**
> • **PR/media**

You can take a major step toward solving any problem by asking the right questions. Finding the answers to the questions posed by this three-step process will move your start-up's marketing plan to the testing stage, where you can then ask the one question only your market can answer: "Will they buy our product?"

Marketing Assumptions Used for a Start-Up's Financial Projections

At an early point in the life of your start-up, financial projections will (or have already been) made. And incorporated in these financial projections are generalized **marketing response** assumptions. These are the marketing and sales goals set forth in your start-up's financial projections—the most important measure of any start-up.

Because all products, businesses, and industries are different from each other, it's always a very risky business to make broad market response generalizations, as in: "Our mailings will generate 3% response." It is a fool's game to attempt to predict the response to a mailing, or to predict how many inquiries a print advertisement will generate for your start-up, if your company doesn't have any prior track record in its market.

The best way to determine market response is to test. This is why most of the discussion of marketing for start-ups and new product launches in this book centers around market testing.

In a perfect world, truly enlightened venture capitalists (or corporate decision-makers in new product launches) would not make all-or-nothing decisions to fund start-ups. Instead, they would "stage" their funding to a new venture or product launch, with a relatively modest up-front investment to fund an initial market test, used to measure the market response to the product. In some cases, this market testing can be done, in a limited way, *even before the product is developed*, using product mockups in direct mailings.

The response to a market test can yield viable measures of a product's appeal. A positive test result can dramatically strengthen the confidence of investors and management teams alike; a negative result can save millions of dollars for investors.

Even "grey area" results—a test that generates some positive response, but is not a strong "win," teaches important marketing lessons that can lead to eventual success, as the start-up's founders change their product, its price, or their marketing approach in response to the lessons learned from the initial test results. Usually, the next market test yields a better result.

Estimating Market Response Before Market-Testing Your Product

However, many start-ups (or new product launches) don't have the opportunity to market-test their products when they draft their first business plans. At some point, the start-up's management team is asked to produce a business plan, along with 5-

year financial projections incorporating critical market response assumptions. The start-up's business plan is then used by investors (or, in the case of a new product launch in an established company, by the company's executive management) as the basis for its funding decision. In addition to influencing the initial decision to fund the start-up, the plan becomes the benchmark used to evaluate the early performance of the start-up's management team. But without the benefit of market testing, the start-up's management team must essentially make its best guess on market response.

Here are some key "plug numbers" often used as market response assumptions in financial projections for new venture and product launch business plans:

- **Direct mail response:** What percentage or individuals who receive our direct mailings will contact our company?

    Rule of thumb: *Mailings designed to generate inquiries (for follow-up by your start-up's sales reps) will produce response rates ranging from 2% to 10%, depending on the mailing lists used. Generally, highly targeted or self-compiled lists (such as those created by your own telephone canvassing methods) generate results closer to the high end of this range;*

- **Advertising response:** What percentage of a publication's total readers will respond to our advertising by contacting our company to inquire about our product?

    Rule of thumb: *A good benchmark to use is to project (best case) that 1/10 of 1% of the publication's average monthly reader base will respond to your ad, each time the ad is run. For example, in a publication with 500,000 subscribers, a trade ad placement that generates 500 inquiries from readers (500,000 X .001)—by phone, mail, or access to your company's Web site—is considered to be an excellent response for a single ad placement;*

- **Sales conversions:** What percentage of the inquiries generated by mailings and advertising can be converted to sales by our start-up's sales force?

    Rule of thumb: *In a successful marketing program, a company's sales force can close 5% to 10% of the inquiries generated by its marketing efforts—mailings, advertising, and other marketing programs. This conversion rate is often higher for lower-priced products (i.e., products priced under $1,000);*

- **Average unit purchase:** What is the average unit purchase made by a customer as a result of our start-up's marketing and sales efforts?

    Rule of thumb: *Here, you'll have to make your own best assumptions, based on the pricing of your own start-up's product or service.*

Again, these "rules of thumb" are highly subjective, and may or may not apply to your start-up or product launch. In fact, any untested assumption is probably wrong. But they're a starting point from where you can more thoughtfully develop your own initial market response assumptions and, hopefully, test them as soon as possible.

Step 1: Market Gap Analysis

To be successful, any product or service developed by a company must fill a **market gap**. A **market gap analysis** is the process of uncovering problems and brainstorming product or service ideas that solve these problems.

A market gap is the key problem that is solved by your company's product or service. The resulting solution, represented by this product or service, is your company's reason for being in business.

Market gap examples: It's likely that you and your start-up's management team have already analyzed your start-up's market gaps—after all, discovering or identifying market gaps is what entrepreneurs do.

For example, the emergence of high-technology companies, the new, more efficient manufacturing and distribution systems put in place by many companies in the 1970s, and the need for all of these companies to rapidly ship small-sized components anywhere, overnight, was one of the market gaps identified by Fred Smith when he started Federal Express.

The laborious, repetitive process of filling in, erasing, and, re-calculating accounting ledger sheets by hand was the market gap solved by Dan Bricklin and Bob Frankston, who created VisiCalc, the first electronic spreadsheet program for personal computers, and the first "killer app" that led to the widespread use of the Apple II, the first mass-market personal computer.

The Apple II personal computer was, in its own right, a revolutionary business and consumer product that addressed many individual market gaps. For example, word processing, where a personal computer user gained the benefit of being able to type, correct, and print his/her own documents faster and more efficiently than by using a typewriter—and for less money than by using the more expensive, dedicated word processing systems prevalent at the time. The personal computing revolution itself succeeded largely due to the efforts of software entrepreneurs, who created many other specialized personal computer-based applications, each addressing their own market gaps—by intent, or by accident.

Start-ups that successfully identify and solve the problems revealed by a market gap will generate sales. Start-ups that fail to identify market gaps will also fail to develop coherent or successful marketing plans, leaving them in the hands of ad agencies, marketing consultants, or other outsiders who may not have the know-how to identify or exploit profitable market gaps.

The market gap must also meet your company's objectives: Market gaps addressed by your start-up must also meet other business criteria already agreed upon by your founder's team:

- *The market gap must be addressable by the desired type of product or service to be developed and sold by your start-up;*

- *The price of the product sold must meet a price-to-cost ratio sufficient to allow the start-up to operate profitably;*

- *The market served must be of sufficient size and depth to assure continued sales growth;*

- *The available sales channels and production requirements of the industry must be compatible with the founder's skills, knowledge, and experience;*

- *The market gap must be attractive enough in the current investment environment, so the start-up can obtain sufficient, timely, financing.*

Market gap variations: There can be different kinds of marketing gaps. For example, **customer gaps** can pinpoint opportunities to solve problems by addressing the needs of customers in certain demographic groups, by age, income, consumer preference, or lifestyle. **Distribution gaps** can uncover opportunities to market and deliver existing products in new ways, such as Amazon.com's use of the Internet as a new distribution channel for selling books online.

Step 2: General Market Assessment Checklist

Once you and your start-up's management team have identified the market gaps(s) to be addressed by your company, the general market assessment checklist (see **Figure 16-1**) helps you gather the general marketing and sales information you need, to focus on the markets your plan will address, and to fill in the more specific characteristics of these markets, such as size, competition, sales copy benefits, marketing methods, and sales distribution channels.

This general market assessment asks questions that help you define the general shape, characteristics, and approach to the markets being addressed by your start-up's marketing plan. These questions are also designed to spur your thoughtful consideration of other aspects of marketing that are important to your start-up's success, such as your company's strategic positioning relative to its competitors, and the ways your company can meet the needs of prospects better than the ways your competition is currently serving this market.

Part 2: Start-up Marketing Manager's Analysis and Action Plan

After you and your team have thoughtfully considered, researched, and answered the preliminary questions posed by the general market assessment checklist of **Figure 16-1**, it's now time to gather specific information related to your role as a marketing manager, to establish the shape of your marketing plan and determine the specific marketing deliverables you will need to execute your plan.

There are five sets of questions that help you to focus on the information and action items required to develop your marketing plan for your start-up or new product launch, covered under these five general areas:

- **General Issues;**
- **Background Research and Action Items;**
- **Marketing Deliverables;**
- **Market Testing;**
- **Targets of Opportunity**

1.) General Issues:

These first questions are marketing-related brainstorming questions designed to stimulate your thinking, and to provoke responses from the other members of your start-up's management team. At the very least, they will help you get your current marketing ideas on paper, where you can act on the best of these ideas and include them in your marketing plan, and put other good ideas on the back burner for further consideration:

- *What are our initial ideas for the best marketing and sales methods required to reach these new markets?*

- *Are there products similar to ours that are currently being sold in this market?*

- *If so, should our company duplicate the marketing methods currently being used to sell these products, or would it be more advantageous for us to use new marketing methods and different sales channels?*

- *Are there marketing methods, such as new forms of distribution, that could be highly successful if they were introduced into this new market (i.e., Internet Web site sales direct to the customer, or using direct mail instead of sales calls)?*

- *Can our company afford to make a radical departure from the current ways products like ours are marketed and sold in this market? Would an initial failure hinder us from re-entering these markets with other marketing or distribution methods that might be successful?*

Figure 16-1:

General Marketing Assessment Checklist

- In general, what are the markets and groups of customers to be served by our start-up or new product launch ?
- What "market gap" does our company's product or service fill?
- What are the major market segments where these market gaps exist?
- What are the estimated market sizes of each of these market segments (i.e., make your best estimate on the dollar value of the market being addressed by your start-up, using credible estimates from reliable third-party industry sources, such as trade associations or industry consultants)?
- What prices—and promotional pricing flexibility—will be required in each market?
- What sales and distribution networks are required to penetrate these markets?
- What are the most common ways products are currently promoted and sold in these markets? Personal sales calls? Direct mail? Phone?
- Who are the existing competitors in each market segment?
- What are these to competitors' strengths?
- What are these competitors' weaknesses?
- How will these competitors respond to our entry in the market? How can we anticipate, and counter, these actions?
- Who are probable future competitors that may appear on the scene in the next 2-3 years?
- How many sales calls will be required for each sales close?
- How many of our company's salespeople will be selling in these markets?
- Who are the largest corporate customers in each market segment (if this is a business-to business market)?
- Who is the most likely buyer in each market segment, by job title or responsibility?
- In what ways are present competitors serving these markets well?
- In what ways are these markets poorly served by present competitors?
- What are our company's strengths, and how can we use them to "end run" our competition in these new markets?
- What is the positioning, and the major sales benefit statement, required for each market segment?
- For each market, what is our current "best guess" of the prospect's most likely sales objections, and what sales and copy approaches will be used to overcome these objections?

2.) Background Research and Action Items:

Once you've answered the general marketing issues as best you can, the next set of questions are a list of hard action items to help you match opportunities available in your market with concrete marketing projects and deliverables:

- *Who are our targeted prospect buyer(s)?*
- *What are the top two trade publications these prospective buyers read most often?*
- *What are the top two trade shows these prospective buyers attend each year?*
- *Are mailing lists available for the publications read by these prospects?*
- *Can we locate these prospective buyers on other, high-quality, mailing lists?*
- *What is the level of Internet usage of these prospective buyers?*
- *What top two trade associations do these prospective buyers belong to?*
- *Are the membership rosters of these trade associations available as mailing lists?*
- *What are the top two independent consulting groups and industry newsletters serving this market?*

You can address each of these action items by careful study of the material covered in the previous chapters. For example, by asking a couple of people you may already know who work in your start-up's market, and by checking the Standard Rate and Data Service (SRDS) advertising and mailing list directories, you can readily identify the top publications and mailing lists available in your market. A few hours' worth of Google searches also helps you uncover the top trade associations, consulting firms, and newsletters in these markets.

Visit the library: Visit the business publications and research section of any major public library to review a year or more's back-issues of your market's leading trade publications. Ask the librarian at the business research desk for other relevant resources on your market, such as industry directories, or market/industry forecasts, and other research-oriented publications in your start-up's targeted market. Make copies of the relevant pieces of information and take notes for later review.

As you gather this market information, start the process of collecting the additional information you need, such as publication advertising media kits, trade association materials, such as membership rosters (if available), and other materials.

Get to know the people in your new market: As you begin to immerse yourself in the market for your start-up or new product launch, make a habit of introducing yourself to key contacts who could be prospective customers of your new company's product or service. Your goal here is to develop personal relationships with individuals who are representative of typical customers and prospects in your new company's market. You will be contacting these individuals from time to time during the next, critical phase in the development of your marketing plan—the **market testing phase**, covered in the next chapter.

These contacts will be an important part of your "marketing brain trust," and will provide invaluable advice on your marketing copy ideas, drafts of marketing deliverables, and other important parts of your marketing program during the early life of your start-up or product launch.

3.) Marketing Deliverables

Once you are well underway with your background research, and have completed the information-gathering activities in the previous steps, you are now ready to devote some thought to the marketing methods, tools, and deliverables you need to develop for use in your marketing plan:

- *Based on what I know about this market so far, what is our product's major sales copy benefit?*

- *What are the other major sales benefits that we can use in our company's advertising and marketing promotion?*

- *Should we run print advertising? If so, what publications are best for our market? What sizes and frequencies should we run?*

- *Should we run a direct mail program? If so, what mailing lists look most promising?*

- *What hard-copy marketing deliverables, such as high-quality brochures, lower-quality sales flyers, catalog sheets, direct mail packages, and standard sales presentation info kits, will be required?*

- *What other materials will we need to "educate" our customers, and can these materials be offered as sales premiums in our company's advertising—special reports and booklets, instructional videos, software programs, industry reports, etc.?*

- *What type of Web site should our company have, and how should it promote and sell our company's product?*

- *Among the two major trade publications read by our target prospects, which writers or editors cover, or seem most knowledgeable about, the applications, technologies, or product areas most closely linked to our company's product or service?*

> • *Can our product's story be told effectively in a multimedia format? If so, could it be "packaged" for distribution to broadcast media outlets (i.e. CNN, CNBC)?*

As you acquire more knowledge on your market, and how existing companies, including your competitors, sell their products in this market, the rough outlines of your start-up's marketing program should now be coming into focus. While you are not yet ready to commit your company to either a print ad campaign or direct-mail program—usually the two largest expenditures in any company's marketing budget—you can sketch out the major sales copy points of your start-up's product or service, based on your best impressions so far of how you would sell your company's product in this market.

You should know enough about your product's major sales benefits to write its "Laundry List," "Park Bench Story," and "Elevator Pitch," as detailed in the writing exercises in Chapter 4.

Selecting an ad agency or marketing consultant: Now is also the time to begin the process of selecting an advertising agency or marketing consultant to assist you in the development and execution of company's marketing program.

Development of Rough Marketing Deliverables for Market Testing

The "Rough and Ready" sales brochure: You now should focus on the types of marketing deliverables you will need for your marketing program, and their form and content. Create a semi-finished "Rough and Ready brochure," that sets forth your product's main selling points and tells its sales story, based on the best copy information you have so far.

You will circulate this rough-and-ready brochure during the informal market testing process described in the next chapter. It's your start-up's very first piece of sales collateral, and a very important one, because it makes your start-up look "real," and gives your market test respondents and initial sales prospects a fair idea of what your product or service is all about. By putting your product's sales benefits and features down on paper, this rough brochure is also an ideal platform for eliciting constructive comments, criticisms, and suggestions for improvements to your sales message from knowledgeable insiders in your market.

Since a brochure is often the very first project an ad agency or marketing consultant is asked to produce for a new client, the "rough and ready" brochure is a good way to start off a new working relationship with your newly-retained ad agency or marketing consulting firm. However, if you haven't yet found an ad agency, don't let this interfere with the creation of this very important marketing deliverable: If necessary, work something up on your own, and find a local desktop designer in your area to work it into final form. All you need at this point is a presentable brochure that can be used for the next, informal testing step.

Figure 16-2:

"Rough and Ready" Sales Materials—Help you test your new product's sales appeal to real prospects

The "Rough and Ready Brochure," *and other simple, laser-printed sales materials, help you test the sales appeal and presentation of your start-up or new product launch to a small group of representative prospects in your market.*

These materials can be sent out quickly as laser-printed or color-xeroxed pieces. Here, your goal is to receive feedback from respondents as quickly as possible; this is more important than production quality

Your start-up's Web site: Think about your start-up's Web site (or the Web site that will be used for your new product launch). As you spend time on the Internet researching your start-up's market, its competition, and the online news and research available in the industry and market served by your start-up, bookmark the interesting and relevant Web sites you find.

Some of the more compelling content, layouts, and features you see on these Web sites can give you "inspiration" for your own start-up's site. Reading and bookmarking interesting Web sites in your new market is also a good way to learn the jargon of your industry and, more important, how other companies talk to their audience—i.e., your potential prospects and customers in this market.

Customer "education:" The additional marketing deliverables required to educate prospects about your start-up's product or service can wait until you gain more practical knowledge from the market testing activities to come, but it's never too early to start thinking about any additional, specialized marketing deliverables you believe might be instrumental in helping to sell your start-up's product or service. These include printed booklets, reports or "white papers," an instructional or sales video/DVD, and other materials that can also serve as promotional sales premiums in your company's advertising and direct-mail programs.

Trade publication contacts and broadcast media potential: While your start-up is still operating "under the radar" out of public view, it's not too soon to anticipate, and prepare for, the introduction of your company and its new product or service to your industry and financial markets, by way of trade publications, general business publications, and broadcast/cable outlets. Depending on your budget, the "launch event" that formally announces your start-up's product or service to the media may be as simple as a small press kit mailing to some key trade media contacts, or as elaborate as a big-budget New York City press conference.

Whatever form your company's official launch announcement takes, you should begin your planning by taking notice of writers, editors and correspondents at the business, trade, and industry publications serving your market. Read the articles in these publications covering the topics close to the applications and problems solved by your company's products, and take note of the writers of these articles.

These knowledgeable media contacts will become your company's most interested and receptive audience for news of your start-up's launch of its new product. Just prior to your launch, you can "move your story" to the best one or two of these contacts at these top publications, on an exclusive basis, to increase your chances of receiving media coverage during your launch. The writers and editors you select will appreciate getting the exclusive on coverage of your company and its product, and will be receptive to ongoing news announcements from your company after your launch.

Video distribution: You should also explore your company's potential for utilizing television cable, broadcast, business, and financial news channels for distribution of a video news release (VNR) to news outlets like CNN, CNBC, and MSNBC, as well as satellite distribution to local broadcast news outlets. Additional aspects involved in PR and "free media" are covered in Chapter 14, and video news releases are covered in Chapter 15.

4.) Market testing

During the new venture planning stages, you will also need to consider how, and how much, to test your start-up's marketing program. Testing can be a very informal, inexpensive process, or it can be elaborate, expensive, and time-consuming—never good for a start-up. Here are the testing questions you need to ask:

- *Is there enough time to run a market test, or should we roll out with our market introduction and change course as necessary?*

(If "yes"):

- *How can we test our marketing methods and sales copy ideas in these new markets?*

- *How long will it take for us to run this test, and how much will it cost?*

As a member of the new venture's start-up management team, you will be expected to "drink the Kool-Aid"—that is, to buy into the founder's vision of the company, its product, and the world-changing growth potential of its business. However, as a marketing manager you cannot afford to luxuriate too long in this vision, since you will be held accountable for the company's sales performance, and for the execution of the marketing programs that help to create those sales.

There always needs to be someone in any start-up to ask the question: "Do we have a market?"—and since you will be held most accountable, that someone may as well be you.

Market reality check: Although testing is covered in far greater detail in the next chapter, during the background research and marketing planning stages you must decide if your start-up can devote the extra time and expense necessary to conduct a more formal market test, or if less expensive, informal testing methods can provide you with the answers you need to these very important marketing questions:

- *Do we have a market?—i.e., is the market big enough to sustain our company's financial objectives, and can we afford to reach it?*

- *Are the sales copy approaches we are using in our market test collateral materials the right sales copy benefits, and are they effective enough to turn prospects into customers?*

- *Will the marketing channels we are considering, such as print advertising or direct mail, produce our desired sales results?*

Don't just test—test while moving forward: All start-ups, or anyone involved in a new product or market launch in an established company, must have what management guru Tom Peters calls "a bias for action." More than any other business discipline, market research and testing causes those involved in the process to "think too much." If you're not careful, analysis of test results can often lead to over-analysis and over-intellectualizing of your company's marketing efforts by your start-up's team.

This "paralysis by analysis" not only takes the edge off your start-up's marketing program, it can establish a pattern of undue hesitation and doubt in each and every marketing move made by your company. Bear this in mind as you consider the ways you test your start-up's marketing program, and as you review the testing options available to you in the next chapter. By all means, test, but don't let your testing get in the way of your marketing program's forward motion.

5.) *Targets of Opportunity*

Another critical area to address in your start-up's marketing planning will be the process of uncovering, addressing, and developing the major "targets of opportunity" available to your new venture:

Figure 16-3:

"In-the-Box" Promotions and Premiums—A fast way to boost distribution for start-ups and product launches

Boost Your Start-Up's or New Product's Distribution by linking up with other companies to offer your company's product "in the box" with another company.

"In-the-box" deals, such as this software company's retail tie-in with a major diskette manufacturer (right), give your distribution partner an added sales edge for their product lines, and dramatically increases your company's distribution and prospect base

- Are there major, non-competing companies already serving this market who could be potential joint-venture or distribution partners for our company?

- If so, in what ways could these potential relationships be structured —"In-the-box" deals, private-label marketing, joint marketing and sales relationships, promotional premiums, or other ways?

- What is the best way for us to approach these companies?

- Who should we contact at these companies, and how?

"Targets of opportunity" are marketing and new business development activities that are separate and apart from the day-to-day marketing activities you're executing in your marketing plan. These are the major marketing and sales opportunities for your start-up (or product launch) that involve high-level relationships with larger, well-established companies in the markets your company is entering.

Examples of targets of opportunity available to many start-ups include:

Co-marketing deals: Your new venture can get a major early boost in its first months if you can persuade a much larger company to promote your start-up's product along with one or more of its own products.

Figure 16-4:

Private-Label and Co-Marketing Deals—Think of ways your product could be sold by a much larger company

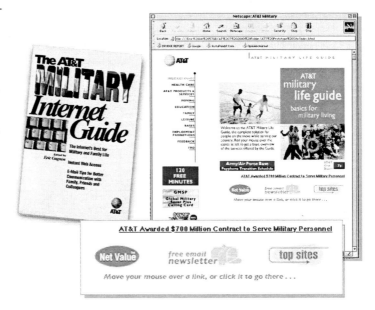

Selling a Specially Branded Version of your company's product, or establishing a joint marketing relationship with a large company, such as this information and private-label promotion service for a major telecom company (right), can give your start-up or new product launch an important early boost in the critical first year of operation

If your start-up's product or service has unique and proprietary features, and its utility would add value to another major company's product, then your product could be offered "in-the-box" with the larger company's product. It could be sold, either directly by the larger company, or by some other field-sales or direct-response method that leads potential buyers back to your company.

Options available here range from the larger company simply including a brochure or coupon for your start-up's product in its own product's packaging, to special promotions, where the larger company offers a scaled-down version of your company's product as a value-added premium to complement its products. These "in-the-box deals" can produce a substantial number of high-quality sales leads in your start-up's early months. These deals can also be inexpensive for your company if they are self-liquidating; for example, if you can convince the larger company to cover your company's out-of-pocket printing, marketing, and product development expenses.

Co-marketing link-ups with a major corporation can offer other interesting opportunities. For example, as a part of your deal, you could ask to retain the rights to the mailing list of sales leads generated by the joint-marketing effort for use in your company's subsequent direct-mail marketing programs. You could also negotiate for promotion of your company's new product along with the major corporation's ongoing advertising programs. There are many other potential opportunities available to you here, that, though seen through the eyes of your larger corporate partner as minor "gimmes," can give your start-up's marketing program a tremendous promotional boost in its early days;

Joint-venture and distribution deals: Major targets of opportunity include private-label deals, where your start-up's product can be sold by a larger company under its own name, or licensing arrangements, where a major partner licenses your product's proprietary applications, patents, or technology, also known as licensing of your product's "reference technology." A major corporate partner can also act as a distributor for your new venture's product, either in certain markets, or in certain product lines;

Strategic deals: Any of these marketing relationships could eventually lead to an exit strategy for you and the other members of your founders team, if the major corporate partner expresses an interest in buying your company. However, in these situations, you must be careful not to disclose any proprietary information during your negotiations for marketing relationships.

Given half a chance, many major corporations would rather steal your start-up's ideas, patents, and other proprietary intellectual property than pay a nickel of their own money to license your patents or acquire your company, so be careful how much you, and the other members of your management team, disclose during these initial business discussions.

Before you initiate any business discussions with large companies who may be potential strategic partners, make sure to have their representatives sign your company's Non-Disclosure Agreement (NDA). Other prior written agreements may also need to be reached prior to strategic discussions with another company. Consult with your company's legal counsel before engaging in any discussions that could disclose your company's patents, trade secrets or other proprietary intellectual property.

Finding contacts for potential targets of opportunity: As a marketing manager you play a central role in identifying your new venture's targets of opportunity, by brainstorming ideas for potential deals, then tapping other members of your start-up team, your company's investors, board members, and venture capital firm to contact people they know at larger companies to set up initial meetings to discuss these new marketing and distribution deals. Here, "friend-of-a-friend" business networking can be very useful for helping you connect with influential people at larger companies who can help your start-up.

Figure 16-5:

Strategic Marketing Relationships

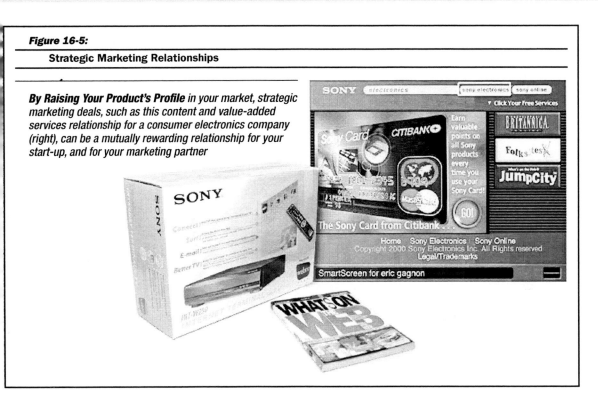

By Raising Your Product's Profile in your market, strategic marketing deals, such as this content and value-added services relationship for a consumer electronics company (right), can be a mutually rewarding relationship for your start-up, and for your marketing partner

---

   An early success can lead to more success, since a major co-marketing or distribution deal done in the first few months of your company's launch can establish your company's reputation and credibility in its industry, making it easier to close similar deals with other companies in your start-up's market.

START-UP TESTING & LAUNCH
CHAPTER 17
MARKET TESTING AND RESPONSE
FOR START-UPS AND
NEW PRODUCT LAUNCHES

Executing market tests during your company's product development stage, and before and during its new product launch, gives you the opportunity to test your sales copy and marketing methods before you commit big dollars to a full-scale marketing program.

The response from a market test almost always improves the quality and effectiveness of your marketing program, and sometimes leads to radical changes in the direction of your entire marketing plan, such as a shift from display advertising to more targeted direct-mail programs, a change in your marketing focus to reach new or different prospects, or more radical changes, such as abandoning one market for another, or changing your product's original distribution approach for an entirely new distribution method.

Testing and Market Research

The value of testing: Market-testing is the marketing manager's most important function during a new venture's early development stages. If well executed, a market test can save a new venture thousands of dollars of expense that otherwise would have been squandered on poorly-conceived ad placements, mailings, or other unsuccessful marketing projects. The feedback received from market tests can dramatically change a start-ups' marketing direction, its product pricing, or its sales and distribution channels; these critical changes in marketing tactics and strategy can mean the difference between success or failure in a start-up's first critical year of operation.

It's easy to gather market feedback, if you have a lot of money to spend. If you don't test, you can buy into the illusion of "branding," and spend your company's entire marketing budget on advertising, rolling your product out first without testing—and failing—just like the dot-coms did during the Internet bubble. Or, you can do it the smart way: Spend a little money up front to run a small market test and learn a lot, and then incorporate these lessons into your next, larger marketing effort.

Failing to test leads to failure: The sad fact is that most start-ups don't market-test their products. Instead, they rely on an outside ad agency to develop "creative" ideas to promote their product just before their product launch, usually involving the placement of many full-page ads in trade and business publications, or mailing too many splashy direct mail pieces to a few, thoughtlessly-chosen rented mailing lists. When the ads and mailings don't pull, the start-up fires the agency, hires a new "Man on a White Horse," and repeats the process until it runs out of money, or pulls back to take a more pragmatic approach (this also happens in established companies launching new products in new markets). Occasionally a start-up will succeed despite a poor marketing program, if it gets lucky, is acquired, or clinches a big distribution deal with a large corporation outside of its normal marketing channels. It can truly be said that marketing budgets for most start-ups are often simply capital transfers from venture investors into the pockets of ad agencies, PR firms, and trade publications.

For companies who don't have bottomless marketing budgets—and this includes every start-up—the testing options described in this section can be executed at low cost, and do not require extensive or specialized knowledge of market research techniques. These testing methods also work for new product or market launches in any established company. They don't require the use of focus groups (more on these further in this section), no special "test methodologies," or the other academic trappings of the marketing research field that distract a company's marketing team from the salesmanship required to sell its products.

Test your copy, your sales message, and deliverables: In market researcher-speak, these testing techniques are qualitative rather than quantitative, relying mostly upon anecdotal results. They require you, not an outside market research consultant, to be involved in their execution, and to form impressions based on the responses you receive. Most of the time, results gathered from these techniques will require you to take corrective action to change and adapt your marketing program to meet the needs of your prospects and the realities of your marketplace.

These techniques have been proven in actual use, and can help you answer the most critical marketing questions for your start-up or new product launch:

- *Are our product's sales copy benefits persuasive to the prospects in our market, and will our product's "story" be well-received by the most likely prospects in our marketplace?*

- *Are the other aspects of our product and its marketing message, such as its price, features, and applications, compelling to the prospects in our market?*

- *Are the "marketing media" we're using—display advertising, direct mail, direct sales, trade shows, or telemarketing—the best, least expensive ways for us to sell to these prospects?*

- *What is the approximate cost-per-sale for the advertising media we are using?*

- *Have other prospects, markets, applications, or "targets of opportunity" for our company's product been uncovered by our tests?*

Two Stages to the Testing Process for Start-Ups and New Product Launches: Informal and Formal Tests

The market testing process has two stages:

- **The initial, "informal" testing stage**, where the sales copy points, positioning, and other key aspects of your marketing program and its sales message are broadly established;

- **The "formal" testing stage**, implemented as a separate, limited market test prior to the launch of your company's product or service. This stage can also be implemented as the first stage in your company's product launch, depending on your start-up's timing requirements, budget constraints, and your confidence in your company's marketing program. These formal tests can be repeated as often as necessary, with the more successful aspects of each test being incorporated into the expanded marketing launch for the start-up, and/or in subsequent market tests.

First Principles: There Is No Such Thing as Failure, Only Failure to Test

As you read the next several pages on testing, keep these two important points in mind:

Mixed test results happen most of the time: The final response to most market tests is usually neither a runaway success nor a dismal failure. Usually, some aspects of a test do better than others. If you can listen to what potential customers in your market tell you about your test, you can "ramp up" the parts of a market test that *were* successful, which will help you open new sales opportunities in your start-up, while you continue to develop and refine your marketing program;

Testing is a continuous process: In a start-up or new product launch, there is no such thing as failure; only *failure to test*. An exploitable sales opportunity exists, and can be found, in *any* market test, but the sales rewards from this opportunity can only be realized by testing again, on a larger scale. And, even as these aspects of your testing program start to show promising sales results, and your marketing program begins to generate good response, you must always test new ways of selling your start-up's product or service on a continuous basis. You must continue your market-testing until you are confident you have found the marketing tools, methods, and media that you believe can be scaled up to build sales for your start-up's product or service.

The "Informal" Market Test: The First Step in Testing Marketing Deliverables and Sales Copy for Your Start-Up or New Product Launch

The first market testing step for a start-up, the "informal" market test, puts your start-up's sales copy—the "story" of your product or service—in front of a handful of actual prospects, the kinds of people in your market whom you must eventually persuade to buy your company's product. The informal market test relies upon your verbal presentation and personal questioning of the individuals who receive your marketing deliverables, to draw out the constructive comments and response necessary to put your start-up's sales message into sharper focus. Informal testing can also be used in an established company launching new products in a new market, in advance of the actual product launch.

This type of market test is in no way scientific; it requires no special research procedures or any of the other specialized skills of the market researcher's trade. It does, however, require you to be a very good—and discriminating—listener, asking questions designed to elicit the constructive responses you need. You must listen very closely so you can separate the valuable "signal"— the information that can improve your marketing efforts—from the "noise," the superfluous comments and criticisms that can throw your sales message off in the wrong direction.

The quality of the results you receive from your initial market test will depend on:

- **The quality, content, and level of detail** of your test marketing deliverables—brochure, ad sample, mailing package, or other printed piece;
- **The questions you ask**, and your skill in listening to and understanding the answers you receive;
- **Your own gut instincts**, based on your own prior experience in dealing with people in selling situations;
- **Your ability to separate the information** you can use (the "signal") from everything else you'll be hearing (the "noise"), as you talk to test respondents.

Informal testing is really informal *selling*: This informal market test has many of the earmarks of a sales presentation, except for the "sales" part. Like any good salesman on a sales call, you'll be providing your "prospects" (test respondents) with your information and persuasive benefits on your company's product, and you'll be listening very intently to the questions they ask you. Most of all, you must be alert to the offhand comment or observation that could cause you to make an important change in your product's sales message, price structure, feature descriptions, or promotion. Your ad agency's account executive or the other marketing consultants who prepared the printed sales materials used for the test should also be participating in the telephone or personal interviews you'll be having with these informal test respondents.

Step 1: Finding Respondents for Your Start-Up's Informal Market Test

During the period your start-up is operating "under the radar"—that is, while your management team is developing the product or service that will eventually be sold by your start-up, you should build your own informal network of people in and around the industry served by your company. You also want to put your test marketing materials in front of individuals who are representative of the prospects you are trying to reach, by their job title and responsibility, and who will be the most likely buyers of your company's product or service.

Here are some good places to develop your own network of contacts for your informal market tests:

> **Trade association contacts,** in addition to being an excellent all-round industry and market information resource for your start-up, can refer you to almost any insider you need to contact at any company in the industries they serve. A call to the association's membership director, research director, or (at larger associations) staff librarian can help you find the right contacts at the companies you need to reach for your test;

> **Trade media contacts,** such as space advertising sales reps for trade publications, can often put you in contact with other executives at the companies you're trying to reach in your marketplace. Ad sales reps get around in your industry, and as long as you don't disclose too much information on your start-up and its product, contacting a publication's ad rep can be an excellent way to get referrals for your test—especially if you let them know that a successful market test might lead to future advertising business from your company;

> **"Second tier" company contacts** at smaller companies in your market are your preferred contacts for your start-up's initial market test. For this initial test, you will be working with the "rough draft" of your product's sales message, so you'll want to do your initial testing with prospects at smaller companies in your market, rather than industry leaders, to avoid the possibility of making a poor first impression on a major potential customer by showing him or her sales copy that may not be as persuasive, or as well developed, as the final versions of your company's marketing deliverables.

> Better to start your informal market testing by staying "Off-Broadway," working out your sales copy and deliverables with contacts at smaller companies, until your start-up's final product rollout. This prevents you from showing an early version of a marketing deliverable that creates a poor first

impression to an influential prospect at a major company. This approach also allows you to respond to the feedback you get from your first set of respondents, by creating a better, more refined second set of deliverables to present to these larger potential customers;

Trade suppliers in your marketplace are another excellent source of contacts. Key vendors, contractors, and other trade suppliers who serve your industry, such as parts and component suppliers, or service providers, work every day with the key contacts at the companies you're trying to reach. The first call to a trade vendor, followed by one or two more calls inside the company, usually puts you in touch with the person who should see your market test materials.

Step 2: Preparing Marketing Deliverables for Your Informal Test

The production value for the printed marketing deliverables you and your ad agency or marketing consultant prepare for the informal test don't have to look as good as their final versions. However, the more "finished" the pieces look—with color photos of your company's product, typeset text, and all other design elements in place—the more credible the impression you'll make with test respondents.

With today's digital printing and color copying technology, you can print very small runs of four-color brochures, flyers, and ad sheets for between $1 to $3 each. If your production schedule allows, take advantage of this new technology and produce your test materials in color, on coated paper stock. If, however, your start-up is under extreme deadline pressure, just print the materials you have in their current form and send them out; time is more important than presentation on your start-up's first market test. Preferably, your test materials should be sent out as hard copy, or (less preferable) by e-mail as Adobe Acrobat .PDF files.

Materials to prepare for the test: The materials to prepare for your test should reflect the marketing media (such as direct mail, or print advertising) and the sales benefits, features, and other content your company plans to use in its marketing deliverables, based on the best marketing information available to you so far. At a minimum, your test should include a mockup of your company's large-format (11 X 17) color brochure, and a sample of your company's proposed advertising, if you are planning to run a print display advertising campaign.

Other useful materials for your test would include a prototype price schedule, a sample promotional order form for your company's product, outlining any promotional offers you are planning to make in your company's sales presentations or direct-mail programs, or any other printed material that tells more about your company's products and their benefits, such as case histories or spec sheets. Sample market test materials are shown in **Figure 17-1**.

Figure 17-1:

Market Testing Sales Materials—Test your sales copy and marketing deliverables as early as possible

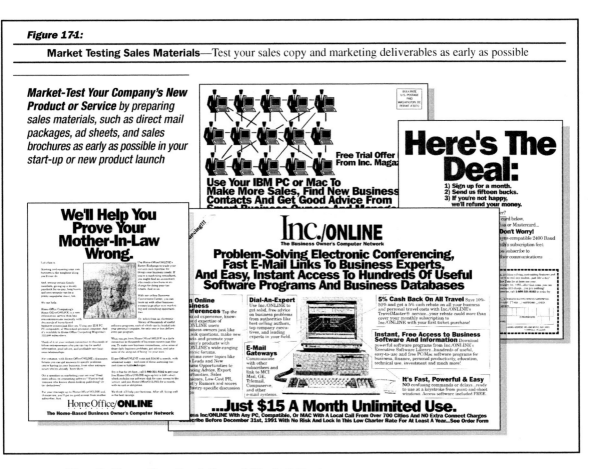

Market-Test Your Company's New Product or Service by preparing sales materials, such as direct mail packages, ad sheets, and sales brochures as early as possible in your start-up or new product launch

Step 3: Executing the Informal Market Test

By now, you should have your list of respondents assembled for this informal market test. Contact approximately ten of these likely prospects for your test by phone. Tell them you and your company are in the process of launching your company's product, and because they are a key executive in this market, you value their opinion. You want to hear their thoughts and comments on your product and how it's being marketed. If they agree to review your test materials, tell them you'll be sending them out in today's mail or Fedex.

In your conversation with them it's very important to let these contacts know there will be no selling pressure. All you are asking for are their opinions and constructive comments on your company's marketing approach; they'll be flattered that you've asked for their help.

Send your marketing collateral materials, along with a brief cover letter telling your contact the purpose of your test, asking him or her to review the enclosed materials. Ask them to read over the enclosed samples (brochure, ad sheets, order form, etc.) as if they were an actual prospect seeing these materials for the first time. Let them know you'll be following up with them by phone in about a week. Your advertising agency's account executive, or the marketing consultant who prepared these printed test materials, should also participate in these follow-up phone calls.

Your telephone follow-up: Give your contacts a few days to review your test marketing deliverables before your follow-up phone call, when you'll ask a series of questions (below). These questions are designed to stimulate useful answers from your test contacts. If you ask these questions more or less in the same way they have been written, they'll help you avoid asking questions that elicit only "yes" or "no" responses, since your goal here is to keep the conversation moving, and to draw out as much useful information as possible.

Ask your test respondents the following questions:

Sales benefits: Do you believe the sales benefits we've featured in our materials are the right benefits for our company's product and market, and have they been organized correctly—i.e., is the most prominent sales benefit the one that's the most important?

Main sales copy benefit (headline used in brochure or ad): What did you find about the headline that was compelling, and how well did it express the main benefit of our product? If you didn't find the headline to be effective, how do you think it could be improved?

Product features: Were the features of our product explained in a clear and convincing way? What features were not explained very well, and how could these be clarified or improved?

Product applications: Of our product's suggested applications, which of these do you believe are more important than others, and why? Also, can you think of any new, additional applications you believe should be included, and why are these applications important in your industry?

Pricing and promotion: Do you think our product's price is too high, too low, or about right? Was there anything about the terms of our promotional offer (if used in the test) that wasn't clearly understood? What are some of the promotional offers you've seen in products like ours offered by other companies? How did these promotional offers motivate you to purchase those products?

The purchasing decision: What individuals at your company, besides yourself, are responsible for making the final purchase decision on our company's product? In general, who, by job title or responsibility, do you think would make the purchasing decision for a product like ours in your industry? Based on the materials we sent you describing our company's product, would you buy it? If so, why? If not, then why not? Here again, you are *not* trying to pressure your contact to buy. You only want to put the question directly to them, and flush out any objections that you might be able to address, and neutralize in revised marketing deliverables.

Overall presentation: What sales copy or other presentation (such as tables, diagrams, etc.) could have been explained more clearly or more persuasively in our deliverables, and how?

Publications and trade shows: What are the most important industry and trade publications you read every month? Of these, what's your favorite industry publication? What are the top trade shows in your industry? If you could only go to one trade show each year, which one would that be?

Wrap up your phone conversation by asking your contact if they have any other comments and observations on the marketing materials you sent to them. Of course, as you wrap up the phone call, thank your contact for their time and let them know you'll be keeping them in the loop as your company continues its development and product launch.

As you conduct these interviews, take detailed notes, and be sure to ask follow-up questions if they will help you gain additional insight from your conversation with the contact.

Step 4: Assessing the Results of Your Informal Market Test, and Adapting Your Marketing Deliverables and Marketing Plan

After you complete a handful of these interviews, you'll begin to get a sense of whether or not the sales benefits you've presented in your marketing deliverables used in your market test are persuasive and understandable in your market. You'll also find that the people in your industry you contact in your test have a knack for discovering confusing sales copy, inaccuracies in your use of technical jargon, and other errors and omissions you'd never find on your own.

When you complete your interviews, the general pattern of the improvements, additions, and deletions you'll have to make to the sales copy in your marketing deliverables becomes apparent. Your own common sense also helps you to weed out the trivial responses that are not useful to your marketing program, such as someone's artistic criticism on the design of your test marketing deliverables, or other off-target comments.

You can incorporate the best of these comments and observations into the final versions of your company's marketing deliverables used for the next step in the process, which is either the "formal" market testing step (covered in the next section), or your start-up's actual product launch.

Strategic shifts in marketing direction: In some cases, the final result of your conversation with market-test respondents may give you the strong impression that your company must radically change the way it markets and sells its products. For example, you may find that the executives you've contacted as likely prospects for your company's product are either "too low" in their company's hierarchy to make a purchasing decision, or too technically-focused to see the strategic business advantages of your company's product.

This often occurs if your company is selling complex, technically-oriented products or processes to technically-focused executives, who may, themselves, have some reason to block the adoption of your company's exciting new approach to their field. Your company's product or process may also meet resistance because it requires a major change in the way the technical executive must run his/her operation. Your company's product or process may suffer from the "Not Invented Here" syndrome prevalent in many larger firms, or may meet with resistance when a technically-oriented prospect decides to nit-pick your product's unimportant technical details to death, or may be resentful because he didn't think of it first.

In these cases, shifting the marketing focus to get your company's product in front of prospects who have a more strategic, results-oriented vision of their company—by changing the point of contact from a "VP of Technology" to a "VP of Business Development" or "VP of Marketing" job responsibility, for example—can often dramatically improve your start-up's sales results.

Targets of opportunity revealed by informal test feedback: In the course of your testing, the other comments you receive from test respondents may put you on the path to some new and very exciting marketing opportunities for your start-up, such as word of a major distributor who might be a good prospect to carry your product, or a large corporation that might be an important potential joint-venture partner. These are but two examples of exciting and potentially profitable new "targets of opportunity" that smart marketing managers will aggressively pursue during their start-up's development stage, and which may necessitate additional new marketing efforts, or even a shift in direction for your company's marketing program.

The "Live" Market Test (or, the First Stage of Your New Product Launch)

Once you've finished your informal market test, and you've taken the time to think through and form impressions from its results, making the necessary changes to your start-up's marketing program, and your product's prime benefits, sales copy, and descriptive product information on your marketing deliverables, you are now ready to move your marketing program to the next step—the "live" market test.

Here, your live market test can be executed as a standalone program, performed for 30-60 days ahead of your product launch, or it can be the product launch itself, occurring during a kind of market launch "probationary period" within the first 30-60 days of your product's actual introduction in the marketplace.

Figure 17-2:

What About Focus Groups?

In theory, focus groups the sound like a marketer's dream: put a representative group of likely prospects in a comfortable meeting room, give them coffee and doughnuts, and ask them a series of "scientifically"-developed questions about your product and its sales appeal, then sit back, analyze the results, and all of your start-up's marketing issues and key copy points come into view.

This is the way it's supposed to happen, but the reality of basing your start-up's entire marketing program on focus group results is often far different. For every accurate focus group that produced a conclusion that was later confirmed by real sales results, there are many focus groups that lull their start-up's management team into a false sense of good-feeling about their products, or threw their company's product positioning and marketing programs in a totally wrong direction.

Focus groups rely too much on academically-based research principles and dynamics, and not nearly enough on street-proven marketing and sales wisdom. Focus groups results bend too far to the whims of focus group participants, and place little reliance upon marketplace leadership and vision. The major product innovations in our daily lives have succeeded due to world-changing innovation and forceful marketing, not focus group results.

If your company has developed a revolutionary new technology or innovation, you'll need to show your market that they need it, and how they can use it, because your potential customers simply have no concept of what your product is, what it does, and what it can really do for them. If focus group participants find your company's product to be unlike any other product they've ever seen before, then how can they possibly have an opinion on it? And, even if they are presented with information on your product and some "yes/no" research questions in a focus group situation, how valuable is any snap judgement they render within a few minutes of their exposure to your product?

A company that relies on focus groups is like a politician who shapes his or her opinion based on poll numbers. Both place themselves in the position of responding to opinions and events, based on the status quo, instead of getting out ahead of the voters (or prospects) and displaying bold leadership to shape events (or to create new markets).

Other problems with focus groups stem from bad group dynamics often occuring within them, such as:

Pleasing the interviewer: Over time, participants begin to sense the result the focus group moderator is aiming for, and, the urge to please being a very human trait, they to tell the focus group moderator what they believe he or she wants to hear. This often leads to rubber-stamping of your product's sales copy benefits and proposed marketing programs as, over time, focus group respondents simply agree to your study's questions to please the moderator;

"Group-think:" Another focus group shortcoming reveals itself when the majority of participants begin to censor and moderate their opinions in response to questions asked by the moderator, to keep their opinion in line with what they feel is the group's consensus opinion, or to avoid giving answers that may be viewed as being too iconoclastic or out of the mainstream. Group-think is the worst result of any focus group, because of its dangerous tendency to dilute and compromise your marketing program's product positioning, your sales copy, and other proposed sales appeals. A too-provocative headline that otherwise could be extremely effective when viewed by a single individual in an ad or a direct-mail package will often be criticized by these same people if discussed openly in a group setting;

"Follow the leader:" Inaccurate and misleading survey results occur when less-assertive participants in the group "follow the leader," gradually molding their own opinions around the group's most vocal, assertive, opinionated, participant. This places the entire focus group at the whim of its most outspoken participant's views, and places your entire marketing program and direction at similar risk, if you allow these results to unduly influence the form and content of your marketing program and deliverables.

Don't ask—sell, and then watch the reaction: Because it requires you to engage each participant on a one-on-one basis as an individual, the informal market-testing process covered in this section neutralizes the group dynamics and personality effects that plague marketing focus groups. You'll get better information from informal, selling-based testing than you get from focus groups, if you keep your respondents focused on your sales presentation, marketing program, and deliverables, and listen closely to, and reflect thoughtfully on, their responses.

Either way, in a "live" market test, you'll be testing the pulling power of your start-up's marketing channels, programs, and deliverables with real marketing programs, such as direct mailing tests, trade show displays, sales force support efforts, and print advertising placements. You'll be spending money in your marketing budget, for sure, but not as much as you'll be spending once you're underway with your company's ongoing marketing program, after you've adapted your marketing program in response to this test.

The time it takes to execute this test is roughly 30-60 days, and it can take place as soon as your start-up is ready to deliver its product or service to its marketplace. A typical "live" market test usually includes one or more of the following marketing activities:

Direct mail test: A test of your product's direct mail/direct response sales potential, with a test mailing to samples of 3-6 of the best available mailing lists of likely prospects in your industry;

Sales force support: If your start-up employs a field sales force (or a network of independent sales reps), as most business-to-business start-ups do, your test would also include all marketing activities required to support your sales staff as they hit the streets, such as development of marketing collateral and other sales materials. Of course, your start-up's sales force will follow up on the inquiries generated by the mailings, ads, or other marketing activities you execute during this test;

Trade show exhibit: If the timing is right, and there is an opportunity for your company to attend a major industry trade show as an exhibitor, then your test should focus on this major marketing opportunity;

Print advertising: Lastly, and if your start-up's marketing budget allows, you can place a limited number of display ads in your industry's leading publications to test the responsiveness of your market to trade print advertising.

Your testing goals: While the goal of the initial, "informal" market test was to test the sales appeal of the benefits, copy, features, and applications used in your start-up's marketing deliverables, the purpose of the "live" market test is to determine the actual response of your marketing program and deliverables in the marketplace, and the level of sales that ultimately can be converted from the inquiries generated by your marketing program. This market test may still be a test, but it's a test that is intended to generate *sales*.

Plan ahead to measure your response: Because of the chaotic nature of most start-ups, procedures are often not put in place to track and measure response to a start-up's first direct mail drop, ad placements, or other, measurable marketing projects. As a marketing manager, you'll have to bear this in mind, and set up a system to accurately measure the inquiries received, and the sales results of your mailings, ad placements, and other marketing programs, in advance.

Be ready for change: As a marketing manager in a start-up, you must be ready to change and improve your marketing program during this initial testing/launch phase, making adjustments to your advertising sales copy, product information, promotional offers and pricing as needed, and in response to the valuable feedback you receive from prospects in your market, who by this time will be making their preferences known to your company's sales reps, or indirectly through your start-up's dealer or distributor network.

From the standpoint of marketing execution, the only two things that count are whether or not the inquiries and sales generated by your live market test meet your desired marketing goals, and, if not—how quickly you can make the necessary changes to your marketing program during the test to improve the results of your marketing program (more on this in the next section).

Execution of Your Start-up's "Live" Market Test

The marketing execution involved in a "live" market test for a start-up or new product launch shares many similarities with the day-to-day execution of conventional marketing programs, except for these key differences:

> **Speed:** while you'll be executing many of the same kinds of marketing projects for a start-up as you would for a more established company, in a start-up—and especially during the initial testing phase—you'll be doing everything much faster. Time is limited during any new venture's market test, and you must not only work faster to develop, execute, and manage your start-up's marketing program, you must also communicate this sense of urgency to the other members of your start-up's marketing team—your ad agency or marketing consultant, and your key vendors, such as your printer, Web site producer, or lettershop.

> This often places you in the position of having to run up and down your marketing program's chain of execution, sweet-talking, cajoling, and twisting arms with printers, publication ad sales reps, mailing houses, Web producers, and the other critical suppliers to your start-up, motivating them to work faster on your behalf when necessary. Most of your suppliers already know that start-up companies can sometimes grow into very large, profitable customers, and they'll work hard to meet the extreme deadlines of your rush marketing projects, as long as you show respect for their work process by not pushing them into rush projects when it's not necessary, or interrupting a supplier's work schedule with his other customers due to a delay caused by your own preoccupation with another project;

Cost: A start-up must conserve its capital at all times, but especially so during the time of your initial live market test. Since it is more likely that initial sales results will force you to substantially revise your marketing program, it's all the more important to spend the minimum dollars necessary to determine whether or not the methods and media you are using in your marketing program will produce the results you hope to achieve. You can keep your marketing execution costs to a minimum by carefully managing your printing, advertising, and other marketing expenses (see below) during your test.

If you decide to place some ads for your test, the same attention to cost also applies to your company's print advertising schedule. Don't run a full page ad if you can make a half-page ad do the job. As already covered in extensive detail in Chapter 9, a half-page (or smaller) size print display ad, if properly executed, often generates the same sales response as a full-page ad. When running a print advertising test in a start-up, the response generated after the second appearance of your ad in any publication should provide enough sales response to tell you whether or not advertising works in your market. During your start-up's test phase, never commit your company to a placement schedule of any more than three consecutive monthly issues in any publication, and be brutal about cancelling any open ad placements if sufficient response isn't generated after your ad's second appearance in a publication;

Scale: Keep marketing costs down during the initial market test by carefully monitoring quantities of all printed materials, such as those used in your direct mailings, the first versions of all of your printed materials for sales kits, product packaging, and any other printed sales collateral pieces. It's likely you will be making substantial changes to all of your printed materials due to market response, so keep your quantities to a minimum to avoid having to discard large numbers of printed marketing materials.

Open for Business: Executing Your Start-Up's First Market Test

Your main goal in your initial marketing test is to execute the test as quickly as possible so that you can generate accurate and reliable sales response from real, live customers in your company's market. For this test, the advertisements, direct mail packages, and other sales collateral you use must be "open for business," so interested prospects can contact your company and buy your start-up's product or service.

This means that all advertising, mailing pieces, your Web site, etc., should be set up to let these prospects call your company's toll-free number, click on a Web link to order, or mail in a coupon to order or request additional information on your product.

You must also set up a system and procedures to accurately record, track and measure inquiries and orders you receive from the mailings, ad placements, and other methods used in your test. These critical test results form the basis of the all-important financial and sales assumptions you will be making as you scale up your start-up's marketing program. Make sure that you have accurately recorded the results of your testing activities, such as telephone calls in response to mailings and ad placements, page views on your company's Web site, or reply cards mailed in by prospects requesting more sales information.

Tools of the Trade: Elements of Your Start-Up's Initial Test Marketing Program

The next two sections cover the key marketing methods used for initial test marketing and product launch marketing programs, the major advantages and drawbacks of each method, and the factors that help you decide which of these marketing tools to use in your company's market testing and launch programs.

Direct Mail

For most start-ups or new product launches, direct mail, in its many, varied forms, is an extremely effective way to test the sales and market response of your product or service, and often becomes an important part of your start-up's ongoing marketing program after you move your start-up past its initial market-testing phases. You can obtain high-quality mailing lists that allow you to reach virtually any type of consumer or business professional, by industry, job title, location, purchase history, or almost any other criteria relevant to the markets you need to reach. You can also obtain phone numbers for these mailing list contacts, for follow-up by your company's direct sales staff after the prospect has received the direct mail piece.

Mailing sizes: For a market test in a start-up, or in a new product launch for an established company, a typical direct-mail test usually consists of a minimum of three mailings to three different lists of 2,500 names each (3 mailings X 2,500 names per list = 7,500 pieces total). A list sample size of 2,500 names is usually the lowest statistically-valid sampling size for testing your start-up's marketing appeal by direct mail, and testing the three best, most representative mailing lists in your industry allows you to reach a reasonably-sized cross section of potential buyers in your market. If you can afford to test higher individual quantities on each list (at 5,000 names for each list), or more lists, this also buys you a higher level of confidence in your test results, but at a minimum, a 7,500-name test across three mailing lists will be sufficient to tell you whether or not a direct mail marketing program will generate inquiries and sales for your company's new product or service.

Mailing list selection: When selecting mailing lists for your test, start with the top three mailing lists available in your market. Usually, these will be the subscriber lists of the top trade publications in your industry, trade association member lists, or, if available, mailing lists of individuals who have already purchased products or services very similar to those offered by your start-up. Ask your mailing list broker to select only lists where a specific individual is identified, by name, along with their job title in the company, ruling out lists lacking names and using only generic titles, such as "President," "Marketing Manager," or "Office Equipment Buyer."

The direct mail piece: Although it's certainly possible to test two or more different mailing packages in your start-up's initial market test, *speed of execution* is more important than the advantage of testing alternative direct mail packages. Work with your ad agency or marketing consultant to create and develop the direct-mail package you and your team think does the very best job of selling your company's product or service, using your best current knowledge, and, of course, incorporating the comments and feedback you received from conducting the "informal" market test covered in the previous section. You will have more opportunities to develop and test different mailing packages in a series of larger, ongoing tests once you have executed this initial market test, or as part of your ongoing marketing activities after the product launch.

Timing and execution: Time is money, especially in a start-up, so send your direct mail tests out by First Class Mail, even though your postage costs will be more expensive than other, slower postal rates. The sooner you can get your test in the mail and on to its recipients, the faster you'll be able to measure the response and reach a conclusion on your test.

Give your mailing test every chance to be successful: Whenever you use direct mail in a market test, do your best to give every element of your direct mail test the best possible chance of success. The sales benefits, product information and overall presentation of your direct mail package must be as effective as you can make them, and your mailing list selection—critical for any test—should focus on the best lists you can obtain in your industry.

Work closely with every member of your marketing team—ad agency or direct mail marketing consultant, printer, mailing list broker, and lettershop—to insure flawless execution in getting direct mail pieces in the mail and on time, without a hitch. The same prompt follow-through on your mailing also applies to your sales staff, when they respond to telephone and Internet inquiries from prospects who respond to your mailings, or when they make their follow-up sales calls, as well as product fulfillment and customer service for those who purchase your product.

Do everything you can to give your direct-mail test every chance of success, and you will go a long way toward eliminating any doubts you might have that you could have done more. If your product won't sell to the best mailing lists you can find, with the best direct mail piece you and your creative team can develop, then it probably won't sell at all, unless you change the product, or find a new market for it. This is why it's important for you and your team to put forth your very best effort to eliminate poor marketing execution as a possible contributor to poor test results. See Chapter 18 for detailed coverage of troubleshooting and solutions to poor response on direct mail programs.

Sales Force Support

If your start-up is marketing a complex product or service with a high purchase price and a long sales cycle, it's also likely your company's sales efforts will depend on a field sales force, who will be using personal, on-site sales calls to present and sell your start-up's products.

In addition to sales lead-generation activities, such as mailings and trial print advertising placements, the initial market test in a start-up or new product launch marks the beginning of a start-up's field selling efforts. Next to the professional selling skills and sales closing abilities of your company's sales staff, the hard-copy marketing collateral your company's sales reps use during their first sales calls—brochures, sales catalog flyers, spec sheets and bound business presentations—leaves a critical, lasting impression on the prospects they call.

Your prospects not only judge your start-up by their first meeting with one of your company's sales reps, they also form an impression of your company and the perceived quality of your product by the sales collateral materials your sales rep leaves behind. Even during the initial market test phase, when your company's sales reps are setting up and making their first sales calls, it's critically important to supply them with solidly-produced, well-written, well-presented printed marketing materials.

The printed marketing collateral used by your sales reps in a market test should be at least equal to—and, preferably, better than—that of your competitors. It should have a highly finished look, and its sales copy, descriptions of benefits, features, and applications, graphics, and other explanatory material must be as good as you can possibly make them for your test.

This is one area where you should invest the money necessary to pay your ad agency or marketing consultant to design, develop and produce these crucial materials to a high production quality. While it's certain that the results of your marketing test will prompt you to make significant changes to these printed materials, the work that's invested in them is not wasted, because once developed, many design elements, like logos, photographs, and other visuals, can be carried over to the revised pieces.

Sales presentation collateral materials: Examples of printed marketing collateral pieces used in most field selling applications include:

Large sales brochure: This is usually a glossy, 11 X 17 four-color brochure, folded to 8-1/2 X 11 size. For some sales applications, this large brochure may consist of multiple 11 X 17 sheets bound together to create a multiple page, catalog-format piece. For market testing purposes, stick with a single 11 X 17 sheet size, folded to 8-1/2 X 11 final size, and, if your product's sales story and applications require more extensive documentation, you can develop smaller, individual color sales flyers (described below). The large brochure is usually the most expensive printed piece to design for your market test, since it is nearly always printed in four-color format. However, by using high-end color digital printing and color copying technology, you can print only the quantities you need, when you need them, at relatively low cost;

Color sales flyers/catalog sheets: While the large-format color brochure describes your company and the general benefits, features, and applications of its products, it's often a good idea to develop one or more smaller, single-sheet 8-1/2 X 11 four-color gloss sales flyers to highlight other aspects of your start-up's product appeal. These color sales flyer sheets, printed on letter-sized 8-1/2 X 11 gloss paper stock, are usually produced as harder-hitting versions of the large brochure, and are often used to drive home a product's key sales benefits, or to cover certain features and applications of your product in greater detail;

Sales flyers can also be produced to tailor your company's marketing appeal to the needs and wants of a specific market segment, or to a group of prospects in a specific industry. This supports your sales reps as they further customize their sales presentations to these key groups during the market test. Since these kinds of sales flyers often serve a highly targeted marketing need, they can be produced in very small quantities on a digital color copier, as needed;

Business presentation materials: The same high production values applied to brochures and sales flyers should also be applied to any customized, printed proposals or other communications with prospects during your test. Companies such as Paper Direct (**www.paperdirect.com**) provide many types of attractive, printed presentation binders, folders, and printable color paper items you and your company's sales reps can use to dress up your printed sales presentations, proposals, price estimates, and other printed deliverables prepared by your company's sales reps and left behind with potential customers;

Sales video: You may also want to consider producing a short (1-2 minute), sales video on DVD for your start-up's sales reps to play for their prospects during this initial market-test period. This need not be an elaborate or expensive project; a simple, slide show-type presentation with audio voiceover is all that is necessary.

Your Start-Up's Web Site

The Internet is so pervasive that a company isn't "real" these days unless it has a Web site. The prospects at the companies you'll be contacting in your start-up's marketing test, whether by mail, by print advertising, or through your company's field sales force, will expect your company to have a Web site, and will link there to learn more about your company, and its new product.

For a market test, however, your company's Web site doesn't have to be an elaborate production. Have your ad agency, marketing consultant, or Web producer create a basic "Web brochure" site, lifting sales and descriptive copy from your company's printed sales materials, and including additional information as needed, such as your company's management profiles, relevant news announcements, and company contact information. Since you'll be very busy on other, more important marketing projects during the market test, don't spend a lot of time on your Web site: Just put together a good-looking, but quick, temporary design for your site, with basic sidebar navigation buttons. Your Web developer has access to standardized, "canned" Web page design templates that they can use to get your Web site in place. Once they know what you want, your Web producer will know what to do to get your site up as quickly as possible.

Web site content for a market test or new product launch: At a minimum, your Web site should contain the following information:

- **Company description;**
- **Promotional product benefits and features;**
- **Company management team and executive profiles;**
- **Company contact information—e-mail, phone numbers, and physical mailing address;**
- **Company news releases (optional)**

Also, if time and ability allows, it's never too soon to start collecting Internet e-mail addresses from interested visitors to your Web site. If possible, ask your Web producer to create a "free e-mail newsletter and updates" link on your site, in its own pop-up window on your site's home page, so your company can start capturing e-mail addresses for later communication with interested, potential prospects, as you continue to develop your company's marketing program.

Trade Shows

Renting booth space at an important conference or trade show in your industry is a wonderful test marketing opportunity for any start-up or new product launch. Trade show opportunities have often served as launching pads for many start-ups who've gone on to become very successful companies, and provide you, your sales staff, and other members of your management team with an unprecedented opportunity to meet face-to-face with hundreds of prime prospects for your company's product or service.

When you can find one, an upcoming trade show is a golden market-testing opportunity. If the date of a major trade show in your industry happens to coincide with the timing for your start-up's initial market test, you should do everything possible to get your company into that show, even if it means diverting marketing dollars from other test projects, such as a direct mailing program.

At a trade show, you and your company's sales staff can try out your product's "sales story," and listen to real questions being asked by real potential customers.

This is an extremely valuable and important experience for members of any start-up, and one that can't be duplicated by a mailing, an ad placement, or any other marketing activity.

Trade show booth and other deliverables: In addition to your company's out-of-pocket costs for renting booth space at the show, plus airfare, lodging, and other travel costs, you will have to create, rent, or buy a booth backdrop, and produce additional signage for your company's booth at the show. For start-ups on limited budgets, there are some very workable, expedient trade show backdrop options that you and your ad agency or marketing consultant can develop; these can generally be executed at a cost of less than $3,000 (see Chapter 13 for more information on expedient trade show booth display options).

Trade show collateral and signage: The other marketing deliverables you develop for your market test, such as color brochures, sales flyers, etc., can also be used in trade show opportunities. Many of the sales headlines and copy benefit bullet points you're using in your printed sales collateral can also be displayed on 28 X 44-inch board-mounted poster signs in your trade show booth. In addition to your booth backdrop, these attention-grabbing signs add extra impact to your booth on the show floor.

Print Display Advertising

Because of its expense and limitations, print advertising has the lowest priority in your initial market test, and should only be executed when your company's marketing budget and schedule allows. Compared to the other market-testing activities already covered, print advertising is more expensive, for results received, than direct-mail, trade shows, or personal sales calls. The second drawback to print advertising is timing: Most trade publications publish on a monthly schedule, which means that there will always be a 3 to 5-week lag between the time you place your ad, and the time the publication reaches its subscribers.

It is very important for any market test to generate accurate results as quickly as possible. A delay of several weeks from insertion to publication of your ad for a test is too much time. You should only run test ads if you can hedge your bets by using other marketing tools, such as direct mail, that generate more immediate results. Also, you can always test the effectiveness of print advertising at a later date, once you have developed other proven, effective methods to sell your company's products, such as direct mail or sales force support.

If you believe that print advertising will play a very important role in your marketing plan, and feel it necessary to test ad placements immediately, keep your expenses down by going with half-page display ads in your industry's top one or two publications. If you have a choice between a publication that is published on a monthly basis, and one published bi-monthly (every two weeks), you'll get results sooner if you select the bi-monthly publication for your test, since ad space placement lead-times for these publications generally run closer to 2 to 3 weeks, instead of 4 to 6 weeks for monthly publications.

Factors Influencing Your Market Testing Decisions

The types of marketing tools and methods you use in your start-up's initial market test are influenced by the following conditions:

Time: All start-ups are in a hurry all the time, and this is always a good thing, because a start-up in its development stage generates no sales revenue while it burns through its seed capital. And since most start-ups underestimate the time required to develop their company's product or service, they will often overshoot their development window by a few, or several, months.

When this happens, even greater time pressure is placed on the start-up's marketing and sales team to develop, test, and execute the company's marketing plan. As a result, the responsibility falls upon the marketing manager to develop and test the start-up's marketing plans using methods that can generate accurate results in the shortest time. The next section of this chapter covers the top market-testing tools, from those providing results in the shortest period of time, to those requiring longer lead times;

Product price: High-priced products often require longer sales cycles, and are often more complex than lower-priced products. This complexity requires marketers to devote a substantial amount of their marketing effort toward "educating" the prospect on the product's uses and applications. This requires a different marketing approach than for lower-priced products, and means you must choose the marketing methods best suited to your product's price level and complexity.

For example, technically-oriented prospects who respond to a mailing or an ad for a complex, expensive product sold by your company will often seek out as much in-depth information on your product as they can find, by first going to your company's Web site, *before* they even contact your company to speak to a sales rep. If you do not anticipate the questions your prospects will be asking about your product, by developing and distributing the background information they want to review before their "first contact" with your company—online FAQ files, technical spec sheets, white papers, and other information—you are needlessly prolonging the sales cycle, and throwing this task onto your company's sales reps, who may do a uneven job of providing this information to their prospects;

Sales force and selling channels: Most start-ups or new product launches selling business-to-business products employ either a field sales force making personal on-site sales calls, an in-house telemarketing sales group, or a network of independent dealers, distributors, or independent sales reps—or, any combination of these selling methods. The market-testing tools you use must support the structure of your start-up's sales staff, and must be compatible with the available sales and distribution channels of the industry served by your start-up.

For example, if your company is selling a costly business-to-business product through a field sales force, a market test using a series of direct mailings that *doesn't include follow-up phone contact with prospects by your start-up's sales reps is bound to yield poor final results.* Likewise, a start-up that spends most of its initial market-testing budget on a splashy trade print advertising campaign, without a provision for driving prospects to its sales reps or key distributors, is not running a market test—they're wasting money.

Your market test cannot work in a vacuum. If your start-up depends upon salespeople to sell its products, then the tools used in your market test must support your sales reps, and the focus, benefits, and content of the personal sales presentation that's used to sell your company's product;

Representative results: You must select the test marketing tool that puts your start-up's product in front of the people who are most representative of those who will buy your company's products. Your market test must also be designed to generate real inquiries that lead to actual sales for your start-up, not meaningless "intention to buy" results.

The sales copy, deliverables, and promotional offers you use in all market tests should not only look like those you'd use in your start-up's ongoing sales and marketing efforts, they should "ask for the order," just as you'd ask for it once your company's marketing and sales operations are firmly established;

Your budget: While you can always find ways to keep your market-testing costs to a minimum, you can't escape the fact that you must spend money to test, and you won't get meaningful results if you don't spend money. Since the deliverables you'll be using in your "live" market test—mailings, sales kits, ads, etc.—must present your company's products at least as well as (and preferably, above) the level of your industry competition, you must pay your ad agency or marketing consultant a fair price for their efforts to develop first-rate marketing deliverables for your test.

No competent ad agency or marketing consultant will work for your start-up "on spec" (for free), so be prepared to spend what it costs to produce high-quality marketing deliverables to make your start-up's market test worthwhile. The creative, copywriting, design, and production costs for developing marketing deliverables for your test, (not including your company's printing, mailing, list rental, trade show and advertising placement costs), generally start at $15,000 for a small test, but usually average $30,000 for many typical market test projects.

Because it's likely that your company's ongoing marketing program will be
utilizing much of the content and creative product of the deliverables you've
used in your test, your ongoing marketing development costs should be lower
down the line, since you've already paid for some of the creative,
development, and production costs in this test.

Market Testing Tools: How to Select the Right Marketing Tools to Use in Your Initial Market Test

Time is the enemy of every new venture. Of all the factors influencing your
market-testing choices, you must be the most concerned with the time required to
execute marketing projects for your company's market test. This section describes the
various marketing tools you can use to test your start-up's product or service, from
the perspective of the *time required* to put each of them into action—from the
marketing projects requiring the shortest execution times, to those requiring longer
execution times.

1.) Trade Shows

Exhibiting at a leading trade show in your industry is the very best marketing tool
to use for testing the marketing and sales response in any new venture or new product
launch, and requires the least amount of lead time to execute, compared to any other
market-testing activity. Trade shows work well for market-testing of nearly any
product or service, if you select a show that clearly targets the most likely prospective
buyers for your product, and, almost as important, if the timing required for your
market test happens to coincide with the date of an upcoming show.

The major benefit of trade shows is that they put your company face-to-face with
hundreds (or thousands) of real-live potential customers. This can be an incredibly
valuable experience for any start-up's marketing and sales team, and especially for
marketing managers. There's no substitute for making your company's sales
presentation, over and over, directly to many people in a single day, seeing and
hearing their reactions to each of your key selling points, and learning what it takes
to persuade a prospect by listening closely to the questions they ask about your
company's product.

In addition to being an excellent market-test experience, a successful appearance
for your company at a trade show is an excellent platform for launching any start-up
or new product. Reporters, trade media contacts, and business development
executives from major corporations always attend major industry shows, and these
contacts can open up many exciting opportunities to boost your start-up or new
product launch in its early growth stages.

From a sales and marketing perspective, the main advantage of trade shows is that
one show can replace hundreds of individual field sales calls, because all of the
prospects come to you. The very best indicator of success in any market test for a

start-up are actual sales: If you are targeting the right market, and you have a good product at a good price, and execute well at the show, there's an excellent chance your start-up will make some early initial sales, in addition to the valuable market feedback you'll receive from real, live prospects.

Trade show interaction improves sales copy and marketing deliverables: Working your company's booth at a trade show is not only an invaluable selling experience for your company's sales reps, it's an excellent way for you to learn which benefits have the most sales appeal to the prospects in your market. As you work a trade show, repeating the process of making your sales presentation to many visitors in your company's trade show booth, you can quickly adapt your sales presentation points and improve the way you tell your product's "story," spending more time emphasizing those sales benefits that seem to resonate best with your prospects, and minimizing less-important ones. You can then incorporate this information into all of your company's marketing deliverables, mailings, advertising campaigns, and other marketing efforts to make your start-up's marketing program more effective.

Trade show drawbacks: Of course, the timing of a trade show works against you if the date of the show doesn't coincide with the time you need to run your market test. And while last-minute opportunities are sometimes available, you may not be able to get into a trade show on short notice (30-45 days), since booth space in many of the most popular trade shows may fill up months beforehand. However, last-minute openings do become available, and you can occasionally get a booth space on short notice, so by all means let the show producers know you're interested in any booth openings that might come up, since this is often the time when a start-up can get into a show with only a couple of weeks' lead time.

Also, the additional expense involved in appearing at a trade show—cost for your booth space, booth backdrop purchase or rental, signage and marketing collateral expense, and related travel and lodging expenses—can get very expensive for a marketing test. But this downside is minimal when compared to the huge potential marketing and sales benefits your company can receive by appearing at the show. So, if necessary, it's always better to divert resources from other planned marketing activities (such as mailings or ad placements) to a major trade show opportunity, if you believe your start-up will find a receptive audience at the show. For detailed coverage of trade show execution, see Chapter 13.

2.) Sales Force Marketing Support

While trade shows may be the best market-testing opportunities for your start-up, a trade show availability may not coincide with your immediate need to execute your market test. In the absence of a trade show opportunity, the next best market-testing method, and the one used most in business-to-business start-ups employing a field sales force, is a market test using targeted direct mailings in support of personal sales calls made by your company's sales reps. This is also usually the "default" market-testing approach for most start-ups and new product launches.

The purpose of the sales force support market test, whether it uses direct mailings, print advertising, or any other form of marketing media, is to either:

1.) **Run "in front of" your sales reps,** by using mailings or ad placements to generate and supply sales leads to your company's in-house or field sales reps, or

2.) **Follow-up a sales rep's initial prospecting and cold calling** during the test, by mailing sales information kits to prospects.

Usually, the goal of a market test in support of a start-up's sales force is to generate a sufficient number of inquiries from prospects who respond to your company's mailings or advertising, as in the case of 1.) above; these inquiries are then passed along to the appropriate sales rep for telephone and in-person follow-up.

Direct mail and sales force support: Market tests to support a field (or in-house) sales force usually involve the development and execution of a direct mail sales piece mailed to 3-6 rented mailing lists and/or to other, self-compiled mailing lists, such as lists of key contacts you've developed through telephone canvassing, compilation of trade association mailing lists, or other sources discovered in your own industry research (see Chapter 7 for more information on mailing lists and list compilation).

When executing mailings for sales support market tests, you must closely coordinate your activities with your start-up's sales manager, making sure to avoid mailing too many pieces, which may overwhelm your company's sales staff with too many sales inquiries, or not mailing enough pieces, which may generate too few responses for sales followup, and unreliable market test results. Additionally, if your company has a network of field sales reps positioned in various parts of the country, you may also need to work with your company's sales manager to key-code the lists used in your market test, by region, state, or type of company, so that inquiries can be routed to the appropriate sales rep in the field.

For testing purposes, you may also want to *exclude* certain major potential prospects from your test mailings. For example, if you or your management team believe your company may still need to refine or improve certain aspects of its product, or if you believe your test may lead to substantial improvements in your marketing message and sales presentation, you may decide to hold off on contacting some of the large corporations who have the potential to be major customers, thereby avoiding a less-than-optimal first contact with prospects in these companies. Accordingly, you'll want to exclude test mailings to these major companies, until you feel your company has improved its product, or sharpened its marketing message.

Implementation: An initial series of test mailings to support an in-house sales staff may start with as few as 100, but usually no more than 10,000, mailing pieces for the entire test, to provide your start-up's sales force with a sufficient number of inbound sales leads, without inundating your sales reps with more leads than they can handle, or more follow-up phone calls than they can make in a timely fashion.

Development, production, and mailing for this market test can usually be implemented, start to finish, in 3-4 weeks at the earliest.

3.) Direct Mail-Only Market Testing

If your start-up offers a low-priced, easy-to-explain product that can be sold directly in business-to-business or consumer markets from a single direct mail piece, such as a consumer electronics product, a software package, or an information product, such as a book, directory, newsletter subscription, or specialized information service, you can use direct mail to test the sales "pull" and responsiveness of your market, without follow-up by sales reps.

Direct mail-only market tests usually consist of test mailings to a half-dozen or more carefully-selected samples of rented mailing lists, such as selections from trade publications in targeted markets, or test selections of "buyer lists" of individuals who have already purchased products or services similar to those offered by your start-up. The direct-mail piece is designed to provide enough sales and product information to the prospect, so they will place an order directly from the mailing, without phone follow-ups by telemarketing sales reps. Since your company will rely almost exclusively on direct mail in its marketing program, your test should include at least 6 (or more) lists, and you should also consider testing more than one direct mail package against these lists.

Make sure your test reflects your entire market: When executing a direct mail-only market test, remember that the available universe of mailing lists in your market *is* your market. Because of this, your initial test should be broad enough so you can make a clear assessment of your product's sales response across a variety of mailing lists. Test a wide cross-section of different mailing lists, of varying quality, using test sample sizes large enough to provide your start-up with results that would be representative of those you'd receive as you ramp up your mailings to larger portions of these lists in your company's ongoing direct mail marketing program. This helps to insure that your product can be sold on a sustainable basis by direct mail to a large base of prospects, by mailing to the many lists available in your market, and not just "cherry picking" the few, most responsive, mailing lists available in your industry.

Implementation: Development, production, and· mailing for a direct mail-only market test can usually be executed, start to finish, in as little as 3-4 weeks. For more information on direct-mail testing, see Chapter 7.

4.) Print Advertising

From every standpoint—timing, cost, and quality of results—print advertising is the least desirable market-testing tool for a start-up or new product launch. If used at all, advertising should only be done in addition to, and only to support, any of the other marketing activities described in this chapter, such as sales support mailing tests, or company trade show appearances.

Print advertising can be very expensive compared to other marketing media, and requires a long lead time (around four to six weeks) from the time ads are placed, until the publication reaches its subscribers. Print advertising is also the least targeted form of marketing, even for vertical-market industry or trade publications. For example, unlike direct-mail, you can't target your print advertising to specific types of prospects, such as job title, geography, or company size in most trade publications.

Exposure danger: Another drawback to using print advertising as a market-testing tool, and one of special concern to start-ups, is exposure. Placing a print advertisement in one of your industry's top publications is a very public act, essentially announcing your start-up's product or service to the world. For many start-ups in the late product development and early market launch phases, such exposure during a market test runs the risk of unnecessarily tipping off your company's competitors by disclosing your company, its product, and its key features—perhaps before your team is confident enough in its sales and marketing execution to reveal itself to the entire marketplace. For an initial market test, it's better to use more discreet marketing tools, such as direct mail, or sales presentations, for your initial market test, deferring your print advertising campaign until your marketing program is on solid ground, making use of the other, more effective (and less expensive) market-testing techniques covered in this chapter.

If you're not concerned about the risk of public exposure, if your marketing budget allows it, and, most important—you believe a print advertising campaign can be a viable sales lead-generation channel for your start-up, you can certainly add a few print advertising placements to test this marketing channel and broaden the scope of your initial market test. For more information on executing trade print advertising campaigns, see Chapter 9.

Executing Your Test and Tracking Results

It generally requires at least 60 days to plan and execute an initial market test for a start-up or a new product launch. This includes the essential planning that must occur before the tools and methods of the test have been determined, such as the "informal" market test, as well as the steps for the actual execution of the marketing deliverables for the test, such as copywriting, design, layout, and production of printed direct mail pieces, development of self-compiled mailing lists, ad media placements, and mailing list rental decisions.

Watch the details: As you execute your start-up's initial market test, you'll be surprised at the number of tasks you'll need to perform that are outside of the marketing manager's usual role. For example, marketing managers in start-ups must often see to it that arrangements for hosting of the company's Web site are made, that the company's toll-free phone numbers are established, postage-paid permits for reply coupons are obtained, and other administrative chores are completed.

These tasks are often overlooked by those who should be responsible for completing them. But they are essential, because they determine whether or not interested prospects will be able to contact your company. If they're not done on time, they will delay a marketing test, so you'll often have to step in and do them yourself.

Tracking Results

As you manage the creation and production of deliverables for your market test, you must also establish systems for logging and tracking the responses your company will be receiving from the test mailings, ad placements, and other marketing programs you will be executing during your test.

Don't forget to key code your mailings: When you and your ad agency or direct mail consultant produce your direct mail pieces, make sure that the address labels and/or reply cards used in your mailings feature a key code identifying the mailing list used for the test. Alternatively, and better yet, you can match the replies you've received from test mailings against the original electronic mailing list files, but this will require some additional database programming to automate the process. Either way it's done, make sure you are able to track responses to each mailing, and by each mailing list you've tested.

Log all responses to all marketing activities: The systems required to track responses to market tests don't have to be complicated. In fact, the simpler, the better, since simple tracking systems tend to be used more often than complicated ones. A xeroxed tally sheet on a pad placed next to those in your company who answer the phone, open the mail, or log Internet responses from the test, with spaces to track inquiries by day, and by the source of marketing activity (key code from mailing list, ad placement, etc.) is usually all that is needed. Enter the results in an Excel spreadsheet on a daily basis for further analysis. If you are sending out mailings that contain mail-back reply cards, make sure you receive these reply cards and tally the responses daily, by their mailing list key codes.

Building a "response curve:" Tracking each day's responses received from a mailing, starting from the first day responses are received, lets you build a response curve for your mailings. Response curves can be an extremely useful tool for predicting total returns from a mailing based on partial early response. Once you have recorded the daily responses from a number of mailings, your response curve can help you project the total response to a mailing based on the first few days, (or, with higher accuracy) the first week's responses.

Response curves are an extremely useful tool for start-ups because they allow you to make a faster decision on whether or not a mailing test was successful, based on early returns, without having to wait the additional two weeks (or more) for all responses to arrive. Once you have developed a few response curves for your mailings, and you are confident that the response curve can accurately project the final response to your mailings, you'll find they improve your marketing execution by giving you the confidence to move ahead with the printing and production steps necessary to ramp up your mailings to larger quantities of your most productive mailing lists (see Chapter 7 for more information on response curves).

Listen Closely to "Anecdotal" Results During Your Test

In addition to sales results, the "anecdotal" response you receive from your start-up's initial market test often has a critical effect on your start-up's marketing program. The comments, criticism, and observations you receive from actual customers in your market can provide your start-up with invaluable feedback on the sales copy used in your advertising and other marketing deliverables, product features and benefits, and your final mix of marketing tools used in your company's ongoing marketing program.

It's true that "everyone has an opinion," and giving every viewpoint the same weight is worse than not listening to your market at all. However, watch out for those instances when you receive enough comments on a specific aspect of your marketing program, such as an ad headline or product feature description that was not well understood by a sizeable number of prospects, or product pricing options that were not well received by a fairly large number of prospects, during your testing and launch activities.

You'll often notice that the most significant comments seem to crop up again and again. If enough of your potential customers have taken time out of their busy workdays to offer their comments, and if many of these comments point to a few key aspects of your marketing program, then these responses require further examination. This often indicates that a change must be made to either your marketing program, your product, its pricing, features, or purchasing options.

As you execute your marketing test, take every possible opportunity to expose yourself to this useful anecdotal information from prospects and customers. Listen in on your company's toll-free inquiry order line during the test, read the e-mail replies that come in to your company's Web site, and take every possible opportunity to listen to what people in your start-up's market are saying about your product, and about the way you are selling it. This feedback will often cause you to make important changes to your marketing program, sales copy, and marketing deliverables as you continue to develop your marketing program.

The Marketing Report Card: Assessing The Final Result of Your Start-Up's Initial Market Test

Generally, the total responses received from an ad or a mailing by the end of the first week's worth of responses will give you a very rough indication of whether or not your start-up's initial market test was a success.

As response comes in from your market tests, compare your actual market test results against the market response assumptions you made previously in the original financial projections for your start-up or new product launch:

- Average response to advertising placements (inquiries generated);

- Average response to mailings (and breakdown by each mailing list tested);

- Sales conversions (inquiries-to-sales);

- Average unit purchase

If your market test results post at or above your goals, then you can ramp up your start-up's marketing program as conservatively or as aggressively as your company's situation and resources allow, by increasing the quantity of your next mailings, extending your advertising schedule, and expanding the scope of the other marketing activities that tested well.

If, however—and this often happens—your results are ambiguous, or fall below (or, even well below) your goals, it's time to look further into your product, and your marketing choices, to assess what to do next. These important tactical and strategic considerations are addressed in the next chapter.

START-UP TURNAROUNDS
CHAPTER 18
WHEN YOUR MARKETING PROGRAM HITS THE WALL: TROUBLESHOOTING AND CORRECTING POOR SALES RESPONSE

It has been said that failure is a better teacher than success. As a marketing manager, it's certain you will experience failure in a marketing project: A new mailing or ad campaign that generates a low number of inquiries, or a marketing program that targets the wrong prospects, or whose sales message is not well-received by your market. For marketing managers, failure can reveal the insights that lead to a successful result on your next marketing effort. <u>Not</u> failing often means not <u>doing</u>.

While this chapter covers the process of uncovering and assessing the causes of poor **market test** response in start-ups and new product launches, many of these techniques also apply to the problems faced by all marketing managers who must deal with the results of poor sales response in marketing projects in any company. The material covered in this chapter is perhaps the most important of this book, because it can help you stage a turnaround in a failed marketing project.

Landing in the Grey Middle

Many times, the marketing projects you execute for your test marketing program, or a marketing project for a new product launch (or any new marketing project, for that matter) falls way short of your expectations. Your mailings, ad placements, sales support follow-up and other marketing activities generate inquiries and sales, but not up to the level of the market response assumptions in your company's business or marketing plan. You must move quickly to assess your marketing program, and take action to save it.

Another common outcome is that some marketing activities, such as print advertising placements, generate far less response than others, such as test mailings to selected mailing lists, or a trade show appearance. All in all, however, overall results fall about halfway between your projections and zero, indicating a clear need for a change in your marketing program, its product, its sales and distribution channels, or all of these.

When the results of a new market test in a start-up indicate neither clear success nor outright failure, falling somewhere down the "grey middle" of sales performance, there will be many immediate reactions to the news; most of them distracting and unconstructive. Some members of your team will begin to panic, and others—especially founders in a start-up, or senior executives in your company—will simply deny the clear facts before them.

These are indeed surprising responses to adversity, since ambiguous sales response is the usual outcome of most market tests. As already stated, the reason a market test is done in the first place is to uncover both the *bad* and the *good* aspects of a product's marketing appeal, and to make the necessary changes to the start-up's marketing program.

When you consider the fact that most start-ups are introducing their products or services for the very first time, in strange and completely untried markets, and with products or services that may require potential customers to change their ways of doing business, it's actually surprising that so many members of a start-up's team react in panic and denial to news of disappointing response to the company's first market test. They should have expected it, and should have been better prepared to face it.

There's Always Something You Can Do

Your first reaction as a marketing manager in a start-up, or in an established company facing sub-par results from any marketing project, is to avoid being swept up in the panic that follows bad news, or to be influenced by the emotional responses of others around you.

Your next reaction should be to remember the words of Lt. General Harold G. "Hal" Moore (Ret.), the American commander in the battle of Ia Drang, who, with 395 men, took on 2,000 North Vietnamese Army regulars during the first major engagement between the North Vietnamese and American troops at the beginning of the Vietnam war:

"Don't say 'there's nothing you can do.' There's always one more thing that you can do."

There's **always** something you can do.

Figure 18-1:

Optimism vs. Reality in a Start-Up: Dealing with the Founder's "Reality Distortion Field"

As a marketing manager executing your start-up's first market test, you must review and assess the results of your market test with a clear eye, and you must accept the final outcome of your test— good, bad, or—as usually occurs—somewhere in between.

Members of start-ups, especially founders, often travel inside their own "reality distortion fields," glossing over any bad news or poor feedback on the start-up, its product, its business conditions or market situation. While a positive mental attitude and a certain amount of denial of adverse events is, indeed, a requirement for overcoming the many obstacles that are faced in getting any new

venture off the ground, as a marketing manager you can't let this cloud your assessment of market test results.

If you receive a less-than-positive overall result from a market test, it is up to you to realistically identify the problems uncovered by the test, with an attitude of stark objectivity, and make the hard choices required to solve these problems. You need to see things as they are, and not how they should be, or—most important—how the other members of your start-up's team want you to see them. Glossing over or denying any obviously negative results, such as poor sales response, or obvious shortcomings discovered in your start-up's product, its performance, or its features, only compounds your company's problems as you continue to expand your marketing program.

The next section will show you how to identify the common marketing problems uncovered by market tests in start-ups, or in any underperforming marketing project, and what *you can do* to correct them.

What Went Right?

Before you examine the causes of a poor initial market market test or any other marketing project, look for those areas where your test or marketing activity did well. These positive indicators often become the keys to showing you what you need to do to change your marketing program and dramatically improve your results, for example, by helping you to change your marketing approach, the types of prospects you are targeting, or your marketing methods.

Here are the areas to examine in market test results:

Sales generated by the test—who bought, and *why:* Look to the sales your test *did* generate, or to the individuals and the companies who look to be the closest to making their decision to buy your company's product or service. Why did these individuals buy, and is there anything about them, such as their job title or responsibility, that makes them different from the majority of prospects you targeted in your test?

Call some of these new customers on the phone and try to find the common threads that led them to buy your company's product or service. What factors motivated them to buy: Cost savings? Fear of becoming technologically obsolete, or of being "left behind" in their business? Dissatisfaction with a similar product sold by a competitor? Can these motivations be turned into better sales copy points for marketing deliverables used in follow-on marketing efforts?

What benefits and features did these buyers find compelling about your company's marketing deliverables (mailings, brochures, sales presentations, advertising, etc.)? What did they find that was lacking, or that confused them, in your marketing deliverables? Perhaps the marketing deliverables (mailings, ads, etc.) you used in your test succeeded with these few buyers in spite of major problems with their sales benefits and content (more on this in the next section);

What kinds of companies bought your product? Also, if you are selling a business-to-business product, closely evaluate the companies who bought from your company during the test: Do they seem to be more, or less, technically innovative than other companies in their industry? If your company is selling a high-tech product or service, such as computer software, hardware, or systems, even a few sales to a handful of smaller companies known to be early adopters of new technology in their industries can be a bright spot in a poor overall market test result. This may mean that, as more sales effort is applied, and as your product proves itself in the field, other companies will follow;

Are the companies who purchased your product smaller than the average company in your field? If so, it's a fact that smaller companies make purchasing decisions faster, and perhaps it's only a matter of time—with additional effort on the part of your company's sales reps—before larger companies decide to buy;

Examine the niches these companies occupy in their fields: Take a closer look at the markets these companies serve, and the specific applications they provide to their own niche markets. Did these companies buy your product to address some very specific applications, or to serve their own special market segments not served by all the other companies in your industry? This fact may be an opportunity for you to promote certain aspects of your product specifically to these market niches, or "sweet spots," in subsequent marketing activities;

Mailing lists: If you tested a variety of different mailing lists for a direct mail test or project, examine the results generated by each list you tested. Did certain mailing lists do better than others? If so, are these mailing lists large enough to make direct mail a viable part of your marketing program, despite the poor performance of other lists?

If you tested a few mailing lists of subscribers to a few of the major trade publications in your industry, did one of these list tests do any better than others? Did it do better by a considerable degree (at least 30% better)? If so, perhaps you can improve your direct mail results on publication mailing lists (and possibly on other mailing lists), by improving the sales impact of your direct mail piece and testing again. Even a mildly positive result on a mailing to an industry's major publication mailing list is a good sign, since subscribers to a major industry publication are often the most representative cross-section of your market.

Examining Where Marketing Projects Go Wrong: Common Causes of Poor Marketing Response

There are four major causes of sub-par market response revealed by market tests, or in other marketing projects:

- **Marketing-related problems;**
- **Product-related problems;**
- **Distribution and market size problems;**
- **Uncontrollable factors (such as inadequate funding or bad market timing)**

The first three causes above can often be corrected by you and your marketing team. Other factors, such as lack of sufficient financing to adequately fund your start-up's marketing activities, or bad timing, also determine the success or failure of a new venture, even if they are not marketing or product-related problems, per se. But even these factors can sometimes be reversed by better marketing methods.

Marketing-Related Problems

Many of the causes of poor marketing results are problems that are directly related to the marketing content, methods, deliverables, or execution of the test or marketing activity. This section covers the most common causes of poor marketing results, and how they can be corrected.

Copy and Deliverable Problems

Inadequate sales copy and poorly-developed marketing deliverables are the leading cause of poor response in any marketing effort. This is the first place to look in the aftermath of a test that generates poor or mixed results. With the benefit of hindsight, and the experience of receiving feedback from prospects in your market who receive your test marketing materials, you can often identify areas in sales copy and presentation that can be improved.

Main benefit missing or is not recognized by the prospect: Of all sales copy-related problems, a main sales benefit that is either missing, or is not recognized by readers as being powerful enough to persuade them to buy your product, is the leading problem in direct mail pieces, ads, sales kits, Web sites, etc. and the major cause of poor marketing response.

The most common example of this problem is when ad agencies lead a mailing piece or a print ad with a clever headline or silly visual pun, instead of a clear, no-nonsense presentation of your product's most compelling benefit to the prospect. Relying on your prospects to even understand, much less be motivated by, a "clever" headline or visual, especially in a market test, is a foolhardy move that nearly always leads to poor sales response.

Main benefit not understood by the prospect: Sometimes a main benefit is presented, but it's not one that prospects can understand or appreciate. For example, a start-up that has developed a revolutionary, low-cost AI-based robotic vision system for manufacturing plants in a specific industrial market may be so proud of its accomplishment that it makes this fact its main benefit. However, most prospects in manufacturing companies won't see the inherent advantages found in a headline claiming "revolutionary, low-cost AI-based robotic vision systems for manufacturing," but *would* understand the benefits of lower reject rates, reduced materials costs, and higher assembly line output provided by using the start-up's vision systems in their plants. Any one of these benefits would be a stronger main benefit, generating more prospect inquiries in a revised marketing deliverable.

Sales copy and benefits poorly organized or not well presented: Usually when the main sales copy benefit is missing or is not well executed, the other, less-important sales copy benefits are also not presented well. Persuasive sales copy should have the same effect as a personal sales presentation, leading the reader through each of the product's key benefits, building a presentation that logically and persuasively moves the reader to the final "action step" required by the marketing deliverable. Most poorly-written marketing deliverables are either not clearly written, don't present their sales benefits in a logical fashion, or don't contain enough sales copy benefits to persuade the reader in the first place.

Prospect not told what to do next, or is not motivated enough to take the next step: The main headline and sales copy of your marketing deliverables may be compelling enough to interest your prospect, but your "call to action," or the contact information you need to provide to get prospects to call you, to fill out and mail a coupon, or link to your company's Web site, may be buried in your ad, brochure, or response coupon—or it may not be there at all.

Or, you may have included the necessary sales contact information, but no additional incentive for the prospect to call—for example, a discount if the prospect orders within 30 days, or an offer for a free sales premium that's highly useful and relevant to the product or service being offered, such as an informative video, a report, software CD, or other item of perceived value.

In either case, some prospects may call your company, but some will put your brochure, ad, or reply coupon aside, making a mental note to call you. But soon the busy tempo of their work lives resumes, and, absent any extra incentive offered by your marketing deliverable to nudge them into action, your prospect's attention shifts somewhere else.

If all other aspects of your marketing deliverables are persuasively written and well produced, a clear "call to action," combined with "something extra," can boost your inquiry response by as much as 30% on a mailing or an ad.

Identifying and solving copy and deliverable problems: You can eliminate sales copy benefit and presentation problems now and in the future by training yourself to look at all of your start-up's marketing deliverables as your prospects do—that is, like a total stranger would.

Start by emptying your mind of all you know about your company's product or service, then view and re-read each marketing deliverable in its final layout version.

Open your direct mail package just like your prospect would, and evaluate the sales headline on the envelope, and the inside brochure and other pieces in a few quick seconds, just like all your potential customers do. Ask yourself: Is the main sales benefit of my product or service "getting through" to me? Do I understand what this product is, what it does, and what it can do for me? Are the other benefits easy to read and understand? Are they convincing? Does this company (yours) look credible? What do I do next, and how can I order?

Perform the same exercise with your company's advertising. Print out the final layout of your ad, and tape it into the middle of the trade publication where it's to appear. Then quickly flip through the pages of the publication from the front, just like your busy prospects do.

Does the layout of your ad stand out from the blur of the other ads? Read the headline, then skim the body text. After a few seconds, do you get the idea of what product's being sold? If not, then your copy needs to be re-written, or your layout needs to be redone and "amped up"—headlines set bigger, or in bolder type, visuals enlarged, more spacing between bolder subheads in body type, etc.

Repeat this process for every marketing deliverable you produce in your company: Sales kit materials, flyers, catalog sheets, your company's Web site. With these "new eyes," you will begin to see how a main headline could be written more persuasively, the missing bold subheads in your sales copy where the benefits should be, the "call to action" that should be at the bottom of your ad, but isn't, or is, but needs to be bigger and bolder so it won't be missed by someone who sees it for the first time.

Even the best, most well-written direct mail packages, print ads, or Web sites can be made even better, and you should look at your development of marketing deliverables as a process of constant examination, adaptation, and improvement. Cultivating the ability to look at all of your marketing deliverables with "new eyes" helps you see how to make a good sales message even better.

Developing this skill, and listening to the feedback you receive from prospects, customers, and sales reps from your initial market test or other marketing activity, generates better response on your next marketing project, and helps you eliminate sales copy and presentation weaknesses as a cause of low response on future marketing projects.

Market and Prospect Selection

If you have carefully examined the sales copy and marketing deliverables used in your prior test or other marketing project, and you are confident they do an effective job of presenting and selling your start-up's product or service, then consider the choices you and your team have made on your market, and your prospect targeting in this market.

After poor marketing copy and deliverables, poor market targeting and prospect selection are the next leading causes of poor sales response. Many times you will discover that you are marketing to the wrong prospects, or trying to sell your product in what turns out to be the wrong market. This is often learned only after running a market test—which, of course, is the reason you are testing in the first place.

Many causes of poor market targeting and prospect selection can be identified and corrected; the most common of these problems will be addressed here, for each of the most common marketing activities in your marketing program.

Direct Mail

Prospects not identified by name, or names out-of-date, on mailing lists: Nothing kills response more than direct mail packages sent to mailing lists where the name of the individual at the company is missing from the mailing list record. Instead, generic, nondescript job titles, such as "Purchasing Manager," "Computer Systems Buyer," "VP Marketing," and the like are used as a substitute for an actual contact name.

Nothing says "junk mail" more than envelopes that do not address a specific individual at the company. Even if direct mail pieces addressed in this way do manage to reach the individual you're trying to reach, their next stop is often a short journey, unopened, from the manager's desktop to their trash can (that is, if the assistant who opens their mail hasn't already trashed it beforehand).

Another common problem with mailing lists are incorrect, out-of-date company contact names, with records containing names of executives who are no longer with the company, or companies that are either no longer in business, or who have moved to another location, and whose mail forwarding order with the Post Office has expired. Sending a mailing piece to someone that's addressed to their predecessor is a bad way to start a business relationship, and in large corporations, these pieces often don't make it past the mailroom.

You'll know you have an outdated list when you see an unusually high number of your own direct mail pieces returned to you by the Post Office, marked as "undeliverable," or with the words "no longer works here" scrawled across the front of your envelopes.

Each of these mailing list problems can be readily solved, and will almost always guarantee better results after they are corrected. In the first case, don't ever send a mailing out to generically identified contacts, no matter how hard your ad agency or mailing list broker tries to sell you on the list.

To avoid mailing to out-of-date lists, ask your ad agency, list broker, or the list owner if they keep their list up-to-date, and how often. Top-quality rented mailing lists, such as trade publication subscriber lists, and especially those of major business publications, are usually updated, or "cleaned," on a regular basis.

The problem with out-of-date contact names is usually found in other types of rental mailing lists, such as buyer lists of contacts who have purchased certain products, or with lower-grade, compiled lists, which are lists created by list brokers from Yellow Pages directories and other data-mining processes. While you will never know if a list is outdated unless you test it (and this is why we test in the first place), a list owner with a good reputation in your industry will also properly maintain and update their mailing lists.

Forgot to get the phone number/no phone numbers available: Another common problem in many companies is failure to view the direct mailing project as a two-step process—first, you send out the mailing, then your company's sales reps follow up by phone to the contacts on the list.

If your start-up (or established company) sells to businesses, and the unit price of your product is high enough to justify employment of a sales staff, then most of your direct mailings should support this two-step process. If your company fits this profile, and it's just sending mailings out and waiting for prospects to call, your company could be losing half, and probably much more, of the mailing's potential response.

While some rentable mailing lists are available with phone number fields, you'll often have to append phone numbers to mailing lists on your own, on both rented lists, and with the self-compiled lists you develop in-house. Commercial services, such as Gannett's TeleMatch (**www.gannettoffset.com**), have extensive databases and automated systems that append business phone numbers to any mailing list you supply to them. However, this service usually finds phone numbers for just 60-70% of database records, and experience has shown that up to 10% of these matched numbers may be incorrect. The best solution, if you are developing your own, smaller, self-compiled mailing lists, using public-source information, such as trade association membership lists, phone directories, or information pulled from Web sites, is to assign this research task to an administrative person or a temp, and compile phone numbers on your own (see Chapter 6 for more on self-complied mailing lists).

Insufficient number of mailing lists tested: Many start-ups and established companies will execute a new direct mail test to just one, two, or three, often haphazardly chosen, mailing lists, and then wonder why they didn't get the response they expected. Your market test should mail to enough lists to give you a reasonable indication of the response you would receive from the market these lists represent. For a start-up's initial market test, a test mailing to at least 6 different mailing list selections, and to at least 2,500 names per list (15,000 pieces total) provides good coverage of any market, and will yield statistically valid results for those lists.

Many mailing list owners and brokers require a 5,000-name order minimum for list rental. If you can afford to mail these many names to each of the half-dozen or more lists you order, you'll get a more statistically valid sampling result, but this is not necessary for your initial test. You can always order 5,000 names, and when you receive the list, have your mailing house, with further processing, select only every other name from the list (an "Nth name select") to mail just 2,500 names from each list.

In addition to giving you a clearer picture of your market's response, testing a sufficient number of mailing lists has other advantages. What generally happens in a test is that one or two of the lists will pull exceptionally well, one or two lists generate poor response, and the response from the other lists fall somewhere in between. Accordingly, if you test enough mailing lists, you'll hedge your bets by giving yourself the option to test your market further, by executing follow-on mailings to the lists that generated the best response in your test.

Now, imagine what would have happened instead if you *only* tested the one or two lists that did very well, or if you *only* tested the one or two lists that were the poorest performers. In the first instance, you'd have come away from your test with the false illusion that your start-up's product was a runaway winner, or, in the latter case, you would have colored your entire market with the same dark brush. In either case, you would have received a completely misleading impression of sales response in your market. Test enough mailing lists and you'll give your marketing program a wider range of options, even if parts of your test yield poor response.

Sales Support

Many common causes of poor response from marketing programs, such as late or non-existent phone follow-up with prospects, stem from poor planning and coordination with the company's in-house sales force. Once identified, however, these problems can often be easily corrected. Other causes of poor test results are revealed by the feedback your company's sales reps receive from prospects as a result of the mailings, ads and other marketing activities you've executed.

Targeted prospect is not the best sales contact: Sometimes, after the test mailings have been sent, and as your company's sales reps begin their follow-up phone calls, it turns out that the prospect who was originally targeted to receive the mailing piece, or who was addressed in the company's advertising, either by job title or responsibility, is not the individual your sales reps should be speaking to, and, therefore, is not the prospect who should be targeted by your start-up's marketing programs.

For example, if you're selling a technically-complex product, such as a software system or other technology, which has demonstrable benefits that are readily understood by non-technical business executives, you may do better to shift the focus of your marketing program from "VP of Technology" or "Chief Information Officer" job titles, to other job titles or responsibilities more closely aligned with the actual problem solved by your start-up's product or service.

For example, if you are selling a software system that improves manufacturing efficiency, manufacturing VPs or plant managers may see and understand the benefits of your product more readily than their company's computer systems executives. These managers might then be more likely to become champions for your product in their companies, as they push for its adoption within their own operations.

An astute sales professional can tell whether or not the person he or she is speaking to is the right person to be contacting within the targeted company. Often, during the initial phone contact, the prospect will even tell your sales rep they're not the right contact at their company, and will refer your rep to the right individual there. If this happens frequently, you need to know about it, so you can target different prospects in your subsequent marketing activities.

No telephone follow-up/late telephone follow-up: As described previously, most marketing programs in companies selling products in business-to-business markets rely on the one-two combination of an outbound marketing activity, followed up by calls from in-house or field sales reps, who contact the prospects who respond to mailings, ads, or other marketing activities.

A prospect who receives a mailing, or sees your ad, and who then takes the time to contact your company should receive a follow-up phone call from your sales rep the same day (or, within 24 hours of his call, at the latest). In most business-to-business marketing programs (and tests), all prospects who receive direct mail packages should also get a follow-up call from your company's sales reps within a week of their receipt of your mailing piece.

If these follow-up calls aren't made in a timely manner, or if they're not made at all, the prospect's interest cools and their memory of your company and its product will fade. When this happens, your marketing project has just been compromised by poor sales execution.

This problem can result from weak coordination between the marketing manager and the sales manager, as more direct mail pieces are mailed than sales reps can reasonably follow up on in a given week. In other cases, this problem is caused by poor discipline among the company's sales reps, or poor sales management. Better communication, along with the implementation of a workable sales contact management system, can produce a dramatic turnaround in inquiry-to-sales close rates.

Print Advertising

In general, print advertising is the one marketing activity most often plagued by the poorest sales response of any other marketing activity executed during a market test or ongoing marketing program. Print advertising is also generally the most expensive marketing activity for most companies, and the riskiest, from the standpoint of generating profitable sales response.

Sales copy and presentation problems: This is the most common cause of poor sales response from ads, and is often caused by the same types of sales copy and presentation problems found in poorly-performing direct mail pieces and other printed deliverables.

These problems are often magnified in print ads because, unlike a direct mail package, which has more space to sell the product, and more ways to do it through the envelope, cover letter, brochure, and reply coupon, a print advertisement has much less time to attract the reader's attention, and far less space to present and sell the product. Because of this, a print ad whose headline doesn't grab the reader, whose sales copy doesn't make the case for the product, and whose call to action is not persuasive, often fails more spectacularly than any other marketing method.

Often this happens when a start-up runs its print advertising schedule too soon, before it has learned the best ways to sell and present its product (see next section).

Ad content: Often, the cause of sales copy problems in advertising is that the key elements of the ad—the headline, subhead, body copy, and call to action—are not written in a plain, direct, salesmanlike way.

How your prospects see your advertising: You have about three seconds to get your reader's attention, and about five seconds after that to hold it once the reader begins to skim-read your ad. During this brief interval, your reader's mind will pick up and absorb a few bits of information about your product—some phrases picked out from the text of your ad, a benefit from your ad's headline, a few more words about your product, a glance at your product shot or visual.

While this is happening, the reader may be matching these pieces of information in your ad to their own thoughts of their problems that the copy points in your ad claim to solve. If there is enough agreement between what the reader absorbs from your ad and what was in his mind before he saw it, he will either:

1.) Store away a few vague concepts about your product in his mind as he turns the page, or;

2.) Be motivated enough to take the next step to contact your company

The outcome in 1.) above is what ad agency types like to call "brand awareness," a kind of weak memory the reader has about a company or a product that relies on some other marketing action to occur for the reader to buy the product—to see it on the shelf at a store, or to see ten more placements of the same ad, so the reader can say he heard about the company when the sales rep calls.

You want *sales response to your product now*, not brand awareness later. The sales content of your print ad must be powerful enough to force the reader to contact your company *now* rather than later. The sales copy elements of your ad must be amplified enough to overcome the reader's inertia, to get him to pick up the phone *now*, or to swing around in his office chair *now* to check your company's Web site, to contact you by e-mail *now*.

What the reader may or may not remember to do later doesn't count in marketing: If you're running print advertising, you've got to put everything you've got into it, or don't advertise at all. This is good advice not just for marketing managers in start-ups, but for marketing managers in larger and more established companies as well.

Does your copy give your prospects what they *want*? Do the sales benefits communicated by the main headline and sales copy of your print ad match the kinds of benefits that prospects respond to in your print advertising? Are those benefits relevant to what the average prospect in your market needs, or better yet, *wants*?

It's always easier to sell something if you know what your prospects *want*, and your product gives it to them; the rest is just good copywriting. However, it's much harder to sell prospects on what they *need*, since prospects often don't know what they need. In this case, your ad's sales copy must also haul the extra baggage of "education," by telling prospects *why* they need your product. Your sales copy must often address this added objective in many marketing situations.

Ad presentation: Another cause of poor ad response is weak presentation. The layout, or presentation, of your ad's key elements (headline, subheads, body copy, call to action, and visuals) must work together as a powerful, cohesive unit to push the reader to action and generate sales response.

Problems in presentation are problems of either **clarity** or **boldness**. Either the words and meaning of the *content* of your ad have not been communicated as well as they should be (clarity), or have not been presented well (boldness). Sometimes, both of these problems plague your company's advertising.

Clarity

Examine your ad, putting yourself in the mind of the person who's seeing it for the first time (with "new eyes"):

- ***Do you understand, within a few seconds,*** *what product is being advertised?*

- ***Do you understand the product's main benefit***—*stated in the ad's headline, or in its headline-and-subhead combination—in the first few seconds after you see the ad?*

- **If so, does this main benefit seem useful and compelling enough** to draw you further into the ad, so you'll keep reading the body copy?

- **Do the key points of the ad's subheads** in its body copy clearly communicate the product's other benefits?

- **Do each of these other features and benefits** in the body copy add to the case for buying the product, by answering a likely question or doubt that you'd have about the product, as a first-time reader?

- **Does the ad make it very clear to you as a reader what to do next:** Call for more info, speak to a sales rep, or visit your Web site?

Boldness

Next, as a first-time reader, examine the overall visual impression given by your ad:

- **Is your ad's headline** set big and bold? Can it be read from well beyond arm's length?

- **If your ad has a subhead** (most ads should), is it tucked up close to the headline, or above the body copy of the ad?

- **Is the leading,** or the space between the lines, of your headline set as tightly as possible?

- **Is the kerning,** or the space between letters of your headline and subheads, set as tightly as possible?

- **Does the total visual impression** given by the ad—layout, visuals, colors, logo—impart a sense of professionalism and credibility to the product or service being presented?

- **Does the ad's "call to action"**—the promotional offer, and the action you want the reader to take next (call your phone number, link to your Web address)—stand out clearly in the ad?

Certain aspects of boldness, such as tight leading and letterspacing (kerning) induce a sense of "dramatic tension" to the text of an ad. This tension infuses a sense of urgency to the headline, subheads, and body copy of the ad that influences the reader to take action and follow up with your company.

Boldness improves sales response: Anything that is lacking in an ad's boldness, as described above, reduces the power of your ad to cut through the haze of your prospect's daily routine, and reduces the sales response to your ad. Any content or visual element that gets in the way of your ad's clarity or boldness dampens sales response.

Bold design can also be good design: Any reader can see and appreciate good design, even when they're not actually noticing it, which is most of the time. Skilled use of bold type that is set tightly and well in your ad, combined with a well-executed visual, such as a product photo or graphic, makes a strong impression on every viewer: It imparts a sense of craftsmanship and quality to the ad that carries over to the product or service being advertised.

Most of your prospects won't ever read all of your ad's sales copy, so the impression of *boldness* created by the ad—the readability and dramatic tension of the headline, subheads, its key copy points, and your company's call-to-action and contact info—do their part to motivate readers to respond to your ad.

Other aspects of skilled ad copywriting and design that contribute to boldness can't be described in words. As the expression goes: "You know it when you see it." And if you're not seeing this boldness in your advertising, it's not helping to improve your ad's sales response, either.

From a design standpoint, this means your ad's design should be judged on how clearly and boldly it delivers your sales message, and not on how "pretty" or "well-designed" it looks, since the "prettiest" ads often aren't the ones that pull in the most inquiries. This is a somewhat undefinable aspect of ad layout, copy and design, but it can be sensed if you develop the ability to see your print advertising with "new eyes."

Print advertising used as the only testing method, or is run too soon: As discussed in the previous chapter, start-ups should avoid running print advertising until they get their sales copy and product presentations "dialed in," by reaping the market feedback advantages available from other, more cost-effective marketing activities in their tests, such as direct mail and trade shows.

Nonetheless, and as a cautionary note, many a start-up's entire market test activities have consisted exclusively of an expensive run of print ads, with no other marketing activity tested. Start-ups who run advertising-only market tests are choosing to lead with the riskiest and weakest-performing method of selling their products, and this fact is nearly always revealed by the final result.

This often occurs in start-ups whose advertising agencies tend to view every marketing problem as one that can be solved by a clever or "creative" print advertising campaign. These ad agencies either can't see the value in using other, more targeted marketing methods, such as direct mail, or they don't have the ability to work in these other marketing media. Another key factor is financial motivation, since ad agencies make a 15% commission on all ad space they place with publications, which certainly doesn't stop them from using a splashy ad campaign as their tool of choice for every marketing project.

The obvious solution to poor print advertising response when no other marketing methods have been used is to cancel the current print ad schedule, and re-deploy those marketing dollars to better sales force support, more direct mail tests, more trade show appearances, and other marketing projects that do a better job of helping a company develop and refine its sales copy benefits and marketing message. A market test using several tools, instead of one, allows your company to experience the sales potential that exists in all of the marketing options available to any new venture, product launch, or new marketing project.

Print ad page size is too large for inquiries received: Many companies buy full-page ads, when a half-page (or even smaller) ad size often pulls just as well, or at least pulls a higher number of inquiries relative to the lower cost of the ad. This often occurs where companies have been unduly influenced by their advertising agencies, who receive a commission on all ad space they place with publications, and, because of this, are financially motivated to place bigger ads for their clients.

In many cases, a full-page ad size is simply too large for the number of inquiries that a publication can produce, but if the same sales copy and layout are scaled down to a smaller page size, the ad will generate almost as many responses, or, will at least improve the cost-per-inquiry rate for the ad placement in the publication.

If you experience a response to a full-page ad placement that is, say, half of what you expected, and you are confident that the ad's sales benefits and presentation are on target for your market, you can produce a new version of the same ad in half-page size (or quarter-page, if possible), and run this new size at the next available insertion opportunity. You may find that the smaller ad size pulls almost as many inquiries as the full-page size. At the very least you will cut substantial unnecessary advertising cost from your company's marketing budget, while generating enough response to make the ad placement worthwhile.

Marketing Execution

As a contributor to poor response in market tests and marketing projects, problems in marketing execution are the easiest problems to identify, and the easiest to correct, if you and your team can learn from experience and avoid repeating the same mistake a second time.

Gross execution errors: These can be an almost unlimited combination of slip-ups, goofs, oversights, and production glitches occurring in marketing projects; any one of which adversely affects sales response.

On direct mailings, for example, processing errors on mailing lists can cause mailing labels to be printed with dropped fields or incorrect Zip Codes. Printed pieces used in your direct mail package may contain major typos or production errors, such as missing product photos. When your mailing house assembles and inserts the individual pieces of your direct mail package, the key printed elements of your mailing piece, such as a sales brochure or reply coupon, may not have been inserted into every mailing piece, or may not be available to insert in all mailing pieces, because they weren't printed in sufficient quantities. A direct mailing can go wrong in an almost infinite number of ways, due to the number of people who are involved: Between you, your ad agency, mailing list broker, printer, and lettershop, there are more than enough people to screw up a mailing at any point, anywhere along the line.

On ad placements, your ad files can be sent incorrectly to publications, causing an ad to be printed with a major, embarrassing production glitch, or this glitch may cause your ad to miss the submission deadline for that issue entirely (having your ad dropped before publication can actually be the merciful outcome, if your ad layout is embarassingly defective).

Sometimes, an undue lack of confidence in your advertising layouts can delay the prompt execution of your marketing projects. Key advertising issue insertion dates are missed or print schedules delayed because an ad layout or sales brochure is endlessly tweaked and revised by a nervous CEO or client (you, perhaps?). Major marketing opportunities are missed, due to too many needless revisions to ads and other marketing deliverables.

Poor execution due to seasonality: Failure to think through the timing of an ad's placement, or when a mailing piece "hits," can have a dramatic effect on the response you receive to any marketing activity.

For example, July and August are generally very bad months to initiate any major business-to-business marketing effort. Your potential customers are either on vacation with their families, or at their desks thinking about their vacations—and not thinking too much about their businesses, or your product. Response to mailings, ad placements, and sales follow-up calls falls off dramatically during this time.

Seasonality effects contribute to poor response during other times of the year as well. In most businesses, the period from Thanksgiving to New Year's Day can also be a poor time for a business mailing to arrive. Other slack seasons occurring in certain industries, such as during a major annual trade show in one market, or a seasonal drop in industrial production in another, may also be poor times to execute major marketing projects.

Overall, the effects of seasonality can reduce the sales response to a mailing or ad placement by 15%, to as much as 50%. If you are experiencing sub-par response to a market test (or a regular marketing activity) that occurred during any of these times of the year, and you've ruled out other problems, such as underperforming sales copy and prospect targeting, consider seasonality as a possible cause.

Sometimes, seasonality is easy to avoid. For example, you can often delay a December mailing for a few weeks so that it drops immediately after New Year's Day. If, however, events force your start-up's major market test into the July/August time window, you can't afford to have your entire marketing program lie idle for a full two months. One option is to run a scaled-down version of your test during these two months, and conserve the bulk of your marketing budget for your big marketing push timed to strike immediately after Labor Day. This way, you can gather critical market response for your product (discounted for seasonality by some degree), and your follow-on marketing program can still benefit from the improvements made to it as a result of your July/August test.

Uncontrollable events affecting execution: Of course, there will always be production and execution problems affecting response that are beyond your control. Mail bags full of your company's direct mail pieces can fall off the back of a USPS truck, a major news event or a weather disaster can kill market response; events both seen and unseen can supress the sales response of your marketing activity.

Solving Execution Problems

While there is often nothing that can be done to reverse the effects of a botched mailing, a missed ad placement, or lack of coordination in sales follow-through, most experienced marketing managers will only make the same mistake once, having learned the hard lessons of poor marketing execution.

For marketing managers, the keys to solving marketing execution problems are awareness, respect for the process, and leadership:

> **Awareness:** As a marketing manager you must not only manage all marketing activities, you must be aware of the individual execution tasks involved in every marketing activity performed by your team, the things that can go wrong as each of these tasks are executed, and as these tasks pass from one member of your team to the next in the process. Much of the material in this book is devoted to helping you understand the many steps involved in marketing execution in these marketing activities.

> Poor execution, missed deadlines, and lack of accountability are often the tangible end result of the marketing manager who doesn't know (or care) about these marketing execution steps, is not engaged in the process of marketing execution, or doesn't have respect for the work that must be done by the other members of his or her marketing team. Your ad agency, marketing consultant, list broker, printer, and lettershop are more likely to tighten up their execution once they "know that you know" what can go wrong, and what needs to be done to prevent a key step from going wrong in a marketing project.

> **Respect for the process:** Another way to avoid marketing execution errors is to have respect for the production process. An unnecessary delay in one step caused by you, or another member of your marketing team, creates problems down the line for others on your team who weren't responsible for the delay. If your printer is delayed for three days because you've been sitting on the final revisions of your brochure, your mailing may be delayed by a week because you missed the scheduled time slot for your mailing at your lettershop. Why should the lettershop manager have to twist his schedule out of shape to accommodate a delay caused by you (or someone else)? How would you feel if you were in his position?

> Respect for the production process also means having respect for the people who perform these tasks for your company. A marketing project that becomes a

fire drill for a vendor because of someone else's poor time management, or a gratuitous, thoughtless, delay, not only shows a lack of personal respect for the vendor, it can often lead to big execution mistakes in the marketing project.

A key to developing a respect for the process is accepting the fact that all the members of your marketing team require a certain amount of time to complete any marketing project on a non-rush basis, and that you must back up the timing of your marketing plan accordingly to avoid making every project a fire drill.

For example, if your ad agency told you they needed 3 weeks to write, produce, and print your direct mail package, arrange your schedule to give them the time they need to create a high-quality product, instead of throwing the project at them in the 11th hour. Don't fall into the habit of making every project a rush project, unless circumstances make it absolutely necessary. While it's unavoidable that some of your company's marketing projects must be executed on a rush or emergency basis (especially in start-up environments), too many rush projects, especially unnecessary ones, are bad for morale and lead to errors in execution.

Leadership: The final cure for execution errors is leadership. Once you've found problems in execution, admit the mistake, be the first to take responsibility for them, and do what you must to correct the problem. Be a square-shooter, and take the blame on behalf of your team, even if you, personally, were not to blame. If someone else was responsible for the execution error, and it's clear to you that they are genuinely sorry about it and are making every effort to correct the problem, let the matter drop and get on with the program. The other members of your marketing team will respect the "bigness" they see in you, and you will have taken a big step toward building a strong, cohesive marketing team.

Product-Related Problems

Many marketing activities generating poor sales response are caused by deficiencies in the products or services being marketed. These product-related problems are not only revealed by poor market-test results, but also by the comments and feedback your company's sales staff receives about the product from prospects in the field, and as a result of the marketing activity.

Some product-related problems can be corrected by the application of marketing skill, but other problems in your product may not be correctable unless your product undergoes substantial modification. Sometimes the product must be refined so that it is less expensive, or it must be made with more, fewer, or different features, or it must be improved in some other way to give your market what it wants.

You must be honest with yourself, and with your management, to discriminate between those product problems that can solved by marketing skill, and the problems that require a retooling of the product. Marketing problems caused by product deficiencies are the most challenging problems for any company, because product retooling efforts often mean a crash program for the product development team to make the necessary changes to the product. This also means you will have to work just as hard to change your marketing program to reflect the newly-modified product's features, benefits, and capabilities.

More and Better Marketing Skill Will Never Save a Bad Product

Experienced marketers who have to sell real products in the real world already know that a different, or more intensive, marketing program will never save a deeply-flawed product, or a product that is wrong for its market. If your market response reveals that your product's poor marketability can only be reversed by improving the product, then the application of your skill to the current version of the product is no better than a band-aid approach.

You may be able to improve sales in the short run, by resorting to a price cut, or by puffing up the product in your sales copy and presentation, or by resorting to the other cheap tricks of marketing illusion in your next marketing effort. But these methods will only further erode market confidence, dampening your sales over time, and will make your company's situation far worse than if your management had straightened out the product in the first place.

Product-related causes of poor market response require you to work closely with your company's product development team to communicate the market response received on the product, and to champion the product changes necessary to increase the product's sales potential in your company's market.

How to Get Product Feedback

Product deficiencies and improvements are usually revealed by the word-of-mouth comments you and your company's field sales staff receive from conversations with prospects during your marketing program. As your company's sales reps make their follow-up calls to prospects who receive your mailings, or they hear from prospects who call your company in response to your ad placements, a picture often forms of the problems inherent in your product. If these problems are significant, they will affect sales response.

The product faults that kill sales tend to repeat themselves over and over again. As your sales reps make their presentations and "go for the close," they will root out the prospect's objections to buying the product. While most skilled sales professionals can effectively counter the most common sales objections raised by a prospect, objections related to major product deficiencies can't be overcome by selling skill. And if the same objections keep getting raised over and over by your prospects, your sales reps will definitely take note—and you will know that your marketing effort is plagued by a major problem with your company's product.

Common Product-Related Causes of Poor Market Response

This section covers the most common product problems, ranging from those that can are relatively easy to solve by marketing techniques, to those that require extensive re-tooling of your company's product or service.

Product is not well explained or understood: This is a common problem for marketers of complex, high technology-related products and services, and is caused by not providing sufficient detail on product features and applications in marketing activities aimed at prospects.

Complicated, expensive products take more time and effort to sell. Part of your function as a marketing manager in a high-tech company is an "educating" task, supplying potential customers with all the information they need to make their purchase decision, *at the time it does your company the most good.*

The latter point is critical in high-tech selling: You don't want to bombard your prospects too soon with too much in-depth product information in the initial mailings, ads, and sales kits you send to them. Providing too much information too early in the sales cycle is self-defeating, because your prospects either won't bother to read it, or, absent any personal interaction with your sales reps, some of the prospects who do read these background materials may begin to develop incorrect impressions of your product, based on their incomplete or misunderstood reading of the sales information supplied to them.

This happens most often among technically-oriented prospects, who will tend to overlook the business benefits of your product, choosing instead to impose their own, incorrect, final judgement on your product's technical features in the manner of a frustrated product engineer.

Product information to give to the prospect right away: As a rule, you'll want to supply just enough product information in your initial marketing activities to get the prospect to contact your company. How much is "not enough" depends on whether or not your prospects keep asking the same questions over and over during their first contact with your company's sales reps.

Here are some examples of questions that, if asked over and over again by prospects in their initial conversations with your sales reps, should have been addressed by the marketing deliverables sent to them previously by your company:

- **Major functionality question:** *"How does your product work?"*

- **Common product misconception clarified:**
  "Do I have to do such-and-so to use your product?"

- **Major application question:**
  "Can your product do _____?"

- **Compatibility with another commonly-used industry product or service:**
  "Is your product compatible with [well-known product, system, standard, or process] ?"

- **Common feature question:**
  "Does your product have [feature 'X']?"

If you're getting a sizeable number of questions like these, important product information is missing from the marketing deliverables—mailings, ads, Web site, etc.—in your marketing program.

For every prospect who asks one of these questions, there's at least one other prospect out there (if not many more) who has also already asked and answered the question himself, but not in your favor. These are the prospects who *aren't* responding to your marketing programs.

Closing product information gaps: These important product information gaps in your marketing executables can be solved by revising the sales copy of your printed marketing deliverables and advertising to provide the needed additional product information. Other product information gaps can be addressed by developing additional printed tip-ins for mailings and sales kits, such as "Answers to Frequently-Asked Questions," or "Product Q & A" sales sheets.

Answer the questions your prospects ask most frequently about your product in your first marketing contact with them (mailing, ad, etc.), and more prospects will respond to your marketing efforts. You'll also clear the field to allow your sales reps to handle the more complex and difficult questions raised by your prospects during phone and in-person sales calls, which are the best times in the sales cycle to address these questions.

Product information your prospect should receive from your sales reps: In-depth, detailed information on your product's technical features and capabilities, its applications, and other information addressing complex aspects of your product should be part of the sales material your sales reps supply to prospects in follow-up mailings and personal sales calls with prospects.

Examples of the kinds of product information that should be accompanied by additional explanation and commentary by your sales reps include:

- *Product case studies;*
- *"White Papers" on specialized product uses and applications;*
- *Third-party technical articles and analysis relating to the product;*
- *Product sales/applications video;*
- *Product instructional use manuals, reports, and specification sheets*

The rule of thumb here is that any issue relating to your company's product that prompts a question from the prospect which threatens the sale, should instead be handled and skillfully neutralized by an on-the-ground sales rep when the sales rep contacts the prospect.

To make distribution of these materials fast and easy by your company's sales reps, many of them can be posted to a dedicated Web URL (i.e., a Web address not otherwise made public by your company) on your company's Web site. Your sales reps can then e-mail this link to their prospects as a follow-up to their contact with them. You should, of course, continue to produce these important deliverables in their printed forms, and your sales reps should continue to distribute them to prospects as needed.

Crisis Marketing: Taking Action When the Product is Ahead of Its Time

Products that require too great a change in the prospect's ways of doing business, or are ahead of their time, represent the toughest product-related problems to solve. This is a very common problem in high-tech start-ups and established companies launching brand-new kinds of products.

A start-up or established company may create and produce a revolutionary new product, process or service with many, very positive attributes: A new metals-finishing process for industrial manufacturers, a new electronic payment system for businesses, a new resume-screening system for personnel managers.

The company's cutting-edge new product or service may well be a quantum leap beyond the current technology, manufacturing processes, or the market's current business practices. But, despite their many positive attributes, and despite a well-conceived and executed product launch, sales response is poor.

The company's management, product development, and marketing staff are stunned to see such a poor reaction to their new product, and rightly so. After all, they say America is the land of the creative innovator, the technology that transforms entire industries, the new way of doing business that creates an entirely new market. *But why aren't we getting traction with our product?*

For every business innovation or technology that changes the world, there are many, perhaps equally significant, new products or services that fail to generate sales response, for one or more of the following reasons:

- *They require users to make disruptive changes in the ways they currently do business, or to run their operations in ways that are too much of a radical departure from their current ways of doing business;*

- *They threaten the prospect's economic livelihood by upsetting traditional, well-established sales and distribution channels in the industry;*

- *The time required for an industry or marketplace to accept and adopt the innovator's new technology is well beyond the innovator's financial staying power.*

Sometimes the "disruptive technology" represented by your company's new product or service is just too disruptive for its market. The smart marketing manager knows it's a losing battle to waste time criticizing the prospect's lack of vision, and to despair in his company's bad fortune.

Action is the antidote to despair, **and a product or its marketing approach can often be changed in ways that increase market acceptance and sales response:** A new day begins for a troubled company as soon as the company's management team snaps out of the shock and despair that comes from the realization that its product is too far ahead of its market, and starts taking action to solve its problem in the "here and now."

Saving a Product That is Ahead of its Time

Staging a turnaround for a company with a product ahead of its time in its market is the most difficult effort any company's management, product development, and marketing teams can undertake. For an established company with other successful product lines, a single new product failure may be a major, but survivable, setback. But for a start-up, failure to save its one and only product can be fatal blow.

Products utilizing technology or processes way beyond the understanding and acceptance of their markets must often be substantially modified to meet the needs and wants of the prospect. For example, a product can sometimes be scaled back in some way, by eliminating certain features or components to reduce its price, and hopefully to improve its market appeal. A product or service can also be reduced in scope down to the one or two essential features that are most useful to its potential customers, or new features may be added to bring the product more in line with market needs.

As a marketing manager with this kind of problem in a start-up or new product launch, you must make drastic changes in how you present and sell the product. Many of these marketing approaches will require a similar "downsizing" of your original marketing plan and deliverables. In the process, you must put aside many of the aspirations you once held in your original vision of the product, in order to make the required changes.

However, if you can keep from losing your sense of idealism in the mission that drove you to join the company or start-up in the first place, and instead, view the inevitable compromises you'll have to make in the product and its marketing goals as a strategic pullback, not a defeat, your start-up's original goals may only be temporarily deferred, and not compromised out of existence. One day, the full version of your product may return to the market and be embraced by it, with all of its exciting technical aspects. But until then, your current marketing efforts can generate sales and keep your company going so that it (and you) may "live to fight another day."

Common Changes to Marketing Strategy and Deliverables When a Product is Retooled

When a start-up or established company undergoes a major product retooling, the sales copy and presentation used in the marketing deliverables of your marketing program also faces a massive revision. As the product is changed to make it more saleable for its market, here are examples of three kinds of changes to sales copy and presentation that frequently occur alongside product retooling efforts:

- **Sell a piece of the product, not the whole:** Focus on the one or two aspects of the product that provide the most benefit to the prospect, instead of overwhelming the prospect with all of its product features and detail. Prospects in your market may more readily accept a simpler product that is positioned as a solution to their one big problem, rather than a product they perceive as a complex new technology or process they will have to install and learn;

- **Talk like an insider:** Adopt the language of your market, describing your product in ways that are analogous to the kinds of products the prospect currently uses in his/her industry, and the ways the prospect currently does business;

- **Hide the hardware:** Shift the focus of your product's sales copy from its technology ("the hardware"), to the *problems your product solves for the user in his or her industry*. Most people—your prospects—don't like to think about having to do the extra work required to learn a better way of doing their jobs, no matter how impressive your technology looks, so cut back on the technospeak and other marketing rhetoric you use to describe your product's technology.

These changes are solid advice for any marketing project. However, many start-up (or new product launch) management teams lose touch with their markets because they have become too attached to the notion of touting their product's advanced technical features. These are the very features that made their product too advanced for their markets in the first place, and this attachment often carries over to the company's marketing program, and the deliverables used to sell the product. When the product is retooled, the marketing deliverables that are used to sell the retooled product must also lose this attachment.

Distribution and Market Size Problems

Wrong distribution channel selected: A market test for a start-up, or a company launching a new product in a new market, sometimes reveals that the method of distribution selected for the company's marketing program will not generate sales at a sufficiently low marketing cost.

For example, a company may discover that selling its product through a network of dealers or distributors is a cumbersome, low-profit process, when instead, its marketing effort could be far more effective if it sold its products directly to end-users in a coordinated direct mail and telemarketing program. Sometimes the exact opposite is true—especially in markets that are controlled by a few major distributors (see below), or if your product has a high sales price and requires extensive support before, during, and after the sale.

Some products can only be sold through distributors: Distribution problems show up quickly in market tests. If your company is attempting to sell directly to end-users when it should be using distributors, your prospects will often tell you that they only buy products such as yours exclusively from a certain distributor, and they just don't buy from individual vendors. For the prospect, this is a choice that's easy to justify: Many company purchasing departments prefer the advantage of having just one vendor to order from, and to pay, for certain types of products, and therefore will only deal with a single, exclusive distributor. Electronic components, food and grocery products, beverages, books, and retail software are examples of product lines usually sold only through established distributors.

Common Distributor Problems

On the other hand, your company may have organized a handful of distributors, dealers, or an independent sales rep firm for your initial market test or new product launch, and it experiences poor sales response. Often, the problem is the dealer, distributor, or rep firm is simply not devoting sufficient time and effort to promote your company's product. Here are some of the other major reasons for poor distributor performance:

> **Product depth:** Your distributor may carry thousands of products, many of which, unlike your company's new product, are proven sellers. Distributors, dealers, and reps will usually spend the most time selling the products that are the easiest to sell, or have the biggest profit margins or sales commissions;

> **Account size:** As a start-up or new customer of the distributor, the distributor sees you as a small account relative to the other, more well-established accounts generating most of his sales volume. While professing an interest to work with your small company, distributors will often push the products of their larger, more influential, suppliers;

> **Inertia:** This is often the most difficult problem to address. Even though the distributor's reps express an interest in your product, it's apparent that they're not working hard enough to sell it. Your product becomes just another item number in the distributor's catalog. Sales reps at the distributor, especially for well-established distributors in mature industries, have become glorified order-takers for their accounts—your potential customers. These kinds of distributors won't push your product by themselves; you must generate

demand on your own (through advertising and other marketing methods) to stimulate prospects at their accounts to buy from your distributor.

Solving Distributor Problems

If you believe you have no other option but to sell your company's product through a dealer, distributor, or independent sales rep network, you can often improve sales by improving, and intensifying, the sales training and support you provide for your product to the on-the-ground (or phone) sales reps at your distributors. This is accomplished by applying more time and effort to improving the distributor's reps' awareness of your product and its benefits, and by showing them the best ways to present and sell your product.

Here are some steps you can take to heighten awareness of your company's product and create a sense of enthusiasm about your product in the minds of your distributor's sales reps.

Sales Meetings

Most distributors offer numerous opportunities for marketing and sales managers at the companies they represent to present their products to their sales reps, at sales meetings held during the year. You should never pass up an opportunity to get in front of the distributor's sales team at these meetings. However, some distributors, especially those in mature industries, will try to limit contacts between their accounts (your company) with their sales reps, because they are concerned that these presentations take selling time away from their reps.

This is not your problem, however, and if you feel that the distributor's reps need more and better sales training to boost your product's sales response, insist that your distributor make special arrangements to allow you to stage your own presentation to his reps, and take that opportunity to present and reinforce your product's story, features, and benefits. If you are experiencing poor sales response in a start-up, this may be your last opportunity to pull your product out of its slump.

At the presentation you make in the sales meeting, you want to highlight the following:

- **Make your product's benefits, advantages and positioning crystal clear:** Explain to the distributor's reps the essential features and benefits that make your product different from and better than similar products in the same class. Use point-by-point comparisons of key product features to make these distinctions crystal clear, to position your product very clearly against competitive products, in the mind of the rep;

- **Go beyond your product's sales pitch:** Don't stop at giving reps your product's standard sales presentation. Equip them to handle what comes next from their prospects: Discuss the common sales questions and objections that prospects have on your product, and thoroughly describe the best methods for responding to and countering each of these questions, and the prospect's most common objections;

• **Tell the rep what your company is doing to help them move your product:** Every distributor's sales rep will push a product harder if they know that your company is helping to make their selling job easier. Detail the marketing efforts your company is making to promote the product: Trade print advertising campaign, direct mail program, trade show appearances, etc. If your company cannot afford to spend money on a significant marketing effort, you can at least execute a trade PR media awareness project at very low cost (see Chapter 14) to get the word out on your product, and mention this during your presentation;

• **Help the rep target their accounts:** Let sales reps know what types of customers would be most likely to buy your product; for example, by their industry or location, by their use of other products sold by the distributor, or by their order volume. This gives the reps an immediate goal to push your product to a few most-likely prospects to get some early sales momentum going for your product;

• **Your door is always open:** Let the distributor's reps know that you and your company's management team are at their disposal, to help them on any problem or issue with your company's product. Distributor sales reps respond well to greater attention and involvement on the part of marketing staffs in their product line companies, so prove it to them by being responsive to their requests for assistance on day-to-day sales and administrative issues;

• **De-brief the distributor's reps:** After the meeting, try to gather additional, informal prospect feedback on your product from the distributor's sales reps, on a one-on-one basis. You want to hear anything and everything the sales rep's accounts say about your product—the good, the bad, and the ugly. Try to do this very discreetly, so that any negative information about your company's product won't be overheard by other reps in the meeting.

Adding and Improving Distributor Sales and Marketing Deliverables

In addition to the sales meeting with distributor reps, You'll need to re-evaluate the sales and marketing deliverables you provide to your distributor's sales reps for the prospects they call on your behalf. Often in the wake of poor marketing results, you will identify improvements to sales copy and presentation of existing marketing deliverables, and you will need to supply these improved sales materials to your distributor's sales reps.

As you plan for your sales meeting with distributors, you should assess the marketing deliverables and sales training aids your distributor's sales reps give to their prospects to help them sell your product, and the sales training materials they will need to keep their selling skills sharp and your product in mind when they talk to their customers.

Here are some examples of sales training aids and marketing deliverables typically produced for a distributor's sales rep force:

Prospect sales deliverables: These are typical sales materials given by your distributor's sales reps to their prospects:

- **Big brochure:** 11" X 17" four-color gloss brochure, folded to 8-1/2" X 11";

- **Sales flyer:** Single sheet, 8-1/2" X 11" four-color gloss flyer;

- **Product technical specification sheets:** 8-1/2" X 11" sheets, offset (black and white) printed one or both sides;

- **Price sheet:** 8-1/2" X 11" sheets, offset (black and white) printed one or both sides;

- **Other:** Specialized pieces as needed (for example, application case histories or "white papers")

Sales training aids: These are sales training materials given to your distributor's sales reps for their personal use and reference:

- **Sales presentation outline**

- **Competitive product features chart** (your product vs. your top competitors)

- **FAQ** (most frequently-asked prospect sales questions) sales flyer

Sales training and marketing videos: Videos also make excellent sales and marketing deliverables and, depending on their content and presentation, can be used in either sales training or prospect selling applications by your distributor's sales reps.

A short, 5-10 minute **sales training video** is an excellent way to get the substance and style of your product's ideal sales presentation across to sales reps, and can also address responses to common questions and prospect sales objections. Likewise, a short, (5 minutes or less) professionally-produced **marketing video** shown by your distributor's sales reps to their prospects insures that no information is left out during the rep's personal sales call to the prospect.

Either of these kinds of videos can be very elaborate, and expensive, but simpler, less expensive versions can also be effective. Often, all you need is a well-written, professionally narrated audio track accompanied by simple images and a few live video shots of your product in action. This type of video can be produced for less than $5,000 and duplicated for distribution on DVD or VHS tape at nominal added cost.

Greater Involvement, Training and Communication Improve Distributor Sales Performance

Most underperforming distributor sales relationships can be improved just by showing your distributor and his sales reps that you want to be more involved in helping the distributor increase sales for your company's product, and sales revenue for the distributor.

The two goals you must meet in working with distributors in any sales turnaround situation are to keep your product foremost in the mind of your distributor's sales reps, and to do everything you can to help their sales reps properly present and sell your company's product to their prospects. More involvement on your part, with skilled sales training and open communication with the distributor's reps, improves your product's market response and sales success.

Uncontrollable Factors Revealed by Your Test

Despite good execution and deliverables with an effective sales message, there are other factors influencing poor marketing results that may be beyond your control as a marketing manager. These include:

Funding: Sometimes you will discover that prospects will buy your company's product, but only in a selling cycle that is much longer than you and your management team anticipated. Mailings and ads pull responses, but prospects take far longer to make their purchase decision than originally hoped. Because of this, your company will need a higher level of funding, both for its marketing budget, and its ongoing operations, to sustain this more prolonged sales and marketing effort;

Timing: While the problem of products that are ahead of their time has been covered previously, there are other "bad timing" factors that influence marketing programs. Industry dynamics, such as a major slump affecting the industry served by your company's product, a deep recession, a natural disaster, or any other factor beyond your company's control may be more than any marketing program can overcome;

Competition: In mature industries, the competition in your field may be dominated by a very few, very large, powerful, and well-entrenched competitors. In some markets, a single company may exercise total dominance. In these situations, not even the most effective conventional marketing program executed by a start-up or new market entrant can compete against large, wealthy competitors in these mature markets;

In The Arena

"It is not the critic who counts: Not the man who points out how the strong man stumbles or where the doer of deeds could have done better. The credit belongs to the man who is actually in the arena, whose face is marred by dust and sweat and blood, who strives valiantly, who errs and comes up short again and again, because there is no effort without error or shortcoming, but who knows the great enthusiasms, the great devotions, who spends himself for a worthy cause; who, at the best, knows, in the end, the triumph of high achievement, and who, at the worst, if he fails, at least he fails while daring greatly, so that his place shall never be with those cold and timid souls who knew neither victory nor defeat."

Theodore Roosevelt,
26th President of the United States
"Citizenship in a Republic,"
Speech at the Sorbonne, Paris, April 23, 1910

Market size: Although the total size of a market, and the total sales generated from it, should always be assessed before a product or service is created for it, Members of a start-up or new product launch will sometimes realize, after some time has elapsed, that their company has entered a market that is too small. Here, a very effective marketing program will often harvest all of the sales that can be made from these markets within a year; after that, the response generated by every additional marketing dollar spent takes a steep drop. When the market has been tapped out, there are no more new mailing lists that can be rented, no more new industry publications in which to advertise, and no ways to reach more prospects in this market, because everyone who can be reached in your market has already been reached.

These are but a few examples of situations that are often beyond your ability to control from a marketing standpoint. A better direct mail piece or a more targeted ad won't generate any more sales when the prospects in the market are highly resistant to buying from a new industry player, or when your biggest entrenched competitor has a virtual lock on the market. These are the times when all of the "positive mental attitude" you can muster will be ineffective, because you are operating inside a negative environment.

Action is the Cure for Adverse Market Conditions

The antidote to any adverse major marketing factor you can't control is _action_. Don't ever give up.

When you are operating inside a negative environment that's resistant to your marketing program, and, after thoughtful assessment, you're convinced that there's nothing wrong with either your product or its marketing program, **_change the environment_**. Think anew about how and where your product could be sold. Do this by trying new options—keep testing new markets, keep making changes to your product or service that you and your team think will make it more attractive to buyers, and keep working all the options available to you.

Taking action always creates more options. And these new options will often lead you to more effective ways of selling your product or service: A new test mailing in a totally new and different market or industry that generates sizeable interest and response; a cheaper spin-off of your product that makes its price point more affordable, and triples your sales volume in a few months; an overnight change in your pricing or distribution methods that removes key sales barriers to buying your product.

Shaking up the perception of your product in the minds of your prospects, or putting your product in front of a whole new set of prospects in a new market are but two examples of _action_ that creates new options.

Keep blasting away and the breaks will come. Every day, the mere fact that your company is active, and "_in the arena_" with its marketing program keeps your product's profile high, and brings good fortune a little closer.

As mentioned earlier in this book, the founders of many successful companies reached their eventual successes in markets, and with products and sales approaches far different than those they started out with. And as a marketing manager, the responsibility for finding these markets, and executing plans to make a success of your company's marketing efforts there, often falls to you.

You will only fail if you quit—so don't quit!

There is _always_ something you can do.

APPENDIX

Books: Highly Suggested Reading

The following list of books will provide you with solid background and inspiration for your work as a marketing manager, and should form the core of your marketing library.

Advertising and Marketing

Caples, John. *Tested Advertising Methods.* Prentice Hall Professional, 1998. The classic book on ad copywriting, this book is a "must" for anyone in advertising or marketing.

Caples, John. *How to Make Your Advertising Make Money.* Prentice Hall Press, 1983. This updated book by advertising copy master John Caples expands on the material covered in *Tested Advertising Methods,* and is a useful companion to this earlier book.

Cotton, Stan. *Anybody Can Be In Advertising....It Beats Working For A Living.* Back 2 Basics Publishers, Inc., 1997. Stan Cotton's "honesty in advertising" approach, and irreverent tales of his exploits in advertising, is a tonic for anyone in the advertising and marketing fields. Excellent and highly recommended.

Hopkins, Claude. *My Life in Advertising/Scientific Advertising.* McGraw-Hill/Contemporary Books, 1986. Claude Hopkins is considered to be the father of modern advertising and promotion. Originally published in 1923, this classic book on advertising and copywriting covers the timeless techniques required to turn readers into buyers.

Landen, Hal. *Marketing with Video.* Oak Tree Press, 1996. A solid primer on all aspects of marketing-oriented video production.

Levinson, Jay Conrad. *Guerrilla Marketing: Secrets for Making Big Profits from Your Small Business.* Mariner Books, 1998. Packed with many solid, practical marketing ideas for start-ups and small businesses.

Reeves, Rosser. *Reality in Advertising.* Random House, 1961. An advertising classic, Rosser Reeves, former chairman of top ad agency Ted Bates & Co., was the creator of the USP (Unique Selling Proposition), and his advertising and presentation techniques generated phenomenally successful results in the 1940s and 1950s.

Ries, Al and Jack Trout. *Positioning: The Battle for Your Mind.* McGraw-Hill Trade, 2000. A modern marketing classic details the essential top-down elements of marketing strategy.

Schwab, Victor. *How to Write a Good Advertisement.* Wilshire Book Co., 1985. Another classic text on the art and craft of creating and writing powerful and persuasive advertising.

Smith, Cynthia S. *How to Get Big Results from a Small Advertising Budget.* Lyle Stuart, 1989. Many useful pointers on all aspects of marketing for industrial and business-to-business marketing managers.

Design

Rand, Paul *Design Form and Chaos.* Yale University Press, 1993. An excellent, visually-arresting design book from one of the world's top corporate designers.

White, Jan. *Graphic Idea Notebook.* Rockport Publishers, 1991. A very useful idea-starter for any visual presentation.

Williams, Robin. *The Non-Designer's Design Book.* Peachpit Press, 1994. An outstanding primer for understanding the elements of clear and effective design presentation for advertising and many other types of print marketing deliverables.

Wurman, Richard Saul, David Sume, and Loring Leifer, *Information Anxiety 2.* Que, 2000. In invaluable guidebook for marketing managers, designers, or anyone responsible for presenting information in a readily understood way, written by the originator of "information architecture." Highly recommended.

General Inspiration

Carnegie, Dale. *How to Win Friends and Influence People.* Pocket Books, 1990. The essential book for improving your relationships with people in business and in life.

Hill, Napoleon, W. Clement Stone. *Success through a Positive Mental Attitude.* Simon & Schuster, 1992. This classic self-help book highlights the importance of developing and maintaining a positive attitude in any business or personal situation. Any book of this type written by Napoleon Hill or W. Clement Stone is worth reading.

Marden, Orison Swett. *Pushing to the Front.* Sun Publishing Company, 1997. This book, originally published in 1894, tells the stories of famous figures throughout history, and the character attibutes that helped them overcome obstacles to acheive greatness in their fields. The forerunner of the modern self-help book, and a true classic.

Moore, Harold, and Joseph L. Galloway. *We Were Soldiers Once...and Young: Ia Drang: The Battle That Changed the War in Vietnam.* Random House, 2002. Gripping story of the first major battle of the Vietnam War. An inspiring tale of leadership, teamwork, and courage in the face of extreme adversity.

Start-Ups and Entrepreneurship

Cook, James. *The Start-Up Entrepreneur.* HarperCollins, 1987. A streetwise entrepreneur shares his wisdom on starting and expanding successful new ventures. Full of enlightening personal anecdotes and useful, proven advice.

White, Richard. *The Entrepreneur's Manual.* Chilton Book Company, 1977. In-depth coverage of hands-on techniques for identifying lucrative market gaps, forming new venture management teams, and raising venture capital. Highly recommended for anyone involved in a start-up venture.

INDEX

About the Author

Eric Gagnon has over 20 years' experience in marketing, product development, consulting and publishing, and is the president of GAA, a marketing and product development firm providing product development, marketing, consulting, and new business development services to a wide variety of clients, ranging from start-ups, to mid-sized industrial and trade companies, and Fortune 500 corporations in the telecommunications, publishing, software, electronics, conference/exhibition, and information services industries.

Gagnon is the editor of the book, *What's On The Internet®*, co-published with Peachpit Press/Addison-Wesley, and two Internet directories, *What's On The Web®*, published by Internet Media, and *The AT&T Military Internet Guide*, published by AT&T. Gagnon holds a U.S. patent, and three overseas patents, for Internet-related systems and services. Gagnon has a B.A. in Business Administration/Marketing from George Washington University.

Author Contact Information:
Eric Gagnon
(888) 505-7447
eric@realmarkets.net
www.realmarkets.net

Ordering Information

To order additional copies of *The Marketing Manager's Handbook*, contact the publisher, Internet Media, at (540) 349-2438, or by e-mail: mail@sellyourproduct.com.

Bulk ordering and educational discounts: Quantity discounts for multiple copies of *The Marketing Manager's Handbook* are available to bookstores, libraries, and educational institutions.